Qualitative RESEARCH

Studies in the
Postmodern Theory of Education

Shirley R. Steinberg
General Editor

Vol. 354

The Counterpoints series is part of the Peter Lang Education list.
Every volume is peer reviewed and meets
the highest quality standards for content and production.

PETER LANG
New York • Washington, D.C./Baltimore • Bern
Frankfurt • Berlin • Brussels • Vienna • Oxford

Qualitative
RESEARCH

*A Reader in
Philosophy,
Core Concepts,
and Practice*

EDITED BY BARBARA DENNIS,
LUCINDA CARSPECKEN, & PHIL FRANCIS CARSPECKEN

PETER LANG
New York • Washington, D.C./Baltimore • Bern
Frankfurt • Berlin • Brussels • Vienna • Oxford

Library of Congress Cataloging-in-Publication Data

Qualitative research: a reader in philosophy, core concepts, and practice /
edited by Barbara Dennis, Lucinda Carspecken, Phil Francis Carspecken.
p. cm. — (Counterpoints: Studies in the Postmodern Theory of Education; v. 354)
Includes bibliographical references and index.
1. Qualitative research. 2. Social sciences—Research—Methodology.
I. Dennis, Barbara. II. Carspecken, Lucinda. III. Carspecken, Phil Francis.
H62.Q3517   001.4'2—dc23   2011040249
ISBN 978-1-4331-0473-2 (hardcover)
ISBN 978-1-4331-0472-5 (paperback)
ISBN 978-1-4539-0197-7 (e-book)
ISSN 1058-1634

Bibliographic information published by **Die Deutsche Nationalbibliothek**.
Die Deutsche Nationalbibliothek lists this publication in the "Deutsche
Nationalbibliografie"; detailed bibliographic data is available
on the Internet at http://dnb.d-nb.de/.

The paper in this book meets the guidelines for permanence and durability
of the Committee on Production Guidelines for Book Longevity
of the Council of Library Resources.

© 2013 Peter Lang Publishing, Inc., New York
29 Broadway, 18th floor, New York, NY 10006
www.peterlang.com

Printed in the United States of America

Contents

Acknowledgments

Putting a book of this magnitude together requires work and support from many people. The authors whose work is included in this book were quick to respond to editorial comments and requests. Cicada Dennis did the formatting and helped with editing the whole text. He worked tirelessly over an enormous amount of material. Ian Arthur supported our organizing and indexing work. Editors at Peter Lang were patient with our delays and provided particularly helpful comments. We would specifically like to acknowledge Bernadette Shade, Phyllis Korper, Chris Myers, and Stephen Mazur from Peter Lang. Shirley Steinberg encouraged our proposal and shepherded it through the process. She has been a source of support for us personally and professionally in this and other endeavors.

Introduction: Philosophy and Qualitative Research

BARBARA DENNIS, LUCINDA CARSPECKEN, & PHIL
CARSPECKEN

If the events of September 11, 2001, have proven anything, it's that the terrorists can attack us, but they can't take away what makes us American—our freedom, our liberty, our civil rights. No, only Attorney General John Ashcroft can do that.—Jon Stewart (after the passage of the Patriot Act) http://www.brainyquote.com/quotes/authors/j/jon_stewart.html

Philosophical rigor and the status quo have always been uneasy companions. In any given time, the less carefully one examines the latter's rallying cries, the safer its existence. Words like "freedom," "meritocracy," "rights," or "security" are more effective weapons when they are left conveniently vague, conveniently malleable. Within qualitative research we have our own rallying cries—terms that carry the weight of the received wisdom of the day—"generalizability," "validity," and "rationality," for example. Given some of the misuses of qualitative research in the past, including the long tendency for the powerful (in academia and elsewhere) to study the powerless (see Trinh T. Minh-ha's work, for example, 2009, as a critique of this tendency), it is important to look carefully at the key concepts and the way these are used in both the practice and theory of qualitative inquiry. What tends to be left out, glossed over, or gone unnoticed in research methods? What is inconsistent or misleading? What has the potential to be empowering or liberating?

We conceived of this book with the idea that critical explorations into the key philosophical issues in qualitative research could throw light on distortions, power relations, hidden assumptions, and possibilities within the field, and could ultimately provide the groundwork for needed conversations. We wanted to do this with rigor, both by building up philosophy and core concepts and by exploring specific practices in qualitative research. The distinction itself between core concepts, philosophy, and specific qualitative inquiry practice is blurred from the outset, as philosophy and practice are merely foregrounded or backgrounded in various papers, not divided.

The book, in a way, then, is a statement of hope. We have seen many promising trends in the last few decades as academics from the groups who have traditionally been studied and been spoken for by others in the past—indigenous peoples, women, minorities, gays and lesbians, for example—make their voices heard, as the "other" speaks back, and as the uses to which research is put receive more attention. We have also seen more scrutiny given to the key concepts that define our methods. We see signs that qualitative research may begin to turn the tables on its own history to become not only a tool for emancipation but an effective one, and we want this book to be a part of that trend.

A further goal for the book is to apply the idea of inclusiveness across disciplines, and to begin some needed dialogue. We had noticed that books and journals on research methods had become somewhat specialized and niche driven. We decided to include articles that covered research methods across a range of subject areas. Thus, our interest in the philosophy of research methods was taken up through scholarship that spans various traditions including anthropology, education, law, counseling, language, queer studies, systems theory, and computer technology. We hoped that this inclusive approach that drew us each out of our own fields would provide an opportunity to think more carefully than usual about the terms we used, the background information we took for granted, and the questions we raised.

These basic purposes for the book reveal the critical underpinnings of our efforts, yet even that word "critical" cannot assume an unproblematic status for us. In broad, general terms, we are inviting and taking a critical perspective on qualitative inquiry, which means precisely that we want to refrain from taking the status-quo knowledge for granted, that we want to encourage questioning and dialogue about core philosophical concepts and methodological practices among both researchers and participants, that we want to contribute to emancipatory pursuits in and through social science, and that we acknowledge the pivotal necessity of reflection for inquiry, most particularly reflection on the doing of social science. This, for us, is a hopeful process, opening up possibilities for liberation on both personal and social levels.

We also wanted to encourage dialogues between qualitative and quantitative methodologists. Many of us work in situations where both approaches are used. Yet, many of us have also been reared in the academic milieu of inquiry separation—where people who engage in qualitative and quantitative inquiry are rarely in the same departments and scholarly conversations, even though similar philosophical problems underlie the two general streams of human research—problems of defining the self, meaning, and "knowledge," for example, or of choosing desirable means and ends for research.

Habermas (1984) has suggested that through any one particular research project, we can gain understanding related to the substantive questions at hand, the metatheoretical principles involved in the conduct of the study, and the methodology that was used to address the substantive interests. In the act of doing qualitative research, as in any social science, we bring all of these elements to the table, so to speak, and our inquiry, then, can reciprocally inform each of these elements. Across all three of these domains, the authors who are included in this text take seriously the opportunity to explore and critique taken-for-granted underpinnings in their own inquiry practices. As already indicated, these explorations traverse an array of interests and disciplines, principles, and methodological designs and approaches.

Criticalists are not a monolithic group. In fact, as Kincheloe and McLaren (2007) so aptly pointed out, "Critical theory should not be treated as a universal grammar of revolutionary thought objectified and reduced to discrete formulaic pronouncements or strategies" (p. 404). Kincheloe and McLaren have been major contributors to the field of critical inquiry and have consistently argued that lively dialogue among criticalists should be encouraged. It is our hope that this book benefits that dialogue.

Some of the important questions that have emerged in critical dialogues of late involve debates about the limits of knowledge, whether and to what extent truth claims can be considered valid, how to represent the voices of "the other," how are socially fluid, cosmopolitan identities to be taken into account in understanding participants, what is the relation between truth and power, and under whose authority can researchers speak. These debates are engaged across the chapters, but do not necessarily find resolution.

We have organized the book in a way that reflects our own principles. Philosophical concepts are explored throughout. In the first section of the book, this is done in a direct and broad way, thinking across qualitative inquiry in general. In the four remaining sections of the book, the examination of core concepts occurs in the context of methodological practices and outcomes. These remaining sections are organized in a fashion that reflects insights from Habermas's *Theory of Communicative Action* (1984, 1987). Habermas makes a theoretical distinction between the coordination of lifeworld activities and the coordination of system-level phenomena. The level of coordination is one of two fundamental ways of distinguishing system from lifeworld. Social integration involves the coordination of action as in a face-to-face context that occurs at one social site (what could be considered a bounded unit), which could be a tribe, a household, a school, a classroom, or an internet blogosphere. This is what many people will think of as "lifeworld"—culture, or that which is intuitively known. Habermas (1984) writes that "Subjects acting communicatively always come to an understanding in the horizon of a lifeworld. Their lifeworld is formed from more or less diffuse, always unproblematic, background convictions" (p. 70). The lifeworld also collects the interpretive work of preceding generations and in this sense is the conservative "counterweight to the risk of disagreement that arises in every actual process of reaching understanding" (p. 70). All activities involve lifeworld milieu, because people monitor themselves as they act, act for values and according to norms and identity commitments, and this we do always. There are two principles for the coordination of action, one based on action orientations and one based on patterns linking large numbers of action consequences to the reproduction, iteration or directional transformation of action conditions. The reason "level" is an appropriate term is that system processes require a macro perspective to be discovered as truly system processes, whereas studies of lifeworld are more micro level (but micro level studies are needed to understand very specifically how system processes associated with cultural reproduction actually occur. According to Habermas (1984, 1987), the system uncouples from the lifeworld in response to the complexities of coordinating social life.

There is always system, but the basis for system *uncoupling* from the lifeworld occurred when "media" like money replaced communication in certain sub-systems of activity like the economy. What makes highly complex social formations distinctive is not that they involve system processes (all societies are also systems) but that systems have uncoupled from lifeworld. The cultural resources necessary for reaching consensus overtax the capacities of social beings in complex societies. For example, we find we cannot bargain for all of our needs by assessing the fair trade of our labor for our consumption. Social integration, then, also involves the coordination of action at a system level, one where the communicative negotiations get fixated through particular formulations. According to Habermas, the system imperatives colonize aspects of the lifeworld, which get turned over to strategic action and a system of causes/effects and action consequences that limit the likelihood of taking yes/no positions. Coordination at this level involves conditions for action, action consequences, and functional relations across actions as effective ways of describing system relations. These three categories capture most conditions for action through which systemic coordination of activity is operationalized within the lifeworld: the distribution of cultural resources/milieu; economic relations; and political relations.

- Cultural Milieu. This has to do with the volition of the actor, but also involves the availability of cultural themes to draw on when acting, the value of the themes identified among cultural others—including the value for one's identity, and the distribution of cultural themes across sites. One's cultural milieu can both resource and constrain action. The distributions of cultural resources and cultural milieu reflect the potential for systemic relations.

- Economic relations. These conditions will primarily be experienced as outside one's volition and they are the basic arrangements involved in how basic needs are distributed and met or not met.

- Political relations. These conditions involve the formalized relations of authority that are widespread in society—laws are the most substantial of these formalized relations.

Habermas's distinction between the lifeworld and the system guides some important distinctions in the conduct of critical qualitative inquiry. Readers will see evidence of this through both the organization and substance of the chapters, though only a few of the chapters specifically advance Habermas's ideas. First off, inquiry into social life varies methodologically between the lifeworld and system levels. When studying the lifeworld, researchers are more inclined to engage in and seek access to the everyday life experiences of participants; but when studying the system, researchers are more inclined to study the distribution of material goods, legal and economic patterns, functions, and unintended consequences of large-scale activities coordinated across time and space. Moreover, there is a difference in the way critique of the status quo is generated. For example, lifeworld critique is facilitated by examining relations of claims to truth made when actors negotiate meaning, whereas system critique is facilitated by examining the ways consequences and effects exceed the intentions of the actors, contradict one another, or limit the potential for understanding. It is also possible to examine the mismatch or relation between analyses of both levels. Habermas (1984, 1987) argues that in complex societies, institutions form a "switching station" between activities coordinated through the lifeworld and activities coordinated through the system. In this text, we do not have system-level analyses, but we have chapters that address the analysis of institutional activities. These chapters provide an opportunity for readers to think about the distinction between lifeworld and system, and the place of institutions in the negotiation of meaning and action-coordination between the lifeworld and the system.

Many social sciences focus, in a privileged way, on either the lifeworld (as hermeneutics and phenomenology do, for examples) or the system (as macroeconomics, macrosociology, or objective sciences do, for examples). When we do social science that focuses on the everyday interactions of people in order to better understand their experiences, we draw on particular methods of data collection and analysis that provide us, as researchers, access to the lifeworld interactions of participants. Sections Two and Three focus on methodological theory and practice involved in understanding the life experiences, interactions, norms, values, distortions, and ideologies entailed in the everyday life engagements of participants. The chapters in Section Two explore core concepts involved in innovative methodologies while wrestling with related problems. For example, focus groups have been considered one of the mainstays of doing qualitative inquiry because of their capacity to elucidate and engage participant experiences. In Chapter 7, Melissa Freeman explores the concept of hermeneutics in relation to focus-group method. The chapters in Section Three focus more specifically on language. The linguistic turn in philosophy and methodology made it clear that social science had often taken language for granted, as if it were merely a tool for communicating knowledge, and as a result, researchers have been looking at language more closely in the last few decades; at its effects on the life experiences of participants, its effects on the researcher's engagement with those life experiences, and its effects on the theoretical resources and constraints embedded in words and word use. In Chapter 12, Benetta Johnson looks closely at the use of the personal pronoun by reconstructing its shifting meaning in personal narratives. Both of these sections concern what we think of as hermeneutic and reconstructive examinations of the culture and experiences of participants. Hermeneutic reconstructive investigations require the researcher to be able to dialogue meaningfully with participants and position-take with them.

The chapters in Section Four involve taking more of a relative outsider, third-person perspective toward institutions, cultural structures, and routines that are not often a part of the horizon of interpretations of which actors might be most immediately aware. This perspective is, in principle, available to participants, but is usually not explicit through the immediate level of face-to-face engagements. It involves reflection on the patterns and routines and effects and conditions of action across time, space, and multiple interactive opportunities. These structures, institutional routines, and conditions for action are drawn upon by actors, but usually in tacit ways. While one instance can constitute and reconstitute cultural structures and systemic effects, no one instance would suffice for capturing the description of these structures and systemic effects as part of a larger process. For example, let's say we are interested in how friends experience their interactions with one another as caring. We might interview the friends and observe them and reconstruct their experiences from the perspectives of how they are experiencing these interactions. However, their experiences will also be riddled with cultural structures, perhaps gendered effects that are not part of the intentional or even experiential awareness of the participants. They might not specifically acknowledge how this was part of their experience. The gendered effects, instead, become visible by looking at how caring actions both function within and are the effects of the interactions. Researchers must engage in different sets of methodological practices in order to get at these functions, consequences, and structures that are situated in specific interactions, but also link interactions across the time and space. We find these are both inclusive and broader than any particular instance of interaction. Thus, the methodological concepts and practices are different from those we see described and exemplified in Sections Two and Three.

In the final section of the book, researchers have explored the possible meaning of doing qualitative research for the participants and for the social world within which inquiry is located. When we first conceived of this section, we thought of it as the "Qualitative Research As…" section. When we engage with participants in researching their lives with them, we are engaging in action that could have meaning for them beyond the goals or questions articulated explicitly as rationale for doing the research. Qualitative research can be particularly mindful of this potential in social science because as researchers we tend to develop relationships with participants, care about them, and take seriously what participating in the research is doing for their lives—not just how the findings of the research will benefit them or the literature. This final section of the book stands as a critique of social science that fails to take into account its own "footprint" in the social worlds through which it treads. For us, the dichotomy between practice and theory is a false one. Exploration into core concepts is not merely an academic pursuit. These concepts are intimately connected to the life experiences of all us. They are substantive concepts in the first place. And, thus, by better understanding them, we better understand our ordinary life experiences. This matters because when we do research, we are not merely examining phenomena of interest, we are making friends, we are conversing, we are sharing concerns, and so forth. As the chapters in this section indicate, our qualitative research can be philosophy, healing, and activism.

In summary, the organization of the book involves highlighting various aspects of the qualitative inquiry process in order to look more closely at its core concepts and practices, encourage dialogue about those concepts and practices, and move toward a more democratic, inclusive, healing, critical social science.

Description of the Text

Philosophical Explorations

Our first section, then, deals with some core philosophical concepts as they pertain to doing qualitative inquiry. The authors whose chapters comprise this section have all pushed on the traditional boundaries of these core concepts, namely, generalizability, intersubjectivity, rationality, reflexivity, validity, and system.

The first chapter is on generalizability, a notably tricky topic in qualitative research. Doctoral students whose dissertations use qualitative methods are often asked to justify their research designs and findings in terms of generalizability by professors on their committees who have quantitative backgrounds. The usual response has been to suggest a new name, originally coined by Lincoln and Guba in 1985—"transferability"—and then provide a few explanations of what transferability entails. In Chapter 2, Staffan Larsson updates and expands upon one of the most widely read journal articles on qualitative research in 2010: "Om generalisering från kvalitativa studier" (On generalization in qualitative research; in Swedish). Larsson carefully explores the concept of generalizability and offers five versions of it that can be applied in qualitative research. It is high time that this difficult concept be given rigorous consideration from the perspective of qualitative social researchers. It is almost a cliché to say that qualitative research involves building relationships. Often times, this claim is left unexamined. In Chapter 3, Michael Gunzenhauser confronts the relational aspects of doing qualitative research by developing the concept of empathy and clarifying its link to both intersubjectivity and knowing. Gunzenhauser takes a philosophical approach to the problematic of understanding how one identifies with their participants through similarity while respecting participant alterity at the same time. He draws our thinking toward what he calls "creative intersubjectivity"—the idea that the research encounter provokes newness of being for all involved (researchers and participants). The encounter carries the possibilities of respecting difference and energizing action. He draws on philosophy (particularly feminist interpretations of philosophy) to address practical aspects of being in relationships with our research participants, even critiquing the idea that emancipatory research goals are sufficient. He uses research exemplars to talk about how subject-to-subject engagements, necessarily involving empathy and care, can produce strong research and concurrently advance knowledge. Gunzenhauser's unapologetic interest in the affective aspects of our work with participants is inspiring. Gunzenhauser challenges us to think more critically about what it means to care, to have empathy, and to be in relationship with our participants.

"Rationality" is a term that has been much contested and critiqued in qualitative social science over the last few decades. Central to these critiques is a concern for the cultural and social conditions within which something is considered rational. These concerns come sharply into focus when researchers try to study marginalized groups and unusual experiences on the participants' own terms. Lucinda Carspecken discusses ways of knowing and relating to the natural world among a group of environmentalists in Indiana as a lens to highlight some of the values and assumptions that underpin what we tend to unthinkingly define as rationality in mainstream North America. Especially in the case of marginalized ritual or spiritual practice in the industrialized world, it is easy to assume or "see" irrationality, set against a familiar backdrop that we take to be rational. Yet, the very perspectives that are commonly dismissed, even in academia, may throw up possibilities for new and liberating forms of rationality, informed by alternative clusters of values.

"Reflexivity" is one of the more popular concepts regularly identified with contemporary qualitative research. It would be difficult to get an article published in today's qualitative journals without demonstrating "reflexivity," and researchers are taught early on that they need to be reflexive. In Chapter 5, Ian Stronach, Dean Garratt, Cathie Pearce, and Heather Piper explore models of reflexivity that have been specifically linked with qualitative research. Their critique of the models involves both philosophical explorations and practical examinations. The authors draw on how their own Ph.D. students use/misuse reflexive practices in writing their theses. The students' lack of fidelity to reflexive principles led the authors to further explore the concept and nature of reflexivity, which leads them to a new account of "reflexivity" as picturing. To do this, the authors used art, ultimately linking the reflexive nature of art to that of research. This new account retains a more open and fluid structure to be navigated, but not prescribed or specifically defined.

Like generalizability, the concept of validity has been bandied about among qualitative researchers for quite some time, with a proliferation of varying definitions and commitments. Barbara Dennis examines the trends in this discourse and then proposes, against the criticism, a move toward a more inclusive, holistic concept of validity. She reviews a few other scholars who have also proposed a more inclusive validity concept in order to examine the grounds on which their particular holistic views are based. Dennis proposes a model that emerges from the scholarship of Habermas and Phil Carspecken. This model links research validity to meaning and understanding in everyday life. The qualities of validity are explicated as part of describing this holistic, inclusive approach to validity. This approach can be unifying in that its basic principles hold across all varieties of methods and it addresses the variety of issues under the umbrella of the term "validity." Moreover, it eliminates the need for some divisions that have perplexed the validity debates (like pitting objectivity against subjectivity).

In Chapter 6, Sunnie Lee Watson and Bill Watson review the emergence of critical systems theory over the past few decades. After Bertalanffy's groundbreaking work of 1968, *General Systems Theory*, concepts of system branched off in several directions, with some branches eventually intersecting with "chaos theory," now more often named "complexity theory." Critical systems theory could be regarded as a distinctive and highly important branch in that it has managed, in the hands of most of its theorists and practitioners, to avoid the entirely objectified notions of system found elsewhere. It is now a version of systems theory that competes with a few others in the fields of management, institutional analysis, and policy. Sunnie and Bill Watson have provided a chapter that gives an important introduction and overview of the field, along with guidelines for its use in social research.

Exploring Methodological Innovations for Critical Inquiry

New philosophical insights beget new methods and this is the focus of our second section. Some of these new methods critically examine the boundary lines between researcher and researched, researcher and reader, partly by making the researcher more visible and partly by exploring the processes through which meaning is constructed. In place of the traditional model of a passive and objective researcher recording information from active respondents with fixed worldviews, the innovations in this section—conversations, collaborative storytelling and focus groups—acknowledge and explicitly include the active presence of the researcher. Even technological information is reframed as something inherently communicative, rather than as a mysterious substance to be imbibed passively through the senses. In each of the chapters, conceptual development is advanced through the interplay of methodological practice and ideas.

Our first two chapters in this section take commonly used methods—focus groups and interviews—and re-examine them from new philosophical perspectives. In "Meaning Making and Understanding in Focus Groups: Affirming Social and Hermeneutic Dialogue," Melissa Freeman explores the history and range of focus-group methodologies in qualitative research while she also looks at the philosophical frames that inform them. She notes that theories about the self alter the way researchers approach meaning. In particular, she traces the shift in methodology from a data-collection strategy that treats participants' perspectives as fixed and separate, to one that recognizes the active construction and negotiation of meanings within focus-group interactions. Freeman argues for recognition of an embodied, relational self rather than an isolated one. She also advocates Gadamer's philosophical hermeneutics as a lens through which to understand the dialogic nature of focus groups, and as a basis for focus-group designs that take full advantage of the potential for critical and reflective engagement within them.

In "Conversations as Research: Philosophies of the Interview," Svend Brinkmann offers a model for qualitative research interviews based on conversation rather than the commonly used therapeutic counseling style (which he simultaneously critiques). He looks at the philosophical assumptions embedded in these two approaches and argues for "epistemic" interviewing as an important complement to current conventions of "doxatic" interviewing. The first is a mutual, dialectical process of expanding knowledge through the exchange of ideas, whereas the second is a unidirectional flow of knowledge or opinions from the respondent to the researcher, who remains passive. Brinkmann points out the dangers of drawing out only superficial "common-sense" responses through doxatic interviewing rather than dealing with the assumptions and inconsistencies behind them. He also points out the implicit power of the researcher in this mode, where his or her own perspectives are invisible in the interview, coming into play only behind the scenes, in the process of interpreting the respondents' words. Using a range of interviewing examples, including excerpts from Socrates, Brinkmann explores the democratic and philosophical potential of the underused epistemic style of interview.

Lai Ma's chapter provides a critique of dominant concepts of information and the limited, misleading, and often erroneous epistemological implications of these concepts. Information science is a burgeoning field for sure and the term "information" has become used within a huge number of fields and contexts. Many physicists, for example, have reconceptualized traditional constructs like physical states and physical systems in terms of information. Social theorists of various colors and stripes discuss contemporary societies and the globalization process as "the information age." Information as a concept informs cognitive psychology, learning science, artificial intelligence, and of course information science itself. But Ma shows that in all contexts this word is used as if information were something objective, and this perspective is, in turn, tied to a fairly naïve empiricist epistemology. Ma's chapter gives a careful critical reconstruction of the concept of information and then offers a much more promising way to understand what information is: in terms of hermeneutics and communicative action theory. Ma outlines a critical qualitative research methodology for studies of information.

In "Telling It Like It Is: Creating New Layers of Meaning in My Collaborative Storytelling Practices," Dan Mahoney describes the process of adopting an interpretive, self-reflexive stance in his research based on collaborative storytelling with gay men. He argues that his willingness to dialogue and interact with the research participants and to be explicit about his own part in the process has enabled him to represent more layers of interpretation in their stories. He describes this as analogous to laying down tracks in a music recording—the tracks or layers ranging from the actual textual voices recorded in the transcripts to his own internal dialogue to his "sociologist" voice. He advocates a shift away from the role of an invisible, authoritative author presenting a single narrative towards an engaged and visible author working with highly contextualized meanings. He also situates his own perspective within pragmatic, interpretive and postmodern traditions. Although Mahoney's storytelling deals with "large" themes like love, belonging, and identity, he aims to slow these down, emphasizing "small" everyday occurrences and thus bringing out intimate, particular details and symbols rather than flattening these out in grander, romanticized accounts.

Exploring Methodological Innovations for the Critical Analysis of Language Use

We devote the next section to the use of language. On the one hand, some of the authors look at the way details of personal language use intersect with broader, tacit relationships of power. Examples of this are African American women's use of personal pronouns in the context of a predominantly white campus and the gendered and racialized discourses and performances in the interactions between white female clients, an African American female counselor, and a white female researcher. On the other hand, narrative is explored. For instance, Yi-Ping Huang and Phil Carspecken discuss the relation of negation and narrative in human identity claims; and Amir Marvasti and Christopher Faircloth look at Romantic influences on narrative genres in ethnography and find within them tacit messages that could serve to justify oppression.

These explorations into the analysis of language develop theoretical and methodological refine-ments necessary to thinking about qualitative inquiry since the linguistic turn (Rorty, 1967).

In the first chapter of this section, "Content Inference Fields in Intersubjective Space," Phil Carspecken and Ran Zhang combine intensive theory development with data analysis illustrating the use of the theoretical advances. Carspecken and Zhang reinterpret concepts we are already familiar with, such as "structure," "illocution," "interactive setting," "objectivation," (and more) within a theory of communicative pragmatics and inferential semantics. They invent quite a few new terms in the process: for example, "temporal compression," "illocution-ary inference fields," and "intersubjective space." The concept of intersubjective space involves a virtual space involving possible subject positions that involve transpersonal illocutionary and content inferential relations. Intersubjective space is a concept relevant to many things, among them the nature of logic, the commitment and entitlement formations that form dur-ing interactions, and recognition and existential needs. Although the theory introduced in this chapter seems very abstract when considered on its own, Carspecken and Zhang show in great detail how this theory captures, in the form of reconstruction, very concrete features of hu-man interaction that participants implicitly understand and make use of. The section on data analysis not only serves to illustrate use of Carspecken and Zhang's theoretical work, it also models various ways of presenting and analyzing recorded human interactions. Back-and-forth displays with columns for different types of codes, nested setting displays, and reconstructed/ graphically represented content inference fields are examples of the contributions to method one can find in this chapter.

In Chapter 12, Benetta Johnson explores the use of personal singular and plural pronouns in the talk of African Americans describing their experiences at a predominately white uni-versity. Johnson develops the concept of descriptive pronouns that invoke narrative relational structure between the pronoun use and the storyteller. Johnson refuses to take linguistic sub-stitutions for granted and instead turns a microscopic look at their use and does so in order to render a more exacting understanding of her participants' experiences. Her close analysis is both subtle and sophisticated. It stands as a linguistic critique and an exemplar in hermeneutics.

Yi-Ping Huang and Phil Carspecken offer some theoretical considerations of human iden-tity that depart from poststructuralist statements about the nonunity and nonintegrated self (even about the "illusion" of subjectivity in some cases), which they say have not been consis-tently formulated in relation to the assumptions about knowledge and knowledge claims made by their formulators. The theoretical discussions provided by Huang and Carspecken relocate some of Hegel's philosophical forms, particularly those of "negation," "the negative," and "de-terminate negation." Unity and integration both are necessarily claimed features of human identity that usually do not manifest as such empirically. The "self" contains a transcending, negative feature that no positive representation can capture. Hegel is put together with Mead, Habermas, Dilthey, and others, and the resulting theoretical themes are then illustrated and further explored through application to self-narrative interviews.

Norm Denzin has pushed symbolic interactionism and pragmatism from inside to develop the concept of performativity and an interest in the performance of meaning for qualitative research. Denzin argues that all meaning is performance and that to understand others is to understand them in the context of performance. These points could be made more precise. This is exactly what Corinne Datchi has done in her chapter on performing identity stories in pyschotherapeutic interactions. Datchi drew on performative theories of meaning to develop analytic tools useful in conducting critical qualitative research. Her chapter illustrates the tight connection between theory and practice as she explores new ways to comprehend the identity negotiations that occurred between therapist and client across the counseling sessions.

In the last chapter of this section, "Narrative and Genre in Qualitative Research: The Case of Romanticism," Amir Marvasti and Christopher Faircloth explore traditions of romanticism that they see as implicit and common in the narrative genres of ethnography. They argue for careful attention to the process of writing in qualitative research, as well as its content. They note that genres are never neutral or detached from history and that relations of power are embedded in the frames that narratives create. In the case of romanticism they draw out three themes—exoticism, authenticity, and moralism—and show that these tend to gloss over power differentials and reinforce a mainstream, modern conception of individualism, overshadowing alternative moral and social possibilities.

Methodological Explorations of Structural and Institutional Phenomena

Drawing on Habermas's distinction between the lifeworld and the system, structures and institutions are the focus of the five chapters in this next section. As mentioned earlier, Habermas (1987) theorizes that institutions are the switching place between the lifeworld and the system.

Structures are lifeworld phenomena, but they inhabit the social coordination of activities in ways that can be identified as media and outcomes of action not necessarily intended by actors. Structures are often taken up by actors as less reflective resources and constraints on their interpretations that are mostly taken for granted. Structures can be reconstructed across a variety of actions over time and space—they do not exist in time and space. They must be inferred not observed. The reconstruction of cultural structures provides researchers with provisional descriptions of cultural material that has assumed objectified form for its participants. For Giddens, who draws on Marx, action and structure presuppose one another. They are not dualisms, but a duality. The duality of structure relates "to the fundamentally recursive character of social life, and expresses the mutual dependence of structure and agency. . . [in other words, the duality means that] structure is both the medium and outcome of the practices involved in social interaction through both society and culture, conditions for acting and acting." (Giddens, 1979/1990, p. 69). "The reasons actors supply discursively for their conduct in the course of practical queries [even those that come through interviews, for example] stand in a relation of some tension to the rationalization of action as actually embodied within the stream of conduct of the actor" (Giddens, 1979/1990, p. 57). Giddens (1979/1990) produces what he calls a stratification model of social action that has the actor engaged in reflexive monitoring of action and the rationalization and motivation of action set within a context of unacknowledged conditions of action and unintended consequences of action.

Moreover, studying institutions provides a way for researchers to see how people are negotiating, navigating, and engaging with system-level imperatives. The authors examine the way states and legal institutions influence everyday life, through laws and legal methods of interpretation, through textbooks/texts, and other cultural products where the coordination of human activity is carried out through institutional, structural, and systematic means. Concomitantly, these authors examine how people draw on and negotiate these influences on their activities. Making these influences, resources, and constraints explicit involves a set of methodological principles, concepts, and tools and it is this with which we find the authors of these chapters wrestling. Two of the chapters—one by J. Debora Hinderliter Ortloff and the other by

Barbara Dennis—involve an analysis of cultural structures). In their respective chapters, Nurit Stadler and Beverly Stoeltje examine complicated authority structures as employed through legal systems and religious texts respectively. In her chapter, Rebecca Riall demonstrates the mutual benefit and necessity of integrating anthropological approaches to qualitative research (reflecting more of a lifeworld account of social life) with legal studies (reflecting more of a structural and systematic account of social life). While these studies all use lifeworld data, they push into provisional descriptions of social coordination. In the first chapter of this section, Nurit Stadler reports on her study of the inner workings of an "ultra-Orthodox Jewish community" called Haredi. She found little methodological literature to guide her, particularly with respect to how fundamentalist community members tend to appropriate spiritual texts. Stadler's honest account of her ethnographic experiences and decisions fills a much needed gap in the scholarship about how one goes about studying fundamentalist institutions in an ethical manner. Honoring the scriptural mode of life emphasized within the community, Stadler collaborated with Haredi yeshiva to develop a canon-infused approach that delivered insights relevant to understanding Haredi. The enforced boundary between outsiders and insiders was traversed and Stadler was able to capture subtle in-group diversity with respect to how texts were interpreted.

Debora Ortloff did a textual analysis of German textbooks with an interest in articulating possible state intentions regarding diversity as they might be expressed both through policy and through state-adopted texts. Ortloff argues that the traditional hermeneutic interests of qualitative researchers are often complicated by concerns that are better grasped at a structural level. She advances framing theory as a way to explicate cultural structures. The structural analysis links the discourse of texts with the cultural milieu and educational messages associated with the specific substance of the texts, illustrating the interpretive basis of textbook analyses. Ortloff wanted to deal with the question of how any given ethnographic or qualitative research example or finding is connected to a systematically coordinated set of activities. To do this, Ortloff reconstructs structures from empirical data instead of fitting data to existing theories about systemic and cultural phenomena of interest.

Beverly Stoeltje uses the example of Asante queen mothers' courts in Ghana to show the importance of context in researching legal institutions. The courts handle conflicts that arise over custom—verbal agreements and commonly held norms and penalties—and frequently deal with claims made by women. The role of customary legal institutions, she argues, tends to be understated in academia. Among the Asante, they provide a voice and an audience for ordinary people, and also often enable women to use traditionally female ways of speaking to their advantage. Stoeltje gives a beautifully detailed description of court procedures, emphasizing local understandings of the process and the roles of the people involved. She also describes some of the specific conventions involved in doing research there. She argues for the importance of understanding Ghana's particular history and its dual-gender traditions of queen mother chieftaincy. Its courts, she claims, offer an essential space for agency and negotiation, despite operating within a formerly colonized state that has adopted many more typically Western models of governance.

Rebecca Riall offers narratives about two researchers—an attorney and a qualitative social researcher, showing the contrasting perspectives assumed in each process. She illustrates her arguments further with examples from Native American treaty law, showing how what are assumed to be the facts of a legal argument often include highly subjective interpretations and definitions, and how legal investigations tend to preclude social contexts and implications because of an emphasis on precedent. As a result, essential information can be lost. In treaty law, the legal documents that still provide precedents were negotiated in contexts of highly uneven power between the Euro-American powers and the Native nations in question. This is reflected in assumptions that rights of various kinds, and even sovereignty itself, have been "given," by European and United States governments to Indian nations, rather than recognized. Riall's chapter vividly shows the impact of research style and research conventions on findings, and she argues that each of the two approaches—legal research and qualitative social research—has something to offer the other. Social research can potentially help fill in some of the injustice and misinformation embedded in legal struggles over native sovereignty, and may also provide groundwork for building new legal theory that is both more emancipatory and more practical.

Barbara Dennis studied a group of friends and their experiences caring for and with one another. Her original analysis provided a thorough description of what the friends would have said they experienced. And yet, there was an un(der)-acknowledged set of patterns that were part of the description of the caring that was not precisely or easily told through the narratives as they were. Articulating these structures is not an explanatory effort, but a descriptive effort. The descriptions move beyond, without excluding, the hermeneutic analysis of the experiences and activities of the friends. This structural analysis gets at the cultural conditions through which the friends interacted, particularly with respect to how they cared for one another through those interactions. The analysis of structures draws on Gidden's (1979/1990) ideas on the analysis of structures and agency as elaborated by Carspecken (1996).

The Critical Engagement of Qualitative Inquiry in the Social World

And finally, we look at what qualitative research does in practice. We look at how it engages with the world and at some of the recent uses to which it has been put. "Inquiry which aspires to the name 'critical' must be connected to an attempt to confront the injustice of a particular society or public sphere within the society. Research thus becomes a transformative endeavor unembarrassed by the label 'political' and unafraid to consummate a relationship with emancipatory consciousness" (Kincheloe and McLaren, 2007, p. 406). This last section of the book addresses the question of "What are the effects of your research for the world?" The chapters in this section exemplify a few of the many possibilities for qualitative research, for example, qualitative research as philosophy and as healing. This section reflects an intersection of metatheoretical principles, substantive interests, and methodological promise. Qualitative inquiry, in its direct engagement with participants, has the special opportunity to be part of a transformative potential. In recent decades, feminists have asked researchers to think about the difference between doing research *on* subjects and doing research *with* participants. Researchers cannot rest content with producing answers to research questions on a substantive level, and must also hold themselves accountable to understanding the effects of their research for the people with whom they are working.

There is not much written on doing qualitative inquiry with children, but the first chapter in this final section is an exception. Alba Lucy Guerrero and Mary Brenner each conducted studies with vulnerable youth using media. It was important to both of them to engage in research that was capable of benefiting their child participants as well as the larger society. By reflecting on their two studies, Guerrero and Brenner are able to locate ways in which their studies had an impact on the lives of the children who participated in their research, including issues that posed challenges for them as researchers.

Grace Giorgio shares with us her personal hope for and experiences with the healing potential of qualitative research. She begins with a story about how her own published research on lesbian relational battering brought her face-to-face with this healing possibility. In this chapter, she explores the characteristics of qualitative research that make it particularly well-suited to healing possibilities. She examines qualitative inquiry with her eye toward healing and trauma. Readers will find this honest and openly compassionate way of thinking about and doing qualitative research is critical in the most personal way. This chapter proposes, by example, an alternative to the aloof, unengaged researcher, with a more positivist approach to inquiry. This inspiring chapter makes it impossible to embark on a qualitative research endeavor without imaging its healing possibilities.

Kip Kline writes on the relationship of philosophy to ethnography, specifically his ethnography of hip hop artistry. As Kline argues, qualitative methodology is unavoidably philosophical. First, Kline carefully details the way metatheoretical concepts were employed ethnographically. Minimally speaking, ethnography will involve philosophical claims about what meaning is and how the social world is conceptualized. Then, of course, there will be philosophical underpinnings related to the substantive interests of inquiry. Kline explores the Habermasian concepts he drew on as metatheory as well as other philosophical concepts that were entailed in the way he was engaging with the data. Then, Kline illustrates how the hip hop artists he worked with were doing philosophy on the street. Kline argues that doing philosophy through critical ethnography is a way to better understand the philosophy of everyday lived experiences.

The book ends with a chapter on participatory action research or PAR, which is explicitly conducted in terms of its meaning for participants. PAR was developed originally through the work of Orlando Fals-Borda in Colombia. Taking issue with dominant views of social research taught in developed nations like Europe and the United States, Fals-Borda formulated a way to do research that combines it with community-based decision making and mobilization for change. PAR has taken root in Australia under the hands of Kemis and McTaggert and also, in different ways, in England. In this chapter, Doris Santos, a fellow Colombian and friend of the late Orlando Fals-Borda, reviews the history of PAR. The breadth of her knowledge and work in the field situates her as uniquely capable to produce this history. Doris Santos has applied PAR in a number of innovative and socially important studies of her own. Her chapter reviews the key tenets of PAR, and its history, and offers a new interpretation of it by making links with the philosophy of Hannah Arendt.

Conclusion

This book reflects a conversation among a diverse collection of scholarship. The authors are united in their insistence on calling the status quo into question and their willingness to reflect on their own practices. In fact, many of the chapters were developed precisely out of such reflections and openness. Peter McLaren (1986) once wrote that researchers should be willing to be "wounded in the field," and one way researchers interpret that call is to examine their research claims, their epistemological beliefs, and their personal commitments in order to better understand what they are doing. One way to encourage such a process among scholars is to invite dialogue across diverse perspectives. As we were editing the various chapters, we found our own ways of thinking called into question. We did not immediately agree even with each other about such things as the extent to which we should use the word "critical." Our work is not equally affiliated with Habermas or feminism or other critical perspectives…. This is true across authors and among ourselves as editors of the text. Our commitments and passions for understanding one another and for locating our social science in a trajectory of hope may find different sources, varied potentials, unfamiliar interests, and all of this is for the good. Inevitably and importantly arguments will emerge. With a concerted focus on philosophical concepts we intend to provide substance for the debates of practice and theory.

References

Carspecken, P. (1996). *Critical Ethnography in Educational Research: A Theoretical and Practical Guide.* London and New York: Routledge.

Giddens, A. (1979/1990). *Central problems in social theory: Action, structure and contradiction in social analysis.* Berkeley and Los Angeles: University of California Press.

Habermas, J. (1984). *The theory of communicative action.* Vol. 1: *Reason and the rationalization of society.* Boston: Beacon.

Habermas, J. (1987). *The theory of communicative action.* Vol. 2: *Lifeworld and system. A critique of functionalist reason.* Boston: Beacon.

Larsson, S. (2010). Om generalisering från kvalitativa studier (On generalization in qualitative research; in Swedish). In I. Eriksson, V. Lindberg, & E. Österlind (Eds.), *Uppdrag undervisning: Kunskap och lärande.* Lund: Studentlitteratur.

Lincoln, Y., and Guba, E. (1985). *Naturalistic Inquiry.* Thousand Oaks, CA: Sage Publications, Inc.

Kincheloe, J., and McLaren, P. (2007). Rethinking critical theory and qualitative research. In N. Denzin and Y. Lincoln (Eds), *The Landscape of Qualitative Research.* Thousand Oaks, CA: Sage Publications Inc.

McLaren, P. (1986). *Schooling as ritual performance: Towards a political economy of educational symbols and gestures.* London: Routledge & Kegan Paul.

Minh-ha, Trinh T. (2009) *Women, Native, Other: Writing Postcoloniality and Feminism.* Bloomington: Indiana University Press.

Rorty, R. (Ed.). (1967). *The linguistic turn: Recent essays in philosophical method.* Chicago: University of Chicago Press.

Philosophical Explorations

CHAPTER ONE

"Validity Crisis" in Qualitative Research

Still? Movement Toward a Unified Approach

BARBARA DENNIS (FORMERLY KORTH)

For a while now, academics have produced a cacophony of validity concepts and anti-validity rhetoric that can be stultifying, confusing, frustrating, infuriating, even (for some) silencing. Dialogue on the topic of validity reaches a fever pitch in journal articles and conference presentations where the choice of words indicates the magnitude with which communities of researchers are both laying stake to their own conceptions of truth and validity and where they are simultaneously wrestling with the uncertainty/promise of understanding one another's research (Schwandt, 1996; Alexander, 1990). Despite this noise, chapters on qualitative research in educational research texts (Onwuegbuzie & Leech, 2005) and research reports themselves (Aguinaldo, 2004) give relatively little attention to validity—the issues seem almost too complicated and too divisive to deal with so people tend to write for an audience that already agrees with them in terms of validity (Polkinghorne, 2007). The traditional definition of validity for qualitative research involved the degree to which the researcher's account of the phenomena matched the participants' reality (Eisner & Peshkin, 2000), but this definition is now totally up for grabs (Rolfe, 2006). Polkinghorne (2007) says that validity is not even properly thought of as a definitional concept and should instead be thought of as a "prototype" concept.

There are moments in the history of doing quantitative social science where validity debates were prominent and where progress was made in clarifying what manner of validity questions arise in the context of doing quantitative inquiry (for examples, see Campbell, 1957; Campbell and Stanley, 1963; Cronbach, 1971; Messick, 1989; Kane, 1992; Shepard, 1997). The debates among quantitative researchers are not as widely scattered as those we find going on among qualitative methodologists, but they do, nonetheless, address some similar definitional and practical complexities (Wolming & Wikström, 2010). According to Wolming and Wikström (2010), the fervent debate among statisticians that occurred in the 1980s and 1990s has come to a recent standstill, with no progress in terms of the debated issues being resolved or more deeply understood (Winter, 2000). Moreover, the validity debates among statisticians have not explicitly called into question the very nature of doing social science inquiry, though there have been significant shifts in validity conceptions. For example, Cronbach (1971) and Messick (1989) invited a shift from talking about the validity of instruments to talking about the validity of interpretations with respect to research that uses tests for data gathering. For qualitative researchers, the "conversation" on validity is a conversation about the nature of understanding, the status of truth, the possibility of justification and rational deliberation, and the purpose of inquiry. In quantitative social science, these sorts of validity concerns lurk behind the definitional reification that has been achieved. The reification has resulted in these basic concerns only surfacing periodically and even then without much of a splash (despite work like Kane, 1992). Efforts among quantitative methodologists to address these more basic questions concerning validity have been largely ignored in practice (Wolming & Wikström, 2010). Despite some theoretical advances toward the development of a more unifying concept of validity (Messick, 1989), the reified notions of construct, content, and criterion validity are still primarily treated as types of validity dependent upon the idea that it is a test that is validated, not a score or an interpretation.

The status of validity conceptualization for qualitative inquiry is contrastingly problematic. The contemporary qualitative research literature poses such a plethora of concepts, ideas, arguments, and approaches to validity that making sense of the literature and weighing into the varied discussions are difficult at best (Seale, 1999; Smith and Deemer, 2000; Lewis & Ritchie, 2003) and contribute to the "crisis in validity" in qualitative research (Gergen & Gergen, 2000; Denzin & Lincoln, 1994, 2000; Lincoln & Denzin, 2000).

While the proliferation of ideas might be inspiring, creative, and insightful, there seems to me a need for bringing the conversations together. The risk is that in the bringing together we lose ideas, we close off conversations, and we end up subjugating some ideas to other ideas for reasons that might not be shared. Another possibility, in light of what we have witnessed among quantitative inquiry practices, is that we end up reifying constructs to such an extent that their intractability produces a paralysis in theory and practice. There is synergy between the lack of judgment over which validity concepts/constructs might be more or less valid and the way the contemporary proliferation continues to churn out new ideas without taking positions capable of settling the question of validity and of validity constructs themselves. For some researchers (Richardson, 1994, 1997; Schwandt, 2000; Lincoln & Guba, 2000; Bochner, 2000; Denzin, 2008) this unwieldy proliferation would be counted as a strength of the literature, but it seems to me that the contemporary conversation is stunted because we are not actually relating these disparate and varied ideas with one another in ways that would lead us to more deeply understand validity (and I am not alone in this view, see also Tracy, 2010; Polkinghorne, 2007; Carspecken, 2003; for examples). We have a flat development and array of ideas that are not gaining in the sort of complexity that many of us envision (Donmoyer, 1996). The validity conversation is, practically speaking, difficult to jump into, maintain, and develop in its current state and this is a problem with ramifications for methodological practices and theory (Tracy, 2010; Creswell & Miller, 2000; Scheurich, 1997).

Typically, the issue of validity is approached by applying one's own community's protocols about what, in its view, is acceptable evidence and appropriate analysis to the other community's research. In these cases, the usual conclusion is that the other community's research is lacking in support for its knowledge claims. I think this cross-community approach is unproductive and leads to a dead end because each community is making different kinds of knowledge claims. (Polkinghorne, 2007, p. 475)

A number of attempts at managing the various validity concepts and practices have been developed (see Maxwell, 1992, 1996; Hammersley, 1992; Winter, 2000; Tracy, 2010) as well as attempts to start anew (see Lather, 1993). These efforts suggest some impetus toward bringing diverse sets of validity ideas and concerns into a common dialogue. Most approaches to doing this start with research practice and definitional criteria that was established through research practice. My approach will be different because I will use ordinary life conceptions of validity as the basis for talking about validity in research (I am directly following Habermas, 1984, and Carspecken, 1996, 2003). The trajectory of this chapter points toward a unifying concept of validity that ought to be relevant for quantitative and qualitative methodology (though the focus here will be on its relevance for qualitative methodological theory and practice). My proposal should be challenged and queried, for in the end, that is what validity is based on. To begin with, I will briefly describe the contemporary state of affairs regarding the validity discourse among qualitative researchers. Then, I will introduce the problems and possibilities of moving toward a unified approach to validity. I establish the basis for a unified concept of validity in our ordinary concepts of validity, then, I demonstrate how this ordinary description of validity is applicable to social science (Habermas, 1984, 1987; Carspecken, 2003; Korth, 2005). These two sections lead to a situated articulation of what this unified concept might look like. This approach to validity is not new with me (see, most particularly, Habermas and Carspecken as cited above), but I am hoping that this detailed examination and explanation will seal its relevancy for the validity crisis and increase its understanding among researchers.

State of Affairs: Cacaphony

Lewis (2009) reviewed validity conceptions according to philosophical eras in an effort to arrive at what validity might look like in this fifth (post-modernist) moment (Denzin & Lincoln, 1994) of conducting qualitative inquiry. His trajectory demonstrates the increasing complexity, divergence, and discontent riddling the scholarship. He suggests that there is unified agreement about the nature and status of validity and reliability for both quantitatively and qualitatively conducted inquiries among positivists and post-positivists, but that constructivists were not content with these constructs and their definitional baggage. Soon new words replaced old ones. Transferability as a kind of generalizability was the more advanced concept meant to supplant constructs oriented toward external validity. Words like "dependability," "consistency," and "accuracy" were, taken all together, a better fit for qualitative research than the quantitative rendition of reliability. Credibility and truthfulness were more acceptable ways of talking about internal validity for qualitative research. And, confirmability replaced objectivity. By the mid-80s:

> [r]esearch was being dispersed in various interpretive forms, with no consensus between the different paradigms within qualitative research (posistivists, postpositivists, naturalists, constructivists, and the orientationalist inquirists) and the internal paradigms of the crisis of representation period (feminists, culturalists, Marxists, etc.) about the standard for validity and reliability (Lewis, 2009, p. 6)

And so the proliferation goes.

Onwuegbuzie and Leech (2005) identified 50 "components of validity or legitimation" in use by qualitative educational researchers. Fifty? Fifty! And since their publication, several more have popped up. One benefit of such a rich conceptual state of affairs is the extent to which the terms provide both the grounds and the substance for dialogue. Schwandt (2000) cogently argued that labeling complicated theoretical and practical ideas as this or that "is dangerous, for it blinds us to enduring issues, shared concerns, and points of tension that cut across the landscape of the movement, issues that each inquirer must come to terms with in developing an identity as a social inquirer" (p. 205) and, indeed, perhaps this has been evidenced in the discourse on validity in quantitative approaches with the tendency to remain tethered to construct, content, and criterion validity. However, failing to bring in some coherency and conciseness across the divergent ways of thinking about validity makes it difficult to figure out how to go about conducting valid qualitative research (Tracy, 2010; Lewis, 2009; Creswell & Miller, 2000). Does one just pick the validity concepts that seem most helpful? How does one determine the extent to which one's inquiry is valid? These are the sorts of questions that Tracy (2010) says cause problems for students of qualitative inquiry. It's no wonder that there are researchers (for examples, Lather 1993; Richardson, 1994, 1997) that purposely strike off on an altogether "transgressive" path (Lather, 1993; Rolfe, 2006).

The cacophony is marked by different approaches that have different sorts of goals. Moving on from the proliferation of constructs, each with their important nuance, I provide a sample of the variety of approaches scholars have taken to deal with validity in qualitative inquiry. I do this in order to demonstrate the breadth and unwieldy nature of the discourse, but the sampling is by no means exhaustive and at best can be thought of as illustrative. I analyzed the literature and have organized it according to various ways validity seems to be conceptualized. Doing this helps to highlight the differing ways that a unified approach might be developed. The review is a simplified rendition of a complicated set of dialogues. Much more emphasis is placed on the proposal that follows than on the breadth of existing literature.

Organizing/Categorizing Validity According to Research Design or Paradigm

Creswell and Miller (2000)[1] argued that the validity criteria to which researchers might hold themselves accountable are dependent upon two attributes of their research; namely, the particular methodological design and the paradigmatic assumptions invoked by the researcher. Thus, Creswell and Miller's approach to validity has been to organize the range of options in the field according to research design or paradigm, locating specific constructs and methods appropriate for different methodologies with their varying paradigmatic assumptions. This approach is well cited and seems particularly useful for novice qualitative researchers. It is nonoffensive and inclusive in the sense that Creswell and Miller refrain from judging the validity of the different designs and paradigms with their concommitment criteria for validity. It serves as a basic description of a simplified set of paradigms and designs.

Design-Specific Criteria

A substantial number of scholars discuss validity concepts from within one particular design or approach. This seems like a spin-off of the tack Creswell and Miller (2000) have taken. Whereas

Creswell and Miller (2000) survey across approaches, scholarship in this design-specific group focuses on one particular theoretical attitude and/or design and addresses validity as a coherent byproduct of that attitude/design.[2] There are many examples of this, such as addressing validity as it applies to a grounded theory study (for instance, Elliott & Lazenblatt, 2005) or narrative study (Polkinghorne, 2007). Sikes and Gale (2006) created a web-based module for learning about narrative inquiry. In that particular module, there is a section on how one might go about evaluating narrative research. Drawing heavily on Richardson's (2000) work, Sikes and Gale propose tentative criteria for evaluating creative, transgressive and nontraditional forms of research such as we find in narrative inquiry. They are hoping to inspire conversations about criteria, acknowledging that validity propositions should be open to criticism. It is informative to look at the substance of the criteria to see what it is they envision as validity standards. They propose that good research: (1) makes a "substantive contribution" to the "understanding of a social and cultural life"; (2) has "aesthetic merit" noticeable through the way it "opens our senses"; (3) addresses the complexities of representation through reflexive and participatory engagement; (4) has a potential impact for its participants; and (5) what they refer to as "experience-near" accounts—accounts that are fair to the participants (Sikes & Gale, 2006). Sikes and Gale also provided a few techniques for addressing these validity criteria. While Sikes and Gale recognize the risks involved in laying out such criteria, for our purposes, the paper serves as an example of how validity criteria are generated within the context of a specific design or approach linking the criteria as closely to the design characteristics and theoretical principles that are the foundation of the design/approach.

Identifying Validity in Terms of Specific Threats

One way of thinking about validity has involved conceptualizing what threats might accrue both in the general sense, as related to the design, and in the specific sense, as related to the specific implementation/conduct of a research project. Maxwell (1992)[3], in an effort to create a dialogue, wrote an article on the topic of validity in qualitative research. He articulated five domains through which validity can be queried in qualitative research. Those five domains include descriptive validity, which involves the extent to which one's descriptions of an objective nature are accurate; interpretational validity, which involves the extent to which one's interpretations articulate the range of plausible, possible interpretations the participants themselves might understand through their interactions with one another; theoretical validity, which involves articulating how well a theoretical explanation fits the data it is meant to explain; evaluative validity, which involves the extent to which an evaluative framework can be appropriately applied to making sense of the data; and lastly two forms of generalizability. Internal generalizability refers to the extent to which particular inferences can be generalized to the group of participants involved in the study and their particular modes of understanding. External generalizability refers to the extent to which particular inferences can be generalized beyond the group, setting, and particular context within which the inferences were derived.

Organizing Validity According to Research Purpose

In a manner that is similar to organizing validity according to research design or paradigm, Cho and Trent (2006) identified two main types of research genres according to their purposes (transactional and transformational). Then, they identified validity approaches appropriate to the underlying assumptions of the two main purposes. Their work stands as a criticism of the approaches that are design specific because they think too much is made of design differences when, instead, the purposes of research are a better way to identify underlying paradigmatic assumptions that would be relevant to matching up with validity tools. Cho and Trent extend Donmoyer's (2001) organization of qualitative research to identify relevant "uses" of validity techniques according to each of the five purposes Donmoyer (2001) identified. For example, Cho and Trent identified the main use of validity for research oriented through "truth-seeking" purposes was to establish the correct answer (Cho & Trent, 2006, p. 326). The specific validity techniques, it is argued, do not ensure the study is valid, but can be engaged holistically—that is, across the entire research process—to address the kind of validity that is useful for the particular purposes of the inquiry.

Counter-validity, Transvalidity, and Transgressive Constructs

Lather (2007) writes of transgressive validity.

> The following [approach to validity] is a dispersion, circulation, and proliferation of counter-practices of authority that take the crisis of representation into account. In creating a nomadic and dispersed validity, I employ a strategy of excess and categorical scandal in the hope of both imploding ideas of policing social science and working against the inscription of "another regime of truth." (Lather, 2007, p. 120).

Lather's work aims to be an antithesis of modern validity strangleholds. In 1993, Lather presented the idea of catalytic validity, which asks researchers to consider how the findings of the research and/or the research process itself contribute to transforming both the community and the researchers who were involved in the study. Catalytic validity is transgressive in two fundamental ways. First, it speaks of a different kind of relationship between researchers and participants. Second, it suggests that the primary meaning of a research endeavor is its transformative potential and worthwhileness. This second point is transgressive in a summative way. That is, it suggests that data collection and analysis are not the focal junctures through which research ought to be assessed as valid.[4] Lather and Smithies's (1997) heart-rendering poststructuralist account of women living with HIV/AIDS is a stunning, bold, unnerving example of how this transgressive and catalytic validity is enacted.

The Problems and Possibilities of a Holistic Approach to Validity: Unifying Without Simplifying?

Campbell and Stanley's (1963) influential scholarship identifying threats to internal and external validity has been importantly consequential in conceptualizing and making practical validity concerns for experimental and quasi-experimental quantitative designs, although it left these concerns less articulated with respect to correlational or descriptive quantitative studies. The debate between Cronbach and his colleagues Cook and Campbell has been revisited for experimental and quasi-experimental designs, but these debates have not been extended or examined with respect to nonexperimental designs (Shadish, Cook, & Campbell, 2002). In an educational age in the U.S. that re-emphasizes randomized control trials as the gold standard of educational research, perhaps this revisitation makes sense despite the limitation it reflects in terms of inquiry as a social scientific field (Denzin & Giardina, 2008).

Messick (1989) (as not the only, but perhaps the most widely cited scholar), encouraged a unitary concept of validity, meant to locate validity concerns variously related to constructs, criterion-related issues, content, and social consequences in one conceptual apparatus or system. Messick's unitary system of validity was also a more expansive notion, unifying and adding to the prominent notions of validity to which researchers using quantitative methods were being held accountable. Other scholars argued that the best way to unify the concepts of validity would be to focus and simplify what was being conceptualized as validity. This would not force researchers to discount important concerns for how research was applied, but the definitional simplification would result in these kinds of concerns not being treated as a matter of validity (Popham, 1997; Mehrens, 1997). It should be noted that there has been difficulty translating these theoretical ideas of a unitary validity into practice (Wolming & Wikström, 2010).

Given that there has been limited progress toward unifying constructs of validity for quantitative inquiry, and we can see that the conversation on validity among qualitative researchers is far from unified, what sort of progress is possible for unifying across quantitative and qualitative methods? One approach to unification basically held that concepts and standards of validity as they had been worked out by quantitative researchers should be thought of as universal to research, in general, and thus applicable to qualitative research directly. To be sure, the work of qualitative research was blatantly misunderstood and misread when the traditional quantitative ways of reading research were simply applied to the practices of qualitative inquiry (Aguinaldo, 2004; Lewis, 2009; Lincoln & Guba, 2000). Qualitative researchers were asked to verify and justify their research methods and findings through questions that did not seem either applicable or appropriate (Aguinaldo, 2004). For example, if the findings of an ethnography of a school were presented, the ethnographer might have been asked: "But how do you know whether or not your findings will generalize to other schools?" as the main validity issue to which the research should be accountable. If this question was not answered in a way that might be similar to the answer a statistician might provide in describing how her research was generalizable from a sample to a population, the qualitative findings would likely be discounted as invalid or irrelevant despite the fact that ethnography was usually conducted for reasons unrelated to this kind of generalizing.

It will come as no surprise to social scientists that there has been little effort to apply concepts and standards of validity developed among qualitative researchers to quantitative approaches. If the approach to unifying validity concepts merely involved subsuming the expectations of qualitative inquiry to those of quantitative inquiry on the technical level or vice versa, an oversimplification and misunderstanding would ensue. This is one important impetus behind Lather's (1993) efforts to problematize the historical taken-for-grantedness of validity in social science.

One is left to wonder what other possibilities there might be for developing a more unified validity theory. Rolfe (2006) argues that any attempt to bring together approaches to validity across the various qualitative methodological traditions will prove futile. But perhaps the proliferation of validity concepts among qualitative researchers opens up new possibilities for exploring unified concepts of validity precisely because traditional knowledge about validity, in this context, cannot be taken for granted (Tracy, 2010). Moreover, it is inevitable that researchers involved in the simultaneous use of both qualitative and quantitative approaches to inquiry will have to confront the tensions across the different terms and concepts through which validity is addressed and this could contribute to a more unified approach to social science validity. There are some efforts toward this end already at work (see Shaffer & Serlin, 2004; Onwuegbuzie & Johnson, 2006; Mertens, 2007).

Among qualitative researchers, I am not the first to suggest movement toward inclusive, unifying validity conceptions. I will begin this section of the chapter by introducing the work of a few scholars whose exemplary efforts at organizing and unifying validity conceptions with respect to qualitative inquiry contribute to the dialogue.

Sarah Tracy

Tracy (2010) drew on her experience as a teacher of qualitative research to propose a twofold schematic for thinking about validity. Her idea can be considered a conceptual advance of approaches that categorize the various ways of thinking about validity across the field of qualitative inquiry. Tracy equates "validity" with "good" in so far as the characteristics she identifies are said to describe good research, and then she assumes that what is meant by "good" is that the research is valid. She suggested that there are eight common markers of goodness (p. 139) that can be examined through a variety of practices (techniques, crafts) that address particular elements specific to each of the common markers. She takes a "big-tent" approach, having reviewed the literature and synthesized it to locate these eight common markers of good qualitative research. She contends that these markers are prevalent regardless of which specific theoretical or design approach one employs. Their particular manifestations may vary. That is, the way the eight markers might actually be put into practice given particular methodological decisions and proclivities will vary. The proposal is a holistic, integrated one. The basis of it is this set of markers assumed to be commonly applicable and that were derived via a review of the validity literature. Given each of those markers, there would be a variety of possible ways to address the common concerns that one might select contingent on one's philosophical orientation. In this way, the markers transcend orientation. Tracy skillfully knits together many of the various constructs of validity within her scheme.

Here is the basic skeleton of a schematic depicting her approach (it's not entirely filled in for want of space):

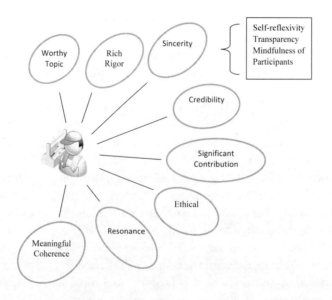

Now let's focus on just the common marker of "Sincerity" to see how Tracy is developing this twofold idea. You can see that for the marker there are qualities that would be involved in the extent to which one would be judged "sincere" through one's research, and there are specific things to do to increase the extent of one's sincerity. The flexibility so noteworthy and appreciative in qualitative research is respected on the level of how one goes about addressing the common markers.

- Assessing biases introspectively
- Include self-reflexivity in field notes
- Self as instrument
- Get feedback from participants

- Auditing (show methodological details)
- Disclosing challenges
- Giving credit where it is due

- Consider the needs of the participants
- Behave earnestly, empathetically, kindly with self-deprecation
- Be vulnerable in the field

To develop this particular marker, Tracy drew together the following validity constructs she found in the field. For example, she refers to Emerson, Fretz, and Shaw's (1995) inclusion of self-reflexivity in their field notes. She could have just as easily made reference to others, Peshkin (1988) and Korth (2005), as examples. My point here is that she identified a key element in the literature and then she showed how to establish criteria related to that element by synthesizing the scholarship—reminding us as qualitative researchers what we are saying about our own work. She refers to Seale (1999) and Creswell and Miller (2000) to talk about the method of auditing (using audit trails) to document the process one engages in as a way of increasing transparency. If you return to Tracy's (2010) article, you will notice that her chart only includes the first two sets of criteria, but her text talks about the third and so I added it to the scheme I created.

She skillfully pulls together the various constructs, ideas, and approaches. She locates them either at the level of criteria related to the eight common markers or at the level of craft (for example, how one goes about achieving sincerity, specifically). Gaps indicate gaps in the existing literature. For example, Tracy has identified criteria for assessing the marker "Worthy Topic," but not necessarily techniques or methods for applying those criteria to pieces of research. Further contributors could build on her work at this point.

Dennis Beach

Beach (2003) assumes a view of validity that is unifying through purpose and transgression. His unifying approach can be interpreted as a conceptual advance on validity discussions described above as related to organizing validity around purpose (e.g., Cho and Trent, 2006) and counter-validity/transgressive validity (Lather, 2007). Rather than acknowledging a set of categories of research linked to varying purposes (as did Cho and Trent, 2006), Beach argues that there is one significant reason for doing education research under the conditions of capitalism and this purpose has consequences for validity. Beach is concerned, fundamentally and solely, with research that serves to promote democracy over and against the pressures and illusions of a capitalist market system. "My suggestion is that because of the inequities of capitalism, education research should be concerned with trying to improve equity and democracy both within and through education and that it also requires a validity form that corresponds with this task" (Beach, 2003, p. 860). Beach goes on to indicate that catalytic validity is the only validity concept up to the task. As Beach has argued, it is most typical that education research reifies and supports the inequities that are the effects of capitalism. Rather than following Lather's (2007) ironic approach to validity as something that names itself in order to erase itself (Rolfe, 2006), Beach takes seriously the concept of catalytic validity—seriously enough to think it can serve as a unifying approach to validity across social science in the capitalistic milieu—ethical social science whose lust for democracy should not be assuaged.

Beach indicates that it is very difficult to conduct research that supports and engages in democratic practices because of contradictions that riddle our research (he is writing specifically about education research, but in a way that suggests his points are applicable regardless of the substantive social domain). These contradictions limit the validity of research in ways that are systematically ignored. The contradictions include:

a. the celebration of distance, objective truth, and neutrality rather than closeness, subjective engagement, and authenticity;

b. the creation of a labor hierarchy and theory-practice distinction that favors the decisions and ideas of theorists over practitioners with respect to truth claims;

c. the presence of a low exchange rate regarding care for the communities researched, where researchers leave the application of findings to others and wash their hands of any responsibility for the consequences of this application;

d. the production of alienating concepts (e.g., Spearman's g) that severely damage the ecology of genuine community and possibilities for equity and solidarity (see, e.g., racially slurring research such as that by Jensen, 1985a, 1985b, 1987). (Beach, 2003, p. 861)

One can see from the list of contradictions that traditional validity requirements for social science inquiry have, themselves, served to structure the contradictions. Beach holds that catalytic validity loosens research dependency on those first terms in the stated contradictions above. In his description of the research situation under capitalism, Beach (2003) argues that democratically valid inquiry, to be valid, must "contribute toward changing education [and other social contexts] in the interests of a more egalitarian form" and that "this can be done by researchers recognizing and showing in theoretical and practical detail what education actually involves for a population, how it occurs within the corrupted forms of symbolic exchange that we currently call schooling, and how class interests are presently disguised in and/or protected by education" (p. 864).

The background schematic that emerges through Beach's conceptualization of validity is vividly described as the practice and promise of research bursting through the capitalist conditions to transform them.

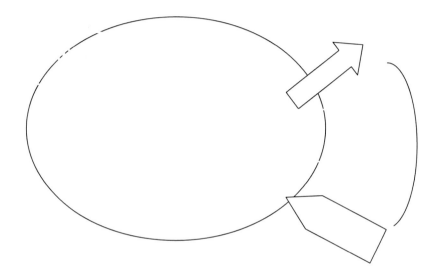

A microscopic view of this background schematic shows us the contrastive nature of the schema through three moments.

The first moment relates to the purposes of research. The first contrast internal to this first moment is a conflict between perpetuating/promoting capitalist economic and ideological conditions versus promoting and establishing democratic opportunities. The second moment relates to validity elements of engaging in democratic inquiry with an internal contrast between the validity requirements of democratic research, which include correspondence validity and catalytic validity. The third moment relates to the practice of democratic research with an internal contrast involving the challenges posed by capitalism, but with the possibilities for transforming the very conditions under which those challenges are sustained.

The internal relations of the contrast sets are not the same across the moments, and this seems to suggest that the moments actually have a trajectory—they are not flat, equivalent phases with characteristics, but rather dynamically evolving moments in the engagement of meaningful social science. The three moments are paradigmatically linked as a trajectory from the purposes to the possibilities. Beach locates validity as the catalyst and lynchpin between the purpose and the possibility of democratic inquiry within capitalist situations.

Practices of
Democratic
Research:
Challenges, but
Promise

Validity ELements
of Democratic
Research: Catalytic
Validity and
Correspondence
Validity

Purposes of
Research: Promote
Capitalism Vs.
Foster Democracy

Beach's unified approach to validity has less to do with specific techniques and more to do with the underlying momentum for social inquiry, most particularly education research.

Laurel Richardson

One way of proposing a unifying concept of validity is to describe the character of validity using a metaphor. This approach shares something in common with the one I will take up: it begins by describing validity itself, rather than by looking at research and trying to locate validity there. Richardson has provided a crucial voice in the scholarship on validity for qualitative inquiry. One of her most cited contributions has been the development of the metaphor "crystallization" for thinking about validity and methodology. The metaphor reflects the (at once) unitary and complicated "nature" of validity for qualitative researchers and expands on the triangulation metaphor that has wide currency in the discourse on validity in qualitative research.

> In postmodern mixed genre texts, we do not triangulate, we *crystallize*.... I propose that the central image for "validity" for postmodern texts is not the triangle—a rigid, fixed two-dimensional object. Rather the central imaginary is the crystal, which combines symmetry and substance with an infinite variety of shapes, substances, transmutations, multidimensionalities, and angles of approach. (Richardson, 2000, p. 934, emphasis in original)

Ellingson (2009) forged Richardson's "crystallization" metaphor into a framework for qualitative researchers to draw upon—putting "crystallization" into the context of a specified methodology for nontraditional qualitative inquiry (Cugno & Thomas, 2009). By developing a metaphor for validity, Richardson is, at base, locating characteristics of both validity and research as if they are really one and the same. Though certainly some evaluative criteria would be presupposed in these descriptive attributes, Richardson's work really stays with locating the characteristics of validity as doubling for characteristics of good research. She then engages people in interacting with those characteristics in studies—for example, encouraging people to use multiple dimensions and modalities. These characteristics enhance the validity of a project because they resist oversimplification, enabling the researcher to both accept and explore the complexities of the field, including one's own position in it, without reducing, masking, or hiding its validity issues.

Another metaphor that has gained some currency among qualitative researchers as a description of validity is the "rhizome." As with the above example, this metaphor doubles both as a description of validity and as a description of research. Rhizomes are interconnected networks or systems that are complex and tangled beneath the ground. "Rather than a linear progress, rhizomatics is a journey among intersections, nodes, and regionalizations through a multicentered complexity" (Lather, 2007, p. 124). This description of research begs for validity conceptions to mirror its principle characteristics, for example, to be inclusive of complexity.

In both of these cases, as with others that might be similar, the metaphor is considered a unifying concept that would apply to social science research in general, on the whole. But the metaphors are also complicated and inviting; inclusive and nondirective. Some people refer to them as ironic because they seem to turn the traditional way of thinking about validity on its head. They require us to recognize the characteristics that might map over to research/validity as a way of conceptualizing validity. Specific combinations of attributes and research decisions would be fit to the metaphor by aligning in saliency and quality.

From http://www.dicts.info/picture-dictionary.php?w=crystal. Accessed January 30, 2011. Used with permission.

Barbara Dennis

The path I want to forge toward a holistic concept of validity is one that has been developed through Habermas's (1984, 1987) critical theory and Carspecken's (2003) postenlightenment methodological theory. It is a path that begins with validity in the ordinary context and then moves into social science. Habermas's (1988) *On the Logic of the Social Sciences* pointed a way toward this unified theory of validity, which becomes more visible in terms of details in Habermas's *The Theory of Communicative Action* (*TCA*) (1984, 1987). In the *Logic of the Social Sciences*, Habermas establishes a procedure for connecting validity to the logic of doing social science across the various disciplines. Through this process, he raises questions that propel the reader toward an increasingly unified view of social science validity. For example, he begins by exploring the field of economics, which he argues has two prominent approaches—one that examines economy as a matter of normalized individual behavior and the other that examines economy as a matter of rational choice and deliberation. Habermas is able to argue that both approaches, when modified, contribute in different ways to a fuller understanding of human economic activities, because together they provide a richer description and explanation of those activities. Habermas explored what in practice seemed like divergent, oppositional approaches to validity with the logics of a given social science, and found convergence and correctives. That is, he used the benefits of one to correct the indulgences of another. More important than the really exciting content of his arguments is the structure and origination of the arguments themselves. Habermas kept making the validity assumptions explicit. That is, he looked at the ordinary context of proposing a particular logic to one's social science in conversation with one's colleagues and he brought out implicit validity conditions through which those arguments might be persuasive. It was on the level of examining these implicit conditions and truth claims that Habermas was able to point toward some unifying validity criteria for the social sciences. Carspecken (2003) took a similar approach in examining the philosophical underpinnings of postenlightenment theories of knowledge and inquiry. Both Habermas (1984, 1987) and Carspecken put into practice on the level of social science critique what we can find at work in the ordinary communicative context, and they both know they are doing this.

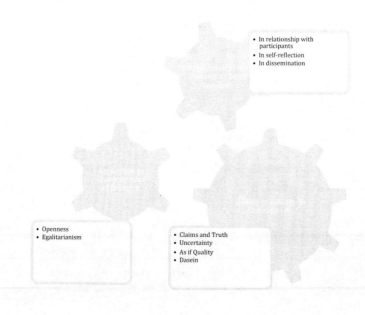

- In relationship with participants
- In self-reflection
- In dissemination

- Openness
- Egalitarianism

- Claims and Truth
- Uncertainty
- As if Quality
- Dasein

This picture illustrates the interactive, communicative nature of the unified proposal for addressing validity. Image from http://www.rmu.edu/web/cms/academics/scis/organizational-studies/Pages/bs-org-studies.aspx. Accessed January 30, 2011. Used with permission.

The proposal I am spreading is this: We can forge a unifying approach to validity by looking first at a description of validity in its ordinary context. The ordinary context is already necessarily a linguistic, social, intersubjective one (Habermas, 1984, 1987 and many others as this is a well-accepted description of ordinary life across myriad philosophical communities). This becomes the starting place because it is the starting place for validity itself.

Ordinary Concepts of Validity

To suggest, as I am doing, that ordinary concepts of validity supply insight for how we think about validity in qualitative research is not novel in either the general or particular way. For example, in general terms, it is common for qualitative researchers to talk about research validity using words like "trustworthiness" and "authenticity" (Lewis, 2009), which are taken in the first place from our experiences with truth in ordinary life contexts. In particular, specific methodologists and methodological theorists have provided detailed accountings and justifications for this (Habermas, 1984; Altheide & Johnson, 1994; Carspecken, 2003), even in the particular way I am advocating. Habermas (1984) made the following comparison between doing research and the ordinary life context:

> In thematizing what the participants merely presuppose [in ordinary life] and assuming a reflective attitude to the interpretandum, one does not place oneself *outside* the communication context under investigation; one deepens and radicalizes it in a way that is in principle open to *all* participants." (p. 130, emphasis in original)

By examining what validity looks like in ordinary life, we learn more about the nature and structure of validity itself. This examination will produce a description of validity rather than a description of how to apply validity to research. While this link between ordinary concepts of validity and research practice is certainly not an idea original to me, its potential as a unifying orientation for validity has not been realized. Thus, it is my hope to move further along in its realization.

Moreover, this link is not simply a heuristic for understanding validity; it is matter of necessity—that is, concepts of research validity cannot really escape a connection with ordinary concepts of validity. This isn't a matter of choosing this approach over others; it means that our very validity discussions and the process of deliberating what validity means for qualitative inquiry, in addition to the practices involved in engaging in valid qualitative research, are dependent upon these ordinary concepts of validity (Habermas, 1984; Carspecken, 2003; Korth, 2002, 2005). The subsections below should adequately illustrate this.

Validity in Everyday Interpretations

"To understand a proposition [in ordinary life] means to know what is the case if it is true. (One can understand it, therefore, without knowing if it is true)" (Wittgenstein, 1974, p. 21). In rather precise form, Habermas's (1984, 1987) *TCA* articulates the everyday manner in which people interacting with one another will grasp the meaning of those interactions by grasping the reasons one might offer to explain the actions. Every meaningful action, for example, a head-nod greeting in the hallway as you pass by someone you know, or a gesture with one's hand indicating to another an available place to sit down, is imbued with claims to truth that one's interactant will draw on, in part, to understand the activity. Let's say I see you walk into the room. The room is bustling with talk, many people (including me) are already seated in chairs around a large conference table. You look at me and I point with my hand to the empty chair next to me. Then, I move my bags from the chair to the floor next to my chair. You nod and come over to sit there. As you lower yourself into the chair, you smile and whisper, "Thanks." You interpreted my pointing at the chair and looking at you as an invitation for you to sit in that chair. You understand the meaning of my pointing at the empty chair within a context of possible things I might mean. In this case, that range of possible meanings would be narrower than is sometimes the case when we act. To ask if your interpretation of my gesture is valid is to ask more than just whether or not your interpretation matches my intended meaning. According to Polkinghorne (2007), "Validity is not inherent in a claim [by which he means not inherent in the fact that it was claimed with particular intentions] but is a characteristic given to a claim by the ones to whom the claim is addressed [or those who assume the claim includes them as addressees]" (p. 475). The assumption of validity implies that the interpretation could be queried and the interpreter would be able, in principle, to provide responses to those queries. For me to intend my gesture to be interpreted in a particular way, I must be able to anticipate what the likely interpretations are. I also must be able to draw on shared understandings of expression, appropriateness, the states of affairs at the time, and so forth. These shared understandings form a background horizon that is implicit in the meaning of my gesture. The background horizon may be made explicit at any point during our interactions, should you have a question or should there be a misunderstanding. In ordinary life, we do not have a simple yes/no experience with the validity of meaning actions. Instead, when we understand something to be true, we understand what it would take to validate that specific claim to truth should queries be raised. We grasp this intuitively. Thus, to understand my gesture is to understand a whole host of plausible validity claims that are assumed to hold if the given interpretation of my action is reasonable.

In this way, truth claims are quickly and intuitively switched over to validity claims, which Habermas has organized according to categories through which the validity is intuitively established. Let's return to the previous example: If you come over to sit in the chair and I say, "Oh, I am sorry, but I was saving that chair for Lucy," we will both realize that there was a misunderstanding in terms of who I meant to be looking at and gesturing toward. You know who Lucy is and you also know that she is my friend. At this point you become aware that Lucy walked into the room right behind you. Both you and I can see how the misunderstanding happened.

The various categories of validity involved in the interpretive process can be demonstrated in this example. The interpretations and my claims to truth are validated through the process of sussing out what the validity claims/claims to truth are. The validity of aspects of the interpretation that assume the existence of things in the external world, as well as cause and effect or functional, mechanical relations among things in the external world, are examined through an articulation of what is and what works given the principle of multiple access. The principle of multiple access means that any one of us (and in principle, any anonymous observer) should be able to utilize the same methods (usually observational in some way) and definitions in order to arrive at the same claim to truth. Habermas refers to this category of validity as objectivity. Some objective validity claims referred to in my comment include (but are not limited to): that there is a chair I am pointing at, that you entered the room, that Lucy also needs a chair, that there are a particular number of chairs, that the room holds a particular number of people, that there are enough chairs for the number of people who will be attending the meeting, and so on. The interpretation that I am saving a chair for Lucy is valid, in part, to the extent that these objective validity claims hold. This is the most recognizable and well-developed validity category in the practices of doing social science. Habermas (1984, 1987) argues against limiting our truth conceptions and validity to this one category, as it defies our ordinary experience with meaning. Another category of validity, according to Habermas, is subjectivity. Subjective claims refer to claims a person makes about his or her own feelings, states of mind, proclivities, and desires—attributes that indicate the existence of a person's internal world. These claims involve the principle of privileged access, which means that each subject has a distinctly privileged way of knowing his or her own feelings, states of mind, proclivities, desires, and matters internal. These claims point to a world internal to the speaker describing the ontology of that internal world on an epistemological basis. We cannot validate these claims about one another primarily through direct observation. Instead we must establish the extent to which the speaker is being honest and authentic; that is, the extent to which the speaker is both aware of his or her feelings and is being open and honest about those feelings. Part of the meaning you might infer from our interactions about the chair would include that I feel sorry about the misunderstanding and/or I feel awkward. Also, you might think that I did have the intention of saving the seat for someone else—namely Lucy. This would mean ruling out that I intended to put you in an awkward situation or snub you—to articulate just a few counter interpretations. The validity of these parts of the interpretation depends on the extent to which I am being honest and self-aware, because they make reference to states of affairs internal to me to which I would have privileged access. According to Habermas, there is a third category of truth claim whose validity is different from both objectivity and subjectivity—Habermas calls this category normativity. Though we will recognize this category immediately in the ordinary context, we rarely see it referred to in a distinct manner in the research literature—its claims are generally lumped in the category of subjectivity. An example of a couple of normative truth assumptions implicit in the interpretations one would articulate for my comment to you about my saving the chair for Lucy includes that people should sit in chairs for meetings when chairs are available, people should sit in one and only one chair, people should not hoard chairs for non-sitting purposes when chairs are in short supply, people should be able to hold chairs for other people, people should rectify misunderstandings when they happen. The validity of normative truth claims is linked to the extent to which people in a given community find the norms worthy of their assent. The social world is referred to (as objective claims refer to an external world and subjective claims refer to an internal personal world). The social world is a linguistically, culturally constituted set of relationships with norms and values as its material.

Four insights from the above exploration of validity in the everyday context will be drawn forward in the subsection to come: (1) That validity is conceptualized in terms of interpretive justification or answers to queries that, regardless of whether such queries are explicated, are always implied in the way interpretations are rendered valid. (2) That validity queries reflect categorical differences across objectivity, subjectivity, and normativity. (3) That validity is intersubjectively structured. (4) That validity is horizonally structured—that is, there will be claims in the foreground and claims in the background and the horizon ever recedes so that it's not possible to fully articulate all claims involved in understanding any particular interaction.

These insights about validity eliminate the need for debates about whether or not: (a) subjective claims can be valid; or (b) objective claims always invoke a positivist/postpositivist paradigm; or (c) subjectivity and objectivity work against each other, as in the more objective something is, the less subjective it is. Realism is implied, though the validity procedures are about the claims related to those implications. This is basically what we mean by "critical"— open to scrutiny on the grounds that it claims as its own.

The Uncertainty of Meaning in Ordinary Life

You can see from this approach to validity that there is not a one-to-one correspondence between the interpretation and the act being interpreted because meaning does not work that way. When I act, the horizon of my act implies that I expect a range of possible interpretations would be likely, but also your response to my act will hone or shape the meaning of my act. As such, there is an openness to the interpretive process—a bounded openness, not free-for-all incoherency. In terms of the character of validity, the interpretive openness implies a continual nature of validity (which also jibes with the idea that validity has a horizon-like shape with respect to meaning) rather than either/or nature (either it is valid or it isn't valid). As we explicitly query particular truth claims, we draw out the reasons that justify particular claims and interpretations. Let's return to the earlier example. If you come to the empty chair near me and begin to sit down, you are implicitly querying an interpretation of my gesture. You are raising your interpretation as valid. I realize this interpretation is valid and I can either leave the interpretation in place and let you sit down without revealing my initial intentions (which involved directing my gesture at Lucy rather than at you) or I might raise the alternative interpretation, which would rely primarily on knowledge of my initial intentions or on the view of the room that included all three of us: you, me, and Lucy. Then Lucy sees you sitting down. She smiles at me because she recognizes the misunderstanding. She walks passed the two of us to an empty chair behind me (which in fact I had not seen). The openness of interpretation is necessarily bounded, but this boundedness is not standardized across various interpretive encounters. It is linked to the context of the action. Every act is both open/flexible and bounded in terms of interpretation and this quality of interpretation is important when thinking about validity. As such, validity must be conceptualized as the process through which people come to understand one another given the bounded range and flexible field of possible interpretations. Both the boundedness and the openness are tethered to the context of the interpretive milieu, not to rules about the correspondence between the referent and the expression. There is no one-to-one correspondence of my gesture to an interpretation that would always hold across all particular instances. It is in this way that we can understand Polkinghorne's (2007) comment that validity does not inhere in the claim, but in the judgment of the claim by the interpreting audience/interactants.

Also, there are always presumably shared assumptions in the interpretation process, but there are reasons for us to be more or less certain of the sharedness of our assumptions. The context of our action sets the background for this aspect of certainty. Do we share a common language and culture? Is the meaning general enough to be warranted, given the level of knowledge and history we have of one another and of our shared context? This layer of certainty is most often called into question on definitional levels, but not only on definitional levels.

The uncertainty of meaning is, also, implicit to the assumption that an act always could have been otherwise (Giddens, 1979). In ordinary life, this means that we would be hard pressed to assume that there was a unidirectional, deterministic cause-effect relation for acting. The more plausible way of thinking about contingencies to which our meaningful action might be partially attributed would be as conditions of action. Conditions of action cannot be used to predict forthcoming action, but would instead be linked to action in terms of how the act might be interpreted (Carspecken, 1996). As just mentioned, the context within which I am acting and within which my action is being interpreted contributes to how the action is understood, but does not determine how the act is understood. In ordinary life we cannot effectively understand one another if we limit what is taken to be a valid interpretation to only those interpretations that have a direct cause/effect relation between the conditions of action and the meaning of the action itself. In fact, it is difficult to talk about ordinary validity in this way. Consider this convoluted description of our example articulated using this cause/effect sense of validity: You walked into the room and this caused me to point out the empty chair beside me. Or, the empty chair beside me caused me to indicate its availability for your use. Or, the social norms of politeness caused me to offer you the empty chair beside me. None of these cause/effect articulations would be considered adequate or even accurate in the everyday world of giving reasons for our actions. If you had approached me and said, "Why did you gesture at this chair when I walked into the room?" none of the above answers would have made sense. However, the above conditions help to provide a context within which interpretations are considered plausible or are ruled out. In the ordinary context, there are some examples in which we think of more deterministic, causative conditions as having more sway over the interpretations than is typical for most claims. For example, when someone gets hit and falls down, we might feel confidence in saying that the force of the hit caused the person to fall down. Even so, this kind of physical description with its focal point on the cause/effect element does not satiate our understanding of the action per se. So while cause/effect relations might be foregrounded in some physical descriptions (he hit her and she fell down) where the range of plausible interpretations is quite narrow, they do not suffice in ordinary life as explanations. We could say that because he hit her, she fell down—but there are assumptions that we must also accept that reveal the partiality of the cause/effect explanation. For example, we must accept that he is stronger than she is and that she was unable to resist the hit; or that he caught her off guard; or that she was, for some reason, unwilling to resist the hit. We would also want to understand why in the world he hit her.

Sometimes in research literature, uncertainty is treated as a concern peculiar to subjectivity—that the procedures of objectivity specifically preclude interpretive uncertainty, but in our ordinary context we recognize that we experience uncertainty across all three types of claims. In other words, the uncertainty of meaning is addressed, but not eliminated, through validity queries of all three types. There will always be some degree of uncertainty. The validity of objective aspects of interpretation is only potentially resolvable through the principle of multiple access. Thus, it seems easier to diminish the extent of uncertainty related to objective claims. Moreover, objective claims can be very easily taken for granted because of a strong sense of certainty ascribed by Westerners to information from their senses, particularly from vision (Carspecken, 2003). For example, we would probably have little reason to question whether or not the chair next to me was empty (an objective claim) or exists—our certainty would be very strong and the level of facticity we ascribe these claims would be high. In fact, it would seem crazy to query such claims in this example. Actually, in this example, it is hard to come up with an objective claim that would even seem sensible to query, but let's look at the crux of the misunderstanding: you did not notice that Lucy was behind you and I did not realize that you were looking at me when I gestured to her. These are objective claims whose uncertainty had to do with the scope of observational and attentional view we each had. In ordinary life, we deal with the uncertainty associated with objective claims by addressing definitions, by making sure our observations are accurate (including in terms of scope), and by establishing procedures for getting information. Certainty about objective claims invokes a distinction between the claim and the "observation" or the way things are/work.

In contrast, with respect to the uncertainty that might be involved in understanding my initial intentions, one will have to trust that I am being honest and sincere and that I know how I feel. I might experience greater certainty about this than you, because you do not have direct access to my intentional states of mind. So certainty about our self-knowledge claims involves a distinction between our claims and our self-awareness and self-expression.

We would establish certainty about the norms involved by pointing to other supportive and backgrounded norms on which we find agreement. For example, if you said to me "Are you saying that it is okay for you to save a chair for someone at this meeting?" then you would be calling the certainty of that validity claim into question. I might be quite certain about the validity of many other normative claims (such as that people should sit in chairs at the meeting and that people should sit one person to a chair), and experience less certainty about the validity of the normative claim that people should be able to hold or save chairs for other people. Your query would indicate some uncertainty about the validity of that particular normative claim.

So while uncertainty is linked to validity claim and while different aspects of certainty reflect different types of validity, uncertainty itself is not solely a product of subjectivity, nor is it totally eliminated when objective claims are offered up. (For a detailed discussion of certainty as it relates to meaning and truth claims, see Carspecken, 2003.) This is important because in the ideology of U.S. life there is a counterintuitive claim that the more certain we are of a truth claim, the more objective it is; the less certain we are of a truth claim, the more subjective it is. This formulation is just not as precise as we actually experience it in our ordinary lives. I am every bit as certain that I love my children (and so are my children)—a subjective claim—as I am that my children exist in observable form—an objective claim.

There is one more aspect of uncertainty that is even more primary than certainty related to the validity of truth claims, and that is the uncertainty linked to never knowing for sure what someone means. This isn't just about never knowing for sure what another intends, but actually never knowing for sure that there is identity of meaning in any given particular interaction (Carspecken, 2003). We at best understand a range of possible meanings. As Rolfe (2000) stated, it is not a matter of "denying the existence of a real(ist) world, nor … necessarily claiming that we can never 'know' that world, simply that we can never know that we know it" (p. 173). The reason we can never know that we know it is because we cannot establish the identity of meaning. Understanding does not require identity of meaning and instead requires intersubjective fields of possible meaning. Validity as an interpretive concept in ordinary life has this same quality.

Three insights about validity given the certainty/uncertainty of meaning are relevant to the discussion applying ordinary concepts of validity to social science. These insights include: (1) that uncertainty is not a fixed commodity, but indicates domains of validity concern; (2) that uncertainty happens at the level of meaning and is, therefore, not solely a matter of method and is always a matter of interpretation (specifically, interpretation is always partial and a person always could have acted otherwise); and (3) that (un)certainty is addressed via query. "Certainty simply has no paradigm, it is rather a telos of a longing for presence" (Carspecken, 2003, p. 1039) that cannot be fully resolved communicatively through validity queries. "When people push on the question of certainty …, then principles that had always been in the background move forward to become problems" (Carspecken, 2003, p. 1039). These insights are about the nature of validity itself and how we might query that uncertainty, though provisionally and incompletely. "No final answer [to the question 'What do you mean?'] can be formulated but we do [in everyday life] understand what conditions would be required" to answer the question in any given instance in which the question of certainty arises (Carspecken, 2003, p. 1039).

The "As If" Character of Ordinary Interpretation

In our ordinary lives, we understand gestures and utterances through an "as if" quality. This as-if character is basic to meaning. It implicates the intersubjective ground of interpretation. Just in the way a person could have always acted otherwise, within a bounded range of possibilities, an interpretation will always indicate that one is interpreting/expressing something as if a particular set of conditions, assumptions, beliefs, attitudes, proclivities, and whole worlds hold as valid truth claims. This as-if quality indicates that we cannot ever fully explicate the meaning of something and must instead make references that cannot be totally cashed in. On some level, we have to allow the as-if character of understanding to remain. The as-if aspect of understanding always takes a propositional form—actually, the as-if nature of interpretation is entirely propositional in structure (Tugendhat, 1986). This is one of the clearest ways to see the necessarily linguistic and representational aspect of understanding—the way understanding always, in part, invokes this as-if quality. This quality also has motivational force underneath it—the desire to be understood or to understand in a particular way.

Let's return to the example. Of course, on the surface, one might interpret my gesture as if it were an invitation. The mode of inviting carries with it a host of claims including the expectation that you would thank me and that I am a nice person. In addition to this layer of as-if clustering, there is also the as-if character that has to do with the pragmatic coordination of our interaction. This could be articulated like this: We act as if we are making entitlements for which we are also implicitly expected to make good on should this be requested of us. "Every time any of us acts meaningfully our expressions tacitly carry 'promissory notes' that others can ask to be redeemed'" (Carpecken, 2003, p. 1023). This as-if character is part of what constitutes the paradigmatic horizon of our understanding one another (Carspecken, 1996). In referring to Habermas's ideas about the normative grounds of understanding, Carspecken (2003) reminds us that "the form of both objective and subjective validity claims may have evolved via metaphoric extension from the normative claim" (p. 1034).

It is this as-if quality that some of the sharpest work on referential semantics elucidates and it is this as-if quality of meaning that we have more particularly focused on since the linguistic turn in philosophy and social science.

Care and Dasein in Ordinary Experience

When we are oriented toward understanding those we are interacting with, we are investing ourselves—we care. We care in a way that brings our own identity into being with others while simultaneously opening up our interest in understanding others in a particular way. This understanding has the potential of changing us, and we realize that when we are in these interactive encounters with others, we may emerge new in the process. Heidegger used the word "Dasein" to mean something like one's particular being there, one's "disclosedness" (paraphrased from Tugendhat, 1986, p. 151). It is through understanding that we are able to understand and be understood—to be recognized. "A core 'interest' to all human beings would be the 'interest' in having and maintaining a self. This is an interest that is wholly intersubjective in constitution" (Carspecken, 2003, p. 1035). Recognizing others and being recognized by others is a fundamental element of understanding and interpretation in our ordinary experiences. Often enough, this recognition is satisfied in quite backgrounded ways. "Meaningful acts are motivated, in part, at varying levels of foregrounding and background[ing], by the identity claims they put at stake" (Carspecken, 2003, p. 1036).

There is a necessary connection between the validity of truth claims we offer up and the sense of self carried by the claim. This connection links the validity accepted of the claim to the sense of one's self as a valid worthwhile truth-sayer. When we are engaged in validity efforts, we are also engaged in identity efforts. In some ways, this helps us better understand why there is such passion and diffusion and proliferation going on in the validity discourse itself. As we have staked ourselves in our research and our research findings, we have linked the validity of our own identities in the validity of the work to which we are associating our "selves" (Korth, 2005).

Applying These Concepts to Social Science

Ordinary concepts of validity seem particularly relevant to the way social scientists make sense or interpret ordinary life. In other words, it does not seem like much a stretch to say that ordinary concepts of validity would apply to the substantive material of ordinary life experience under investigation by social scientists. The interpretation of ordinary life tends to be more directly engaged in qualitative approaches to inquiry because ordinary life tends to be more directly engaged with through qualitative research endeavors. However, ordinary concepts of validity are also applicable in a basic way to understanding social science validity across all sorts of methodological approaches, methods, and designs. This point has been made by others. For example, Carspecken (2003) wrote: "Critical epistemology is a theory of knowledge, truth and power that is exactly this: an articulation of already understood but implicit assumptions and structures used in the course of everyday life" (p. 1040).

This section will largely explore the insights for social science, in general, and qualitative research, most specifically, but will end by troubling this approach. The idea here is to look directly at validity and see how in what ways the concept of validity drawn from ordinary life might have merits for social science.

The Interpretive, Intersubjective Quality of Validity

Validity claiming is a process of articulating what it would take to figure out whether or not something is true (in the objective sense), authentic (in the subjective sense) and right or appropriate (in the normative sense). It is an interpretive process and all interpretation is a manner of position-taking (Mead, 1934; Habermas, 1984; Maxwell, 1996; Carspecken, 2003). This quality of validity holds for all kinds of claims in social science. It is a characteristic of validity, not a characteristic of particular social science methodologies, per se.

We can talk about this with respect to observation. Elements of observation are involved in all forms of social science, whether through direct observation or not. In Western experience, we talk as if "seeing is believing" and so we can easily take for granted the interpretive work involved in "seeing." Historically speaking, the effects of this for Western social science have been to think that objective claims associated with observation primarily rely on our senses and work off of the principle of multiple access and are not, in fact, interpretive. But a similar error is offered up by scholars who claim that qualitative research is subjective and not objective; these scholars fail to acknowledge the observational engagements of qualitative research. These observational elements have objective components to them regardless of the type, manner, or paradigm under which the researcher is attending to her work. When queried, the objective validity will rely upon procedures related to what things are (how they can be measured, observed, and so forth) and how they work (functions and consequences). In any given particular study (even autoethnography), there will be observations and there will be objective claims. But these will not be the only kinds of claim (even in quantitative studies, objective claims may be foregrounded, but they do not operate solely), and all observations are constituted of interpretation and intersubjectivity. Observations are not free of interpretation. While most social scientists will acknowledge this point, the ramifications for it have not been easily admitted into the conceptions of validity held by the social scientists.

The categorical distinctions between objectivity, subjectivity, and normativity are implicit in the interpretive nature of validity because our interpretations are understood through these categories. This distinction would help us talk about validity issues that have surfaced in the literature. For example, there are arguments about whether or not research should be held accountable to criteria of accuracy. In our ordinary lives, if we were interpreting something objectively, we would hold the meaning accountable to accuracy with respect to its descriptive characteristics of things in the external world and how they work. We would do this even if our conversation is primarily about subjective and evaluative interests. Similarly, it would be possible to raise queries about research interests too (Korth, 2005). Transformational research (Cho & Trent, 2006) foregrounds normative claims about what the research itself should accomplish in the real world. Even with normative claims foregrounded, there are objective claims about the way things are for the participants that could be queried, and subjective claims about the experiences of the researcher (research reflections) that can be queried. The point here is that all research projects will involve, to varying degrees, objective, subjective, and normative claims with warrants that necessarily fit the category (criteria of accuracy, honesty, normative rightness, for example). Each of these criteria can be addressed through a variety of validity techniques (which the research literature has abundantly supplied). Qualitative researchers might take Peshkin's (1988) work on subjectivity (which includes both subjective and normative interests) as one approach to articulating the subjectivity involved in the research process. It has been common for researchers to speak of objective and subjective validity in research (though these are often talked about as if their difference is one of magnitude or continuum, rather than category).

This interpretive, intersubjective characteristic of validity can be unifying procedurally (an argument-based approach to validity would be implied) and also in terms of the claim-oriented types of validity that would be amenable to query regardless of the type of research or philosophical paradigm one wants to affiliate with and conduct. Given this characteristic, it doesn't make sense to treat research validity as being either objective or subjective or research projects as being only objective or subjective. Furthermore, it would not make much sense to talk about research as valid without an understanding that this is always a negotiable, consensual process of querying what might be taken for granted in the claims.

The Uncertainty of Meaning and Validity

Uncertainty is one of the characteristics of meaning and validity. Uncertainty related to particular kinds of truth claims will involve querying those claims on grounds related to the type of claim—objective, subjective, normative as has been previously described. This is primarily the kind of uncertainty that social scientists try to eliminate. We know that our truth claims can be fallible and that we must be open to challenge and change. When social scientists thought of their work as noninterpretive, a more limited view of uncertainty made sense. Now, however, even people involved in using very objective, quantitative methods acknowledge the interpretive aspects of their research. And interpretation will always carry an element of uncertainty that is not merely about the content of the truth claims—full and complete understanding is not possible to articulate. This insight, also, speaks to the goals of research. The idea of accumulating accurate information about the world (internal and external) can, at best, be a provisional and secondary one: provisional in the sense that our research will constantly be updated by new information, but also by new ways of interpreting old information; secondary in the sense that how people interpret, utilize, care about, change, and engage with the information is more primarily of interest.

The uncertainty character compels us to move past thinking of research as either valid or not. "Either it is/or it isn't" nature of validity has been challenged by others. For example, Aguinaldo (2004) proposed that qualitative researchers should not be asking "is this valid research? Yes or No"; but should instead be asking "What is this research valid for?" However, the nature of validity even in this second question seems to reside in the either/or proposition. For example, if we answer the second of Aguinaldo's questions with the proposition "This research is valid for better understanding the way children read difficult texts," we have still assumed it either is or is not valid for this purpose. We don't assume it is or is not valid in general, but in particular, given a context. Scheurich (1997) also argued against this either/or way of thinking of validity. In the place of this either/or conceptualization, Scheurich proposed an approach to validity that is dialogic specifically across difference. Conversations across difference help researchers address the uncertainty related to content of truth claims in part because the difference requires us not to take certainty (or identity/sameness of meaning) for granted. Conversations across difference can help researchers face the limits of understanding and interpretation.

What we can be certain about is the conditions under which we could query (Carspecken, 2003).

In research, we need to toggle between the limits of knowledge and the conditions of knowledge. We also need to address the content fallibility, which is the result of never being surely able to reach full consensus on the level of content. This quality of validity seems to require that researchers (1) leave their work open to scrutiny and (2) recognize the boundaries of their work, particularly across difference. Postmodern and poststructuralist forms of research foreground this necessary uncertainty, but often times the insights have been treated as if this is uncertainty rules out the possibility of knowledge or truth all together. In contrast, the insights of ordinary life teach us that even though uncertainty is necessary, it only means our capacity to understand is partial, not eliminated. Our will to knowledge is strong and our capacity for learning and coming to better understand one another is ongoing. This uncertainty does not rule out the possibility for truth; it rules out the concept of totalizing and complete truth at any one given time. Keeping the dialogue of difference at play is one way of taking seriously the uncertainty that inheres in meaning and validity. Scheurich's proposal is one that not only applies to postmodern forms of research, but to all research precisely because uncertainty is a characteristic of all validity and, therefore, all inquiry.

"As if" Quality of Validity

Searle's (1970) speech act theory helped to illustrate the illocutionary force of utterances—the action that was accomplished in speaking. For example, if I say "Girls do well in mathematics," the illocutionary force is something like "I AM SAYING that girls do well in mathematics" and "I ASSERT that I KNOW girls do well in mathematics" The as-if quality of the validity comes to play in the relation between my speech action as a claim (the illocutionary force) and the claim itself. The as-if quality of validity indicates that social science approaches to validity that solely depend on the idea of a match between referent and object are not tenable.

This as-if quality is found foregrounded in approaches to social science that theorize language as the fundamental basis for validity. For example, Lakoff and Johnson (1980) proposed the idea that all language is metaphorical and this has implications for how research claims are interpreted (for example, one might look at the ways the claims themselves are metaphorically contingent) and how research claims are established (for example, one might examine metaphors like inside/outside as applied to research positionality). Minh-ha (1989) voiced a strongly representational view of social science that also foregrounds the as-if quality of validity. With respect to validity, she concludes that no universal validity is possible, only fractured, momentary structures of meaning that do not or need not hold up to particular validity tests. The most important validity issue for her is how the researcher acts as if she is a knower, an interpreter, an articulator, and so forth. Here the metaphorical nature is located between the researcher and how she positions herself. In other words, the as if quality is about the relation between the I in the illocutionary force and the pragmatic positionality one would find in that force. I—the sayer; I—the knower; and so forth.

Earlier in the chapter, I described some metaphorical approaches to the description of validity—namely, Richardson's crystallization. The metaphorical approaches to validity recognize that validity itself has an as-if quality that defies being fully articulated, but can be alluded to and referenced through metaphors. The metaphors can invoke subtleties for the interpreters that might be difficult to convey straight up. Though this difficulty speaks to the practical problem of describing validity, at its heart, those who have been drawn to describing validity in this way recognize that validity might best be understood and enacted through proximal metaphors that unite particular characteristics and demonstrate particular uses.

The Dasein Quality of Validity

This aspect of validity links both the doing and producing of research to the praxis needs of the researcher (Carspecken, 2002) and to the researcher's relationship with participants. Ultimately, the researchers, as with persons in their ordinary life experiences, must win the free assent of rational colleagues regarding the validity of their work as part of what it means to be recognized as a worthwhile and valid scholar. One's passion must be engaged, but also opened to others and reflected upon. In some research, this aspect of validity might be more highly backgrounded than in other types of studies (perhaps this is the case with the natural sciences in comparison with autoethnography, for example). Nevertheless, it isn't really the type of research that makes this an issue; rather, it is always at issue. I remember reading about the scientist Maurice Wilkins (Nobel Laureate) who was involved in research that contributed to the atomic bombs dropped on Nagasaki and Hiroshima. He felt remorse when the bomb worked. He spent much of the rest of his life trying to engage in science in ways that contributed to making the world a better place. He led a group called the British Society for Social Responsibility in Science, which was formed in 1969 in order to pose questions about the social effects of science (Rose & Rose, 1976). Rose and Rose (1976) describe a natural science that is moving increasingly toward an articulation of this insight in the way it accounts self-reflectively for its own worth.

Cho and Trent (2006) distinguished between transactional and transformational qualitative research, suggesting that transactional researchers were those who looked at validity in terms of their interactions, interpretations, and understandings with/of participants; while transformational qualitative researchers are those who associate the validity of their work with eventual ideals regarding transformational outcomes. This distinction suggests that the Dasein quality of validity is more directly drawn out in some instances, namely when transformational orientations are foregrounded or explicated. But every act of inquiry is an act whereby the researcher is risking herself and the effects for this on validity have been variously named (catalytic validity is one example). McLaren (1993) described this as "being wounded in the field." When one enters a research project, one does so open-minded not only with respect to the substance of one's research questions, but also with regards to one's cares for others and for the self, one's identity so to speak. The basic validity issue at question has to do with worthwhileness and this issue gets at the heart of intersubjectivity and the normative claim. Every critical effort questioning claims to truth, that is, every validity effort, involves the problem of identifying who we are and who we can be through the critique.

The Trouble with Ordinary Validity in Practice:
Must Social Science Be Truer Than True?

Our ordinary validity-ensuring processes have problems. In practice, our orientations toward understanding are deeply riddled with oppressive hangovers that go masked in terms of our orientations and intentionalities (Beach, 2003; Carspecken, 2003). Power can distort our capacity to reach consensus and understand truth. But good research ought not perpetuate such masks; rather, research ought to contribute to making the world a better place.

Woodhouse, Hess, Breyman, and Martin (2002) remind us that all research is troubled:

> Because all inquiries and knowledge claims occur in social contexts by persons with cognitive, emotional, interpersonal, and other commitments, biases, and ideologies, all research can, of course, be said to have a normative component. (p. 298)

Woodhouse includes biases and ideologies in the category of normative, but I think we can safely say (given Habermas's refinements of the terms "objective," "subjective," and "normative") that "social" would be an adequate substitution. The point here is that ordinary interactions have problems in terms of validity. How then can we loosen research from the ordinary binds that limit our understanding of one another (Beach, 2003; Lather, 1993)?

Habermas (1987) has suggested that validity queries can be and regularly are violated on a procedural level because of power, other forms of inequity, and structural distortions.

The answer to this question draws researchers back to the ordinary context of validity. Habermas (1984 and elsewhere) has suggested that validity queries can be violated on a procedural level. These violations take the fundamental form of breaching with principles of egalitarianism and openness, losing sight of the ideal that is implicit to every critical act. Carspecken (1996) ends his practical, methodological guide with the principle of egalitarianism, stating that the best way to limit potential harm to participants is to engage in as democratic a research process as possible. Beach (2003) and Korth (2002) would echo these sentiments. Openness involves coming to the dialogue with an open mind, willing to learn from those with whom you are conversing. The point has already been made that this is best facilitated by encouraging a dialogue across difference. Wilkins (1999), in referring to the strong working relationship among his colleagues Watson and Crick, concluded that "dialogue between scientists who do not share views might be the most important vehicle for keeping science accountable for its social effects" (Dennis, 2009). Power distorts our capacities to freely assent and dissent by damaging the possibilities for egalitarian and open conditions. This happens both in our research and in the ordinary context. We must work against this in both spheres. However, the added complication of the power wielded by science and publication results in the likelihood that the claims rendered by social scientists will be interpreted as "more true" than claims offered up in everyday interactions. For this reason, and because such interpretive distortions have effects on the social world, researchers must be extra careful to encourage conditions of egalitarianism and openness, at the heart of which is self-reflection and freedom from power.

> The knowledge gained by a social scientist in research can and should follow the principles of the ideal speech situation [referencing Habermas's notion and the principle just identified] to invite the voices of those "being studied" into the research process and to allow those voices to change the pre-existing ideas of the researchers. This theory gives us standards by which to design and undertake research that will result in well-supported claims and well-articulated articulations of the research limitations. (Carspecken, 2003, p. 1027)

Also, we should not forget that one of the first layers of transformation comes in the shape of consciousness raising. Research always has this potential at its disposal (Korth, 2002).

A Unifying Approach to Validity: Conclusion

Rather than approach the problem of complexity by proposing a proliferation of different, divergent, and even contradictory constructs that might each in some nuanced way contribute to thinking of research as valid, the approach I have been establishing involves characterizing the nature of validity in ordinary life from which we might be able to discuss the validity of particular research efforts. In other words, I am starting with the nature of validity rather than with the nature of research; though the two are like sides of the same coin. In this conclusion, I briefly locate an approach to validity that shares many similarities with this proposal and then sketch out the proposal using the schematic presented earlier in the paper.

Argument-Based Validity

Moghaddam (2007), like Carspecken (2003), argued that "validity refers to the reasons we have for believing truth claims" (p. 236). This approach matches up with an approach known as the argument-based validity—an idea that has currency among methodologists of both quantitative and qualitative inquiry (Kane, 1992; Polkinghorne, 2007). Kane (1992), who writes on validity in the quantitative tradition, suggested that validity is an interpretive accomplishment (he drew on Cronbach, 1971, and Messick, 1989, to develop these ideas) whose inferences must hold up to queries. He proposed the idea that argument-based validity "adopts the interpretation as the framework for collecting and presenting validity evidence and explicitly associates validity with the plausibility of the various assumptions and inferences involved in the interpretation" (p. 528). Kane goes further to indicate that the validity argument is actually inherent in the interpretation itself. He proposes (1992), for the context of research that analyzes test scores, that interpretations be analyzed according to "the arguments associated with the interpretations" and that validity be defined "in terms of the overall justification of those arguments" (p. 528). According to Kane, the kinds of evidence needed for validation is determined by the content of the interpretive argument itself. "The validity of an interpretation can be defined in terms of the degree to which the interpretive argument is plausible and appropriate" (p. 532). The validity argument functions as a meta-argument, making the interpretive argument more explicit.

Kane et al. (1999) identified five types of inference made in quantitative research, particularly when using tests as a way of gathering data. These five types of inference include evaluation, generalization, extrapolation, explanation, and decision. Others have been developing this argument-based approach even further (see Kim, 2010; Bachman, 2003; Mislevy, Steinberg, & Almond, 2003). This particular group of scholars makes reference to the argument-based validity work of Toulmin (1969). They have this in common with Habermas. This synergy might indicate some common starting points for forging a unifying conceptualization of validity across the traditional quantitative/qualitative divide.

Polkinghorne (2007) argued that validity is a "prototype" concept rather than a "definitional" concept. He was also arguing for a more unified approach to validity across research communities and he built his position up in much the same way I have done here—by looking at validity directly and then talking about its application for social science. "A conclusion is valid when there is sufficient evidence and/or reasons to reasonably believe it is so… . A degree of validity or confidence is given to a claim that is proportionate to the strength and power of the argument" (p. 475). He goes on to say, "In spite of differing assumptions, I expect that both social science communities adhere to the general notion that judgments about the validity of a knowledge claim depend on the force and soundness of the argument [not in a rule-based way, but following Habermas in a communicative-rationality way] in support of the claim" (Polkinghorne, 2007, p. 476). What divides the communities, according to Polkinghorne, are disagreements about what counts as evidence and reasonable argument. I think a way through this division is Habermas's categorization of the three types of validity claim, which corresponds with how we resolve validity concerns in ordinary life experiences.

We can look at the structure of arguments to get an idea of how these might apply to social science. Toulmin (1969) proposed that a good argument makes explicit the connection between the conclusion and the evidence, examples of the evidence, justification for the link between the evidence and the conclusions, and rationale for the justification. Perelman (1982) described arguments as (1) having an informal structure (not the formal or strict structure of induction or deduction); (2) addressing an audience ideal or concrete; (3) involving ambiguity; and (4) seeking a measure of acceptance (not total acceptance). These descriptions are compatible with what we learned about validity in ordinary life.

The New Proposal: Following Habermas

The argument-based approach is in line with the insights we garnered from the everyday context of validity and it demonstrates a potential line of synergy among researchers who engage in both quantitative and qualitative inquiry. We can locate this argument-based approach in the unifying proposal that I am advocating here. The procedural similarities might make it seem that my proposal is redundant to the argument-based approach; these other approaches do not maximize their own insights because they stop short in identifying the intuitive criteria for assessing the validity of objective, subjective, and normative claims, which would be the same regardless of whether one is conducting a study that employs qualitative or quantitative methods and regardless of the type of paradigm to which one ascribes. The following schematic is a representation of that proposal—a proposal that focuses on the nature of validity as its orienting force with explicit correctives for possible ideological distortions and the force of power.

Qualities/Characteristics of Validity. This proposal involves describing the characteristics of validity in the ordinary contexts. I did that by identifying four main elements of the characteristics that emerge from already assumed social, intersubjective ways of understanding meaning.

These characteristics of validity have been well described in the chapter. They provide the ground for saying an argument-based approach to validity is, in fact, valid. They also supply the ground for critique that would enable researchers to move toward making claims that are in some ways liberated from the ideologies and distortions that can riddle truth in the ordinary milieu. Though, this same potential for critique is also accessible to participants. There is no reason why these emergent characteristics of validity would not be relevant to all forms of social science regardless of whether quantitative or qualitative methods are being utilized

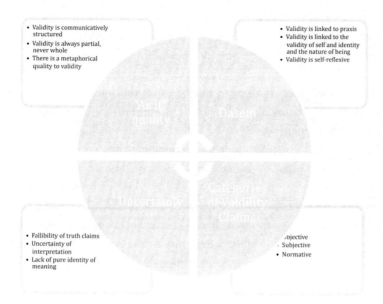

- Validity is communicatively structured
- Validity is always partial, never whole
- There is a metaphorical quality to validity

- Validity is linked to praxis
- Validity is linked to the validity of self and identity and the nature of being
- Validity is self-reflexive

As-if quality

Dasein

Uncertainty

Categories of validity claims

- Fallibility of truth claims
- Uncertainty of interpretation
- Lack of pure identity of meaning

- Objective
- Subjective
- Normative

Applications to Characteristics of Research. Habermas's ideal speech situation is a limit case description of the basic underlying assumptions of coming to understand one another through communication. The fundamental principles of this are (1) openness (both in terms of one's expression and in terms of one willingness to hear and be persuaded by others' perspectives) and (2) egalitarianism (all people having equal opportunity to voice and listen to the various ideas that are expressed). These principles set the conditions to best engage the above characteristics of validity. This is no different than in ordinary contexts, but in our research projects we should be explicit about accounting for these conditions. Argument-based approaches to validity make the most sense when these conditions are actualized to the best of our abilities. This holds regardless of whether we are talking about qualitative or quantitative approaches to inquiry. Dialogue across difference and democratic research practices seem to be the most fruitful way to engage these conditions in the conduct of social science.

Openness

Egalitarianism

Applications to the Domains of Doing Research. In every social science effort, ordinary validity concepts come into play across at least three recursive domains. One domain involves understanding participants. Another domain involves the researcher's self-reflective understanding of his or her own involvement in the activities of participants. A third domain has to do with how the dialogue about those findings is rendered public. In all cases, the validity issues are related to the insights garnered from looking at validity in the ordinary context: We can liken the first domain to the experience of witnessing an interaction and being involved in the same interaction. We can liken the second domain to the experience of reflecting on our interactions with others. We can liken the third domain to the experience of telling someone else a story or an account of the interactions. We do these things all the time in ordinary life. For researchers involved in more fixed, designed, quantitative studies, these three domains are quite distinct from one another in ways that are abstracted from, but not unrelated to, the more recursive nature of the domains in ordinary life.[5] The characteristics of validity are not shifted because of the domain involved. Each of the characteristics would apply, but the specificity of the relevant questions would, of course, be different. For example, the second domain would really focus on questions about the researcher's perspectives, while the third domain would focus more on questions of representation; but the process of examining the validity would be the same.

Like Beach (2003), I would argue that validity is the catalyst that infuses the three domains and holds the three domains together. The experiences in all three domains should be recursively returned to participants in order to maximize egalitarianism and openness.

In Summary

I have provided an argument for an approach to validity that is grounded in our everyday experience with validity. This approach can be unifying in that its basic principles hold across all varieties of methods. Moreover, it eliminates the need for some divisions that have perplexed the validity debates (like pitting objectivity against subjectivity). Remaining true to the underlying argument itself, this proposal should be queried, interrogated, challenged, added to, and developed. The idea is to get the conversation on validity moving in a productive, complicated, and inclusive manner.

Notes

1. Creswell and Miller's (2000) approach, on the surface, is antithetical to a movement toward a unified concept because they assume that people from differing paradigms would not be able to agree on what validity means and how it might best be established. The best-case scenario from this perspective is to be sure that one has taken up the validity challenges appropriate to the paradigm or design one is utilizing. It is a utilitarian approach that might be, in the end, the principle upon which a unified vision of validity could be forged from their work.

2. Criteria in these examples are meant to explicate and clarify validity concepts and procedures within very particular fields of qualitative research conduct. There is an abundance of such validity conversations going on within particular design/approach categories. Often, scholars taking this approach assume that validity is such a specified, contingent concept that conversations across designs and paradigms are moot. (Polkinghorne, 2007, is a counter-example of this.) The unifying concept here would have to be something like validity as a paradigmatic-contingent concept—and then one would need to argue (in general, philosophic terms) how validity and paradigm are internally linked.

3. Maxwell's proposal is a strong one, but there are problems in terms of how it has been utilized. One problem with this scheme is that the domains themselves are distinct from the decisions one must make to fit or use the domains in their research (Tracy, 2010). Another problem involves how to link Maxwell's five domains with what others who are approaching the validity problem in the same way are writing (this is a problem related not specifically to Maxwell's ideas, but to the state of the cacophony). For example, Greenwood and Levin (2000) distinguish between credibility, validity, and reliability in ways that Maxwell subsumes into validity.

4. The prospect of a unified concept of validity would be particularly suspect from this perspective because unification is generally the result of power subordination and ideology rather than the force of the better argument. And yet the idea that research ought to be accountable to its ends is a unifying claim itself applicable to any research endeavor.

5. For example, a quantitative researcher might examine the factors correlated with recidivism in juveniles. The researcher seeks to understand the participants by providing some sort of stimulus (a test maybe) for the participants to use to report their experiences with the juvenile justice system as well as their experiences with criminal activity. The researcher's interest in correlation is at its heart an interest in understanding what conditions and characteristics seem to be involved in the person's recidivism. The test and test responses are an abstraction of a possible conversation about recidivism that a researcher and a participant might, in principle, hold. If the participant does not understand the questions on the test or does not have a way to adequately express an honest response or does not think it's appropriate to interact with the researcher, then a misunderstanding akin to the first domain is likely. Also, issues related to how test scores are interpreted have to do with how the researchers are understanding their participants. When the researcher reflects on her decisions (for example, choice of tests and inclusion of particular variables), her commitment to juveniles, her concern for recidivism, or even her discussions of her own objective perspective—these fall into the second domain. The third domain is involved when researchers include particular literature in their scholarship, publish in particular journals, or return findings to participants.

References

Aguinaldo, J. (2004). Rethinking validity in qualitative research from a social constructionist perspective: From "Is this valid research?" to "What is this research valid for?" *The Qualitative Report, 9*(1), 127–136.

Alexander, J. C. (1990). Beyond the epistemological dilemma. General theory in a postpositivist mode. *Sociological Forum, 5*(4), 531–544.

Altheide, D., & Johnson, J. (1994). Criteria for assessing interpretive validity in qualitative research. In N. Denzin & Y. Lincoln (Eds.), *Sage handbook of qualitative research* (2nd ed.). (pp. 485–499). Newbury Park, CA: Sage.

Bachman, L. (2003). Constructing an assessment use argument and supporting claims about the test-taker assessment task interactions in evidence-centered assessment design. *Measurement: Interdisciplinary Research and Perspectives 1*(1), 63–65.

Beach, D. (2003). A problem of validity in education research. *Qualitative Inquiry, 9*(6), 859–873.

Bochner, A. (2000). Criteria against ourselves. *Qualitative Inquiry, 6*(2), 266–272

Campbell, D. T. (1957). Factors relevant to the validity of experiments in social settings. *Psychological Bulletin,* 54, 297–312.

Campbell, D. T., & Stanley, J. C. (1963). *Experimental and quasi-experimental designs for research.* Chicago: Rand McNally.

Carspecken, P. (1996). *Critical ethnography in educational research: A theoretical and practical guide.* New York & London: Routledge.

Carspecken, P. (2002). The hidden history of praxis theory within critical ethnography and the criticalism/postmodernism problematic. In Y. Zou & E. H. Trueba (Eds.), *Ethnography and schools: Qualitative approaches to the study of education* (pp. 55–86). Lanham, MD: Rowman & Littlefield.

Carspecken, P. (2003). Ocularcentrism, phonocentrism, and the counter-enlightenment problematic: Clarifying contest terrain in our schools of education. *Teachers College Record, 105*(6), 978–1047.

Cho, J., & Trent, A. (2006). Validity in qualitative research revisited. *Qualitative Research, 6*(3), 319–340.

Creswell, J,. & Miller, D. (2000). Determining validity in qualitative research. *Theory into Practice, 39*(3), 124–134.

Cronbach, L. (1971). Test validation. In R. Thorndike (Ed.), *Educational measurement,* Vol. 2 (pp. 443–507). Washington, DC: American Council on Education.

Cugno, R., & Thomas, K. (2009). A book review of Laura Ellingson's "Engaging Crystallization in Qualitative Research: An Introduction." *The Weekly Qualitative Report, 2*(19), 111–115. Accessed January 24, 2011 at http://www.nova.edu/ssss/QR/WQR/ellingson.pdf.

Dennis, B. (2009). Theory of the margins: Liberating research in education. In R. Winkle- Wagner , C. Hunter, & D. Hinderliter Ortloff. *Bridging the gap between theory and practice in educational research: Methods at the margins* (pp. 63–79). New York: Palgrave Macmillan.

Denzin, N. (2008). The new paradigm dialogs and qualitative inquiry. *International Journal of Qualitative Studies in Education, 21*(4), 315–325.

Denzin, N., & Giardina, (2008). *Qualitative inquiry and the politics of evidence.* Walnut Creek, CA: Left Coast Press.

Denzin, N., & Lincoln, Y. (Eds.). (1994). *Sage handbook of qualitative research* (1st ed.). Thousand Oaks, CA: Sage.

Dicts.info. (2003–2011). *Picture Dictionary: Crystal; crystallization.* Accessed January 30, 2011 at http://www.dicts.info/picture-dictionary.php?w=crystal.

Donmoyer, R. (1996). Educational research in an era of paradigm proliferation: What is a journal editor to do? *Educational Research, 25*(2), 19–25.

Donmoyer, R. (2001). Paradigm talk reconsidered. In V. Richardson (Ed.), *Handbook of Research on Teaching* (4th ed.) (pp. 174–197). Washington DC: American Educational Research Association.

Eisner, J., & Peshkin, A. (Eds.). (2000). *Qualitative inquiry in education: The continuing debate.* New York: Teachers College Press.

Ellingson, L. (2009). *Engaging crystallization in qualitative research. An introduction.* Thousand Oaks, CA: Sage.

Elliott, N., & Lazenblatt, A. (2005). How to recognize a quality grounded theory research study. *Australian Journal of Advanced Nursing, 22*(3), 48–52.

Emerson, R., Fretz, R. and Shaw, L. (1995). *Writing ethnographic fieldnotes.* Chicago: University Chicago Press.

Gergen, M., & Gergen K. (2000). Qualitative inquiry: Tensions and transformations. In N. K. Denzin & Y. S. Lincoln (Eds.), *Sage handbook of qualitative research* (2nd ed.) (pp. 1025–1046). Thousand Oaks, CA: Sage.

Giddens, A. (1979). *Central Problems in Social Theory. Action, Structure, and Contradiction in Social Analysis.* Berkeley: University of California Press.

Greenwood, D.J. & Levin, M. (2000). Reconstructing the relationship between universities and society through action research. In N.K. Denzin & Y.S. Lincoln (Eds.), *Handbook of qualitative research* (2nd ed., pp. 85–106). Thousand Oaks, CA: Sage Publications

Habermas, J. (1984). *The theory of communicative action.* Vol. 1: *Reason and the rationalization of society.* Boston: Beacon Press.

Habermas, J. (1987). *The theory of communicative action.* Vol. 2: *Lifeworld and system. A critique of functionalist reason.* Boston: Beacon Press.

Habermas, J. (1988). *On the logic of the social sciences.* Cambridge, MA: MIT Press.

Hammersley, M. (1992). *What's wrong with ethnography!* London: Routledge.

Kane, M. (1992). An argument-based approach to validity. *Psychological Bulletin, 112*(3), 527–535.

Kane, M. T., Crooks, T. J., & Cohen, A. S. (1999). Validating measures of performance. *Educational Measurement: Issues and Practice, 18*(2), 5-17.

Kim, Y. (2010). An argument-based validity inquiry into the Empirically-Derived Descriptor-Based Diagnostic (EDD) assessment in ESL academic writing. Unpublished thesis submitted to the faculty of The Ontario Institute for Studies in Education, University of Toronto for completion of the degree Ph.D. in the Department of Curriculum, Teaching and Learning.

Korth, B. (2002). Critical qualitative research as consciousness-raising: The dialogic texts of researcher/researchee interactions." *Qualitative Inquiry 8*(3), 381–403.

Korth, B. (2005). Choice, necessity, or narcissism. A feminist does feminist ethnography. In G. Troman, B. Jeffrey, & G. Walford (Eds.), *Methodological issues and practices in ethnography. Studies in educational ethnography*, Vol. 11 (pp. 131–167). Oxford and London: Elsevier Ltd.

Lakoff, G., & Johnson, M, (1980) *Metaphors we live by.* Chicago: University of Chicago Press.

Lather, P. (1993). Fertile obsession: Validity after poststructuralism. *Sociological Quarterly, 34,* 673–693.

Lather, P. (2007). *Getting lost: Feminist efforts at a doubled science* (Suny Series, Second Thoughts: New Theoretical Formations; Suny Series in Philosophy of Social Science). Albany: State University of New York Press.

Lather, P., & Smithies, C. (1997). *Troubling the angels: Women living with HIV/AIDS.* Boulder, CO: Westview.

Lewis, J. (2009). Redefining qualitative methods: Believability in the fifth moment. *International Journal of Qualitative Methods, 8*(2).

Lewis, J., & Ritchie, J. (2003). Generalising from qualitative research. In J. Ritchie, & J. Lewis (Eds.), *Qualitative research practice: A guide for social science students and researchers* (pp. 263–286). London, Thousand Oaks, New Delhi: Sage.

Lincoln, Y., & Guba, E. (2000). Paradigmatic controversies, contradictions, and emerging confluences. In. N. K. Denzin & Y. S. Lincoln (Eds), *Sage Handbook of qualitative research* (2nd ed.) (pp. 163–188). Thousand Oaks, CA: Sage.

Lincoln, Y., & Denzin, N. (2000). The seventh moment: Out of the past. In. N. K. Denzin & Y. S. Lincoln (Eds.), *Sage handbook of qualitative research* (2nd ed.) (pp. 1047–1065). Thousand Oaks, CA: Sage.

Maxwell, J. (1992). Understanding and validity in qualitative research. *Harvard Educational Review, 62,* 279–300.

Maxwell, J. (1996). *Qualitative research design: An interactive approach.* Thousand Oaks, CA: Sage.

Mead, G.H. (1934). *Mind, Self, and Society. From the Standpoint of a Social Behaviorist.* Chicago: University of Chicago Press.

Mehrens, W. (1997). The consequences of consequential validity. *Educational Measurement: Issues and Practice, 16*(2), 16–28.

Mertens, D. M. (2007). Transformative paradigm: Mixed methods and social justice. *Journal of Mixed Methods Research, 2007, 1 (3),* 212–225.

Messick, S. (1989). Validity. In R.L. Linn (Ed.), *Educational measurement*, Vol. 3 (pp. 13–103). New York: American Council on Education, Macmillan.

McLaren, P. (1993). *Schooling as ritual performance: Towards a political economy of educational symbols and gestures* (2nd ed.). New York: Routledge.

Minh-ha, T. (1989). *Women, native, and other: Writing postcoloniality and feminism.* Bloomington: University of Indiana Press.

Mislevy, R., Steinberg, L., & Almond, R. (2003). On the structure of educational assessments. *Measurement: Interdisciplinary Research and Perspectives, 1*(1), 3–62.

Moghaddam, A. (2007). Action research: A spiral inquiry for valid and useful knowledge. *Alberta Journal of Educational Research, 53*(2), 228–239.

Onwuegbuzie, A., & Johnson, A. (2006). The validity issues in mixed research. *Research in Schools 13*(1), 48–63.

Onwuegbuzie, A., & Leech, N. (2005, March 10). A typology of errors and myths perpetuated in educational research textbooks. *Current Issues in Education* [online], *8*(7). Accessed July 11, 2010 at http://cie.ed.asu.edu/volume8/number7/.

Peshkin, A. (1988). In search of subjectivity. One's own. *Educational Researcher, 17*(7), 17–21.

Perelman, C. (1982). *The Realm of Rhetoric.* Notre Dame, IN: University of Notre Dame.

Polkinghorne, D. (2007). Validity issues in narrative research. *Qualitative Inquiry, 13*(4), 471–486.

Popham, W. (1997). Consequential validity: right concern—wrong concept. *Educational Measurement: Issues and Practice, 16*(2), 9–13.

Richardson, L. (1994). Writing: A method of inquiry. In N. K. Denzin & Y. S. Lincoln (Eds.), *Sage handbook on qualitative research* (1st ed.) (pp.516–529). Thousand Oaks, CA: Sage.

Richardson, L. (1997). *Fields of play: Constructing an academic life.* New Brunswick, NJ: Rutgers University Press.

Richardson, L. (2000). Evaluating ethnography. *Qualitative Inquiry, 6,* 253–256.

Rolfe, G. (2000). *Research, truth and authority: Postmodern perspectives on nursing.* Basingstoke, UK: Macmillan.

Rolfe, G. (2006) Judgment without rules: Towards a postmodernist ironist concept of research validity. *Nursing Inquiry, 13*(1), 7–15.

Rose, H., & Rose, S. (1976). The radicalisation of science. In H. Rose & S. Rose (Eds.), *The radicalisation of science: Ideology of/in the natural sciences* (pp. 1–32). London: Macmillan.

Scheurich, J. (1997). *Research Method in the Postmodern.* London: Falmer.

Schwandt, T. (1996). Farewell to criteriology. *Qualitative Inquiry 2*(1), 58–72.

Schwandt, T. (2000). Three epistemological stances for qualitative inquiry: Interpretivism, hermeneutics, and social constructionism. In. N. K. Denzin & Y. S. Lincoln (Eds.), *Sage handbook of qualitative research* (2nd ed.) (pp. 189–214). Thousand Oaks, CA: Sage.

Seale, C. (1999). Quality in qualitative research. *Qualitative Inquiry, 5*(4), 465–478.

Searle, J. (1970). *Speech acts: An essay in the philosophy of language.* Cambridge, UK: Cambridge University Press.

Shadish, W. R., Cook, T. D., & Campbell, D. T. (2002). *Experimental and quasi-experimental designs for generalized causal inference.* Boston: Houghton-Mifflin.

Shaffer, D. & Serlin, R. (2004). What good are statistics that don't generalize? *Educational Researcher, 33*(9), 14–25.

Shepard, L. (1997). The centrality of test use and consequences for test validity. *Educational Measurement: Issues and Practice, 16*(2), 13–24.

Sikes, P., & Gale, K. (2006). *Narrative Approaches to Education Research.* Accessed January 24, 2011 at http://www.edu.plymouth.ac.uk/resined/narrative/narrativehome.htm.

Smith, J., & Deemer, D. (2000). The problem of criteria in the age of relativism. In. N. K. Denzin & Y. S. Lincoln (Eds), *Sage handbook of qualitative research* (2nd ed.). (pp. 877–896). Thousand Oaks, CA: Sage.

Toulmin, S. (1969). *The use of argument.* Cambridge, UK: Cambridge University Press.

Tugendhat, E. (1986). *Self-consciousness and self-determination.* (Paul Stern, Trans.) Cambridge, MA: MIT Press.

Tracy, S. (2010). Qualitative quality: Eight "big-tent"criteria for excellent qualitative research. *Qualitative Inquiry, 16*(10), 837–851.

Wilkins, M. (1999, May 11). *Social responsibility in science.* Paper presented at the Institute of Science in Society, London.

Winter, G. (2000). A comparative discussion of the notion of validity in qualitative and quantitative research. *Qualitative Report, 4*(3&4). Retrieved January 24, 2011 from http://www.nova.edu/ssss/QR/QR4-3/winter.html.

Wittgenstein, L. (1974). *Tractatus logico-philosophicus.* London: Routledge Humanities Press International.

Wolming, S., & Wikström, C. (2010). The concept of validity in theory and practice. *Assessment in Education: Principles, Policies and Practice, 17*(2), 117–132.

Woodhouse, E., Hess, D., Breyman, S. & Martin, B. (2002). Science studies and activism: Possibilities and problems for reconstructivist agendas. *Social Studies of Science, 32*(2), 297–319.

CHAPTER TWO

Generalizability

STAFFAN LARSSON

What's the Point?

Generalizing talk is rife in everyday life: citizens discuss the morals of politicians, politicians give speeches evaluating the standards of schools. Such talk habitually expresses assumptions that all politicians are the same or that schools nowadays in some general sense are different from schools in earlier times. The personal knowledge behind these opinions might be limited to what has been reported on television and personal experiences, while the speakers' knowledge of schools in earlier times is fragmented to say the least. The shaky support for general judgments is often striking.

However, it's difficult to avoid making generalizations. Our language is permeated with taken-for-granted generalizations. As soon as we open our mouths, we cannot avoid generalizing. We cannot abstain from adopting standpoints for which we do not have empirical data. We would be severely handicapped as citizens and as persons. Consider this: every piece of data immediately becomes data from an earlier time—we have to think that it has a meaning, even if it is, in principle, already the next day, a new situation. We generalize from one moment to the next. Generalizations are therefore not only dubious; they are also useful to the degree that we might say is necessary in human life. Researchers also generalize and actually have difficulties avoiding it, even if they want to. The issue of generalization is thus complicated, and absolute answers tend to be difficult to defend. However, in research, generalization is also a profoundly practical question. It is not a very good idea to flee from the issue—the question doesn't disappear by avoiding it. Readers and other audiences might ask themselves: Where and when are these interpretations useful? Questions about generalizability are present not only for researchers, but often even more so for the interested general public, even if their understanding is not very sophisticated. It might be better if researchers had a more reflected view, rather than leaving it to the reader.

This chapter focuses on problems of generalization in qualitative research. It is common to divide social science into quantitative and qualitative research. One can identify qualitative research as certain practices and the intellectual discourses related to these practices, which are at least in certain respects different from those under the heading of quantitative. The division is sometimes contested and the dividing line is not clear cut. I agree with the last proposition—behind the two labels are a number of different research approaches, genres, or traditions; that is, the division between qualitative and quantitative is crude but useful, bearing the lack of precision in mind. However, I find it unwarranted to argue that there are no differences or that differences are gradual, which means I find the argument of a dimension between quantitative and qualitative completely misleading (e.g., Ercikan & Roth, 2006). It is not a case of dimensionality, but rather one of qualitative differences between a number of lines of reasoning. The dimension argument would blur the logic that resides within various research traditions in terms of the knowledge interest, the philosophical underpinning, and other aspects that belong to methodology. Such relations should be brought to light and developed rather than made invisible.

Furthermore, my argument is that there are several lines of reasoning; that is, more than the two that the pragmatic divide between quantitative and qualitative would suggest. Qualitative research can be seen as a family name for several rather different lines of reasoning with consequences for how generalization is to be conceived. This is also the case with quantitative research. It is not one coherent methodology, but also a family—researchers using experimental designs often have to use other lines of generalization reasoning than those working with descriptive statistics. Showing this pluralism in the case of qualitative research is the first aim of this chapter.

My second task is to discern and describe a number of lines of reasoning about generalization substantially in order to contribute to identifying possible variants in the thinking about generalization.

Scholars doing qualitative research often demonstrate a lack of enthusiasm for the issue of generalization. The limited number of elaborated texts on generalization—or transferability or external validation, whatever words are used about the topic—suggests a pattern of avoidance. One reason might be a feeling among qualitative researchers that they have an inferior hand in an imaginary poker game with those using quantitative approaches. The concept of generalization is actually dismissed altogether by some qualitative researchers, such as Usher (1996, p. 14). Scheurich finds the concept useless on philosophical grounds when he declares that his postmodernist orientation explicitly links the word to a modernist realism: "While these generalizations are said to represent reality, in my mind they mostly represent the mindset of the researcher" (Schuerich, 1997, p. 64). Scheurich is in fact making a generalization, while at the same time rejecting the use of it. This illustrates the difficulty of escaping the "mindset," which is signified by the word.

Greenwood and Levin (2005) are, on the other hand, critical of the universal critique of generalization; it is "without any sense of social or moral responsibility" (p. 55). Carspecken (Carspecken & Walford, 2001) is also critical against a general dismissal of methodology and finds a totalizing relativism "absolutely debilitating for most of us" (p. 2). Social science researchers do sometimes justify their profession by contributing to public debates. If they content themselves with a denial of the need to answer questions about the potentials and limits of the claims, they might not be taken seriously. Deliberating on possible meanings of generalization instead of dismissing it might therefore be a good idea—even if concepts are only "usable." Social responsibility and usefulness might be valid arguments, but at the heart of the matter are adequate conceptualizations of generalization as a human practice in academic contexts.

One can note that the dismissals operate on the assumption that the word "generalization" has a clear, singular meaning. I think this is a mistake and will actually base my text on showing an alternative view; that is, the possibility of discerning a number of different lines of reasoning concerning generalization. Beyond a crude commonsense singular meaning to signify the practice we call generalization, there are a number of different logics and practices hiding, which can be illuminated.

I will therefore argue for the need to elaborate the conceptual meaning instead of marginalizing the issue of generalization. Such an elaborated discourse is not limited to pointing out how to generalize; it also involves identifying lines of reasoning when generalization is not possible or even unnecessary. A third "thesis" is that specific kinds of research are faced with particular problems of generalization, which means that there is an issue concerning which line of reasoning on generalization is appropriate in relation to a particular piece of research.

What is the use of such an elaboration of the meanings of generalization? The point is not primarily to identify the best, but rather to communicate a repertoire of different lines of reasoning. Awareness of a repertoire of possible meanings will hopefully make arguments about generalization more precise and rational: you need a number of tools in order to be able to choose what is appropriate for various tasks.

Words and What They Signify

Words are difficult in the sense of the relation between words and what they signify. In our case, the word "generalization" competes, so to speak, with other words that seem to bear at least a family resemblance, e.g., "transferability" (Lincoln & Guba, 1999) or external validity (Campbell & Stanley, 1963). On the other hand, it is not easy to delimit the practices which are pointed at, i.e., what the words signify. As a consequence, there is no clear relation between words and what they refer to. However, this is not a unique case; it is rather common, and our trouble might be allayed by Wittgenstein's remark on the worries about the lack of exact concepts when he points out the usefulness of a rough indication of something: "If I tell someone 'Stand roughly here'—may not this explanation work perfectly?" (Wittgenstein, 1958, p. 41). If concepts lack an exact meaning, they can still be useful. I therefore suggest that we accept a rough but useful point of departure in order to arrive later at a more elaborated, still not exact, but even more useful understanding.

Sometimes it's fun to look at a Latin dictionary, even if it does not prove anything. The word "generalization" seems to have a root in that language and we can find its branches in various modern languages: in French, Spanish and Italian, it is basically the same word signifying the phenomenon we are looking for. The Latin word "gener" is given the meaning "a daughter's husband, son-in-law" (Lewis & Short, 1966, p. 806) and "generalis" refers to: "I. Of or belonging to a kind or species, generic (very rare)" and "II. Of or relating to all, general" (ibid, p. 806). Generalization obviously has to do with relations between individual cases: what are the "relatives" of the classroom that was investigated? Are all classrooms in the same family or do they belong to the same species? However, the metaphor and its roots might betray the proper meaning of generalization in our research context: sons-in-law are often rather different from the rest of the family, i.e., the contemporary use is quite different, not least since we expect more similarity between the individual cases, which are studied, and other cases, which are generalized to. Metaphors should obviously be handled with care—they point to something, but in this case they must not be understood literally. In the end, we must find the meaning in the contemporary use of words or we could persuade readers to use familiar words in some new way. This latter possibility is the challenge.

What's Wrong with a Uniform Meaning?

The view that generalization has one uniform meaning is not only expressed in everyday contexts, there are also researchers who take this view. We saw it in Usher's (1996) and Scheurich's (1997) dismissals, and in a dictionary of statistics and methodology defining generalization, one can see the same singular view: in this case, it is the idea of sampling from a population, which resides in the definition: "The extent to which you can come to conclusions about one thing (often a population) based on information about another (often a sample)" (Vogt, 1993). The idea of sampling becomes the model. These two examples share what can be called a "monist view" of generalization, even if they are at opposite ends—for or against the use of the concept. They do not distinguish between various alternatives of meaning.

If we want to be more precise about the meaning of generalization and what is an acceptable way to argue on the issue, there are several problems with such a monist view. The most hard-hitting flaw is if the concept gives a particular aspect of generalization a universal position. If representation through strict sampling of a defined population is pointed out as a prototypical way of defining generalization, other ways of reasoning on generalization will be invisible. Since sampling of this kind is limited to certain kinds of research, the definition will not illuminate the question for a wide range of research: it is, for instance, not very useful for qualitative research, where its logic is different, such as understanding something in its context, rather than as relations between variables.[1] Thinking in terms of sampling from populations is actually of limited use for a lot of research based on experimental design—such research has developed a habit of thinking in terms of replications, that is, a conclusion will be met with skepticism until it is replicated in other laboratories (Shadish, Cook & Campbell, 2002). This line of reasoning is also not included in the monist discourse on generalization.

The view in Vogt's definition thus seems to make important lines of reasoning about generalization invisible. The logic of sampling from a population with its foundation in the theory of probability and the calculable relation between sample and population has no doubt a certain aesthetic elegance that is attractive. It might also be very useful within certain assumptions about the meaning of the categories, often units, which represents something in a uniform way (male/female, etc.) in relation to other units (grades, etc.). However, it also has its limits in such cases, where the logic of a sample from a population seems most suited. Shulman (1997, p. 14) argues that even very ambitious large-scale experiments or quasi-experiments will face the same question from skeptics concerning other populations than those from which the sample was drawn (Shulman, 1997, p. 14). All existing populations might be investigated, but it is not very practical—researchers will therefore routinely accept conclusions and apply them to populations that were not sampled, and not least are that every investigation is used in another time than when the data were collected. There is therefore something practical about generalizations—one has to judge whether something makes sense, rather than making mechanical calculations.

Quantitative Versus Qualitative Research?

Most of the discussion on generalization among qualitative researchers distinguishes between quantitative and qualitative research and then allocates different notions to each. Some find the word "generalization" polluted and therefore propose an alternative word. Denzin and Lincoln (1994), for example, propose "transferability," to be used when researchers have a constructivist or postmodern conviction. On a certain level, it makes sense—we need more distinctions, not fewer. However, the success of this neologism seems to be limited. I would argue that the main problem is the idea that there is one universal notion for all kinds of qualitative research. Even if it differs from the one used in quantitative research, it is in my mind still a mistake. Also Schofield (1993) creates such a dualism in her discussion on generalization. She argues that generalization from a case can be made by considering the similarities of the context between a researched case and the cases that can be generalized to. However, these ideas of a dualism, that is, two meanings of generalization linked respectively to qualitative or quantitative research, can be challenged.

Both monist and dualist answers underestimate the complexity of the problem. Rather, there are good reasons for operating with a plurality, discerning not only arguments for different ways of doing generalization, but also for cases when generalization with good reason is not an important issue. A plurality of lines of reasoning about generalization is needed in order to address a variation of generalization problems. In order to illuminate the issue, different lines of reasoning are presented. Here, the notion of a line of reasoning stands for a certain kind of practical logic. Five qualitatively different lines of reasoning in qualitative research are suggested. I do not claim these five to be the only ones possible, but they should at least illustrate my arguments for a plurality of lines of reasoning. Hopefully, they will also point to the dialectic between the specific research design and what will become warranted reasoning about generalization—different research designs having different kinds of generalization problems.

A pluralism in notions of generalization is not only warranted in qualitative research, it is also argued for concerning quantitative methodology. Shadish, Cook, and Campbell (2002) discern two completely different lines of reasoning on generalization in their textbook on quantitative research. One is linked to description, that is, sampling from populations. Sampling provides suggestions about the distribution of something in the population from which the sample is drawn, but also a technique where the accuracy of the results can be calculated. It is thus a very elegant and strong line of reasoning about generalization. However, it is limited to research where samples from populations can be drawn, in that it does not provide much help for laboratory experiments: "However, in actual experimental practice few researchers ever randomly sample items when constructing measures. Nor do they do so when choosing manipulations or settings" (ibid., p. 23). They therefore argue for a different logic in relation to research, which aims at causal explanations. It turns out that the practice of such experimental designs is not very comfortable with the criteria for generalization that suits descriptive statistics.

To conclude: I hope to show that a number of qualitatively different lines of reasoning on generalization can be demonstrated; that is, the idea of a dimension is a mistake. I will also show that there are kinds of research where generalization is not called for, but that it is also a mistake to dismiss the idea of generalization altogether. I have discerned five different logics in thinking about generalization in qualitative research. These, together with the two logics that are discussed in the literature on quantitative methods, would make seven qualitatively different lines of reasoning about generalization. The knowledge of these seven ways of thinking can be seen as a repertoire that researchers can use in their work: doing, criticizing, or defending research.

Lines of Reasoning on Generalization

Since this text is about qualitative research, it is focused on the five lines of reasoning linked to such research. The reasoning in quantitative and experimental designs will not be presented in full, but will be discussed where appropriate as comparison.

The presentation starts with cases where there is arguably no need for generalization; for example, certain kinds of empirical research are meaningful without any claims of generalization. These cases seem to be of two different kinds. One is typically the one we find in history, where a unique chain of events is investigated. The other kind is quite different—here, it is about single cases that undermine what were believed to be universal truths. Even if it is not necessary to do generalization, it might be wise to be able to warrant the lack of generalization claims in specific pieces of research.

However, many cases of qualitative research cannot dismiss generalization, but must instead formulate positive solutions to the challenge of generalization. One such line of reasoning takes variation of cases as its point of departure. Another has the similarity between the context of the researched case and other cases as the platform for the reasoning. The third argues that the interpretation as a whole, its gestalt, must be seen as a potential for generalization. If the potential is realized, it is then in the eye of the reader, who tries it out on specific cases, to decide if it makes sense in these cases.

1. The Logic of an Ideographic Study

In order to generalize, one must have the assumption that a number of similar cases exist, such that a study of one of them tells us something that is related to the others. The idea of generalization therefore becomes superfluous in an ideographic study since it in principle focuses on unique events. Wright (1971) defines it as: "the descriptive study of individuality" (p. 5). The thought of an ideographic study takes as its starting point a specific metaphor of pieces put together in a pattern. One can use the metaphor of a jigsaw puzzle. The role of a study of this kind is not to say something about other contexts, but to contribute to the broader picture by filling a "hole" in the whole. Let me exemplify. An investigation of Paulo Freire's writings and conceptual inspiration would be justified even if it only interprets the work of one person. Why? One argument could be that it will contribute to the understanding of the tapestry of educational philosophy, for example, how Freire's views connect to various thoughts in philosophy. The study will be like a piece in the big puzzle of the history of ideas. It's also easy to find examples from research on the history of educational reforms when they are conceived as parts of national history.

Wilhelm Windelbrand, a German anti-positivist philosopher at the end of the 19th century, coined the term "idiographic" to describe this kind of research (Wright, 1971, p. 5). Its opposite is "nomothetic," where research aims at discovering universal laws that must be generally applicable. This distinction is still needed since the idea of what research is aiming at is often based on the assumption that the investigated phenomenon is uniform or predictable, that is, as if it was following a law. It is the rule in experimental designs, even in those texts that are sophisticated, when it comes to epistemologies (Shadish et al., 2002). This is also the case in many studies using qualitative approaches, not seldom as an implicit assumption. Audiences reading about case studies often also interpret the case as having universal claims, as if it were nomothetic. The idea of the piece in a puzzle is fundamentally different from the idea that a case is an example of a universal process or of what is typical; it is the idea that each event is different but fits together. It is therefore only applicable, when this logic is reasonable, in certain kinds of history or the study of unique or similar events. This late-19th-century anti-positivism rejected methodological monism; that is, the idea that there was only one uniform method of producing scientific knowledge—an idea advocated by the positivistic philosophers of science. The celebration of the ideographic was part of a revival of hermeneutics as a method for human science. Hermeneutics, the methodology of interpretation, is based on the interplay between pieces and wholes, where the meaning of a piece of data is based on the meaning of the whole and, which is significant, vice versa—the meaning of the whole is based on the meaning of the pieces. A practical example is the interpretation of daily acts. If someone winks, we can interpret it as a sign, but also as a reflex (Geertz, 1999). If it is seen as a sign, it can furthermore be interpreted as an invitation to closer contact. Each interpretation is plausible, but the meaning of the piece of data varies according to what is used as context. Context here can also be other pieces of data, for example, indicating in what culture the winker has grown up, but it can also be broader alternative assumptions such as reflex or message. The choice of interpretation has completely different consequences for action. In academic work, hermeneutics can point to the problem that the interpretation of data can depend on in the chosen context, such as interpretational theory: The same event can be interpreted differently by an economist and a sociologist. However, the idea of the ideographic study was an aspect of the thinking in hermeneutics and is an idea in its own right. One has to ask oneself prior to a study: is this a case, where I expect other similar cases or is the study important as a piece that can complement other studies in a larger pattern?

In history, it is easy to see how investigations into certain events are motivated, not because they represent similar events but because each event is linked to other different events. Talking about generalization in this context is thus a mistake, since it would denote a lack of understanding of the fundamental logic of such research. However, I do not think that all kinds of qualitative research have this logic. In spite of this disagreement, these late-19th-century philosophers' ways of portraying the practice of research are useful in relation to a considerable number of cases. It is therefore perfectly legitimate to investigate the emergence of educational systems in a specific country, without any aim of generalizing the interpretation, as in Durkheim's work about the development of secondary education in France (1985). Even though historical studies or biographies could be seen as prototypical of the first line of reasoning, there are certainly historical investigations that are based on a logic where generalization problems are at the forefront and therefore follow a different kind of logic. Social history, when the purpose is to describe general patterns among the population based on limited information about a number of persons, is one example. We can also think about biographies, which trigger questions about generalization, for example, a schoolteacher representing others of his kind.

Sometimes there are studies that have parts that don't call for generalization, and other parts where questions of generalization arise. Policy ethnographies can be an example. Generalizing from the production of a specific political agenda on education in the EU administration might not be necessary, but when the consequences on the local level are studied, the issue of generalization will be brought up.

Critical comments: One difficulty with this line of reasoning is that the significance of the case becomes crucial. The philosopher or the reform must be important in some way to the broader context. The significance has to be convincingly argued for. The focus on the significance of the single case places certain phenomena in the foreground and others in the background. It is easy to argue that decision making among elites in central positions are important single cases, but it is difficult when the focus is on the local level. Another similar effect is that it is easy to argue that dramatic events are significant cases, while changes in everyday routines are less easy to use as important single cases, where generalization is not needed. So this line of reasoning is limited in use and can only be applied where appropriate; the German philosophers' claims were a contribution, but when they argued that there was only one alternative to the logic of natural science, they overrated the idiographic notion.

2. Studies That Undermine Established Universal "Truths"

The first line of reasoning operated on the assumption that each event had in principle a unique position in history or society. The aim of research work was to construct a weaving of the threads. The second line of reasoning is quite different. The assumption here is more of a liberating kind—to critically scrutinize ideas that have "totalitarian" claims about something. Such universal claims are very common. They can have different origins; some are just taken-for-granted notions in a specific cultural context, e.g., religious convictions; some emanate from science, e.g., biological ideas about what is "natural." In the latter case, they are based on the idea of laws of nature, which are universal. Such claims can be challenged with the aim of undermining unwarranted claims and with the aim of widening the horizon of what is possible.

The focus here is on "negative" cases; that is, where the research creates doubt about something that is generally thought of as true. Each single case that deviates from the established truth will be of vital importance, since it falsifies one essential aspect—the universalistic claim. After such a study has created doubt, the reach of a claim is reduced. This way of arguing can be found in many poststructural approaches. Söndergaard (2002) describes the ambition to "contradict the obvious, to think against the stream of what is taken for granted" (p. 191). Cases that break the rule, which are not in accordance with the available discourses, will do the job of troubling or destabilizing the taken-for-granted. What seemed to be essential is contingent, that is, true in some cases, but not always. The undermining effect is enough to make the research meaningful. The line of reasoning here goes like this: all cases must be included if something is universal, i.e., any deviant case undermines the universalism. This does not mean that the numbers per se are not interesting and meaningful, but it is a completely different question, irrelevant in relation to the claim of universalism. An example: in a study by Brown, Cervero, and Johnson-Bailey (2000), we can discern an undermining effect on the idea that it is progressive to have a pedagogy that gives students a strong position in the classroom. They describe how students challenge the authority of black, female math teachers. Students' image of a "genuine" math teacher is a white male; thus their challenge is based on race and gender constructions, and the conclusion will undermine a dominating idea about the political implications of pedagogy where students are influential. This case shows that such pedagogy could support racism and sexism. Phoenix (2004) presents findings undermining critical pedagogy's claim of liberating from oppression, showing how such pedagogy operates in relation to black students' views of masculinity. Such studies invite reconsideration of the formulation of pedagogies in these cases.

That universal claims about human nature have been undermined by case studies is nothing new. Mead's work on cultural variation of gender constructions is a classic example from social anthropology, giving rise to doubt about something being "natural" (Mead, 1963). Undermining universal claims when it is possible is extremely important, since false universal claims are used to delimit human understanding of the possible range of being—that is, they suppress possibilities and place false limits on freedom. History is full of examples where science has presented arguments about human nature that have been used to legitimate racism, sexism, etc. What was believed to be universal becomes contingent. It is easy to see it as parallel with Popper's (1963 focus on falsifying as the central attitude in research. The underlying assumption is, in his case, that science is about universals, however preliminary. Social or human science strives towards universals only to a limited degree. We probably encounter more universalisms in the public debate, where citizens' opinions are influenced.

Critical comments: This line of reasoning is limited insofar as it presupposes that there are universal claims to investigate. In contemporary human and social science, such grand ambitions are often not put forward. To some extent, this is based on the fact that these parts of academia view human action as socially and culturally constructed and thus do not follow universal laws. However, humans are also the legitimate objects of natural science, as well as social or human science, which creates a fruitful area of debate on questions about human nature.

When Generalization Claims Are Called For: Three Lines of Reasoning

I would argue that qualitative studies, with the above exceptions in mind, on the whole have difficulties in avoiding making claims about generalization. The phrase "one cannot draw any conclusions about any other situation than the investigated cases" is sometimes used in defense of qualitative studies. Taken seriously, it reduces the interest in many qualitative studies to practically nothing. If someone has made a study of a classroom in the spring of 2005, it is difficult to take it seriously if there are no ambitions to say something that can be of use outside this situation in time and space and the persons involved: "...there must be a *capacity* for generalization; otherwise there would be no point to giving such careful attention to the single case" (Wolcott, 1994, p. 113, emphasis in original). I want to show possible solutions that can be used when appropriate, and add three qualitatively different lines of reasoning to the two already presented.

3. Enhancing the Generalization Potential by Maximizing Variation
This line of reasoning is useful in studies where a number of cases constitute the empirical basis. Qualitative interview studies are examples. This logic is based on the fact that a sample

is drawn, but the logic of sampling is opposite to the standard of statistical sampling. Instead of relying on random chance in order to calculate the representativeness, one wants to cover a variation of qualitatively different cases of a phenomenon. To understand how pupils experience learning about religions, one might get a fuller understanding by choosing pupils of as many different religious backgrounds as possible instead of a representative sample. Covering more of the variation in qualitative different views will enhance the generalizability of the study. In an interview study based on random sampling, the most common answer would be really well represented, and unusual answers would be less or not at all represented. In order to maximize the differences, a sample should be based on qualified guesses about how to achieve this broad variation.

This thought has a certain similarity with "theoretical sampling" (Glaser & Strauss, 1967): sampling should be based on what was already known and what was needed next in order to push the understanding of the researched phenomenon further. The variation of a phenomenon should be investigated. The idea of maximizing variation has been most explicitly expressed in the tradition called phenomenography (Marton, 1994), where the focus is on describing variation in ways of seeing a phenomenon. It is often used in studies of learning, for example in science education. In order to generalize from a certain study, one needs to optimize the probability that as many qualitatively different cases or categories as possible will be possible to describe. This means that the uncommon case is as important as the most common case.

In this kind of reasoning, one cannot generalize from one specific category or case but only from the whole set—the variation in the study should be expected to also exist in relevant situations that one wants to generalize to. If the researcher has made a wide selection of persons or cases that could be expected to be diverse, one could expect to have covered the variation relatively well. Kennedy (1979) summarizes this line of reasoning: "The range of characteristics included in a sample increases the range of population characteristics to which generalization is possible" (p. 665). This line of reasoning is actually also present in Shadish et al.'s text about generalization from experiments: "purposive sampling of heterogeneous instances is most commonly used" (2002, p. 23).

Critical comments: The usefulness of this line of reasoning is limited to such studies where one operates with not too few cases, as for instance with qualitative interviews. It is really not an option for traditional case studies, where concentration on one or two cases is often recommended in order to conduct an in-depth study. Another problem is the choice of cases or persons: It is not easy to predict the real difference on the basis of surface impression or formal characteristics. This presupposes a deterministic logic, which is often not realistic—cases often turn out not to be what they looked like or persons with certain social characteristics do not follow prejudices about how such persons should think. A third problem is the lack of knowledge about the real breadth of the variation: in terms of generalization, it is impossible to know how many undetected variants there are in real life.

4. Generalization Through Context Similarity

The similarity between a researched context and other contexts is in the focus of some texts on generalization. Thorne's (1993) study of how gender identities are shaped by everyday interaction in schoolyards should, according to this logic, be possible to generalize to similar schoolyards. Schofield (1993) argues that this conception should be the foundation of a view of generalization that is adapted to the essence of qualitative research. She refers to a number of authors who have developed such arguments about context similarity. The concept "transferability" has been defined as similarity between contexts: Lincoln and Guba (1999) define the constructivist or postmodern version as something that is related to abstracted results, "the transferability of which is an empirical matter, depending on the degree of similarity between sending and receiving contexts" (p. 404). The focus of attention here is obviously on context and on the similarity between contexts. Strauss and Corbin (1990) suggest that "explanatory power" should replace generalizability. In this case, prediction is a key factor: "Therefore, in writing the theoretical formulations that evolved from our study, we specify the conditions that give rise to certain phenomena" (p. 267). One is given the impression that they operate with causality as a presupposition; that is, if conditions are known, the consequences should be possible to predict. I judge this to be a variant of context similarity, even if they do not express it in such a way.

Hammersley (1992), whose line of reasoning about empirical generalizations is about similarity of settings, views similarity as an open question that has to be answered by means of empirical support, e.g., survey data. Lincoln and Guba (1999) point out that judgments about generalizability presuppose that contexts are known, which often means that those who want to use the research are better able to judge than the researchers. Consequently, they draw the conclusion that "the responsibility of the original investigator ends in providing sufficient descriptive data to make such similarity judgments possible" (p. 404).

Here, I want to stress that something quite different, which has important consequences, is introduced. When they argue that the researcher is not necessarily the person with the obligation to judge the generalizability, they change the power relation between the researcher and his audience. It is the audience who are often in the best position to judge the similarity of a context with the one portrayed in the research work. The role of the researcher then changes into one where the description of the context of the interpretations is given this new function: to communicate a context to an audience, which has the role of judging whether some context they know about is similar to the researched context. They refer to Ryle's (1968) and Geertz's (1999) concept of "thick description" as a foundation for drawing conclusions about context similarity. Geertz's text discusses the validity of descriptions in terms of thin and thick: thin is a description that only describes behavior, while a thick description also includes actors' interpretation of the world. A wink of the eye could be seen as something that has a meaning (thick) or as a reflex without any message (thin). If I interpret Lincoln and Guba with the help of Geertz's text, it could be concluded that the concept of "context" should not only refer to descriptions of material circumstances and actors' behavior but also to the interpretational world, such as a similar culture.

Critical comments: Descriptive statistics' way of dealing with generalization is based on probability theory. This is not an option in qualitative research, which is normally based on one case or a limited number of interviews or observed sites. Instead, the focus must be on what is empirically known rather than theoretical assumptions. The focus on similarity between the research context and other similar contexts becomes a kind of parallel to the relation between sample and population. Instead of operating with a similarity that is an a priori assumption, as in traditional sampling, one must judge the similarity empirically and a posteriori. One problem here is the difficulties in judging when a similarity is present. It is obvious that the varying exactness in describing a case points to varying numbers of similar cases. The exactness of similarity searched for in order to draw conclusions about unresearched cases often seems to be unknown to both the researcher and the reader of a study.

Another problem concerns a more theoretical aspect. Generalization via context similarity presupposes that the context determines the phenomenon or pattern. It's the idea that a specific context will always have the same qualities in a phenomenon or pattern. It is not difficult to imagine cases where persons act differently in the same context or even that the same person acts differently in the same context on different occasions. The assumption that qualities are determined is, to say the least, an underestimation of the complexities of human action. One is reminded of the fact that the same person is able to operate with different interpretations of the same phenomenon. Different persons act differently in the same context, not least because of different personal histories. Normally, it is not practical to check such things in order to judge the possibility of drawing conclusions about generalization. One limitation in regards to this conception is that it is suited to case studies where there is an abundance of context data. It is less suited to, for instance, qualitative interviews where context data are less prominent.

5. Generalization Through Recognition of Patterns

Research texts can communicate ways of seeing something, often with the ambition of transcending old or taken-for-granted ways of understanding the studied phenomena—this is the "heuristic validity" of interpretational research (Larsson, 2005). Qualitative research often produces such interpretations—theoretical constructions, concepts, or descriptions, i.e., patterns or configurations—that can be recognized in the empirical world. The reader is invited to notice something they did not see before. We can view this as a variant of generalization: the communicated pattern is recognized in new cases. The fundamental role of the act of communication has also been stressed in research: theoretical constructions are often metaphorical, terms like "social capital" or when society is depicted as an organism (Atkinson, 1990). We might understand social science as something that can be interpreted as rhetorical and persuasive. Lee (2009) has pointed out how doctoral students' training can be seen from such a perspective. This rhetorical side is not necessarily a problem or something "false," but can be the fundamental output of a piece of research: the formulation in words of a process will be the important thing. Using words as tools, new aspects of something become noticeable.

An example: Gamble (2001) describes the "pedagogy" of a South African furniture carpenter introducing a novice into the trade using wordless communication. Her description cannot be generalized in a simple way to all other carpenters introducing novices, but knowing Gamble's description and interpretation of the case, one may recognize similar wordless pedagogy in teaching, which can be similar, but also different in varying degrees from the original case. Since in this case it is a process, not a person or a context that is the focus of her research, it is very difficult to predict when or where something similar will happen. On the other hand, we can be alert to the potential use of Gamble's study when we are observing situations and persons that are roughly similar. Gamble's words provide a bridge from her case to readers' ways of noticing processes in similar contexts. But such context similarity is only a potential for recognizing the process. There is a loose relation between process and context. The description might not make sense to processes in similar contexts—it is only a potential.

Another familiar example: In a study of a North American university, a "hidden curriculum" is described (Snyder, 1971). With the help of the analysis of the hidden curriculum and the description of it, it becomes possible to recognize similar patterns in other educational in-stitutions. This pattern has reached a huge audience at least indirectly; many can recognize the pattern of a hidden curriculum in various contexts. However, it would be too much to expect such a description or interpretation to be appropriate in all other similar contexts—it is also here only potentially useful in other cases.

The line of reasoning here is that generalization is about the potential use of a piece of research: generalization is an act, which is completed when someone can make sense of situa-tions or processes or other phenomena with the help of the interpretations that emanate from research texts. A lot of educational research describes and interprets processes which emerge in situations and human actions, but only as a potential. You cannot claim that they always emerge in these situations or when these persons act. This creates special challenges for gener-alization claims. We can compare the use of a substantial portion of qualitative research with the development of a diagnostic repertoire: interpretational tools for identifying patterns in the everyday world and making better sense of the world around us. We can compare with nosography in medicine: the systematic description of diseases.

Here, I will explore the limitations of a focus on context in more detail, as a basis for generalization. There are two ways of problematizing such a generalization concept. The first argues that context similarity does not imply that the interpretation of one context must be useful in another similar context—it might, but does not have to. The other argument is that interpretations of a context transcend the original context; they can be and often are useful in interpreting other contexts that are not necessarily strikingly similar. We even use interpreta-tions, which were originally about one kind of practice, to understand a different kind of prac-tice. I would suggest that there is a logic here that is quite different from the reasoning based on "context similarity."

According to the first argument—interpretations might, but do not have to be, useful in another similar context—context similarity only indicates a pragmatic potentiality. It can be practical to be alert to the possibility that an interpretation from a research study makes sense also in this new case. However, being able to generalize from a researched case to this new case is a matter of how the interpretation fits the whole case. It is the whole configuration—interpretation in context—that is the basis of generalization, an experience of recognition of something. Here, there is no a priori assumption that an interpretation can be generalized to similar contexts: it is not enough. The generalization is loosely related to contexts in the sense that the researcher cannot predict in which cases the interpretation is useful, only suspect in which contexts one might look for it. It is often more a matter of "realization"—someone who is familiar with a piece of research realizes that the original interpretation "fits" cases they have met. The metaphor of diagnoses can again serve to illustrate the point: the task for medical doctors is to recognize patterns that turn up during the examination and in conversation with a patient, where all the pieces form a configuration, a specific diagnosis. They realize that they have a case of x.

In one way, this line of reasoning operates with the same assumption that some of the authors in the "context similarity" category worked with: that the task of generalization is shifted from the researcher to the audience. However, it is not only about the context, but also the interpreted context; a convincing interpretation will emerge when the original text is used to interpret a new context. I operate here with the assumption that no context can be identified without interpreting it as something. A piece of qualitative research "offers" a way of interpreting other cases than the original.

A difficulty for generalization through context similarity is a hidden assumption about homogeneity within a context. It is a trivial fact that different students or groups of students in the same classroom act differently. To return to the comparison with the medical doctor: simply saying that a certain context determines a specific illness is not accepted; rather, the specific qualities in the patient's state come together with more peripheral information about circumstances and history, etc. In this case, it is also the user of knowledge who determines when a description (interpretation) is useful and applicable. Kennedy makes this point, discussing evaluation: "The evaluator should produce and share the information, but the receivers of the information must determine whether it applies to their own situation" (Kennedy, 1979, p. 672). She also points to law and clinical medicine as fields where this is an established way of generalizing. Stake (1995) touches on this line of reasoning in a text on "naturalistic generalizations": "Naturalistic generalizations are conclusions arrived at through personal engagement in life's affairs or by vicarious experience so well constructed that the person feels as if it happened to themselves" (p. 85). It seems as if Stake focuses on description with very thick descriptions—as if it were lived experience that was described. I think this is an unnecessary limitation of this line of reasoning. It is as if language, metaphors, constructions, were not valid parts of humans' ways of making sense of their world (Atkinson, 1990). The ideology of naturalism has without doubt been subjected to criticism (for instance, Clifford & Marcus, 1986). In spite of this, Stake operates with a variant of "generalization through recognition of patterns."

Schofield (1993), who seems to focus on context similarity, transcends the focus on the case as representing the typical by suggesting the choice of cases, which can be the leading edge of change (p. 103). She also discusses the choice of exemplary cases, thus giving it a normative role as an ideal (pp. 106–107). It is obvious from her suggestion that generalization here is focused on what the audience can learn from it, but it is not generalization through recognition of patterns in the empirical world. Wolcott (1994) might be closer when he gives the reader the role of "completing" the researcher's contribution: "The art of descriptive research, I believe, is in portraying the case at hand so well that readers themselves make the generalizations for us. They fill in or complete the pattern work that we outline only faintly" (p. 113). Generalization by recognizing a pattern can happen even if the context to be understood is different from the original study, as long as the pattern is recognizable—a somewhat odd consequence of this line of reasoning.

Critical comments: The strength of this case is that it can deal with research, where there is a loose relation between context and the phenomenon in focus. I think this line of reasoning is more realistic than context similarity in many cases, not least when the objects of study are processes. Giving the user "responsibility" for generalizations highlights the issue of authority: the researcher loses authority or at least control and the audience becomes the judge of the meaningfulness of a piece of research.

The audience might be other academics or practitioners—both with varying degrees of knowledge and experience of the studied phenomena. Audiences are not necessarily very sophisticated, which risks corrupting the original qualities of a study when it is generalized and used. On the other hand, serious practitioners working in relevant contexts can be the audience researchers are hoping for, since they can be the actors, who should be mobilized by the research. This should not least be the case for critical researchers, with aspirations to make nonresearchers form opinions, and eventually also political action to organize something differently.

The lack of a clear claim on which to generalize contexts might reduce the possibility for researchers to act as experts when facing a skeptical audience. This might be a blessing when it reduces the halo effect of academic authority, for example when scholars judge in cases they do not know more about than anyone else. On the other hand, having carried out a study is supposed to generate expertise and respect for that expertise—it is on the whole a fundamental argument for doing research at all.

The researcher's skill in persuading the audience (as well fellow researchers and the general public) becomes a cornerstone of a generalization of an interpretation. An effective rhetoric and the precise use of language become necessary. This is nothing new—effective metaphors have always been part of successful social science and aesthetic qualities are very much highlighted as key qualities in qualitative research (Atkinson, 1990; Denzin, 2000; Richardson, 2000). However, this invites difficult questions about the boundaries between warranted claims and seductive language, which will not wane since there seems to be no convincing demarcation line (Phillips, 1987). The dialectic in a debate about the validity of an interpretational pattern might help to expose the usefulness of it.

I think "institutionalized dialectics" is underestimated in the discussion about quality in academic claims. We all know about various institutions where rhetoric combined with dialectics are used: in courts the conflictual positions of prosecutors and advocates are institutionalized and the qualities of the arguments put forward by rhetorical skills on both sides will be judged through the argumentative conflict. Every claim will be met by arguments, which are searching for the weak point, etc. Universities have the same in seminars, in disputations, which were for a long time the place where academic skill was shown; it was not writing a dissertation, but defending it that was evaluated. Durkheim (1985) claimed, writing about the medieval university in Paris, that disputations were the method to gain knowledge in empirical matters, while lectures should be held only in subjects where truth was necessary, such as logic and mathematics. Through the dialectic struggle of trying to put forward the best arguments, the public could get a better grasp of the issue. Critical examination in such a deliberation might enhance the precision in generalization. It also contextualizes rhetoric in a way that makes it a valuable tool rather than a problem. However, skilled rhetoric without a counterpart is a problem, since it makes it possible to get away with poor claims. If such institutionalized dialectic processes exist within academia, this is not obvious in the case of readers outside academia, those involved with practice or decision making. The argument about the power of rhetoric being "disciplined" by a context of dialectic debates is therefore limited in this respect.

Final Remarks

I hope I've convinced the readers about the possibility of discerning a number of qualitatively different lines of reasoning. This should also show the fruitfulness of making different distinctions in order to identify the proper kind of argument in relation to the specific case and approach.

The argument that there is a dimension between quantitative and qualitative, as described by Ercikan and Roth (2006), should also be refuted by the same demonstration, even if those using experimental design can have the same kind of generalization problem. However, even in this case, it is not fruitful to think about a dimension, but rather to distinguish between different lines of reasoning. It is difficult to identify what the dimension should be and what the poles should represent.

It seems that reasoning about cases, when generalizations are not necessary, have escaped being described in texts on generalization. I have not found any text on this issue yet, but that certainly does not prove that such texts do not exist. I think it is important to elaborate the reasons also in these cases. It sharpens the academic sensitivity about when it is warranted to abstain from generalization claims. It might also make writers and readers more aware of the kind of logic that legitimate such research.

Is There Something Behind the Pluralism?

Another issue: Is the pluralism in generalization reasoning a consequence of some other variation? If we look carefully at the five lines I have discerned, we can notice differences on the level of epistemology or knowledge interest, to borrow Habermas's term. The idiographic line of reasoning is focused on a coherent tapestry of pieces, creating an interpretational whole of pieces and whole constituting each other, according to the hermeneutic methodological tradition. Habermas relates this to the 19th-century interest in building national identities through a common interpretation of history. Nowadays, we can see how interpretations are used in similar ways to construct consensus and identities, which have other motives than a nationalistic one.

The "undermining" logic is actually the enemy of the latter project. Here, it is linked to a knowledge interest, which is turned against consensus and universalisms, often based on the assumption that the latter is totalitarian and oppressive. However, they both escape the call for generalization.

The "variation" line of reasoning seems to be based on the assumption that it is important to focus on variation, since precision is the consequence of being able to relate differences and communalities. To maximize variation is an effort to develop the potential in qualitative research to describe rich and nuanced meanings. It therefore seems to be something technical, like a tool. A similar line of reasoning is used in experimental methodology.

The "similar context" variant assumes in principle that context is overarching and produces the "thing" in focus, which is to be generalized. This is a special kind of assumption of the role of the context.

The last line of reasoning is based on an assumption that the social world is complex and, at least on a practical level, in a flux, so that precise prediction is often not possible. It also contains the view that language, that is, the description of a phenomenon, is at least often a prerequisite for noticing or discerning something or even producing the existence of something. The assumption here is that research can produce conceptions or interpretational tools, which might become part of the perceptions and ordinary talk also outside of academia.

As can be seen from this section, each of the five lines of reasoning is imbedded in different notions of what academic knowledge might be. However, in my mind there is also a pragmatic level: once someone has decided to do a certain kind of qualitative research, limitations emerge in what kind reasoning makes sense.

A Repertoire of Possible Lines of Reasoning as Intellectual Tools

It has not been my aim in this text to reach a conclusion about a single best line of reasoning. Rather, I wanted to make the point that there are several different lines of reasoning that can be used. The usefulness of each resides in the specific circumstances and purposes of each piece of research. Qualitative researchers therefore need a repertoire of possible lines of reasoning. Researchers have to find out which line of reasoning makes sense in the specific study they are conducting. Pluralism is underscored by my understanding that in some cases several lines of reasoning on generalization can be applicable to different parts of the same work. Another aspect is also the need to elaborate the reasons, when claiming that generalization is not necessary.

However, nothing is perfect: I have tried to point to problems related to each of the five lines of reasoning. In *Nicomachean Ethics*, Aristotle (1984, pp. 1800–1801) discusses the intellectual virtue of practical wisdom, which I think is important to consider. The notion is about how to deliberate about what is good, but not through the knowledge of universal principles. We might translate it to the virtue of individual cases, taking into account all relevant aspects of the case. A text like mine, discussing something in principle, can invite readers to draw overstated conclusions.

I hope the arguments presented here support the need for a repertoire of lines of reasoning. It can be seen as tools in a toolbox to be used in various situations: doing research, criticizing research, drawing conclusions from a study about the consequences for practice, evaluating research proposals, and so on.

However, there is no reason to believe that there are not more ways of thinking about generalizations.

Campbell and Stanley (1963) wrote that generalization in a strictly logical sense is not possible and that one has to guess: "guesses as to what factors lawfully interact with our treatment variables, and, by implication, guesses as to what can be disregarded" (p. 187). Any study will face the fact that it was performed in the past when it is published—it seems to be difficult to argue in a strictly logical sense that nothing has changed. Generalization is a pragmatic matter where perfection has no place. Case studies and experiments share the problem that they were performed with a limited number of persons and in specific contexts. In spite of this, the academic community accepts them as ways of gaining knowledge. A long time ago, Cronbach criticized the possibility of drawing conclusions from experiments in teaching: "When we give proper weight to local conditions, any generalization is a working hypothesis, not a conclusion" (Cronbach, 1975, p. 125). These examples show the general fragility of conclusions about human social life.

On a more fundamental level, the problem in social science is caused by the fact that human beings are not only nature but also culture, objects of both natural science and human science. What we are investigating are creations of the human mind, formed by interpretations that are not static but dynamic. Giddens (1990) points to a "double hermeneutics"; that is, researchers study humans who are acting on interpretations, which are sometimes produced by researchers. In the final analysis, every researcher as well as every reader must strive for wise estimates of or sophisticated discussions on the limits of the use of a specific study. Rules are collective wisdom in universalistic form, but they must be subordinated to wise judgments about the specific case. In the case of making generalizations, these wise judgments about how to deal with the specific case seem to be in great demand.[2]

Notes

1.   When Glaser and Strauss (1967), in a classic text on the importance of qualitative research, use the expression "theoretical sampling," one should not be confused, since they mean something completely different from the reasoning in descriptive statistics.

2   A first text on generalization in qualitative research was written in Swedish (Larsson, 2010). A different text in English elaborated the theme (Larsson, 2009). The present text is reworded for a broader audience and has also added an extensive section on the nature of differences within research methodology, which is missing from the journal article.

References

Aristotle. (1984). *The complete works of Aristotle*, Vol. 2 (J. Barnes, Ed.). Princeton, NJ: Princeton University Press.

Atkinson, P. (1990). *The ethnographic imagination. Textual constructions of reality.* London: Routledge.

Brown, A. H., Cervero, R. M., & Johnson-Bailey, J. (2000). Making the invisible visible: Race, gender and teaching in adult education. *Adult Education Quarterly, 50*(4), 273–288.

Campbell, D., & Stanley, J. (1963). Experimental and quasi-experimental designs for research on teaching. In N. Gage (Ed.), *Handbook of research on teaching* (pp. 171–246). Chicago: Rand McNally.

Carspecken, P. F., & Walford G. (Eds.). (2001). *Critical ethnography and education* (Studies in Educational Ethnography, Vol. 5). Amsterdam: JAI.

Clifford, J., & Marcus, G. (Eds.). (1986). *Writing culture: The poetics and politics of ethnography.* Berkeley: University of California Press.

Cronbach, L. J. (1975). Beyond the two disciplines of scientific psychology. *The American Psychologist, 30*(2), 16–27.

Denzin, N. K., (2000). Aesthetics and the practice of qualitative inquiry. *Qualitative Inquiry, 6*(2), 256–265.

Denzin, N. K., & Lincoln, Y. S. (Eds.). (1994). *Sage handbook of qualitative research* (1st ed.). Thousand Oaks, CA: Sage.

Durkheim, E. (1985). *The evolution of educational thought. Lectures on the formation and development of secondary education in France.* London: Routledge & Kegan Paul.

Ercikan, K., & Roth, W. M. (2006). What good is polarizing research into qualitative and quantitative? *Educational Researcher, 35*(5), 14–23.

Gamble, J. (2001). Modeling the invisible: The pedagogy of craft apprenticeship. *Studies in Continuing Education, 23*(2), 185–200.

Geertz, C. (1999). Thick description: Toward an interpretive theory of culture. In A. Bryman & R. G. Burgess (Eds.), *Qualitative research*, Vol. 3 (pp. 346–368). London, New York, New Dehli: Sage.

Giddens, A. (1990). *Consequences of modernity*. Cambridge: Polity.

Glaser, B. G., & Strauss, A. L. (1967). *The discovery of grounded theory: Strategies for qualitative research.* New York: Aldine.

Greenwood, D. J., & Levin, M. (2005). Reform of the social sciences, and of universities through action research. In N. Denzin & Y. Lincoln (Eds.), *Sage handbook of qualitative research* (3rd ed.) (pp. 43–64). Thousand Oaks, CA: Sage.

Hammersley, M. (1992). *What's wrong with ethnography? Methodological explorations.* London & New York: Routledge.

Kennedy, M. M. (1979). Generalising from single case studies. *Evaluation Review, 3*(4), 661–678.

Larsson, S. (2005). Om kvalitet i kvalitativ forskning (On quality in qualitative research; in Swedish). *Nordisk Pedagogik, 25*(1), 16–35.

Larsson, S. (2009). A pluralist view of generalisation in qualitative studies. *International Journal of Research & Method in Education, 32*(1), 25–38.

Larsson, S. (2010). Om generalisering från kvalitativa studier (On generalization in qualitative research; in Swedish). In I. Eriksson, V. Lindberg, & E. Österlind (Eds.), *Uppdrag undervisning: Kunskap och lärande*. Lund: Studentlitteratur.

Lee, A. (2009). When the article *is* the dissertation: Pedagogies for a PhD by publication. In C. Aitchison, B. Kamler, & A. Lee (Eds.), *Publishing pedagogies for the doctorate and beyond* (pp. 12–29). London: Routledge.

Lewis, C. T., & Short, C. (1966). *A Latin dictionary*. London: Oxford University Press.

Lincoln, Y., & Guba, E. (1999). Establishing trustworthiness. In A. Bryman & R.G. Burgess (Eds.), *Qualitative Research* (Vol. 3) (pp. 397–444). London: Sage.

Marton, F. (1994). Phenomenograhy. In T. Husén & T. N. Postlethwait (Eds.), *The International encyclopedia of education* (2nd ed.) (pp. 4424–4429). Oxford: Pergamon.

Mead, M. (1963). Sex and temperament in three primitive societies (2nd ed.) New York: Morrow Quill

Phillips, D. C. (1987). Validity in qualitative research. Why the worry about warrant will not wane. *Education and Urban Society, 20*(1), 9–24.

Phoenix, A. (2004). Using informal pedagogy to oppress themselves and each other. *Nordisk Pedagogik, 24*, 19–38.

Popper, K. (1963). *Conjectures and Refutations: The Growth of Scientific Knowledge.* London: Routledge.

Richardson, L. (2000). Evaluating ethnography. *Qualitative Inquiry, 6*(2), 253–255.

Ryle, G. (1968). The thinking of thoughts. What is Le Penseur doing? *University Lectures Number 18.* Saskatoon, SK, Canada: University of Saskatchewan Press.

Scheurich, J. J. (1997). *Research method in the postmodern.* London & Washington DC: Falmer.

Schofield, J.W. (1993). Increasing the generalizability of qualitative research. In M. Hammersley (Ed.), *Educational research: Current issues* (pp. 91–113). London: Paul Chapman.

Shadish, W. Cook, T. D., & Campbell, D. T. (2002). *Experimental and quasi-experimental designs for generalized causal inference.* Boston: Houghton Mifflin.

Shulman, L. S. (1997). Disciplines of inquiry in education: A new overview. In R. M. Jaeger (Ed.), *Complementary methods for research in education* (2nd ed.) (pp. 3–19). Washington DC: American Educational Research Association.

Snyder, B. R. (1971). *The hidden curriculum.* New York: Knopf.

Söndergaard, D. M. (2002). Post-structural approaches to empirical analysis. *Qualitative Studies in Education, 15*(2), 187–204.

Stake, R. E. (1995). *The art of case study research.* Thousand Oaks, CA: Sage.

Strauss, A., & Corbin, J. (1990). *Basics of qualitative research.* Thousand Oaks, CA: Sage.

Thorne, B. (1993). *Gender play: Girls and boys in school.* Buckingham: Open University Press.

Usher, R. (1996). A critique of the neglected epistemological assumptions of educational research. In D. Scott & R. Usher (Eds.), *Understanding educational research* (pp. 9–32). London & New York: Routledge.

Vogt, W. P. (1999). *Dictionary of statistics and methodology* (2nd ed.). Thousand Oaks, CA: Sage.

Wittgenstein. L. (1958). *Philosophical investigations.* Oxford, UK: Basil Blackwell.

Wolcott, H. F. (1994). *Transforming qualitatived data: Description, analysis, and interpretation.* Thousand Oaks, CA: Sage.

Wright, G. H. von (1971). *Explanation and understanding.* Ithaca, NY: Cornell University Press.

CHAPTER THREE

From Empathy to Creative Intersubjectivity in Qualitative Research

MICHAEL G. GUNZENHAUSER

January 31, 2010
I am convinced Pam knew I was not ready for her class. My beard and longish hair, my leftist tendencies, my lack of experience with children, and my job as a professor all attested to this. Yet she took me anyway. She showed me and told me what she knew—and watched my world shake and crumble. (Noblit, 1999, p. 213)

In this passage, George Noblit (1999) captures the beginning of a knowing relation he developed with Pam Knight, a second-grade teacher and a subject in a collaborative research project on caring in elementary schools. Noblit positions himself in the role of student to Knight's teacher, learning from her to challenge his preconceived notion about the pristine quality of caring. He came to understand that caring and power are bound together, and in Knight's case, her performative, teacher-centered power was her route to caring, because in her practice, her teacher-directed instruction enabled her to make connections with individual students and to establish a collective in the classroom.

The knowing relation between Noblit and Knight is the unexpected insight; for through his engagement with Knight over the course of a school year, Noblit came to appreciate her form of caring, which contrasted sharply with his prior understanding of the democratic classroom, critical pedagogy, and caring practice to which he had become attached (especially following Noddings, 1984). In his article, Noblit focuses on the varied power relations between him and Knight during his time in her classroom, and how Knight exercised her power to break the rules of research. As Noblit explains, Knight, "in many ways, chose me to be in her classroom for the caring study, rather than the other way around" (p. 209), inviting him into her constructed moral space and taking responsibility for the success of the study as much as she took responsibility for the success of her second graders. For example, Knight did not intervene in Noblit's struggle to present story time to the children in the classroom by himself, aiding him over time to become more effective as a teacher during the brief period he was solely responsible for them. The arrangement placed him squarely in the role of Knight's student, subject to her moral authority and receiving her caring.

As evidenced by Noblit's essay about his relation with Knight, some of the most compelling insights from qualitative research emerge when research subjects challenge the taken-for-granted notions of the researcher and assert themselves as what Lorraine Code (1995) calls "knowing subjects." I argued in a previous article that qualitative research is most helpfully characterized as an interaction between knowing subjects, a series of knowing relations that have simultaneously ethical and epistemological dimensions (Gunzenhauser, 2006). Echoing Code, to know another well is to come to know the other's cares and concerns, and vice versa. Echoing another feminist philosopher, Sharon Welch (2000), to know another well is also to subject oneself to critique and to build a solidarity across difference. In these manners, ethics and epistemology intertwine in relation, providing a moral epistemological grounding for inquiry, a rationale and agenda for qualitative research that seeks to be transformative (Gunzenhauser, 2006).

In this chapter, I seek to expand my focus to all qualitative research that claims to be interpretive and to complicate the role of relation in qualitative research for its ontological dimension—the nature of being that is called into play for the researcher and research subjects. Specifically, I am interested here in the nature of relation between the researcher and research subjects. What does it mean to interact with others to produce knowledge in a research setting? The question arises from consideration of empathy, an important aspect of an encounter with another, particularly in what Sharon Todd (2003) refers to as "relations across difference," wherein knowers interact. I argue that a relation across difference occurs whenever a qualitative research studies another knowing subject.

To craft an argument, I turn to theorists who have named empathy as a problematic relational construct, and use that discussion to rest upon a form of intersubjectivity, influenced by Maurice Merleau-Ponty, and as articulated in relation to empathy by Matthew Schertz (2007) and Eva Johansson (2007). To do so, I will walk a fine line between alterity and sameness, which Todd, drawing from a different set of philosophical traditions, warns against. I wish to argue that interpretive qualitative research should be understood as a series of sites of creative intersubjectivity, with empathy as one characteristic of that relation that has potential for creating new forms of being, resulting at times in compelling knowledge and ethical action, but also with the potential for violence and apathy. Of further significance in qualitative research is that the sites for creative intersubjectivity include not only the researcher-researched relation in the field, but also relations that emerge with readers through representations in text.

Relation

It has become a theoretical commonplace to argue that qualitative research has complicated ethical dimensions. Multiple methodologists have been telling us for years that we need to return to our ethical theorizing for understanding the power of qualitative research, whether we are speaking of power in its positive, negative, or ambivalent connotations (Smith & Deemer, 2003). Knowing across difference is a complicated enterprise, amounting to no less than a crisis of representation (Marcus & Fisher, 1986). The potential violence inherent in representing the lives of others has raised legitimate ethical concerns for many qualitative researchers. As Patricia Hill Collins (1998) helps us to see, it is important to act mindful of the dangers, because while we are contemplating whether or not to act or to make our knowledge claims, others will certainly act and make knowledge claims in our place if we do not. If we do not act, then we are faced with learning the new conditions of subjugation rather than creatively participating in the construction of knowledge.

The concern for violence in qualitative research highlights the importance of turning to ethics as an alternative to paralysis, or what Welch (2000) refers to as middle-class despair. I posit that as social science researchers, we cannot act from positions of purity, innocence, or impunity, the quest for which gets in the way of ethical reasoning. Despair speaks perhaps to the limitations of our ethical frames, since as Welch argues, despair is a position of privilege, the despair of a comfortable, middle-class population that is used to receiving whatever it wishes, mostly through nominal effort. As social scientists, educators, and those concerned with acting in the world, the relations we seek and how we respond to them are crucial areas for attention.

Particularly relevant is Patti Lather's (2007) conclusion about what relations across difference mean for social research in a postmodern era:

> It is the encounter with difference that is the motor of history in postmodernism. To use that encounter toward not being so sure of ourselves is ethics in postmodernism. Western knowledge systems assume the innocence of knowing, grasping, understanding. Levinas taught us this is a betrayal of the other into the same. The other who refuses to give itself over to such knowledge is our best teacher. This is the other of our own reformulated thinking as well as those we other and those who other us. Our inability to comprehend makes ethics possible. (p. 160)

Herein Lather speaks of the value of radical alterity, and for qualitative researchers, how one responds to the insight of alterity prefigures one's ethical positioning. Related areas of theorizing provide much support for ethical bases to inquiry. One line of argumentation has been for the need of the fearless speech of *parrhesia* (Burch, 2009; Foucault, 1983/2001), to combat ignorance and victimization. A related line of argumentation has been around the hermeneutics of the subject, wherein the postfoundational self works to constitute itself in multiple and conflicting power relations (Foucault, 2001/2005; Scott, 1991). Another important consideration is the significance of engagement with others, particularly those who are different from ourselves, so that we might embrace our prejudicial nature and listen to others, witness their struggle, and cultivate a rich, ongoing self (Garrison, 1996; Greene, 1988; Ritter, 2008).

I offer creative intersubjectivity as a relational emphasis of interaction between researcher and researched as knowing subjects. Inquiry that aspires to particular knowing is my focus here. Qualitative research that seeks fundamentally to verify existing knowledge, to test hypotheses drawn deductively from prior research, or to search for nomothetic explanations of human phenomena is not my concern in this chapter. I would argue that these forms of research, what most authors term "postpositivist" forms of qualitative research, cannot avoid the ethical issues of relationality and intersubjectivity, and indeed, it could be argued that the subjugation of those concerns is its main limitation.

Nevertheless, in this chapter, my approach will be to focus on empathy as a concept around which many problems of relation revolve. Empathy has recently been addressed as a troubled concept in theorizing. As an emotion, an aspect of communication, and a motivator for ethical action, empathy has been found lacking, an unreliable impulse, something that we cannot demand others to feel, and even potentially dangerous, because the tendency of empathetic feelings is refocus on the one feeling empathetic (the researcher), rather than the others, whose experience draws empathy. Below, I explain these dangers more fully and explain how they come about; but first I explain the draw to relation and empathy as important contributors to ethics, knowing, and being.

Empathy

Generally, empathy is considered to be a phenomenon of projecting one's feelings into the experience of another with the presumption of understanding (Egan, 1986). It is distinct from the related concept of sympathy, which retains a notion of common feeling but does not carry the same connotation of understanding that empathy does. As psychologist Gerard Egan defines it, "Sympathy…denotes agreement, whereas empathy denotes understanding and acceptance of the *person* of the client" (p. 139; emphasis in original). Empathy retains an uncomfortable link to sympathy, but even in the distinction, evident in the definition of empathy is both the strength and limitation of the conception, for as theorists have identified, the notion of projection can be highly problematic.

A contemporary definition of empathy, from the Merriam-Webster Online Dictionary (2010), captures the tension in empathy without including the concept of projection. Empathy here is:

> the action of understanding, being aware of, being sensitive to, and vicariously experiencing the feelings, thoughts, and experience of another of either the past or present without having the feelings, thoughts, and experience fully communicated in an objectively explicit manner. (http://www.merriam-webster.com/dictionary/empathy)

Merriam-Webster highlights a seemingly ineffable connection between one and another, linking emotionally without fully communicating the details of experience. The interesting distinction made between objective communication and vicarious emotional experience is intriguing when considered in the context of qualitative research, with the implication that an encounter with another has the potential for generating understanding not only of the facts of another's experience, but the thoughts and feelings of another as well. This definition taps into what qualitative researchers might consider the ideal outcome of their inquiry. Surely a qualitative research study that is able to tap into subjects' thoughts and feelings (and convey them to a waiting audience) is of tremendous value. Further consideration might be given to what might be considered empathetic representations, wherein a reader of a qualitative research study might experience empathy for the research subjects through a textual representation that conveys feelings, thoughts, and experiences in manners other than "objectively explicit."

Egan's (1986) model of the skilled helper is a counseling model that makes the communication of empathy a central construct, drawing from Carl Rogers and others on the importance of developing empathic relationships with clients. Beginning with the assumption of impossibility of empathy between two persons, Egan also assumes that neither person in a relation has a monopoly on the truth of the situation, paraphrasing Robert Burns about it being a gift to see ourselves as others see us (and we should also keep in mind that we all receive unwanted gifts at times, sometimes from people who misunderstand us or perhaps want us to be a certain way). A counselor who communicates empathy is to be attentive, and empathetic statements back to the client are labels, "interpretations rather than understandings of the client's experience" (p. 126).

Egan (1986) distinguishes between basic empathy and accurate (or advanced) empathy, the former largely denoting the affirmation of an emotion when it is heard expressed, and the latter coming about through interpretation grounded in extended engagement between conversational partners. As Egan explains, basic empathy involves simply acknowledging that a person has conveyed an emotion and a reason for the emotion. Advanced empathy, on the other hand, is available to the skilled helper after some time, when the helper comes to piece together interpretations and make connections that the client has not yet (or cannot) make. Both basic and advanced empathy are important, I would argue, for the relation between the researcher and research subject. Part of being an effective qualitative researcher is building trust with respondents, and active listening is an important tactic for encouraging respondents to keep talking, to give extended responses, and to open up (Rubin & Rubin, 2005). It may be effective to communicate understanding by the way of empathetic responses—respondents may tell the researcher more than they ordinarily would tell a stranger. As a powerful research tool, however, basic empathy is prone to abuse and exploitation—treating research subjects as means to the end of acquiring their knowledge. As Rubin and Rubin (2005) remind us in their model for qualitative interviewing, however, the goal should be relationship building.

To build that relation, basic empathy is inadequate; advanced empathy is more characteristic of engagement between knowing subjects. To use different language, advanced empathy is a responsibility borne out of the relation over time. In qualitative research, advanced empathy comes in at least two places. First, a researcher who engages with a research subject over time eventually begins to make connections that the research subject may or may not have openly discussed. Communicated to the research subject, this interpretation becomes the basis for further dialogue between the researcher and the research subject (some would call it verification, others would refer to it as member checking). In any event, it is understood as an opportunity for meaning. That it is a responsibility as well became clear to me as a novice researcher studying the implementation of an arts integration program at an urban elementary school, wherein I held in too long my interpretations about the challenges the school faced and the principal's frustration with seemingly intractable problems (Gunzenhauser, 1999). A total-quality-management reviewer visiting the school saw nearly immediately what I had been reluctant to explore (his interpretation that the program at the time "was not working" caught me flat-footed, for it was also clear in my data, collected over a semester, but I was reluctant to broach it with the principal). Only when I conveyed my more specific interpretations with the principal did I deepen the relation.

The second place where advanced empathy comes in is in representation. As one responsible for representing another to an audience, the researcher-as-writer presents another with as much integrity as possible. Not only is the representation an enactment of respect for another's perspective, but also careful consideration of how an audience may perceive another's perspective. And further, a faithful representation of the meaning of another's experience, to include thoughts and emotions, actively contributes to understanding of phenomena. For instance, an empathetic portrayal of an ineffective leader avoids demonizing the leader and instead explains some of the motivations and intentions that can lead to ineffective leadership. Flat characters, in other words, are no more respectable or beneficial to understanding in a qualitative study than they are in a novel or film.

In sum, I believe it makes sense to think of qualitative research as including and making use of several aspects or forms of empathy: trust building, depth of interpretation, integrity of representation, audience interpretation, and meaning generation. However, that is a lot to expect from a concept that has such ineffable qualities.

Enactments of Empathy

In one of the earliest examples of encounters with empathy in this period of new awareness of the value of the researcher-researched relation, anthropologist Ruth Behar (1993) wrote in *Translated Woman: Crossing the Border with Esperanza's Story* about the ways in which her life intersected (both real and imagined) with the ostensible subject of her research, a Mexican woman called Esperanza Hernández struggling to craft a healthy, independent, and nonviolent existence, despite her social class. The working-class hero role seemed primed for the study, but that did not work out for Behar:

> I jumped on her as an alluring image of Mexican womanhood, ready to create my own exotic portrait of her, but the image turned around and spoke back to me, questioning my project and daring me to carry it out. (p. 4)

Hernández seems to have no intention of being an obedient research subject, drawing the much wealthier (by comparison) Behar family into her life with expectations of subtle and explicit patronage. The text has all the complications of empathy, and at times the linkages between Hernández and Behar are incomplete (to Behar's admission), suggesting that Behar is actively engaging with the perils of projection. The reader is treated to extensive stories about Behar that seem largely separate and at times draw attention away from the relation, except in the sense that the connections arise in Behar's imagination and family history.

In another text, *Bad Boys: Public Schools in the Making of Black Masculinity* by Ann Arnett Ferguson (2001), the relation between researcher and research subjects is also richly conveyed. The subjects are African American boys in an elementary school who are constructed as dangerous and delinquent by school personnel. Befriending the boys as an adult woman and taking on their point of view as the reason for the study, Ferguson successfully conveys a counter-story of the boys' lives in the midst of their subjection. Further, she employs a novel representational strategy at one point to convey an extended field note. She represents in poetic verse a mother's story of frustration with her 10-year-old son's disobedience, exacerbated by humiliating arrest (and subsequent two-year probation) for publicly whipping him for skipping school to sell drugs. The mother's desperation is palpable, especially if the reader takes Ferguson's advice and reads the passage aloud, saying "You cannot understand it unless you hear the words" (p. 135). The extended length of the verse takes the reader through an excruciating, prolonged story of frustration and institutional indifference, clearly scarred from her arrest and subsequent surveillance by child services, which ironically undermines her ability to discipline her child effectively. The verse commands the reader's attention, and its form conveys Ferguson's confidence that her experience of the story will translate to the reader. (Beyond the scope of this chapter, but worth mentioning here, are the ways in which researchers may aesthetically create relations with an audience to create meaning.)

In another remarkable study, Mitchell Duneier (1999) in *Sidewalk* represents ethnographic data collection over five years of Greenwich Village street vendors, many but not all unhoused and many operating within a whisper of local law. Among the many relevant aspects of the work, Duneier captures how vendors rely upon carefully negotiated relations of respect with local police. As I explain in a previous article, Duneier succeeds in one of the chapters by walking the reader through multiple tangled relations associated with a breach of those carefully negotiated relations of respect. Adding complexity for Duneier and readers are enactments of race privilege that draw the reader into a complicated, empathetic understanding of one of the officers in particular, a black officer who complies with a white superior's quest to breach his respectful stance toward the street vendors and then loses the support of the white superior when Duneier challenges the legality of his actions (Gunzenhauser, 2006). (Again, in this case, multiple aesthetic choices by Duneier actively contribute to conveying and facilitating empathy.) There are multiple additional examples where both strong relations and multiple relations lead to richly textured analysis, because of empathetic portrayals of participants in a research setting. They are particularly significant for critical, emancipatory, or transformative research over the years, leading to nuanced portrayals of those in superior power positions. Notably, Angela Valenzuela (1999) conveys not only the students' perspectives in *Subtractive Schooling: U.S.–Mexican Youth and the Politics of Caring,* but also the educators' to give a more compelling sense of how and why subtractive schooling happens in diverse high school settings.

In her case studies of families in one metropolitan arena at different socioeconomic locations, *Unequal Childhoods: Class, Race, and Family Life,* Annette Lareau (2003) largely succeeds conveying empathetic portrayals of families whose views of childhood and childrearing vary tremendously, positioning them inequitably for interactions with health care providers and school personnel. Readers get unromanticized portrayals of middle- and working-class families, and despite the clear advantages in status cultivated in the middle-class children in the study, the integrity of all families and their forms of childrearing are retained. The relative value of childrearing practices is left appropriately ambiguous, even if the middle-class children's in-school advantage is clearly superior in the immediate time of the study. If there's room for greater empathetic work in Lareau's depictions, it's in the portrayals of school personnel; without extensive engagement with the school personnel, the educators' perspectives reinforce the families' perspectives and experiences and provide only limited understanding of why and how educators expect all parents to behave as middle-class parents. As a possible extension to her thorough and purposive selection of cases, the views of educators with competent knowledge of working-class and poor families could be explored; adding them would provide complexity regarding school-family relations.

These examples show the contribution of intensive relations to qualitative research, akin to the advice for prolonged engagement, dialogue, reflexivity, and other methods that build rapport with research subjects (for other examples, see Foley, 1990; Roman, 1993; Weis, 2004; for further discussion on this point, see Noblit, Flores, & Murillo, 2004). Empathetic portrayals are not without their challenges and limitations. For example, Duneier (1999) warns against taking personal accounts at face value, because he "would have concluded that their lives and problems were wholly of their own making" (p. 343). In the same volume, collaborator and book vendor Hakim Hasan warns, "In the end, any sociologist who simply believes that time spent in the field qualifies him as 'one of the boys' is not only sadly mistaken but in grave trouble" (p. 326). While extensive engagement and attention to multiple relations provide texture and complexity to analysis, as the next section demonstrates, the concept of empathy itself has its theoretical limitations, which are reflected in the challenges of research practice.

Dangerous Knowing

Philosopher Sharon Todd (2003) challenges the rhetorical claim that superior forms of knowing arise from emancipatory commitments. Indeed, if we consider knowledge as superior merely because the research engaged in it has the stated intentions for emancipation, we are forgetting that such claims are rhetorical in quality as well as moral, and if the moral grounding is undeveloped, we have only the rhetoric to fall back upon (Gunzenhauser, 2004). Needed is a clearly articulated rationale for how emancipatory commitments contribute to emancipatory research projects (Carspecken, 1996; Hammersley, 1992). Instead of the options that Martyn Hammersley suggests, I have in prior work chosen to focus on feminist standpoint theory and feminist moral epistemology, wherein knowing through relation means coming to know and care about the life-projects of those with whom one is engaged as knowing subjects and engaging in a process of mutual critique to build an ethic of solidarity and difference (Code, 1991, 1995; Gunzenhauser, 2003, 2006; Welch, 2000).

Knowing through relation also demands much of a researcher (Gunzenhauser, 2006), particularly in terms of empathy, and Todd (2003) is not the only one concerned that the demand is more than can be possibly demanded. Others argue against a too-simple sense that a feminist commitment to others would reasonably provide the basis for a morally defensible research practice. Early on, in response to the crisis of representation in anthropology, George Marcus (1995), noting the critique of ethnography's rhetoric, advocated a number of redesigns of both the observer and the observed, advocating a more dialogical and bifocal entanglement. Kimala Visweswaran (1994) is similarly concerned with this rhetorical claim of feminist scholarship, naming it as one of the fictions of feminist ethnography. Steiner Kvale (2006) likewise expresses concern about the power dynamics that are often left unarticulated in qualitative interviewing. In his article, Kvale is concerned with the ways in which the interpretive quality of the interview is obviated only in some forms of interview studies, particularly in postpositivist and market research. However, his critique can rather easily be expanded to include all claims of interpretive work. His argument is that researchers assume they know a research subject through the interview well ahead of any point where it would be reasonable to claim so.

For interpretive research, the dangers of knowing happen when researchers overestimate their success in relations across difference, what Code (1995) refers to as engaging in impersonal caring. The phrase "relation across difference" comes from Todd's (2003) directive to "explore how ethics and education might be rethought together as a relation across difference" (p. 2). Todd exclusively focuses on pedagogical relations and sets up her project by arguing this: "For it's precisely in the context of the educational struggle for more just social relations—where an encounter with difference, or otherness, is the *sine qua non* of pedagogical practice—that an elaboration of ethics as a relation to otherness becomes integral to its very project" (p. 3).

In interpretive research, the danger is when a researcher acts in a manner that substitutes understanding for the respondents' needs with an abstracted, generalized knowing. Code (1995) explains how knowing relations may systematically lead to impersonal caring. Her moral epistemology is a response to what she sees in social inquiry as the inappropriate adaptation of conventions in traditional epistemological theory regarding propositional knowledge. In relations across difference built on this insight, Code's moral epistemology forms what she terms enhanced subjectivity. In previous work, I used examples of what I found to be rich, empathetic forms of research by Duneier, *Sidewalk* (1999), mentioned above, and *Slim's Table: Race, Respectability, and Masculinity* (1992); and *Troubling the Angels: Women Living with HIV/AIDS,* by Patti Lather and Chris Smithies (1997). I named some implications of attending to relation, namely what it means to commit to knowing to care, the significance of multiple empathetic relations in a research setting, the illusions of closeness, and problematic issues associated with representation of relational knowing.

I named this research as empathetic and noted in a footnote that what I had in mind for empathy was not the emotional notion of empathy that I found was being written about (and critiqued) at the time. I suggested that "empathy matters most [to me] as a form of communication of understanding (however partial)" (p. 645n), drawing on Egan's (1986) model of empathetic listening for counselors as skilled helpers. While now I would still argue that communicating partial understanding is an important aspect of empathy, in this chapter I wish to place greater emphasis on the construction and cultivation of the relation between the two knowing subjects that are implied by both the emotional and communicative aspects of empathy.

Thoughtful considerations of the strengths and weaknesses of empathy provide an appropriately complicated context for this discussion. For many years, the concept of empathy has been an important but contested construct for critical and feminist theorizing, pedagogy, and inquiry. The role of empathy in relations across difference in interpretive qualitative inquiry is not a context for which empathy is very often discussed, so I need to draw out some of the limitations of empathy to identify what is at stake in empathic relations for constructing knowledge and confronting the potential violence of impersonal caring, colonization, and misrepresentation of others.

Teasing out the emotional and cognitive aspects of empathy turns out to be the first problem. In much of the discourse about empathy in philosophy and psychology, there is attention to both the affective and cognitive aspects of empathy. Debate centers around whether empathy is the emotional response to others' emotional lives, the cognitive acquisition of understanding of the lives of others, or some articulated relation between the emotional and cognitive.

The tendency in theorizing is to separate the emotional and the cognitive and then articulate their problematic relation. Doing so encourages theorists to consider the emotional to be too unreliable (particularly in contrast to the supposedly more reliable cognitive). Taken by itself, the emotional aspect of empathy seems too self-focused to matter much ethically. As discussed previously, in a situation in which one experiences empathy, the concept focuses upon the one coming to feel. The concept itself seems to be the self-absorbed aspect of ethicality.

This linkage is particularly problematic for the qualitative researcher who acts based on the self-focused emotion. This could be quite dangerous. If an actor experiences empathetic feelings in reference to another's experience, the impetus may be to act to assuage those self-focused feelings, rather than doing something more relevant to the other's experience (as I discuss below, there are some in developmental psychology who suggest that this is the impulse behind empathy). The resulting egoism or narcissism may damage the relation. This may be particularly dangerous if the actor uses the experience of empathy to claim to have acted ethically (or perhaps to use the empathy as an epistemological basis for a knowledge claim). Worse, the researcher may allow his or her egoism or narcissism to take over, missing or misrepresenting lingering pain among the research subjects.

One of the clearest examples of this danger from the literature on empathy comes not from interpretive research but from film criticism. In her analysis of *Monster's Ball* (Daniels & Forster, 2001), Aimee Carrillo Rowe (2007) demonstrates the ways in which feelings of empathy can effectively recenter the experience of dominant individuals in relations across difference. Most troubling for Rowe is how empathy can be employed to reproduce (rather forcefully) the hegemony of the multicultural logic of liberal pluralism. Two central black male characters in the film are killed (the first husband and son of the character played by Halle Berry). The white protagonist is the husband's executioner (the character played by Billy Bob Thornton), who is redeemed of his violence and racism by experiencing his own son's death and Berry's character's sexual acquiescence to him, which implies forgiveness, Rowe suggests, melting her into a role as intermediary between white racism and black subjugation.

Rowe sees productive empathy submersed in its narcissistic form in the film. Empathy becomes "color-blind, apolitical, ahistorical" (paraphrase, p. 125). "This logic of white disadvantage serves what Henry Giroux (1995) calls a 'pedagogic' function, teaching audiences how to read race relations through a lens of benign multiculturalism and to frame the stories of individuals outside history, politics, and power" (pp. 125–126). Rowe finds such narcissistic empathetic forms in some philosophical treatments of empathy, specifically Martha Nussbaum's unproblematic appeal to compassion for getting inside the experiences of others.

The aesthetic forms of film and qualitative research representation are no doubt significantly distinct. First of all, successful films tend to succeed for the ways in which they align themselves with dominant cultural themes, such as benign multiculturalism, as Rowe explains in her analysis. *Monster's Ball* certainly disrupts the audience through novel aesthetic means (by juxtaposing violence and interracial sexuality), but ultimately it resolves itself through detachment from action. (The film *Crash* [Haggis, 2005] continually enacts and disrupts empathy. Similarly to *Monster's Ball*, it executes novelty—intensity through vignette and implausible coincidence—then resolves itself through a calculated balance of racist equity wherein nearly every victim of racism is in a different scenario a purveyor of presumably equal racism.)

Todd (2003) goes further along this line of critique, arguing that empathy can paradoxically lead to violence. She makes the troubled linkage between empathy and moral action to support her argument that empathy is ethically insufficient. Her reasoning is that the demand for empathy (in pedagogy, her context of consideration) is neither something one can control, nor the reliable basis for action:

> [E]ven if we accept that the demand for empathy is a worthy one, we nonetheless cannot ignore how empathic feelings are within no one's sphere of control, neither the one who wishes to encourage empathy in others nor the one who actually feels empathy. Thus the unpredictability and nonintentionality that characterize the experience of being—for turn the demand for empathy into an impossibility. Insofar as a demand has intention and purpose, the demand for empathy ironically becomes a demand for that which we cannot be demanded. (p. 49)

One response is to combine these two concerns to carve out a particular kind of desirable empathy that meets some criteria for moral action. Susan Verducci (1999) is likewise concerned with the gap between the emotional aspect of empathy and the cognitive, but in her case, the contrast plays itself out most importantly in the distinction between emotion and moral action. To resolve the gap, her approach is to argue for a distinct moral empathy, "the form of empathy that is likely to trigger moral action" (p. 336), and she argues that it must have three features: "resonating emotion of the same valence," intersubjectivity, and "dialogic confirmation" (p. 336).

The criterion that moral empathy must include "resonating emotion of the same valence" calls to mind the difficulty that privileged researchers have in appreciating the historicity and depth of pain that subjugated persons experience, but there is no reason to believe that this criterion would only apply in such situations. This is a key problematic aspect of empathy, because of the divide between individuals' historical locations and the inherently subjective experience of emotion, not only between persons, but within the same person at different moments in time. One could also imagine, for instance, overestimating the depth of another's emotion. As a researcher, I may be moved deeply by what my respondent finds an ordinary or insignificant occurrence, yet be simultaneously oblivious to an emotion that I underestimate, finding melodrama in the familiar.

Verducci's call for dialogic confirmation is compelling and consistent with Code's notion of enhanced subjectivity. Whether the confirmation needs to be explicitly dialogic is debatable, since it seems to place a high premium upon rational confirmation of subjective experience. Duneier (1999) demonstrates well the value of what in other contexts is referred to as member checking. Especially since real names and faces appear in *Sidewalk*, his effort to read through with his subjects every line of text that relates to them reflects a thorough concern for dialogic confirmation. This is in contrast to typical uses of member checking, where respondents are handed thick pages of interviews and asked to fix errors (which strikes some as asking research subjects to do the researcher's work).

In her response to Verducci, Suzanne Rice (1999) expresses concern that rather than distinguishing moral empathy from mere empathy, "one alternative is to view empathy as a capacity that does not necessarily lead to moral response, but that makes moral response possible" (p. 345). Further, it's not clear that Verducci's moral empathy effectively resolves the problems with the concept of empathy itself. The moral action might not have much to do with the cared-for's needs and interests, or it might result from a tragic misunderstanding of the cared-for's needs and interests.

The turn to intersubjectivity is important in Verducci's formulation, since at this point, Verducci has held to a distinction between the emotional and actionable aspects of empathy. I do think it holds promise for addressing the challenges of empathy as impersonal caring. I do think it makes sense to speak of both empathy as an emotional construct and moral action that might be characterized as empathetic—action that is triggered by empathy, emotional and/or cognitive, such that we might refer to it as an empathetic action.

Intersubjectivity

Help on this point comes from a philosophical critique of some of the leading developmental psychological theory on empathy, wherein the affective and cognitive are separated. Eva Johansson (2007) argues that the link between emotional empathy and moral action is always tenuous (and would presumably be, even with moral empathy being distinct). She summarizes Martin Hoffman's theory of empathy as initially a biological, instinctual process, exemplified by the infant who cries when it hears other infants crying in a nursery. It grows to become empathetic and sympathetic affect, basically a sympathetic pain that is only relieved when the other's pain is relieved. For Hoffman, children over time develop greater capacity for empathy through stages. The biological roots provide an important basis for moral action, according to Hoffman, but Johansson is not so sure.

Johansson is here moving toward the point that the emotive feeling is somewhat beside the moral point.

> A feeling of distress in the presence of another person's distress could be an important emotion, but not always necessary to understand the other person's feelings and to develop morality. Instead of regarding empathy as the basis of morality, we could view empathy as one of many ways of understanding others, where emotions and, to some extent, also cognitions are assumed to play a central role. (p. 45)

Significant here is that Johansson's work focuses on the limits of psychological frames of reference for her study of empathy among preschool-age children. She reveals Hoffman's currently dominant psychological theory about empathy to be lacking in appreciation of the ambiguity of one's ability to access another's experience. Following Maurice Merleau-Ponty, Johansson argues that the ambiguity is unavoidable. Drawing from her studies of preschool children, she argues that the impulse for what Hoffman would call empathy does not necessarily have anything to do with moral outrage or any moral sentiment at all. She concludes that these observations show how it doesn't make sense to make a facile linkage between empathy as an emotional response and then a moral sense. It could instead get the child to focus back on his or her own pain or remind the child of some previous (and even unrelated) transgression.

Johansson turns to Merleau-Ponty's notion of intersubjectivity. (Significantly, Verducci's intersubjectivity is grounded in a prior formulation from Edmund Husserl, which relies upon a notion of verification). She arrives at this interpretation of the children's experience as the children becoming attuned to the vulnerability of others through relation, which she finds more significant than the debate about whether they feel empathy. Through relation, the child begins to appreciate "a moral demand which the other, with his trust, implicitly places on us" (p. 44). As an intersubjective experience via Merleau-Ponty (wherein mind and body are of the same existence), "that concern for the other children is integrated, lived and shaped in the children's bodily existence" (p. 44, with cf. to Merleau-Ponty, 1962, pp. 77–92, 136–147). Emotions are part of the relation, but so are other forms of experience. The relation is what's important.

For Johansson, greater emphasis in moral development should then be placed on "encounters between children…., and what takes place between the children can tell us about how they understand and care for others" (p. 45). Applying this insight to qualitative inquiry brings us back to Rice's (1999) point about empathy being an important emotional experience that makes moral action possible. For qualitative inquiry, then, the relation is what is of significance when empathy is at play, and so it makes more sense from an ethical standpoint to focus upon what happens in the relation.

Also working with Merleau-Ponty, Matthew Schertz (2007) also finds value in empathy as intersubjectivity, with empathy part of continual, intersubjective self-constitution through relation. The affective/cognitive disjunction of empathy resolves itself through intersubjective being, which is always fluid and dialectical. With intersubjectivity, "empathy's ambiguities would dissipate" (p. 165). Schertz argues the following:

As a result of this reformulation, empathy can be understood as an aspect of an event of interaction between body-consciousnesses. Feeling is no longer transferred between one subject and another, whether through projective mechanisms or cognitive decentration. We are no longer "inside" another or "imagining" another's feeling: we are now participating in an anonymous, affective field—the gestalt—produced by the event of our meeting. Empathy can now be understood as a primary condition of human intersubjectivity. (p. 172)

Intersubjective being effectively redefines objectivity; the received notion of the dispassionate researcher is neither possible nor coherent. As Schertz argues, "being-in-the-world" suggests very clearly that it does not make sense to place oneself apart from the world, able to see the world apart from being in it. With the separation of the self and another theoretically arbitrary, the relation is what remains (p. 171).

This formulation of intersubjectivity, when applied to pedagogy, places greater emphasis on the pedagogic encounter, between educators and students and between and among students. Applied to research, relations in research not only take on greater significance, but the relations take their place as the site of meaning. Schertz's recommendations for education include "[asking] ourselves what kinds of subjects we hope to perpetuate through the experience of schooling" (p. 177). Similarly for qualitative research relationships, the concern is for the kinds of subjects created through the research encounter. Following Schertz and his interpretation of Merleau-Ponty, part of the answer would have to be that we wish to have relations of trust, without the expectation that one would know the other, but that the relation would be the source for meaning generation, and that empathy would be a crucial part of that relation.

In other words, we seek a relation with empathy as a component, but which retains what Todd (2003) refers to as the "radical alterity of the Other" (p. 51), because in the encounter between two knowing subjects, "the encounter must always refuse reducing the Other to a common ground with the self" (p. 51). This criterion should cause us to reject some formulations of intersubjectivity, such as the one that Verducci (1999) draws from Husserl. While Verducci's criterion of dialogic confirmation may be a compelling ideal (and indeed, Verducci refers to it as a regulative ideal), the component of verifiability that Verducci wants to maintain does not quite fit. In the notion of intersubjectivity drawn from Merleau-Ponty, there is no ideal to which to compare our knowledge. The point is a subtle one, but it shifts attention from the knowledge generated through intersubjective relations to the relation itself; in other words, instead of generating knowledge through an encounter with another, I would like us to focus more attention upon generating meaning about an encounter with another.

Todd (2003) is drawing from Levinas instead of Merleau-Ponty, and Levinas critiqued Merleau-Ponty's intersubjectivity as retaining essentialized Western notions of separate subjects, specifically "reducing the other to the same" (Busch, 1992, p. 195). Thomas Busch suspects that even though Levinas disagreed with Merleau-Ponty, their positions on the relation between ethics and ontology may not be all that different when it comes down to defining what it means to have a moral obligation to the Other. Busch argues that Merleau-Ponty's combining of ethics and ontology in the relation of intersubjectivity makes being and ethicality always intertwined with each other. For Levinas, ethics is prior to being, because the obligation that one has to the Other exists prior to the encounter with the Other. Busch argues that since in neither formulation does it make sense to speak of moral obligation with a specific encounter in mind, the differences seem to melt away. I find Busch's argument compelling enough to support linking Johansson's and Schertz's discussions of empathy with Todd's. This distinction between the theorists is significant at this point in my argument, because it explains why Todd, using Levinas, is fundamentally concerned with the dangers associated with empathy.

The notion of intersubjectivity drawn from Johansson and Schertz is a suitable way to think about what happens when knowing subjects encounter each other in qualitative inquiry, as long as we pay attention to the lingering dangers associated with relations across difference, even if these relations are understood through the lens of intersubjectivity. Lingering still is Todd's concern about the potential for violence.

By making a distinction between learning about another and learning from another, Todd is encountering the difficulties associated with empathy directly. Todd's main problem with conventional ethics is the presumption of how tightly connected it is with knowledge. Her concern is that ethics in education (or most theorizing about the moral roles of educators) is built upon the assumption that teachers act based upon their knowledge: knowledge of the good, knowledge of the best outcomes, or (in Code's [1995] terms) knowledge of others and their concerns. Todd explains her goal in these terms:

> to pose the possibility that ethics might have a different relation to education…is to put into question a foundational idea of much of ethical philosophy: that our moral actions, our capacity for acting in the name of what is right, good, or simply better, are premised on our knowledge of what is right, good, or simply better. (p. 7)

We come back to the point that the potential for violence comes about with the presumption of knowledge. Rather than leaving knowledge of the Other as a regulative ideal, Todd suggests that the relation between knowledge and ethics is the problem. Understanding the Other is "exercising my knowledge over the Other…., [and the] Other becomes an object of *my* comprehension, *my* world, *my* narrative, reducing the Other to me" (p. 15; emphasis in original). Instead, Todd advocates an alternative understanding, learning from rather than about the other. She says: "if I am exposed to the Other, I can listen, attend, and be surprised; the Other can affect me" (p. 15). Todd goes on to develop an ethical theory for social justice pedagogy that makes use of attentiveness, listening, and communicative openness with the Other.

Significant for my interest in intersubjectivity, Todd's ethics are in the relation, rather than embedded in knowledge about the other. Responsibility for the Other is certainly situational for Todd, without universalizable principles to be applied to all contexts. Instead, she wants "a mindfulness and a sensitivity to the ways in which we participate in attending to difference within institutional contexts" (p. 142).

Attending to difference is a significant part of the ontological project, "the continual renewal of the self in relation to another" (p. 146). Todd envisions a role for empathy, wherein one who acts does not assume that his or her feelings in relation to another arise from understanding, connection, or oneness with the Other. One who feels empathy should be vigilant:

> Our vigilance to attend to our attentiveness is an approach to communication that takes responsibility for itself *as* we encounter another person. Listening to the ways our own affect, as well as that of others, infuses our encounters makes listening to stories of suffering extremely difficult, but it also makes learning from them possible…. Every emotional response is pedagogically fruitful, since it reveals an implicit struggle with the ethical aspects of encountering difference. (p. 146)

Todd suggests that engaging the Other is an everyday practice, and emotions such as empathy are opportunities to consider our own "implications in the lives of others" (p. 146), in other words, an opportunity to explore connection, which may be a lot more complicated than we at first believe it to be. For Todd, teaching is the cultivation of relations to otherness, and I would argue that the practice of interpretive qualitative research is a quite similar thing. If we also follow her in this statement—"Turning our attention to the conditions for ethical possibility means giving up on the idea that learning about others is an appropriate ethical response to difference" (p. 9)—we must think about what this means for research.

The distinction between learning from and about, and the implications for qualitative research, comes from this passage, in which Todd could easily be talking about qualitative research:

> Instead, learning *from* as opposed to *about* allows us an engagement with difference across space and time, it focuses on the here and now of communication while gesturing toward the future and acknowledging the past; it allows for attentiveness to singularity and specificity within the plurality that is our social life. It is only when we learn *from* others that we can respond with the very humility necessary for assuming responsibility (p. 16; emphasis in original).

Creative Intersubjectivity

For Todd, the value of empathy is as a component of communicative openness with the Other and the revelation of alterity. Projection, the problematic aspect of empathy that so many others identify, is the impulse to overcome difference, an understandable but potentially dangerous impulse:

> learning through empathy cannot but mask, despite our best intentions, the Other's radically different feelings…. Empathy necessarily leads to questionable assumptions that the Other is ultimately somewhat like me, that what I feel *is* the same as (or at least approximates) the Other's feelings, whether I project or identify or not. (p. 63)

Much like Johansson, Todd argues that in pedagogical situations, students' feelings of empathy are not necessarily moral empathy in Verducci's sense, but an indication of how students are relating across difference. In my view, this offers a direct transfer to the role of the researcher, for whom empathy as feeling should be recognized as feeling and meaning, not necessarily understanding.

What I propose we have instead to draw from is what I am calling creative intersubjectivity. The relation between the researcher and the research subject I believe should be understood as a moment for the creation of new forms of being. The research encounter is a relation across difference created as a site and a space for action. Coming together, knowing subjects interact around knowledge, emotion, cares, concerns, and aesthetic experiences.

The report of the interaction is further opportunity for creative intersubjectivity. Writing qualitative research is a process of making meaning anew, with the additional intersubjectivity of the audience to contend with. As I mentioned previously, complete engagement with the aesthetic contributions of creative intersubjectivity are beyond the scope of this chapter, but at this point, it should be clear that representing relational knowing both brings greater urgency to the enterprise but also invites new dangers.

I want to end with what I think empathic knowing is: knowing that emerges from relation; the relation itself has qualities, texture, time, history, and above all tension and limitations; inherently intersubjective (not a co-construction but an interaction, built upon commitment);

done in recognition of alterity—there is difference, but neither side of the relation has a priority of truth; the potential for violence is not controllable, to be taken seriously, but not to be avoided at all costs. Further, empathic knowing participates in the continual creation of self. To help someone with her project is not necessarily to understand it.

As Egan (1986) suggests, empathy when communicated can help build the relationship, stimulate self-exploration, check understandings, provide support, lubricate communication, focus attention, restrain the helper (and get it back to the client right away), and pave the way (for deeper engagement and stronger interventions possible later on in the intervention model) (p. 135). Drawing from Todd (2003), a researcher who experiences feelings of empathy is advised to learn from their projection of their feelings. The researcher should question: Why am I so drawn emotionally to my respondent's experience? Why am I in this situation believing I now understand the person better? What might my respondent tell me about her experience when I share my empathetic feelings? Perhaps a straightforward dialogic confirmation may result, but sometimes confirmation is not what is needed in a dialogue; sometimes conflict and further dialogue is needed, particularly if respondents feel misunderstood, mocked, or trivialized (Cozart, Gordon, Gunzenhauser, McKinney, & Patterson, 2003). More importantly, the researcher is furthering an intersubjective experience of self-creating in action. My formulation suggests that the journey for additional interaction is worthwhile.

Again, I return to my point about what it means to communicate empathic knowing to a reader. Here's where I think we can develop a more sophisticated understanding of the crisis of representation. Creative intersubjectivity gives us a greater sense of the moral nature of the crisis of representation, certainly. In an interview several years after his book was published, Duneier said this to interviewer Les Back (Duneier & Back, 2006):

> If you are going to get at the humanity of people, you can't just have a bunch of disembodied thoughts that come out of subjects' mouths in interviews without ever developing characters and trying to show people as full human beings. (p. 554)

Here Duneier is concerned both with the humane treatment of research subjects and the explanatory value of qualitative research practice. Embedded in his comment is a belief about the responsibility of a social science researcher. The work of a social science writer—generating descriptions, explanations, and theories about social phenomena—carries with it a danger of violence, in Todd's sense, so taking relation seriously is imperative.

Qualitative research that pays greater attention to the relation as a site of creative intersubjectivity would look more like Duneier's (1992, 1999) work than it currently does and more like the other exemplars I've mentioned in this chapter. Learning from others, as Noblit (1999) did from Knight, is a viable alternative to learning from others. Respondents would be presented as rounded characters as much as possible. Researchers would seek empathetic explanations for participants' beliefs and behaviors. They would be attentive to the emotional quality of their field work and their representations. While not taking responsibility for everyone and everything, the qualitative researcher is responsibly creating.

References

Behar, R. (1993). *Translated woman: Crossing the border with Esperanza's story.* Boston: Beacon Press.

Burch, K. (2009). *Parrhesia* as a principle of democratic pedagogy. *Philosophical Studies in Education, 40,* 71–82.

Busch, T. (1992). Ethics and ontology: Levinas and Merleau-Ponty. *Man and World, 25*(2), 195–202.

Carspecken, P. F. (1996).*Critical ethnography in educational research: A theoretical and practical guide.* New York: Routledge.

Code, L. (1991). *What can she know? Feminist theory and the construction of knowledge.* Ithaca, NY: Cornell University Press.

Code, L. (1995). *Rhetorical spaces: Essays on gendered locations.* New York: Routledge.

Collins, P. H. (1998). *Fighting words: Black women and the search for justice.* Minneapolis: University of Minnesota Press.

Cozart, S. C., Gordon, J., Gunzenhauser, M. G., McKinney, M. B., & Patterson, J. (2003). Disrupting dialogue: Envisioning performance ethnography for research and evaluation. *Educational Foundations, 17*(2), 53–69.

Daniels, L. (Producer), & Forster, M. (Director). (2001). *Monster's ball* [motion picture]. United States: Lionsgate.

Duneier, M. (1992). *Slim's table: Race, respectability, and masculinity.* Chicago: University of Chicago Press.

Duneier, M. (1999). *Sidewalk.* New York: Farrar, Straus, & Giroux.

Duneier, M., & Back, L. (2006). Voices from the sidewalk: Ethnography and writing race. *Ethnic and Racial Studies, 29*(3), 543–565.

Egan, G. (1986). *The skilled helper: A systematic approach to effective helping* (3rd ed.). Pacific Grove, CA: Brooks/Cole Publishing.

Ferguson, A. A. (2001). *Bad boys: Public schools in the making of black masculinity.* Ann Arbor: University of Michigan Press.

Foley, D. E. (1990). *Learning capitalist culture: Deep in the heart of Tejas.* Philadelphia: University of Pennsylvania Press.

Foucault, M. (1983/2001). *Fearless speech* (Joseph Pearson, ed.). Los Angeles, CA: Semiotext(e). (Original lectures recorded 1983)

Foucault, M. (2001/2005). *The hermeneutics of the subject: Lectures at the Collège de France, 1981–82* (Graham Burchell, Trans.). New York: Picador. (Original work published 2001)

Garrison, J. W. (1996).A Deweyan theory of democratic listening. *Educational Theory, 46*(4), 429–451.

Greene, M. (1988). *The dialectic of freedom.* New York: Teachers College Press.

Gunzenhauser, M. G. (1999). *Knowledge claims and ethical commitments: Toward a moral epistemology for critical ethnography in education.* Unpublished doctoral dissertation. University of North Carolina at Chapel Hill.

Gunzenhauser, M. G. (2003). Solidarity and risk in Welch's feminist ethics. In E. S. Fletcher (Ed.), *Philosophy of education 2002: Proceedings of the fifty-eighth annual meeting of the Philosophy of Education Society* (pp. 101–109). Urbana, IL: Philosophy of Education Society.

Gunzenhauser, M. G. (2004). Promising rhetoric for postcritical ethnography. In G. W. Noblit, S. Y. Flores, & E. G. Murillo, Jr. (Eds.), *Postcritical ethnography: Reinscribing critique* (pp. 77–94). Cresskill, NJ: Hampton.

Gunzenhauser, M. G. (2006). A moral epistemology of knowing subjects: Theorizing a relational turn for qualitative research. *Qualitative Inquiry, 12*(3), 621–647.

Haggis, P. (Producer & Director). (2005). *Crash* [motion picture]. United States: Lionsgate.

Hammersley, M. (1992). *What's wrong with ethnography?* New York: Routledge.

Johansson, E. (2007). Empathy as intersubjectivity? Understanding the origins of morality in young children. *Studies in Philosophy and Education, 27*(1), 33–47.

Kvale, S. (2006). Dominance through interviews and dialogues. *Qualitative Inquiry, 12*(3), 480–500.

Lareau, A. (2003). *Unequal childhoods: Class, race, and family life.* Berkeley: University of California Press.

Lather, P. (2007). *Getting lost: Feminist efforts toward a double(d) science.* Albany: State University of New York Press.

Lather, P., & Smithies, C. (1997). *Troubling the angels: Women living with HIV/AIDS.* Boulder, CO: Westview.

Marcus, G. E. (1995). The redesign of ethnography after the critique of its rhetoric. In R. F. Goodman, & W. R. Fisher (Eds.), *Rethinking knowledge: Reflections across the disciplines* (pp. 103–121). Albany: State University of New York Press.

Marcus, G. E., & Fischer, M. M. J. (1986). *Anthropology as cultural critique: An experimental moment in the human sciences.* Chicago: University of Chicago Press.

Merriam-Webster. (2010). Empathy. *Merriam-Webster Online Dictionary.* [Online] http://www.merriam-webster.com/dictionary/empathy, Accessed January 5, 2010.

Noblit, G. W. (1999). *Particularities: Collected essays on ethnography and education.* New York: Peter Lang.

Noblit, G. W., Flores, S. Y., & Murillo, Jr., E. G. (Eds.) (2004). *Postcritical ethnography: Reinscribing critique.* Cresskill, NJ: Hampton-.

Noddings, N. (1984). *Caring: A feminine approach to ethics and moral education.* Berkeley: University of California Press.

Rice, S. (1999). Paying empathy its due. In S. Tozer (Ed.), *Philosophy of education 1998: Proceedings of the annual meeting of the Philosophy of Education Society* (pp. 344–346). Urbana, IL: Philosophy of Education Society.

Ritter, M. (2008). The significance of finding a witness in liberatory education. In B. Stengel (Ed.), *Philosophy of education, 2008: Proceedings of the annual meeting of the Philosophy of Education Society* (pp. 359–366). Urbana: University of Illinois.

Roman, L. G. (1993). Double exposure: The politics of feminist materialist ethnography. *Educational Theory, 43*(3), 279–308.

Rowe, A. C. (2007). Feeling in the dark: Empathy, whiteness, and miscegenation in Monster's Ball. *Hypatia, 22*(2), 122–142.

Rubin, H. J., & Rubin, I. S. (2005).*Qualitative interviewing: The art of hearing data* (2nd ed.). Thousand Oaks, CA: Sage.

Schertz, M. V. (2007). Empathy as intersubjectivity: Resolving Hume's and Smith's divide. *Studies in Philosophy and Education, 26*(2), 165–178.

Scott, J. W. (1991). The evidence of experience. *Critical Inquiry, 17*(4), 773–797.

Smith, J. K., & Deemer, D.K. (2003). The problem of criteria in the age of relativism. In N. K. Denzin & Y. S. Lincoln (Eds.), *Collecting and interpreting qualitative materials* (2nd ed.) (pp. 427–457). Thousand Oaks, CA: Sage.

Todd, S. (2003). *Learning from the other: Levinas, psychoanalysis, and ethical possibilities in education.* Albany: State University of New York Press.

Valenzuela, A. (1999). *Subtractive schooling: U.S.–Mexican youth and the politics of caring.* Albany: State University of New York Press.

Verducci, S. (1999). Moral empathy: The necessity of intersubjectivity and dialogic confirmation. In S. Tozer (Ed.), *Philosophy of education 1998: Proceedings of the annual meeting of the Philosophy of Education Society* (pp. 335–343). Urbana, IL: Philosophy of Education Society.

Visweswaran, K. (1994). *Fictions of feminist ethnography.* Minneapolis: University of Minnesota Press.

Weis, L. (2004). *Class reunion: The remaking of the American white working class.* New York: Routledge.

Welch, S. D. (2000). *A feminist ethic of risk (Other feminist voices).* Minneapolis, MN: Fortress.

CHAPTER FOUR

Unusual Experience as Demystification

Ethics and Rationality at the Green Margins

LUCINDA CARSPECKEN

I know that nature is not just plants and animals, nature includes rocks and dirt and us… People are at the core animals. (Conney, 2008, www.elvinhome.org)

Many people take the safe stance, not taking the risk of believing in something that might be wrong, or that might cause others to think they're crazy. We are crazy, crazy to be willing to live in the misery, cut off from our roots. (Interview with Bright, 2010)

I began dissertation fieldwork at Lothlorien Nature Sanctuary in southern Indiana in early 2006 and kept visiting there long after my research ended, to maintain the friendships I had developed and to do occasional volunteer work. Besides being a forest sanctuary, a collectively owned residential community, and an experiment in sustainable stewardship, Lothlorien is a festival site with (loose) contemporary Pagan associations. It hosts Full Moon ceremonies and celebrations related to the stations of the sun, like Solstices and Equinoxes. Spirituality was not my focus, however. Few people offered information on this topic in the first few months and I was more interested in the garden, the buildings, the organization, and the environmentalist ethic—all of which seemed to present, on a small scale, possibilities for alternative ways to live in North America.

A common element among participants at Lothlorien is that most visitors have some degree of ecological sensitivity (which is why I use the phrase "green" margins in the title of this chapter). Other than that, there is no such thing as a typical participant, nor is there a typical belief system. The community tends to accept a wide range of people with a variety of mainstream and nonmainstream perspectives and lifestyles, some of which are unacceptable, or at least raise eyebrows, in most contexts in the world beyond its gates. (A former resident called the place "The Land of Misfit Toys.") And when, in the first few years, people talked to me about religion, ritual, or spirituality, it often seemed to come as much from a desire to avoid being defined or labeled as from a desire to be understood in any other way. Comments like "I tend to run from labels" and "I'm not really anything" were common, and kept me from asking further questions. Sometimes I was given paradoxical descriptions, like "agnostic yet person- ally devoted" or mixed descriptions, like "Christian Pagan," "pantheistic Taoist with hedonistic tendencies" or "agnostic forest freak." Overall, people's spiritual or religious identifications seemed none of my business. I didn't want to define people in ways that they themselves didn't want to be defined.

Trying to define Lothlorien as a whole was problematic enough as I did my research. It was sometimes confounding. Was the place an intentional community or a forest preserva- tion project or something else? Whatever angle I tried to take up, I would meet with refuta- tions, like "We're not an intentional community," or "It's not really a Pagan place." The name Lothlorien means "dream flower" in J. R. R. Tolkien's invented language, and Conney, who has lived on the land since it was purchased in 1987, describes this flower as, "Something that just keeps opening and it has more and more layers, and it changes, and it's not quite finished blooming ever but it's always in some stage of change." A few people live there full-time, but most people come in and out in the course of a year, to attend festivals or to camp or to work for a weekend. Change and fluidity pervade the very heart of the place. All of this has made sense to me, (frustrating as it was at times when I was doing research), since I also dislike being defined, described, or even photographed; and I have tried to incorporate the ambiguity into my writing.

Part of Lothlorien participants' reluctance to define themselves, too, came from the fact that even a loose association with Paganism, or to a lesser extent, communalism, can be seen as suspect in the wider world, especially outside of the major cities and the East and West Coasts. Lothlorien has frequently been vandalized by neighbors, members of the family at the front gate have been threatened—once even with a shotgun—and several people I interviewed had had their associations with Paganism used against them in child custody cases, at work, and (less formally) in school. The community ethos makes it stand out from its neighborhood in several stark ways; its stewardship, its economics, its lifestyle norms, its material culture, the clothing styles of its members, its rituals. It is marginal and therefore vulnerable.

Even within academia, marginal pockets of experimentation within industrialized coun- tries—like communes and new religious movements (NRMs)—are easily dismissed. Research on contemporary intentional communities has been mainly the preserve of sociologists,[1] and has been oriented towards a search for predictive social laws to explain their existence. Surveys and comparative studies that looked for recurring patterns have been the most common ap- proach (for example, Wallace, 1956; Kanter, 1972; Zablocki, 1980.) Such communities, from this perspective, appear as phenomena that operate on their individual members as if from the outside—through social stress, for example—rather than being created or chosen by them. Hence the potential subversion and utopian visions implicit in unusual lifestyle choices have rarely been explored. There are signs, however, that this may be changing. Anthropologist Susan Brown, in her edited book *Intentional Community* (2002), describes participants' choices to form or join intentional communities as "a non-elitist form of critique available to privi- leged and underprivileged alike" (p. 158.)

In the case of NRMs, Elijah Siegler (2007) observes that among academic publications, "Either they assume that NRMs are a sociological problem to be solved…or else they describe NRMs one by one in an alphabetical or chronological list…. The sociological approach can

imply that NRMs are something that has 'happened' to the Western world since the 1960s…
the encyclopedic approach can reduce NRMs to exotic curiosities." (p. 8).

As for contemporary Paganism, as recently as 1989 a study of magicians in London took
as its explicit aim the desire to find out why seemingly rational people would develop irrational beliefs (Lurhmann, 1989.) And at a job talk I attended among anthropologists at
Indiana University three years ago, a reference to "Goddess worshippers" raised a collective
(perhaps inadvertent) giggle among the audience, an amused discomfort in spite of the respect
anthropology claims to have for diverse communities. Paganism has been taken up in a less
dismissive way as a topic of scholarship in the last decade or so,[2] but at some professional risk
to its researchers. The historian Ronald Hutton (2003) describes the scorn and misperception
he encountered among other academics, towards both Paganism and himself, while working
on a (skeptical and thoroughly researched) history of British Paganism, *The Triumph of the
Moon* (1999). He acknowledges, however, that the reaction against scholars of living Paganism
has been stronger, characterized in many cases by what he refers to as, "hostility, derision and
neglect" (2009, p. 221.) As Amy Hale argues in "White Men Can't Dance" (2009), white
people who pursue spiritual experiences outside of mainstream religion are an embarrassment
to most academics. And the scholars who study them are often considered suspect themselves
by association.

While a very large majority of people in the U.S.—about 93 percent, according to a 2008
Gallup Poll—believes in a God or a universal spirit, Euro-Americans manage somehow to
maintain a self-image of secularity, of untainted objectivity. However far from accurate this
portrait may be, it is an entrenched part of what Clifford Geertz (1973) called "the story we
tell ourselves about ourselves." Hale points out the implicit racism in assuming that nonmainstream, especially ecstatic, religion and ritual ("irrationality") are, or should be, the domain of
non-Westerners. She also describes an experience she had as a graduate student in a class on ritual. All the students did presentations on contemporary rituals, showing videos and analyzing
the symbolism. All the traditions were syncretic. But she was the only one whose participants
were white Americans—in a Pagan wedding ceremony—and she was also the only one whose
presentation was received with laughter. ("Hilarity" was the word she used.)

Why do Euro-Americans regard ourselves as secular, and why, even in academia, do we
find the practitioners of marginal religions or rituals in our midst so suspect, so embarrassing,
so funny? Almost all of us (according to the Gallup Poll cited above), have beliefs that go beyond the scope of what can be measured. Christianity, for one, is entrenched by virtue of its
long history, and weaves invisibly through our landscapes of thought. Nobody at a job talk or
conference, I think, would snicker at a God worshipper, although it is neither more nor less
rational, neither more nor less strange, to worship a God than a Goddess. But in the case of
marginalized religion, ritual, or spiritual practice among Euro-Americans in the industrialized
world, it is easy to assume or "see" irrationality, set against a familiar backdrop that we take
to be rational. Just as close examinations of the terms "insanity" and "crime" show up social
norms, taboos, and power structures, there is much to be learned from looking at the kinds of
experiences we marginalize—the lines we commonly draw between rationality and irrationality, normality and weirdness. Marginal pockets within North America reveal our shadow side,
the parts of ourselves that we are unwilling to acknowledge or to give credence to at any given
point in time.

In the last year or so at Lothlorien, I talked to people who were very forthcoming about their unusual spiritual and ritual experiences, and some of these people were kind enough to be interviewed. A few were long-time friends. One or two were new friends. The interviewee who talked in the most detail about his spiritual life was Bright, a man who had regular experiences of connection and communication with plants, animals, people, and spirits. At Starwood, a Pagan festival in New York state, he had met and fallen in love with a long-time Lothlorien sponsor named Leslie, and she brought him back to Indiana with her on her return home. I first got to know him over the course of a few festivals in the autumn of 2010.

In this paper I will explore the experiences, practices, and interpretations of Bright and a few other Lothlorien participants. Some of these went beyond what is usually considered ordinary or rational, yet also at times showed up some of the irrationality and hierarchy in mainstream ways of thinking, and expanded my own sense of what "rational" meant. They are unique experiences (rather than experiences typical of Lothlorien's visitors and volunteers), although Lothlorien provided a space for them. My argument is that there are emancipatory aspects and utopian possibilities among at least some marginalized spiritual paths, unusual individual experiences and experimental communities in North America, and that there is much to learn from them once this subject matter can be addressed respectfully, with attention to context and meaning. Many of the descriptions have an upside-down quality to them, reversing, questioning, or showing up assumptions and norms in mainstream thinking.

Humans, Animals and Plants

Within a pre-19th-century Christian worldview in Europe and North America, humans were set above other species, and were seen as separate and as having a right to dominion.[3] To be animalistic or "bestial" was something to be avoided—the opposite of holiness and humanity. This scheme also provided a framework in which people could be ranked, and that subtly justified hierarchies of power, since animality, instinct, the senses, and the emotions were associated with nonwhite races, the lower classes, and women. After Darwin and Lamarck's ideas spread, this sharp division between humans and the rest of the natural world was questioned. Evolutionary theories postulated a continuum ranging from bacteria to plants, animals, and humans. But interestingly, until recently[4] this link has been framed as a kind of disenchantment with humans rather than as an appreciation of other species. Sociobiology and evolutionary psychology in particular draw on the link to question the existence of qualities like generosity, kindness, even malleability in humans. Books like *The Selfish Gene* (Dawkins, 1976) and *The Blank Slate* (Pinker, 2002) depict us as "hardwired" to be aggressive, unequal,[5] and sexually selfish, however much we might want to delude ourselves that this is not the case. The evolutionary frame, then, shares some assumptions with the earlier view. In both, the animal world is defined negatively—by selfishness and brutality. The difference is that in the evolutionary view, these traits are seen as inevitable for humans as well as animals; whereas in most early Christian thinking "animal nature" is something that can and should be overcome. In both views, humans are above the other species. For traditional Christians, humans are closer to God, or have the capacity to be so, since God made man in his own image. For evolutionary theorists, there is also an implicit (or sometimes explicit) teleology—a trajectory from single-celled organisms to human beings (rather than, say, to coral reef ecosystems, or banyan trees, or sperm whales[6]).

Most contemporary Pagans, among others, take a third position. On the one hand they agree with the evolutionists that we share qualities with plants and, more so, with animals—that we are linked rather than essentially different. However, for Pagans and for many people at Lothlorien, it is the plants, animals, and even the elements that have something to teach the humans. The hierarchy, when there is one, goes in the other direction. To be associated with animals, with plants, and with air, fire, water, and earth is a good and sacred thing. To be "wild" is a good thing. To be "green" is a good thing. These qualities are revered, and the inanimate world too is revered; figures or symbols of the elements are placed on shrines and are used in most rituals. Sabina Magliocco (2004, pp. 185–204) points to the "oppositional" nature of Pagan spirituality and ritual, where the concept of holiness itself is opened up and questioned. Besides the nature/human dichotomy being blurred, gender stratification and class-related concepts of high and low culture are undermined as femininity, sensuality, humor, and mundane objects are all included in sacred imagery.

A few people I interviewed at Lothlorien—Pagan sympathizers rather than Pagans in most cases—experience the links between humans and other species quite directly. Laura strives for growth and improved social relationships by first finding a connection with the land. She does this through listening and feeling:

> I think about empathizing with people instead of controlling them or avoiding them, and trying to be compassionate and…trying to hear what's going on around me in nature and the land. And I'm outside right now listening to crickets and tree frogs and trying to remember how to feel like I'm a part of that, like I did when I was four. And then doing that and crossing it over and doing that with people. (Interview with Laura, 2010)

Most regular participants at Lothlorien see the animal and plant worlds not only as alive but as conscious. Rather than showing humanity to be bestial, they humanize other species, or at least point to their wisdom. Braze, who lived at Lothlorien for nine years, once gave a guest lecture for my class at Indiana University. He talked in detail about the relationships between plant and insect species in the community garden. "Decoy" plants that distract destructive insects from other plants, insects that pollinate, and "companion" plants all worked together to make the garden closer to a self-sustaining ecosystem—a system that cares for itself and improves its own soil. From this perspective, there is wisdom among plants, insects, and earth that manifests in their relationships with one another.

Bright communicates with individual plants and animals, and for him they are sentient or conscious beings. His experiences are sensory, but sometimes they go beyond what is normally sensed. He talks, for example, about light and music among plants:

> Each flower has its own little being of light, and they sing, and together the plant makes a song, and the other plants are singing nearby, too. To hear this is to hear your soul fly. I don't know how else to say it. (Interview with Bright, 2010)

Bright regards plants as teachers, with an "ancient and deep wisdom, from a way different time-perspective." Further, like Laura, he sees a therapeutic value in making the effort to communicate, and in conceiving of spirits and consciousness in other species:

> If anyone is reading this and they feel lonely and disconnected from nature, open to the possibility that there are spirits in every plant, like the ones in your yard, and your soil, and the plants you may have in

your house. They are all loving you, trying to help you. Just try a little bit to be aware of their presence, and extend pleasant energy to them, love and gratitude for what they do for us, appreciation of their beauty. (That is a strong doorway for communication.) (Interview with Bright, 2010)

Conney expresses the link and the essential sameness between humans, other species, even rocks and clay, in a fairly down-to-earth way. For her it is through feeling—this time the impressionistic sense of being "submerged"—that we can know the connection. This feeling is as effortless as any other direct sensation because it reflects something real:

I know that nature is not just plants and animals, nature includes rocks and dirt and us. Nature is a force that works and moves through everything. It is possible to walk in the forest or along a beach and become submerged in nature with no more effort than breath. People are at the core animals; the same force that tells geese when to fly south or tells spiders how to spin can guide us if we allow it. (Conney, 2008, www.elvinhome.org)

The people quoted above offer a view of the world where there is less of an experiential break between humans on the one hand and nature on the other, than is usual in the United States (or Europe). This follows in part from more optimistic assumptions about both nature and human nature. Yet neither a sense of connection with nature, nor a sense of disconnection from it is inherently rational or irrational. Rather they are both value-infused positions, interpretive, and even sensory perceptions of the world, which have the potential to inform rationality in different ways. I will discuss these different approaches to rationality at greater length below.

A different set of values also, of course, leads to a different set of actions, and this was one of the features that had originally drawn me to Lothlorien. The land comprises 109 acres, over 90 of which are forested. A great deal of experimentation with sustainable building and gardening goes on there in the area reserved for camping and festivals. It is done on a shoestring budget and entirely through volunteer labor. Given these constraints, the composting privies, showers, hall, sustainable camping facilities, forest care, and gardening are impressive.

"Living Backwards"

Ritual at Lothlorien often has a childlike, humorous quality to it. It is more playful than reverent in the usual sense.[7] At Witches' Ball in 2009 (one of the smaller festivals, celebrating *Samhein*, or Halloween), a papier mâché "mummy" was burned at midnight in a large outdoor community fire pit in the woods, amidst drumming. It needed a name and there was some humorous banter about this. Someone suggested "Toot'nCommon." Eventually it was named "Bubba Ho tep."[8]

Jason describes the way all-night drumming sessions end at festivals. First there is an ode to the sun, as it rises. But then, instead of a solemn "Amen" or its equivalent:

…You just really scream out "Bull!" and just make as much noise as you can. It's kind of an alarm clock for the rest of the land. "Alright, we've done our part. We've stayed up all night, we've made sure the sun comes back up. This is your information, this is your info-gram that the world will go on, that the sun has risen, and everything's all good," and we continue to drink a little bit more and be silly, and then we stumble off to bed. (Interview with Jason, 2008)

Some participants honor childlike qualities in individual life as well as in ritual. Just as in the previous section where Laura talks about her growth in terms of "trying to remember," trying to recapture the experiences and insights that she had as a four-year-old child, Bright describes his life in terms of a journey from adulthood to childhood. He occasionally uses the phrase "living backwards," which has two meanings for him. One refers to flashes of precognition, where he experiences the future in the present. He describes one such (shared) flash in the following example:

> River, my ex-wife, had been previously having visions of Arkansas also before we went. I know that was because we were feeling the impact of the experience, backwards in time like a ripple in a pond going out in all directions. (Bright, 2010)

The other meaning of the phrase "living backwards" is a process of letting go of the analytic or controlled parts of the mind in order to reclaim a child's perspective. For him, adulthood is associated with distance from the body, emotions, and spirit. Childhood is the goal.

> I grew up as a little child very cerebral, very disconnected from my body, my emotions, and somewhat disconnected from my spirit…. I was very adult-like as a child. It's been a long journey for me to get to the point where I'm carefree and childlike, at least to a decent degree. I worked hard for it. (Interview with Bright, 2010)

Learning or growing, then, becomes a process of remembering forgotten things, especially spiritual experiences, undoing suppression and regaining lost abilities, as well as a process of discovering new things:

> I know people have always said it's our imaginations, when we were children, so we to some degree suppressed it for fear of disapproval. Kids can sometimes see into other worlds. We have the ability, we can regain it. (Interview with Bright, 2010)

Children, along with animals, are the ones who can perceive and acknowledge expressions from the heart or the soul. They are, in a sense then, the real elders and teachers:

> Animals and little children will notice and want to come closer when the adult humans FINALLY let their hair down and let the soul out. I learned this being a street musician. I began to just close my eyes, play and sing from my heart. Occasionally, I would feel some other soul up higher above our heads with me, dancing in the music, and I would open my eyes and look and it was often a small child stopped in its tracks staring at me, smiling, maybe dancing, sometimes just mesmerized. (Interview with Bright, 2010)

Connections

The theme of connection between people and nature has already been discussed above and is an ideal that is used in many mainstream and environmentalist contexts (where it is often referred to metaphorically, as "the web of life," for example.). Connection between people is also important at Lothlorien, and both kinds of connection provide the foundation for other kinds of experience and ritual. However, as in the above examples about humans and nature, most of my interviewees talked about them in more concrete ways than is usual. First there is emotion or sensation. Laura, who does not identify with any particular set of beliefs, describes a shift in feelings during rituals at Lothlorien:

If we were there during a festival and there was a full moon, and Jef and Vickie did stand up and do a full moon ritual, you could feel the connectedness in that group of people gathered there. When Lisa came down and did the opening ceremony, for Elf Fest[9]... everybody was down there, you could feel—there was community there...and no matter how low you might feel in other parts...there's this expansiveness that happens. Everybody's included, nobody is special, and we're all just part of this group. (Interview with Laura, 2010)

PJ used to choreograph large rituals around the central fire at Lothlorien's festivals. She stopped attending from the late 1990s until 2009. Her connection with the land and community, particularly with the area around the central fire, remained so strong, however, that she could sense activity there, even at a physical distance:

For many years after I left, I would wake up in the middle of the night and say, "there's someone drumming," on some random evening, and I would call sometimes and say, "Were there people down there last night?" and they'd say, "Yes, of course," and I knew when there were people there, and I knew when someone was doing something, and I could feel it. (Interview with PJ, 2010)

Besides PJ feeling connections across space, she also felt them across time. She perceived the many different festivals as one continuous experience:

To me it's all one fire. People will say, "When did that happen?" Well, it happened at a festival, one festival goes into the next into the next. It's all the continuous stream to me, it's like dipping your toes in the water, and then you just keep going back to the river again and again. It's the same river, it's the same flow, it's the same fire, every fire that we kindle is the same, it's the same fire. Because people ask me, "So when did that happen?" I don't know. It happened. If I really had to think hard I could tell you when certain things occurred, but it's all the same. (Interview with PJ, 2010)

Neither from PJ's perspective nor from Bright's would these time-shifting and long-distance experiences seem particularly strange. Bright believes in a basic solidarity and unity between human beings, as well as other species, which underlies the "illusion of separateness" in everyday life. Because there is something more real, in his view, about connection than disconnection, experiences that most people would think of as magical are to be expected, and because connection reflects a natural part of human psychology, it is associated both with longing and, potentially, with bliss, a kind of homecoming:

Am I really a shaman, am I really a witch, am I really a wizard? Or do I just *want* to be really bad. But yes, we want to be so bad because we all are. The natural state of our souls is bliss. We all know that, and long for the connection again. (Interview with Bright, 2010)

Fluidity

If humans are connected, if humans and other species are connected, this suggests porous boundaries and a fluid self.[10] There are several different levels on which to understand this kind of fluidity. I will take the cultural level first. Possibilities for changing roles, changing activities, and changing self-image vary from community to community. Lothlorien allows for a lot of flexibility. I mentioned earlier that the place itself is perpetually changing and that the individuals within its boundaries were reluctant to be defined. Lothlorien also has an unusually accepting and nonrestrictive culture and it was often described by interview participants as an environment that enabled them to risk expressing new sides of themselves and thus to stay fluid on a personal level.

Teal's words express this kind of fluidity perfectly. In her view, feeling accepted and affirmed, and also feeling free from most normative restrictions, had led to the possibility of making personal changes and of experimenting with new identities:

> I think it's actually two things which may even sort of contradict in a way. I mean on the one hand you felt like you could completely be yourself. You didn't have to put on a different face. You didn't have to pretend that you were someone else or something else. And if you had ideas about things that were not quite what everyone else thought, you know… So it was okay to be different….
>
> And also I think that on the opposite side of that you also had the freedom to experiment with who you were—just start to learn things about yourself that maybe you didn't even have the context for in your regular mundane life. Like people play around with new names and they play around with—and not play as in like it's a game but in trying to understand themselves better—then they try it here in a safe place and then a lot of people may extend it to their mundane life…. I've had some of the best conversations with people here about things; and healthy debates, not crazy arguments you know, but healthy debates where we try to challenge each other to think in different ways, or at least consider a different perspective. (Interview with Teal, 2007)

This coexistence of individual freedom and community feeling contradicts at least some of the recent writing in social research on communitarianism. Clifford Christians (2008), for example, describes a feminist communitarian point of view as arguing that, "The total opposite of an ethics of individual autonomy is universal human solidarity…. The primal sacredness of all, without exception, is the heart of the moral order" (p. 206). I have no quarrel at all with the second of these sentences, but I disagree with the first. Connection and solidarity at Lothlorien on the social level would be more superficial without respect for the choices and voices of each of its individuals.[11] In "the Land of Misfit Toys," it is partly because it is more acceptable and comfortable than usual to be a gay person, an atheist, Pagan, or Christian, a woman, an environmentalist, a member of an ethnic minority, an elder—and to keep defining and combining these categories in new ways, that people tend to develop strong social connections there. It is partly because people are free to come and go and because they feel free to make a range of lifestyle choices, without the expectation of being judged negatively, that they develop loyalty to the place and people. This is not to say that solidarity and community do not develop in highly disciplined and stratified communities too—clearly they do. But individual autonomy and solidarity can not only coexist but, at Lothlorien at least, seem to enhance one another. Community culture there does not fix the individual into some reified form, nor define her, but enables growth, change, and fluidity.

In Lothlorien's early years, rituals were more dramatic and choreographed than they are now, and active members often took on "elvin" identities, connected with fantasy literature. This kind of enactment took fluidity to a further level. Shifts in identity were literal, and involved the expectation that one would "become a character," as PJ says:

> It was very theatrical, very literary-based. The costuming was a big draw for me, because any excuse to sew and make costumes and then become a character, for me, when I had just got done with theater school—I just thought it was a paradise then, you know, because I was eighteen years old, and it was the perfect place to be. (Interview with PJ, 2010)

Bright has experiences that take the fluid self a stage beyond this theatrical level too. He often channels beings that he experiences as both "higher" and other than himself. The internal shifts are characterized by feelings of joy or inspiration or intuitive senses about what to do. The beings range from spirits to animals. One is a wolf. Changes in consciousness like this happened on a number of occasions while I was interviewing him or talking to him. He describes the process thus:

> I tend to classify the word "channeling" as at least to a small degree the higher being is speaking through my mouth. I tend to fluctuate between levels of consciousness. As my Spirits surface, I allow my conscious mind to surrender to the back a bit. This proportion of my mind to theirs fluctuates in waves. I love this…. By staying somewhat conscious, I get to hear what they are saying, sometimes see visions they are communicating with, and all that wonderful and inspiring stuff. (Interview with Bright, 2010)

His sense of self, then, is not as one being but literally as a number of beings focalized into one place, characterized by varying feelings and varying degrees of conscious control. Usually one part of himself sees, feels, and hears what another part is communicating. One could describe this, perhaps, as a variety of discourses, but it is feelings rather than clusters of thoughts or words that seem to distinguish them from one another. Channeling enables him to embody radically different kinds of consciousness, from animal to divine.

I have written here about three layers of fluidity, and all are somewhat unusual. First, because Lothlorien is both a marginal community and an accepting community, which provides a kind of sanctuary for people who may or may not fit comfortably in the mainstream, there is more space than in the mainstream for experimentation with individual identities and roles. Second, the drama of some Pagan rituals allows for even greater shifts in personas. Finally, Bright experiences internal shifts that are diverse and marked enough to give him the sense that a variety of beings are expressing themselves through him.

In these examples, both individual nature and "human nature" are fluid. Usually the commonsense assumptions about human nature in any given time bolster mainstream social formations, and this is one of the reasons why intentional communities and marginal groups often become bones of fierce contention.[12] At Lothlorien, people can expand beyond the generally accepted limits in their individual identities, in the ways they interact with one another and the natural world, and in some cases in their interaction with supernatural beings.

Knowing

After my second interview with Bright, I read Svend Brinkman's chapter for this book, and decided to pursue episteme (shared knowledge) as well as doxa (personal impressions) in the third interview by asking more probing questions than I usually do. "How do you know that?" was a question I asked and rephrased numerous times (to the extent I began to feel that I was being annoying[13]). But I was genuinely curious about the way Bright distinguished some of his unusual experiences—channeling, connecting with plants—from his everyday ones, and about what this might say about knowing, and about rationality and validity in general. Looking back later, even over the first two interviews, I noticed that he had already answered my question in several different ways.

The kind of knowing that he referred to most often was expressed as a form of bodily experience, combined with a sense of familiarity. Here, for example, he is describing a conversation about past-life experiences with his ex-wife. When he heard her words,

> I felt it ripple through my being, complete with chills, as if she was telling me something that I already knew but had forgotten. (Interview with Bright, 2010)

In this next quotation, Bright is reaching out into a range of common experiences that readers might have, in order to communicate what it is like to connect with the sacred. It is expressed here as something that is accessible through positive emotional and physical feelings, some of which relate to religion, some of which are sensual, some aesthetic:

> Most of us know that sacred feeling. Even people who don't find it through meditation or prayer, they know it in other ways, like making love to someone you really love, or childbirth, or a sunset—experiencing anything beautiful, like snowboarding or skiing. People know what that sacred feeling feels like, when they feel connected and alive. (Interview with Bright, 2010)

In this context, he refers to childhood again, too:

> It's like voices filled with happy childhood feelings. Yeah, it's light and happy, blissful contentment. We all know this feeling, it's no mystery. (Interview with Bright, 2010)

Sometimes he talks about knowing as a more subtle process, something faintly perceived but not fully recognized. In this next example, he is describing precognitive experiences. Again there is a reference to familiarity:

> Visions and stuff like that are often at first so subtle that they are occurring on the outskirts of our conscious awareness, and it seems like idle daydreaming sometimes, so faint and flowy. As we learn to pay more attention to that kind of awareness, it grows stronger and stronger. But until then, and even then sometimes, it's not until the event occurs that we suddenly realize that we had already sensed it coming and didn't pay attention to it much. (Interview with Bright, 2010)

The "rational, controlling part of the mind" is what tends to filter out unusual experience, and dismiss experiences of connection beyond the individual self. For Bright, there is another important aspect to this too—that the kinds of knowing he describes are accessible to all people rather than being esoteric. He wants to avoid distinguishing or ranking people based on the types of experience they have.

> I'm talking about direct experience without trying to make it happen with the rational, controlling part of the mind. We all know it. We all know who it is on the phone sometimes. How do we explain that? The idea of separation between some people who aren't spiritual and some who are is an illusion. (Interview with Bright, 2010)

Finally, there are times when he talks in terms that are more reminiscent of the mainstream, of finding validation through the fact that other people have shared his experiences:

> I have had a lot of experiences that other people witnessed. I need that "objective" validation. Objectivity is pretty much an illusion, but it's a good illusion. (Interview with Bright, 2010)

For the most part, among these descriptions, "knowing" is something that is experienced internally, through the body and emotions, rather than through analysis, deduction, or even through validation from others. This links up with the earlier sections about children and the natural world. Children and animals (as far as we know in the latter case, which is not very far) orient themselves through their bodies and emotions to a greater extent than do adult humans. They "know" more empirically and experientially. The other common component of the descriptions is a sense of recognition, familiarity, or remembering.

At points in the third interview, Bright brought the conscious mind into the picture more by talking about thoughts creating reality. In this view, a range of realities could be experienced by different people at different times. Truth too would become a fluid thing as multiple perspectives would have to be allowed for:

> With arguments of a philosophical or spiritual nature, both sides are usually right, just seeing a different perspective. It's nice, like a win-win situation. The more I learn to see from the soul perspective, the more I see how both arguments are true in more and more situations. (Interview with Bright, 2010)

Another interviewee, Sarah, whom I met in my first year at Lothlorien, expresses something similar to this last idea of thoughts creating reality. She describes the enchanted view of the land at Lothlorien as a construction and a choice—a choice to see the world in ways, or through metaphors, that lead to new, sometimes shared "realities," and that provide an alternative to instrumentalist thinking:

> The people try to hold on to some of that magic, even if it seems totally ridiculous or totally outlandish. If you can think it, then you've kind of created that existence with your own mind, because perception is reality in a sense. And if you have enough people pulling energy into one idea or thought or place, then it becomes a lot more real, because a lot more people are thinking it. And I just—it's great that people want to keep magic and things like that alive, because there's not enough of it in the world. There's just commercialism and industry and you know, G.E. and Nike and Abercrombie and Fitch and all those things. (Interview with Sarah, 2006)

Others at Lothlorien avoid talking about spirituality altogether, although they might share some of the sentiments expressed in earlier parts of this paper about connections with the natural world. Bonedaddy, for example, describes himself as an agnostic, and was originally drawn to the land partly because people there were open-minded. He trusts his sense impressions and emotions rather than any metaphysical scheme. He says,

> I freely admit that I don't have the slightest idea where we came from or where we're going. I'm one of those people who requires proof. I believe in the earth because I'm standing on it. I believe in my friends and the people I love. I believe in my emotions. (Interview with Bonedaddy, 2006)

Bonedaddy, like Bright and several other people quoted in this chapter, uses the body and emotions as a reference point most of the time rather than some more indirect or deductive process. Otherwise, he is more secular than most of his Midwestern neighbors, both within and outside Lothlorien's gates. Yet his life is highly unusual. He has lived in a tipi in the woods there for the best part of 15 years (actually, a "tipi complex" since he built an extra tipi as a bathroom, complete, at present, with a purchase from a used-furniture store—a marble bathtub!). He is an empiricist and a skeptic whose values happen to be out of sync with mainstream values:

[At Lothlorien] I didn't feel so alone. I found people cared about the planet…. It's a better way to live life than "Consume, consume, gimme, gimme, greed, greed…" Society teaches respect but it doesn't teach respect for the environment. Not enough yet. (Interview with Bonedaddy, 2006)

All of these overlapping ways of knowing are marginal worldviews within the context of the United States. But the sharpest contrast between these and mainstream views is not between rationality and irrationality, Reason and Faith. The contrast is between two clusters of values that inform rationality in different ways. Some divergent perspectives on animal and human nature were noted above. I will add two more examples of entrenched differences.

First, mainstream instrumentalist discourses reflect a preoccupation with profit, loss, and measurability that is itself infused with values and assumptions. In *The Protestant Work Ethic and the Spirit of Capitalism* (1904/1958), Weber wrote about the mutually sustaining themes within European Protestant working life—noting the particular influence of Calvinism. Calvin preached that only an elect few were chosen by God for an afterlife in heaven and that there was nothing the rest of the population could do to ensure such a future. From this perspective, wealth accumulation was a visible indication of God's favor, while work was a way to honor God's creation here on earth. God himself, however, was wholly transcendent and separate from the material world. Profit calculations were associated with the quest for prosperity, but material and sensual enjoyment of goods were not, since human sensuality and emotion were sites of "the corruption of everything pertaining to the flesh." The influence of Calvinism lingered long after the religion itself had waned in influence, through a continuing focus on what can be measured, specifically monetary profit.

Second, some of modern North America's more disconnected and disenchanted views can be traced back to everyday experiences of distance, which have grown since the Industrial Revolution through lives spent largely, by necessity, among human artifacts. From our vantage points on the inside of cars, buses, houses, offices, factories, stores, and increasingly preoccupied as we are, in the last two decades, by electronic screens and by survival through money, the natural world and even our emotions and senses can seem somehow unreal, even irrelevant.

At Lothlorien, perceptions of connection between people and nature, people and one another, reflect in some cases a deliberate move beyond instrumentalism into intentional re-enchantment, and in other cases an acknowledgment of sensations that are not often noticed or honored. From these points of view, the sense of being separate, qualitatively different or cut off from the rest of the natural world and from each other would be the irrational position. Laura, for example, questions…

…this idea that we are born into the world from outside, and it's a place where things have to be controlled and overcome. And it's just part of the mindset that we're raised with over here in the West…. It's creating a false view, almost a hallucination. (Interview with Laura, 2010)

Conclusions

At Lothlorien and among the people I talked to, there was much that seemed to me to be demystifying in the paradigms of connection, with nature and with humans, and of honoring the senses and emotions (even when these convey something unexpected). According to this worldview, it made sense to live backwards, to unlearn the "collective hallucination," in Laura's words, of disconnection, and to unlearn the need for top down control over the natural world, our minds, or each other. There was a need to see with new eyes. This paradigm also translated into action—in ecologically sensitive stewardship of the forest and campgrounds, in collective ownership, and in a culture of acceptance.

I have noted that many people at Lothlorien are wary of being defined, and that the culture of the place enables a great deal of flexibility in behavior and identity. Often the very choice to be part of an intentional or marginalized community implies a refusal to accept limitations in the first place. Once such a community is in place, these refusals are reinforced further. Wilma Mankiller made this point when she wrote about the 1969–1971 occupation of Alcatraz by the Indians of All Tribes:

> The Alcatraz experience nurtured a sense among us that anything was possible—even, perhaps, justice for Native people. (Mankiller & Wallis, 1993, p. 192)

Bright, in his channeling, is in a sense refusing to accept limitations on an individual level too, refusing to limit himself to being a single personality. He cultivates states of mind where he can let in more than this—the wiser, more blissful, or more primal perspectives of animals and spirits.

Across the board, the existence of each intentional community and each minority spiritual path offers the statement, "Yours is not the only way to live." We stand to lose a lot if, in our research, we are not willing to look respectfully at the marginalized pockets and unusual experiences within our own societies, and to try to understand them on their own terms. They represent what is pushed away. Sometimes they upturn hierarchies. They present examples of change. They offer hope. Krishan Kumar argues for the importance of utopian thinking, and his words also apply aptly to alternative communities and belief systems:

> Our historical condition—one in which life itself is threatened with insupportable damage, perhaps even extinction—is unprecedented. There is nothing to guarantee that we will find our way out of this mess. But at the very least we can think about, we must think about alternatives to the system that has got us into it. (Kumar & Bann 1993, p. 80)

Notes

1. Historical examples of experimental communities have been described more interpretively and in more depth. See for example the excellent collection of essays in Donald Pitzer's edited collection, *Utopian Communities* (1997.)

2. See for example Hutton (1999); Berger (1999); Greenwood (2000); Harvey (2000); Pike (2001); Salomonsen (2002); Magliocco (2004); Clifton (2006) .

3. I recognize that this view does not apply to Christianity across the board. There are plenty of exceptions, especially among contemporary Christians. "Green Christians" constitute a growing movement and many Christians are conscientious in their role as planetary stewards.

4. Recent exceptions to this framework are works by Jeffrey Moussaieff Masson and Susan McCarthy (1996) and Frans de Waal (1996) on the emotional and moral lives of nonhuman animals.

5. Arguments for inevitable inequality along gender lines come up frequently among these works.

6. Of all animal species, sperm whales have the largest brains.

7. Sarah Pike writes about playfulness at Lothlorien and other Pagan festival sites in her book, *Earthly Bodies, Magical Selves*, (2001, pp. 182–219.)

8. The name "Bubba Ho tep" came from a comedy horror film of the same name, produced in 2002 by Jason Savage and directed by Don Coscarelli.

9. Elf Fest is Lothlorien's largest festival, held annually in May.

10. The alternative to this would be to see each person in a distinct but fixed role, like components of some perfectly calibrated machine.

11. I also think it is misleading to describe the ideal of respect for individual autonomy as an essentially (or typically) Western construct, even though, like secularity, it is one of the stories we tell ourselves about ourselves. There are numerous examples of non-European societies that have held and continue to hold to this ideal (see for example, Mann, 2005, and Samson, 2003); and many critiques both of European and Euro-American societies, and of colonialism, are based precisely on the direct and indirect curtailment of individual freedom, and on the ways this curtailment is disguised. This issue could and perhaps will be the topic of a whole book, but meanwhile for a slightly more detailed (although still embryonic) discussion, see Carspecken (2011), An Unreal Estate: Sustainability and Freedom in an Evolving Community.

12. Carspecken, 2011 (Chapter 2).

13. This reflects on my lack of experience with epistemic interviewing rather than the method itself!

References

Berger, H. (1999). *A community of witches.* Columbia: University of South Carolina Press.

Brown, S. L. (2002). Community as cultural critique. In S. L. Brown (Ed.), *Intentional Community.* Syracuse,NY: Syracuse University Press.

Carspecken, L. (2011). *An unreal estate: Sustainability and freedom in an evolving community.* Bloomington: Indiana University Press.

Christians, C. (2008). Ethics and politics in qualitative research. In N. Denzin, & Y. Lincoln (Eds.), *The Landscape of Qualitative Research.* Thousand Oaks, CA: Sage

Clifton, C. (2006). *Her hidden children: The rise of Wicca and Paganism in America.* Lanham, MD: AltaMira Press.

Dawkins, R. (1976). *The selfish gene.* New York: Oxford University Press

De Waal, F. (1996). *Good natured: The origins of right and wrong in humans and other animals.* Cambridge, MA: Harvard University Press

Gallup Poll. (2008). http://www.gallup.com/video/109111/Majority-Americans-Believe-God.aspx

Geertz, C. (1973). *The interpretation of cultures.* New York: Basic Books.

Greenwood, S. (2000). *Magic, witchcraft and the otherworld: An anthropology.* Oxford & New York: Berg.

Hale, A. (2009). White men can't dance. In D. Evans, D. Green, & R. Hutton (Eds.), *Ten years of triumph of the moon* (pp.76–95). Harpenden, UK: Hidden Publishing.

Harvey, G. (2000) *Contemporary paganism: Listening people, speaking earth.* New York: New York University Press.

Hutton, R. (1999) *The triumph of the moon: A history of modern Pagan witchcraft.* Oxford: Oxford University Press.

Hutton, R. (2003). *Witches, Druids and King Arthur.* London: Hambledon Continuum.

Hutton, R. (2009). Afterword, In D. Evans, D. Green, & R. Hutton (Eds.)., *Ten years of triumph of the moon* (pp.215–227). Harpenden, UK: Hidden Publishing.

Kanter, R. M. (1972). *Commitment and community.* Cambridge, MA: Harvard University Press.

Kumar, K., & Bann, S. (Eds.). (1993). *Utopias and the millenium.* London: Reaktion Books.

Lurhmann, T. (1989). *Persuasions of the witch's craft,* Cambridge, MA: Harvard University Press.

Magliocco, S. (2004). *Witching culture: Folklore and neopaganism in America.* Philadelphia: University of Pennsylvania Press.

Mankiller, W., & Wallis, M. (1993). *Mankiller: A chief and her people.* New York: St Martin's Griffin.

Mann, C. (2005). *1491.* New York: Vintage.

Masson, J. M., & MacCarthy, S. (1996) *When elephants weep: The emotional lives of animals.* New York: Delta.

Pike, S. (2001). *Earthly bodies, magical selves.* Berkeley: University of California Press.

Pinker, S. (2002). *The blank slate.* New York: Viking

Pitzer, D. E., (Ed.). (1997). *America's communal utopias.* Chapel Hill & London: University of North Carolina Press.

Salomonsen, J. (2002). *Enchanted feminism: The reclaiming witches of San Francisco.* London: Routledge.

Samson, C. (2003). *A way of life that does not exist: Canada and the extinguishment of the Innu.* London: Verso.

Siegler, E. (2007). *New religious movements.* Upper Saddle River, NJ: Prentice Hall.

Wallace, A. (1956). Revitalization movements: Some theoretical considerations for their comparative study. *American Anthropologist, 58*(2), 264–281.

Weber, M. (1904/1958). *The Protestant work ethic and the spirit of capitalism.* New York: Charles Scribner's Sons.

Zablocki, B. (1980). *Alienation and charisma: A study of contemporary American communes.* New York: Free Press.

CHAPTER FIVE

Reflexivity, Picturing Selves, and the Reforging of Method

IAN STRONACH, DEAN GARRATT, CATHIE PEARCE, & HEATHER PIPER[1]

The apparatus of reason would not be complete unless it swept itself into its own analysis of the field of experience. (Mead, 1934/1962, p. 138)

There are two styles of philosophers: eg and ie philosophers—illustrators and explicators. Illustrators trust, first and foremost, striking examples, in contrast with explicators, who trust, first and foremost, definitions and general principles. (Margalit, 2002, ix)

The histories of reflexivity are many and various. There is a ghostly "positivist" account that seeks origins in scientific warrants, analogically derived (for example, as Heisenberg might have intended). If the scientific observer has to be regarded as part of the experiment, then all the more complicit will be the observer bent on social inquiry. Then there is the reflexivity that would seek to locate itself within a community of researchers, including scientists. In this version, promoted by the Social Scientific Knowledge group (for examples, see Latour, 1988; Woolgar, 1988; Ashmore, 1989), the socially constructed nature of all knowledge, including scientific knowledge, requires that we introduce a reflexive dimension to accounts of its "discovery," and indeed that we regard metaphors of "discovery" as themselves the epistemological deceptions of an implicit correspondence theory, or at least a naïve realism. Again, we might turn to Macbeth's (2001) analytic notion of "positional reflexivity" (p. 37) wherein attempts are made—often confessionally—to align "methodological rigor with a critically disciplined subjectivity" (p. 39). Macbeth also considers a contrasting "textual reflexivity" that reflects the well-known "linguistic turn" in anthropology (e.g., Marcus & Cushman, 1982; Clifford & Marcus, 1986; Rosaldo, 1987). A fourth alternative is offered in relation to an ethnomethodological return to "essential indexicality" (Macbeth, 2001, p. 49), whereby reflexivity is identified as the everyday resource of individuals in society. Foley (2002), indeed, offers a typology of various reflexive approaches even though such an analytical strategy is itself a way of taking sides, epistemologically speaking. Denzin (2003) opts for a more decidedly performative reflexivity. All of these approaches differ, but as both Macbeth and Foley concede, they are not always distinct. Our approach in this chapter will be eclectic, combining aspects of textualist and performative approaches, and avoiding static labeling. We envisage reflexivity as dynamic, a Deleuzian "concept," or signature, as we eventually argue it. More practically, we will be looking at the "ambivalent practices of reflexivity" (Davies et al., 2004, pp. 360–389; Stronach, 2010b). Unlike Davies et al., however, we will draw not on ourselves as evidence of reflexive practice, but on the reflexive practices of doctoral candidates whose theses reflect the ways in which they chose to appropriate reflexive methodological texts. To our knowledge, reflexivity has not been studied "empirically" in this way. Finally, we will return to the problem of reflexive "modality": if there cannot be a model, or models for reflexivity, then what can be said about the enterprise in terms of "sensitizing" rather than "prescribing" (Guillemin & Gillam, 2004, p. 278)? Can reflexivity be made to perform in heuristic ways, even if it cannot be de- or prescribed? In the fluid metaphors of Deleuze (1995), "[t]he only question is how anything works, with its intensities, flows, processes, partial objects..." (p. 22).

Constructing Reflexive Selves

We begin by offering a brief sketch of three different "models" of reflexivity, offered to educational researchers at Manchester Metropolitan University between 1996 and 2008, and subsequently at Liverpool John Moores University, as methodological warrants and methodical guides. These are somewhat encapsulated and no doubt parodic, but we are interested here in how these reflexive positions were appropriated by doctoral "users" rather than in the detail of the original arguments. The progenitor of the reflexive series of seminars for present purposes was Peshkin, who in 1988 offered an account of the reflexive researcher as comprising, in his case, six segments. These "multiple I's" offered access to founding prejudices or dispositions that could be addressed by the researcher in ongoing self-scrutiny. An obvious criticism was that these various perspectives also depended on an unexplicated transcendental position that allowed him to look down on these selves from nowhere, as it were. Arguably this was a rather masculinist and mechanistic management of reflexivity, based on a realist option. In doctoral workshop, it was dubbed the Clockwork Orange. Heshusius (1994, p. 18) later criticized this model. Instead of segments, she proposed a fusion of I and Thou, the "selfother" (sic) of a "participatory consciousness." To workshop participants, this often seemed a better mnemonic than it was a heuristic. Clearly it was more of a phenomenological option, and one we nicknamed the Ontological Omelette. The final commentator in the series was Lenzo (1994). She offered neither a segmentary self nor a self-other fusion. Instead, she invoked a kind of anti-model, talking the language of transgression and incompletion by citing Lather (1993). This was certainly a poststructuralist option with some version of a "fractured-I" (Deleuze & Guattari, 1994, p. 145)—we called it Humpty Dumpty. Arguably there are many other "reflexive" papers we could have referred to, but we are concerned with those that most strongly resonated with, and were appropriated by, our doctoral students. How were these various methodological texts taken up? If we are to be reflexive about reflexivity, and there seems no choice, then we need to ask "what does reflexivity do, as well as mean?" (an illocutionary concern in Austin's terms, 1962/1989), and "what would be a reflexive approach to such enactments?" (a prescriptive rather than descriptive ambition). A neglected way of getting into these issues is empirical (compare Young, 2001)—that is, to look at the ways in which doctoral students, exposed to reflexive prescriptions such as Peshkin, Heshusius, and Lenzo, have responded.

The first surprise is the great range of legitimating strategies engendered by these founding texts, given that each aims to prescribe and proscribe "approaches" to reflexive educational inquiry. Starting from Peshkin's "multiple-I," which posited a segmented self, managing its various manifestations within the research process, several students launched a retrospective and ongoing search for the self engaged in the creation of data and text. In some cases, the researcher was seen as an "emerging" self (Plummer, 1996, p. 1; Bibi-Nawaz, Grant & Stronach, 2010), the youngest of the "voices" (Plummer, 1996, p. 3). Accordingly, Plummer also learned from overlapping selves, such as the "counselor" and the "teacher," or the "mother" and "principal" in Ërculj's case (2003). There was also a dutiful scrutiny of segmented selves whose "thwarting biases" (Plummer, 1996, p. 9) were subject to retrospective analysis, such as Koren's (2002) self-diagnosis of a "professional-I" making assumptions about interpretation ahead of the data. The latter expressed the disabling ghosts of familiarity in relation to the subject of the inquiry, while the former amounted to the sorts of "enabling" selves that Peshkin largely had in mind. Others interpreted Peshkin rather differently by identifying the conscious generation of a series of research selves within the acts of research itself, rather than as accompanying selves to that process. For Allan (1995, p. 52) "the marginal/subversive" role was an ongoing Garfinkel-like subterfuge, a style of research engagement necessary for the generation of a Foucauldian perspective on inclusion while simultaneously conducting government-funded empirical evaluation. The perspective dictated a certain ethical duplicity, or so she intended. This self was generative, strategically both open and closed to its interlocutors, and eventually in the thesis a self-confessed "undercover agent."

So segmented selves were all subject to some kind of inventory, constructed by authors looking over their shoulders via research diaries, data, and theoretical excursions. Such "selving" could provoke more ontological sorts of tension in the authors' inquiries. Selves offered a simultaneously dangerous and productive contamination of each other. This is evidenced in the work of Trunk-Širca. As director of a tertiary college, and researching her own institution, her balancing of a managing self and a research self was always a precarious "question of power exercised for and against itself" (Trunk-Širca, 2002, p. 72). Her selves inhabited a cuckoo's nest of truth and power. She was part of the "power" that the "truth" of her inquiry tried to interrogate, and in such inherently conflicted accounts there was always an obvious double risk: that Truth into Power Won't Go, and that Power into Truth Won't Stop.

Still others shifted the debate more firmly away from roles and selves to standpoints, translating Peshkin's pluralities into such things as a "multiple-centred standpoint epistemology" (Jones, 1997, p. 131) while claiming a "mutually dependent" relationship between teacher and researcher selves. In this account, Peshkin is chewed over, but not swallowed: "It is interesting that Peshkin did not acknowledge a seventh self, the 'academic-I' that constructed the entire account" (Jones, 1997, p. 100). Others sought to undermine the notion of selves in an attempt to tell a "journey" of a self that aimed for a "wily versatility that will allow me to think and speak both 'as if' the lesbian self does exist and 'as if' it does not" (Riding, 2002, pp. 47, 79). Riding inserted selves not as retrospective "discoveries," but as tactics to produce a divided political epistemology where perspectives might productively conflict—a crossroads where poststructuralism encountered standpoint epistemology or critical realism (Lewis, 2002; Roberts, 2004). Such a versatility allowed the researcher, for example, to make signing up statements in regard to methodological stances—"I align my own position to that of Heshushius" (Englad, 2003, p. 52), while simultaneously generating a range of poststructuralist and hermeneutic affiliations that made such an arrangement promiscuous in terms of the "authentic" ambitions of a Heshusius. A rationale for such promiscuity was belatedly offered by Stronach (2010a) in terms of "critical adjacency" or "near-miss narratives" (pp. 178–182).

Thus selves could be engendered in the real as "discovered" past roles at work in the inquiry or transformed into personated epistemologies, as a dialogue of ideas generative of a "research self"—such as the "black researcher," the "lesbian researcher," the minority ethnic "lone mother." Ěrculj (2003) added another mobility by casting doubt on the permanence of any of these divisions, opting for a more occasional, emergent, and situated sense of research consciousnesses, drawing particular attention to a "theory-laden-I" whose emergence recontoured the configurations of management and organizational issues in contra-distinction to a "tradition-laden-I" steeped in a Slovenian professional and national culture. This was an ongoing reframing of the research self as an emerging but unrealizable synthesis, an "unsettled hybrid" as another doctoral author put it (Hanley, 2001, p. 170). For several, there was a partly unresolved problem in telling, as it were, realist stories about their poststructuralist selves. Finally, Jones (1997) offered an iconoclastic attack on all such selves and selving. Starting from Lenzo's Lather-based notion of a "transgressive self" (p. 130), he attacked the telling of methodological stories (in the style of Ashmore, 1989) and reported such narratives as plotlines, mocking the solemnity of methodological narrative within a Mickey Spillane genre in which academic credentials were interrogated and dispatched:

> His high-pitched pleading annoyed me but I let him whine, "There are many teachers' voices, not just one" (1997: 13). I stubbed my cigarette out on the collar and helped him towards the broken window. What the hell was that supposed to mean? … "There are other voices worth articulating, hearing, and sponsoring as well as those of teachers." I let him drop. (Jones, 1997 p. 208)

This perspectival, ironic approach culminated in supervisors, subjects, and author being required to enact in his thesis a triple "play" of reflexive meaning (play as drama, as fun, as looseness), a play with a possible sting in the tale for accounts such as this. There is "little point in outlining a handbook of reflexivity because as soon as it was created its processes would need to be subverted by the truly reflexive researcher" (Jones, 1997, p. 87). Selves, in his account, are eventually realized as fiction—within a play that addresses issues of performativity rather than claiming to represent any "real" situation in itself, or "real" selves, whether segmented or participatory in nature.

There are many other ways in which doctoral authors drew on their "founding" methodologies in order to construct research selves. In the first section of this paper, we have attended most closely to the tightest of the three prescriptions, the managed research selves of Peshkin. Yet that text was appropriated in a great variety of ways. Its indeterminations are more impressive than its determinations. It was "provocative" when it intended to be "realist," "transgressive" when it sought fidelity. And the translations seemed most interesting and creative the more unfaithful they were to the original text. They provoked a range of realist, hermeneutic, poststructuralist, and postmodernist interrogations. But perhaps we have said enough about their diverse strategies to encourage us to think in more interesting ways about what is going on when one reading enters another, and then re-emerges with a claim to methodological warrant. We came to call such "translations" and "appropriations" revisionary, in order to point to the creative infidelities and apparent inversions involved. That takes us to the next step in this reflexive exploration: what questions can we cull from the way these texts were so differently read and rewritten in their journey—"trip" might be better—from academic reading to enacted methodological text? What can we say of this "doctoring" of the text? Of the picturing of selves that went on in each author's encounter with the Methodologists of Reflexivity? Finally, the nightmare question: if methodology can't account for itself methodologically, then where does that leave us?

Picturing Selves

Each reflexive author sought to figure herself from the "ground" of research practice, as well as the "air" of reflexive theory. That double extraction involves, of course, crucial metaphorical decisions. The perceptual play of figure/ground? The punning "mine" of extraction? The ways in which we relate such articulations of self "systematically" to the practices of inquiry are crucial. In the light of our preliminary empirical study of such (dis)articulations, we propose here the notion of "grounded metaphor" (see, for example, Stronach & Piper, 2008). We seek to explore precisely those indeterminations in methodological texts that appear to undermine/ outgrow their claims to legitimacy and the possibility of systematicity (Stronach & MacLure, 1997). Such indeterminations still seem both important and neglected. Methodology seeks to contain indeterminacies, whereas we prefer to explore and mobilize them as far as possible.

In deciding which metaphors to deploy in order to develop a feel for reflexivity, we intend accordingly to avoid those metaphors that carry a realist or positivist implication, such as the "mirror."[2] As we have shown, the reflexive picturing of our authors was much more performative than that, and suggested a more loosely coupled articulation of one text upon the other, a kind of fruitful miscegenation. Their methodologies were not "applied" instances of the general so much as singular variations on an underlying theme. A necessary improvisation? Further, their idiosyncrasy underpinned claims to originality. Where doctoral candidates stuck most closely to the prescriptions of the methodology, creativity was least. The least conceivable metaphors for this sort of process were "science," "application," and "representation," In Peshkin's terms, it was the "untamed" self that seemed to be the necessary precondition for good thinking, and we need to consider what it was about that indiscipline that made thinking the "self" creative.

Such serial infidelity reminded us of the ways in which artworks (themselves inquiries into meaning's meaning) sometimes give birth to a series of reinterpretations, as in the visual commentaries on Velázquez's *Las Meñinas* by Picasso, Manet, Dégas, and so on. These were not, of course, replications so much as they were responses, which raised interesting questions about what qualities in the "original" called forth subsequent evocations, and in what ways these "exceeded" the former. Were these "representations," "dialogues," "transformations," or "developments"? What tropes did we need to deploy here, and with what justification? And what meanings could be given to such processes? In addition there was commentary on the meaning of such "picturing" that might provoke new thinking. Such commentary offered us a double entry into visual and textual registers concerning acts[3] of reflexive performance. A review of indetermination in relation both to accounts of theory and narrative suggested some provocative possibilities. For example, we asked: what was the composition of such "picturing"? There were elements of narrative, logic, figure, "scene" (Rosaldo 1978), emotional tone, and philosophy.

In all these aspects there are good reasons for expecting imprecision. Just to illustrate, Primo Levi (1991), discusses the "secrets of the trade, indeed, the non-trade" of narrative writing that expresses and contains all these aspects:

> They exist, I cannot deny it, but luckily they have no general validity; I say "luckily" because, if they did, all writers would write in the same way, thus generating such an enormous mass of boredom. (Levi, 1991, p. 207)

Research accounts, then, in so far as they are narratives, demand "novel selves." Such a view would inform the sorts of research selves envisaged by Denzin (1997) in terms of a "reflexive poetic" (p. 223), a kind of affective crafting. Kamuf takes the argument further, arguing that the impossibility of a self present to itself (foreground and background always being hidden from each other) is in itself productive, "it is these very limits, demarcating intention, that produce it, and allow it to function as such" (Kamuf, 1991, p. 81). Elsewhere: "The difference is inscribed at the limit; it is the difference, or *différance* of that limit—its division—that holds I-we apart together and thus opens each to the other" (Kamuf, 1997, p. 122). Accordingly Kamuf denies the possibility of reproduction, fidelity, and stability, arguing instead for "the graphic of iterability rather than the logic of repetition" (1991, p. 86). It is, then, reflexivity's impossibility that makes it work, as "impossibility" is part of the creative process. We should aspire only to a "restless ontology" (Watson, 2008, p. 11), and to a "terminology [as] the properly poetic thought" (Agamben, 2005, p. 4). This is a familiar Derridean kind of thinking where meaning is constantly displaced and deferred, but Polanyi earlier made a similar point in relation to "tacit knowing," concerning the impossibility of formalizing such knowledge:

> If such formalization of tacit knowing were possible, it would convert all arts into mathematically pre-scribed operations, and thus destroy them as works of art. (Polanyi, 1962, in Grene, 1969, p. 164)

That seems to recall Calvino's suspicion of "trade secrets." Finally, we might acknowledge Heidegger (1962):

> The more genuinely a methodological concept is worked out and the more comprehensively it determines the principles on which a science is conducted, all the more primordially is it rooted in the way we come to terms with the things themselves, and the farther is it removed from what we call "technical devices," though there are many such devices in the theoretical disciplines. (Heidegger, 1962, p. 50)

We do not wish to present these arguments against technical reduction and rule-bound specification as refutations of Peshkin or Heshusius, or recommendations for Lenzo, so much as reasons why methodological writers have had their texts appropriated in ways they did not prescribe and presumably would not approve. Nor do we wish to instigate a different paradigm with new slogans: "Iterability not Repetition!"; "Indiscipline your Thinking!"; "Indetermination (Mis) Rules!"; and so on. Instead, we want to experiment with the concept of reflexivity in a different way, suspending any notion of further definition and looking instead for "striking examples" of performative reflexivity, forged in the sort of philosophizing that Deleuze and Guattari (1994) recommend, one dedicated to "fabricating concepts" (p. 2), to "double paradigms" (Agamben, 2005, p. 73), or indeed "multiple ontologies" (Stronach & Smears, 2010). Such a fabrication, with its "anarchic principle" (Rancière, 2010, p. 53) offers a dynamic that links the visual, textual, and performative in a hybridity whose becoming is its only possibility of coherence.[4]

In this thought experiment, we intend to explore "picturing" as a grounded metaphor that addresses (though never exhaustively) the business of reflexivity. First, we need to remember that we mean this metaphor to be for reflexivity (as a project) rather than a metaphor of reflexivity (as a definition). This is important in that the metaphor should exhaust itself in relation to its end, and not its representational means. Second, it is clear from the reflexive accounts we have examined that methodological application, procedural specification, and so on, rather mistake the appropriations that doctoral authors made from founding texts. Instead, we wanted to explore empirically how authors "pictured themselves" in their accounts, bringing in theory, method, biography, introspection, retrospection, witness and so on. But at the same time, we don't want to create a kind of negative theology, or a kind of anything-goes relativism. We need to be able to say, somehow, what will count as good "picturing" rather than inadequate "picturing," while at the same time refusing a contextual specification or universal criterial judgment. We say more about this later, but meanwhile reinvoke Margalit's distinction between "e.g." and "i.e." approaches to philosophical inquiry. The former is founded on illustration, the latter on explication.[5] Our claim is that our doctoral colleagues by and large invoked the latter and performed the former in relation to their methodological "extractions." The extent to which their "warrants" were unwarranted, or even unwarrantable, was neglected. Such a distinction overlaps with "inside-out" and "outside-in" ethical claims (Dawson, 1994), and also with the kinds of distinction that Rancière makes between "policing" and "politics."[6] In each case, an element of "free play" is essential. We later explore that overlap as a potential political space—relating indetermination (etc.) to notions of trust and freedom (etc.). First, however, we turn to a more detailed study of how such illustration, such picturing, works.

Figuring Pictures

Our strategy in this section, then, is to proceed by example rather than rule. Our examples are two very different artists. One is a Zairean street artist, Tshibumba, whose pictorial history of Zaire has been studied by the anthropologist Johannes Fabian (1996). The second is Velázquez and in particular, the ways in which his painting *Las Meñinas* has been analyzed by Foucault, Searle, and Snyder, as well as reiterated by later painters, from Degas to Picasso. However, both Velázquez and Tshibumba comment reflexively on the relation of artist to society, the business of representation, and the nature of sovereignty.

At first sight, Tshibumba offers a series of naive realist representations of major political events in the history of the Congo/Zaire, from the arrival of the Portuguese in the 15th century, through colonial rule, independence, and the dictatorship of Mobutu. But a closer reading suggests a more transgressive self. Tshibumba lived in an era of ethnically fraught despotic regime, and so the themes of his painting pay tribute to rulers while subtly presenting national heroes like Lumumba as crucified oppositional figures who continue to stand for lost ideals of government, unity, civilization, friendship, and collective identity. (For a more detailed consideration of Tshibumba and the dark metaphor of the Congo, see Stronach, 2006; Stronach 2010a). The themes of his paintings (this one and others) are simultaneously the record of a bloody past and a mnemonics of an ideal: they point forwards just as much as they point backwards. In creating this allegorical political space, his paintings indicate that which cannot safely be named.[7] Fabian (1996) refers to this as a "vociferous silence" (p. 306). We might also note that there is an interesting similarity between Tshibumba's tactics of representation and those employed by Conrad in *Heart of Darkness* (1910/1980), another Congolese commentary that had to be careful of its readership (in this case Victorian, middle-class, and British) and yet that succeeded in offering a multilayered account "in order to question the reader's positioning of themselves in relation to the narrative" (Hampson, in Conrad, 1910/1980, p. xxvi). Both conclude, or offer the possible conclusion, that "darkness is located at the heart of the 'civilising" mission'" (p. xxxvi). According to Fabian (1996), these paintings are also "[p]erformative acts that create or intensify co-presence" (p. 253). We would rather express that co-presence in terms of an "I-We" relation that underlies his paintings as communications. The collective "We" is black, colonized, oppressed and Congolese, and the paintings are "weapons of the weak" (p. 279), "articulating popular memory" (p. 276) by way of allegorical critique.

Fabian's account is entitled *Remembering the Present*, but we could just as easily see Tshibumba as opening up a space where past and future can also be contemplated from the perspective of the collective "we." That "we" is national rather than ethnic, and clearly articulated to communal values such as peace, community, and order. The subversive need to remember is suggestive of Kundera's early novels, and is carried by much the same covert politics of resistance[8]—against the "scandal of forgetting" (Kundera, 1982, p. 37). What seems immovable in Tshibumba's work is the determined nature of the relation between artist and viewers, the "I–We" relation. It emplots a story of collective loss, and of friendship betrayed. Features like these frame his series of paintings, and fix readings within certain limits.

Figure 1: *Colonie Belge* by Tshibumba Kanda Matulu
(courtesy of Professor Johannes Fabian)

Other features of his picturing, however, open up more plural possibilities. First, there is the multilayered nature of the paintings. They can be read as "realist" paintings of "real" historical events—and criticized on both grounds (for example, faulty chronology, wrong birthplaces, illogical or impossible representations). But as Fabian (1996) argues: "His [Tshibumba's] paintings are thoughts… that constitute his history, not illustrations of a pre-existing text" (p. 295). He is picturing a certain kind of political thinking, and knows it, as "an artist who paints history" (p. 261). The allegorical nature of the paintings allows Tshibumba to foreshorten chronology so that Portuguese and Belgian stand side by side, and *Colonie Belge* stands for the Mobutu regime and its covert indictment. This is strategic compression rather than error. Tshibumba paints in order to say something with "We the people," and as Lee and LiPuma (2002) point out in another context, such a combination prioritizes the performative "We" over the constative "the people" (p. 193). The story is mainly told in terms of blacks/whites, although again it is implied that white oppression can be made to stand as a disguise for postcolonial oppressions as well. In such a telling, Tshibumba's "I-Me" relation is rather like that envisaged by Mead. The "me" is fixed, historical, relatively unmoving, and for Tshibumba much subordinate to the "we"; while the "I," as Mead (1934/1962) indicates, is "uncertain," shifting, somewhat ambivalent, and in Tshibumba's case tactically mobile (p. 176). Finally, these paintings belong within an oral culture of storytelling, and cannot therefore be read entirely as political acts on their own: a context of tradition is involved that informs local readings of the series.

If we return to the picture with a "methodological" frame in mind, we can see how a surface naive realism works as a cover for a more transgressive politics (cf. Allan above, 1995). Allan's text has its own "vociferous silences." In another doctoral text a standpoint epistemology recurrently works a "civilization–oppression" polarity, inverting the many-sided claims of the former, and implying that oppression is a constant of the current context (see doctorates of Rider and Lewis above). In a further instance, the doctoral "painter" deploys indetermination in order to open up a political and defensible space for thinking, inviting a kind of solidarity from his audience through strategic indirection rather than representation (see R. Jones in his "abuse" of methodological genre). The aim is a transgressive validity (Lather, 1993) rather than any direct representation, either in terms of chronology, or strict historical "fact." The appeal is to an oppressed "we" relation that can be inferred, but may not be directly referred to. In the more reflexively radical of the theses such "oppression" is also a marker of the "doctoral regime." If not resistance to the spirit of Mobutu, this time, then perhaps Papa Doc? The act of resistance is an act of remembering, of condensing and visualizing the less public and more traditional genres of storytelling. It is a remembering of the past as a political resource for a possible future. And as such it operates as a kind of public *samizdat*.[9] Put in another way: methodology is an accident waiting to happen.

"Picturing," then, may be a performative metaphor for reflexivity. If so, it is picturing that includes its own frame, embodies itself, and anticipates its audience. But in each case reflexivity may require a different "picturing" of the agentic self in acts of (self-) creation.

Velázquez's *Las Meñinas* will also help us explore how different such picturing can be, and therefore how contingent and malleable reflexive practices can be, and have to be. We then try to work out what features of picturing may translate back across to research methodology.

A first thought would be that Velázquez takes Mead's advice at the beginning of this chapter—he sweeps himself into the picture in an act of apparently perfect reflexivity. There he is, looking out at us, brush in hand, the back of the canvas facing us, painting what we take to be the King and Queen who seem to stand where we also view the picture. This is where Velázquez himself must "really" have stood in order to paint himself painting, not the King and Queen

Figure 2: *Las Meñinas* by Diego Velasquez
(courtesy of the Prado Museum, Madrid)

(though they are in the mirror), but some of the rest of the royal family and court, in particular the Infanta and her entourage. The paradox is that "the viewer *cannot* be there where logically he must be" (Bal, in Pollock, 1996, p. 30)—"he is painting the picture we see, but he can't be because he is in the picture" Megill (1985, p. 486). It is the instability of these perspectives that animates the picture by forcing onlookers into reflective and reflexive action. They have to work out what is going on. That working out suggests that Velázquez, like Tshibumba but in different ways, offers pictures that exceed the real. Indeed, we might claim that Tshibumba's "excess" lies behind the picture in their coded and contextual nuances, whereas Velázquez's "excess" lies in front of the picture as a paradoxically crowded absence.

Like Tshibumba's, this reflexive painting also addresses issues of sovereignty, but simultaneously pictures the role of the artist, and indeed the whole business of "classical" representation. Unlike Tshibumba, it is dominated by an astonishing "I-me" relation. It's as if Velázquez were saying, "I, the Painter of Kings, am also the King of Painters." But the self-portrayal cannot be dismissed as narcissistic because it is the painterly nature of its production that is being emphasized. The "original I-me" relation passes (in both directions), through the brush of the painter and in turn the pen of the critics in its doubled journey from "scene" to "emplotment," also with each movement the scene changes and is rewritten. "I," "thou," "we," "them," and "us" are all caught up in an instantaneous circulation of reflexive meaning (Stronach 2002).[10] These figures enact and picture something like Kamuf's (1997) earlier cited "I/we apart together" (p. 122).

What is also framed in *Las Meñinas* is the act of framing. Velázquez empties Painter, the philosophy of Royalty, the technology of painting, the paradoxes of representation, as well as the impossibility of a settled perspective, across the canvas. Just as Tshibumba invoked an "I-We" relation in his spectators, so too does this painting insist on the participation of the spectator, an "I-Thou" instability of relation that provokes later painters to rework its reflexive magic in their own, very different ways. Velázquez draws us towards the spectacle that is observation itself. That is the fecundity of its reflexive ambition. In the mirroring of an "I-me" relation, the painter also points to, and performs, the highly significant metaphor of the mirror.

This time we can relate our reflexive theses to a double educative axis in the painting.[11] The double sovereignty of painterly technique and royal education run orthogonal axes across the picture from left to right, and also from back (mirror) to front (the invisible ideal of a royal education for the *Infanta* located in the center of the picture). In this doubling, Velázquez is a match for the King. So too in the reflexive theses: each in its own way works out an education of the researching self, while displaying (in some form or another) the tools of its trade whereby such selves are constructed, displayed, and left "open" to interpretation and criticism.

Picturing Figures

One cannot see God from the back, because if he is not watching us, he is not God. (Gell, 1998, p. 192)

There are a number of emergent themes in relation to reflexivity that we now wish to make more explicit and develop further. They comprise singularity, comprehensiveness, articulation, mobilization, and fecundity. Together they point to a version, a constellation, of reflexivity not as a prescription or model capable of typologization and prioritization in the ways Macbeth or Foley undertake, but more as a kind of Derridean or Deleuzian exemplarity whereby exactness and replication constitute the "transcendental illusion" (Deleuze & Guattari, 1994, p. 265).

The first cluster imbricates singularity, comprehensiveness, and articulation. Between the artists' pictures there are significant differences—one is more solidary than the other. It addresses "We" more than it addresses "Thou." Each establishes a different "I-me" relation, the one self-effacing, the other aggrandizing. Velázquez shows his face yet hides his work, while Tshibumba hides his face in showing his work allegorically—as our doctoral authors variously emplotted themselves in their own narratives. Yet both artists look at the world in order to picture it, paint the world in order to see it, and in doing so "draw in" the observer as partic-ipant—a Thou—rather than leaving them merely to gaze. Both suggest a form for reflexivity that denies the closure of a "model." These relations have parallels in the literature on reflexiv-ity. Marcus (2001) imagines the contemporary Other as "counterparts"—an interactive, ago-nistic version of the I-Thou relation (p. 453) dependent on "renegotiations and reboundings" (p. 523), a kind of "drawing in" of the Thou. Others formulate an I-Me relation in terms of "positionality(ies)" or "assignment" (Dixson, Chapman & Hill, 2005, p. 20; Macbeth, 2001; Alexander, 2003, p. 418, citing Butler), rather as Velasquez does in drawing himself, in pun-ning with the figure in the doorway at the back of the picture.[12] In Macbeth's terms, this is an act of "positional reflexivity." Still others work at the I-We relation in terms of "collective biog-raphy" (Davies et al., 2004, pp. 360–389), or "reciprocal reflexivity" (Lather, 1991, p. 63), just as Tshibumba does. We might agree with Marcus, therefore, that in order to read, we need to acknowledge a "theater of complicit reflexivities," variously emplotted (Marcus, 2001, p. 524).

That theatre does not comprise a universal set for reflexivity. Indeed we might return here to Margalit's distinction between "i.e." and "e.g." thinking by pointing out that each "reflexion" combines depiction and exemplification in different proportions and ways. Embarking on this kind of "picturing" venture, then, is always taking a singular leap into the unknown. Nancy (1993) echoes the Derrida of "Force of Law" when he writes: "Decision, or freedom, is the ethos at the groundless ground of every ethics. We have to decide on laws, exceptions, cases, negotiations: but there is neither law or exception for decision" (see Stronach, 2010a, p. 183ff)

Methodology may deny decision, but method can't. The disjunction of the substantive and the methodological is different in each case—because it has to be crafted both by the individual who writes/paints/thinks, and the reader who interprets the necessary incompletions of the project. It involves the risk of the new, not merely the promise of the incremental. It follows that a methodology determined in advance—the absolute convention of our times—is self-defeating for any research that wishes to chance this kind of radical educational move.[13] Worse, it is a form of policing. Reflexivity becomes through the processes of performing, exemplifying, deconstructing, and so on.

The figure of reflexivity, we argue, is singular. Yet it articulates a number of subject perspec-tives, which may be more or less comprehensive, and sets them off against each other. It can be an achievement, but not a prescription or an application. It has no possible model. It is a working out that contains a productive contradiction that, working from the actual, exceeds the "real" just as Tshibumba and Velázquez do in their different ways. Reflexivity, then, is the working out, and in, of a kind of supra-representation of actuality(ies). We now turn to the nature of that working out, and to characterize it (gesturally) as a kind of mobilization, or better, lability,[14] most aptly approached through the metaphor of the signature. This is the reflexive text as a traveling methodology, a kinetic epistemology, a "kenomatic state" of an es-sential emptiness (Agamben, 2005, p. 6) instead of the arrested convention (think Glaser & Strauss, 1967; Peshkin, 1988) whose "classic" features resist change precisely as a guarantor of their enduring worth.

First, consider that productive contradiction we referred to earlier. When Velázquez looks us in the eye, he is of course playing a trick. He's not "there" in a number of obvious senses. The same might be said of "models" of reflexivity, all of which presume to "look the other/ self in the eye." They play the same trick—Mead's total reflexivity, or God's back, both impos-sible as an accomplishment of the "I" as Gasché indicates.[15] So those reflexivities that through alleged method look you in the eye, lie. That is the false closure of the Model. "Picturing" on the other hand, proceeds through the I, Thou, and We (etc.) as a kind of signature that can be deciphered—and made educative—by the reader. It is a ludic move, but it makes us look ourselves in the "I," impossibilities notwithstanding. It says, it writes writing's impossibility: "You and I, we will never be here, and yet here we are" (Stronach, 2002, p. 294).

This paradoxical unsettlement of the perspectival and the real involves both writer and reader, artist and interpreter, in oscillations that are a necessary condition of indeterminacy. Just as in reflexive novels such as *Tristram Shandy*, "self-awareness arises out of a background of indeterminacy in the encounter with the other" (Swearingen, 1977, p. 82). The requirement for writer and reader is a kind of ideal movement: "His ideal [Sterne] requires that both he and his reader abandon themselves and their methods of procedure to the free play of the event in which new meanings unpredictably occur" (Swearingen, 1977, p. 12). Let us call that a kind of signature relationship—invoked, necessary, and yet incapable of prescription because subject to the multifaceted requirement of a situated yet ideal "play." It is the necessary forgery of a reflexive thinking that would seek to include readers rather than just perform in front of them.

After all, that is writing's sleight-of-hand. It is also a kind of writing, a signature, that we always know to be an imposture as well as a deception—like Velázquez's "presence" in the picture. It brings together communal, personal, and dialogic possibilities. Each is a possible vantage point, a perspectival difference. They contrast rather than collude, and they contradict productively. That bringing together is an increase, an exceeding of the real. In that sort of way, we approve of the allegorical projects of Tshibumba and of R. Jones's thesis: they prohibit explication while nevertheless framing—illustrating—the sorts of creative responses they hope to engender. They avoid despoiling the reflexive project with a modernist intolerance of contradiction; they intend to exemplify. In the reflexive literature such plurality is often portrayed as static—between entities (segments of selves, assignments, others), subject of course to modification and alteration in a language of "fluidity" and "shift." Useful as such local mobilizations are, they can trap us within root metaphors of relations between neighbors—"negotiation," "boundary," "in-betweenness," and so on. These boundaries are specific, dichotomous, and to an extent atomistic. We have in mind movements that are locally negotiated in those ways, but also are articulated more comprehensively or globally to each other by the "signature." The signature is not so much a matter of boundary as a relation of one for all and all for one, on a plane of immanence distinct from dualistic boundary negotiation. Such a signature is not a holism, let alone a model-as-precipitate (in terms of a chemical analogy), but an event of lability subject to a mobilization of singularities, comprehensiveness, and articulation. But what does that mobilization mean?

Conclusion

The last section of this chapter offers an account of the sorts of conceptual movement inherent in the notion of reflexivity we wish to explore. Gell's (1998) reading of Marcel Duchamp is instructive here. Drawing on the early work of Husserl, he mobilizes the work of art, setting it in motion with concepts of "retention" and "protension" (p. 242). All such works look forward and backward, and are part of a series. Each changes its meaning, is redefined, as time moves on. Bibi-Nawaz et al.'s (2010) attempt at reciprocal reflexivity has that same layered, provisional, revisable desire. The work of art is inherently transitional, in a kind of motion that makes each appropriation of it unique, a work of the individual and of the moment.[16] But at the same time, part of a style, still a signature, the still of a signed object. Yet nothing stays the same in the "durée" of time. Redefinition is written into the oeuvre as a necessary aspect of its qualities. Gell (1998) relates that motion (which is indeterminate in the way we're reaching towards) to "lineages" (p. 253), in relation to a certain kind of reflexivity. His account, based on Husserl's "law of modification" (p. 244), is however too linear for our ambitions here. Whatever its rhetorical tolerance for radical change, it is founded diagrammatically and hence epistemologically on the line, the series A, B, C, etc., with their prospective and retrospective allegiances as a guarantor of change. This is perspectival knowledge, serially envisaged. But disjunctive change, transformational change, is not envisaged epistemologically in such a model, which remains radically unradical. Nevertheless, Gell does refer in passing to a more labile notion of "perchings" emanating from a folk belief:

> Everything as it moves, now and then, here and there, makes stops. The bird as it flies stops in one place to make its nest, and in another to rest in its flight. A man when he goes forth stops when he wills. So the god has stopped. The sun, which is so bright and beautiful, is one place where he has stopped. The moon, the stars, the winds, he has been with. The trees, the animals, are all where he has stopped, and the Indian thinks of these places and sends his prayers there to reach the place where the god has stopped and win help and a blessing. (Durkheim, quoted in Levi-Strauss, *Totemism*, and cited in Gell 1998, pp. 248–249)

This is valuable. It introduces the concept of change as more idiosyncratically motivated, or in the words of Benjamin (1997) "knowledge comes by way of thinking in images from 'lightning flashes'—the text is the long roll of thunder that follows" (p. 457).[17] Yet, we need still more movement. Gell envisages a kind of historical mobility for concepts. But Deleuze and Guattari (1994) see a "signature" as a different kind of mobilization, as in their discussion of the Cartesian *cogito ergo sum*. Envisaging a concept as a plural thing, made up of zones, bridges, and movement, they offer the following definition: "The concept is defined by *the inseparability of a finite number of heterogeneous components traversed by a point of absolute survey at infinite speed*" (p. 21, emphasis in original). The Cartesian concept has movements like "doubting," "thinking," and "being" and it is the articulation of all of these (the "survey" or "survol" in their terms) that yields the concept. In a similar way, we envisage the "survol" of "reflexivity" as a sweeping through various mobilizations of "I," "me," "thou," "we," and "them" in the singular articulation of a deliberative reflexion that is nevertheless a distributed object.

Reflexivity, in that instance, is a chance rather than a model (Garratt, 2003), whose serendipity is the paradoxical promise of its achievement. Marcus (2001) invokes the "rhetoric of serendipity" as an expert preserve (p. 527), but we wish to extend that preserve. We don't apply reflexivity: we make it happen in the instance, a task for novice and "expert" alike. The double movement, both serial and looping like the writing of a signature, constitutes not a methodological guarantee[18] (compare with Peshkin, 1988, and Heshusius, 1994) so much as a promise, as indeed a signature promises, even as it forges the "reality" that is compromised. It is contradictory, in that it is and it isn't, it both exceeds and disappoints the reality that it addresses. That is the promise of the signature (Stronach, Piper & Piper, 2004). The reflexive injunction, thus constituted, remains a "thin" text (in Margalit's terms, 2002) engaged in the provocation of "thick" texts of reflexive practice.[19]

To conclude, we argue that such a notion of reflexivity opens up qualitative research to creative, nonarbitrary development: and takes us away from the current obsessions (which are more extra-professional than professional) with universalistic prescription and a priori methodological specification. They are a kind of educational death—a sentence perhaps commuted to a life imprisonment—that educational research must resist. Current efforts to "nationalize" educational research (as evidence-based practice, as ethically proper, as nationalized research training and universally prescribed methodologies such as random-controlled trials) are all educationally backward in that they trail behind similar homogenizations in U.K. schooling, at least, that are already failing because of the ways in which they destroy creativity, originality, trust, and experimentation. They are, above all, an exercise in symbolic violence. As Butler (2005) has recently put it, such universalizing fantasies operate a "false unity" that both performs an "anachronism" while perpetrating an "ethical violence" (p. 4, 5). To return for a last time to the generative metaphors of "art" that inform this account, these approaches can be characterized as "painting by numbers." Such movements are recurrent in the West, and a century ago Frazer noted the ideological closure: "the element of chance and of accident are banished from the course of nature" (Tambiah, 1990, p. 68). Almost as long ago, Robert Musil in *The Man without Qualities* (1997), began to mock such modernist and scientistic ambitions as "the utopia of exact living" (p. 395). Not only is it wrong to elevate Science as *pharmakon* in this way, it is doubly wrong to characterize "Science" in such reductive ways, because if Tambiah is right in his definition of science, it is what we propose—"a self-conscious, reflexive, open-ended process of knowledge construction" (p. 395).

> A concept is a brick. It can be used to build the courthouse of reason. Or it can be thrown through the window. (Deleuze & Guattari, 1988, p. xii)

Notes

1. An earlier version of this chapter was published under a similar title ("re-forging" rather than "forging" marks the update) in 2007: *Qualitative Inquiry 13*(2), 179–203. The account has been updated by Ian Stronach.

    Ian Stronach is professor of Educational Research at Liverpool John Moores University, UK. Dean Garratt, Cathie Pearce, and Heather Piper were doctoral students involved in "reflexivity" workshops at MMU. Garratt is now reader at the University of Chester. Pearce is a research fellow. Piper is professorial research fellow at MMU. Most but not all of the doctoral students cited in the chapter were supervised by Stronach, and their diverse responses perhaps reflect less of a party line than a party nonalignment. The first of the MMU doctoral training sessions, "Reflexivity Workshop," in June 1996, featured the following readings, some of which were articles, some single chapters or excerpts: McRobbie, 1993; Meyerhoff & Ruby, 1992; Peshkin, 1988; Heshusius, 1994; Frankel, 1991; Ashmore, 1989; Cassell, 1991; Lenzo, 1994; Escobar, 1993; Calvino, 1965/1993; Lather, 1993; Plummer, 1996; Allan, 1995; Ball, 1993. Participants were asked to select and read beforehand one or two texts; small-group sessions shared knowledge of, and insight into, the texts; plenary sessions developed overall themes and possible "positions." The sample of users comprised completed doctoral dissertations from those attending such seminars since 1996. These workshop sessions spanned the period until Stronach's departure in 2008, also disseminating elsewhere as part of an unintended doctoral diaspora. The account here represents the divergence of responses rather than any typicality. It does so because we are interested in how the chosen methodological texts were deployed, in a range of appropriations.

2. The "mirror" has a long and distinguished history as a metaphor of self-regard, from Narcissus through to the work of Gasché (1986) on the "tain" of the mirror. We do not wish to imply that such a metaphor takes us nowhere, but we suspect that it will not take us anywhere new, and therefore seek to cast around the reflexive stories in order to provoke new possibilities. "The 'matrix' produces the matrix and nothing else" (Letiche & Malci, 2001, p. 5)—or perhaps the mirror all too easily becomes metonymic rather than metaphoric.

3. "Acts" are a misnomer in so far as they imply conscious and intentional implementation. We would rather regard reflexivity as an event in which we somewhat intentionally participate, but nevertheless acknowledge inescapable remainders of the unconscious and the unintended.

4. There are many such calls for plural, interpolated, hybridic, anarchic (etc.) conceptualisations of adjacency and interconnection. As Rancière (2005) has it, a "new regime of meaning" requires new accounts of association, for both concepts and for people—"intertwinings" (p. 168). These are usually modernist criticisms and often postmodernist invocations but we should note that "triple disquisition" has long had its advocates, skeptical ones at that: "to speak the language of a rope-work [...] again twined together into one indistinguishable string of confusion" (Scott, 1816/1998, pp. 150, 152). In order at least to indicate the possibility of very different ontologies, consider this from Bachelard (1958/1994): "two perspectives that could be said to be in reciprocal anamorphosis" (p. 119).

5. Tarde put this slightly differently: "So far all the philosophy has been founded on the verb To be.... One may say that, if only philosophy had been founded on the verb To have, many... slowdown of the mind, would have been avoided" (Tarde quoted in Latour, 2001, p. 17). Tambiah makes a similar point in distinguishing between "denotation" and "exemplification" (Tambiah, 1990, p. 104). Stronach (2010a), on the other hand, wants a philosophy of prepositions (p. 181), while others wish to summon a "philosopher of adjectives" (Bachelard, 1958/1994, p. 180).

6. Dawson (2005) argues for a distinction between Aristotelian "inside-out" professionalism as opposed to the externally regulated version—"outside-in" professionalism, as encouraged, for example, by the audit culture. An exemplary rather than a definitive ethics is proposed. See also, Stronach, Corbin, McNamara, Stark, & Warne, 2002. Rancière (2010) opposes the two notions (p. 36), but later extends that "anarchic principle" to "the disjunctive relation between three terms: police, politics and the political" (p. 53).

7. This appeal to excess parallels Lather's (1993) notion of voluptuous validity or a validity of excess.

8. We have in mind Kundera's *The Joke* (1970) and *The Book of Laughter and Forgetting* (1982). A further parallel is that Kundera's stories are also the deliberate and sardonic emplotment of political thought within a totalitarian regime. In the light of recent "states of exemption," we might well extend that thought to the ways in which "democratic" and "modern" states exempt themselves from their own laws (Agamben, 2005; Amoore & Goede, 2008).

9. A clandestine copying and distribution of literature especially in the formerly communist countries of the Soviet Union and Eastern Europe.

10. The "I-me" relation is literal to the painting, if we take the figure illuminated in the doorway—another Velasquez—to be a further signature by the artist (Stoichita, 1997). Velasquez thereby "triangulates" himself in his representation and his commentary on representation.

11. Gill (2000), after Polanyi, argues that the notion of the "axis" is a useful one: "For the image of an axis suggests anchoring that is not fixed and in need of further support" (p. 57). This too, then, can be part of a certain constellation of metaphors with which we attempt to mobilize the notion of reflexivity and connect it to the nature of contemporary educational knowledge—in that "patchwork of metaphors" that Sfard (1998, p. 12) recommends.

12. The figure in the doorway is also a "Velasquez"; his crooked elbow signs the "V"; his role as Chamberlain is the role to which the artist aspires. Or the figure can be read as unveiling the scene—ambivalence and indeterminacy are inevitable.

13. The resurrected positivism of evidence-based practice and effectiveness/improvement studies exemplifies this current convention. David Hargreaves (2001) is a leading UK exponent. His most recent writing on "capital theory" (p. 489) employs the "Johari window" cliché in order to typify teacher "inputs" and "outputs," idealizing "high leverage" as opposed to other states, such as "cynical tokenism" and "short-term effectiveness by burn out." This style of low-level categorization was popular in the 70s. Indeed Haraway (1992) has effectively mocked the very same "infamous semiotic square" as "this clackety, structuralist meaning-making machine." See also, Shavelson and Towne (2002) for U.S. examples of "scientific" educational research. Such confident quantification of the social has of course met—without much political recognition—its nemesis in the Great Recession. The "quants" had removed risk from their equations via a normative statistical procedure that went badly wrong in 2007–2008. It is interesting to watch the erasure of this methodological disaster, and its parallel displacement of blame from the private to the public sector. In contemporary capitalism and its attendant wars, it is the victims who get arrested, and the criminals exonerated (Stronach & Clarke, 2010).

14. We take the metaphor of mobilization to indicate different and plural positionalities. It therefore relates to a kind of "base" language based on identities that, sure enough, are redrawn as plural or shifting, or arrived at through "tensive negotiation" of selves, and so on (Alexander, 2003, p. 430). The language of the "fluid"is invoked (Knight, Beentley, Norton & Dixon, 2004, p. 392); yet as Macbeth (2001) argues, each of these disclaimers still appeals to a more fixed territory of ideas: "The move [towards positional or textual reflexivity] promises new ground to stand on, shifting and unstable but, for that reason, possessing a field of view that could delineate the order and structure of first worlds and the conditions of their possibility" (p. 48). We take "lability" to imply a turning away from such a register of implicit grounding, since it goes beyond arguments about "boundaries" and "in-betweens" in order to posit singular fluidities as "anti-ground" rather than extensions that fail to note that they conspire with their opposites.

15. It might seem at first that such "total" reflexivity falls prey to the dilemma that Gasché (1986) outlines: "Thus anyone who sets reflection into motion must already be both the knower and the known. The subject of reflection on its own thereby satisfies the whole equation 'I=I.' Yet reflection alone was supposed to bring about this equation" (p. 99). We raise a number of arguments against such a dilemma: that the impossibility is productive, that Gasché neglects the "detour" of the self through the other, as well as the impact of "I-We" relations on self-knowledge.

16. Picasso's *Guernica* is a good example of this. Its positioning in relation to American art is as labile as its relation to U.S. politics. It is shifted around as an icon of European art's supremacy, just as it is rewritten as a "Communist" statement from its prior status as an anti-Fascist discursive object. It is rewritten in a series that then prefaces the transformations of Pollock and Rothko (Hensbergen, 2004).

17. The flash? When Sterne (1995) lets Tristram Shandy attempt to tell us the truth about a lady, in three words, which he does not write down.

18. Calls for a looser "methodology" in qualitative inquiries are now subject to the kinds of analogical scientism that often typifies epistemological rhetoric in quantitative educational inquiry. Such approaches in their reductive, simplistic, and normative approaches to educational events and meanings, automatically shortchange the possibilities of new and creative educational options. They are a form of self-regulated discipline that would surely entertain Foucault. They "civilize" educational research through methodological narrowing and pre-specification—that is the darkness at the heart of the U.K. government's current mission.

19. "Thick descriptions are culturally bound and historically sensitive, whereas thin descriptions are more context-independent" (Margalit, 2002, p. 38).

References

Agamben, G. (2005). *State of exception*. (K. Attell, Trans.). Chicago: University of Chicago Press.

Alexander, B. (2003). (Re)visioning the ethnographic site: Interpretive ethnography as a method of pedagogical reflexivity and scholarly production. *Qualitative Inquiry 9*(3), 416–441.

Allan, J. (1995). *Pupils with special educational needs in mainstream schools: A Foucauldian analysis of discourses* (Unpublished PhD dissertation). University of Stirling, Scotland.

Amoore, L., & de Goede, M. (2008). *Risk and the war on terror*. London: Routldge.

Ashmore, M. (1989). *The reflexive thesis: Wrighting sociology of scientific knowledge*. Chicago: University of Chicago Press.

Austin, J. (1962/1989). *How to do things with words*. Oxford, UK: Oxford University Press.

Bachelard, G. (1958/1994). *The poetics of space*. (M. Jolas, Trans.). Boston: Beacon Press.

Ball, S. (1993). Self doubt and soft data: Social and technical trajectories in ethnographic fieldwork. In M. Hammersley (Ed.). *Educational research: Current issues* (pp. 32–48). Buckingham, UK: Open University Press.

Benjamin, W. (1997). *The arcades project*. (H. Eiland & K. McLaughlin, Trans.). Cambridge, MA: Harvard University Press.

Bibi-Nawaz, S., Grant, D., & Stronach, I. (2010). Lone mother, lone researcher: Making a reflexive start. (Working Paper), Liverpool, UK: John Moores University.

Butler, J. (2005). *Giving an account of oneself*. New York: Fordham University Press.

Calvino, I. (1965/93) From the opaque. In I. Calvino, *The road to San Giovanni* (T. Parks, Trans.). London: Picador.

Cassell, J. (1991). Subtle manipulation and deception in fieldwork: Opportunism knocks. *International Journal of Social and Moral Studies 6*(3), 269–274.

Clifford, J., & Marcus, G. (1986). *Writing culture*. Berkeley: University of California Press.

Conquergood, D. (1998). Beyond the text: Toward a performative cultural politics. In S. Dailey, (Ed.), *The future of performance studies; Visions and revisions* (pp. 25–36). Washington, DC: National Communication Association.

Conrad, J. (1910/1980). *Heart of darkness and the secret sharer*. New York: Harper and Brothers.

Davies, B., Browne, J., Gannon, S., Honan, E., Laws, C., Mueller-Rockstroh, B., & Petersen, E. (2004). The ambivalent practices of reflexivity. *Qualitative Inquiry 10*(3), 360–389.

Dawson, A. (1994). Professional codes of practice and ethical conduct. *Journal of Applied Philosophy 11*(2), 145–153.

Deleuze, G. (1995). *Difference and repetition* (P. Patton, Trans.). London: Athlone.

Deleuze, G. (1995). *Negotiations 1972–1990*. (M. Joughin, Trans.). New York: Columbia University Press.

Deleuze, G., & Guattari, F. (1988). *A thousand plateaus: Capitalism and schizophrenia*. London: Athlone.

Deleuze, G., & Guattari, F. (1994). *What is philosophy?* (G. Burchell & H. Tomlinson, Trans.). London and New York: Verso.

Denzin, N. (1997). *Interpretive ethnography: Ethnographic practices for the 21st century*. Thousand Oaks, London, New Delhi: Sage.

Denzin, N. (2003). *Performance ethnography. Critical pedagogy and the politics of culture*. Thousand Oaks, CA: Sage.

Dixson, A., Chapman, T., & Hill, D. (2005). Research as an aesthetic process: Extending the portraiture methodology. *Qualitative Inquiry 11*(1), 16–26.

Ěrculj', J. (2003). *School culture in Slovene primary schools: Aspects of the local and the global* (unpublished PhD dissertation). Manchester Metropolitan University, Manchester.

Englad, J. (2003). *Promoting inclusivity of disaffected pupils*. Unpublished Ph.D. Thesis. Manchester Metrpolitan University.

Escobar, A. (1993). The limits of reflexivity: Politics in anthropology's post-writing culture era. *Journal of Anthropological Research 49*, 377–391.

Fabian, J. (1996). *Remembering the present: Painting and popular history in Zaire*. Berkeley: University of California Press.

Foley, D. (2002). Critical ethnography: The reflexive turn. *International Journal of Qualitative Studies in Education 15*(4), 469–490.

Frankel, B. (1991). The bartered self: Negotiating a role in a field situation. *International Journal of Moral and Social Studies 6*(3), 246–256.

Gasché, R. (1986). *The tain of the mirror: Derrida and the philosophy of reflection*. Cambridge, MA: Harvard University Press.

Garratt, D. (2003). *My qualitative research journey: Researching against the rules*. Cresskill, NJ: Hampton.

Gell, A. (1998). *Art and agency: An anthropological theory*. Oxford, UK: Clarendon.

Gill, J. (2000). *The tacit mode: Michael Polanyi's postmodern philosophy*. Albany: State University of New York Press.

Glaser, B., & Strauss, A. (1967). *The discovery of grounded theory*. Chicago: Aldine.

Grene, M. Ed. (1969). *Toward a unity of knowledge*. Study Group on Foundations of Cultural Unity. New York : International Universities Press. Guillemin, M., & Gillam, L. (2004). Ethics, reflexivity, and "ethically important moments" in research. *Qualitative Inquiry 10*(2), 261–280.

Hanley, U. (2001). *Facing another way* (Unpublished PhD dissertation). Manchester Metropolitan University, Manchester.

Haraway, D. (1992). The promises of monsters: A regenerative politics for inappropriate/d others. In L. Grossberg, C. Nelson, & P. A. Treichler, (Eds.), *Cultural studies* (pp. 295–337). New York: Routledge. Retrieved 2/12/02 from http://www.stanford.edu/dept/HPS/Haraway/monsters.html.

Hargreaves, D. (2001). A capital theory of school effectiveness and improvement. *British Educational Research Journal 27*(4), 503.

Heidegger, M. (1962). *Being and time*. (J. McQuarrie & E. Robinson, Trans.). London: SCM Press.

Hensbergen, G. van (2004). *Guernica: The biography of a 20th-century icon*. London: Bloomsbury.

Heshusius, L. (1994). Freeing ourselves from objectivity: Managing subjectivity or turning toward a participatory mode of consciousness? *Educational Researcher 23*(3), 15–22.

Jones, R. (1997). *Deafening silence: Telling stories of beginning teachers' understandings of ethnicity* (Unpublished PhD dissertation). Manchester Metropolitan University, Manchester.

Kamuf, P. (1991). *The Derrida reader*. New York: Columbia University Press.

Kamuf, P. (1997). Deconstruction and feminism. A repetition. In *Feminist interpretations of Jacques Derrida*. Philadelphia: Pennsylvania State University Press.

Knight, M., Beentley, C., Norton, N., & Dixon, I. (2004). (De)constructing (in)visible parent/guardian consent forms: Negotiating power, reflexivity, and the collective within qualitative research. *Qualitative Inquiry10*(3), 390–411.

Koren, A. (2002). *Decentralisation—centralisation and autonomy in the Slovenian school system: A case study of "constructed" views* (Unpublished PhD dissertation). Manchester Metropolitan University, Manchester.

Kundera, M. (1970). *The joke.* (M.H. Heim, Trans.). New York: Penguin.

Kundera, M (1982). *The book of laughter and forgetting.* (M. H. Heim, Trans.). London: Faber & Faber.

Lather, P. (1991) *Getting smart: Feminist research and pedagogy with/in the postmodern*. New York: Routledge.

Lather, P. (1993). Fertile obsession: Validity after poststructuralism. *The Sociological Quarterly 34*(4), 573–693.

Latour, B. (1988). The politics of explanation: An alternative. In S. Woolgar (Ed.), *Knowledge and reflexivity*. London: Sage.

Latour, B. (2001). Gabriel Tarde and the end of the social. In P. Joyce (Ed.), *The social and its problems.* London: Routledge.

Lee, B., & LiPuma, E. (2002). Cultures of circulation: The imaginations of modernity. *Public Culture 14*(1), 191–213.

Lenzo, K. (1994). Validity and self-reflexivity meet poststructuralism: Scientific ethos and the transgressive self. *Educational Researcher 14*(4), 17–45.

Letiche H., & Maier J. (2001). *The "self" in self-organization.* Working Paper 2001-5b earlier version of this paper 2001-5, presented at the EGOS conference in Lyon July 5–7, 2001.

Levi, P. (1991). *Other people's trades.* (R. Rosenthal, Trans.). London: Abacus.

Lewis, L. (2002). Khepra: cultural developmental groupwork: An evaluation (Unpublished PhD dissertation). Manchester Metropolitan University, Manchester.

Macbeth, D. (2001). On "reflexivity" in qualitative research: Two readings and a third. *Qualitative Inquiry 7*(1), 35–68.

Marcus, G. (2001). From rapport under erasure to theatres of complicit reflexivity. *Qualitative Inquiry 7*(4), 519–528.

Marcus, G., & Cushman, D. (1982). Ethnographies as texts. *Annual Review of Anthropology 11*, 25–69.

Margalit, A. (2002). *The ethics of memory.* Cambridge, MA: Harvard University Press.

McRobbie, A. (1993). Feminism, postmodernism and the real me. *Theory, Culture, Society 10*, 127–142.

Mead, G. H. (1934/1962). *Mind, self and society: From the standpoint of a social behaviourist.* Chicago: University of Chicago Press.

Megill, A. (1985). *Prophets of extremity: Nietzsche, Heidegger, Foucault, Derrida.* Berkeley: University of California Press.

Meyerhoff, B., & Ruby, J. (1992). A crack in the mirror: Reflexive perspectives in anthropology. In B. Meyerhoff, D. Metzger, J. Ruby, and V. Tufte (Eds.), *Remembered lives: The work of ritual, storytelling, and growing older.* Ann Arbor: University of Michigan Press.

Musil R. (1997). *The man without qualities.* (S. Wilkins & B. Pike, Trans.). London: Picador.

Nancy, J. L. (1993). *The birth to presence.* (B. Holmes, Trans.). Palo Alto, CA: Stanford University Press.

Peshkin A. (1988). In search of subjectivity—one's own. *Educational Researcher 17*(7), 17–21.

Plummer, G. (1996). *Making connections with students in at-risk situations: Reflections and interpretations* (Unpublished PhD dissertation). University of Stirling, Scotland.

Polanyi, M. (1962). *Personal Knowledge; Towards a Post-critical Philosophy.* New York: Harper.

Pollock, G. (1996). *Generations and geographies in the visual arts: Feminist readings.* London: Routledge.

Rancière, J. (2010). *Dissensus: On politics and aesthetics.* (S. Corcoran, Ed. and Trans.). London: Continuum.

Riding, H. (2002). *The annihilation of the lesbian self: An event without witness* (unpublished PhD dissertation). Manchester Metropolitan University, Manchester.

Roberts, L. (2004). *Shifting identities. An investigation into trainee and novice teachers' evolving professional identity* (submitted PhD dissertation). Manchester Metropolitan University, Manchester.

Rosaldo, R. (1978). The rhetoric of control: Ilongots viewed as bandits and wild Indians. In Babcock, B. (Ed.). *The reversible world: Symbolic inversion in art and society.* Ithaca, NY: Cornell.

Rosaldo, R. (1987). Where objectivity lies: The rhetoric of anthropology. In J. Nelson, A. Megill, & D. McCloskey (Eds.), *The rhetoric of the human sciences* (pp. 87–110). Madison: University of Wisconsin Press.

Scott, Sir W. (1816/1998). *The antiquary.* (D. Hewitt, Ed.). London: Penguin.

Sfard, A. (1998). On two metaphors for learning and the dangers of just choosing one. *Educational Researcher 27*(2), 4–13.

Shavelson, R., & Towne, L. (2002). *Scientific research in education.* Committee on Scientific Principles for Educational Research. Washington DC: National Academic Press.

Sterne, L. (1995). *Tristram Shandy.* London: Everyman's Library.

Stoichita, V. (1997). *The self-aware image.* Cambridge, UK: Cambridge University Press.

Stronach, I., & MacClure, M. (1997). *Education Research Undone: The Postmodern Embrace.* Milton Keynes, UK: Open University Press.

Stronach, I. (2002). This space is not yet blank. *Educational Action Research 10*(2), 291–307.

Stronach, I. (2006). Enlightenment and the heart of darkness: (Neo)imperialism in the Congo, and elsewhere. *International Journal of Qualitiative Studies 19*(6), 757–768.

Stronach, I. (2010a). *Globalizing education, educating the local: How method made us mad.* London: Routledge.

Stronach, I. (2010b). How to fail successfully: An autobiographical reprise. In A. Sparkes (Ed.), *Yearbook of auto/biography.* London: British Sociological Association.

Stronach, I., & Clarke, J. (2010). Bring back Das Kapital punishment! The credit crunch and the fall of the knowledge economy. *Forum 52*(1), 119–124.

Stronach, I., Corbin, B., McNamara, O., Stark, S., & Warne, T. (2002). Towards an uncertain politics of professionalism: Teacher and nurse identities in flux. *Journal of Educational Policy 17*(1), 109–138.

Stronach, I., & Piper, H. (2008). Can liberal education make a comeback? The case of "relational touch" at Summerhill School. *American Educational Research Journal 45*(1), 6–37.

Stronach, I., Piper, H., & Piper J. (2004). Re-performing crises of representation. In Piper, H. & Stronach, I. (Eds.), *Educational research. Difference and diversity* (pp. 129–154). Aldershot: Ashgate.

Stronach, I., & Smears, L. (2010). Dual ontologies and new ecologies of knowledge: Rethinking the politics and poetics of "touch." In S. Hillyard (Ed.), *New frontiers in ethnography* (Studies in qualitative methodology, Vol. 11, pp. 81–100). London: Emerald. To be published in extended form in a Special Edition of the *International Review of Qualitative Research* (I. Stronach, Ed.), forthcoming.

Swearingen, J. (1977). *Reflexivity in "Tristram Shandy": An essay in phenomenological criticism.* New Haven, CT: Yale University Press.

Tambiah, S. (1990). *Magic, science, religion and the scope of rationality.* Cambridge: Cambridge University Press.

Trunk-Širca, N. (2002). *Understanding the interwoven processes of institutional evaluation and continuous improvement: An action research study.* (unpublished PhD dissertation), Manchester Metropolitan University, Manchester.

Watson, C. (2008). *Reflexive research and the (re)turn to the Baroque. (Or, how I learned to stop worrying and love the university).* Rotterdam, Netherlands: Sense.

Woolgar, S. (1988). Reflexivity is the ethnographer of the text. In S. Woolgar (Ed.), *Knowledge and reflexivity: New frontiers in the sociology of knowledge.* Newbury Park, CA: Sage.

Young, L. (2001). Border crossings and other journeys: Re-envisioning the doctoral preparation of education researchers. *Educational Researcher 30*(5), 3–5.

CHAPTER SIX

Critical Systems Theory for Qualitative Research Methodology

SUNNIE LEE WATSON & WILLIAM R. WATSON

Critical systems theory (CST) is derived from the ideas of systems theory and critical social theory. In the mid-20th century, systems theory was established by a multidisciplinary group of researchers who shared the view that science had become increasingly reductionist and the various disciplines isolated. Bertalanffy (1968) was among the first to establish a general systems theory, which noted the existence of principles and laws that could be generalized across systems and their components. The term "system" has been defined in various ways by different systems researchers, but the core concept is one of an organization of interacting or interdependent parts forming an integrated whole. In other words, systems thinking entails identifying the components making up a system and understanding their relations and how they impact the larger system, external systems, supra-systems, and vice versa.

Systems theory became a large influence in management sciences and research over the last half of the 20th century with the development of hard- and soft-systems thinking for understanding various kinds of systems, including natural systems, engineering systems, and human social systems. However, while applying systems thinking in human systems in the early 1980s, a number of systems-thinking researchers felt the need for systems theory to evolve towards a more critical, socially aware approach to systems thinking and practice (Mingers, 1980; Jackson, 1982). These scholars developed their critical approach to systems thinking based on the epistemological and ontological views of Habermas (Flood & Jackson, 1991; Jackson, 1991a, 1991b), and today CST is defined by its commitment to three core values and commitments: critique, emancipation, and pluralism (Schecter, 1991; Flood & Jackson, 1991).

With decades of research and practice in the management and operational sciences, CST's approach to research methodology, and its core concepts of critique, emancipation, and pluralism, offer considerable insight to qualitative researchers in many disciplines. This chapter examines CST and its methods as applied to and informing qualitative research and its goals and methods. The chapter begins with a discussion of the development and philosophical perspectives of CST, and then moves on to a more practicable discussion of the application of CST's system of systems methodologies framework in light of qualitative research and practice.

CST Development and Epistemological Perspectives

Metaphors for Understanding Systems

As discussed earlier, the term "system" is defined in various ways by many systems researchers. However, in general, it encompasses the concept of an organization of interacting or interdependent parts forming an integrated whole. Systems thinking went through significant developments over the last half of the 20th century, including the evolution of the core metaphors used for representing various systems concepts. Flood and Jackson (1991) discuss the progression of five systemic metaphors for understanding human social systems and phenomena, which represent the gist of management and organizational theory. These metaphors demonstrate the evolution in systems thinking that took place: machine, organic, neurocybernetic (brain), cultural, and political.

In the beginning, human social phenomenon was thought of as if it was a naturally forming physical system such as the solar system, and a "machine" metaphor was used to explain this hard-systems approach. In this closed system view, a system is understood to be comprised of parts, each with its own clearly defined function and it is assumed to operate routinely and repetitively towards efficiently meeting predetermined goals. The machine metaphor is highly appropriate for understanding human-designed physical systems such as machines, and some machine-like systems that have humans as parts of the system, such as factories, armies or fast-food chains. However, the social systems researcher who studies human and social phenomena finds the machine metaphor inadequate in applying it in the works of social sciences, such as understanding problem situations in schools, labor unions, or communities of learning.

In addressing this inadequacy, the organic metaphor was put forward by social systems researchers. The organic metaphor is a more open systems view and represents the initial state of modern systems thinking about human social phenomena. This view looks at an organization as a self-regulating and self-maintaining organic or ecological system such as animals or plants: a "complex network of elements and relationships that interact forming highly organized feedback loops, existing in an environment from which it draws inputs and to which it dispenses outputs" (Flood & Jackson, 1991, p. 10). Some examples of systems that fit this systems view could be the ways that small businesses or schools work to adapt and survive in today's unstable economic times. This metaphor however views relations of the components of the system as only harmonious and does not recognize the conflict that exists within the system.

The neurocybernetic view sees a system as a brain that depends upon the ability to communicate and learn. It focuses on active learning and control rather than passive adaptability of systems and has led to systems work in information processing and viability. This view adds to the importance of accepting dynamic rather than static objectives of systems and self-questioning more than self-regulating in systems thinking. Examples of systems that fit this view would be consulting firms, research and development institutions, or knowledge groups. However the neurocybernetic view lacks the viewpoint of seeing the system as constructed by the individuals, and often overlooks that the purposes of the parts may differ from those of the whole.

The cultural metaphor focuses on the "often unspoken but familiar ways of thinking and acting that exist" in organizations; in other words, the "various nebulous, shared characteristics at all levels of organization: societal, corporate, group, etc." (Flood & Jackson, 1991, p. 11). This metaphor's use of the word "culture" can be quite misleading to qualitative researchers, as it is focusing on culture as being "engineered" by the decision makers in the system, and is used in ways of promoting an official, collaborative, and community-like spirit in an organization. A cutting-edge computer technology research laboratory that emphasizes not only the technology and structure of its organization, but also the changing perceptions and values of the employees would be a good example in describing this metaphor. This view recognizes the social nature of human systems, but does not consider the differing opinions in the system, and therefore pushing an engineered culture can lead to attempts at ideological control that can promote mistrust or resentment in an organization.

Finally, there is the political metaphor that highlights all organizational activity as interest based. It views a human system as one in which everyone is an individual who pursues his or her own interests and is always potentially in competition with other individuals, forming a system. This approach looks at problem situations that are unitary, pluralist, or coercive as competitive relations between individuals and groups over the pursuit of power. These situations can be seen as representing a team, coalition, or prison type of relations, respectively. For example, we can think about the situation of a nonunionized nursing workforce in a hospital. Let's say the hospital is facing budget cuts and lays off numerous staff. Working long hours in a down economy, nurses and medical assistants feel a lack of power to seek better compensation and working conditions. Furthermore, individual nurses feel compelled to compete with their peers in an attempt to improve their standing with administration in order to gain any measure of job security possible, while the hospital administration is taking advantage of this competition to further cut income and benefits. A political metaphor views this system as being comprised of individuals and possibly groups of individuals (doctors, nurses, patients, administration) who are in conflict over issues of power and ultimately focusing on satisfying their own interests. The three types of relations, unitary, pluralist, or coercive, will be discussed further later in this chapter when discussing appropriate systems methodologies. This viewpoint is more critical in nature in that it recognizes the key role of power in systems; although this focus on power can have the potential to lead to generating unnecessarily undesirable effects such as mistrust or cynicism regarding all human social phenomena.

It is important to note that all metaphors discussed above by Flood and Jackson (1991) are helpful, valid perspectives on different kinds of systems and systems problems, and not one metaphor is more accurate or true. However, some systems views and metaphors are more useful than others to the qualitative researcher who is likely to be studying social and cultural systems and phenomena. The following discussion on the development of systems thinking will explain why a CST is an appropriate approach to consider for qualitative researchers.

Hard-Systems Approaches to Systems Thinking

Early systems thinking represented a hard-systems approach, which reflects a positivist epistemology with the methods focusing on prediction and control inspired by the natural sciences. While this approach was valuable in understanding systems such as machines, armies, and factories as we discussed earlier, social researchers faced challenges in applying hard-systems thinking to understand human social phenomena. Systems researchers found it difficult to apply this hard-systems view to understanding complex human problems, such as poverty, high-school drop-out rates, or conflicts between business owners and labor unions. Checkland (1981) argued that the engineering-inspired, hard-systems focus on identifying objectives and optimal solutions for meeting those objectives represented an inaccurate view of the reality of human systems. He further argued that hard-systems thinking did not recognize the conflict that can exist in social systems that makes the setting of clear, correct objectives and desirable end points impossible. Systems researchers agreed that social systems are too complex for the black and white methodologies of hard-systems thinking, resulting in reductionist, inaccurate, and unsuitable approaches to solving social problems. Jackson (1985) discussed how the engineering focus of hard-systems thinking presupposes that system objectives can be determined from outside the system, while in reality, objectives originate from individuals and groups within social systems and can often vary or conflict. This false assumption by hard-systems thinking means that success from designed interventions can only take place if there is agreement on objectives across the entire system, which is unlikely, or that objectives of the system are determined by those in power and without the input of others in the system, which is more likely. The hard-systems philosophy of identifying an "optimal" solution regardless of the viewpoints or values of individuals in the system was a big challenge in understanding human social systems (Jackson, 1985).

Soft-Systems Approaches to Systems Thinking

In elaborating on the challenges of the application of hard-systems methods to human social systems work, researchers (namely Churchman, Ackoff, and Checkland) turned to soft systems approaches and a more interpretive and subjective approach (Jackson, 1982).

Both ontological and epistemological distinctions exist between the two approaches of hard- and soft-systems thinking: what a social system is ontologically, and how we gain knowledge about them epistemologically. Soft-systems thinking's understanding of human systems includes the cultural, psychological aspects of human activity as well as the objective, hard systems approach. It views social systems as constructed by individuals and strives to understand and respect the perspectives of those individuals rather than studying the system as if observed from an outsiders' perspective. Given the differing viewpoints that individuals bring with them, soft systems does not seek an "optimal solutions" as even understanding of the problem will be "subjective" to all individuals in the system. Instead, soft-systems thinking seeks a dialogue between individuals and decision makers in the systems in order to reach agreement (albeit temporary) about the nature of the system. The systems analyst then works with the different individuals involved in the process to identify potential changes that they can agree are possible and will be beneficial.

Despite the move away from hard-systems approaches, soft systems itself saw criticism. Jackson (1982) argued that meaningful change is unlikely through soft-systems approaches as soft-systems practitioners are typically working at the ideological rather than practical levels. The lack of understanding of social facts and constraints, as well as the likely unwillingness of individuals in positions of power to fully participate in the required dialogue among stakeholders also make significant change difficult. Jackson (1982) further argued that the "subjective" approaches of soft-systems thinking constrain soft-systems practitioners' ability to intervene and make meaningful change in situations of fundamental conflict or unequal power, as soft-systems thinking only gathered the "subjective" opinions in a system. He discussed how "soft systems thinking either has to walk away or fly in the face of its own philosophical principles and acquiesce in proposed changes emerging from limited debates characterized by distorted communication" (p. 236).

Critical Systems Approach to Systems Thinking

So while hard-systems approaches are suitable for closed, engineered systems, and soft-systems approaches are better suited for human systems, systems thinkers still identified the challenges of hard- and soft-systems thinking as not being able to capture and reconstruct holistic meaning that is shared within the system, and argued for an approach that will help understand a collective, shared meaning of a system rather than merely collecting the various opinions in a system. And the need for a critical systems approach was identified for "situations where there is little common interest shared between stakeholders, there is fundamental conflict, and the only consensus that can be achieved arises from the exercise of power" (Jackson, 2001, p. 237). A focus on critical analysis of systems, particularly in regard to issues of power, oppression, and emancipation, became highlighted as a requirement in using systems approaches. As Ulrich (2003) stated, "Systems thinking without critique is blind with respect to its underpinning boundary judgments and their normative implications" (p. 327). Furthermore, beyond the issues of power and emancipation, which became a defining characteristic of CST, the strengths and weaknesses of different systems methods led to a focus on pluralism of methodologies, recognizing these strengths and weaknesses and using approaches in combination for different contexts and purposes. Accordingly, the commitment to critique, emancipation, and pluralism form the three core values and philosophy of CST.

CST Philosophy and Core Principles

Development and Epistemological Perspectives

The philosophical underpinnings of a critical approach to systems theory were initially established by Churchman (1970). In his discussion of operations research and management science, he identified the need to move away from the approaches of the natural sciences inherent in what he called the rational operational approach and its foundation of rationalism and empiricism. He noted that these approaches did not fit with the actual realities of operational research and its human components, particularly the messy nature of social systems and the anxieties of such social issues as political power, poverty, crime, or pollution. It was Churchman's (1970) view that the rational tradition of systems thinking could not address these issues. He called for an irrational systems approach founded on the philosophy of Kant's discussion of "systemic judgments" necessary for understanding and making data meaningful. Along with this, he incorporated Hegel's view of additional "alternative systemic judgments," which lead to a "learning process" of understanding that there can be no one absolutely right judgment or solution to a system problem (p. 42). Through this argument, he established a need for critique in systems thinking by pointing to the need to view systems thinking as a system itself and one that should therefore be open to systems analysis. Checkland (1985) later distinguished between these approaches as a hard-systems approach versus a soft-systems approach, the critiques of which we discussed in the previous section. The further development from the soft-systems approach to a critical approach founded on emancipatory principles can be seen in Jackson's (1985) criticism of soft systems and call for a critical approach. In his criticism of the interpretive nature of soft-system approaches and their shortcomings, Jackson draws heavily on Habermas's (1973, 1984, 1987) epistemological theory of universal human participation in work and interaction and his theory of knowledge-constitutive interests. These theories respectively deal with the concepts of communication free from distortion and communication competence through an ideal speech situation where validity claims are respected, and the authentication of the knowledge produced in communication by a process of enlightenment of where the actors in communication attain self-understanding and recognize the account of their communication as acceptable. Systems researchers find these concepts of particular importance when considering systems wherein inequality of power exists in relation to opportunity, authority, and control. Through this development and epistemological heritage that CST holds, from hard-, soft-, and to critical systems thinking, CST's three core principles can be identified as critique, emancipation, and pluralism as we discuss in the following section (Schecter, 1991; Flood & Jackson, 1991).

Commitment to Critique

The first core principle of CST is a commitment to critique and is reflected in the previous discussion of hard- and soft-systems approaches. The notion of critique facilitates the researcher to critically consider the methods, practice, and underlying theory that she brings to her research. In applying a systems-thinking approach, the researcher should be critical of the chosen methods and the theories they reflect when planning her research. It intends to be cautionary against the lack of focus on theory that "pragmatists" invoke in putting together a toolkit of "proven" methods, and is also watchful against the choice of "isolationists" who pick a single theory as solely legitimate (Flood & Jackson, 1991). Instead, an understanding of the theory behind different methodologies is necessary with an effort to uncover hidden assumptions and conceptual traps that a researcher might have.

For example, a researcher using soft-systems methodology seeks above all to generate mutual understanding by exploring worldviews; however, theoretically this process could be endless and therefore the process typically will allow the dominant culture to specify when this exploration is over. As a result, the theory behind a soft-systems approach can be inappropriate in a system where different groups have different power. A steadfast focus on dialogue for understanding can be pointless if the group in power has no interest and sees no benefit in recognizing or conceding a weaker group's point of view. Thus the concept of mutual understanding through dialogue is a conceptual trap to the practical solving of problems in systems where inequality of power does not allow for mutual respect (Flood & Jackson, 1991).

A commitment to the critique of the underlying ethics and a questioning of understanding, particularly in regards to normative content and the value of rigor, is necessary in order to ensure that traditional approaches do not import existing "baggage" into the research study. This commitment is especially important in discussing the issues of power and barriers to communication that may exist in systems, as we discuss in the next core commitment.

Commitment to Emancipation

A second key commitment of CST is the commitment to emancipation, which includes the notions of freeing of the system and system's individuals from any kind oppression that disables them to critique and fully develop their potential. It also includes the idea of freeing systems researchers and practitioners from the control of research methodologies in power.

This directs the researcher to recognize the barriers to human emancipation: the unequal power relations and the conceptual traps, which exist and can be easily overlooked. Jackson (1985) explicitly called for an emancipatory systems approach, and Flood (1990) identified his discussion of CST as liberating systems theory that calls to "liberate and critique." Oliga's (1991) examination of stability and change in social systems, which he calls "empower and transform" (Schecter, 1991) as well as Ulrich's (1987, 2003) critical systems discourse are all considered as a commitment to emancipation in order to work towards full human potential development via free and equal participation in community. Examples of systems that are emancipatory would be small groups that make decisions together and have a highly reflective group culture, being fully self-monitoring, self-critiquing, and self-guiding, although these small systems are usually embedded within dominant larger systems in ways that can limit the emancipatory potential of that smaller system.

Commitment to Pluralism

The final core value of CST is pluralism, focusing on the notion that researchers should employ a creative design of methods by appreciating all methods and using multiple methods, grounded in appropriate theory. Schecter (1991) argues for taking on a pluralistic approach over isolationist, imperialist, or pragmatic approaches to systems thinking. This pluralistic approach does not agree with the "pragmatists" trend of using a toolkit of only "proven" methods, and also disagrees with the "isolationists" who pick one theory as solely acceptable (Flood & Jackson, 1991). It rather strives to liberate researchers from these prevailing approaches of using methodology and help them to create a meta-language that can properly locate the researcher's own intentions and have crosscultural understanding and communications with others. By doing this, the researcher will support the environmental compatibility of the chosen methods. Ulrich (2003, 2006) is another systems researcher who discusses how methodological pluralism and complementarism is indispensable. However he also warns against shallow pluralistic approaches in that prevailing notions of complementarism "rely on a positivistic concept of methodology choice" and that "systemic boundary critique and other forms of emancipatory reflection and discourse are subordinated to the choice of the intervention purpose (and of a corresponding methodology)" (Ulrich, 2003, p. 340). He calls for "deep complementarism" that distinguishes itself from prevailing, shallow conceptions of methodological pluralism "by not subordinating emancipatory reflection and boundary critique to methodology choice" (2003, p. 340). The notion here is to be cautionary against relying on a positivistic trend of methodology choice, which disallows the researcher from engaging in boundary critique, a process that permits her to gain accurate understanding of the scope and design of the system and what members, facts, and norms are to be considered relevant in that particular system. Boundary critique is a key notion in critical systems thinking that helps keep boundary judgments explicit by revealing the current state of the system (what it is) and the just or desired state of the system (what it should be). The detailed process of boundary critique will be further described later in our section on critical systems heuristics.

CST in Research and Practice

While systems theory has decades of research and practice in the management sciences, its impact on qualitative research outside of the field of management science has been minimal.

However, critical systems science has significant similarities with qualitative research, as both research areas are heavily influenced by Habermasian social and epistemological theory and perspectives (Carspecken, 1996; Jackson, 1985). By combining this critical view and the systems-thinking approach to the study of social systems, CST and its methodologies can contribute valuable methods and guidance for qualitative researchers. Jackson (2001) argues that social scientists are often well grounded in theory, but seldom can provide specific guidance for how society or organizations can be changed; while systems scientists commonly are focused on practice, but do not ground it in theory. CST seeks to bring these disciplines together to provide practical means, which remain grounded in established theory. When applying CST in research and practice, a researcher is utilizing a system of system methodologies (SOSM).

The Systems of Systems Methodologies

The SOSM approach arises from the established base of research on the application of systems thinking in the design of social systems, systems analysis, soft systems, the management sciences, the information sciences, and operational research, among others. It addresses the notion that different systems methodologies have different strengths and weaknesses, making them suitable for application in different circumstances. So by applying SOSM, the researcher strives to recognize the type of the problem context being examined and understand what systems methodology might be most appropriate for applying to the problem context. It is important to note that the SOSM is not meant to be used as a rulebook to be followed systematically, and rather that it should be regarded as a framework that facilitates critical reflection on methodology choice in systems research and practice (Midgley, 1997).

SOSM has been explained in a number of different ways, but Flood and Jackson's (1991) SOSM is the most widely utilized. By examining the varied systems approaches, each informed by their own theoretical influences and phenomenological perspective, Flood and Jackson (1991) illustrate what view of problem contexts each takes. The systems problem contexts are categorized through two different categories: System and Participant. System refers to the perspectives on complexity of the problem situation. Participant refers to the perspectives of the relations between participants in the problem situation.

The Participant category is categorized into three different groups, and is grouped by the relations of participants being unitary, pluralist, or coercive. In the case of participants in unitary relations, participants have shared interests, values, common agreement on ends and means, and engage in participatory decision making. Referring back to our example situation, a unitary example would be a context where the medical staff reach consensus on issues through a democratic decision-making process. In the case of the pluralist relations, participants have compatible interests among them. There are differences of opinion in values and means, but with a possibility of compromise in between, and some participants are excluded from decision-making process. In the case of coercive relations, participants do not have any common goals or interests, have conflicting values, and have strong disagreement on the ends and means without the room for compromise. Clearly, many are coerced to accept the decisions made by those in power. A good example would be the case of our hypothetical nurses in competition for keeping their jobs.

The second category, System, includes only two states: simple or complex. Simple systems have a small number of elements and interactions between them that are easy to comprehend. These simple systems are highly structured and organized, with well-defined laws and highly

	Simple	**Complex**
Unitary	An automated factory assembly line seeking to improve efficiency and quality ratings.	A volunteer chaplain group at the hospital dividing up counseling hours through a democratic decision-making process.
Pluralistic	Members of a unionized janitorial staff who must determine which members will change from day to night shifts for a new client.	A small group of nonmedical and medical staff working together to find a solution for improving customer satisfaction in order to meet the hospital authority's request.
Coercive	Factory assembly line or fast-food chain workers and administration in conflict over wage cuts.	Hospital administration cutting benefits of nonunionized hospital staff already working overly long hours with no compensation due to the down economy.

Table 1. Examples of Problem Situations

structured interaction. They do not change over time. Complex systems are not highly structured, and have a great number of elements with complicated interactions between them; these interactions are loose, and the system changes constantly over time (Flood & Jackson, 1991). The SOSM comes to a cross-referencing of the two categories and three different groups, and therefore groups the problem contexts into six categories: simple-unitary, complex-unitary, simple-pluralist, complex-pluralist, simple-coercive, and complex-coercive.

The first category, simple-unitary methodologies, includes methods such as systems engineering, systems analysis, or operational research for machines or highly structured teams. This problem group assumes that the system analyst or researcher can establish the goals of a system and accomplish those goals by using new operational conditions, which are often quantitative or highly structured. Second, complex-unitary methodologies are for addressing situations that are generally supported by all participants in the system. This problem group views systems as if they were organic or ecological systems and works with methods such as general systems theory, sociotechnical-systems thinking, and viable system diagnosis. Third, the simple-pluralist methodologies assume that systems can be dealt with as machine-type approaches once the existing disagreement is resolved. Therefore this problem group focuses on overcoming the conflict by using methods such as group formation, stakeholder analysis, assumption rating, dialectical debate, and synthesis. Fourth, the complex-pluralist methodologies are for tackling problem situations where participants have differences of opinion in values and means but with a possibility of compromise. Examples of methods of this problem group include interactive planning and soft-systems methodology. Finally both simple-coercive and complex-coercive methodologies consider problem situations where the participants have diverse interests, objectives, and values, and are likely to use any kind of power they have to force their preferred perspectives on others (Flood & Jackson, 1991). A number of CST approaches have arisen out of attention to knowledge-powers issues, such as critical systems heuristics, community operational research, and action research methodologies. In the following section, we will discuss the methodologies grounded in power issues and how through their application in a CST-driven approach, they can inform qualitative research.

Critical Systems Heuristics

Critical systems heuristics (CSH) is a practical critical systems methodology tool that brings an emancipatory systems approach to coercive contexts (Flood & Jackson, 1991). It systematically exposes the assumptions of decision makers and planners to reveal whose interests are being served by encouraging critical thinking about the value judgments that underlie planning decisions. It seeks to help people, particularly those not included in the design process, reflect on the system design and how it affects them (Ulrich, 1983).

The basic idea of CSH is to support a systematic effort of handling boundary judgments critically with boundary critique. A system is a concept, not a concrete entity. While the boundaries of a system may be influenced by such attributes as physical or geographical boundaries, ultimately it is defined by the preconceptions of the designers within the system or the lens the researcher brings to her view of the system. Boundaries therefore are inherently an issue of judgment. Any view of a system requires boundary judgments about the scope of the system or system design effort and what is included or excluded. Design participants, experts, and researchers can all have inherent prejudices or biases—including what data is important and what is not—that must be identified through a systematic and critical process. Boundary critique makes boundary judgments explicit by applying twelve concepts divided into four groups, which question the current state of the system (what is) with the just or desired state of the system (what should be). It facilitates the examination of the limits or boundaries of decision making. So in the nonunionized nursing workforce example we mentioned earlier, CSH can work as a tool to facilitate the understanding of which groups of people and what kinds of information have been considered related or important to a decision-making process and which have been considered unrelated and therefore excluded or marginalized. Using our previous example, who among these stakeholders has a voice in decision making: patients, doctors, nonmedical staff, pharmaceutical companies, pharmacies, insurance companies, or family members of the nurses? This understanding could then be contrasted with what information or who should be involved in the process and therefore inform the decisions on what kind of interventions should be beneficial.

Specifically, the twelve boundary categories focus on people and their social roles in the decision-making process, as it is the people who determine what is an improvement. Ulrich (1993) groups the categories around four different social roles, three of them regarding the people involved in the decision process and the fourth regarding people who are affected but not involved. The first group examines sources of motivation (client, purpose, measure of success); the second, sources of control (decision maker, resources, environment); the third, sources of expertise (designer, expert, guarantor); and, the fourth, sources of legitimation (witnesses, emancipation, world view).

For each column in the table, there are three questions to consider. And for each question, there are two realities to consider: what is and what should be. The first question is about who occupies or ought to occupy what role. So it is necessary to ask who is or ought to be the client, decision maker, designer, or witness.

The second question is about what these roles contribute to establishing what is considered an improvement, and what concerns must be considered: what is and what should be the system's purpose; what resources or conditions are or should be controlled by the decision maker; who is or should be the expert; and what is or should be the level of emancipation of the witnesses?

The third question considers issues that arise if there is conflict with other social actors about the key concern associated with that role: what is or should be the measure of success, system environment (not controlled by decision maker), guarantee of success, and underlying system world view? The way such conflicts are handled contributes to the establishment of what is considered to be "improvement."

Social Roles/ Stakeholder	Major Concern	Main Difficulty	Sources of:
1. Client	2. Purpose	3. Measure of Success	Motivation
4. Decision Maker	5. Resources	6. Environment	Control / Power
7. Designer	8. Expert	9. Guarantee	Expertise / Knowledge
10. Witnesses	11. Emancipation	12. World View	Legitimation

Table 2. Twelve Boundary Categories and Questions of CSH

By answering each of these questions, hidden boundary judgments can be recognized and stakeholders can be empowered (Ulrich, 1993).CSH argues that participants and researchers need to be self-critical and open themselves to external critique from witnesses or nonparticipants in the system in order to ensure that critique of boundary judgments has occurred. For example, whether we were considering a context where a researcher is brought in to improve the efficiency and quality of an automated assembly line, or a context where hospital administration is cutting benefits from a nonunionized work staff that consistently works overly long hours with no additional compensation due to their fear of job loss in a down economy, in order to ensure a systematic critique of the boundary judgments, these twelve questions should be asked and answered in terms of what is and what should be. Furthermore, these answers should be shared and open to further critique from all stakeholders in order to ensure that a proper critique has occurred and all hidden boundary judgments have been recognized and addressed. By asking these questions, hidden bias about the goals of the redesign of the assembly line or about what resources are available for change might be uncovered in the first example. Likewise the role of the hospital staffs' world views and desire for emancipation, or the hospital administration's obfuscation of accurate data that they do not want to acknowledge might emerge in the second example.

Ulrich claims that CSH can and should be applied to any given situation and can guide researchers and participants with boundary critique. However, criticisms of CSH argue that while CSH makes it possible to reveal the system design and all that it implies, it is not evident how to integrate these findings in intervention. They argue that the liability or weakness of CSH methodology is that it makes an assumption that communication between various interest groups is possible, or at the least that mediation by an external authority is possible if communication process is broken down (Midgley, 1997). Midgley (1997) discusses how "coercion, by definition, involves people disengaging from debate and exhibiting dogmatic intransigence, or even violence. Once people have taken a coercive path, they are unlikely to submit to negotiation or arbitration as long as their interests are satisfied through the continuation of coercive activity" (p. 38). Some CST researchers argue that, while CSH proves to be effective in its ability to deal with simple cases of coercion, this assumption of CSH makes it difficult to address complex forms of coercion and needs to be complemented with multiple, pluralistic methodologies that address the problems of false consciousness (Jackson, 1985), along with political action and active campaigning in the larger society (Midgley, 1997).

Despite such criticisms, CSH continues to be applied in systems research. Ulrich and Reynolds (2010) discuss two examples of the application of CSH to natural resources planning and management in Reynolds' (1998) examination of rural development in Botswana, and Berardi et al.'s (2006) and Reynolds et al.'s (2007) look at environmental decision making in Guyana.

Action Research and Critical Systems Methodology

Action research comes from the roots of the work of Kurt Lewin in the 1940s, attempting to understand how to go about changing social systems based on a scientific methodology. Although the two traditions do not share a common-ground-based literature, the complementary relation between action research and critical systems thinking is a strong one (Levin, 1994; Flood, 1998). Researchers from both disciplines consider that the value systems and practice of the professionals within both research areas are similar, as both strands of thinkers are highly committed to solving practical and useful problems that will assist in the larger project of progressive social change. Both disciplines also seek to support liberation and emancipation through theory and knowledge construction based on a critical dialogue between participants and researchers. There are several strands of emancipatory action research approaches that focus on understanding systems of knowledge-power dynamics with a purpose of bringing fairer practice: cooperative inquiry and self-reliant participatory action research.

Cooperative inquiry. Cooperative inquiry, also known as collaborative inquiry, is a good example of a systems research methodology inspired by critical theory and concerned with emancipation. First proposed by Heron (1971) and expanded in the 1980s within the area of action research, cooperative inquiry's main notion is to research "with" rather than "on" the people. It puts an emphasis on having all active participants fully involved in the research process as co-researchers. Researchers and participants design, manage, and draw conclusions from the inquiry, and they go through the experience and action that is being explored.

So for example, returning to our previous example of a nonunionized hospital, perhaps a dysfunctional atmosphere in the hospital has prompted a study of the problems in the workforce. In the case of an outsider coming to study the people and processes within the hospital, it could be quite possible the researcher is viewed by suspicion by some groups, particularly those not used to being asked their opinion, such as the nurses and medical assistants who are working long hours in an uncertain job market. By applying cooperative inquiry, the researcher collaborates with participants in the research process rather than conducting research on the participants, so the nurses and medical assistants come as co-researchers to explore the problems in the hospital. This can gain trust while also encouraging future participation by these marginalized groups.

Cooperative inquiry researchers collaborate with individuals to develop communities with an eye towards future participation (Flood, 1998). Heron (1988a, 1988b, 1996) describes the iterative cycle of four phases of reflection and action in cooperative inquiry: (a) as co-researchers share knowledge, ideas, and goals, problematize power, and come to consensus on actions; (b) record their process and outcomes; (c) immerse themselves in their experience; and (d) continue the cycle of action and reflection until questions are answered in practice.

In the first phase, a group of co-researchers come together and agree to explore a certain topic of human activity and agree on a focus of their inquiry. Co-researchers present knowledge and ideas as well as their view of the purpose of the inquiry; this involves problematizing power (Flood, 1998). Then together they develop a set of questions they wish to investigate and plan a methodology for exploring this idea through practical action. In the second phase, the co-researchers, now working together as co-subjects, engage in the agreed-upon practical actions and observe and record the process and findings of their experience. They seek to observe the subtleties of the experience so that they are able to see how practice does or does not conform to their original conceptual ideas (Heron, 1988a, 1988b, 1996; Flood, 1998). This is followed by further engagement in the third phase, where co-subjects become fully immersed in their experience, so that ideas are further elaborated or developed into unpredicted actions or creative insights. In the final phase, the co-researchers reassemble and reconsider the original propositions and consider modifications and questions. Action and reflection continue until they feel questions are fully answered. They further develop or revise these ideas or reject them and put forward a new set of questions or inquiry methods. Through this process, cooperative inquiry strives to discover better and fairer ways for people to live together in human social systems (Flood, 1998).

Co-operative inquiry methods have been utilized in a variety of research contexts, from social work research involving older lesbians and gay men (Fenge, 2010), to exploring how black women managers learn to thrive as well as survive in the workplace (Douglas, 2002), to studies on in the medical field such as nurses in the mental health field (Tee et al., 2007), and diabetes in a midwestern American Indian community (Mendenhall et al., 2010).

Self-reliant participatory action research. Another good example of the emancipatory systems methodology in action research family is self-reliant participatory action research (Flood, 1998). Focusing on disadvantaged populations (Flood, 1998), the main idea of self-reliant participatory action research is to stimulate and raise awareness of the capacity to transform the relations of knowledge and consciously "shift patterns of power that are buttressed by forms of knowledge creation" (p. 85).

The process involves challenging top-down forms of knowledge relationship. Self-development of participants and researchers begins by engaging in socioeconomic activities that help to transform relations of traditional knowledge relationship and production. This process involves challenging the ways in which support is obtained from other powerful organizations. The ultimate goal of self-reliant participatory action research is to defend "multiple and cherished ways of life" (pp. 85–86), and in doing so, resist against homogenization (Flood, 1998).

Fals-Borda (1996) suggests four techniques of self-reliant participatory action research that may develop people's countervailing power: (1) collective research, (2) critical rediscovery of history through collective memory in defense of the interests of the oppressed, (3) valuing and applying folk culture, such as art, music, drama, myths, storytelling, etc., and (4) production and diffusion of new knowledge within the concept of knowledge ownership, arguing for a systematic way of returning the knowledge to the community so it can maintain the ownership. Rahman (1991) argues for Freire's (1986) notion of conscientization, a process of self-awareness raising for empowerment through collective self-inquiry and reflection taking forms of dialogues, investigations, and knowledge generation. Ultimately, the goal of participatory research methodology is to defend against the monopoly and domination of science and culture led by upper-class elites. Through this process of collective research, people's movements for progress are supported, their influence in sociopolitical systems are increased, and popular knowledge, which they call "a knowledge of life," is stimulated and developed (Rahman, 1991).

For example, perhaps in our hospital situation, the medical staff is seeing a trend of miscommunication between a local ethic minority group and the hospital's doctors, which is resulting in misdiagnoses. This method could be used to work with the minority community in order to help them gain access to the information they need to be better empowered and to understand what information they will need to possess that could help the hospital better serve them. Through the process of the minority group gaining ownership of a knowledge base on health issues and also having their culture better reflected in the hospital, the community could become more empowered and self-reliant while improving the hospital's understanding of their needs and culture, thereby improving the community's overall health and ability to operate effectively within the health system. In literature, self-reliant participatory research methods have been used for training development staff who work with rural poor in developing nations (Burkey, 1993; Rahman, 1990).

Community Operational Research

Schecter (1991) discusses how emancipatory practice in critical systems thinking has mainly centered on community operational research in the United Kingdom. Community operational research method has been a response to Rosenhead (1986, 1987) and Keys' (1987) argument that the classical operational research traditions are largely unsuitable for use in the "community" context. In their view, classic operational research supports the interests that managers have in control, centralization, and de-skilling. In contrast, community organizations are usually smaller, lack resources, do not have a clear administrative hierarchy, and often possess participative decision-making processes (Jackson, 1987). So the unique characteristic of community operational research is the clients or beneficiaries. Community operational research is a movement to serve these untraditional groups, for example, trade unions like the nursing workforce union that we discussed in the previous examples, tenant unions, nonprofits, women's and other social groups as opposed to the traditional clientele of businesses, the military, and government populations (Rosenhead, 1986).

So for example, a systems researcher might come in to the previously described hospital system in order to address the issue of the nursing workforce seeking to unionize. As an unempowered group, the nurses may be doubtful of the systems analyst's motives or of her being able to represent their views accurately and bring meaningful change. By involving all participants actively in the entire process of community operational research, and promoting a reflective, transparent, and participatory decision-making process, the analyst and client relationship can develop into an emancipatory relationship that can transform an oppressive social system.

These groups typically have far fewer resources, are impatient with technical solutions, make decisions using consensus decision making and democratic debate, and are likely to be suspicious and untrusting of expert opinion (Schecter, 1991). They favor a participatory approach to solving problems, are surrounded by complex situations, and usually have to compete for resources that are made available by other powerful organizations (Jackson, 1987).

Within the process of engaging in community operational research, Jackson (1987) notes that no autocratic decision maker can enforce an analyst's recommendation on the rest of the organization, and Schecter (1991) cites Spear (1987, 1989) in pointing out "emancipatory practice must demystify the analytical process and constrain the use of expert power by the analyst" (p. 219), explaining that the analyst and client relationship must develop into an overtly emancipatory relationship. He further argues for having explicit goals for liberation and social justice, supporting those who are directly concerned with problematic situations, not just professional consultants; and being relevant to the task of transforming oppressive social systems, as the requirements for an emancipatory operational research. Finally, Rosenhead (1986, 1987) proposes re-skilling, decentralization, liberation, nonoptimizing, use of analysis to support but not replace judgment, treatment of people as active subjects, acceptance of conflict over goals, bottom-up problem formulation, and acceptance of uncertainty as requirements of community operational research.

Community operational research methods have been employed in a variety of contexts as well. Herron and Bendek (2007) reflect on their experiences working with a framework on active learning for active citizenship in the U.K. Walsh and Hostick (2005) describe two different applications of community operational research to improving health services. Ritchie, Taket, and Bryant (1994) review 26 case studies that utilize community operational research.

Conclusion

This chapter examined critical systems theory and its methods as applied to and informing qualitative research. The chapter looked at the history, development, and epistemological perspectives of CST, presented the core principles and finally examined some of the practical applications of CST in research and practice. Although CST's developmental history has largely been within the management sciences, its core commitment to the concepts of critique, emancipation, and pluralism have a strong connection with qualitative researchers in many disciplines. CST offers tools for evaluating boundaries, recognizing relations, and involving all stakeholders when conducting critical and emancipatory qualitative research. Furthermore, CST provides guidelines and a commitment to deep pluralism to help the qualitative researcher critically reflect on the best tools. With such shared epistemologies and core commitments, we believe that qualitative researchers have much to gain in incorporating CST and its lens of systems thinking into their research practices, and that the field of qualitative research as a whole can be strengthened by incorporating CST and its systemic viewpoint. As Ulrich (2003) argues: "Critique without systems thinking is boundless, and ultimately empty, in that its object and context of valid application remain arbitrary" (p. 327).

References

Bertalanffy, L. V. (1968). *General systems theory*. New York: George Braziller.

Berardi, A., Bernard, C., Buckingham-Shum, S., Ganapathy, S., Mistry, J., Reynolds, M., & Ulrich, W. (2006). The ECOSENSUS project: Co-evolving tools, practices and open content for participatory natural resource management. Proceedings from the *International Conference on e-Social Science*. Manchester, U.K. Retrieved from: http://www.ncess.ac.uk/research/sgp/ecocensus.

Burkey, S. (1993) *People First: A Guide to Self-reliant, Participatory Rural Development*. London: Zed Books.

Carspecken, P. (1996). *Critical ethnography in educational research: A theoretical and practical guide*. New York: Routledge.

Checkland, P. (1981). *Systems thinking, systems practice*. Chichester, UK: Wiley.

Checkland, P. (1985). From optimizing to learning: A development of systems thinking for the 1990s. *Journal of the Operational Research Society, 36*, 757–767.

Churchman, C.W. (1970). Operations research as a profession. *Management Science, 17*(2), 37–53.

Douglas, C. (2002). Using co-operative inquiry with black women managers: Exploring possibilities for moving from surviving to thriving. *Systemic Practice and Action Research, 15*(3), 249–262.

Fals-Borda, O. (1996) "Power/Knowledge and Emancipation" systems. *Practice 9*(2), 177–181.

Fenge, L. A. (2010). Striving towards inclusive research: An example of participatory action research with older lesbians and gay men. *British Journal of Social Work, 40*(3), 878-894.

Flood, R. L. (1990). Liberating systems theory: Toward critical systems thinking. *Human Relations, 43*(1), 49–75.

Flood, R. L. (1998). Action research and the management and systems sciences. *Systemic Practice and Action Research, 11*, 79–101.

Flood, R. L.,& Jackson, M. C. (1991). *Creative problem solving: Total systems intervention*. New York: Wiley.

Freire, P. (1986). *Pedagogy of the oppressed*. New York: Continuum.

Habermas, J. (1973). *Theory and practice* (J. Viertel, Trans.). Boston: Beacon.

Habermas, J. (1984). *The theory of communicative action: Reason and the rationalization of society* (T. McCarthy, Trans.). Boston: Beacon.

Habermas, J. (1987). *The theory of communicative action: Lifeworld and system. A critique of functional reason* (T. McCarthy, Trans.). Boston: Beacon.

Heron, J. (1971). *Experience and method*. Guildford, UK: University of Surrey.

Heron, J. (1988a).Validity in co-operative inquiry. In P. Reason (Ed.), *Human inquiry in action* (pp. 40–59). London: Sage.

Heron, J. (1988b). Impressions of the other reality: A cooperative inquiry into altered states of consciousness. In P. Reason (Ed.), *Human inquiry in action* (pp. 182–198). London: Sage.

Heron, J. (1996).*Co-operative inquiry: Research into the human condition*. London: Sage.

Herron, R., & Bendek, Z. M. (2007). Take part: Active learning for active citizenship contributing to community O.R. reflections and practices. *Operational Research Insight, 20*(2), 3–7.

Jackson, M. C. (1982). The nature of soft systems thinking: The work of Churchman, Ackoff, and Checkland. *Journal of Applied Systems Analysis, 9*, 17–29.

Jackson, M. C. (1985). Social systems theory and practice: The need for a critical approach. *International Journal of General Systems, 10*, 136–151.

Jackson, M. C. (1987) Community operational research: Purposes, theory, and practice. *Dragon 2*, 47–73.

Jackson, M. C. (1991a). The origins and nature of critical systems thinking. *Systems Practice, 4*, 131–149.

Jackson, M. C. (1991b). Post-modernism and contemporary systems thinking. In R. C. Flood, & M. C. Jackson (Eds.), *Critical systems thinking* (pp. 287–302). New York: Wiley.

Jackson, M. C. (2001). Critical systems thinking and practice. *European Journal of Operational Research, 128*, 233–244.

Keys, P. (1987) Management and management support in community service agencies. *Dragon 2*, 19–45.

Levin, M. (1994): Action research and critical systems thinking: Two icons carved out of the same log? *Systemic Practice and Action Research, 7*(1), 25–41.

Mendenhall, T. J., Berge, J. M., Harper, P., GreenCrow, B., LittleWalker, N., WhiteEagle, S., et al. (2010) The Family Education Diabetes Series (FEDS): Community-based participatory research with a midwestern American Indian community. *Nursing Inquiry, 17*(4), 359–372.

Midgley, G. (1997). Mixing methods: Developing systemic intervention. In J. Mingers & A. Gill (Eds.), *Multimethodology: The theory and practice of combining management science methodologies.* Chichester, UK: Wiley.

Mingers, J. (1980). Towards an appropriate social theory for applied systems thinking: Critical theory and soft systems methodology. *Journal of Applied Systems Analysis, 7,* 41–49.

Oliga, J. C. (1991). Power-ideology matrix in social systems control. In Flood, R. L., & Jackson, M. C. (Eds.), *Critical systems thinking: Directed readings* (pp. 269–286). Chichester, UK: Wiley.

Rahman, M. A., (1990), The case of the third world: People's self-development.*Community Development Journal, 25*(4), 307–314.

Rahman, M. A. (1991). The theoretical Standpoint of PAR. In O. Fals-Borda, & M. A. Rahman (Eds.), *Action and knowledge: Breaking the monopoly with participatory action research* (pp. 13–24). New York: Apex.

Reynolds, M. (1998). "Unfolding" natural resource-use information systems: Fieldwork in Botswana. *Systemic Practice and Action Research 11*(2), 127–152.

Reynolds, M., Berardi, A., Bernard, C., Bachler, M., Buckingham-Shum, S., Mistry, J., Ulrich, W. (2007). ECO-SENSUS: developing collaborative learning systems for stakeholding development in environmental planning. Curriculum, Teaching & Student Support Conference, The Open University, Milton Keynes, 1–2 May 2007. Paper available in the Open University's Open Research Online site, http://oro.open.ac.uk/8580

http://oro.open.ac.uk/view/faculty_dept/kmi.html Ritchie, C., Taket, A., & Bryant, J. (1994). Community works: 26 case studies showing community operational research in action. Sheffield, UK: Pavic Publications.

Rosenhead, J. (1986). Custom and practice. *Journal of Operational Research Society, 37,* 335–343.

Rosenhead, J. (1987). From management science to workers' science. In R. Flood, & M. C. Jackson (Eds.), *New directions in management science* (pp. 109–13). Aldershot, UK: Gower Press.

Schecter, D. (1991). Critical systems thinking in the 1980s: A connective summary. In R. L. Flood, & M. C. Jackson (Eds.), *Critical systems thinking: Directed readings* (pp. 213–226).Chichester, UK: Wiley.

Spear, R. (1987). Towards a critical systems approach. In *Proceedings (supplement) of the 31ˢᵗ Annual Meeting of the International Society for General Systems Research*, Budapest, Hungary.

Spear, R. (1989). *Some issues in a critical systems approach.* Paper presented at the 33ʳᵈ annual meeting of the International Society for Systems Science, Edinburgh, Scotland.

Tee, S., Lathlean, J., Herbert, L., Coldham, T., East, B., & Johnson, T. J. (2007). User participation in mental health nurse decision-making: A co-operative enquiry. *Journal of Advanced Nursing, 60*(2), 135–145.

Ulrich, W. (1983). *Critical heuristics of social planning a new approach to practical philosophy.* Berne, Switzerland: Paul Haupt.

Ulrich, W. (1987). Critical heuristics of social systems design. *European Journal of Operational Research 31*(3), 276–283.

Ulrich, W. (1993) Some difficulties of ecological thinking, considered from a critical systems perspective: A plea for critical holism. *Systems Practice, 6*(6), 583–611.

Ulrich, W. (2003). Beyond methodology choice: Critical systems thinking as critically systemic discourse. *Journal of the Operational Research Society, 54,* 325–342.

Ulrich, W. (2006). Rethinking critically reflective research practice: Beyond Popper's critical rationalism. *Journal of Research Practice, 2*(2), Article P1. Retrieved from http://jrp.icaap.org/index.php/jrp/article/view/64/63.

Ulrich, W., & Reynolds, M. (2010). Critical systems heuristics. In Reynolds, M. and Holwell, S. (Eds.), *Systems Approaches to Managing Change: A Practical Guide.* (pp. 243–292). London: Springer.

Walsh, M., & Hostick, T. (2005). Improving health care through community OR. *Journal of the Operational Research Society, 56,* 193–201.

Exploring Methodological Innovations for Critical Inquiry

CHAPTER SEVEN

Meaning Making and Understanding in Focus Groups

Affirming Social and Hermeneutic Dialogue

MELISSA FREEMAN

How the individual or self is theorized in social science research alters the way human meaning is collected and interpreted. At the core of debates over meaning is, on the one hand, an autonomous, agentic self who can speak for him or herself separate from the social and cultural discourses in which he or she lives, and, on the other, an embodied, relational, and dialogical self that speaks with, and through, the voices of society (Taylor, 1991; Hermans, Kempen, & van Loon, 1992). In the first conception of self, developed within logical positivism, is a "strict separation of questions of being…from matters of knowing" (Schwandt, 2004, p. 35, n. 21), where what counts as knowledge is construed separately from the contexts and experiences of the individual or individuals in question. Heidegger's (1962) seminal work *Being and Time*, which prioritized being and the study of being or ontology, has helped theorists articulate the second conception, where humans are believed to have been born into an already interpreted world, and are therefore constituted in interactions with the meaning structures made available to them. Whereas most social scientists acknowledge the influence of the environment and social contexts on people's beliefs, understandings, and attitudes, a desire for objectivism pushes many of them to work within the first conception. Studies that utilize focus-group discussions that seek to exploit the social and relational basis of our understandings are no different. In a simplified way, these studies can be characterized, for example, as either (1) objectivist and positivist in that the focus groups are intended to create a more natural, social condition, but individuals are thought to hold separate identities and opinions; or (2) constructionist and hermeneutic in that the focus group is the social dialogue within which identities and understandings are constructed. This chapter provides an overview of focus-group methodologies with emphasis on its transformation from a data-collection strategy to a form of engagement over meaning. Then drawing more specifically on the theoretical tradition of philosophical hermeneutics, it explores how a hermeneutic perspective can inform this meaning-making process. I conclude by arguing that the premise suggested in philosophical hermeneutics of the dialogic and historical nature of all understanding provides a useful framework for researchers using focus groups in their work.

A Unique, Under-Theorized Method

Focus-group discussions emerged as a data-collection method in sociology during the late 1930s, at a time when more nondirective and flexible approaches emphasizing respondent or participant voices were being developed (Krueger & Casey, 2009). Originally described as a "focused interview" (Merton & Kendall, 1946; Merton, Fiske, & Kendall, 1956) designed to be used in conjunction with quantitative data to assess the subjective responses "of persons exposed to a situation previously analyzed by the investigator" (Merton & Kendall, 1946, p. 541), it has since evolved into a stand-alone method carried out in a variety of ways and for a variety of purposes (Barbour, 2007). Whether conducted as part of positivistic mixed-methods studies or as the primary method in feminist research, what all focus groups have in common is an interest in collecting or generating data through group interaction or dialogue (Morgan, 1997). Kitzinger and Barbour (1999) go so far as to state: "Any group discussion may be called a 'focus group' as long as the researcher is actively encouraging of, and attentive to, the group interaction" (pp. 4–5). Typically, however, a focus group is described as an interview conducted on a specific topic with a small group of people who share certain experiences or backgrounds (Krueger & Casey, 2009). Participants are selected based on their interest and experience with the topic of inquiry as well as on demographic characteristics that are thought to represent a certain perspective, life situation, or background.

> The rationale for the method is to provide a socially-oriented interaction, similar to a real life situation, in which participants freely influence one another, build on one-another's responses, and thus stimulate collective and synergistically generated thoughts, feelings, and experiences. (Smit & Cilliers, 2006, p. 303)

When Robert Merton was invited to assist Paul Lazarsfeld at the Bureau of Applied Social Research at Columbia University to assess audience responses to radio broadcasts or propaganda films during World War II, he considered the qualitatively generated interview data as providing the experiential information necessary to better understand the trends and effects measured quantitatively (Morrison, 1998). In his view, both were necessary to provide a detailed and enlarged understanding of human experience. Focus-group data were not considered rigorous enough to stand alone as evidence of the effects of the propaganda or media material, but were a necessary part of their study. "Qualitative focused group-interviews were taken as sources of new ideas and new hypotheses, not as demonstrated findings" (Merton & Kendall, 1946, p. 558). What Merton theorized is that simply collecting and matching audience negative and positive responses to specific media messages or collecting forced-response survey responses were insufficient for understanding the way individuals and groups simultaneously acted as objects and receptors of media messages and as their co-interpreters and transmitters (Morrison, 1998). In other words, people both respond to and act upon media images and messages, making their meaning far more complex and contextually dependent. The focused interview was intended to re-create as much as possible a naturally occurring social interaction or context where these interpretations and meanings would be shared, defended, interpreted, and constructed so as to better understand the way people's lived experiences affected their responses (Morrison, 1998). For Merton and his colleagues, the primary advantage of generating data in groups was the opportunity to increase the range and variability of participants' responses because of the influence of ideas and opinions offered by others in the group (Merton et al., 1956; Kidd & Parshall, 2000). By speaking with and against the meanings provided by others, focus groups were thought to "produce data and insights that would be less accessible without the interaction found in the groups" (Morgan, 1988, p. 12). An idea I will return to.

It is important to understand, however, that the role Merton gave to participants' subjective meanings is guided by the positivistic logic to which he ascribed. From a positivistic perspective, the focus-group moderator is expected to have a good grasp of the theoretical themes in a given domain, and "tests" these with various audiences in anticipation of further refining a theory. Merton and Kendall (1946, p. 541) considered this process to be systematic and methodologically sound. It involved selecting participants who had or would be "involved in a *particular concrete situation*" like hearing the same radio program or reading the same article; developing "an *interview guide*, setting forth the major areas of inquiry and the hypotheses which locate the pertinence of data to be obtained in the interview," focusing the interview "on the *subjective experiences* of persons exposed to the pre-analyzed situation," and finally analyzing their responses to "test the validity of hypotheses derived from content analysis" …[and] "to ascertain unanticipated responses to the situation, thus giving rise to fresh hypotheses."

I quote the original work at length because it provides the foundational concepts behind focus-group research and helps us understand what has changed or remained the same. Merton (1987) explains: "[The qualitative] information moved beyond the *net effects* of 'the films'—a most complex set of evocative stimuli—to identify, at least provisionally, the elements and configurations of that complex experience which might have led to those effects" (p. 557). This purpose—to focus on individual meanings in relation to a predetermined theoretical landscape—is still very prominent in focus-group research.

Although most theorists acknowledge Merton's seminal work as the precursor to focus-group discussions, influences today include more than half a century of application within market research, and development in critical pedagogy and feminist research (Kamberelis & Dimitriadis, 2005). As a result, focus-group research incorporates an eclectic mix of methodological strategies depending on the theoretical framework used and the purpose of the research. This section reviews the literature on focus-group discussions. It is not a guide for conducting focus groups (see for example, Morgan, 1997; Bloor, Frankland, Thomas, & Robson, 2001; Barbour, 2007; Stewart, Shamdasani, & Rook, 2007; Krueger & Casey, 2009), but an examination of the challenges and benefits interviewing in groups are thought to offer social research and society. Regardless of theoretical perspective, most researchers using focus groups must determine the overall purpose of the research for which the groups are a part, the make-up or composition of the groups, the role of the moderator, and the intended outcome of the discussion (i.e., what the researcher hopes to say and do as a result of analyzing this data). I will address each in turn.

From Groups That Focus to a Focus on Groups

A central assumption of focus-group methodologies is that group interactions are thought to elicit data that are "less accessible" (Morgan, 1988) without the group effect. What is it that groups make accessible?

What Merton and his colleagues theorized about the relationship between individual opinions and culture was that public attitudes and opinions were best articulated in groups because it was in the social dynamics of groups that these were most likely conceived of and expressed. It was not that individual opinions couldn't be elicited in individual interviews, but that social and cultural norms and behaviors were best developed in a specific context and that the contextually based expressions would, therefore, be different in groups made up of middle-class housewives, wealthy male bankers, construction workers, college students, or other homogeneous or heterogeneous group compositions. Bringing culturally similar people together is believed to elicit an in-depth understanding of how members of a particular segment of the population experience or perceive an issue or topic. Bringing together culturally different people, on the other hand, is intended to encourage a wider variation of responses (Stewart et al., 2007). Either way, the presence and influence of others is considered the essential asset of this method (Kitzinger, 1994; Robinson, 1999; Barbour, 2007).

This assumption has been applied in a variety of ways in focus-group research and is what differentiates how focus-group data are considered and analyzed. On one end of the spectrum is the idea that group interactions create a more natural setting (Morgan, 1988) in which individuals can share their opinions and ideas about a topic. The focus-group discussion is presented as an important social context that needs to be controlled to prevent unwanted biases and influences; the desired data are the content of people's statements, their opinions and thoughts, not on how other statements might have contributed to these. Data produced in groups are believed to be higher quality because participants feel pressured to elaborate their responses when questioned by other group members or challenged by others' expressed opinions (Merton, 1987; Wilkinson, 1998a). Furthermore, the data are thought to be more representative of the emic perspective of the participants because "*their* language and concepts, *their* frameworks for understanding the world" (Wilkinson, 1998a, p. 117, italics in original) are prioritized. From this perspective, focus groups provide a way to observe cultural values and group norms in action, while maintaining a focus on the views that are expressed as a result. For example, in their focus group with drug-experienced young people, Agar and MacDonald (1995) learned of topics and issues that hadn't been expressed in interviews or observations but emerged as a significant issue in the group interaction. Nevertheless, the group interaction also raises concern that individual opinions may become distorted, biased, or silenced as a result of wanting to conform to the group's expressed opinions (Carey, 1995). From a positivistic perspective this influence is seen as undesirable, since individual opinions are still considered to be the product of individuals. The group is meant to enhance the articulation of individual opinion, not create it.

On the other end of the spectrum is the idea that focus-group data cannot be considered naturally occurring talk of another kind, but has to be understood as "jointly produce[d] accounts about proposed topics in a socially organized situation" (Smithson, 2000, p. 105; see also Madriz, 2000; Wilkinson, 1998a). In other words, the focus group is its own kind of social interaction and its analysis is representative of itself, not some other social interaction. In this view, the focus group is considered "'a discursive production' serving a particular function in the context of a given interchange" (Wilkinson, 1998a, p. 120); the group's influence, including the moderator's questions and comments, becomes part of the co-constructed dialogue. Whether it is deemed to be negative or positive would be theorized during analysis. From this perspective, individual opinions expressed cannot be considered the province of any individual, but are thought to be part of the discourses constructed through the group's inter-actions (Smithson, 2000).

Between these two endpoints lie a variety of uses and perspectives. For example, the focus group can be used to "probe the underlying assumptions that gave rise to particular views and opinions…. New information, or a question re-phrased within the group, allows the researcher to observe when opinions shift and under what influences and circumstances" (Robinson, 1999, p. 906). This kind of process information can be the primary focus of a study or com-bined with either a thematic or a discursive approach. Another perspective is to consider the whole as a collective human achievement or anti-oppressive statement for a particular group of people (Madriz, 2000). For example in feminist work, individual experiences and stories shared in focus groups are understood as "collective testimonies and group resistance narra-tives" (Madriz, 2000, p. 836).

A group, then, can be understood as the taken-for-granted context for eliciting individual responses on a topic of importance, one that allows participants to bring up dimensions not previously thought of by the researcher; it can be the focal point of the analysis, how meaning was constructed dialogically; or it can provide data for theoretical development of group com-munication norms, how the presence and influence of others affect the responses of individu-als. Knowing the underlying reason for bringing a group of people together alters the choice of participants, their assumed relationship to the topic, and the role of the moderator.

Focusing the Groups

A central feature of focus-group design is the perceived relationship of focus-group partici-pants to the research topic. From the beginning, focus-group methods were conceptualized around the idea that responses elicited about a common topic or shared experience would provide a conduit to human-meaning schemas or meaning-making processes. When Merton and Kendall (1946) recruited participants who had experienced a "particular concrete situa-tion" (p. 541), they saw each focus group as contributing to an already well-established record of empirical work on a particular topic, such as negative responses to certain media messages. Although different theoretical frameworks consider the group and its relation to the topic dif-ferently, in most cases, the intent is to focus the conversation on "a particular stimulus object, event or situation" (Millward, 1994, p. 281). Later I discuss the essential role the topic plays in hermeneutic engagement. Here I examine how the topic has been discussed in the focus-group literature generally.

The primary means for keeping a group focused on the target topic or event is to develop a protocol. Krueger and Casey (2009, p. 38) describe two examples: a "topic guide" that outlines the issues to be covered, or a "questioning route" that provides a more detailed and sequential list of questions to be entertained. Although open-ended, they are focused on some aspect of the shared concrete situation (the topic that brought the participants together), which greatly facilitates the ability of researchers to compare responses across groups. For example, in a study seeking to elicit the beliefs of Vietnamese people regarding tuberculosis (TB), Long, Johansson, Diwan, and Winkvist (1999) conducted 16 focus groups in four different regions. In each region, perceptions were sought out by using the same thematic guide covering general and specific TB issues with four homogeneous groups (male TB patients, female TB patients, non-TB males and non-TB females). In this way, comparisons were possible by gender, condi-tion, and region.

More recently, however, the "topic" has been more loosely conceived and the practice of using a variety of elicitation strategies including art and photography suggests that focus-group designs are covering new ground. For example, in their study of 4- to 12-year-olds' perspectives on physical activity, Darbyshire, MacDougall, and Schiller (2005) used games, drawings, and photography to focus the conversation and maintain interest. Maintaining a clear focus on the topic was less important to these authors than finding ways to encourage the children to interact openly about physical activity in general. They found that these activities provided ways for the children to articulate themes not previously considered by the researchers. Freeman (2006) in her research on parent perceptions of testing and involvement, also used alternative methods to promote a more critical and engaged conversation than might be achieved in a typical moderator-run session. She reorganized data from one focus group into brief poetic transcript segments and read these segments in other focus groups to elicit a responsive engagement on the topic. Similarly, Miles and Kaplan (2005) found that the use of uncaptioned photographs to elicit responses from children, parents, and teachers, encouraged a reflective and active dialogue that went beyond the target topic of inclusion and disability, and offered insight into issues related to the topic, suggesting that there is much to be learned from altering the expected norms of researcher-run group conversations.

Composing the Groups

Different purposes for focus groups have resulted in different types of group composition. The most common argument is that the group should be homogeneous and made up of individuals who share a common background, although not necessarily the same attitudes (Morgan, 1988). Social economic status, level of education, ethnic and racial backgrounds, age, gender, and occupation are all considered to be more or less important as criteria of homogeneity. Millward (1994) suggests selecting people who "will provide the most meaningful information in terms of the project objective" (p. 279). What Millward is talking about is purposive sampling; "that is, a sample which is not representative of the total population, but of some distinct population drawn on the basis of particular characteristics one wishes to examine" (Morrison, 1998, p. 198). Being a parent, for example, may not be enough to be selected for a focus group on homework practice; being a parent who has something to say about homework would be.

The primary rationale provided for homogeneity is to reduce the silencing and distorting effects that power and status differences are thought to produce as they may negatively influence how people respond and what they feel comfortable saying (Morgan, 1997). When a group shares a similar background or experience, there is a synergistic effect of ending each other's sentences and contributing to the development of a shared perspective through the give and take of the discussion. For example, in a discussion about homework involving five working parents, their common belief that parents should help children with homework coupled with their shared experiences as working parents who grapple with finding time to fulfill this responsibility, contributed to a joint articulation of this struggle (Freeman, 2006). A heterogeneous group might have resulted in one parent feeling defensive in relation to other parents on issues where a lack of shared circumstances or linguistic style might have constrained this kind of co-construction. Another way that homogeneity is seen as particularly beneficial is when conducting discussions with marginalized people (Madriz, 2000; Koppelman & Bourjolly, 2001; Barbour 2007). The group situation is thought to contribute to a feeling of safety and solidarity as well as to reduce the authority and influence of the researcher or moderator (Madriz, 2000). For example, Madriz (2000) found that "homogeneous groups in terms of age, class, and race" were important for establishing a safe place for women "to express their ideas about images and cultural representations of crime, criminals, and victims" (p. 845).

Another reason homogeneous groups are favored is that they are believed to assist in generalizability. "Focus group research reveals its historical association with marketing research by using the term 'segmentation' to capture sampling strategies that consciously vary the composition of groups" (Morgan, 1996, p. 143). From this perspective, the focus groups are made up of a sample thought to represent a segment of a particular population. Perhaps they hold different positions in regard to a topic, such as teachers as opposed to administrators, parents, or students, to investigate perspectives on a new curriculum. Segmentation can also vary demographically depending on the purpose and context. In an investigation of patient satisfaction with medical care, Schwarz, Landis, Rowe, Janer, and Pullman (2000) conducted five focus groups, each targeting a specific population: (a) healthcare employees who were also patients (as a way to pilot the focus group questions), (b) pregnant women and families with children, (c) working adults or professionals under 65 with private insurances, (d) people 65 and over, or with disabilities, and (e) African Americans (as a way to elicit African Americans' experiences with the health care facility). Race was not listed as a criterion for selection in the other categories so the racial make-up of those groups is unclear. Groups were chosen because they represented patient characteristics of interest to the healthcare workers. In another context, arguably, different groups would make sense. Segmentation assumes some kind of identifiable whole, of which each segment is a part. In the healthcare example just mentioned, each group represents a segment of the patient population served and it is theorized that the perspectives shared by each group results from the common trait or experience that led to the segment. Many theorists, however, are cautious about assuming that having children, for example, is sufficient for creating homogeneity of perspective; having children, however, provides a common experience from which to discuss the topic of interest. The group becomes the basis for the joint articulation of one or several perspectives but is not considered representative of any segment of the population.

Depending on the research purpose, creating heterogeneous groups is also thought to be valuable. Although less talked about in the literature, researchers are finding that heterogeneous groups can be more innovative, enhance the sharing of explanatory detail of experience, and contribute to the development of the topic in important ways (Stewart et al., 2007). The researcher, however, makes the decision to assess a group of people as heterogeneous or homogeneous, since these categorizations are social constructs and cannot predetermine similarity of response or experience. Furthermore, there is a false assumption that any shared trait or experience creates the conditions for a meaningful conversation. Certainly interest in the topic and a willingness to engage with others are necessary, but it is important to understand which assumptions about people guide our work and not just blindly adopt any one strategy.

Although marketing research guidelines recommend that focus groups should be made up of unacquainted members in order to better observe the development of attitudes and perceptions on a particular topic, most studies using focus groups are small scale and localized, making it more likely that a group will contain some previously acquainted people. Nevertheless, many focus-group theorists find that working with acquainted groups, people who work or live together, brings its own rewards (Wilkinson, 1998a; Bloor et al., 2001; Warr, 2005). Since individual opinions and perspective are thought to be formed by talking and interacting with others during everyday activities, it follows that much could be learned about this process by observing pre-existing social groups (Wilkinson, 1998a). Bloor et al. (2001) explain:

> Where groups are composed of members drawn from pre-existing social groups, it is both inevitable and desirable that the group interactions in the focus group reflect the group interactions in the pre-existing group: one group member may be more forceful than others, another may be the group humorist, and so on.... Nevertheless, all group life possesses some variability and fluidity on which a skilled facilitator can build, in order to ensure that 'the quiet one' makes a relatively more substantial contribution, and so on. (p. 50)

Pre-existing groups are also found to assist the moderator with the development of themes and with clarification of meaning and facts. For example, Kitzinger (1994) found that her participants "often challenged each other on contradictions between what they were *professing* to believe and how they actually behaved" (p. 105). Even in groups where participants don't know each other prior to meeting in the groups, different members of the group contribute to the direction of the discussion. They do this by asking clarifying or supplemental questions that prompt participants to add information to their original account. Sometimes a very outspoken participant can help break the ice for other, more inhibited members, especially around sensitive topics (Kitzinger, 1994).

It is important to understand that many of the decisions made about sampling and grouping come from preconceived assumptions about human nature and the purpose of social research, which are typically informed by dominant theoretical perspectives. Even with the best of planning, humans can be unpredictable, presumed compatibility because of homogeneity can prove unwarranted (Stewart et al., 2007), participants can come to the group uninformed (Agar & MacDonald, 1995), or not show up at all. Therefore, researchers must come to the group discussion prepared to listen, attend to the group, and modify their plans if necessary.

Moderating the Groups

Just as interviewing is often depicted as being as much of an art as a science (Rubin & Rubin, 2005), focus-group moderating can best be understood as a spontaneous form of choreography. This is because the moderator must facilitate the emergent nature of the discussion, while also gently routing it in important ways (Bloor et al., 2001). Whether the moderator conceives of the focus group as a communicative event "in which the interplay of the personal and the social can by systematically explored" (Millward, 1994, p. 280), or a "collective voice" (Smithson, 2000), the moderator needs to attend to multiple occurring events at the same time. These include:

- the ability to convey the purpose of the study and discussion to focus-group participants and assist them in keeping the discussion attuned to those purposes;

- the social and intuitive skills to interpret the verbal and nonverbal behaviors of participants and intervene in ways that assist group processes but does not stifle, control, direct, or in other ways interfere with the internal direction of the discussion, unless the obvious discomfort or distress of a participant suggests otherwise;

- the moderating skills to draw out quieter participants, restrain dominant ones, especially from speaking first, and in other ways facilitate "equal" participation in the unfolding dialogue;

- the interpretive awareness of rhetorical and performative displays so as to enable the elaboration of the themes and ideas that seem conducive to understanding the research topic, while reducing those that seem to be about "something else";

- the ability to see a picture of the whole discussion, a sense of the time passed and the time remaining, and an idea of whether or not to introduce topics not yet covered by a particular group; and

- an understanding of one's own particular style or strength and weakness as a moderator and the desire to work to develop or repress these.

From these bulleted points, it is obvious that one of the assumptions of focus-group designs is that the less controlling or involved the moderator, the more authentic the data will be. For example, Agar and MacDonald (1995) thought that by co-moderating their focus groups, they could lessen their authority in relation to the youth they were working with. Instead they found that they each displayed different styles and each style had the potential to be problematic.

> [The first author] took on a more conversational role. The problem here is that moderator formulations and comments can be taken as conclusive, ending the flow of talk, rather than as invitations to continue the topic, as would be the case in actual conversations. [The second author] plays a more directive role by asking questions. The problem here is that questions can highlight the authority of the moderator and place youths in a performing and evaluative mode. (Agar & MacDonald, 1995, p. 81)

Best to acknowledge the important role played by the moderator and consider in what way he or she can become a contributing member of the socially constructed event. The moderator is a member of the group, whether his or her role is considered to be objectivist and detached or constructionist and engaged. How he or she acknowledges his or her presence is an important component of the design and the subsequent analysis. Smithson (2000) makes this point clear in her discussion of several procedural issues moderators should pay attention to. For example when discussing the issue of dominant voices, she suggests homogeneous grouping as a design strategy, and inviting silent participants to speak as a moderating strategy. However, she states that this does not really resolve the analytical issue.

> This moderator technique may encourage silent individuals to speak within the group, but does not resolve the underlying question of how focus group analysis can treat the group as the primary unit of analysis, when it is not always clear whether the emerging "dominant voice" may over-represent the opinions of one or two vociferous members. (pp. 108–109)

Another issue that is gaining more attention is how all groups are sites of normative influences and that these may not be the same for all groups (Smithson, 2000). Normative influences are dominant social constructions that reflect the way people perceive and understand the world around them (Bloor et al., 2001). Although eliciting and understanding these is a core goal for focus-group research, it is equally important to understand how the presence of certain individuals, including the moderator, might potentially affect the content of the discussion. For example, Allen (2005) revisited the transcripts of focus groups conducted as part of a study on young people's views of sexuality, especially two of the groups composed only of young men between the ages of 17 and 19. She explains that she failed to pay attention to the way the young men performed their masculinities during the focus groups, and now seeks to examine "the 'identity work' young men undertake in front of their peers and myself as a female facilitator" (Allen, 2005, p. 36). In response to being shown an advertisement in a magazine depicting a scantily clad lingerie model, Allen (2005) notes that the "constitution of a hegemonic masculine identity necessitates the sexualization and objectification of a feminine subject" (p. 44). Smithson (2000) argues that moderators need to pay closer attention to how the "other" is constructed in the normative discourse of the focus group. She suggests ways in which the moderator, both in terms of who he or she is in relation to participants and in terms of possible moderating techniques, might contribute to these processes. In other words, focus-group discussions may play a role in maintaining normative values that are denigrating, or they may contribute to challenging those views.

Ethical Considerations

Ethical decision making is an inherent component in all research (Preissle, 2008). Research that uses focus groups must adhere to the same Institutional Review Board guidelines and codes of conduct as other studies targeting human subjects. Every method, however, presents shared and unique ethical challenges. What primarily differentiates focus groups from other methods are, of course, the group dynamics and the open and unpredictable nature of the discussion. While it should be noted that some of the challenges that arise in focus groups may also arise during participant observation or interview studies (e.g., witnessing racist or other oppressive or denigrating comments; facing shy individuals or emotional responses), specific goals, such as having the group take control of its own discussion or wanting participants to question or challenge each other, makes the presence of ethical situations more likely.

> In a group…the issues are wider-ranging and more complex, insofar as group participants can collaborate or collude effectively to intimidate and/or silence a particular member, or to create a silence around a particular topic or issue, in a way that could not occur in a one-to-one interview. (Wilkinson, 1998a, p. 116)

Of particular concern for researchers using focus groups is the possibility for participants to overdisclose sensitive or personal information (Smith, 1995). However, this is not always the case, as individuals can sometimes say more than they intend in an individual interview (possibly feeling as if they need to fill the silence) and be more comfortable sitting back during a group discussion (Smith, 1995). Overdisclosure can lead to emotional upset, embarrassment, and other social and psychological responses either during or after the focus group (Smith, 1995). As a result, many researchers suggest developing strategies for helping participants understand and cope with these possible effects, for example, providing a clear understanding of the nature of focus groups during informed consent, specific guidelines at the beginning of focus-group discussions, and individual or group debriefing at its conclusion (Smith, 1995; Smit & Cilliers, 2006). When group members are already acquainted, special care should be taken to reinforce a sense of group responsibility for keeping information shared during the conversations confidential (Smit & Cilliers, 2006).

The interpretive turn presents new concerns for focus-group researchers by altering the relationship between researcher and researched (Howe & Moses, 1999). For example, Madriz (2000) considers how focus groups can effectively support the informational needs of researchers while also being sites of anti-oppressive work for participants. Furthermore, how are ethical issues to be resolved when focus groups are considered to be the result of the interactive event itself and not the statements of individuals? The uncertain and open-ended nature of interpretive and dialogical work opens up new areas for thought and concern. Howe and Moses (1999) provide an overview of ethical theories and procedures in light of the complexity of these relationships. They describe a variety of theoretical frameworks (e.g., communitarianism, care theory, postmodernism, and others) to offer ways of thinking about the moral and political arena all researchers enter and must consider.

Analyzing Focus-Group Data

Although focus-group methodologies have expanded considerably in terms of their possibilities as a data-collection procedure, they lag further behind in discussions of analysis (Kitzinger, 1994; Wilkinson, 1998a). Coding and categorizing for themes and trends within the content is by far the most common analytic approach, and little discussion, if any, is given to the dynamic interactions that constituted this content in the first place. Krueger and Casey (2009) state that focus-group analysis should be "systematic, verifiable, sequential and continuous" (p. 115). Their emphasis is on the transparency and validity of the analysis and on getting the data you want for the purposes you need it for. Analysis can focus on each individual's responses in a group or consider each group a unit of analysis. Often both forms of analysis are conducted to compare both within and across group responses. Krueger and Casey (2009) offer various frameworks for conducting analyses. These involve grouping data by patterns and themes, identifying critical events that stood out for individuals or whole groups, tracking individual responses to identify changes of opinion influenced by the group interaction, and common forms of thinking or problem solving within and across groups.

One issue with this kind of comparative and thematic analysis is determining whether "an issue constitutes a theme for the group or merely a strongly held viewpoint of one or a few members" (Kidd & Parshall, 2000, p. 301). Another issue is whether or not focus-group data is sufficient for the analytic purposes of the study. For example, Agar and MacDonald (1995) found that ethnographic information collected before the focus groups greatly assisted in its interpretation.

> Without prior knowledge of the folk models as a base, there's nothing to evaluate the group exchanges against, nothing in terms of which to register and interpret the surprises that occur. A focus group can show a researcher some new territory, but it can't tell you much about what it is you've just seen. (Agar & MacDonald, 1995, p. 85)

Depending on what a study is examining, it becomes more or less important to consider the larger context in which the focus-group conversations are located.

More recently, attention has been given to what can be learned about human nature by analyzing focus-group data as dynamic talk or as a co-constructed event. From this perspective, "language is viewed not as a neutral conveyor of information, but as functional and constructive, as a medium which people use to achieve a variety of actions" (Smithson, 2000, p. 105). Departing from the usual content, thematic, or inductive analyses of focus group data, researchers look at how the data is constructed and under what circumstances (Kitzinger 1994; Barbour and Kitzinger, 1999; Matoesian and Coldren, 2002). "What focus groups tell us is how people communicate with others" (Hollander, 2004, p. 628), which means attending to "*the relationships among the participants and between the participants and the facilitator, as well as the larger social structures within which the discussion takes place*" (Hollander, 2004, p. 604, italics in original). Focus groups can provide data for examining what a group contributes to a topic, as well as information about group processes, such as how group interactions might be inhibiting information sharing or providing group support for individual self-disclosure, and the way in which individuals participate, and the attitudes and feelings they share (Kitzinger, 1994; Millward, 1994; Carey, 1995).

The analytic lens and possibilities are multiple. "People engage in any number of activities when they talk, and talk on or about a topic is only one of them" (Matoesian and Coldren, 2002, p. 472). Hollander (2004) examines her focus groups by looking at the influences of four different contexts: the associational contexts, the status contexts, the conversational contexts, and the relational contexts. Hollander and Gordon (2006) take this analysis one step further and consider the processes through which meaning is socially constructed in dialogue. They identify three categories and nine tools through which speakers construct meaning: (1) "building blocks," which form the basic units of construction and consist of categorizing and symbolizing; (2) "linking devices," which place these building blocks in relation to each other, and consist of explaining, storytelling, and forecasting; and (3) "finishing devices," which suggest preferred interpretations (i.e., how hearers should orient toward the meaning under construction) and consist of framing, evaluating, emoting, and rhetorical devices (pp. 187–188). Alternatively, Brannen and Pattman (2005) in their analyses of parents' experiences balancing work and family responsibilities found that the group context played a role in the way participants' negotiated meaning together or in competition with each other, took control of the group, or developed alliances. According to Brannen and Pattman (2005), this kind of analytic focus can "suggest ways in which group dynamics provide a lens upon social and emotional relations within workplaces" (p. 524).

A common approach to gaining entry into relational and dialogic data is by looking at "complementary interactions," which highlight points of agreement, and "argumentative interactions," which focus on points of disagreement between participants (Kitzinger, 1994). Where theorists differ is on what role they give these interactional actions. For some, such as Kidd and Parshall (2000), understanding the effect these interactions have on participants' perspectives is necessary prior to further analysis. In their words,

> before one can make statements with any confidence about what a focus group or series of groups had to say on a given topic, one needs to assess the extent to which responses may have arisen from conformance or censoring…coercion, conflict avoidance, or just plain fickleness. (p. 294).

For others, however, this approach contradicts the performative nature of the focus-group interaction. Although important, group interactions are best understood as situated activities that produce an effect: a co-constructed, discursive display of meaning. Trying to match up a cause-and-effect relationship based on the assessment of an individual's behavior sends the analysis back into the psychologizing that social constructionists seek to avoid. Other approaches such as discourse and conversation analysis are being applied and are proving promising as ways that both contribute to the development of more open-ended, participant-directed conversations and give researchers an analytic lens to make sense of them (Myers & Macnaghten, 1999; Wilkinson, 2006). These approaches have much to offer researchers interested in dialogic theories of understanding, a perspective I now turn to.

Focus Groups as Social and Hermeneutic Dialogue

In the foreword to the second edition of *Truth and Method*, Gadamer (1989a) clarifies that he is not advancing a new hermeneutic method. Rather, he argues that an examination is needed on how the focus on method in the natural and human sciences has resulted in covering up and neglecting the ontological basis of all understanding. What Gadamer asks is a philosophical question about the nature of understanding and how its concealment due to the "'objectifying' effect of science and technology" (Harrington, 2001, p. 1) has negatively affected human consciousness and relations. Gadamer (1989a) proposes instead a hermeneutic "theory of the real experience that thinking is" (p. xxxvi), that moves beyond an objectivist or subjectivist orientation to one focused on being and understanding.

Philosophical hermeneutics begins with the notion that interpretation or the interpretive condition of humankind is a fundamental problem (Grondin, 1994). In response, Gadamer (1989a) advances a dialogical conception of human knowledge and understanding, one which has important consequences for researchers interested in better understanding the "co-construction of meaning in action" (Wilkinson, 1998b, p. 338), such as those working with focus groups. Hermeneutic reflection and understanding are constituted in language, and, according to Gadamer, language is at its most productive in dialogue. This is because dialogue offers an experiential as well as an historical and linguistic basis for meaning making, and all are essential for engaging our interpretive faculties or hermeneutic consciousness. By developing the hermeneutic and conversational qualities described by Gadamer, focus-group participants can contribute actively to their own and to others' (including the researcher's) understanding of a topic (Schwandt, 2004).

Gadamer believes that to participate with others in a genuine or hermeneutic conversation on a meaningful topic or concrete problem requires a stance of openness, risk-taking, and critical reflection. A hermeneutic conversation requires openness to learning, to listening to others, especially those who hold different perspectives on the topic. Sometimes this reflective engagement challenges an individual's preconceptions, other times it extends his or her understanding of these, but in all cases the engagement is with others and the focus is on a topic.

Hermeneutic understanding works with people's preconceptions, prejudices, languages, cultures, and histories, what Gadamer calls our traditions, to identify and uncover their effect upon everyday human action and interaction. This kind of participation requires that we consider how it is that we say the things we say and what, if anything, they contribute to our understanding of self and other.

> The real event of understanding goes beyond what we can bring to the understanding of the other person's words through methodical effort and critical self-control. Indeed, it goes far beyond what we ourselves can become aware of. Through every dialogue something different comes to be.... It is not really we ourselves who understand: it is always a past that allows us to say, "I have understood." (Gadamer, 1976, p. 58)

As described in the previous section, developments of theory and practice in focus-group research are active and productive. This section illustrates how a better understanding of Gadamer's philosophical hermeneutics can serve as a theoretical framework for focus-group research.

A Speech-Partner Model of Interpretation

One way of thinking about hermeneutics and dialogue is to consider the process of interpretation. Taylor (1982) states that "a successful interpretation is one which makes clear the meaning originally present in a confused, fragmentary, cloudy form" (p. 155). He explains that if at first there is confusion or misunderstanding and then there is clarity and understanding, there must be a qualitative difference between these two states. How we get from one state to the other is a hermeneutic concern. Taylor suggests that to convince others of the adequacy of the meaning we have made requires that we take the other through the process, the fragments of our thinking, the points of confusion and clarity, the stops and starts of our expressiveness, the connections and disconnections achieved, and then our final, tentative interpretation. In other words, coming to an understanding is like engaging in dialogue.

An issue for Gadamer is that scientific research rooted in positivism and empiricism seeks to minimize or eliminate altogether the messiness of interpretation, and in doing so has severely disabled humans' capacity to comprehend, deliberate about, and find answers to the complex social and cultural issues affecting our world (Taylor, 1982). When understanding is construed as a scientific or methodological endeavor, "meaning tends to be abstracted from the context of the ongoing communicative practices of the speakers and actors who generate it in ordinary life" (Harrington, 2001, p. 24). Gadamer proposes instead a speech-partner model (Gadamer, 1989a; Taylor, 2002; Schwandt, 2004) for the human sciences. A speech-partner approach values the essentialness of the interpretive process and works with the reality of our historically effected stances when these are put into play in the concrete experience of understanding (Gadamer, 1989a; Harrington, 2001). In this conception of understanding, validity is achieved when partners in the speech event gain a better understanding of the historical preconceptions that have contributed to their and their speech partners' perceptions and statements (Harrington, 2001). This achievement is not akin to one of correspondence between an interpretation and a focal object, nor is this achievement something that can be "measured" as a sort of pre-post condition; it is instead one where partners have been successfully transformed by the event of understanding.

> In the speech-partner model the process of inquiry and its aim are intimately related. Inquiry is not a tool that brings about understanding as an accomplishment external to the act of inquiry. Rather, the process itself is implicated in what can be understood, and the process actually transforms one's way of seeing the world in relation to one's self. (Schwandt, 2004, p. 37)

Language and Tradition

To understand the importance of dialogue in understanding, one needs to understand the hermeneutic problem of language. Gadamer's (2006) central thesis is that "reaching an understanding is a process that must succeed or fail in the medium of language" (p. 13). It is not simply that language is the medium of communication, but that language alone constitutes meaning (Gadamer, 2006). As we try to understand, we develop the object of our understanding in the words we choose. This is not a straightforward process, however, because language is a dynamic, ambiguous medium that means more than we intend, while also leaving us unsatisfied with the quality of our expression.

> Language is such that, whatever particular meaning a word may possess, words do not have a single unchanging meaning; rather, they possess a fluctuating range of meaning, and precisely this fluctuation

constitutes the peculiar risk of speaking. Only in the process of speaking, as we speak further, as we build up the fabric of a linguistic context, do we come to fix the meanings in the moments of meaning of our speaking, only in this way do we mutually agree on what we mean. (Gadamer, 2006, p. 25)

We are always in dialogue in our quest to understand (Grondin, 1994). This understanding, Gadamer explains, is not about fixing or finding the intended meaning, but rather seeking for what aims at being said, beyond the words (Gadamer, 1989b). "The art of nailing someone down to something he or she said is not hermeneutics. Rather, hermeneutics is the art of grasping what someone has really wanted to say" (Gadamer, 1989b, p. 118), which is more about intuiting what is absent from a statement and of uncovering the traces of history and culture shaping the statement, then taking at face value what is stated.

Gadamer explains that our preconceptions or traditions enable us to form a preliminary connection with the meaning structures around us, whether in the form of text, speech, or other symbols, because we, consciously or unconsciously, use what we already know. We limit our ability to understand and develop, however, when we accept these anticipatory responses as understanding. Gadamer (1989a) states that in order to achieve genuine understanding, we have to be able to put our prejudices and preconceptions at risk. This means revealing them to ourselves and to others. In order to open ourselves up to new truths, we have to open ourselves up to the possibility that what the other says has something to tell us and that our preconception might be flawed. We have to challenge tradition, not in the sense of blindly rejecting it, but rather engaging in a process of question and answer (Grondin, 1994) with it. Through this fusion between past and present or between self and other, the essence of the subject matter being interpreted is brought forth.

The Importance of the Topic

Gadamer explains that we are drawn to a text or a conversation because something about the topic or subject matter calls us to it and we feel compelled to respond (Gadamer, 1989a; Binding & Tapp, 2008). The kind of conversation that Gadamer is talking about then is about matters of importance to us, of which we want to know more, and that matter to our lives and world. Interpretation is never someone's, however, nor does it reside in the other or the topic. It is in dialogue that the subject matter becomes known. Opening ourselves up to the views and experiences of others and active questioning are essential aspects of dialogue because its interactive qualities create the condition for the interplay and fusion of competing perspectives (Binding & Tapp, 2008).

We question in order to learn about the topic, which remains central to the discourse. We question because the topic addressed us, to which we are attuned and already attached, because of our history, and because of who we are. When we are prepared to be in a genuine dialogue, we open up the world of human experience. (Binding & Tapp, 2008, p. 129)

Furthermore, these cannot be predetermined questions arising from a different text or previous experience, but must arise by letting the conversation take us up into it. Understanding a text or a topic does not mean understanding what an author intends or what the topic meant historically. Meaning is performed in dialogue, and whatever is understood about the topic is something we live and experience; it can't be given to us. Our traditions, however, have made this letting go difficult. In other words, we need to fight our tendencies to explain, to generalize, to abstract, to use our scientific ways of theorizing, and let the words themselves reveal our traditions to ourselves. Only then can we open ourselves up to the hermeneutic task of understanding and to alternative understandings of that which we seek to know (Gadamer, 1989a; Taylor, 2002).

Understanding as Dialogue

Hermeneutics begins with the problem of language, which is that it both conceals and reveals meaning and leaves interpretation and understanding incomplete. Language, however, is our very way of being in the world, and, as Gadamer's philosophical hermeneutics shows, it is only by participating in language as a living, developing, constituting entity that we are truly ourselves, and that language is at its most productive. Focus groups conceived through the lens of philosophical hermeneutics substantiate constructionist approaches that seek to understand how tradition is put into play in the formation of meaning (Wilkinson, 2006). Furthermore, combining focus groups and hermeneutics encourages participation with understanding of self and others, a way of being, that promotes hermeneutic consciousness and requires that we engage with language not as a statement of our existence but as the means by which we exist. A focus on objectivity and the individual has kept humans from understanding how to engage with the reality of their circumstance, which is one of residing in an already interpreted world, where dominant scientific and technological discourses have succeeded in distancing ourselves from our own interpretive capacities. By resituating our attention on tradition and its productive and counterproductive effects, Gadamer brings together our experiential capacities for experiencing and relating with our hermeneutic capacities for interpreting. Being and knowing are inescapably connected and are brought forth in dialogue.

References

Agar, M., & MacDonald, J. (1995). Focus groups and ethnography. *Human Organization, 54*(1), 78–86.

Allen, L. (2005). Managing masculinity: Young men's identity work in focus groups. *Qualitative Research, 5*(1), 35–57.

Barbour, R. (2007). *Doing focus groups.* Thousand Oaks, CA: Sage.

Barbour, R. S., & Kitzinger, J. (1999). *Developing focus group research: Politics, theory and practice.* London: Sage.

Binding, L. L., & Tapp, D. M. (2008). Human understanding in dialogue: Gadamer's recovery of the genuine. *Nursing Philosophy, 9,* 121–130.

Bloor, M., Frankland, J., Thomas, M., & Robson, K. (2001). *Focus groups in social research.* Thousand Oaks, CA: Sage.

Brannen, J., & Pattman, R. (2005). Work-family matters in the workplace: The use of focus groups in a study of a UK social services department. *Qualitative Research, 5*(4), 523–542.

Carey, M. A. (1995). Comment: Concerns in the analysis of focus group data. *Qualitative Health Research, 5,* 487–495.

Darbyshire, P., MacDougall, C., & Schiller, W. (2005). Multiple methods in qualitative research with children: More insight or just more? *Qualitative Research, 5*(4), 417–436.

Freeman, M. (2006). Nurturing dialogic hermeneutics and the deliberative capacities of communities in focus groups. *Qualitative Inquiry, 12*(1), 81–95.

Gadamer, H. G. (1976). *Philosophical hermeneutics.* (D. E. Linge, Trans. and Ed.). Berkeley: University of California Press.

Gadamer, H. G. (1989a). *Truth and method* (2nd revised ed., J. Weinsheimer & D. G. Marshall, Trans.). New York: Continuum.

Gadamer, H. G. (1989b). Hermeneutics and logocentrism. In D. P. Michelfelder & R. E. Palmer (Eds.), *Dialogue and deconstruction: The Gadamer-Derrida encounter* (pp. 114–125, R. Palmer and D. Michelfelder, Trans.). Albany: State University of New York Press.

Gadamer, H. G. (2006). Language and understanding. *Theory, Culture & Society, 23*(1), 13–27.

Grondin, J. (1994). *Introduction to philosophical hermeneutics* (J. Weinsheimer, Trans.). New Haven, CT: Yale University Press.

Harrington, A. (2001). *Hermeneutic dialogue and social science: A critique of Gadamer and Habermas.* New York: Routledge.

Heidegger, M. (1962). *Being and time.* (J. Macquarrie & E. Robinson, Trans.). Oxford: Blackwell.

Hermans, H. J. M., Kempen, H. J. G., & van Loon, R. J. P. (1992). The dialogic self: Beyond individualism and rationalism. *American Psychologist, 47*(1), 23–33.

Hollander, J. A. (2004). The social contexts of focus groups. *Journal of Contemporary Ethnography, 33*(5), 602–637.

Hollander, J. A., & Gordon, H. R. (2006). The processes of social construction in talk. *Symbolic Interaction, 29*(2), 183–212.

Howe, K. R., & Moses, M. S. (1999). Ethics in educational research. *Review of Research in Education, 24,* 21–59.

Kamberelis, G., & Dimitriadis, G. (2005). Focus groups: Strategic articulations of pedagogy, politics, and inquiry. In N. K. Denzin & Y. S. Lincoln (Eds.), *Sage handbook of qualitative research* (3rd ed., pp. 887–907). Thousand Oaks, CA: Sage.

Kidd, P. S., & Parshall, M. B. (2000). Getting the focus and the group: Enhancing analytical rigor in focus group research. *Qualitative Health Research, 10*(3), 293–308.

Kitzinger, J. (1994). The methodology of focus groups: The importance of interaction between research participants. *Sociology of Health & Illness, 16*(1), 103–121.

Kitzinger, J., & Barbour, R. S. (1999). Introduction: The challenge and promise of focus groups. In R. S. Barbour & J. Kitzinger (Eds.), *Developing focus group research: Politics, theory and practice* (pp. 1–20). Thousand Oaks, CA: Sage.

Koppelman, N. F., & Bourjolly, J. N. (2001). Conducting focus groups with women with severe psychiatric disabilities: A methodological overview. *Psychiatric Rehabilitation Journal, 25*(2), 142–151.

Krueger, R., & Casey, M. A. (2009). *Focus groups: A practical guide for applied research* (4th ed.). Thousand Oaks, CA: Sage.

Long, N. H., Johansson, E., Diwan, V. K., & Winkvist, A. (1999). Different tuberculosis in men and women: beliefs from focus groups in Vietnam. *Social Science & Medicine, 49*(6), 815–822.

Madriz, E. (2000). Focus groups in feminist research. In N. K. Denzin & Y. S. Lincoln (Eds.), *Sage handbook of qualitative research* (2nd ed., pp. 835–850). Thousand Oaks, CA: Sage.

Matoesian, G. M., & Coldren, J. R. (2002). Language and bodily conduct in focus group evaluations of legal policy. *Discourse and Society, 13*(4), 469–493.

Merton, R. K. (1987). The focused interview and focus groups: Continuities and discontinuities. *Public Opinion Quarterly, 51,* 550–566.

Merton, R. K., Fiske, M., & Kendall, P. L. (1956). *The focused interview: A manual of problems and procedures.* New York: Free Press.

Merton, R. K., & Kendall, P. L. (1946). The focused interview. *American Journal of Sociology, 51*(6), 541–557.

Miles, S., & Kaplan, I. (2005). Using images to promote reflection: An action research study in Zambia and Tanzania. *Journal of Research in Special Educational Needs, 5*(2), 77–83.

Millward, L. J. (1994). Focus groups. In G. M. Breakwell, S. Hammond, C. Fife-Schaw, & J.A. Smith (Eds), *Research methods in psychology* (3rd ed.) (pp. 274–298). Thousand Oaks, CA: Sage.

Morgan, D. L. (1988). *Focus groups as qualitative research.* Thousand Oaks, CA: Sage.

Morgan, D. L. (1996). Focus groups. *Annual Review of Sociology, 22,* 129–152.

Morgan, D. L. (1997). *Focus groups as qualitative research* (2nd ed.). Thousand Oaks, CA: Sage.

Morrison, D. E. (1998). *The search for a method: Focus groups and the development of mass communication research.* Bedfordshire, UK: University of Luton Press.

Myers, G., & Macnaghten, P. (1999). Can focus groups be analysed as talk? In R. S. Barbour & J. Kitzinger (Eds.), *Developing focus group research: Politics, theory, and practice* (pp. 173–185). Thousand Oaks, CA: Sage.

Preissle, J. (2008). Ethical issues in qualitative research. In L. M. Given (Ed.), *The Sage encyclopedia of qualitative research methods* (pp. 276–277). Thousand Oaks, CA: Sage.

Robinson, N. (1999). The use of focus group methodology—with selected examples from sexual health research. *Journal of Advanced Nursing, 29*(4), 905–913.

Rubin, H. J., & Rubin, I. S. (2005). *Qualitative interviewing: The art of hearing data* (2nd ed.). Thousand Oaks, CA: Sage.

Schwandt, T. A. (2004). Hermeneutics: A poetics of inquiry versus a methodology for research. In H. Piper & I. Stronach (Eds.), *Educational research: Difference and diversity* (pp. 31–44). Burlington, VT: Ashgate.

Schwarz, M., Landis, S. E., Rowe, J. E., Janer, C. L., & Pullman, N. (2000). Using focus groups to assess primary care patients' satisfaction. *Evaluation and the Health Professions, 23*(1), 58–71.

Smit, B., & Cilliers, F. (2006). Understanding implicit texts in focus groups from a systems psychodynamic perspective. *The Qualitative Report, 11*(2), 302–316.

Smith, M. W. (1995). Ethics in focus groups: A few concerns. *Qualitative Health Research, 5*(4), 478–486.

Smithson, J. (2000). Using and analyzing focus groups: Limitations and possibilities. *International Journal of Social Research Methodology, 3*(2), 103–119.

Stewart, D. W., Shamdasani, P. N., & Rook, D. W. (2007). *Focus groups: Theory and practice* (2nd ed.). Thousand Oaks, CA: Sage.

Taylor, C. (1982). Interpretation and the sciences of man. In E. Bredo & W. Feinberg (Eds.), *Knowledge and values in social and educational research* (pp. 153–186). Philadelphia, PA: Temple University Press.

Taylor, C. (1991). The dialogical self. In D. R. Hiley, J. F. Bohman, & R. Shusterman (Eds.), *The interpretive turn: Philosophy, science, culture* (pp. 304–314). Ithaca, NY: Cornell University Press.

Taylor, C. (2002). Gadamer on the human sciences. In R. J. Dostal (Ed.), *The Cambridge companion to Gadamer* (pp. 126–142). New York: Cambridge University Press.

Warr, D. J. (2005). "It was fun … but we don't usually talk about these things": Analyzing sociable interaction in focus groups. *Qualitative Inquiry, 11*(2), 200–225.

Wilkinson, S. (1998a). Focus groups in feminist research: Power, interaction, and the co-construction of meaning. *Women's Studies International Forum, 21*(1), 111–125.

Wilkinson, S.. (1998b). Focus groups in health research: Exploring the meanings of health and illness. *Journal of Health Psychology, 3*(3), 329–348.

Wilkinson, S.. (2006). Analysing interaction in focus groups. In P. Drew, G. Raymond, and D. Weinberg (Eds.), *Talk and interaction in social research methods* (pp. 50–62). Thousand Oaks, CA: Sage.

CHAPTER EIGHT

Conversations as Research

Philosophies of the Interview[1]

SVEND BRINKMANN

As someone who is attracted to the use of conversations for research purposes, I am often struck by the magic of interviewing. Interviewing is magical because it enables researchers to study domains of human experience that no other research approaches are capable of. Asking people questions about their lives, opinions, and experiences, and allowing them freedom of expression in telling their stories, is a powerful method of understanding people's life worlds (Kvale & Brinkmann, 2008). Interviewing others can open up intimate aspects of people's lives in a way that is often taken for granted by interviewers as well as interviewees. Many interviewers will recognize the experience of having made an appointment with an interviewee, showing up in her home, and then, after a few minutes, witnessing the interviewee telling formerly untold stories and secrets that she may have never told anyone before. After an hour or two, the interviewer leaves, perhaps after giving the interviewee a box of chocolates, and the two conversationalists may never see each other again. The interviewee may be thrilled to have been given a chance to talk about intimate aspects of life to a complete stranger, or she may be shattered after having discovered previously unknown truths about her life.

This, to me, is pure magic. It can be white magic, when no one is harmed and everyone is in good faith, and it can be black magic if the interviewer, for example, engages in a "faking of friendship" in order to quickly establish "rapport" so that important information can be elicited to serve the researcher's purposes (Duncombe & Jessop, 2002). The qualitative research interviewer must strike a balance between the aim of producing knowledge and ethical respect for the integrity of the interviewee. The tension of the quest for knowledge and ethics in research interviewing has been well expressed by Richard Sennett:

> In-depth interviewing is a distinctive, often frustrating craft. Unlike a pollster asking questions, the in-depth interviewer wants to probe the responses people give. To probe, the interviewer cannot be stonily impersonal; he or she has to give something of himself or herself in order to merit an open response. Yet the conversation lists in one direction; the point is not to talk the way friends do. The interviewer all too frequently finds that he or she has offended subjects, transgressing a line over which only friends or intimates can cross. The craft consists in calibrating social distances without making the subject feel like an insect under the microscope. (Sennett, 2004, pp. 37–38).

Based on readings of current interview reports, and supported by Sennett's observations, it is my impression that qualitative interviewers today are often acting as either pollsters, by passively recording people's attitudes, opinions, and experiences, or as probers aiming to enter the private worlds of the interviewees to uncover concealed aspects of their lives, for example by working with what has been called "a method of friendship" (Fontana & Frey, 2005). In the first case of the pollster, a receptive, nondirective practice is followed, where the implicit model of the interviewer often resembles Carl Rogers, who developed client-centered therapy and nondirective interviewing (Rogers, 1945). In postmodern approaches, this practice is sometimes conceptualized as polyphonic interviewing "where the voices of the respondents are recorded with minimal influence from the researcher" (Fontana & Prokos, 2007, p. 53). In the second case of the prober, a therapeutic practice of intimacy is followed, where the probing interviewer sometimes appears in the guise of a psychoanalyst. Both forms are, as I shall explain, quite psychologistic, in being concerned with the individual's experiences, opinions, and narratives.

There are risks involved in both roles of pollster and prober: The pollster risks producing research that is trivial; that is, research that merely reproduces common knowledge and opinions and does not take advantage of the potentials inherent in human conversations, where both parties have a chance of getting wiser through talking. The prober, on the other hand, constantly risks transgressing the line of intimacy, as pointed out by Sennett.

In this chapter, I wish to develop an understanding of interviewing, where the interviewer appears neither as a quasi-quantitative pollster nor as a quasi-therapeutic prober. I do not mean to suggest that these are counterproductive or unethical practices per se. Indeed, important and ethically decent research projects have been conducted based on both of these models. But I do wish to suggest that both models are overused in qualitative inquiry today. Both models work with an implicit view of knowledge as *doxa* (a Greek word for opinion), whereas I am interested in how conversations can help us produce knowledge in the sense of *episteme* (the Greek term for knowledge that has been arrived at through dialectical processes of questioning).

The greatest epistemic interviewer in history was no doubt Socrates, who will serve as my main source of inspiration for an alternative to nondirective and therapeutic forms of interviewing. Along the way, my goal will be to explore four different philosophies of interviewing that differ on two axes: First in terms of interviewer style—nondirective versus confronting style—or receptive versus assertive, to use Wengraf's terminology (2001). And second in terms of epistemic ambitions, and I here introduce the continuum of doxastic versus epistemic interviewing (Brinkmann, 2007), which I have depicted in Figure 1, below. The different forms of interviewing are connected to different philosophical positions, face diverse ethical and methodological challenges, invite participants into different kinds of subject positions, and draw on different social practices.

Interviews and Conversational Realities

Conversations have been used for research purposes at least since Thucydides interviewed the participants from the Peloponnesian Wars in order to write their history (Kvale & Brinkmann, 2008). In a philosophical sense, all human research is conversational, since we are linguistic creatures and language is best understood in terms of the figure of conversation (Mulhall, 2007). Since the late 19th century (in journalism) and the early 20th century (in the social sciences), the conversational process of knowing has been conceptualized and refined under the name of "interviewing." Like "dialogue" and "conversation," the very term "interview" testifies to the dialogical and interactional nature of human life. An interview is literally an inter-view, an interchange of views between two persons, conversing about a theme of mutual interest. "Con-versation" in its Latin root means "dwelling with someone" or "wandering together with," and the root sense of "dia-logue" is that of talk (logos) that goes back and forth (dia-) between persons (Mannheim & Tedlock, 1995, p. 4). Thus conceived, the concept of conversation in the human and social sciences is much broader than simply referring to interviewing as yet another empirical method. Conversations are indeed a set of techniques, but also a mode of knowing and a fundamental ontology of persons, which I will now briefly address.

First, the research interview can be treated as a specific professional form of conversational technique in which knowledge is constructed through the interaction of interviewer and interviewee (Kvale & Brinkmann, 2008). In contrast to the reciprocal interchanges of everyday life, it is normally the interviewer who, as a professional, asks and the interviewee who answers. Second, the conversation may be conceived of as a basic mode of knowing. The certainty of our social knowledge is a matter of conversation between persons, rather than a matter of interaction with a nonhuman reality. Third, on an ontological level, human reality itself may be understood as conversational. As Rom Harré has put it: "The primary human reality is persons in conversation" (Harré, 1983, p. 58). Cultures are constantly produced, reproduced, and revised in dialogues among their members (Mannheim & Tedlock, 1995, p. 2). This also goes for the cultural investigation of social phenomena, or what we call social science. We should see language and culture as emergent properties of dialogues rather than the other way around. Conversations—dialogues—are not several monologues added together, but the basic, primordial form of associated human life. In other words, "we live our daily social lives within an ambience of conversation, discussion, argumentation, negotiation, criticism and justification; much of it to do with problems of intelligibility and the legitimation of claims to truth" (Shotter, 1993, p. 29).

Not only is our interpersonal social reality constituted by conversations, so is the self. Charles Taylor argues that the self exists only within what he calls "webs of interlocution" (Taylor, 1989, p. 36). We are selves only in relation to certain interlocutors with whom we are in conversation and from whom we gain a language of self-understanding. In referring to Heidegger's concept of Dasein—or human existence—philosopher Stephen Mulhall, author of the aptly entitled book *The Conversation of Humanity*, states that "Dasein is not just the locus and the precondition for the conversation of humankind; it is itself, because humankind is, a kind of enacted conversation" (Mulhall, 2007, p. 58). We understand ourselves as well as others only because we can speak, and "being able to speak involves being able to converse" (p. 26). Human reality is a conversational reality.

From these philosophers, psychologists, and social theorists, we get the idea that the conversation is not only a specific empirical method: It also involves a view of the self and the human world. The idea that humankind is a kind of enacted conversation gives the interview a privileged position in producing knowledge about the conversational world. The processes of our lives—actions, thoughts, and emotions—are nothing but physiology if considered as isolated elements outside of conversations and interpretative contexts. A life, as Paul Ricoeur has said, "is no more than a biological phenomenon as long as it has not been interpreted" (Ricoeur, 1991, p. 28). The phenomena of our lives must be seen as *responses* to people, situations, and events. As responses, they are conversational and dialogical, for, to quote Alasdair MacIntyre, "conversation, understood widely enough, is the form of human transactions in general" (MacIntyre, 1985, p. 211). When people are talking, as in research interviews, they are not simply putting preconceived ideas into words, but are dialogically responding to each other's expressions and trying to make sense by using the narratives and discourses that are available (Shotter, 1993, p. 1).

However, if conversations are the stuff that human life is made of, it becomes pertinent to study the specific qualities of our conversations and ask what kinds of persons we become through different forms of conversation. What forms of life and subject positions do interviews create and reproduce? These are some of the questions that I will address in the remaining parts of this chapter.

Varieties of Research Interviewing

One reason behind the current popularity of interviewing is that it is rightly regarded as a powerful method for investigating people's lives, and many see it as a democratic and emancipatory form of social research (however, see Kvale, 2006, and Brinkmann & Kvale, 2005, for a critique of the emancipatory potentials of interviews). Another reason may be that the practice of interviewing is close to something that everyone masters, viz. everyday conversations, which gives it an air of simplicity. Interviewing seems easy to do, at least easier than working with statistical analyses. We all know how to talk with others, don't we? I believe that the simplicity of interviewing is illusory. It is tempting to start interviewing without any preceding preparation or reflection. A novice researcher may have a good idea, grab a sound recorder, go out and find some research participants, and start questioning them. The recorded interviews are transcribed and then, during the analysis of the many pages of transcripts, a multitude of problems about the purpose and content of the interviews surface. The likelihood that such spontaneous interview studies lead to worthwhile information is meager; rather than producing new substantial knowledge about a topic, such interviews may be reproducing common opinions and prejudices (Kvale & Brinkmann, 2008).

The outcome of many such studies is—to use the classical Greek term—"doxa." It can be interesting and important to learn about opinions and attitudes, but when viewed through the lenses of classical philosophy, the outcome will rarely constitute knowledge in the sense of "episteme," that is, knowledge that has been found to be valid through conversational and dialectical questioning. By recording their respondents' experiences and opinions (the doxa), interview researchers are often engaged in what seems like a time-consuming kind of opinion-polling, for which quantitative instruments such as questionnaires often appear to be much more efficient. But let me explain in greater detail how interviews today are frequently "doxastic."

Doxastic Interviews

Several approaches may illustrate the doxastic aspect of current forms of interviewing. Empirical phenomenology is one example. It has long been advocated and brought to considerable sophistication by Amedeo Giorgi (Giorgi & Giorgi, 2003), among others. The first step in the descriptive phenomenological method, according to Giorgi, is to obtain "descriptions of experiences from others" (p. 247), before entering into a scientific phenomenological reduction, ending up with "the essential structure of the experience" (p. 247). Clearly, Giorgi's starting point is in the respondents' experiences, the doxa, although the goal of phenomenological interviewing is to arrive at knowledge in the sense of episteme. The point is, however, that the central part of the process of reaching episteme is confined to what happens after the interview conversation, when the interviewer can engage in scientific analysis of the material (by employing the phenomenological reduction and the epoché). During the interview, the phenomenological interviewer will ask for descriptions of concrete experiences such as "Please describe for me a time in your life when you experienced internalized homophobia" (p. 263). The interviewer follows up on the descriptions by asking the respondent to "tell more," and "what happened next?" etc. (p. 264). Usually, there will not be questions that concern the meaning of internalized homophobia, for example, and very few questions where the respondent is challenged and asked for justifications or reflections.

Others have found inspiration in psychotherapy proper, for example psychoanalysis. Wendy Hollway and Tony Jefferson's psychoanalytic idea of "the defended subject" is a case in point (Hollway & Jefferson, 2000). In their eyes, the qualitative interview researcher is always closer to the truth than the research subject, for "subjects are motivated *not* to know certain aspects of themselves and…they *produce* biographical accounts which avoid such knowledge" (p. 169, italics in the original text). In this perspective, the respondents can give away only doxa and the researcher-therapists are in a unique position to obtain episteme, given their superior theoretical knowledge and psychoanalytic training. This, I would say, is a psychologistic framing of the interview, which states that we only know what is going on in human conversations because of special psychological training. The model for the relation between interviewer and interviewee consequently becomes that of psychotherapist and patient, where the patient is cast in the experiencing, suffering position, and the therapist in the knowing position.

There are many other schools of psychotherapy, however, and a quite different psychologization of the interview is found in Carl Rogers' early "non-directive method as a technique for social research," as mentioned above (Rogers, 1945). As Rogers explained, the goal of this kind of therapy/research is to sample the respondent's attitudes toward herself: "Through the non-directive interview we have an unbiased method by which we may plumb these private thoughts and perceptions of the individual" (p. 282). In contrast to psychoanalytic practice, the respondent in client-centered therapy/research is a client rather than a patient, and the client is the expert. Although often framed in different terms, I believe that many contemporary interview researchers conceptualize the research interview in line with Rogers' humanistic, nondirective approach, valorizing the respondents' private experiences, narratives, opinions, beliefs, and attitudes, which can be captured with the concept of doxa. "Empathetic interviewing" (Fontana & Frey, 2005), for example, involves taking a stance in favor of the persons being studied, not unlike the positive regard displayed by Rogerian therapists, and the approach is depicted as at once a "method of friendship" and a humanistic "method of morality because it attempts to restore the sacredness of humans before addressing any theoretical or methodological concerns" (p. 697). In line with an implicit therapeutic metaphor, the interview is turned "into a walking stick to help some people get on their feet" (p. 695). This is a laudable intention that is often fruitful, but there seems to be significant limitations to such forms of interviewing as well, not least that it becomes difficult to interview people with whom one disagrees and does not want to help (e.g., neo-Nazis).

Attempts to include the researcher's experience in interview research, for example as described by Ellis and Berger (2003), also often focus on doxastic experience, and the interviewer is presented in a therapeutic vein as someone who "listens empathically" and "identifies with participants, and shows respect for participants' emotionality" (pp. 469–470). Ellis and Berger also refer to a number of interview researchers who "emphasize the positive therapeutic benefits that can accrue to respondents and interviewers who participate in interactive interviews" (p. 470), and one experiential form of qualitative inquiry in particular, "mediated co-constructed narratives," is presented as "similar to conjoint marital therapy" (p. 477) where a couple jointly constructs an epiphany in their relationship, with the interviewer/therapist acting as moderator. In doxastic interviews that focus on experiences, opinions, and attitudes, knowing the experiencing self is seen as presupposed in knowing as such. For a key point in these forms of interviewing is that "*Understanding ourselves is part of the process of understanding others*" (Ellis & Berger, 2003, p. 486, italics in the original text). This can be interpreted as analogous to therapists' own need for therapy in their professional development.

As Rogers knew, the most efficient way of eliciting private doxastic elements is by engaging in a warm and accepting relationship, in line with the principles of client-centered psychotherapy (Rogers advocated what he called unconditional positive regard). A clear example of this is found in *Becoming Qualitative Researchers* (Glesne & Peshkin, 1992), which also implicitly illustrates what I take to be an ethical challenge inherent in the client-centered approach: That human feelings are instrumentalized in order to achieve a successful outcome, viz. a "full disclosure" of the respondent's private world (the ethical problems of this are discussed in Brinkmann & Kvale, 2005; and Duncombe & Jessop, 2002):

> trust is the foundation for acquiring the fullest, most accurate disclosure a respondent is able to make.... In an effective interview, both researcher and respondent feel good, rewarded and satisfied by the process and the outcomes. The warm and caring researcher is on the way to achieving such effectiveness. (Glesne & Peshkin, 1992, pp. 79, 87). Trust and empathy are positive properties in relationships, but they can also be used instrumentally in an "effective interview" to obtain a "disclosure."

I believe we may read the spread of psychologistic or doxastic interviews as a reflection of the contemporary consumer society where the client is always right, where his or her experiences and narratives are always interesting because they are some individual's experiences and narratives, and where the interviewer (or therapist) merely acts as a mirror of the respondent's feelings, attitudes, and beliefs. We live in an "experience society" to quote the German sociologist Gerhard Schulze (1992), and the interview is a central technology for sampling and circulating experiences, not just in research contexts, but also in confessional talk-shows and marketized focus groups (Kvale, 2006). The experience society is also an "interview society" (Atkinson & Silverman, 1997), where the interview serves as a social technique for the public construction of the self. Obviously, there is no direct link between the Rogerian interview (or other doxastic interview forms) and confessional talk shows in current consumer societies, and Rogers and other pioneers cannot be held responsible for how this conversational technique has developed and is used today. In fact, we can say that there is as big a gulf between Rogers' original ideas and a confessional talk show or marketized focus group as there is between a Socratic dialogue and a confrontational Bill O'Reilly interview on television.[2] All conversational practices can be used in productive as well as doubtful ways. The point should therefore not be to discard the doxastic interview in light of certain questionable societal developments, but simply to question the fact that this specific construction of the interview is so often taken for granted as the only relevant form. A nondirective, caring, and empathetic approach to interviews is neither ethical nor unethical per se.

It is thus possible to question an unreflective use of doxastic interviews for ethical reasons (more on this below), but equally so for epistemic reasons. In the 1950s, David Riesman warned against the tendency to use the level of "rapport" in an interview to judge its qualities concerning knowledge. He thought it was a prejudice, "often based on psychoanalytic stereotypes, to assume the more rapport-filled and intimate the relation, the more 'truth' the respondent will vouchsafe" (Riesman & Benney, 1956, p. 10). Rapport-filled interviews often spill over with "the flow of legend and cliché" (p. 11), according to Riesman's verdict, where interviewees adapt their responses to what they take the interviewer expects from them (see Lee, 2008; and for a related analysis that puts weight on participants' objections during the interview, see Tanggaard, 2008). The researcher is unavoidably, yet subtly, playing a part in the interview, even in its most nondirective forms, and there are certain advantages to making the interviewer's influence more visible in the conversation, which is one ambition of the more epistemic versions of interviewing.

What, then, are the alternatives to doxastic interviews? In the coordinate system below, I have tried to plot four approaches to interviewing that differ on two axes. The term "receptive" comes from Wengraf (2001), who opposes it to "assertive" styles. He explicitly aligns the receptive practice with Rogers's model of psychotherapy, which seeks to empower the informant (p. 154), and the assertive practice with legal interrogations where the interviewer is in control and seeks to provoke and illuminate self-contradictions (p. 155). Wengraf cites Holstein and Gubrium's (1995) "active interviewing" as a form of assertive interviewing practice (but, like most researchers, he favors the receptive style).

So far, I have mainly addressed the two approaches at the bottom, which are both varieties of the receptive style. One form, the "nondirective," Rogerian, or polyphonic form, clearly advocates a receptive interviewer style, and the knowledge ambitions are doxastic. The other phenomenological form of interviewing (e.g., Giorgi's) does have epistemic ambitions, in the sense of arriving at knowledge about general features of human experience (phenomenological "essences"), but the epistemic process is confined to what happens after, rather than during, the interview. For that reason, I have placed it on the epistemic side, although it frames the interview situation itself as doxastic.

Below, I shall deal in greater detail with the assertive, epistemic practice of interviewing, *in casu* the Socratic form. However, there is also the fourth quadrant of the assertive, doxastic form, where Holstein and Gubrium probably belong. Interviews are, as they have argued, unavoidably interpretively active, meaning-making practices (Holstein & Gubrium, 1995). Nevertheless, the Socratic approach goes beyond the experiential focus that still dominates

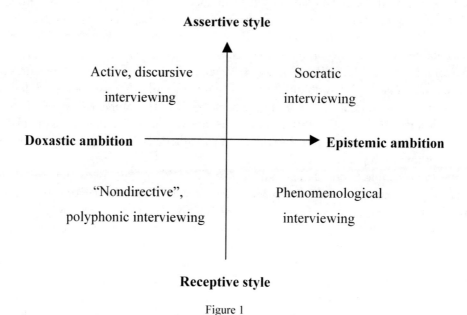

Figure 1

active interviewing, including the practices of those researchers that experiment "with alternative representational forms that they believe can convey respondents' experience more on, if not in, their own terms" (Holstein & Gubrium, 2003, p. 20). Unlike Holstein and Gubrium's active interviews, epistemic interviews are not primarily about conveying experience (doxa) at all, but a practice of developing knowledge (episteme). Discourse analysts such as Potter and Wetherell can also be placed in the upper-left quadrant. In a classic text, they describe the active, constructive role of the interview researcher and summarize discourse analytic interviewing as follows:

> First, variation in response is as important as consistency. Second, techniques which allow diversity rather than those which eliminate it are emphasized, resulting in more informal conversational exchanges and, third, interviewers are seen as active participants rather than like speaking questionnaires. (Potter & Wetherell 1987, p. 165)

Variation, diversity, informality, and an active interviewer are the key words, but the process is nonetheless seen as resulting in doxa, that is, in articulations of the "interpretative repertoires" of the interviewees, but without the interviewer necessarily investigating the legitimacy of these repertoires in the interview situation or the respondent's ways of justifying them.

Epistemic Interviews

Before moving on to characterize epistemic interviews, I need to address the dangerous word "knowledge" without getting entangled in endless epistemological debates; for if doxa concerns our opinions and beliefs, episteme concerns our knowledge. But what does it mean to know something? The term "knowledge" is immensely complex, and the search for necessary and sufficient conditions for knowing is probably futile. "Knowledge" is most likely a concept with a family resemblance structure such as that described by Wittgenstein in the *Philosophical Investigations* (1953). Yet I believe that an essential normativity runs through the processes and states that we refer to as "knowing." When we characterize an episode or a state as one of knowing, philosopher Wilfrid Sellars argued, "we are not giving an empirical description of that episode or state; we are placing it in the logical space of reasons, of justifying and being able to justify what one says" (Sellars, 1956/1997, p. 76).

With this, Sellars wanted to emphasize that when we talk about an episode as one of knowing, we necessarily raise the issue of its normative status. Thus, in order for something to count as knowledge, we have to be able to justify what we think we know. That a belief is true is not enough for it to count as knowledge, for the true belief may be the result of a lucky guess. So saying that something is knowledge does not involve describing it empirically, or placing it in what Sellars called "the space of causation." A belief may be caused by many different processes in my brain, my mind, or my social group, but when we call it "knowledge," we are not talking about what caused it empirically, but whether it can be *justified* normatively. That is, we place it in what Sellars called "the logical space of reasons"—a space of justification and accounting practices.

That knowledge is a normative concept that involves reference to a shared "space of reasons" is old news in philosophy. Plato's dialogues were precisely designed as ways of testing whether the conversation partners have knowledge, that is, whether they are capable of adequately justifying their beliefs, and if they cannot (which is normally the case), if their beliefs are unwarranted, the dialogues unfold as dialectical processes of refining their beliefs—their doxa—in light of good reasons, in order to approach episteme. In Plato's dialogues, knowledge is produced discursively as the conversation partners test each other's beliefs. I am aware that the Platonic notion of the realm of eternal ideas is unsupportable today, and I have no intention of rehabilitating it. I believe, however, that the discursive practice of producing knowledge through conversations, represented in the Platonic dialogues, can fruitfully serve as inspiration for doing research interviews today, particularly when freed from the heavy metaphysics developed in Plato's writings (and it is indeed an open question to what extent Socrates would endorse Plato's philosophical machinery; after all, we should bear in mind that Socrates was a philosopher who did not write but engaged in "performative philosophy" through the spoken word in the present, whereas Plato possibly wanted to "freeze" knowledge for all eternity due to his ideational conception of knowledge).

In order to illustrate more concretely what I mean by epistemic interviews, I shall give a simple and very short example from Plato's *The Republic*. It very elegantly demonstrates epistemically that no moral rules are self-applying or self-interpreting, but must always be understood contextually. Socrates is in a conversation with Cephalus, who believes that justice— "dikaiosune," here meaning "doing right"—can be stated in universal rules, such as "tell the truth" and "return borrowed items":

> 'That's fair enough, Cephalus,' I [Socrates] said. 'But are we really to say that doing right consists simply and solely in truthfulness and returning anything we have borrowed? Are those not actions that can be sometimes right and sometimes wrong? For instance, if one borrowed a weapon from a friend who subsequently went out of his mind and then asked for it back, surely it would be generally agreed that one ought not to return it, and that it would not be right to do so, not to consent to tell the strict truth to a madman?'

'That is true,' he [Cephalus] replied.

'Well then, I [Socrates] said, 'telling the truth and returning what we have borrowed is not the definition of doing right.' (Plato, 1987, pp. 65–66)

Here, the conversation is interrupted by Polemarchus, who disagrees with Socrates's preliminary conclusion, and Cephalus quickly leaves in order to go to a sacrifice. Then Polemarchus takes Cephalus's position as Socrates's discussion partner and the conversation continues as if no substitution had happened.

Initially, we may notice that Socrates violates almost every standard principle of qualitative research interviewing. First, we can see that he talks much more than his respondent. There is some variety across the dialogues concerning how much Socrates talks in comparison with the other participants, but the example given here, where Socrates develops an absurd conclusion from the initial belief voiced by Cephalus, is not unusual, although the balance is much more equal in other places. Second, Socrates has not asked Cephalus to "describe a situation in which he has experienced justice" or "tell a story about doing right from his own experience" or a similar concretely descriptive question, probing for "lived experience." Instead, they are talking about the definition of an important general concept. Third, Socrates contradicts and challenges his respondent's view. He is not a warm and caring conversationalist, working with "a methodology of friendship." Fourth, there is no debriefing or attempt to make sure that the interaction was "a pleasant experience" for Cephalus. Fifth, the interview is conducted in public rather than private, and the topic is not private experiences or biographical details, but justice, a theme of common human interest, at least of interest to all citizens of Athens.

Sixth, and perhaps most importantly, the interview here is radically anti-psychologistic. Interestingly, it does not make much of a difference whether the conversation partner is Cephalus or Polemarchus—and the discussion continues in exactly the same way after Cephalus has left. The crux of the discussion is whether the participants are able to give good reasons for their belief in a public discussion, not whether they have this or that biographical background or defense mechanism, for example. The focus is on what they say—and whether it can be normatively justified—not on dubious psychological interpretations concerning why they say it, neither during the conversation, nor in some process of analysis after the conversation. In the words of Norwegian philosopher Hans Skjervheim (1957), the "researcher" (Socrates) is a participant, who takes seriously what his fellow citizen says—seriously enough to disagree with it, in fact. He is not a spectator who objectifies the conversation partner and his arguments by ignoring the normative claims of the statements, or looks at them in terms of the causes (psychological or sociological) that may have brought the person to entertain such beliefs. To use Sellars's concepts introduced above: The conversation is conducted with reference to the normative space of reasons rather than the space of causation.

With the help of Christine Sorrell Dinkins, we can outline the general principles of Socratic, epistemic interviewing, which Dinkins refers to as "Socratic-hermeneutic interpre-viewing" (Dinkins, 2005). Dinkins is dissatisfied with "phenomenological interviewing," which "calls forth long narratives from the respondent, with few interruptions or prompts from the interviewer, in order to allow the respondents' stories to unfold naturally" (p. 112). Although not couched in exactly these terms, I believe that Dinkins here has in mind what I call doxastic interviewing, and her Socratic alternative corresponds quite closely to my epistemic version of interviewing. Socrates' "method" is not a method in the conventional sense, as Dinkins makes clear, but an "elenchus," a Greek term that means examining a person and considering his or her statements normatively. The Socratic conversation is a mode of understanding, rather than a method in any mechanical sense (cf. Gadamer, 1960/2000). In Dinkins's rendition, the elenchus proceeds as follows (and we can bear in mind the small excerpt from *The Republic* cited above):

> Socrates encounters someone who takes an action or makes a statement into which Socrates wishes to inquire.
>
> Socrates asks the person for a definition of the relevant central concept, which is then offered.
>
> Together, Socrates and the respondent [or "co-inquirer" to use Dinkins's term] deduce some consequences of the definition.
>
> Socrates points out a possible conflict between the deduced consequences and another belief held by the respondent. The respondent is then given the choice of rejecting the belief or the definition.
>
> Usually, the respondent rejects the definition, because the belief is too central—epistemically or existentially—to be given up.
>
> A new definition is offered, and the steps are repeated (adapted from Dinkins, 2005, p. 124).

Sometimes, the conversation partners in the Platonic dialogues settle on a definition, but more often the dialogue ends without any final, unarguable definition of the central concept (e.g., justice, virtue, love). This lack of resolution—"aporia" in Greek—can be interpreted as illustrating the open-ended character of our conversational reality, including the open-ended character of the discursively produced knowledge of human social and historical life generated by (what we today call) the social sciences. If humankind is a kind of enacted conversation, the goal of social science should not be to arrive at "fixed knowledge" once and for all, but to help human beings improve the quality of their conversational reality, to help them know their own society and social practices and debate the goals and values that are important in their lives (Flyvbjerg, 2001). This is what Robert Bellah has called social science as public philosophy (Bellah, Madsen, Sullivan, Swidler, & Tipton, 1985).

Michel Foucault (2001) also discussed Socrates's conversational practices in some of his last writings, and the quotation below nicely brings out the normative and epistemic dimensions of Socratic interviewing. When Socrates asks people to give accounts, "what is involved is not a confessional autobiography," Foucault makes clear (p. 97). Instead:

> In Plato's or Xenophon's portrayals of him, we never see Socrates requiring an examination of conscience or a confession of sins. Here, giving an account of your life, your *bios*, is also not to give a narrative of the historical events that have taken place in your life, but rather to demonstrate whether you are able to show that there is a relation between the rational discourse, the *logos*, you are able to use, and the way that you live. Socrates is inquiring into the way that *logos* gives form to a person's style of life. (Foucault, 2001, p. 97)

Socrates was engaged in conversational practices where people, in giving accounts of themselves, exhibited the logos by which they lived (Butler, 2005, p. 126). The conversation partners were thus positioned as responsible citizens, accountable to each other with reference to the normative order in which they acted, and the conversational topic would therefore not be the narrative of the individual's life, or his or her experiences, but rather people's epistemic practices of justification.

Also the hermeneutic philosopher Gadamer drew inspiration from the Socratic art of asking questions. We begin to question, Gadamer argued, not simply for fun, but when "we are shocked by things that do not accord with our expectations. Thus questioning too is more a passion than an action. A question presses itself on us; we can no longer avoid it and persist in our accustomed opinion" (1960/2000, p. 366). We use conversations exactly to move away from mere opinion to arrive at something more trustworthy. And Gadamer goes on to describe the Socratic dialectic as an art of questioning that is not a simple technique that can be taught as such. It is an art, Gadamer says, which is "reserved to the person who wants to know—i.e., who already has questions" (p. 366). And further, consider the following precise articulation of what is involved in the art of questioning:

> The art of dialectic is not the art of being able to win every argument. On the contrary, it is possible that someone practicing the art of dialectic—i.e., the art of questioning and of seeking truth—comes off worse in the argument in the eyes of those listening to it. As the art of asking questions, dialectic proves its value because only the person who knows how to ask questions is able to persist in his questioning, which involves being able to preserve his orientation toward openness. The art of questioning is the art of questioning even further—i.e., the art of thinking. It is called dialectic because it is the art of conducting a real dialogue. (Gadamer, 1960/2000, p. 367)

According to Socrates and hermeneuticists such as Gadamer, the capacity to converse goes hand in hand with the possibility of growth in our understanding (see also Mulhall, 2007, p. 22).

Epistemic Interviews Today

After having characterized in some detail the philosophical ideas behind epistemic interviewing, it seems pertinent to ask whether this approach to interviewing is possible today, or whether it should be considered as an ancient Hellenic practice that is no longer viable. I support the former idea, and I believe that it is possible to point to a number of significant interview studies that have employed some version of the Socratic approach, perhaps not in a pure form, but nonetheless in a form that seeks to distance itself from doxastic interviewing.

In *Habits of the Heart*, Bellah and co-writers (1985) refer to "active interviews," which correspond quite well to epistemic interviews, and represent one worked-out alternative to the standard doxastic interviews that probe for private meanings and opinions. In the appendix to their classic study of North American values and character, the researchers spell out their view of social science and its methodology, summarized as "social science as public philosophy." The empirical material for their book consisted of interviews with more than 200 participants, of which some were interviewed more than once. In contrast to the interviewer as a friend or therapist, probing deep in the private psyche of the interviewee, Bellah and co-workers practiced active interviews, which were intended to generate public conversation about societal values and goals. Such active interviews do not necessarily aim for agreement between interviewer and interviewee, and there is consequently no danger of instrumentalization of the researcher's feelings in order to obtain good rapport. The interviewer is allowed to question and challenge what the interviewee says. In one of the examples cited, the interviewer, Ann Swidler, is trying to get the respondent to clarify the basis of his moral judgments crystallized in his statement that "lying is one of the things I want to regulate." Swidler asks him why:

A: Well, it's a kind of thing that is a habit you get into. Kind of self-perpetuating. It's like digging a hole. You just keep digging and digging.

Q: So why is it wrong?

A: Why is integrity important and lying bad? I don't know. It just is. It's just so basic. I don't want to be bothered with challenging that. It's part of me. I don't know where it came from, but it's very important.

Q: When you think about what's right and what's wrong, are things bad because they are bad for people, or are they right and wrong in themselves, and if so how do you know?

A: Well some things are bad because... I guess I feel like everybody on this planet is entitled to have a little bit of space, and things that detract from other people's space are kind of bad... (Bellah et al., 1985, pp. 304–305).

Swidler challenges the respondent to examine why lying is wrong, which is quite a hard philosophical question, and the final question cited—concerning why wrong things are wrong—seems very complex, and, in standard textbooks on interviewing, the question could appear as an example of how not to pose an interview question. The question is abstract and invites high conceptual reflection rather than concrete description. It very much resembles Socrates's questions in the dialogues. In the next example, the interviewer, Steven Tipton, tries to discover at what point the respondent would take responsibility for another human being:

Q: So what are you responsible for?

A: I'm responsible for my acts and for what I do.

Q: Does that mean you're responsible for others, too?

A: No.

Q: Are you your sister's keeper?

A: No.

Q: Your brother's keeper?

A: No.

Q: Are you responsible for your husband?

A: I'm not. He makes his own decisions. He is his own person. He acts his own acts. I can agree with them or I can disagree with them. If I ever find them nauseous enough, I have a responsibility to leave and not deal with it any more.

Q: What about children?

A: I… I would say I have a legal responsibility for them, but in a sense I think they in turn are responsible for their own acts (Bellah et al., 1985, p. 304).

Here, Tipton repeatedly challenges the respondent's claim of not being responsible for other human beings. With the Socratic principles in mind, we can see the interviewer pressing for a contradiction between the respondent's definition of responsibility, involving the idea that she is only responsible for herself, and her likely feeling of at least some (legal) responsibility for her children. The individualist notion of responsibility is almost driven ad absurdum, but the definition apparently plays such a central role in the person's life that she is unwilling to give it up. I would argue that this way of interviewing, although not asking for concrete descriptions or narratives, gives us important knowledge primarily about the doxastic individualist beliefs of Americans in the mid-eighties, but secondarily about the idea of responsibility in a normative-epistemic sense. For most readers would appreciate the above sequence as implying the argument that the respondent is wrong—she *is* responsible for other people, most clearly her children. At the very least, the reader is invited into an epistemic discussion not just about beliefs, but also about citizenship, virtue, responsibility, and ethics. The authors of *Habits of the Heart* conclude that unlike "poll data" generated by fixed questions that "sum up the *private* opinions," active (epistemic) interviews "create the possibility of *public* conversation and argument" (Bellah et al., 1985, p. 305). We are far away from the pollster and the traditional doxastic view of social science interviews, portraying these as ways of understanding what people privately think, feel, and want.

Few interview studies that incorporate epistemic aspects do so in a pure form. Normally, studies will have epistemic aspects side by side with more doxastic ones. Many doxastic interviews will also include probing questions that resemble some of the questions found in the Socratic interviews above, so in most cases there is not a clear boundary between doxastic and epistemic elements. This also characterizes my own research practice. In a study of clinical psychologists' moral experiences, I tried consciously to employ a combination (Brinkmann, 2006). I found inspiration in Socrates's practice and asked the respondents challenging questions about how to understand and define the concept of ethics:

INTERVIEWER: How do you understand the words morality and ethics? What do they mean?

PSYCHOLOGIST: Well, morality is something invented by us humans, right. It is a kind of rules about how to relate to one another, so to say. That is what I think about it.

I also asked them about concrete experiences of ethical dilemmas, as in the following excerpt (concerning a client's romantic attraction to the psychotherapist) where the psychologist continues:

PSYCHOLOGIST: Then, suddenly, one feels the ethical dilemma, right.

INTERVIEWER: Do you feel it?

PSYCHOLOGIST: I do feel it. I feel it immediately, right. That—oops—now you have to be careful, right. What is it you are about to do in this instance?

Across the interviews more generally, morality was conceptualized reflectively with words like "timetable," "set of directions," "basic rules," "rules of behavior," and "regulating values." This contrasts with the practitioners' moral narratives, where they talk about "intuition," "feelings," and notably "the stomach" as an ethical indicator, as in "sometimes I can feel it in my stomach what is right and wrong" and "sometimes I definitely have a feeling, it's a sensation in the stomach like: ouch! That was bad!" On a conceptual level, ethics was overwhelmingly described as "rules for behavior," whereas reference to rules was absent when concrete examples were given, and respondents talked very often about the importance of gut feelings, rather than guidelines, principles, and rules in their stories of dealing with concrete moral problems. I used these contradictions in the psychotherapists' statements to investigate in a mildly confronting manner the dissimilarity between the theoretical and the practical understanding of morality in their practice, and I tried to challenge them concerning their implicit and explicit definitions of ethics (for further details, see Brinkmann, 2006; and for more analyses of recent epistemic interviewing practices, see Brinkmann, 2007).

Ethico-Political Issues

The project of developing the epistemic potentials of interviewing is allied, I believe, with other recent explorations of alternative interview forms, for example Norman Denzin's (2001) idea of performance interviews in the "cinematic-interview society." Denzin formulates "a utopian project," searching for a new form of the interview, which he calls "the reflexive, dialogic, or performative interview" (p. 24). The "utopian project" of epistemic interviewing outlined above, however, has a more explicit emphasis on civic responsibility. Qualitative researchers are increasingly becoming aware that interviewing, as Charles Briggs (2003, p. 497) has argued, is "a 'technology' that invents both notions of individual subjectivities and collective social and political patterns." Different conversational practices, including research interviews, produce and activate different forms of subjectivity. Thus, ethico-political issues are always internal to practices of interviewing. Epistemic interviews position respondents as accountable, responsible citizens, which I have presented as an alternative to experience-focused, psychologized interviews that position respondents as clients or patients.

Qualitative research in social science serves—and should serve—many different purposes. One legitimate purpose is to throw light on people's private experiences and opinions. It is difficult to learn about lived experience in prisons, schools, and factories, for example, without the use of experience-focused interviewing. But according to an older view of social science that goes back to Plato and notably Aristotle (1976), the social sciences are practical sciences that should ideally enable the creation of a knowledgeable citizenry capable of discussing matters of communal value (this was also John Dewey's view; see Brinkmann, 2004). Social science should serve the political community in the sense of engaging this community in conversations about ethical, political, and other normative issues. Qualitative social science, according to this view, should not just serve to bring forth privatized narratives or other intimate aspects of people's lives. It should also serve the *Res Publica*, that is, the ethical and political relations between human beings that are not constituted by intimacy (Sennett, 1977).

In *The Fall of Public Man*, Richard Sennett warned against seeing society as a grand, psychological system (Sennett, 1977/2003, p. 4), where the question "who am I?" is constantly pursued, and where psychological categories invade and destroy public life, making us forget that political questions cannot be dealt with alone through trust, empathy, warmth and a disclosure of private opinions (p. xvii). Under the conditions Sennett describes as "the tyranny of intimacy," public, social, civic, and political phenomena are transformed into questions of personality, biography, and individual narratives (p. 219). As an antidote, Sennett calls for more "impersonal" forms of action in public arenas (p. 340).

My worry is that some of the social science interviews, which I have referred to as doxastic, can be said to uncritically reproduce and reinforce the view of social life as reducible to "psychology" in the form of people's experiences and opinions. What Sennett said of contemporary life in general also applies to much interview research: "Each person's self has become his principle burden; to know oneself has become an end, instead of a means through which one knows the world" (Sennett, 1977/2003, p. 4). Current doxastic interviews are often about getting to know people's selves, which is often portrayed as an end in itself in the contemporary "interview society" (Atkinson & Silverman, 1997), and I would echo Sennett's claim that we need a forum "in which it becomes meaningful to join with other persons without the compulsion to know them as persons" (Sennett, 1977/2003, p. 340)—also in the contexts of qualitative interview research. No doubt, we also often need to know others "as persons," and here doxastic interviews have proved to be very efficient, but if we genuinely want to examine ethical and political issues for the sake of the public good, one way could be to add epistemic interviews to the repertoire of qualitative inquiry to a larger extent.

Still, we may ask if the practice of Socratic interviews is not ethically problematic, when it involves challenging respondents, and confronting them with the task of giving reasons and normative accounts. I would counter this objection by arguing that epistemic interviews have the potential for at least as great a transparency of its power relations as doxastic interviews, and do not commodify or instrumentalize human feeling, friendship, and empathy (Brinkmann & Kvale, 2005). Certainly, like all other human practices, epistemic interviews come with certain ethical challenges that should be taken into consideration. For one thing, participants should know what they agree to. And there are perhaps ethical and not just epistemic reasons why actively confronting interviews should be conducted with particular care vis-à-vis children. Nevertheless, I believe that the active and assertive style in epistemic interviews in many ways enables researchers to proceed ethically in qualitative knowledge production. As testified in some of the epistemic interviews discussed above, the interviewers do not try to suck as much private information out of the respondents as possible, without themselves engaging in the conversation with all the risks that are involved in this.

Conclusion

In conclusion, I want to make clear that the distinction outlined in this chapter between doxastic and epistemic interviews is intended as analytical and as a matter of degree. I have not intended to provide "diagnostic criteria" for interviews to count as either epistemic or doxastic. Furthermore, the purpose of this paper has definitely not been to invalidate the use of phenomenological or narrative interviews that focus on experiences and opinions—the doxa. Rather, my aim has been to argue that other kinds of human conversations can also be practiced with the goal of reaching knowledge, as classically illustrated by Socrates in the role of epistemic interviewer. Socrates is never content to hear what people believe or how they experience the world. He is always interested in examining whether people's beliefs and experiences can be justified, and his dialectical "method" (his elenchus) was developed to bring human beings from a state of being opinionated to a state of knowing.

I have argued that knowledge is a normative concept and that a basic interpersonal attitude in human encounters is the participant mode, where we meet others as accountable agents that can give reasons for their actions, feelings, and beliefs. Not that people can always do so, of course (often we have trouble coming up with reasons for our beliefs), but most people have at least the important ethical and political potential to engage in such conversations. In what I have called epistemic interviews, the analysis is in principle carried out in the conversation, together with the accountable respondents involved, since the analysis mainly consists of testing, questioning, and justifying what people say. Such interviews involve a co-construction of conversational reality *in situ*. In Plato's dialogues, we do not hear about Socrates continuing his analyses in solitude after the public meetings. In conventional research interviews, on the other hand, the analysis is typically carried out after the interview has taken place, often informed by the researcher's theoretical preferences that may be totally alien to the participants. I do not think that one of these methods is automatically better, but I do think that researchers could experiment more with testing their own and their respondents' statements in public discussion in the course of the interview, rather than just seeing this as something to be carried out behind closed doors. I believe that this could often improve the validity of the analyses, and it could perhaps also create more interesting interviews. Often, the use of challenging and confronting questions in epistemic interviews generates more readable interview reports compared with the long monologues that sometimes result from phenomenological and narrative approaches.

In short, the epistemic interview is based both on an epistemology, the idea that knowing something involves reference to a normative "space of reasons," but also on an approach to interview style, which recommends a more widespread use of active and confronting questions that challenge respondents to give reasons for what they say. The epistemic interviewer's "intrusion" into the conversation is not thought of as a source of error, or as something unnatural. On the contrary, if knowledge and subjectivity are produced in conversations, it is an epistemic virtue to become visible as a questioner in the interview, and I believe that (without wanting to get entangled in the impossible debate concerning the naturalness of different conversational styles) it is at least as natural for an interviewer to become involved in the conversation as a participant, as it is to act as a passive mirror (a pollster) or a therapeutic analyst (a prober), where the respondent is left to guess what use the researcher will make of his or her lengthy descriptions and narratives after the interview has taken place.

Notes

1. Central parts of this chapter build on a manuscript that was previously published in the journal *Qualitative Inquiry*, Sage Publications, vol. 13, pp. 1116–1138, entitled "Could interviews be epistemic? An alternative to qualitative opinion polling." I would like to thank Lene Tanggaard and Lucinda Carspecken for valuable feedback on different versions of this chapter.
2. I am grateful to Lucinda Carspecken for pointing this out to me.

References

Aristotle (1976). *Nichomachean Ethics*. London: Penguin.

Atkinson, P., & Silverman, D. (1997). Kundera's immortality: The interview society and the invention of the self. *Qualitative Inquiry, 3*, 304–325.

Bellah, R. N., Madsen, R., Sullivan, W. M., Swidler, A., & Tipton, S. M. (1985). *Habits of the heart: Individualism and commitment in American life.* Berkeley: University of California Press.

Briggs, C. L. (2003). Interviewing, power/knowledge, and social inequality. In J. A. Holstein & J. F. Gubrium (Eds.), *Inside interviewing: New lenses, new concerns* (pp. 495–506). Thousand Oaks, CA: Sage.

Brinkmann, S. (2004). Psychology as a moral science: Aspects of John Dewey's psychology. *History of the Human Sciences, 17,* 128.

Brinkmann, S. (2006). *Psychology as a moral science* (Doctoral dissertation). University of Aarhus Department of Psychology, Denmark.

Brinkmann, S. (2007). Could interviews be epistemic? An alternative to qualitative opinion-polling. *Qualitative Inquiry, 13,* 1116–1138.

Brinkmann, S., & Kvale, S. (2005). Confronting the ethics of qualitative research. *Journal of Constructivist Psychology, 18,* 157–181.

Butler, J. (2005). *Giving an account of oneself.* New York: Fordham University Press.

Denzin, N. K. (2001). The reflexive interview and a performative social science. *Qualitative Research, 1,* 23–46.

Dinkins, C. S. (2005). Shared inquiry: Socratic-hermeneutic interpre-viewing. In P. Ironside (Ed.), *Beyond method: Philosophical conversations in healthcare research and scholarship* (pp. 111–147). Madison: University of Wisconsin Press.

Duncombe, J., & Jessop, J. (2002). "Doing rapport" and the ethics of "faking friendship." In M. Mauther, M. Birch, J. Jessop, & T. Miller (Eds.), *Ethics in Qualitative Research* (pp. 107–122). London: Sage.

Ellis, C., & Berger, L. (2003). Their story/my story/our story: Including the researcher's experience in interview research. In J. A. Holstein & J. F. Gubrium (Eds.), *Inside interviewing: New lenses, new concerns* (pp. 467–493). Thousand Oaks, CA: Sage.

Flyvbjerg, B. (2001). *Making social science matter: Why social inquiry fails and how it can succeed again.* Cambridge: Cambridge University Press.

Fontana, A., & Frey, J. H. (2005). The interview: From neutral stance to political involvement. In N. K. Denzin & Y. S. Lincoln (Eds.), *Sage handbook of qualitative research* (3rd ed.) (pp. 695–727). Thousand Oaks, CA: Sage.

Fontana, A., & Prokos, A. H. (2007). *The interview: From formal to postmodern.* Walnut Creek, CA: Left Coast Press.

Foucault, M. (2001). *Fearless speech.* (J. Pearson, Ed.). New York: Semiotext(e).

Gadamer, H. G. (1960/2000). *Truth and method.* New York: Continuum.

Giorgi, A., & Giorgi, B. (2003). The descriptive phenomenological psychological method. In P. M. Camic, J. E. Rhodes, & L. Yardley (Eds.), *Qualitative research in psychology: Expanding perspectives in methodology and design* (pp. 243–273). Washington, DC: American Psychological Association.

Glesne, C., & Peshkin, A. (1992). *Becoming qualitative researchers: An introduction.* New York: Longman.

Harré, R. (1983). *Personal being.* Oxford: Basil Blackwell.

Hollway, W., & Jefferson, T. (2000). Biography, anxiety and the experience of locality. In P. Chamberlayne, J. Bornat, & T. Wengraf (Eds.), *The turn to biographical methods in social science* (pp. 167–180). London: Routledge.

Holstein, J. A., & Gubrium, J. F. (1995). *The active interview.* London: Sage.

Holstein, J. A., & Gubrium, J. F. (2003). Inside interviewing: New lenses, new concerns. In J. A. Holstein & J. F. Gubrium (Eds.), *Inside interviewing: New lenses, new concerns* (pp. 3–30). Thousand Oaks, CA: Sage.

Kvale, S. (2006). Dominance through interviews and dialogues. *Qualitative Inquiry, 12,* 480–500.

Kvale, S., & Brinkmann, S. (2008). *InterViews: Learning the craft of qualitative research interviewing.* Thousand Oaks, CA: Sage.

Lee, R. M. (2008). David Riesman and the sociology of the interview. *The Sociological Quarterly, 49,* 285–307.

MacIntyre, A. (1985). *After virtue* (2nd ed. with postscript). London: Duckworth.

Mannheim, B., & Tedlock, B. (1995). Introduction. In D. Tedlock & B. Mannheim (Eds.), *The dialogic emergence of culture* (pp. 1–32). Urbana: University of Illinois Press.

Mulhall, S. (2007). *The conversation of humanity.* Charlottesville: University of Virginia Press.

Plato (1987). *The republic.* London: Penguin.

Potter, J., & Wetherell, M. (1987). *Discourse and social psychology.* London: Sage.

Ricoeur, P. (1991). Life in quest of narrative. In D. Wood (Ed.), *On Paul Ricoeur: Narrative and interpretation* (pp. 20–33). London: Routledge.

Riesman, D., & Benney, M. (1956). The sociology of the interview. *Midwestern Sociologist, 18,* 3–15

Rogers, C. (1945). The non-directive method as a technique for social research. *The American Journal of Sociology, 50*, 279–283

Schulze, G. (1992). *Die erlebnisgesellschaft: Kultursoziologie der gegenwart* [The experience society: A cultural sociology of the present]. Frankfurt: Campus.

Sellars, W. (1956/1997). *Empiricism and the philosophy of mind.* Cambridge, MA: Harvard University Press.

Sennett, R. (1977/2003). *The fall of public man.* London: Penguin.

Sennett, R. (2004). *Respect.* London: Penguin Books.

Shotter, J. (1993). *Conversational realities: Constructing life through language.* London: Sage.

Skjervheim, H. (1957). *Deltaker og tilskodar* [Participant and spectator]. Oslo, Norway: Oslo University Press.

Tanggaard, L. (2008). Objections in research interviewing. *International Journal of Qualitative Methods, 7*, 15–29

Taylor, C. (1989). *Sources of the self.* Cambridge: Cambridge University Press.

Wengraf, T. (2001). *Qualitative research interviewing.* Thousand Oaks, CA: Sage.

Wittgenstein, L. (1953). *Philosophical investigations.* Oxford: Basil Blackwell.

CHAPTER NINE

Critical Methodology and the Reconceptualization of Information

LAI MA

What is information? Is a newspaper information? Or should we consider the news itself to be information? If we get lost in London and ask the paperboy for directions, is his verbal direction information? Is a pebble information—in a parable, in a museum, at the newspaper stand?

When awarded the Nobel Prize in Physics, Professor Charles Kao responded, "Fiber optics has changed the world of *information* so much in these last forty years. It certainly is due to the fiber optical networks that the news has traveled so fast" (NPR, 2009, emphasis added). What is the relationship between news and information? Or, shall we describe information in terms of "electric rain" (von Baeyer, 2003) in which we immerse ourselves in hallways, lecture halls, coffee shops, and state parks while sending and receiving "information" through our radios, e-readers, and smart phones?

With the advances in information and communication technologies (ICTs), our lives hinge on information. We can say that we need information to get to a new store, to compare prices among different brands of laptops, or to invest in the stock market. Braman (2009) suggests that information can be interpreted as a resource, a commodity, a basin of possibility, and perhaps most importantly, as a constitutive force of society. We have heard terms such as "information age" and "information highway" in the past decade; recently, more and more terms begin with the letter "i"—for example, iSociety, iSchools, iPulse—which presumably stands for information. It is no surprise that the study of information has become inevitable and has attracted scholars and researchers in many different disciplines. Information science, rooted in documentation and librarianship and closely related to computer science, has become a common ground for both technological and sociological discussions concerning information.

The concept of information, however, is controversial in information science (see, for example, Bar-Hillel & Carnap, 1953; Brookes, 1980; Buckland, 1991; Day, 2001; Bates, 2005, 2006; Frohmann, 2004; Hjørland, 2007; Zins, 2007; Ekbia & Evans, 2009). Nonetheless, most discussions of the concept of information have placed "information" within an empiricist framework, prominently in the DIKW (Data-Information-Knowledge-Wisdom) model and the Shannon-Weaver model (also known as information theory). The empiricist understanding of information and the desire to situate information science as a "science" (Brookes, 1980; Bates, 2006) have privileged the use of scientific methods and have largely disregarded humanistic, interpretive, and critical methodologies in information science research. The interplay between the empiricist understanding of information and scientific methodologies not only consolidates a reified notion of information, but also obstructs the understanding of "information" in cultural and social systems.

It is thus important for us to investigate the epistemological assumptions of the influential conceptions of information; until then may we suggest the necessity of critical methodology for intervening in and applying to the ways "information" is studied, and more importantly, for reconceptualizing information in a communicative-action framework.

Information

The word "information" has a long history. According to Capurro and Hjørland (2003), early references to the use of "informo" can be found in a text written in a biological context by Varro (116–27 BC). According to von Baeyer (2003), "information" originates from the word "form," as do "deformation," "conformation," "transformation," and "reformation." If we look in the *Oxford English Dictionary* (2009), the word "information" has multiple meanings; moreover, explanations of compounds such as "information centre," "information flow," and "information-seeking" are also provided.

If the meaning of the word "information" seems elusive, what actually is the object of study in information science and how can and should "information" be studied? While Cronin (2009) suggests that research areas such as knowledge representation, user needs and behavior, information retrieval, bibliometrics, and scholarly communication are central to information science (p. 1), the concept of information has not been agreed upon over the decades. Frohmann (2004) suggests that information has been used either as an umbrella term for "very loosely bounded sets of studies" (p. 55) or "a singular kind of thing conveyed by the many channels of communication" (p. 56). Furner (2004) even suggests that information studies could be done without the word "information."

Dictionaries and encyclopedias of library and information science suggest an alternative view. While taking into account the diverse meanings of the term "information," they all share that information is derived from data (Keenan & Johnston, 2000; Feather & Sturges, 2003; Reitz, 2006; Khosrowpour, 2007). For example, the *International Encyclopedia of Information and Library Science* (Feather & Sturges, 2003) states,

> Information is data that has been processed into a meaningful form. Seen in this way, information is an assemblage of data in a comprehensible form capable of communication and use; the essence of it is that a meaning has been attached to the raw facts. (p. 244)

Dictionaries and encyclopedias of library and information science begin with a nearly synonymous definition of information, and when asked, some researchers and scholars also provide similar definitions (Zins, 2007).

Despite the controversies over the concept of information, there seems to be an agreement that the term "information" refers to something objectified as a result of empirical observations. Despite the fact that the term has diverse meanings in academic, professional, and popular discourses, it seems that "information" can be studied without clarification and justification of the meaning of the term.

As has been noted, the influential DIKW model and Shannon-Weaver model have shaped the common conception of information as well as the methodological choices of information studies. Let's begin with an analysis of the two models.

Data-Information-Knowledge-Wisdom (DIKW)

There is not a theory behind the DIKW model, but the model has definitely shaped the conception of data, information, and knowledge in information science and cognate fields, as shown in dictionaries and encyclopedias of library and information science (Johnston, 2000; Feather & Sturges, 2003; Reitz, 2006; Khosrowpour, 2007) and a survey of researchers and scholars worldwide (Zins, 2007). While scholars and researchers in knowledge management generally regard R. L. Ackoff's presidential address to the International Society for General Systems Research (Ackoff, 1989) as the origins of the model (for example, Rowley, 2006; Frické, 2009), it is believed that the model dates back to at least the 1960s (Buckland, 2008). Some even suggest that it originates from T. S. Eliot's (1934) "The Rock":

> Where is Life we have lost in living?
> Where is the wisdom we have lost in knowledge?
> Where is the knowledge we have lost in information?

While Eliot laments the progressive loss of knowledge and wisdom, the DIKW model suggests otherwise. In fact, the model reverses the progression to the opposite direction from information to knowledge to wisdom.

The DIKW model is usually illustrated in a triangular hierarchy with data at the bottom and wisdom at the top (Figure 1). The model represents the progression of data to information, knowledge, and last, wisdom in human minds. According to Ackoff (1989), "Data are symbols that represent properties of objects, events, and their environments. They are products of *observation*. To observe is to sense" (p. 3, emphasis in original). He then adds, "Information, as noted, is extracted from data by analysis in many aspects of which computers are adept"; also, "information is inferred from data" (p. 3).

It is not difficult to realize that the DIKW model is analogous to the empiricist theory of knowledge. The concept of information is defined as processed data or meaningful data. The model thus suggests that observation is the only way of knowing and the only way knowledge can be attained. In this formulation, "information" must be data that are observable, then objectified and processed. That is to say, information in the sense of imparting knowledge, of "information-as-process" (Buckland, 1991) or in other intangible forms, is not considered as information in this model. The predetermined progression from data to information and knowledge, let alone wisdom, simplifies knowing to naïve empiricism in which "data" is mainly an unexamined assumption; "information" and "knowledge" are then built upon this simplistic, positivistic view of data. It is clear that the DIKW model is a reduction of a complex philosophical question concerning knowing and knowledge to a poorly theorized objectification: "information."

At the same time, the DIKW model also portrays human minds as if they are information processors like digital computers. The analogy of human mind and digital computer is based upon an unexamined notion of data and data/information processing in human learning, and a notion of knowledge based on representation. The function of information processing in human minds implicated in the model demonstrates a distorted view of cognition that is also based upon a taken-for-granted empiricist epistemology.

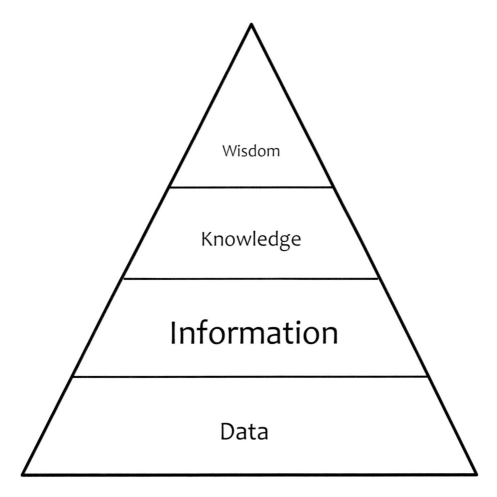

Figure 1 DIKW Model

Shannon-Weaver Model (Information Theory)
Claude Shannon's essay "The Mathematical Theory of Communication" was first published in the *Bell System Technical Journal*, in July and October, 1948. It was then reprinted in a book with the same title , supplemented with an essay by Warren Weaver, "Recent Contributions to

the Mathematical Theory of Communication" (Shannon & Weaver, 1964). Shannon's essay deals with the engineering problems of transmission of messages, whereas Weaver attempts to expand Shannon's theory into a general theory of communication.

Shannon's theory is commonly known as "information theory" for its invention of the measure of information in a message, without defining information and without a physical measurement apparatus, but a conceptual tool—"bit" (von Baeyer, 2003). This concept of information is very influential in theoretical physics, from John Wheeler and colleagues' suggested interpretation of quantum physics (Wheeler & Ford, 1998) to concepts such as qubit and quantum information, to the recent work on the development of quantum computers. However, theoretical physicists seldom refer to Weaver's essay, if at all, while the information theory is often regarded as the "Shannon-Weaver model" in information science. It may be because most information scientists are not familiar with Shannon's mathematical language and hence prefer Weaver's textual discussion. In any case, we must be aware that Weaver's elaboration of the concept of information, although intended to be loyal to that of Shannon's theory, is placed within a general theory of communication. In fact, "information" becomes something essential and necessary in all kinds of communication in Weaver's discussion.

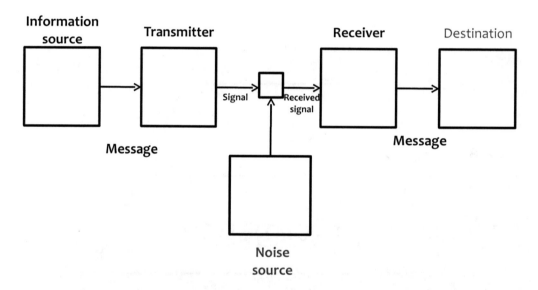

Figure 2 Graphic Representation of the Information Theory

Figure 2 is a graphic representation of the information theory. In his essay, Shannon proposes a model for the transmission of messages from one machine to another. In the introduction, Shannon explicitly states that "semantic aspects of communication are irrelevant to the engineering problem" (Shannon & Weaver, 1964, p. 31). Weaver's essay, however, attempts to expand this model into a general theory of communication; that is, a communication model for both humans and machines. Although Weaver states that semantic problems are essential for a general theory of communication, they are largely neglected in his discussion, because, for Weaver, the purpose of communication is expressed as eliciting effects through planning and procedures. He states that human communication is a matter of "all the procedures by which one mind may affect another" (ibid., p. 3). Communication is not dialogical, not even in the sense of transmission in Shannon's theory, but a causal relationship between information source and destination, the sender and the receiver. In Weaver's elaboration of information theory ("Shannon-Weaver model" hereafter), successful communication can only be evaluated by the receiver's performance of "desired conduct" (ibid., p. 5). In other words, semantic problems are understood as deciphering or decoding messages. Negotiation of meanings between the sender and the receiver is absent; multiple meanings or different interpretations of messages (sometimes known as "information") for the sender and the receiver is impossible in this one-way, one-meaning communication model.[1]

Shannon's "information" is not intended to be interpreted in a general theory of communication, and after all, he clearly states that the engineering problems are not concerned with meanings. So Weaver writes, "*information* must not be confused with meaning" (ibid., p. 8, emphasis in original). However, the concept of information in Weaver's discussion is rather confusing since the term sometimes refers to a concept as in Shannon's theory, but sometimes means "messages." Weaver writes, "two messages, one of which is heavily loaded with meaning and the other of which is pure nonsense, can be exactly equivalent, from the present viewpoint, as regards information" (ibid., p.8). Information in this latter formulation is thus viewed as some objectified entity that can be transmitted for the purpose of eliciting "desired conduct" in communication, and is later interpreted as having causal powers to change "knowledge structure" or "mental states" in human minds. This concept of "information" has become a prevalent one in both academic and popular discourses.

Conception of Information and Its Assumptions

The Shannon-Weaver model is a model of communication, for machines, or humans, or both. The DIKW model depicts a simplified model of cognition. Both models deal with "information" despite their different frameworks and different meanings of the term "information." The implicit assumptions shared by the two models, however, are strikingly similar and should not be neglected, for the conventional conception of information is largely shaped by these assumptions, which in turn shapes the study of information in information science.

First, information is conceptualized as something objectified—as messages or processed data—that has causal powers upon human minds . Information is understood as essential for eliciting effects in communication (eliciting "desired conduct" in the Shannon-Weaver model) and learning (attaining knowledge and wisdom in the DIKW model).

Second, the process of understanding is neglected. Interpretation is not involved in either communication or learning. It is as if we can only understand whatever is told by an information source and behave accordingly; and it is as if we can attain knowledge simply by observation and collecting data. Information is largely understood as objectified sense data as in the empiricist theory of knowledge. Information is conceptualized as things like rocks and trees in the physical world that can be studied by observation and data analyses without negotiation of meanings. In other words, information is not a result of mutual understanding of meanings between two or more subjects; rather, information is conceptualized as entities that have causal powers upon human minds (although the causal relationships in the DIKW and the Shannon-Weaver model are different).

Third, information in both models is intended for instrumental purposes and for increasing effectiveness. For Weaver, effectiveness is achieved when the receiver behaves according to the sender without interruption: "The effectiveness problems are concerned with the success with which the meaning conveyed to the receiver leads to the desired conduct on his part" (Shannon & Weaver, 1964, p. 5). For Ackoff, the "critical point" of the DIKW model is that *"wisdom is the ability to increase effectiveness"* (Ackoff, 1989, p. 5, emphasis in original). Effectiveness seems to be the sole purpose of communication and learning in which information plays a major role, despite the fact that information, whether understood as messages or processed data, could be interpreted broadly and variably.

Information does not have a fixed physical form—it can be studied as books in a library, documents in an archive, images on a web page, services provided by a community clinic, sometimes even a surrogate for many different things combined together. Indeed, the term "information" can be used for a wide range of things and/or phenomena, but, ironically, information is seldom the actual object of study in information science. Instead, studies are usually concerned with the production, access, and use of information, focusing particularly on the effectiveness problems such as the usefulness of algorithms, modeling of information behavior, and collection of factual evidence of information use, with little concern about the constituents of "information," their possible cultural and social implications, and the potential for positive social change. Information, objective and deprived of meanings, moves swiftly across different areas of research and goes through various "turns" (Cronin, 2008) of information science.

Critical Methodology

To understand human-human or human-computer interactions, their relations with cultural rituals and practices, institutional standards and laws, and economic and political functions, and to make explicit the tacit beliefs, norms, and values of the cultural and social systems, one cannot give way to experimental and quantitative research methods that mainly generate results from the manipulation of variables in controlled environments or by mere observations. Rather, one needs the conceptual and instrumental tools for the analyses of phenomena concerning human agency, culture, and society. Critical methodology, one of the diverse research methodologies labeled "qualitative research," is well suited for such kind of study. While it shares the instruments with other qualitative research methodologies such as observations, interviews (structured and unstructured), and focus-group study, critical methodology distinguishes itself from other qualitative methodology in terms of its epistemology and social ontology. Also, critical methodology works toward positive social change with the aim of refining social theory and is not limited to mere descriptions of social life.

Critical Epistemology

How do we know a research study is telling the truth? How could we determine the validity of a study? Could we trust results generated by statistical analyses in regard to (1) racial distribution of a population, (2) factors contributing to the library use of African Americans, and (3) attributes of "information behavior" of African Americans?

If we have five African American students out of a total of 100 students in an academic program, we will all agree that 5 percent of the student population is African American. If we disagree because one researcher counted five and another counted six, we can verify the answer by counting all over again. The validity of the statement is based on the fact that we can all access and verify the data and that we share the understanding of the number system and the category "African American."

But to answer questions such as what factors contribute to library use or what are the attributes of "information behavior" of African Americans, we are not satisfied with statistics, for these questions concern a wide range of issues such as cultural norms and traditions, class structure, racial identity, organizational goals, and not the least, each individual's personal experience and pre-understanding of a library. For critical researchers, the validity of this kind of study depends upon the agreement between the researcher and the community studied as well as among researchers. Critical researchers are not expected to be an "outsider" or a "neutral" observer at all times; rather, they are expected to attain a "virtual participant" view as much as possible during the interpretive and reconstructive process.

That is to say, critical researchers take positions and make use of the hermeneutic circle to attain intersubjective insider views during the interpretive and reconstructive process. The circular feature of the hermeneutic circle alters the initial framework of researchers while they acquire norms, concepts, and implicit rules of a community, which in turn enable them to act communicatively with the people they seek to understand, and more importantly, to explicate the norms, beliefs, and values that escape the explicit awareness of these people. The aim is to have the holistic experience of the intended meanings of the actors and expected responses that actors in the group may provide.

Hence, a research study concerning the "information behavior" of African American students requires the researcher to immerse in the community in order to understand their academic life, social life, study habits, identity, and so on. The critical researcher strives to understand the meanings of actions, linguistic or otherwise, until s/he is confident that s/he knows, to borrow Wittgenstein's (1958) words, "how to go on" in particular contexts and interact with members of the group s/he studies, as they themselves would "go on" with each other. The validity of the study can be justified when the researcher's understandings are agreed upon and recognized by the members of the group, in this example, the African American students.

Position-Taking, Reflection, and Truth

One might then ask: Could there be a universal truth in our understanding of peoples, cultures, and meaning? Is a critical ethnographic study merely the subjective interpretation of the researcher? Carspecken (1996) has discussed the relationship between validity claims and ontological realms (see also Kincheloe & McLaren, 2003); he has also debunked the dichotomy of the universal and the particular in validity claims in his discussion of the relationship between reflection and position-taking (Carspecken, 1999). Let's elaborate his main points using the example of the African American students.

A meaningful act always carries one or more validity claim(s)—of objective facts, of norms, and/or of feelings, desires, and intentions. These validity claims reference three ontological realms, namely, objective, normative, and subjective realms. A statement claiming that 5 percent of the student population is African American is an objective claim because the number can be verified by counting and recounting the number of African American students by anyone. A statement claiming that library services should be tailored for African American students is a normative claim because it states a normative judgment of good, bad, right, or wrong that is expected to be agreed by a community grouping. A statement claiming that unwelcoming attitudes are felt by African American students is a subjective claim because the feelings of these students can only be known by the student her/himself.

Normative and subjective claims cannot be completely understood by the manipulation of variables and have different validity criteria from those of objective claims. The critical researcher must position-take in order to grasp the explicit and implicit meanings of every act. By taking the first- and second-person position, the researcher comes to understand the implicit structures through which people reference their subjective states, norms, values, and beliefs, and the norms of a community grouping through continuous interactions with the community members. The researcher may also continuously alter her/his original frame of analysis during the interactive process. This is what we mean by making use of the hermeneutic circle. At the same time, the researcher also maintains a third-person position in order to access the functions of meaning structures, beliefs, ideologies, and so on in relation to other aspects of the social system. Hence, the reconstructive analysis in critical methodology is not subjective, but rather intersubjective. The nature of intersubjectivity in human communication also implies that the interactive and reconstructive process always involves a third-person position.

Taking both the second- and third-person position means that the researcher is engaging in reflection during the interactive process. When interacting with others, the researcher is taking the first- and second-person position while at the same time making use of pre-understood typifications to understand certain situations, behaviors, etc. The making use of typifications means that a third-person position is involved, although we usually take it for granted and may not be aware of it. When a typification is altered through the interactive processes, that is, when a pre-understanding has changed, an instance of reflection has occurred. Each time a typification is altered, the pre-understanding of the peoples and cultures is also altered.

The relationship between reflection and validity claims discussed above guides us to question the dichotomy of the universal and the particular views of validity claims. Carspecken (1999) writes,

> No validity claims are truly universal because a cultural and contingent side can always be found with respect to each and every claim. But no validity claims are purely relative to culture and circumstances because all such claims include a claim to universality. (p. 264)

The universality grasped by the critical researcher is a result of taking the second- and third-person positions simultaneously and reflectively. Yet, universality is contingent on culture and circumstances. That is to say, universality may be altered over time in terms of its content due to the changes in cultural forms and social practices, while every validity claim, every meaningful act, includes the claim to universality that can remain invisible for extended periods of historical time. When its cultural contingency is discovered, a new claim to universality at least tacitly emerges. The dichotomy of the universal and the particular is thus a false one; instead, they are moments that are dialectically related.[2]

Social Ontology

Once the critical researcher grasps the norms, practices, implicit beliefs, and values, other questions arise: what might be the constituents that give rise to these norms, practices, beliefs, and values? Are all norms and practices culturally and communicatively structured? How might the researcher analyze norms and practices that may not be communicatively structured?

Social phenomena in critical methodology are understood as coordinated human activities. Critical researchers attempt to understand the conditions of action coordination and the human experiences of their social lives and conditions. Conditions of action are of many types:

some conditions of action are culturally and communicatively structured, whereas some confront actors "externally" in the sense that they are usually negotiated and/or planned or otherwise formed outside of community members' daily lives. Markets, laws, formal standards, institutional structures, and physical environments fall into this latter category.

In this social ontology, the social world is not demarcated from human activities; on the contrary, social phenomena are closely related to human agency and are largely produced, maintained, and reproduced through human activities. In other words, communicative-coordinated actions occur continuously when people act, interact, and communicate to follow or challenge norms, values, and beliefs of a culture in ways for which they can provide reasons. Many of these cultural conditions of action, including those that are communicatively structured and those that are "external" to daily lives, escape full awareness of the community members and carry biases and ideologies. One task of critical methodology is to make those implicit and barely noticed cultural assumptions and values explicit such that actors will have more awareness of what had been taken for granted, and thus have more freedom in relation to their future activities.

Critical Methodology, Reconceptualization of Information

As has been noted, "information" is commonly conceptualized as something that has causal powers upon human minds operating within an empiricist framework. With this conceptualization, particularly in the cognitive viewpoint of information science, when we say that we need information to get to a new store, to compare prices among different brands of laptops, or to invest in the stock market, "information" is viewed as something that changes human's knowledge structure and/or mental states—human beings are viewed as passive receiver, not an active agent being informed. The human mind is viewed as a mechanism, like a digital computer, that processes information for attaining knowledge, for decision making, and for improving effectiveness in every aspect of our daily lives. Information is self-evident. The term is often used without explanation or clarification, and not the least without references to human negotiation and communication or socio-economic structures. This empiricist concept of information may have also constituted the reified notion of information, including the views that information has the nature of commodities and market values, that information can be managed, that information can be transmitted, and so on and so forth. Simply put, information is objectified and operationalized with the aim of improving effectiveness.

Information, however, is not self-evident; rather, it is intersubjectively and socially constructed. Some constructions are communicatively structured, whereas some are products of "external" factors such as market and laws. Hence, the question "What is information?" entails questioning the communication structures and/or the external factors that afford the agreement upon the information in question. The epistemology and social ontology of critical methodology provide the framework for this reconceptualization of information.

On the one hand, critical methodology does not equate sensing with knowing. Human beings do not act as a result of processing sense data and we do not react merely to our senses. Rather, we often consider our roles and identities, moral and ethical issues, possible consequences of actions, and many other things when we act. Our choices of action depend upon, among many other things, our experience and our identity. Issues of memory and identity, however, are complex. Although a computer is capable of performing some tasks that a human does, we are far from understanding the actual working of the human brain, particularly in domains such as emotions, moral judgment, and memory, not to mention that a conscious computer is yet to be made. Critical methodology does not provide a typical model of learning, but it argues against epistemologies that depend solely on sensual experiences (Carspecken, 2003). More importantly, it suggests that action is largely communicatively structured. That is to say, a researcher needs to investigate the working of rules, norms, and values, explicit and implicit, for the understanding of social phenomena and personal feelings (although feelings can never be fully grasped) in a community grouping.

Information (whatever it refers to) becomes information when a person is informed and when the piece of information is communicable to other persons. Conceptualizing information as processed and meaningful data implies that only sense data can become information (and knowledge) and that any data sensed by a human being can become information. This conceptualization of information neglects the negotiation and agreement operating within a cultural group and the cultural and social constituents that construct what may be called "information." As a result, study of information is often restricted to engineering problems and modeling of information needs/behavior.

By studying information as communicatively and socially constructed phenomena, critical methodology provides the framework for overcoming this empiricist-influenced concept of information and a reconceptualization of information. Critical methodology opens up questions concerning information in relation to communicative structure, organizational rules, economic and political conditions, and so on. In this type of investigation, the terms "data," "information," and "knowledge" are not taken for granted as self-evident; rather, they require the investigation into their constructions. Also, information is not a product as a result of data-processing, but conceptualized within a communicative-action framework.

On the other hand, critical methodology does not view human and social phenomena in causal relationship. As discussed, the critical researcher makes use of the hermeneutic circle to grasp meaning of interactions and the beliefs and values of community members. The critical researcher also investigates the institutional structures and socio-economic conditions that may give rise to certain beliefs, values, and system structures. These beliefs, norms, and the other external factors are considered as constituents of cultural and social phenomena. They are subject to change over time and across different locales. That is to say, these factors are dynamic and thus cannot have a causal relationship with behaviors of community members or events in a community. A critical reconstructive analysis suggests the most possible reasons of certain behaviors of community members or events in a community. These reasons, however, are not viewed as causes as in the physical sciences because they are subject to change and they are open for negotiations between the researcher and the community studied. More importantly, these reasons are explicated for the purposes of reflection and emancipation of the community, including the explication of ideologically distorted rules and norms such that the community members can overcome them and seek freedom in future activities.

The rejection of causal relationship means that there is not one thing that may cause certain behaviors or events. It also means that "information" cannot be viewed as a cause or an active agent that makes changes in knowledge structures and mental states, or elicits certain kinds of "desired conduct" (Shannon-Weaver model). Changes in our actions may be due to certain types of information; but we have to be careful that this is not because "information" causes the changes in our minds; rather, it is because we are informed in a certain cultural and social context. Information does not do anything. Humans have to do something to it or with it (Buckland, 1991). Devoid of viewing causal relationships between "information" and human behaviors (Shannon-Weaver model) or human minds (DIKW model), questions concerning information can instead be directed to, for example, how certain types of information is produced, stored, and organized in organizations and institutions, how certain things are being recognized as information, and how the production and use of certain types of information shape communication structures.

Critical Study of Information and Critical Methodology

Historically, information science is concerned with the progress of science and is closely related to the development of information technology. Paul Otlet and Henry La Fontaine's dream of the Universal Bibliographic Repertory (Rayward, 1997), Suzanne Briet's establishment of the Salle des Catalogues et Bibliographies at the Bibliothèque Nationale and her endorsement of the American special (science) libraries (Briet, 2006), the development of the American Documentation Institute, now American Society for Information Science and Technology (Farkas-Conn, 1990) are all concerned with the storage, organization, and dissemination of scientific knowledge. The major concern has always been the effectiveness of the information system, be it a local card catalog or a cooperative online retrieval system, with the aim of facilitating the progress of science. With the development of information technology, effectiveness has been drastically improved, particularly by the use of computers and the internet. Consequently, effectiveness problems are usually seen as computer or technological problems.

It is no surprise that experimental and quantitative research methods have been preferred in information science, for its strong relations with computer science as well as the desire for the label of "science" (Brookes, 1980). These methods have been particularly useful for devising new algorithms and solving engineering problems, prominently Gerard Salton's design of information retrieval models (see, for example, Salton, Wong & Yang, 1975). It did not take long, however, for information scientists to realize that information retrieval systems must take user perspectives into account, reflected in the so-called cognitive turn of information science (see, for example, Belkin, 1990; Ingwersen & Järvelin, 2007; Cronin, 2008). The cognitive viewpoint is not only influential in information retrieval research, but also user studies and research in so-called information-seeking behavior (see, for example, Wilson, 1984; Kuhlthau, 1993; Pettigrew, Fidel & Bruce, 2001; see also Case, 2007 for a comprehensive review of research in this area), incorporating concepts such as uncertainty, information, and knowledge in the Shannon-Weaver model and the DIKW model, although often without clarification or justification. Qualitative research methods are more commonly used since then (Fisher, Erdelez & McKechnie, 2005). However, neither the conception of the objective, reified notion of information nor the purposes of increasing effectiveness have been altered or questioned. In most studies, human, cultural, and social factors have been viewed as "background" or "variables" of the effectiveness problems; human-human and human-computer interactions have been understood based on the "conduit metaphor" (Reddy, 1993; Day, 2000) of the Shannon-Weaver model.

The production, access, and use of information are processes associated with professional practices operating within cultural and social milieu while serving certain institutional, economic, and political functions. The effectiveness of a system cannot be evaluated without addressing their practices, standards, and norms. Agre (1997) has suggested that the working of a system is a discursive construct and it "succeeds only if the community assents" (p. 14). Indeed, the design of any kind of interactive system requires a deep understanding of communication, particularly the process of understanding meanings, including interpretation of texts, and mutual understanding of different forms of expression, including linguistic expression, gesture, intonation, and so on. For example, one of the biggest challenges of information retrieval systems is to grasp the "real" meaning of the user's query; for instance, what kind of results does one expect when inserting the word "Vancouver" in a search box? The process of understanding meaning cannot be studied solely by experimental and quantitative methods, if at all. Rather, it requires a methodology rooted in theories of communication and meaning that provides the framework for critical reconstructive analyses.

More importantly, studies concerning information should not be limited to effectiveness problems; rather, they should question the cultural and social constituents and implications of the production, access, and use of information. "Information," after all, is discursively constructed in our daily discourse.[3] Whether the news, the newspaper, the verbal instruction of the paper boy, or the pebble may be considered as information cannot be evaluated by a scientific equation or an individual's opinion or feeling; rather, the construction of information depends upon the consent of a particular community grouping. A pebble becomes information when it is recorded, stored, and displayed in a museum. Why? How is it different from a pebble at the newspaper stand? One main reason is that when the pebble is placed in a museum, we agree that the pebble is, at least potentially, informational to some people in our community. At the same time, we also trust the authority of the museum that the pebble is something worthwhile to be stored and displayed. To consider something "potentially informational" and to trust other people to decide the informational quality involves an anticipated agreement of the community members.

Moreover, the agreement about what may be information, like many other social phenomena, may be influenced or distorted by the exercise of power implicated in economic and social structures. Thus, information demands investigation beyond the effectiveness problems. For example, we may investigate the manner in which information is produced, the types of information produced, as well as the possible types of information that are not produced. Also, information use can be studied as socially constructed needs, in terms of "overt use" as well as "covert/latent" uses that escape the awareness of users but serve various functions. In other words, the production and use of information can be studied in terms of the cultures of producers and users and the relation of these cultures to the economic and social location of production and use.

The question concerning information should be approached from the cultural and social construction of information. Instead of asking what information is, we may investigate the constituents of information in particular organizational, cultural, or social settings. We question: what makes information "information," be it tangible or intangible, measurable or immeasurable, consumable or non-consumable? What are the differences among the information stored by a library, a government agency, a bank, and Facebook? And how do the constituents of information affect the dynamics of power relations in organizations, cultural and professional groups, and the global economy? Studies concerned with the understanding of cultural and social constituents and implications of information, as well as the roles of information in organizations and cultural and professional groups, may be described as the critical study of information.

Information is intersubjectively and socially constructed. It is objective in the sense that it could be observed and studied by taking the third-person position in social situations. However, questions concerning information cannot be based on causal models of communication and learning and should not be limited to effectiveness problems. Meanings, understanding, and interpretation are essential for improving effectiveness of information systems, and more importantly, for the critical study of information. Critical methodology not only provides the framework for rich descriptions of phenomena, but also explicates tacit norms and practices, ideologies, and power relations for critical analyses of the constitution of information.

Notes

1. Reddy (1993) has used the term "conduit metaphor" for describing this communication model. See also Day (2000) for his discussion of "conduit metaphor" in information science research.
2. See "Essay Four: Five Third Person Positions" (Carspecken, 1999) for an in-depth and insightful analysis of the relationship between position-taking and reflection.
3. See Aspray (1985) and von Baeyer (2003) for discussions of the scientific concept of information.

References

Ackoff, R. L. (1989). From data to wisdom: Presidential address to ISGSR, June 1988. *Journal of Applied Systems Analysis, 16*, 3–9.

Agre, P. E. (1997). *Computation and human experience.* New York: Cambridge University Press.

Aspray, W. (1985). The scientific conceptualization of information: A survey. *IEEE Annals of the History of Computing, 7*(2), 117–140.

Bar-Hillel, Y., & Carnap, R. (1953). Semantic information. *British Journal for the Philosophy of Science, 4*(13/16), 147–157.

Bates, M. J. (2005). Information and knowledge: An evolutionary framework for information science. *Information Research, 10*(4).

Bates, M. J. (2006). Fundamental forms of information. *Journal of the American Society for Information Science and Technology, 57*(8), 1033–1045.

Belkin, N. J. (1990). The cognitive viewpoint in information science. *Journal of Information Science, 16*, 11–15.

Braman, S. (2009). *Change of state: Information, policy, and power.* Cambridge, MA: MIT Press.

Briet, S. (2006). What is documentation? (R. E. Day & L. Martinet, Trans.). In R. E. Day & L. Martinet (Eds.), *What is documentation? English translation of the classic French text* (pp. 9–46). Lanham, MD: Scarecrow.

Brookes, B. C. (1980). The foundations of information science: Part I, Philosophical aspects. *Journal of Information Science, 2*, 125–133.

Buckland, M. K. (1991). Information as thing. *Journal of the American Society for Information Science, 42*(5), 351–360.

Buckland, M. K. (2008). Personal communication.

Capurro, R., & Hjørland, B. (2003). The concept of information. *Annual Review of Information Science and Technology, 37*, 343–411.

Carspecken, P. F. (1996). *Critical ethnography in education research: A theoretical and practical guide.* New York: Routledge.

Carspecken, P. F. (1999). *Four scenes for posing the question of meaning and other essays in critical philosophy and critical methodology.* New York: Peter Lang.

Carspecken, P. F. (2003). Ocularcentrism, phonocentrism and the counter enlightenment problematic: Clarifying contested terrain in our schools of education. *Teachers College Record, 105*(6), 978–1047.

Case, D. O. (2007). *Looking for information: A survey of research on information seeking, needs, and behavior* (2nd ed.). Boston: Elsevier.

Cronin, B. (2008). The sociological turn in information science. *Journal of Information Science, 34*(4), 465–475.

Cronin, B. (2009). Changing of the guard. *Journal of the American Society for Information Science and Technology, 60*(1), 1–2.

Day, R. E. (2000). The "conduit metaphor" and the nature and politics of information studies. *Journal of the American Society for Information Science and Technology, 51*(9), 805–811.

Day, R. E. (2001). *The modern invention of information: Discourse, history, and power.* Carbondale, IL: Southern Illinois University Press.

Eliot, T. S. (1934). The rock. Retrieved September 15, 2011, from http://www.wisdomportal.com/Technology/TSEliot-TheRock.html

Ekbia, H. R., & Evans, T. P. (2009). Regimes of information: Land use, management, and policy. *The Information Society, 25*, 328–343.

Farkas-Conn, I. S. (1990). *From documentation to information science: The beginnings and early development of the American documentation institute—American Society for Information Science.* New York: Greenwood.

Feather, J., & Sturges, P. (Eds.). (2003). *International encyclopedia of information and library science.* New York: Routledge.

Fisher, K. E., Erdelez, S., & McKechnie, L. E. F. (Eds.). (2005). *Theories of information behavior.* Medford, NJ: Information Today.

Frické, M. (2009). The knowledge pyramid: A critique of the DIKW hierarchy. *Journal of Information Science, 35*(2), 131–142.

Frohmann, B. (2004). *Deflating information: From science studies to documentation.* Toronto, Canada: University of Toronto Press.

Furner, J. (2004). Information studies without information. *Library Trends, 52*(3), 427–446.

Hjørland, B. (2007). Information: Objective or subjective/situational? *Journal of the American Society for Information Science and Technology, 58*(10), 1448–1456.

Ingwersen, P., & Järvelin, K. (2007). The cognitive framework for information. In P. Ingwersen & K Järvelin's *The turn: Integration of information seeking and retrieval in context* (pp. 23–54). Dordreckt, Netherlands: Springer.

Keenan, S., & Johnston, C. (2000). *Concise dictionary of library and information science.* New Providence, NJ: Bowker-Saur.

Khosrowpour, M. (Ed.). (2007). *Dictionary of information science and technology.* Hershey, PA: Idea Group Reference.

Kincheloe, J. L., & McLaren, P. (2003). Rethinking critical theory and qualitative research. In N. K. Denzin & Y. S. Lincoln (Eds.), *The landscape of qualitative research: Theories and issues* (pp. 433–488). Thousand Oaks, CA: Sage.

Kuhlthau, C. C. (1993). A principle of uncertainty for information seeking. *Journal of Documentation, 49*(4), 339–355.

NPR. (2009). Fiber optics, imaging pioneers win physics Nobel. Retrieved December 8, 2009, from http://www.npr.org/templates/story/story.php?storyId=113527362.

Oxford English Dictionary. (2009). Accessed December 8, 2009: http://www.oed.com

Pettigrew, K. E., Fidel, R., & Bruce, H. (2001). Conceptual frameworks in information behavior. *Annual Review of Information Science and Technology, 35*, 43–78.

Rayward, W. B. (1997). The origins of information science and the International Institute of Bibliography/International Federation for Information and Documentation (FID). *Journal of the American Society for Information Science, 48*, 289–300.

Reddy, M. J. (1993). The conduit metaphor: A case of frame conflict in our language about language. In Ortony, A. (Ed.), *Metaphor and Thought* (2nd ed.) (pp. 164–201). Cambridge: Cambridge University Press.

Reitz, J. M. (2006). *ODLIS—Online dictionary for library and information science.* Retrieved September 7, 2009, from http://lu.com/odlis/about.cfm.

Rowley, J. (2006). The wisdom hierarchy: representations of the DIKW hierarchy. *Journal of Information Science, 33*(2), 163–180.

Salton, G., Wong, A., & Yang, C. S. (1975). A vector space model for automatic indexing. *Communications of the ACM, 18*(11), 613–620.

Shannon, C. E., & Weaver, W. (1964). *The mathematical theory of communication*. Urbana: University of Illinois Press.

von Baeyer, H. C. (2003). *Information: The new language of science*. Cambridge, MA: Harvard University Press.

Wheeler, J. A., & Ford, K. (1998). *Geons, black holes, and quantum foam: A life in physics*. New York: W. W. Norton.

Wilson, T. D. (1984). The cognitive approach to information-seeking behavior and information use. *Social Science Information Studies, 4*, 197–204.

Wittgenstein, L. (1958). *Philsophical investigations* (G. E. M. Anscombe, Trans.). Upper Saddle River, NJ: Prentice Hall.

Zins, C. (2007). Conceptual approaches for defining data, information, and knowledge. *Journal of the American Society for Information Science and Technology, 58*(4), 479–493.

CHAPTER TEN

Telling It Like It Is

Creating New Layers of Meaning in
My Collaborative Storytelling Practices

DAN MAHONEY

My reflexive storytelling practices continue to evolve and change as I pursue my research interests on intimacy construction and storytelling in the 21st century. Using a collaborative storytelling methodology (Mahoney, 2007), I have documented the ordinary occurrences, practices, and emotive experiences gay men face in their interpersonal relationships. It is my way of understanding how gay men go about framing the context of their intimate spheres in their daily lives. What also makes these reflexive tales so remarkable is their ability to offer a glimpse at the private, more personal accounts of gay intimacy. Very rarely do we have such privileged access to the private stories of gay men. Within each of these storylines, I explore a number of interpretive practices, by addressing such issues as voice; self-reflexivity; representation; and authorial presence in the text (Hertz, 1997; Barbour, 1998). I also want to write new stories based on specific substantive themes about love, identity, and belonging.

Silverman (1999) refers to my style of "minority storytelling" as having a distinct aesthetic in sociological inquiry. The author "slows down its narrative" by detailing the mundane in an effort to appreciate the everyday incidences in lived experience. As such, you won't find the excitement of the car chase, the spectacle of special effects, the quick fix, the happy ending, or even the melodramatic representations of life in these collaborative stories. Nor will these tales necessarily keep you on the edge of your seat. Rather, these narratives are about what it's like to maintain ongoing, interpersonal relationships with the people we love—in all of its guises, complexities, and contradictions—and the identities and sense of belonging that get constructed as a result of staying connected to these individuals. In this sense, the "slowness" of my everyday gay tales is a "counter strategy" to the larger and more popular romantic versions of intimacy and belonging. They are "small" representations of life described slowly, carefully, and with some clarity.

This chapter presents an opportunity to take stock of the epistemological, theoretical, and analytical traditions that inform my narrative representations of everyday life. These disciplinary frameworks have greatly impacted how my personal narratives get discovered, structured, and co-developed along the way. As such I will attempt to locate and contextualize my self-reflexive fieldwork practices within interpretive, postmodern, and pragmatic traditions. This exercise will bring to the forefront the underlying assumptions, expectations, and personal belief systems associated with these stylistic ethnographies. Discussing these analytical frameworks and methodological practices will also shed more light on my own reflexive "doings" in the field; and should provide a means of better understanding how my self-reflexive stories were best accomplished.

The discussion will begin with a very personal statement about my everyday, principled, and pragmatic storytelling approach, which is the ethical and methodological basis for my fieldwork collaborations. The conversation then turns to the contextualization of my interpretive frameworks and the sensibilities that inform these traditions. Lastly, I will speak about the importance of using self-reflexive narrative to create more contextual, more meaningful and textually diverse representations of lived experience. In doing so, I will consider my own interpretive ownership of the material and what affect it has had on knowledge construction and my presentation of the everyday lives of gay men.

Everyday, Principled, and Pragmatic Storytelling Approach

My fieldwork collaborations advocate the need for an everyday, principled and pragmatic approach to storytelling in the 21st century. The adoption of such a perspective requires us to shift our gaze (and emphasis) away from the grand narratives of the past and document the specific cultural perspectives and meanings individuals and communities bring to their everyday intimate arrangements (Plummer, 2001). This approach values the need to connect ourselves to the new stories that are being told about contemporary life and understand how these newly constructed identities and experiences help to reshape our understandings and change our worlds. In a sense, it will mean understanding how these newer forms of storytelling are constructed within what Jamieson (1998) calls the "gap" between the internal processes of personal identity, individual responsibility, and human agency and the external social, cultural, and political institutions that help shape the way we live our lives.

As Plummer (2001) suggests, we need to make the case for constructing everyday methodological practices that use principled ways of thinking as "starting points" in guiding individuals and researchers through their ethical, intimate, and moral gaze. "These patterns should be seen as growing out of, and fitting in some useful way, to the lives of the various individuals and groups who share a history, culture and social structural position" (p. 192). What is most valuable about this pragmatic ethical stance is that it presupposes a minimum level of respect and understanding for the cultural conventions of any one group. In doing so, it begins to construct an even playing field where all social identities can coexist and be respected. It is in this "knowledgeable" understanding of these practices and conventions, as Seidman (1992) suggests, that we can begin to see how these practices fit into the lives of a particular group, while grasping the meaning and expectation individuals bring to these conventions in their specific context.

My everyday-storytelling approach understands that all researchers need to be conscious about how their own ideological positions and personal politics come to shape their methodological practices. In doing so, I take the epistemological stance that all scientific inquiry is largely embedded in a sociohistorical context, whether or not they are acknowledged. I also understand all knowledge claims to be reflections of the research process, preferred theoretical assumptions and the social context of the researcher and his or her research collaborators. Belenky, Clinchy, Goldberger and Tarule (1986) suggest that knowledge is best constructed when the interviewer weaves together what he or she knows from personal experiences with what the interviewer learns from his or her subjects. As such, my narrated form of knowledge construction involves connecting reason, emotion, intuition, and analytic thought. I attend to this construction of knowledge by acquiring firsthand from the subjects what they want to talk about; giving equal weight to their personal experience as well as my own; and finding ways to make connections between myself and my collaborators and the subject matter.

Lastly, I take the stance that I cannot separate myself from the narrative subject matter. Rather then trying to bracket ourselves, we should use our personal experience and judgments as part of generating new knowledge. By paying attention to others and being rigorously aware of ourselves, we can create knowledge that is as close to social reality as possible. To this end, the relationship between me and my narrative collaborators is always one of mutuality and reflexivity. This dialectic approach to the co-construction of knowledge allows for an integration of experiences.

My Own Self-Reflexive Project

Self-reflexivity is an essential part of the interpretive ethnographic fieldwork. Self-reflexivity is broadly understood in the literature as a dialectic process, composed of ongoing conversations between the self and the broader social context. These dialectic conversations allow the self to be negotiated through linked processes of self-exploration, shared history, and the development of intimacy with the other. It is a process of understanding not simply "what you know," but also "how you come to know it." The use of reflexivity in narrative research is widespread and can be characterized in many different ways and in various intensities. For my collaborative fieldwork projects, I prefer to use Wasserfall's (1997) reading of reflexivity, which she broadly defines as:

> a continued self-awareness about the ongoing relationship between a researcher and informants, which is certainly epistemologically useful; the researcher becomes more aware of constructing knowledge and of the influences of her beliefs, backgrounds and feelings in the process of research. Reflexivity is a position of a certain kind of praxis where there is a continuous checking on the accomplishment of understanding. (p. 151)

Self-reflexivity, in this sense, implies both a distancing and a unity with the other at the same time. It makes the ethnographer aware of him- or herself as both subject and object, and the process that constructs the knowledge between the two. Having an understanding of these locations in the interaction allows me to be able to "situate" myself in the knowledge construction. As Greer (1990) suggests, you get a sense of who you are and from what position you write, observe, and speak. In doing so, it acknowledges that in the representation of lived experiences, we are editing in some realities while editing out others. This process of "self-awareness" questions the traditional borders between biographical-subject and researcher-object and makes the case for promoting the "purposeful trespassing" (Gottschalk, 1998) of such artificial boundaries—thus replacing the objective authoritative voice with a more democratic representation. Such trespassing of boundaries emphasizes the need for reflexive ethnographic fieldwork to develop their "own ways of knowing" and interpreting lived experience.

For me, this dialectic process happens both in and outside of the interview context—often through reflexive conversations I have with myself and my collaborators. The first interpretive "turn" usually happens during breaks in the interviews when I think about what I have experienced and how best to proceed forward. However, my "continued self-awareness" also happens later that night when writing up my field notes, or even weeks later when I return to my audiotapes and transcripts searching for more analytical understandings of these experiences. Most notably, these reflexive turns allow me to better understand the meanings and processes behind my study collaborator's actions and disclosures.

These reflexive turns have also made me more aware of my own "emotional work" (Kleinman & Copp, 1993) in these fieldwork collaborations. In a few instances, I was confronted with the realization that I had little empathy for the persons I was interviewing. For example, in my collaboration with Richard, I could not relate to his need to control and silence me; I could not relate to his snobbery; and I certainly could not relate to a person who was not more upfront about his feelings. After much reflection and journal writing, I was able to openly acknowledge my discomfort. This examination of my feelings allowed me to ask why I felt so uncomfortable, removed, or even detached from this study participant. Most importantly, this reflexivity helped me evaluate the assumptions, expectations, and belief systems I had brought to the experience. My "continued self-awareness" became an important opportunity to act on these feelings in the research context, and in turn, use them as important analytical tools. In Richard's case, I used my emotional reaction to his snobbery to delve deeper and better understand why Richard was presenting himself in such an unsympathetic manner.

Contextualizing My Interpretive, Self-Reflexive, Ethnographic Practice

At its most basic level, interpretive ethnography is committed to achieving an intimate familiarity with the life-worlds of the other (Burgess, 1984). Ethnographers are generally involved in observing and participating in the daily lives of those they wish to study over an extended period of time. As Hammersley and Atkinson (1993) suggest, ethnographic practice is about "watching what happens, listening to what is said, asking questions—in fact, collecting whatever data are available to throw light on the issues that are the focus of the research" (p. 1). This style of qualitative methodology is based on a combination of open-ended inquiry, observation, and participant observation.

However, in order to create newer forms of self-reflexive storylines about gay men, my interpretive ethnographic approach needed to go beyond the traditional ethnographic fieldwork techniques of observing, participating, and "taking on the role of the other." Such a stance requires me to adopt a postmodern turn to my interpretive ethnographic practice. This postmodern turn asks that we begin to produce new ways of thinking and writing about subjective experience. This movement dares us to engage in self-reflexive narrative, performance text, standpoint epistemology, and poetics as a means of creating new presentations—and hence newer understanding—about lived experience. These new representations locate the researcher and his or her collaborators subjectively in the narrative, and allow for a more creative process for the discovery of knowing (Richardson, 1994). These storied accounts place as much emphasis on documenting the interpretive practice through which social realities are created as it does on observing and describing social life in detail.

The aim of my interpretive, self-reflexive ethnographic practice is to help create a context for authenticity and deeper understanding of the complex nature of everyday intimacies of gay men. These new formats include investigating a hybrid of textual genres—both in content and style—and features self-reflexive storytelling, poly-vocal texts, and new textual repositioning. These experimental styles of inquiries are caught up in the invention rather than the representation of lived experience. It is about the art of producing experience that is shaped by genre, narrative, and stylistic, personal, cultural, and paradigmatic conventions. At its very core, my stylistic, ethnographic ambitions can be centrally located within a symbolic interactionist tradition.

Core Position: Symbolic Interactionism

There are of course a number of epistemological and methodological variations within interpretive ethnographic research; my fieldwork practice is principally informed by the symbolic interactionist tradition, which values face-to-face social interaction, participation, and joint meaning construction between researcher and collaborators. "Taking on the role of the other" (Mead, 1934) is at the heart of my interactionist practice. Symbolic interactionism studies the ways people make sense of their lives and the ways they go about their activities, in conjunction with others. It is a "down-to-earth" (Blumer, 1969) approach to the study of human group life, whereby the natural world of such group life becomes the empirical setting in which day-to-day practices and experiences are observed, understood, and interpreted. This tradition is broadly informed by a number of social science traditions: (1) hermeneutics, the "sharedness of understandings" in group life (Prus, 1996); (2) American pragmatism, which emphasizes a plurality of truths grounded in practical and everyday experiences and language, and appraises truths in relation to their consequences or use value (Meltzer, Petras & Reynolds 1975); and (3) the Chicago style ethnographic research method, an interpretive approach to the study of lived experience and the engagement with the practical, everyday empirical world (Blumer, 1969). A key concern for interactionism is:

> ...the manner through which human beings go about the task of assembling meaning: how we define ourselves, our bodies and impulses, our feelings and emotions, our behaviours and acts; how we define the situations we are in, develop perspectives on the wider social order, produce "accounts" to explain our actions in lives; how such meanings are constantly being built up through interaction with others, and how these meanings are handled, modified and hence evolve through encounters. In the world of the interactionist, meaning is never fixed and immutable; rather, it is always shifting, emergent and ultimately ambiguous. Though we regularly create habitual, routine, and shared meanings, these are always open to reappraisals and further adjustments. (Plummer, 1996, pp. 223–224)

At the heart of my interactionist enterprise are two main assumptions: (1) lived experience is best understood within the larger community context; and (2) the study of human experience cannot be reduced to individual properties. In other words, there can be no self without the other. Humans derive a sense of themselves and their lives from the communities in which they are located, and those communities are contingent on the development of a shared language, symbols, and ongoing social processes. In this way, lifeworlds are understood as both symboli-cally and linguistically constructed. As researchers like myself begin to adopt the viewpoints of the other, it allows us the capacity to become self-reflective beings, capable of distinguishing ourselves from others in their environments (acquiring a sense of self) and developing ways of viewing and understanding others; monitoring and adjusting behavior over time; and acting and interacting towards other people and ourselves (Mead, 1934). Mead understood this open-ness to the other as a process of role taking; whereby the role of the "generalized other" allows for different perspectives and meanings of the self to be contested and negotiated, and perhaps more importantly, serves as a form of social control and self regulation.

Most importantly, symbolic interactionism provides me with a framework upon which to investigate the intimate lifeworlds of gay men. These lifeworlds are best understood as "worlds of activity" and "multiple social realities." The diverse meaning that gay men bring to these sets of experiences requires a particular sensitivity or awareness to the ways in which meaning is assigned in any social context. As such I make the following assertions about meaning con-struction in fieldwork collaborations: (1) meanings are never fixed or inherent, but rather are context specific and based on the ways in which people define, act toward, or attend to them; (2) meanings are also constructed between the self and the other and the joint acts that emerge between them; and (3) meanings are modified through a collective social process. As Plummer (1996) suggests, such a framework allows me to focus upon the strategies of acquiring a sense of self, of developing a biography, of adjusting to others, of organizing a sense of time, of negotiating order, and of constructing civilizations. The emphasis for me is then on the study of ongoing productions of action, collective behavior, and the joint acts through which their gay lives and societies are constructed. The stories I write about gay men can then be situated within a social text, which is shaped by our emergent social conditions (beliefs, myths, and ideologies) of gay male experience.

The centrality of this core position in my ethnographic practice has had important impli-cations for my own reflexive storytelling. Primarily, it has allowed me to construct some shared understandings and experiences with my research collaborators—which are essential to the sto-rytelling process. These shared meanings, language, and symbolism between us then become the basis upon which knowledge gets constructed between us—and ultimately affects how the story is interpreted, presented, and written in my personal narratives. These processes are the ethical, moral, epistemological, and methodological basis for my fieldwork collaborations. They also create a roadmap for my "ways of knowing" in interpretive ethnography, which are more transparent and accountable to the reader.

Lastly, my interactionist perspectives have allowed me some theoretical space to pursue recent developments within the social science literature that are very sympathetic to the in-tersubjective nature of my fieldwork relationships. These developments include: postmodern ethnography; personal narrative as sociology; poly-vocal ethnography; and meaning-making and storytelling.

Development 1: Postmodern Ethnography

My interpretive self-reflexive ethnographic practices have also been greatly influenced by the rise of postmodernism in the social sciences. Often referred to as the "postmodern sensibility" (Richardson, 1991), this movement in the arts and social sciences heralded in a new moment of modernism that defines itself against an immediate past set of assumptions and conventions

(Lyotard, 1984). Although there are a number of perspectives and viewpoints that fall under the umbrella of postmodernism, at the center of this movement is a skepticism of, and disbelief in, the viability of all forms of knowledge claims and practice. Postmodernism argues against the notion of any real absolutes in the human condition and suggests that all knowledge claims are arbitrary and situational and cannot be judged beyond their own context.

Postmodernism rejects grand theories and metanarratives, and makes the case that all universal knowledge claims of the social should be replaced with more local narratives, small-scale ethnographies, storytelling, and life histories. This position stresses the mythical and illusory qualities of a modernist objective scientific truth. Seidman (1994), like many of his postmodernist contemporaries, suggests that the notion of one real truth located outside of the place, history, class, and sexual location of the knower is a "view from nowhere" (p. 316). By doing so, postmodernists stress the uncertainty of our judgments and the contestability of modernist knowledge claims. Taken to extreme (relativism), postmodernism asserts that no one knowledge claim should be privileged over another, and one is no more viable than any other narrative, fictional story, account, or myth.

This postmodern sensibility brought about a "crisis of representation" in traditional realist ethnographic research (Clifford & Marcus, 1986; Clifford, 1988; Denzin, 1997). This crisis questioned the authorial "gaze" and the epistemological assumptions of gender, race, and class implicit in the earlier text. As a result, new forms of creative, self-reflexive ethnographic representations are sought to replace the classical criteria and claims to authority. Postmodern ethnographic practice is keen to produce a plurality of texts that are sensitive to the complex, interactive, and often contradictory experiences of everyday life. In this sense, these postmodern renderings of lived experience are often understood as "fragmented" partial truths (Clifford, 1988 embedded in "messy" text, whereby the authors of these ethnographies locate themselves and the storylines within a moving and ever-evolving biographical landscape. The postmodern ethnographer is then alerted to and guided by the local, tentative, and performative truths, and is sensitive to those linguistic strategies that best describe it. As Gottschalk (1998) suggests, a "compelling affinity" exists between the site, its culture, and the ethnographer's reflexive self.

There is a lot about the postmodern ethnography that fits nicely into my fieldwork practice. I have pursued a multiplicity of approaches, methodologies, and textual genres in my research on gay men. And in doing so, these narratives have produced new interpretive ways of thinking and writing about subjective experience, which are self-reflexive, emancipatory, and based on critically interpretive frameworks. Clifford & Marcus (1986) best describe this style of fieldwork inquiry as the "poetics and politics of ethnography." In this sense, my project is caught up in the invention rather than the representation of culture. However, when incorporating a postmodern approach to the representation of lived experience, there are certain aspects to postmodernism that make fieldwork research somewhat impractical. For example, the postmodern relativistic viewpoint that no one "way of knowing" should be privileged over another is particularly difficult to manage when collecting data in the field. The reality is, when making decisions about methodology, one does end up having to privilege one set of investigative procedures over another; and in doing so, one not only privileges a particular set of data-collection procedures, but also an ethnographic stance and accounts of the lifeworlds of the other (Prus, 1996). It can't be helped.

Furthermore, relativism also takes the position that all universal knowledge claims should be considered no more viable than other stories, narratives, or fictions. Implicit in this argument is the need to dispense with all abstract and obscure sociological theory. However, if we are unable to make some distinctions between more rigorous approaches to understanding lived experience and coffee conversation, then what is the point of engaging in empirical research? I would take a slightly more moderate postmodern point of view. Similarly to Stone (1998), I would argue that there is a lot in the postmodern argument that is attractive and useful; however, as Stone suggests:

> Where we can't agree with Seidman, and postmodernism more generally, is in his belief that developing a more engaged and socially relevant sociology means dispensing with theory and all its concerns, including its concerns with truth. There is no necessary connection between a concern with theory and truth, on the one hand, and becoming cut off from social and practical issues, on the other. For me and for all those who wish to retain the notion of social science, the opposite is true. When we grapple with practical social and empirical issues we often need to decide which is the more accurate picture; or which sketchily imagined picture of something, someone, can be backed up empirically, and to what extent; we need to be aware—and this is a theoretical concern—that some pictures seem to emerge coherently (one part of the jigsaw fitting with the others) and that others seem to be inherently inconsistent...and so on. (p. 6)

When adopting a more moderate postmodern ethnographic stance, which includes grappling with empirical and theoretical truths, the question then becomes how do we go about deciding which narrative, ethnography, or myth is the more accurate picture of lived experience? Plummer (1999) makes the suggestion that the "new" ethnographies in the 21st century can best be judged by a set of guidelines (or critically aware set of standards) that are based on a array of moral, political, and ethical dimensions. He posits that these tales should be evaluated based on a set of questions that address these ethical and moral concerns. For instance: What right do I have to tell the story? Does my ethnography create new cultural insights? What are the truth claims being made through the ethnography? Whose voices are being privileged or silenced by the author? In his view, those new ethnographies that don't meet these critical dimensions should be seriously challenged or understood for what they are.

Plummer's call for the development of an ethical and more socially responsible set of standards for ethnographic inquiry is in fact a very useful and pragmatic incorporation of postmodern sensibilities. These standards are derived from the poststructuralist critiques of realist ethnography, which made us more critically aware of the political, ethical, and textual dimensions of lived experience. In keeping within this argument, I would also suggest that postmodernism's real usefulness is in its ability to provide us with such a critical framework for ethnography—so that we may distinguish between "the more accurate picture" and the "sketchily imagined picture" of lived experience. The application of a moderate postmodern sensibility provides me with a sophisticated set of tools by which my interpretive ethnography can be understood, challenged, or made more accountable.

Development 2: Personal Narrative as Sociology

The introduction of personal narrative to social science inquiry brought about an important shift in focus and textual style to my interpretive ethnography. This epistemological shift introduced a new genre in sociological writing by blurring the traditional boundaries between social science writing and other literary forms, such as fictionalized accounts, autobiography, and personal writing (Banks & Banks, 1998). In doing so, personal narrative provides a unique perspective on the intersection of the individual, the collectivity, and the social (Laslett, 1999). In this way, the self becomes both the subject of the study and the narrator; and self-knowledge, personal experiences, and autobiographical narratives become a rich source of sociological insight into the lifeworld of the other. The sociological meanings embedded in these personal writings are told rather than inferred. Most importantly, these personal narratives allow the self to be understood in relation to their social networks of people (Stanley, 1993).

My self-reflexive narratives about gay men are both experimental and personal in nature. It is my opportunity to write more contextual, more meaningful, and more textually diverse representations of gay male intimacy. These endeavors require me to go beyond the modernist narrative cannons that often situate a cast of characters in time, space, and place. As such I experiment with such written genres as personal narrative, postmodern ethnography, self-reflexivity, emotionality, and multi-vocality—in my case, study narratives. These storytelling formats were in essence my way of breaking away from the grand narratives of the day to begin to think differently about representing lived experience. Creating experimental, interpretive, postmodern, less storied narratives about the everyday are by there very nature somewhat dissociated from the conventions of locality and geography as we know it.

I also wanted to try my hand at writing narrative constructions that intersected the personal with the sociological. This style of storytelling is founded on the assumption that through the personal, the social, and the intersection of the two, one can learn about "individual and collection actions and meanings, as well as the social process by which social life and human relationships are made and changed" (Laslett, 1999, p. 392). I write these storylines in an effort to explore how my own perspectives and interpretive lenses might affect the articulation of the story and my ways of making sense of lived experience. In this way, I become the subject of the study and the narrator; and my self-knowledge, personal experience, and auto/biography becomes a rich source of sociological insight into the world of gay men. My principal ambition in this regard is to create a more transparent reflexive process through first-person narrative.

The arrival of these personal narrative projects has important implications for my own work. Primarily, these projects encourage writers like me to find ways to let my own presence and experiences be felt in the ethnographic text; second, it allows for the recognition of my own perspectives in social science writing; and third, it argues for an increased understanding of how one's own self can greatly facilitate the analysis of the data (Krieger, 1991). My personal narratives about gay men challenge me to think about the rules, methods, and writing techniques I choose when I represent myself and others in research. For example, the difficulties I may have experienced with a collaborator presented me with an important opportunity to let my presence be felt and explored in social science writing. It was also an opportunity to explore a new genre of writing that might "unearth" the emotions I had learned so well to hide, and use these emotional experiences as way of understanding the social. These emotional responses were initially explored as diary entries in my fieldwork journal. However, as I continued to document these feelings, I slowly acquired a deeper sense of the situation under scrutiny and was moved by how my emotions and personal history had greatly facilitated my interpretation of my collaborators and the analysis of the data. I was moved enough by these revelations that I decided to a write a personal narrative by working with difficult collaborators and its implications for knowledge and meaning-making in storytelling.

It is also important to be mindful of the reason for incorporating self-awareness into these personal narratives. It is quite easy to produce self-reflexive texts that do little to acknowledge the presence of the other, or indeed, illuminate my "ways of knowing" in the production of knowledge. Some ethnographers have been quick to label such reflexive writings as "self-indulgent" (Atkinson & Hammersley, 1994) or as mere exercises in intellectual narcissism. There is certainly no guarantee that by changing the presentation rules, we will always produce evocative ethnographic renderings. However, I would agree with Charmaz & Mitchell (1997) when they say that a self-reflexive voice should always be used to communicate the fullness of the fieldwork phenomenon. In their view, "voice forms another dimension of the ethnographic report; voice is one more source of insight from which readers can construct images of the goings-on" (p. 208). With this in mind, I need to ensure that my own reflexive voice helps to illuminate the lifeworld of the other by giving us a deeper sense of the situation under scrutiny. Gottschalk and his contemporaries get it right when they speak about the makings of good self-reflexive ethnography: "Successful ethnographies are those which can self-reflexively connect private troubles to public issues, evoke recognition and empathy, promote action… [and], facilitate healing in some cases…" (Gottschalk, 1998, p. 209).

Development 3: Poly-Vocal Ethnography

Self-reflexive voices have always been an integral part of my interpretive storytelling. It is often a struggle for me to figure out how to represent my own voice while simultaneously writing the respondents' accounts and representing their selves. How voices and identities get constructed in reflexive narrative becomes an important epistemological and methodological consideration for me. The following questions are central to these concerns: Whose voice? Whose points of view? And whose vested interests are being expressed? The literature identifies the inescapable consequences of the author's voice in these social texts (Denzin & Lincoln, 1994; Richardson, 1994; Ellis & Bochner, 1996; Hertz, 1997). It argues that the participant's voice is mostly filtered through the richness of the author's own experiences, understandings, and observation, and as such, textual representations of subjective experiences are always the author's recreations of those experiences—privileging some accounts over others by deciding whose stories or which quotes get included into the text. In this way, my narrative representations are often argued to be "stand-ins" or indirect textual representations of the actual experiences being described and analyzed.

My storylines about gay men were an attempt to capture the multiplicity of voices, locations, and experiences that took place between me and my collaborators in the story construction. Writing poly-vocal narratives is also my way of making public sense of the writers' narrator-interpreter relations (Personal Narrative Group, 1989) in these narratives. I want the reader to become more informed about how I made sense of the storytelling that took place in the interview process. In short, create new ways of articulating my "authorial presence" (Tierney, 1995) and the power relations surrounding the production of narrative.

An interesting contribution of my poly-vocal accounts is my ability to identify the different narrative perspectives in the storytelling. In my fieldwork collaborations, all voices are heard, located, and interpreted in the storyline; and came alive and interacted with each other. I purposely set about the task of selecting storied vignettes from our interview conversations that best exemplify our understanding of the events and occasions that define our fieldwork relationship. Quite often throughout the narrative, the reader is exposed to interactive and collaborating voices in an effort to understand how the storytelling was constructed and presented in the interview context.

My voice in the narrative can be thought of as having three different locations in the text: (1) my interviewer voice; (2) my reflexive journal voice; and (3) my writing voice. My first voice in this narrative construction draws largely from the transcripts—as it relates to the actual questions and interview conversations I have with my collaborators. The second voice is constituted from my fieldwork journal and incorporates what I am thinking, feeling, emoting, and wondering while listening and probing during the interview conversations. My third location is my wondering reflexive sociologist voice that happens while I am writing up the case-study narrative. This third voice brings new insight and interpretation to the storyline as the narrative unfolds on the page. It locates itself squarely in the present tense and takes old voices and perspectives and makes new meaning of them. The historical nature of this position allows me to reconceptualize out loud in the narrative, and re-story previously held views and understandings.

It is important to note that these past and present locations coexist in the narrative. While constructing this poly-vocal account, it is almost like being in a music studio laying down individual tracks for a new song. Each track represents the layering of a different voice, thought, feeling, experience, or perspective to the storyline. The first tracks to be laid are the actual textual voices from the transcripts. The second tracks are my inner voices missing from the transcripts. The third tracks are my wondering reflexive sociologist voice—all of which when strung together represent the totality of the storytelling experience from all perspectives and historical vantage points. Charmaz and Mitchell (1997) would have us think of these voices as several selves—at once reflecting, witnessing, wondering, and accepting. Indeed this is the case. I take these several selves—both past and present—and bring them together in a highly contextualized narrative. What I am trying to do is represent conventional gay lives in less conventional ways, by recreating the interactions, reflexivity, and interpretations that take place around the actual storytelling.

Development 4: Meaning Making and Storytelling

Adopting an interpretive, self-reflexive stance has important implications for creation of knowledge and meaning-making in my narratives. This practice orients the researcher to the interactional construction of meaning. Through entering into dialogue with the meaning systems of my collaborators, I'm enabled as a researcher to discover, understand, and write their stories (Ronai, 1992). Understanding the interactional dimensions in which these stories get told also allows me to lay claim to the process that has allowed me to know what I know.

Riessman (1993) best describes this narrative practice as "a teller in a conversation takes a listener into a past time or world and recapitulates what happened to them to make a point, a moral one" (p. 3). It is the solution to the problem of how to translate knowing into telling. The literature makes the analytical point that individuals use narrative links to construct meaning in their lives (Bruner, 1986; Mishler, 1986; Gubrium & Holstein, 1995). It is through these linkages that individuals piece together bits of experiences in order to specify subjective meaning. Bruner (1986) argues that narrative gives structure, organizes memory, and provides a purpose to the events of everyday life. Central to this argument is the notion that narrative creates plots from disordered and fragmented experiences. The stories people tell do not necessarily represent facts of how things actually were, but rather are meaning-making systems that make sense and give unity to past perceptions and experiences (Riessman, 1993). My storytelling becomes an exercise in reframing a story in order to construct value and meaning-making out of the past. As Josselson (1995) suggests, "in understanding ourselves, we chose those facets of our experience that lead to the present and render our life story coherent" (p. 35).

Implicit in these arguments of narrative and meaning-making are the interactionist assumptions that the social world is negotiated via symbolic orders and social interaction. Storytelling allows us to be reflexive, invent identities for ourselves and others, and create communities of concern. Dialogue and conversation becomes the site where meaning is created, re-negotiated, and contested over time. Plummer (1995) refers to the interactions that emerge around storytelling as "joint actions" of interpretation between the producers of stories, the texts themselves, and the consumers of these told narratives. By understanding interpretative practice as the means through which lives are constructed, we direct our attention back to how persons articulate the stories they tell about themselves and construct biographies centered on the presentation of those realities (Gubrium & Holstein, 1995).

Directing our attentions back to how individuals constructed their own stories and give meaning to these experiences has important implications for interpretive ethnographic practice more generally, and for my work specifically. It allows me to understand storytelling as "situationally constructed communications" whereby individuals actively construct their own stories in collaboration with me—as researcher—and with the aid of locally promoted ways of interpreting experience (Gubrium & Holstein, 1995). These ways of knowing include local cultures and their shared meanings; community-based vocabularies; and the physical settings that subjects use to construct content and give shape to their experience (p. 50). The task of the interpretive ethnographer then becomes to encourage the teller of these tales to actively use these localized, recognizable resources as tools for meaning-making in narrative construction.

Finally, in keeping with these situated narrative constructions, it is important to go one step further and connect my narrative practice and meaning-making to identity construction. The presentation of self (Goffman, 1959), in narrative form, can determine what the teller will include or exclude in the narrativization; how events will be plotted; and how others will interpret us and our personal experiences. Authors of these situated tales create versions of themselves that will be liked by others. Rosenwald & Ochberg (1992) comment on the importance of identity construction in storytelling:

> How individuals recount their histories—what they emphasize and omit, their stance as protagonists or victims, the relationship the story establishes between teller and audience—all shape what individuals can claim of their own lives. Personal stories are not merely a way of telling someone (or oneself) about one's life; they are the means by which identities may be fashioned. (p. 1)

Developing My Interpretive, Self-Reflexive Fieldwork Practice

Writing reflexive narratives about gay men was an opportunity for me to "try on for size" some of the more recent developments in interpretive ethnography, which encourage us to be more experimental with narrative representations of personal experience. The application of these ethnographic practices would be my "doings" of reflexive storytelling in sociology. As such, I go to great lengths to understand what I know and how I came to know it; I struggled to get closer to the experiencing "other"; and in a very practical way, I become very aware of my situated, temporal, and embodied selves in the field and in the research write-up. In the process, I discovered that my reflexivity illuminates my ways of knowing in the research process—and in doing so, materially sheds light on my understanding of gay men's everyday intimate lives.

It is important to note that these representations are not created in a vacuum. In spite of the meaningful interaction that took place between us, I continue to struggle with the presentation of these narratives. Undoubtedly, my authorial sensibilities were a contributing factor in the ways my narratives are constructed. What gets written into the storyline is always problematic and it raises questions about the limitations of textual representations of lived experience. Even in highly contextualized narratives, the reader must continue to rely on the writer's own interpretations and goodwill to represent the story fairly. As is always the case, these attempts to identify and contextualize the author's authority in the text is an imperfect enterprise. When trying to create "better" representations of the experiencing, we ultimately control the representations of those we study. Hertz (1997) points out that the issue of textual authority is particularly problematic in interpretive ethnography. There will always be a tension between giving meaning to the lives of the people we work with through narrative, and our own political vision and the choices we make on their behalf. As Wasserfall (1997) states when speaking about feminist ethnographers:

> While they may contextualize the study they do not erase the tension stemming from the fact that the ultimate responsibility toward the written work lies with the ethnographer. At best these identifications construct another frame of authority, another story, they do not erase it. Authority is an unavoidable even if difficult issue for feminist ethnographers. (p. 153)

I also have to make some ethical decisions about the extent to which I actively take ownership of my interpretive presentations. In such cases where there was either little collaboration or little reflexivity in the original fieldwork collaboration, I have to impose my own thematic storyline to the narrative. The imposition of these themes raises ethical questions about the exploitation of my own reflexivity through narrative. My defense to these ethical dilemmas is to be as transparent as I can about the thematic liberties I took when representing in the storylines. These transparencies in the storyline are my public struggle to contextualize issues of representation, exploitation, and authorial presence. In the end, Charmaz's (1996) "candor" is the best ethical defense when writing up interpretive ethnography. She states that such an endeavor creates the possibility for the author to be up front and open about what he/she brings to, aims for, and does with the material; for as she says, the "ways of viewing the material shape what is viewed and as well as the voice of the viewer.... voice becomes interactive and emergent" (p. 206).

I will continue to develop my interpretive reflexive practice. It has much to recommend it. In doing so, I will endeavor to incorporate many of the negotiated boundaries that take place in the project, when researcher and collaborator blur the lines between public identities and our private intimate selves. I also expect to deal with the singular dimension of the interview process by locating our interview conversations within a larger ethnographic biography. The larger situational storylines often involve many other players, locales, and different versions of these events. I get to see my collaborators acting out roles and identities in ways that a traditional interview could never begin to reveal—lived biographies in the present tense, warts and all.

Going "native" may allow me to locate subjectivity in real life. I get to take my participants off their pedestals, altars—or out of the hell holes I may have built for them during the collaboration. I also get to think of them in less singular ways. They are not just saints, sinners, victims, survivors, heroes, mavericks, or jerks. They are ordinary people who have responded in very extraordinary ways to what life has handed them. In these ethnographic narratives, my collaborators may regain their humanity.

References

Atkinson, P., & Hammersley, M. (1994). Ethnography and participant observation. In N. K. Denzin & Y. S. Lincoln (Eds.), *Sage handbook of Qualitative Research* (1st ed). Thousand Oaks, CA: Sage.

Banks A., & Banks, S. (1998). *Fiction and social research.* London: Sage.

Barbour, R. (1998). Engagement, representation and presentation in research practice. In R. Barbour & G. Huby (Eds.), *Meddling with mythology: AIDS and the social construction of knowledge.* London: Routledge.

Belenky, M., Clinchy, B. Goldberger, N., & Tarule, J. (1986). *Women's ways of knowing: The development of self.* New York: Basic Books.

Blumer, H. (1969). *Symbolic interactionism: Perspective and method.* Berkeley: University of California Press.

Bruner, J. (1986). *Actual minds, possible words.* Cambridge, MA: Harvard University Press.

Burgess, R. (1984). *In the field: An introduction to field research.* London: Routledge.

Charmaz, K. (1996). Forward. In R. Prus, *Symbolic interaction and ethnographic research: Intersubjectivity and the study of human lived experience.* Albany: State of University of New York Press.

Charmaz, K., & Mitchell, R. (1997). The myth of silent authorship: Self, substance, and style in ethnographic writing. In R. Hertz (Ed.), *Reflexivity and voice.* Thousand Oaks, CA: Sage.

Clifford, J. (1988). *The predicament of culture.* Cambridge, MA: Harvard University Press.

Clifford, J., & Marcus, G. (1986). *Writing culture: The poetics and politics of ethnography.* Berkeley: University of California Press.

Denzin, N. (1997). *Interpretive ethnography: Ethnographic practices for the 21st century.* Thousand Oaks, CA: Sage.

Denzin, N., & Lincoln, Y. (1994). *Sage handbook of qualitative research* (1st ed). Thousand Oaks, CA: Sage.

Ellis, C., & Bochner, A. (1996). *Composing ethnography: Alternative forms of qualitative writing.* Walnut Creek, CA: AltaMira Press.

Goffman, E. (1959). *The presentation of self in everyday life.* New York: Doubleday.

Gottschalk, S. (1998). Postmodern sensibilities and ethnographic possibilities. In A. Banks & S. Banks (Eds.), *Fiction and social research.* London: Sage.

Greer, M. (1990). Rewriting culture: Poststructuralism, cultural theory, and ethnography: *Studies in Symbolic Interaction,* 11, Greenwich, CT: JAI Press.

Gubrium J., & Holstein, J. (1995). Biographical work and new ethnography. In R. Josselson & A. Lieblich (Eds.), *Interpreting experience: The narrative study of lives* (Vol. 3). Thousand Oaks, CA: Sage.

Hammersley, M., & Atkinson, P. (1993). *Ethnography: Principles in practice* (2nd ed.). London: Routledge.

Hertz, R. (1997). *Reflexivity and voice.* Thousand Oaks, CA: Sage.

Jamieson, L. (1998) *Intimacy: Personal relationships in modern societies.* Cambridge: Polity.

Josselson, R. (1995). Imagining the real: Empathy, narrative, and the dialogic self. In R. Josselson & A. Lieblich (Eds.), *Interpretive experience: The narrative study of lives* (Vol. 3). Thousand Oaks, CA: Sage.

Kleinman, S., & Copp, M. (1993). *Emotions and fieldwork: Qualitative research methods, Series 28.* Newbury Park, CA: Sage.

Krieger, S. (1991). *Social science and the self: Personal essays on an art form.* New Brunswick, NJ: Rutgers University Press.

Laslett, B. (1999). Personal narratives as sociology. *Contemporary sociology: A journal of reviews, 28*(4), 391–401.

Lyotard, J. (1984). *The postmodern condition.* Minneapolis: University of Minnesota Press.

Mahoney, D. (2007). Constructing reflexive fieldwork relationships: Narrating my collaborative storytelling methodology. *Qualitative Inquiry, 13*(4), 573–594.

Mead, G. H. (1934). *Mind, self and society.* Chicago: University of Chicago Press.

Meltzer, B., Petras, J., & Reynolds, L. (1975). *Symbolic interactionism: Genesis, varieties and criticism.* London: Routledge & Kegan Paul.

Mishler, E. (1986). *Research interviewing: Context and narrative.* Cambridge, MA: Harvard University Press.

Personal Narrative Group (1989). *Interpreting women's lives: Feminist theory and personal narrative.* Bloomington: Indiana University Press.

Plummer, K. (1995). *Telling sexual stories: Power, change and social worlds.* London: Routledge.

Plummer, K. (1996). Symbolic interactionism in the twentieth century: The rise of empirical social theory. In B. Turner (Ed.), *The Blackwell companion to social theory.* Oxford: Blackwell.

Plummer, K. (1999). The "ethnographic society" at century's end: Clarifying the role of public ethnography. *Journal of Contemporary Ethnography, 28*(6), 641–649.

Plummer, K. (2001). *Documents of life-2: An invitation to a critical humanism.* London: Sage.

Prus, R. (1996). *Symbolic interaction and ethnographic research: Intersubjectivity and the study of human lived experience.* Albany: State University of New York Press.

Richardson, L. (1991).The poetic representation of life: Writing a postmodernist sociology. *Studies in Symbolic Interaction* 13. Greenwich, CT: JAI Press.

Richardson, L. (1994). Writing: A method of inquiry. In N. Denzin & Y. Lincoln (Eds.), *Sage handbook of qualitative research* (1st ed.). Thousand Oaks, CA: Sage.

Riessman, C. (1993). *Narrative analysis.* Newbury Park, CA: Sage.

Ronai, C. (1992). The reflexive self through narrative. In C. Ellis & M. Flaherty (Eds.), *Investigating subjectivity: Research on lived experience.* London: Sage.

Rosenwald, G., & Ochberg, R. (1992). Introduction: Life stories, cultural politics, and self-understanding. In G. Rosenwald & R. Ochberg (Eds.) *Storied lives: The cultural politics of self-understanding.* New Haven, CT: Yale University Press.

Seidman, S. (1992). *Embattled eros: Sexual politics and ethics in contemporary America.* London: Routledge.

Seidman, S. (1994). *The postmodern turn: New perspectives on social theory.* Cambridge: Cambridge University Press.

Silverman, D. (1999). The pleasures of slowness. In B. Glassner & R. Hertz (Eds.), *Qualitative sociology as everyday life.* Thousand Oaks, CA: Sage.

Stanley, L. (1993). On auto/biography in sociology. *Sociology, 27*(1), 41–52.

Stone, R. (1998). Social theory: Beyond blind date with the felt and plastic bird kit. In M. Haralambos (Ed.), *Developments in Sociology: An Annual Review* (Vol. 14).

Tierney, W. (1995). (Re)Presentation and voice. *Qualitative Inquiry, 1*(4), 379–390.

Wasserfall, R. (1997). Reflexivity, feminism and difference. In R. Hertz (Ed.), *Reflexivity and voice.* Thousand Oaks, CA: Sage.

Exploring Methodological Innovations for the Critical Analysis of Language Use

CHAPTER ELEVEN

Content Inference Fields in Intersubjective Space

Transpersonal Position, Illocution, and Logic in the Analysis of Human Interactions

RAN ZHANG & PHIL CARSPECKEN

A public school teacher in Tacoma, Washington, has had twelve years of exemplary performance in her profession. Maria is a lesbian but has hidden her sexual orientation in all domains of her life aside from her most intimate relationships. At last she decides to be open about her lesbian identity with other adults, and comes out. Not long afterwards she is fired from her job. With respect to the laws of the United States, of the state of Washington, of the city of Tacoma, and according to school board policies and precedents in case law, was this decision just or not?

In this chapter, we introduce the concept of "content inference field" through an examination of a mock debate on the legality of Maria's dismissal. The mock debate took place between graduate students of educational law at a midwestern university in the United States. We undertook this project out of an interest in the difference between logic and what has been called "illocutionary force." Logical relations, we supposed, are related to human interactions via meaningful contents rather than the interaction infrastructures, the "settings" (explained below) through which people coordinate their actions and communications with each other. The latter pertains to illocutionary force, although we will soon dispense with the word "force" and write instead about illocutionary "structures," "infrastructures," and "inferences." We begin with some theory and then illustrate the reconstruction of content inference fields from the mock debate over Maria's dismissal. We explain the concept of content inference field and show its relevance for understanding human interactions.

I. Theory of Meaning, Structure and Field

Illocutionary Inference Structures

The expression "illocutionary force" can be traced back to a famous book by John Austin, *How to Do Things with Words* (1975). Austin took interest in the fact that speech acts not only convey meanings, but also "do" things. Speech acts represent or signify, but they also result in changed states of affairs within the social world. Hence when an appropriate official, minister, or priest pronounces two people to be married within the proper context, they are from then on married. When a person issues a promise to another, accepts a request, makes a confession, then meaningful actions are clearly more than ways to talk about or represent something else; they change social reality. Austin began his analysis by examining special kinds of speech acts, those whose explicit point is to make a change in human relationships such as providing a guarantee, issuing a declaration, making an avowal, and so on. Because speech acts like these affect social reality rather than merely represent something that has an ontological status independent of speech acts, Austin thought it appropriate to use the term "force" in describing them. He called speech acts whose main point is to convey representations or ideas "locutionary," and these special speech acts that do something were called "illocutionary" and said to possess illocutionary "force."

But with further examination of Austin's insight, it became clear that all speech acts will have an illocutionary component because simply to interact with another human being is to do so through a co-constructed intersubjective infrastructure. When people talk about something, they do so with assumedly shared understandings about how they should be talking with each other, what power relations ought to be recognized as appropriate in their relationship, about how frequently each should talk before receiving a response from the other, and many other things that are implicitly claimed, accepted, rejected, negotiated between them. People take on commitments and issue entitlements, claim and endorse norms of interaction when they communicate and otherwise coordinate their actions together. Hence use of the word "force" in connection to illocution can be extremely misleading, since illocution involves claims made by actors that can in principle be rejected and that can be, in principle, rationally argued for or against. Illocution is not really a matter of "force," but of the capacity human beings have for taking on commitments with and for reasons. And all human interactions will involve illocutionary claims and structures, not just some.

Illocutionary claims are discussed by Robert Brandom (1998) in terms of commitments and entitlements that people in interaction keep track of on a "deontic scoreboard," to use Brandom's metaphor. With the term "deontic," Brandom designates obligations that people commit to while interacting together; and "scoreboard" refers to an assumedly shared intersubjective "record" of the commitments and entitlements that are undertaken and issued continuously while people interact. Brandom does not use the term "illocutionary force" or even "illocution," but he is clearly writing about the same phenomenon that Austin did. "Deontic scorekeeping" is in fact a more precise way to conceptualize what illocution consists of.

Jurgen Habermas (1984) does use the term "illocutionary force" while interpreting it along lines similar to Brandom (see especially Habermas, 1984, Chapter 3, and also his essay "What Is Universal Pragmatics" in *On the Pragmatics of Communication*, 2000). Habermas and Brandom alike link illocution to "rational motivations," consensus based in the end on reasons, which should be contrasted with "force," "persuasion," "utility," and other such terms. A rational motivation is something unique to the intersubjectivity that arises with normed symbolic systems like language. An actor is motivated to act with reasons and sometimes for reasons that are claimed to be transpersonally valid. It feels "right" to act with justifiable reasons and "wrong" to fail to do so. It feels "free" to act for reasons that are claimed to have transpersonal validity. Rational motivation is deeply linked to personhood, to being an accountable, responsible, and free subject rather than to being an object within the play of various causes and forces.

Habermas goes further than Brandom by articulating a theme we explore here in more detail than Habermas and yet still only partially. This is the idea that human understanding involves a "moment of mutuality" as he calls it, that could be interpreted in the direction of a kind of momentary non-self-differentiation, a moment of non-individuation within what we call "intersubjective space." For Habermas this pertains to his quasi-ontology of "social relations," based on identity-relevant, thus existentially relevant and identity-securing, commitments of deep relevance to the "practical I" (rather than the epistemic "I") and therefore to identity maintenance and ontological security. The quasi-ontology of social relationships is one that cannot be captured through concepts and lexical terms pertaining to objects and events. Personhood, self, human identity are constituted by the commitments endorsed or rejected, with and/or for reasons, that people take on in their relations with others.

Because "illocutionary force" is better understood as a specialized domain of deontic validity claims (claims made implicitly, negotiated implicitly, and honored or broken usually implicitly by actors during their interactions), it has some resemblance to logic. The relations are inferential, not causal, in both cases. For example, a commitment implicitly undertaken during an interaction to remain in the role of a good and sympathetic listener while a friend makes herself vulnerable, revealing intimate personal problems, entails a whole structure of other commitments, inferentially related. To be in this role entails not suddenly becoming judgmental and negating, not making a joke at the friend's expense, not responding to a sensitive confession by talking about a football game, and so on. The inferences will be specific in particulars to the context of an interaction; the extent to which the participants already know each other, the cultural milieu they share, and other things. They will also have levels of inferential relations, some of which are less contingent on personal history and localized cultural milieu than others. They are inferentially connected such that one participant can in principle articulate what may be inferred from a commitment taken on by the other to critique an action, or express disappointment or lack of trust if the illocutionary structure seems to be violated at some point. And violations of illocutionary commitments have implications for the identity of the one making the violations. The kind of person one claims to be and wishes to be is at stake during interactions. Honoring illocutionary commitments will maintain such identity claims and even at times develop and enrich them. Dishonoring them will at bottom risk the person's trustworthiness, integrity, dignity, and accountability. Illocutionary commitments are commitments to entire structures whose components are linked inferentially. To commit to being a good and supportive listener in an interaction is to commit to not acting flippantly, to not change the topic at an inappropriate time, and many other things.

Instantiated Structure, Temporal Compression, Possible Subject-Subject Relations in Intersubjective Space

Both logical relations between locutionary contents and illocutionary relations pertaining to interaction infrastructures allow participants in an interaction to anticipate the boundaries within which other persons will or should act next. In terms of illocutionary infrastructure, a commitment to, for example, talk with another within an understanding of equalized status and power allows the other to anticipate the form that actions will take from the former: the acts ought not be, in this example, in the form of an authority figure interacting with a subordinate. Logical relations constitutive of locutionary contents also inform the expected boundaries within which next acts will come. In a discussion of the surprising fact that our moon has very little iron in its soil when our earth has significant amounts, it would be startling to hear one participant suggest that predator-prey systems in nature are a relevant matter to bring up. People in interactions work with assumedly shared structures whose components are inferentially related, such that each participant may act in relation to an inference she (usually implicitly) assumes the other(s) are also aware of.

In both the case of logic and illocution, we find structures whose components are linked inferentially. And this is how we will use the term "structure" in this chapter. A structure is unlike a system because systems are best conceptualized has having time and space differentiations between components. We can speak of "economic systems" because aggregate patterns of buying during one period of time will have an effect on prices at a later time, which will in turn have an effect on new aggregate patterns of buying during an even later period of time. It is a system for this reason. Conditions of action are related to patterns of action; the patterns of action have consequences; and the aggregate action consequences either reproduce or change the relevant conditions of action. Economic events in China will have effects on later economic events in the United States because of an economic system linking events separated by time and space. There are many kinds of social systems, but all of them have time and space differentiations between components.

Inferential relations pertaining to what we call "structures," by contrast, link components of a structure all at once. The concept of "structure" here is that used by structuralists. But whereas structuralists like Levi-Strauss (1974) thought of structures in terms of the determinants of action, we follow Anthony Giddens by thinking of structures as the medium and outcome of action. Structures do not determine actions, but rather enable them and are reproduced or modified as one of the action outcomes. In addition, we add the notions of claiming and inferential relation to Giddens's insight. Structures are instantiated by meaningful actions all at once. The foregrounded meaning of meaningful actions can be broken into constitutive validity claims, and the structures instantiated as what makes such meaning intelligible are themselves "claimed." Responses to meaningful actions can challenge or negotiate the claimed structures that constituted the meaning as well as the validity claims that are more specifically foregrounded within the meaning. The best discussion of the difference between structure and system along these lines that we are aware of was written by Anthony Giddens many years ago, in his essay "Structuralism and the Theory of the Subject," published in his influential book, *Central Problems in Social Theory* (1979). Here Giddens also introduces his now widely used term "structuration." Structures of the sort we are talking about here do not determine actions or thoughts, but rather enable them and are reproduced, modified, iterated through the actions that instantiate them.

We endorse Giddens not only because of the distinction he makes between structure and system, but also the shift he makes from an entity frame to a process frame, from structure to structuration; we regard the possible responses of other actors to a meaningful act as being crucial to any concept of the internal nature of meaning. The anticipated response of another actor to one's own act is learned and then temporally "squeezed" to the simultaneous inferential relations between components of a structure. The meaning of "Please hand me the red apple" pertains to expected possible responses: an action of handing the red apple, a verbal response like "Why, certainly," a verbal response like, "Get it yourself," a verbal response like, "Do you mean the orange apple? I see no red apple here," and so on. The boundaries of acceptable responses constitute the meaning. And this is where inferential relations within structures come from.

Meaning-constitutive structures are of various types and involve different levels such that every meaningful act instantiates many structures simultaneously. "Please hand me the red apple" instantiates structures pertaining to the request form of the act. Requests are structurally distinguished from commands, "You must give me the red apple"; assertions, "You will hand me the red apple"; questions, "Are you going to hand me the red apple?" such that an under-standing of the differences between several such forms is necessary to understand our act as a request. Another structure here pertains to understanding what an apple is and is not. Another pertains to color. Another pertains to assumedly shared norms that demarcate the conditions within which a request like this should be complied with in contrast with conditions within which this same request should be rejected. When we make this request, "Please hand me the red apple," we instantiate these various structures as claims that can be questioned. The fore-grounded validity claims in this request include, "I wish you to hand me the apple," "There is a red apple within the knowledge of us both," "You are requested, not commanded, to hand me the apple." The request for the red apple "draws upon" assumedly shared structures, instantiates them as claims, and one of the outcomes of the request will be the reproduction or slight altera-tion of those same structures. Structure is the medium and outcome of action, as Giddens says.

We do not have space in this chapter to develop many of the theoretical points we make, including this one about how to conceive of structure. Relating structure to learning processes that take temporally separated relations between an act and its consequences and put them into simultaneous, inferential, relations within meaning is much the way that Piaget thought of "structure." Cognition, argued Piaget, is based on "abstractions" from action-consequence relations (see his *Genetic Epistemology*, 1971). But Piaget's work seems to be limited by insuf-ficient attention to the different sort of action that is communicative in nature and that is therefore not oriented towards tangible consequences but towards a possible (but not neces-sarily intended or desired) mutual understanding with another subject. Learning processes that are subject-subject based result in structures by generating intersubjective space: a space of possible other subject positions. This compresses, via learning, specifically communicative experiences that take place during interactions within time to simultaneous structural rela-tions between possible subject positions. And this is where our "inference field" concept comes from: an analysis that could be called "communicative structuration theory," which also could be called "communicative pragmatism." In classical pragmatism, and much of Piagetian cogni-tive theory, learning relates actions to anticipated tangible consequences. With communicative pragmatism, learning relates the communicative experience of another possible subject posi-tion to the position from which one acts. It is not the objective response of another actor that is learned in association with one's own act, it is the place in intersubjective space from which that response comes. We will discuss this idea just a bit more in a section far below on anticipa-tion and its relation to meaning.

Every meaningful act claims the validity of the inferential relations implicitly constitut-ing the meaning of this act, and at bottom these inferential relations are compressions of subject-subject relations originally separated in time, through interactions resulting in com-municative experiences, to simultaneous constituents of meaning. Inferential relations of this sort are relations between multiple possible subject positions within a claimed transpersonal, intersubjective, space.[1] And these inferential relations can have features that are newly claimed and unexpected, which then will either be accepted in the response of other actors or not. This is why we have structuration: a process of instantiating meaning-constituting structures in action that will involve constant changes, modifications, innovations, and so on.

Objectivation

Two ways of objectivating meaning-constituting structures are of special interest to us at this time: content-logical and illocutionary. As already mentioned, both logical relations between meaningful contents and inferential relations between illocutionary commitments and entitlements make it possible to predict next possible actions from other subjects, and understand the boundaries within which next possible acts will most likely come. In the case of logical-content relations, the relevant inferential structures are features of objectivations: the topics that people talk about, and the "propositional contents" of their meaningful actions. These are objectivated at some level although not necessarily thematized. By "objectivated" we mean that actors are in the process of acting communicatively in relation to something distinguished from their communicative actions. By thematizied we mean foregrounded for consideration and usually with explicit linguistic representations. There will always be plenty of nonforegrounded and thus nonthematized implicated contents that people are talking about when they interact communicatively. We are here more concerned with the process of objectivation rather than thematization. The latter, thematization, is a special kind of objectivation that, however, depends upon other implicated contents being objectivated while not thematized. So when talking about an apple and whether it is red or orange, the color of this apple is thematized as well as objectivated; the color spectrum, apples in general, fruits and many other things are now objectivated by thematizing the color of one particular apple, but as background structure, non-thematized backgrounded assumptions and claims making the foreground intelligible and inferentially related to this foreground. They are ready to be brought up in thematized form, if necessary, by following a content-inferential relation.

So in our example, if one person argues against another that an apple the latter had called "red" is actually "orange," then the discussion is about colors and apples and perhaps could move into what is implied logically and contentfully: the perceptual process, colorblindness, color definitions, and so on. In this example, we have talk about something that is not the talk itself. It is not talk about talking, talk about norms of talking, etc.

Illocutionary structures, by contrast, work within the doing of communicating. They can be objectivated so as to be contents with logical and logical-like relations constituting the objectivation; but if objectivated, the talk then simply makes use of new, nonobjectivated illocutionary structures. So in our example of one person challenging the content-claim of another about the color of an apple, it is possible in principle for the first person to respond to this challenge in ways pertaining to illocutionary infrastructure rather than logical and logic-like content structure: "How dare you question my judgment on this!" would be an example. Or, "Should we really be discussing apples just now when we have this pressing deadline to meet?" In cases like these, illocutionary infrastructure, what many sociologists call "settings" and "setting definitions," can become objectivated and the inferential relations that had been at work are now made the content of a new topic for discussion. In this example, the person who questioned "red" and suggested "orange" and was next castigated for violating assumed illocutionary commitments could argue against this castigation: "But I thought you really made it clear that you wished to talk with me as an equal by the way you greeted me today and asked me to correct you about your biological knowledge if I find you to make errors. That is what you implied! You had invited me to talk with you as an equal and now you are acting inconsistently, violating an implicit commitment you made." Here illocutionary structures become objectivated as contents for a discussion. In the process, a new illocutionary structure is bid for. If the other actor accepts the bid and responds with, say, "You clearly misinterpreted me. What on earth gave you the impression that I wished to speak to you as an equal?" then a new illocutionary structure is in place, one within which a previously assumed structure is objectivated for discussion. The new illocutionary structure, in fact, is close to that of two equals debating something rationally.

Identity-Securing Stakes

Hence, both logical-content inferential relations and illocutionary inferential relations are capable of binding persons in interaction to commitments and to acting with reasons rather than according to arbitrary caprice. Identity-securing concerns underlie the way that both logic and illocution place boundaries about next possible acts. If a person violates an illocutionary commitment and cannot give acceptable reasons for doing so, then the identity of that person is at risk at least in relation to the particular partner(s) in question. True, partners in an interaction are not always identity-significant, existentially significant, to each other. And when they are not, then violating illocutionary commitments may not feel important to people in some or even many contexts. But in cases like that there will remain an internalized, generalized possible other-subject audience to which these persons do find it necessary to maintain some degree of trustworthiness or lose their sense of self, dignity, and personal esteem. At bottom, we "lose ourselves" when we cannot trust ourselves: when we cannot make a commitment to ourselves as if we had two parts, "I" and "me" actually, and keep the commitment. We begin to lose our personhood as in the case of an addict who time after time sincerely takes on the commitment to stop using some substance or stop stealing to support her habit only to later break this commitment. The self-relation requires intersubjective space because it is a type of position-taking with a possible other subject position that is of existential significance, in relation to one's self. We cannot elaborate on this interesting and important existential feature of illocutionary commitments here.

If a person violates a logical relation, on the other hand, selfhood is at risk only if the illocutionary infrastructure is of a certain type. If a person says that red apples are good and always preferable to orange apples, but then chooses an orange apple over a red one for eating, and cannot explain why when asked, while still maintaining her belief that she prefers red apples, then her identity as a subject in general could be at risk. She seems irrational, maybe mentally impaired, or not capable of understanding basic logical inferences. If a person argues that the earth is flat, gives an accepted definition of flat, and then continues to maintain the claim about the earth after being exposed to a large amount of information testifying to the global structure of the earth, then again, unless new reasons are provided, the basic subject-status of the person can be at risk. This person puts some sort of inexplicable compulsion, urge, or dogmatic attachment ahead of logic and reason.[2] But in all such cases, the illocutionary infrastructure must be composed of commitments to discussing an issue seriously and for the sake of arriving at an agreement about something pertaining to the contents of the discussion. It cannot include joking, "messing with someone's head," or strategic actions designed to affect other people in certain ways such as to get them to feel perplexed, confused, self-doubting, or something like that. There is only an existential risk to violating logical relations if the illocutionary infrastructure commits one to being logical.

The subject-status of a person is something that has to be renewed and maintained constantly and it is deeply related to our capacity for acting with and for reasons instead of being caused to act. Our individuation as separate selves is a process that takes place within intersubjective milieus, and it is a process that is very much related to the difference between caused events and actions for which an actor can take responsibility. In interactions with other humans, we can experience individuation as if it happens over and over with moments of nondifferentiation, "moments of mutuality," always already just gone. The human self does not "exist" as a finite entity in space and time, but rather as a pattern of more or less stable and integrated individuations that take place within intersubjective space: a space that is culturally contingent in many of its structures, but that is transindividual, pure intersubjectivity, pure movements from "me," "I," "we," and interpenetrating possible-subject positions. Processes of individuating as well as forming collective "we" identifications link the capacity to take on commitments with existential, identity-securing needs.

Inferences, Structures, Fields: Possible Other
Subject Positions Arrayed Within Intersubjective Space

How is it that structures with inferential relations between components exist? From the discussion above we have one way to conceptualize the ontology of these things, through the notion of instantiation. In the case of illocutionary structures, all meaningful acts include, as part of their meaning, some illocutionary claims having to do with the interaction actually going on at the moment. It is not as if an interaction infrastructure is put into place such that it "stays there" in some sort of way. Rather, within the meaning of each meaningful act that takes place within an infrastructure are included new endorsements of that infrastructure. And foregrounded meanings exchanged in an interaction are not fully separable from the illocutionary claims that feature, along with other sorts of claims, within their meaning horizons. Often the illocutionary structures and claims will be backgrounded within meaning horizons (see Carspecken 1996 and 2003 for more on meaning horizons). But they are part of the holistic meaning just the same, and the response to a meaningful act can always objectivate them and thematize aspects of them. In the case of logical-content structures, the meaning of anything foregrounded by a meaningful act has to be understood by understanding entire structures pertinent to the intelligibility of this content that will be more backgrounded.

Understanding meaningful acts is itself a "field" phenomenon in that actors can always doubt an interpretation they make of the act of another. And in many cases, actors experience the actions of others as a field of possible meanings. Structures both enable the field of possible meanings and constitute any particular meaning within such a field. The foregrounded meaning of "Don't you mean the orange apple" could include "You're not very smart," or "You're not very perceptive," or "I like you and really want to be helpful," and many other things. Paralinguistics help to convey one sort of nuanced foreground over others, but often we cannot be sure. When the content of a foreground is pretty clear and unambiguous, there will usually be a field of different possible nuances. Sometimes the content foregrounded is also not clear and unambiguous. A professor sincerely complimenting the work of a student to another professor who also read this work could get the response, "Oh yes, that was really insightful, wasn't it?" in a tone of voice that does not indicate whether sarcasm or sincerity is meant. In a case like this, the meaning field has a hard disjunction: it can mean "I agree, that was very good work" or it could mean "Are you kidding? That was horrible work." And each of these would have a spread of different possible nuances too.[3]

Meaningful acts instantiate structures within possible meanings that are usually understood within a field. Within each field, the possible meanings are each constituted structurally, and responses can differentiate different types of structures and different levels of structure as a process of objectivating: moving what one had been acting within into something one is acting in relation to. What, then, do we mean by "inference fields"?

So far we have a possible ontology of structures that makes use of the idea of instantiation. Possible meanings are constituted by structures and thus instantiated by meaningful acts delivering or opening up those possible meanings. Structures are found to be of different types and to have diverse levels when they are objectivated in order to make components and relations between them explicit, and each type is instantiated. Instantiations of structure are within processes of structuration because the response of another actor can always challenge a structure constitutive of the act responded to; and also because every meaningful act can claim structures in new forms, involving new relations. Hence if one asks the question, "In what mode or manner do structures exist?" the answer would come with the help of the term "instantiation." They do not exist the way that rocks and trees exist, in space and time. They exist rather as instantiations and claims. Giddens therefore proposed the concept of "virtual existence" for structures in the same publication of his that we mention above (1979).

But there is something about inferential relations that suggests another way to conceptualize their existence. We experience them in interactions with others as well as when pursuing thoughts (which, we argue, are communicatively structured in human beings) as if they were in a "world" or a "space" of their own. These metaphors can be misleading, but we nevertheless find them useful. We find them useful because meaningful actions instantiate structures, as we have seen. And a good many of the components of a structure reside within the tacit awareness of the actor. The process of articulating "validity horizons" in qualitative data analysis (Carspecken 1996) involves moving inferentially connected portions of the background of a meaning horizon into explicit articulation. It is a useful method for qualitative data analysis. However, the structures that are instantiated by meaningful acts have inferential implications that exceed even the tacit awareness of an actor. They can be discovered during the course of an interaction if one actor brings them to light so that another actor will be able to "see" them. They can also be noticed and articulated by an outside observer in ways that none of the actual participants have any awareness of (if the observer takes a performative position, i.e., is a virtual participant). Plus, when interacting with other people, we sometimes feel we can "see" more than the others in terms of inference relations, but that we can bring others to greater awareness of the inference fields with respect to which the interactions are taking place. And the contrary is true: we can feel that another person "sees more" that we do of the inferential relations in relation to which our interaction is taking place.

For these reasons, the metaphor of a transpersonal, intersubjective "space" suggests itself. The widely used concept of "lifeworld" is related to what we have in mind. But a lifeworld is metaphorically populated by a great diversity of components and structures. "Intersubjective space" as we use this expression would be one kind of lifeworld structure. We are now ready to explore the concept of "intersubjective space" in more detail.

II. Intersubjective Space

Setting Integration

We are now going to shift from using the term "illocutionary infrastructure" and "interaction infrastructure" to the sociological term "setting." Setting is to be considered synonymous with the other two expressions: illocutionary or interaction infrastructure (both used synonymously in this chapter). Thus a setting is not a "site," not a physical and temporal place where interactions occur, but rather an intersubjective co-construction that can be understood only by taking a participant's position and noticing what commitments and entitlements, norms, and so on are assumedly shared by the actors so that their interaction can take place. When a person goes to a friend to seek solace after some misfortune, she will initially "bid" for a setting in which she is a friend in need and the other is a comforter, listener, advice giver. If this bid is accepted, then the interactions will proceed within a shared understanding that involves many things: the topic to be talked about, the different and distinct roles to be taken on, about how long the interaction will go, whether humor or seriousness should dominate the tone, and so on. That is a setting. It is something that has to be grasped from within intersubjective space. It is an implicit, assumedly shared understanding with many components in inferential relations with each other.

Settings are always assumedly shared by people in interaction, and the degree to which the infrastructure assumptions actually are shared varies a great deal. This gives us the concept of "setting integration," something we have coined ourselves. To interact with another human being at all it is necessary for both participants to assume that an interaction of some kind is intended from both sides. Beyond this minimal requirement we find settings to fall along a continuum from barely integrated to very highly integrated.

The degree of integration has to do with two things: the extent to which assumptions about the interaction infrastructure are in match, and the amount of detail encompassed by those assumptions. People who know each other very well are more likely to coproduce richly detailed and well-matched settings than people who do not know each other at all, especially if they come from different cultures. A common understanding of norms pertaining to an institution will help with setting integration even if people do not know each other and even if they are from diverse cultures, as long as the institution has formal aspects understood by all participants (e.g., a court situation, a lecture hall, a police station). Purposes of an interaction will also be a factor in setting integration. If there is a clearly and explicitly defined purpose, such as negotiating a contract or discussing ideas from a book, integration can be fairly high.

The Concept of Position-Taking

Our interest has to do with the way in which settings make it possible for participants to "position-take" with other possible subject positions delineated and/or bounded by the setting. The expression "position-taking" is a bit tricky and we don't feel compelled to stick with it forever, but we will use it until and unless we discover something better. It is a fairly widely used expression, but for us it refers to our particular theory of understanding meaningful action. Understanding the meaningful act of another person is equivalent to being able to appropriately act next, in response, within three modes simultaneously: being able to respond to the other person in an appropriate manner (acting from a second-person position in relation to the other as shaped by the setting), being able to roughly imitate or repeat the act that the other just made (acting from the first-person position from which the initial act came), and being able to talk about the act from a third-person position. Skill levels vary with respect to these competencies, but understanding meaning has to do with the bare potentiality, the bare capacity, to act or think in all three ways in relation to the meaningful act that is understood. When a person feels she has understood the meaningful act of another, she then has the competency to act next in an indefinite number of ways, but within these three modes. Of course, she does not have to act next at all, nor act next in relation to her understanding of the act in question, but the point is that understanding meaning is having on hand an indefinite number of next possible acts that, however, will each fall within one of the modes we have distinguished (related to the formal speech positions of first, second, and third person).

Being able to talk about the meaningful act of another includes being able to articulate some of the reasons that the other actor would provide for her act, some of the assumptions upon which the act's meaning depends, and some of the inferential relations and structures that the act carries. And the same holds for our own meaningful acts. Others with whom we interact assume we have the competence to be able to describe our own actions, give reasons for them, and articulate some of the assumptions and inferential relations/structures carried by our own acts.

Anticipations and Meaning

A person will feel understood by another if the next act of the other is recognizable to them as being an appropriate response. When communicating with other people, we anticipate possible next acts from them in the form of fields, in that we anticipate the next act to fall within implicitly understood boundaries. We can be surprised by the responses of other people, but when surprised it is usually possible to better take their position so that their response to our action will be found to make sense. And when we are able to find reasons for why it is that we were surprised and why the other person acted as she did, we then have on hand possible next acts of our own that we believe the person who surprised us would recognize as being true to the meaning of their act (the one that surprised us).

Settings make it possible to anticipate next actions and even psychological states that are not moved into expressions. For example, a person can insult another person in a subtle manner and in a situation where the pain caused by the insult would not be something the injured participant would wish to express, but rather hide. And this can be anticipated by all who have a grasp of the setting within which the insult took place. Anticipations involve:

- Anticipating the form and style of the next act but not the content.

- Anticipating the content of the next act but not the form.

- Anticipating both.

- Anticipating psychological states brought about by previous acts and whether or not these will be expressed by the person experiencing them.

This expands upon an earlier discussion: the nature of structure. Inferential relations that constitute meaning and enable interactions via their infrastructures "squeeze" anticipations constituted by the ideal of a possible mutual understanding with possible other subjects into simultaneous relations. Relations learned by having communicative experiences during the course of an interaction in time become incorporated as inferential relations within the meaning of speech acts. The structures are structures of possible subject positions within an array. It is the capacity to anticipate associated with communicative competence that makes this possible. Anticipated, expected, next actions from another subject, as understood from the subject position in intersubjective space from which those responses could come, become inferences within a structure specifying boundaries for possible next actions as meaning-constituting formations.

Whole-Part Relations

Anticipations involve whole-to-part relations. So whether it is form and style, or content, or psychological state, the anticipation will catch general structures more easily than particulars. So when bantering with another person, we can anticipate that the response will conform to the "shape" of bantering without anticipating how it will do so. Or it can include a lot of detail on the how, particularly if we know the person well or if the two of us are using a widely distributed discourse we are both familiar with. The same goes for content. When mentioning an event that has been in the news recently to a person we know, we can anticipate the content of her response in broad terms (it will be about the news event and, perhaps, it will express concern), which may or may not be rich in detail (anticipating the precise points made by the other person, the words used, and so on).

Misunderstandings occur when assumedly shared interaction infrastructures are not in fact much shared. When this happens, assumptions one person has about the setting through which she is interacting with another do not overlap well enough with the assumptions of the other person. Position-taking is going on for both participants, but position-taking is always a matter of taking *possible* other subject positions. Misunderstandings, then, occur when a possible other subject positions assumed to be occupied by another subject is not in fact occupied by that other subject. What often happens with misunderstandings can be described with the help of the model of the hermeneutic circle. Anticipations involve broad and general categories that will be filled in with detail to a degree dependent upon the degree of setting integration. Human interactions involve whole-part relations projected as forestructures of anticipation. When anticipations are not met, the original forestructures are altered and we have the movement famously described as the hermeneutic circle. In the case of human interaction, successful movements through the hermeneutic circle on the part of all participants result in greater setting integration.

Possible Subject Positions and the "Intersubjective Space" Metaphor

Understanding meaningful actions involves the capacity to take possible other subject positions that are enabled by a setting. The higher the setting integration, the more the possible other subject positions are actually shared within the awareness of the participants. Anticipations of next acts improve in accuracy as well as detail with higher setting integration. And it looks as if highly integrated intersubjectivity can be thought of as sharing or occupying regions within what we are calling "intersubjective space."

We find this to be a potent metaphor for guiding us on deeper explorations of intersubjectivity, the constitution and differentiation of subjects as individual persons as processes, experiences of "mutuality" or nonindividuation that last for brief moments in some conversations, and much more. When logic is brought into the picture, it seems as if intersubjective space has some sort of intimate relation with a transsubjective space: a space rather like Karl Popper's "world three"[4] that is not entirely constructed because it contains discoverable structures, entities, relations, and points associated with potentialities for the scope and depth of modes of awareness. Intersubjective spaces display degrees of integration varying between particular, empirical human interactions. Yet it seems that all such interactively constructed spaces involve features that are in some sense "always there." Certain structures, perhaps best conceptualized as generative structures without specific contents, seem to be transsubjective such that they give rise to content-specific arrays of possible subject positions in actual human communicative processes: arrays that can and often do exceed the full awareness of the actors who make use of them in anticipating responses from the other participants and coming up with new responses themselves. The idea should be explored in future work that probes more deeply into universals constituting all possible subject-subject interactions. Logical relations seem to come down to content claims, based on inferences from other content claims that another subject has to agree with to maintain subject-status. Logical relations do not force or cause the response of another person, but if they are tightly logical, then they do, in the limit-case, totally constrain the response of a possible other subject if that other subject is to respond for reasons rather than for some other motivation (reasons are the not the same as motivations, most human action occurring *with* reasons rather than *for* reasons—the difference is partly covered elsewhere in this chapter with the concept of "rational motivation"). Illocutionary structures are related to logical relations, but are more open and less constraining in part because talking about them requires using new forms of them at the same time; and these new forms can always escape any rationally necessary next acts through transcendence and the claiming into being of a new illocutionary structure. Logical structures involve monological closure in that the appropriate response of another subject is the response appropriate for any and all other subjects and thus the response from a universal "I" position similar to the third person position. Illocutionary structures have a necessary openness to them, for they are oriented towards a mutual understanding that cannot be absolutely specified in advance; they involve the necessary unknowable features of all other subjects.

In summary, this is what we are calling intersubjective space at this time. The metaphor is helpful for understanding human social relations, because the human self is intersubjectively constituted and process based. Intersubjective space is emergent from normed symbol use, the use of normed symbols to mediate interactions by allowing for position-taking. Intersubjective space is an array of possible subject positions from which acts come and to which acts are addressed. Personhood is dependent upon intersubjective space; and it suffers, exalts, loves, oppresses, affirms, and negates within forms of the subject-subject relation.

Within intersubjective space, we can find the following forms of subject-subject relation:

a.   taking other possible subject positions results in varying degrees of accurate anticipations of the next acts that come forth from other participants in an interaction;

b.   and these anticipations are related to an implicit understanding of assumptions and inference relations/structures carried by acts, related to the reasons an actor would give for her act;

c.   but actors can vary in terms of how extensive their awareness is of the inferential relations, implications, structures, and assumptions that are associated with an act coming from a particular possible other subject position;

d. so it is as if something transpersonal is in play, and acting next during a conversation or any sort of interaction involves finding a place in this transpersonal space from which the next act comes;

e. mutual understandings between people are often, it seems to us, experienced as if the same place within an intersubjective space has been found;

f. but we can experience "being beyond" another subject in that we understand more of what is implicated, assumed, and otherwise carried by their act than they do: it is as if we have a "higher view," can "see more" of intersubjective space than they do;

g. and we can experience others "being beyond" ourselves in this same way;

h. we can experience moving to higher points in intersubjective space, learning, and expanding our awareness in this manner.

In Figure 1 below, we present some limit-case experiences of understanding other people and being understood by other people and interpret each through the imagery of intersubjective space:

SELF-OTHER RELATIONS	INTERSUBJECTIVE ANTICIPATIONS	INTERSUBJECTIVE SPACE
I understand you, but you do not understand me.	I am able to anticipate your next actions and the reasons you would provide for them; you cannot do this as well in relation to me: recognition is asymmetrical	I have more awareness of our intersubjective space than you do and can find more inferentially connected positions than you can; in extreme cases, I could negate your subject-status by knowing your possible next acts and the reasons for or against them better than you do.
I feel understood by you, but I don't fully understand you nor even "myself" as well as you do.	I cannot anticipate your next actions nor the reasons you would give for them very well, but I know you can do this in relation to me: recognition is asymmetrical.	You are beyond me and have more awareness of our intersubjective space than I do; you can find more positions than I; in extreme cases, you could negate my subject-status knowing my next acts and the reasons for or against them better than I do.
We understand each other well.	Recognition is roughly mutual, anticipations roughly equivalent between us.	We share positions in intersubjective space and move through it together; we mutually recognize each other.
We do not understand each other.	Neither one of us anticipates actions of the other well.	Intersubjective space is minimal and impoverished between us; little more than a shared understanding that we are trying, so far unsuccessfully, to reach an understanding .

Figure 1: Self-other relations in intersubjective space

In the rest of this chapter, we present only one main initial discovery related to intersubjective space: content inference fields. There is still much more to discover. And yet quite a bit is involved with content-inference fields, as readers will see.

III. Content Inference Fields in the Debate over Maria's Dismissal

To explore these issues, we examined qualitative observational data that was video- and audiotaped by Ran Zhang on a mock legal debate for students of educational law. Ran also interviewed participants and collected written briefs, plus observed the instructions given to different groups taking part in the debate. Ran and Phil together conducted a stimulated recall session with some of the debaters, asking them to watch a videotape of the debate with us, and stop it in various places to comment on what they had been thinking at the time or on anything else they wished to say. This stimulated recall session was also videotaped and analyzed.

We have already introduced the topic that was debated. It was fictional yet based on a real case.[5] In the fictional case, Maria had been an exemplary, highly regarded school teacher for 12 years in Tacoma, Washington. When she came out as lesbian, not to her students but to adults in the community, she was fired. These graduate students were divided into three groups: a group taking the side of Maria, a group taking the side of the school board, and a panel of judges.

In-class preparation times were given to each team and one of these was recorded and observed. During the oral debate, the teacher's side and the school district's side each gave a ten-minute brief and a three-minute rebuttal separately, and the judges could interrupt at any point and ask questions. The teacher's side presented first, followed by the school board, followed by a teacher's side rebuttal, followed by a school board rebuttal. Legal debates occurred between the judges and each side separately, not between the teacher's side and the school board's side. In the next class meeting, the judges delivered their decision, which was in favor of the teacher's side in this case, although the judges reported some difficulty in arriving at this decision.

Twelve weeks after this mock debate had taken place, one student from each side agreed to participate in the stimulated recall session. The three participants were chosen based on their leadership role in each side, their articulateness, and availability. In the recall, the videotape for the oral debate was played back, and the participants and researchers were allowed to stop the tape at any time, to ask others for comments about their strategies, thinking, anticipations, and interpretations during the period of the debate at which the video was stopped.[6]

Analysis Procedures

We both analyzed this data in multiple ways, producing diverse sets of codes and dialogically interacting with each other many times to decide on an angle for the final analysis. Eventually we decided to map out the debate interactions in specialized ways, illustrated below, to look for "interaction dynamics."

We wanted to explore illocutionary infrastructures in relation to logical inference fields. Our hunch was that we would find interesting relations between these two types of fields because homosexuality is still fairly controversial in the United States. Taking a position on homosexuality is identity-significant and potentially identity-risking. Yet in this debate, purely logical arguments about laws and circumstances were supposed to be employed. The interaction infrastructure, unlike more common settings in everyday life, was formally defined with explicit rules. Hence we thought we might find subtle negotiations of the setting structures due to concerns about identity claims. And such negotiations would have to balance between logical relations constituting the contents of discussion, identity-securing strategies, illocutionary commitments, and entitlements pertaining to setting structure.

Alas, what we found was different than expected. Precisely because the setting was strictly and formally defined and precisely because students took on roles understood by all others to be fictional and not representative of their true views about gay and lesbian sexual orientations, illocutionary features of the interactions were not as interesting as we had thought they would be.

But nevertheless, because participants did engage in logically structured legal debates fixed within formal settings, we found the relation of logical-content fields to the interactions very interesting indeed. Let us say more about what readers need to understand in order to best understand the results of our analysis:

1. The settings through which this debate took place were distinguishable primarily by the following criteria:

   a. *Topic*: what content is to be discussed.

   b. *Form*: is the content to be presented as a list of points or as an extended discussion of a point?

   c. *Side*: who is allowed to speak, Maria's representatives in dialogue with judges or the school board representatives in dialogue with judges?

2. The type of interaction overall was strategic. School board representatives and Maria's representatives had the goal of winning over the judges. They used logic to do so, but also many other devices *in relation to logic* to do so. This is where our reconstruction of logical-content inference fields became very helpful in analyzing the data. Participants had varying degrees of awareness of logical-content inference fields that they and those they were debating with could have shared access to. Hence, to act strategically, participants would avoid, mask, and dodge arguments against their side that they were aware of. We present the ways we found participants to make use of the logical-content inference fields below.

Settings

We found it helpful to divide settings by four levels and then represent them in two forms of graphic display that we present later in this chapter. The setting levels are:

Setting level
- 1: = Major setting
- 2: = Sub-setting
- 3: = Sub-sub-setting
- 4: = Sub-sub-sub-setting

Sub-settings are nested within larger settings. In the case of a debate like this, nesting was often based on the topic under discussion. For example, there could be an interaction infrastructure in which it was understood that case law is to be presented sequentially by case, that the current case under discussion is such and such a case, and that the current discussion is about the meaning of a key term that comes up within this case in terms of its applicability to Maria's case. That can be represented as three nested settings, distinguished by topic and sub-topic. All of these, in turn, would be within a major setting that specified who talks, Maria's representatives or school board representatives. The entire mock debate falls into four major settings as follows:

MAJOR SETTING NUMBER	FORMAL PERIOD OF DEBATE	NUMBER OF SPEECH ACTS
I.	Teacher's counsel presentation	42
II.	School board's presentation	35
III.	Teacher's counsel rebuttal	14
IV.	School board's rebuttal	22

Figure 2: Major settings in the mock legal debate

Interactions within each of the four formal and major settings above were reconstructed according to the concepts of setting, setting bids, setting negotiations, and "setting slides" (a term we coined). We present examples of our graphic representations of these setting dynamics we found next. What the reader will see in them includes the following:

- "Full settings" that retained form over many interactions (all level-1 and -2 settings below are of this kind, many level -3 and some level -4 are of this kind);

- "Very short-lived settings" that held form for as little as two or three interactions;

- A few "implicit settings" where actors actually have changed topics but not explicitly and probably not consciously (the significance of these will only come out later in this chapter);

- And "mere setting bids" that were clearly bid by actors but not accepted as bids by other actors and thus left as bids (many level-3 and -4 setting names below were mere bids). We include mere bids because often they correlate with the content inference fields we discuss in the next main section of this chapter.

Figure 3 illustrates one of the graphic display forms we employed, the "back-and-forth display." Speech acts and responses are separated by columns, representatives of Maria on the left and judges on the right. Other columns are used to keep track of settings and sub-settings at different levels. Commentary in the columns farthest to the right is specialized and color-coded.

Blue-colored commentary reconstructs the main purpose of the act (asking for clarification, bringing in legal evidence, outlining an argument, and so on).

Brown-colored commentary pertains to setting issues (making bids, accepting bids, type of setting bid for or accepted, and so on).

Green-colored commentary captures strategic moves made by the actors (dodges, smuggling in predispositions through word choice, smuggling in assumptions by not mentioning them but stating something that presupposes them, halting a path of logic to shift to a new one, and so on).

The green-colored commentary will become more interesting when considered in relation to reconstructed inference fields in later sections of this chapter. Meanwhile, here is Figure 3, an example of a back-and-forth display. We chose to show this display from speech act 31 to the beginning of the second major setting, speech act 22, to speech act 31, although we produced this sort of display for the entire mock debate.

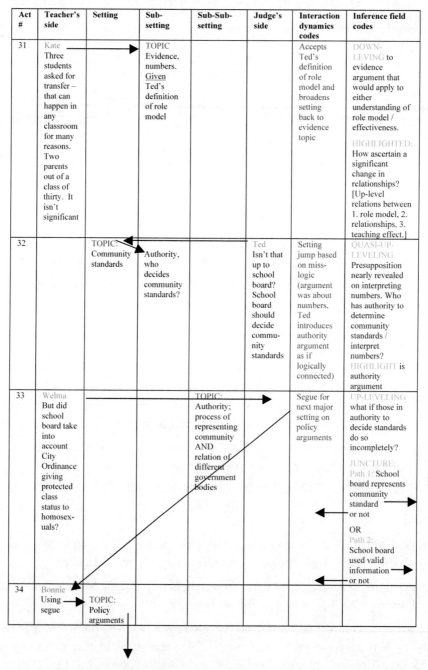

Act #	Teacher's side	Setting	Sub-setting	Sub-Sub-setting	Judge's side	Interaction dynamics codes	Inference field codes
31	Kate Three students asked for transfer – that can happen in any classroom for many reasons. Two parents out of a class of thirty. It isn't significant		TOPIC Evidence, numbers. Given Ted's definition of role model			Accepts Ted's definition of role model and broadens setting back to evidence topic	DOWN-LEVING to evidence argument that would apply to either understanding of role model / effectiveness. HIGHLIGHTED: How ascertain a significant change in relationships? [Up-level relations between 1. role model, 2. relationships, 3. teaching effect.]
32		TOPIC: Community standards	Authority, who decides community standards?		Ted Isn't that up to school board? School board should decide commu-nity standards	Setting jump based on miss-logic (argument was about numbers, Ted introduces authority argument as if logically connected)	QUASI-UP-LEVELING Presupposition nearly revealed on interpreting numbers. Who has authority to determine community standards / interpret numbers? HIGHLIGHT is authority argument
33	Welma But did school board take into account City Ordinance giving protected class status to homosex-uals?			TOPIC: Authority; process of representing community AND relation of different government bodies		Segue for next major setting on policy arguments	UP-LEVELING what if those in authority to decide standards do so incompletely? JUNCTURE: Path 1: School board represents community standard or not OR Path 2: School board used valid information or not
34	Bonnie Using segue	TOPIC: Policy arguments					

Figure 3: Back and forth display with codes for interaction dynamics and inference fields

We also displayed the interactions a different way, with a "nested setting display." Below we excerpt speech acts 1.1 through 42 to give readers the basic idea.

FORMAL PERIOD						SETTINGS
I: Teacher's Side Presentation	Level 1					
	1. (#1.1)	Provide constitutional arguments				
		Level 2				
		1. (#1.1)	"List" arguments without argumentative elaboration			
			Level 3			
			1. (#2)	Freedom of Association		
			2. (#5)	Establishment Clause		
			3. (#9)	Privacy rights, 14th and 9th Amendments		
			4. (#10)	Due Process # one		
			5. (#13)	Due Process # two = the nexus argument		
				Level 4		
				1. (#14) Historical effects on evidence		
			6. (#19)	Privacy rights		
	2. (#22)	Provide case law argumentation				
		Level 2				
		1. (#22)	Case law: describe/list cases and provide arguments			
			Level 3			
			1. (#22)	Bowers and Lawrence cases		
				Level 4		
				1. (#23)	Application argument; Criminal vs. Civil law;	
		2. (#25)	Teaching effectiveness and nexus arguments			
			Level 3			
			1. (#25)	Evidence of nexus arguments		
			2. (#27)	Evidence nuanced by temporal / historical factors		
			3. (#28)	"Role model" topic		
				Level 4		
				1. (#30)	Role model definition	
			4. (#31)	Role model, evidence = numbers argument		
		3. (#32)	Community standards arguments			
			Level 3			
			1. (#32)	Authority issues, who has right to decide standards?		
				Level 4		
				1. (#33)	Criteria for decision	
	3. (#34)	Provide policy argumentation				
		Level 2				
		1. (#34)	Overview			
		2. (#34)	Washington State Common School Provisions			
			Level 3			
			1. (#34)	Why was Maria dismissed?		
		3. (#36)	Tinker case, fear of disruption vs. actual disruption			
			Level 3			
			1. (#37)	Redefine disruption issue, evidence		
				Level 4		
				1. (#38)	Disruption vs. objection	
				2. (#42)	Prevalence of disruption	
		4. (#42)	Nexus issue			
		6. (#42)	Human rights			
		7. (#42)	Community standard issue			

Figure 4; Nested setting display for speech acts 1.1 through 42

The above figure illustrates the nesting of settings as they were constructed by participants in this debate, through the four formal periods of teacher's case presentation, school board case presentation, teacher's rebuttal, and school board's rebuttal. There is a lot of information in this diagram. We can see, for example, that in the teacher's presentation period of the first major setting, three settings were established in a logical sequence:

1. Constitutional arguments presented in list form

2. Case law was provided argumentatively

3. Policy arguments were provided, also argumentatively

Also, in looking at speech acts from 1.1 through 19, we find many very temporally short sub-sub-settings. When seeing a pattern like this, one is directed back to the transcribed data to find out why and how the pattern came about. What we found was the use of illocutionary infrastructure to lead logic-content inference fields and build an illocutionary defense against having certain arguments debated too much. We won't get into the details of this strategy used by the side representing Maria here. Our main purpose so far is to illustrate the two ways of displaying interaction data and to give in gist-form some idea about the insights that can result from such displays.

Content Inference Fields

As explained in the first major sections of this chapter, by "content inference field" we refer to the inferential, largely logical, structures implicated by locutionary contents: the topics discussed. Such fields pertain to the logic of internal connections between categories, principles, implicated grounds, implicated needs for evidence and other backing, definitions and more. Clearly, content inference fields and illocutionary infrastructures, that is, settings, often intersect and are related to each other in ways that we are not fully clear about—for it is precisely that set of relations that are under exploration in our unfinished project. The norms and commitment claims that constitute settings can be objectivated, articulated, and argued for or against rationally, in the process producing content inference fields related to normative structures. Settings are also frequently changed in everyday life through bids and their acceptance, which can quickly render irrelevant the logical structure of contents under discussion. But the content inference fields associated with a legal debate have certain fixed features that are not characteristic of everyday interactive settings. In particular, there are laws that have a fairly fixed form even though laws must always be interpreted. There are facts, "evidence" pertaining to a case that can be argued about but that have an objective or quasi-objective status. Hence we can, from the outset, indicate some of the features of a content inference field that distinguish it from illocutionary infrastructures before we actually bring the concept to bear upon our analysis of this debate.

We gave a number of terms special meanings to articulate the things we found with reconstructive analysis. We highlight some of them in an explanation of inference fields next.

A content inference field cannot be freely constructed, created, or discarded by actors to the extent that illocutionary structures and norms of interaction can. Rather, content inference fields can be articulated in different ways to highlight some regions and obscure others. One actor may bring another actor into awareness of regions within the relevant content inference field that she previously had been blind to, or keep another actor ignorant of such regions if this suits strategic purposes, by obscuring inference field regions. There are also paths that can be taken within content inference fields that an actor has some control over.

Content inference fields have levels, such that paths of argumentation on one level must presuppose agreements on a higher level—a level of presuppositions. "Up-leveling" a content inference field is a process of articulating previously assumed principles, definitions, or truths in order to problematize them. In fact, most assertions made in argumentation will be found to have implicit inference chains associated with them: their claim to be valid or true depends upon several levels of assumptions that constitute part of the field. Up-leveling is usually a process of articulating inference chains. Examples of up-leveling from our debate will be presented in a section later on.

"Down-leveling" is the opposite sort of process, ignoring unresolved issues of a certain generality in order to highlight more particular issues. Down-leveling can occur to smuggle presuppositions back into the picture, hiding their problematical status behind a particular topic presented as of pressing importance during a debate (but a topic that depends upon taking a certain position with respect to a presupposition or cluster of presuppositions). For example, in our debate, at one point the teacher's side makes the argument that precedents exist in case law that support the argument that judgments of immorality for behaviors conducted outside the workplace are not sufficient grounds to fire an employee. The argument is up-leveled by a judge who points out that the cases cited were criminal cases and Maria's case is not a criminal case: so there are problems of application involved with citing such cases for support. The teacher's side responds by simply repeating the assertion that these cases show immorality to be an insufficient reason for dismissal, smuggling back in the assumption that such cases apply to Maria's. This is down-leveling, because the problem of whether or not criminal cases apply has not been resolved. If expressed with the right sorts of pragmatics and illocutionary force, a down-leveling effort of this nature can obscure the lack of resolution on the presuppositions. One position on such higher-level issues can be smuggled in through strategies like this (in our example, however, the judges did not fall for the trick).

On the other hand, down-leveling can operate with a "no matter which position you take on these other matters, this particular issue would apply in either case." For example, our debaters engaged for a time on the topic of whether or not the school board made its decision to dismiss Maria based on valid community beliefs about homosexuality or erroneous community beliefs. Suddenly one representative of the school board said, in reconstruction, that parents have the right to determine their community values regardless of whether their reasons are valid or not. This is down-leveling in an open way. Up-level to this claim is the fact that community standards will be based on beliefs that will either have good support or not, but this argument makes the issue irrelevant—it need only be presupposed that the community has beliefs that will lead them to continue along this path, for the conclusions reached by this path will hold no matter what is determined about the validity of community beliefs.

Content inference fields accompany all human interactions, but in the case of legal argumentation, or any other form of argumentation, their distinction from settings becomes very marked. This is because in argumentation, propositional contents and what they implicate are emphasized in a way that is not as common to other forms of communicative interaction. Setting structures will constrain or enable the articulation of content inference fields, but they will be distinct from them. Figure 4, which displays settings and setting bids in nested structures, gives some clues to the constraining and enabling roles played by interaction infrastructures in the argumentation. "List" settings constrain argumentation because their norms are for one side to list out arguments without much elaboration, and the other side to listen and allow the list to be completed.

Content inference fields sharpen, broaden, highlight, up-level, down-level, branch, juncture, become obscured, unpack, Balkanize, take on ambiguity, and otherwise change "size, shape, and focus" as an interaction proceeds. They contain regions and relations to other content inference fields.

The concept of a content inference field will become clearer as we use it in our analysis of this legal debate over Maria's dismissal. First we'll introduce another set of specialized codes we produced as part of our analysis of the content inference fields. The chart below gives names and explanations for these special codes, many of which have been highlighted in our discussion above:

BLUE = communicative acts

GREEN = strategic acts

YELLOW = could be either communicative or strategic

Processes related to content inference field	Description	Some types of action that can bring this process about
Field development	The movement of implicit portions of a field into articulation and consciousness	Clarifications, presupposition articulation, Inference clarification, asking questions, listing issues
Paths	Linked regions of a field forming the basis of an extended argument	A structure, rather than a process
Junctures	Junctures occur when an argument could be developed along two or more paths; or when successful arguments along two or more paths are necessary to back an assertion	A structure, rather than a process
Sequencing	Focusing on part of a field with the understanding that other, related parts will be discussed subsequently	Taking up part of field with the intersubjective understanding that other parts will follow in an order
Articulation of argument	Bringing several related field elements together to back an assertion	Co-opting parts of opponents' language or argumentation for one's own purposes
Articulation of counter-argument	Bringing several related field elements together to undermine an assertion	Co-opting parts of opponents' language or argumentation for one's own purposes
Path selection	Taking one of several possible argumentative paths, or getting an opponent to do so	Trap setting, meaning smuggling = implicitly changing the meaning of a term Articulating a logical direction to take, or simply acting on a choice of paths
Path termination	Bringing a clear end to a line of argumentation either logically or pragmatically	Halt with identity stroking, intimidation = e.g., acting as if other's point is absurd Logically ending a path, or ending a path for articulated reasons
Narrowing	Reducing a field in terms of what is relevant to an argument. For example, ruling out, through argumentation, an entire issue or path	Inference smuggling, assumption smuggling Ruling out the relevance of field regions for clear reasons
Expanding	Bringing more realms of a field into relevance for an argument or assertion	Articulating implications horizontally
Highlighting	Bringing just part of a field into focus and relevance	Use of analogies to clarify
Obscuring	Acting in ways to hide paths or regions of relevance from other actors	Disposition smuggling, coating, halting, identity stroking, repeating point already made without addressing arguments against it, moral cloaking, use of analogies to obscure
Breaks	When interactions shift settings in a major way, to change the topic and break off development of an inference field	Halting, followed by a shift
Field anticipation	Acts that reveal anticipations on the actor's part that other actors have certain features of a field in mind and are about to make use of them	Dodges, pre-emptive strikes

Figure 5: Relations between actions and content inference fields

Figure 6 presents a back-and-forth display with the far column on the right displaying codes pertinent to content inference fields. The actions presented in this figure are 71–77, showing an inference juncture that resulted in a pattern of level-3 setting bids, a bid from one side of the debate for moving along one path from the juncture, followed by a bid from the other side to move along the other path from the juncture, repeated several times without acceptance of any bid.

Act	Teacher's Side	Sub-setting	Sub-sub-setting	Judges	Interactive dynamics	Inference field
71	Lily / We also want to point to the Washington Bill 2174 and Aden is expert on that	Washington Bill / The Washington Bill			Setting bid for relevance of Washington Bill / Halt and shift function. New setting without ending above arguments logically; introducing Aden helps HALT because we don't know whether this will relate to previous arguments or not	BREAK / Introduction to new field as yet not clarified
72	Aden / Washington Bill states you cannot promote nor denigrate homosexuality. To not fire Maria would promote.	TOPIC: Washington Bill remains +	SUB-TOPIC: Not firing would promote		New major setting in place with two nested and alternate sub-setting bids	ARGUMENTS / Argumentation about promotion / denigration effects of dismissal
72	Given that school board can neither promote nor denigrate, School board must use its own policy 5280 = deciding the need of community and continuity of educational program for ALL students		+ SUB-TOPIC: school board policy 5280 applies			Argumentation about why school board policy must prevail [with implicit emphasis on nexus] / NEXUS / Path 1: argument; / Path 2: argument;
73			TOPIC: First of Aden's points: Promotion / denigration	Vivian / So do I hear you saying you only hire heterosexual teachers?	Taking promotion / denigration topic / Exaggeration to push logic. Said as if absurd	SELECTION OF PATH 1 (counter argument) / If consistent, you would only hire heterosexual teacher (fallacious)
74	Lily / No, when the school board meets it cannot counter State Bill. We cannot. [and therefore we must follow board policy 5280]		TOPIC: Second of Aden's points Why board policy prevails		Bid for setting on why board policy prevails / Confusing because Aden's two points were not clear, his first point is hard to defend and Lily seems to shift to the second AS IF that is the only point.	SELECTION OF PATH 2 IMPLICITLY (but as if responding to counter argument above) / HIGHLIGHTING 1. Does Washington Bill entail prevalence of School board policy? 2. Does school board policy justify dismissal? 3. What is link between Washington Bill and School Board Policy?
75			TOPIC: First of Aden's points Effects of dismissal on promotion / denigration	Sally / How do you balance state bill with city ordinance that extends protected class status?	Bid rejected or not understood, back to effects of dismissal on promotion / denigration	PATH SELECTED IMPLICITLY (Path of highlighted argument in previous speech act) / HIGHLIGHTED Issues of legal authority and hierarchy
76	Greg / The state bill states NO denigration nor promotion. Again this is about effects, not about homosexuality		TOPIC: Second of Aden's points. State bill forces attention to effects, and School Board policy applies here.		Shift back to second of Aden's points / Dodge, Sally's point not directly addressed and change of topic not explicit because Greg refers to the State Bill as if responding to her question directly. Asserts that being true to state bill, we must concentrate on effects	SELECTION OF PATH 2 bid (responding to above question) / HIGHLIGHTED Interpretation of the Washington Bill? Relevance to this case / OBSCURING Balance between ordinance and state bill
77			TOPIC: First of Aden's points	Ted / How does retaining her present homosexuality as an appropriate behavior?	Shift back to first of Aden's points.	SELECTION OF PATH 1 (counter argument) / HIGHLIGHTED Argumentation about promotion / denigration effects of dismissal

Figure 6: Inference juncture resulting in pattern of to-and-fro level-3 bids

Speech act 72 resulted in an inference juncture with two possible paths involving two difference arguments. In speech act 73, a judge, Vivian, bid (at setting level 3) for argumentation along path one that has to do with whether employing an openly lesbian teacher would or would not result in promoting homosexual lifestyles or denigrate a legally defined class. This path is based on law that prohibits school boards from either promoting or denigrating.

Vivian's bid was not accepted; instead Lily, in speech act 74, responds as if accepting the bid but elaborating a point that would take participants along path two: a debate about whether school board policy should prevail over state law. It is in effect a new bid at level 3, but disguised as acceptance of a previous bid. Lily either did not understand the relation of speech act 73 to the inference juncture or she did understand but was strategically trying to take participants along path two instead of path one. Acts 75, 76, and 77 are all bids for the opposite inference path from the juncture opened by speech act 72. The pattern looks like the following with a nested setting display:

FORMAL PERIOD	SETTINGS			
II: School board Presentation	Level 1			
	1. (#43)	Outline full set of arguments in favor of dismissal		
		Level 2		
		1. (#44)	Evidence	
			Level 3	
			1. (#45)	Interpretation of evidence supported by school board policy
			2. (#46)	Comparisons of transfers in school; is homosexuality treated differently?
		2. (#47)	**Reasons for transfers from Maria's classroom**	
		3. (#48)	**Explanation of expression "Open and Notorious"**	
	2. (#53)	Fit with 14th Amendment		
		Level 2		
		1. (#53)	Lack of fit with 1st Amendment	
		2. (#53)	Link to Lawrence vs. Texas case	
		3. (#54)	Nexus argument	
		4. (#55)	Relation between nexus argument and 14th Amendment	
			Level 3	
			1. #58	Community beliefs in relation to nexus
			2. #58	Scientific evidence / community beliefs
			3. #60	Distinguishing behaviors from identities
		5. (#61)	**Implicit bid for nexus setting**	
		6. (#62)	**Community Standards**	
	3. (#64)	Purposes of schooling		
		Level 2		
		1. (#64)	School-community relations	
			Level 3	
			1. (#66)	Appropriate decision-making procedures
		2. (#70)	**Teaching effectiveness**	
		3. (#71)	**Washington Bill 2174**	
			Level 3	
			1. (#72)	Not firing would promote homosexuality
			2. (#72)	Bill 2174 means School board bill 5280 applies
			3. (#73)	Not firing would promote homosexuality
			4. (#74)	Bill 2174 means School board bill 5280 applies
			5. (#75)	Not firing would promote homosexuality
			6. (#76)	Bill 2174 means School board bill 5280 applies
			7. (#77)	Not firing would promote homosexuality

Figure 7: Inference juncture (#72) resulting in pattern of level-3 bids (#72-77)

The pattern of many level-3 bids shows up in the nested display prominently, in the high-lighted area (acts 72–77). The inference juncture with two paths helps us to understand how this pattern occurred.

Illustrating Content Inference Fields: The "Effectiveness/Nexus" field

A number of distinct content inference fields emerged during the debate, and each can be named by the researchers. For example, at times a field having to do with the purposes of education and school-community relations manifested. Fields just barely began to manifest with respect to freedom of association and privacy rights, but were never developed very far.[7] The field that is of most interest to us because of its clear importance to the case and to our debaters is the effectiveness and nexus content inference field.

We find this content inference field manifesting for the first time during the first major interactive setting led by Anne and analyzed in terms of setting dynamics above. Describing its manifestation will make its nature clear to the reader. As we have already discussed, during the first major setting, the setting norms constrained development of the content inference field. Responses from judges that were true to the field of inferences and called for Anne to further articulate and support what she had in mind were not taken up by Anne. Anne's responses in fact built resistance potential about the setting norms such that pushing harder for argumentation came to require almost full explication of setting norms in order to challenge them explicitly. The judges were not willing to do this, partly because part of their formal charge as judges was to ask questions and stimulate arguments, but in general to defer to the side presenting in terms of what is to be talked about and how. Such norms regarding the appropriate activities for judges made it all the easier for Anne to build resistance potential about the setting norms she wished to be in place.[8]

The excerpt from our data display below (figure 8) shows interactions taking place within the first major setting, along with the commentary on how the acts made use of content inference fields (far right column). We have this column of commentary for the entire data set. In the case of the first major setting, reading down that column on the content inference field will show little content development. Inference possibilities in the fields are nonarticulated and highly general given Anne's mere statements of relevant constitutional amendments, without argumentation. Maureen's questions affect the fields through sequencing, up-leveling, and path selection, each of which are correlated with requests for more reasons and arguments. Anne's responses keep the content inference fields undeveloped. Acts 13 through 17, however, do bring out what we call "the effectiveness-nexus content field" for the first time.

Speech Act	Teacher's Side	Setting	Sub-setting	Sub-sub-setting	Judges	Interactive dynamics	Inference field
1.1	Anne 1st, 9th, and 14th amendments	List setting, PROCESS	Overview			Setting bid Overview given	Fit of each with case, any priorities [Up-level; importance of constitutional arguments to this case]
2			Freedom of Association TOPIC		Maureen Rationale for freedom of association?	Setting accepted, Sub-setting bid Request for reasoning	SEQUENCING Freedom of association: arguments of fit with case
3	Anne No compelling gov. interest to curtail freedom of association AND We argue for its extension to romantic associations					Sub-setting accepted Statement of position with argumentation implicitly promised 1. Partial dodge: Short and simple assertion after expression of surprise for request 2. Disposition smuggling, "Romantic association"	ARTICULATION OF ARGUMENT No compelling government interest AND Expansion to romantic associations JUNCTURE: Paths possible Arguments for 1. or 2 / arguments in terms of legal categories or use of case law precedents as evidence
4					Maureen Ask for case law	Same sub-setting Request for legal evidence	PATH SELECTION: Evidence OR No evidence
5	Anne No case law, repeats short assertion for extension rationale					Dodge: Short and simple assertion, immediate flow to new setting bid Argumentation implicitly promised	FIELD NARROWED: No evidence HIGHLIGHTED: Good reasons for extension, Poor reasons for extension [Up-level; significance of reasoning without case law precedent]
5	Anne Also, Establishment clause; principal's own morality and is not the only morality because only a few parents objected		Establishment clause TOPIC			Sub-setting bid Partial coating Argument from evidence provided	FIELD BREAK, next in sequence Immorality decision, Represents community, Doesn't represent community [Up-level: 1. connection to religion and 1st amend, 2. factual evidence?,]
6					Maureen Decision to dismiss was simply based on estab. clause violation of principals own morality?	Sub-setting accepted Request for reasoning "simply based" as if not a convincing argument	UP-LEVELING to assumption Was decision based solely on morality issue? Yes OR No [Up-level: Is decision based on individual's moral judgment covered by 1st Amend?]
7	Anne "It could be, yeah"					1. Dodge: Short and simple assertion 2. Implicit acknowledgement that argument is speculative on evidence	Field unchanged
8					Maureen So do you have evidence?	Request for evidence Challenge to dodge	Factual evidence OR no evidence

Figure 8; Lack of inference field development in first major setting (pg. 1)

Speech Act	Teacher's Side	Setting	Sub-setting	Sub-sub-setting	Judges	Interactive dynamics	Inference field
9	Anne That information hasn't been available to us,					1. Dodge: Short and simple assertion; immediate flow to new sub-setting bid 2. implication that evidence could exist	Field unchanged
9	Also, 9th and 14th Amend. right to privacy		Right to privacy under 9th and 14th, TOPIC			Sub-setting bid Mere statement of link to 9th and 14th, implication that rationale will come later	BREAK, rest in sequence 9th and 14th both for privacy, fit?, connection between two? Due process issues (14th)
10			14th Amend only	Due process TOPIC	Maureen A procedural violation?	Refracted sub-setting bid with nested sub-sub-setting (14th also involves due process: restriction of liberty only after due process); Request for clarification	SEQUENCING, due process first How is due process related to this case?
11	Anne "Yeah"					Sub-setting nest accepted, focus on the sub-sub-setting Dodge: Short and simple assertion	Same field
12					Maureen Due process, a violation of due process under the 14th?	Request for clarification repeated, implication that more reasoning should be provided	Same field
13	Anne Right, that's part of it					Dodge, short and simple assertion with immediate setting bid in speech flow	Same field
13	Also, when dismissing a homosexual teacher, a nexus must be shown between homosexuality and reduced teaching effectiveness, AND she had 12 years' teaching experience			Due process 2, Nexus, TOPIC		Sub- sub setting bid Assertion with evidence argument linked	BREAK, shift to other due process argument NEXUS CLUSTER [Up-levels to nexus cluster = effectiveness vs. performance, effectiveness in general, and school-community relations]
14				Before / After ARGUMENT	Sally Was that exemplary performance BEFORE public knowledge of her homosexuality?	Bid accepted and focused to evidence Request for defense of evidence by up-leveling to presupposition	UP-LEVELING, presupposition articulation Effectiveness distinguished from performance: Effectiveness = teacher's performance OR Effectiveness = relationships JUNCTURE: Path: base arguments on this distinction, Path 2: provide evidence that 'effectiveness' is not compromised
15	Anne This is speculative, but we do know only small number complained					Logical response; defending with presupposition acknowledged	DOWN-LEVELING, through path selection Numbers argument on post-public knowledge performance or effectiveness Small number complaining = not significant vs. Any number is significant
16	Welma Two parents, three students					Teaming Clarifying evidence to back teammate's point	Same field
17	Anne Right						Same field
18	Kate Concerning case law….	Case law TOPIC				Setting bid Introducing case law	
19		List setting maintained	Privacy TOPIC		Maureen Privacy rights under 9th. or 14th as well?	Counter-bid to maintain list, with nested sub-setting on privacy Clarification with implication that reasons should be given.	BREAK, return to completion of bid / privacy Rationale for and relation between 9th & 14th 9th & 14th
20	Anne: Both					Dodge: Short and simple assertion	Same field
21					Maureen: Okay	Closure to first large setting	Same field

Figure 8; Lack of inference field development in first major setting (pg. 2)

Many of the terms we invented for reconstructing inference-field-related phenomena are concretely illustrated in the figure above. There are examples of sequencing (#2), juncture (#3), path selection (#4), up-leveling (#6), down-leveling (#15), and elsewhere there are field breaks and highlighting.

In this first major setting there was little "field development" because Anne continuously bid for new sub-topics in the form of a list rather than engaging with the judges on arguments. If she had engaged with arguments, we would see inference fields emerge with actions made in relation to it. There are different inference fields for different topics. As an illustration of the basic idea, the field we will reconstruct is called "the effectiveness/nexus inference field." This concerns the legal requirement of establishing a "nexus" of influence between Maria's homosexuality and her teaching effectiveness. The term "nexus" is used in this way within legal discourses. Anne introduces the field in act #13 above.

To illustrate the idea of content inference fields, we first reconstruct the field abstractly. And this is how inference fields are effectively used in analyzing human interactions: reconstruct a field of interest abstractly first and then look at the interactions that took place whereby participants clearly had an understanding of the field and used it to position-take with each other and interact with each other. Participants will not all be aware of everything in a field, and they will vary in terms of how much of the field they each are aware of. Differences in awareness levels also help to understand the interactions. And inference fields can be extended indefinitely because the logical relations involved extend in all directions. Hence the researcher needs to reconstruct as much of the field as is necessary to help understand those interactions that took place, as well as to understand those interactions that could have taken place but did not. Figure 9 gives our abstract reconstruction of the effectiveness / nexus inference field.

EFFECTIVENESS	IS INDICATED BY		DUE TO		DURING TEMPORAL PERIOD		AFFECTING	AS DETERMINED BY		WITH AUTHORITY OF
	Criteria	How measured?	Performance/ actions of teacher in role of teacher		Before	After	Individual students	School board		Legal / organizational rights
	Efficiency				Public knowledge of sexual orientation	Public knowledge of sexual orientation	Classroom	Some (any) parents		Correct procedures
	Disruption or complaint levels		Relationships with:	Students			Entire school	Community		Valid underlying beliefs
	Influence or role modeling			Parents				City		
	Amount of academic learning			Community				State of Washington		
								Educational professionals:		
								Practitioners	Researchers	

Figure 9: The effectiveness / nexus inference field

Anne introduced the nexus argument in act 13. A condensation of the argument as she introduced it and as it was subsequently used by the relevant actions would look like this: First Effectiveness/Nexus Argument (Acts 13–17)

1. Maria had **12 years' exemplary teaching performance,** therefore no nexus [Anne]
   a. But that was **before homosexuality became public knowledge** [Sally]
      i. **Only small number** of students transferred, small number parents complained [Anne and Welma]
      ii. END

The short debate seems to leave participants with these conclusions: Evidence for diminished teaching effectiveness after public knowledge of homosexuality is only three student transfers and two parent complaints. Remaining possible arguments on this same path would revolve around:

Such numbers are not significant

OR

Such numbers are significant

In Figure 10, this same short argument is diagrammed on the effectiveness and nexus content inference field. We can see from Figure 10 how challenge and response argumentation moves from some portions of the content inference field to others, articulating and highlighting portions that were implicated from the outset; as soon as Anne asserted her argument in speech act 13.

BLUE = arguments from the teacher's side
RED = arguments from the judges
Arguments are given in order of their appearance during the debate.

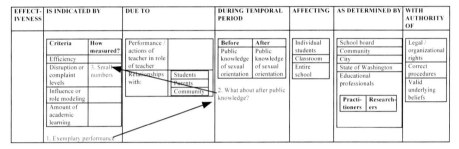

Figure 10: The first effectiveness argument

The second time arguments over effectiveness and nexus take place, we find a more generous use of the content inference field by participants. The relevant speech acts can be found in Figure 11, which follows the present discussion. Readers may wish to consult Figure 11 as they read our description of this argument.

Kate begins case law arguments with speech act #22 by taking what looks like a preemptive strike on the Bowers case.[9] The decision in the Bowers case did not favor liberties for homosexual people, but the Bowers case was basically overturned by a later case: Lawrence vs. Texas.[10]

Sally challenges this path in argumentation by pointing out that both Bowers and Lawrence were criminal cases, whereas the case under consideration is not. Kate's response is not satisfactory—she simply says that the Lawrence case shows that "immorality was not a sufficient reason." We call this a "dodge" because Kate acts as if important issues within the content inference field are simply not there. Many dodges are used throughout this debate for the same reason: to avoid taking a path on the content inference field that will not favor one's case. A dodge is a strategic act that can only make sense in light of the concept of content inference field. Dodges are one example of where setting dynamics, interactive norms, and content inference fields bear clear relations to each other.

Kate goes on, as part of her dodge: "The individual with privacy at their home can decide what kind of behaviors they choose to engage in." Ted now stops this path of argumentation in the following way:

> Maria is not denied the right to do whatever she wants in her home. She is being denied a position as a teacher because she would influence her students. This is the argument the other side is making, and

> her teaching efficiency is in question. So her privacy rights in this instance are not being threatened. She continues to live a private life she desires, isn't that true? (#25)

Ted's ending "isn't that true?" is typical of his argumentative style, which frequently presents people with "yes or no" type questions squarely within one articulated segment of the content inference field. He forces people, in this way, to address themselves to logical force and give him the response he needs to bring them down a path toward his own point of view. We coded a number of Ted's acts as "traps" where he clearly had a path of argumentation in mind and where he wished to force the other side to take the path themselves, bowing to logical force so that they would articulate an argument against their own position in the end. The above argument by Ted is not one of his traps, but it does use a "yes or no" question to force the other person logically in a certain direction.

Ted points out that Maria's case is not a matter of privacy rights for a citizen; it is a matter of professional effectiveness for a teacher. Thus we have the effectiveness/nexus field emerging for the second time.

Welma next gives the counterargument that there is no evidence Maria's teaching has been impacted in any way by her lifestyle (#26).

Then the post-public-knowledge point is raised again, followed by a role-model argument. After public knowledge, judge Vivian argues, Maria becomes a negative role model for students in the classroom.

Kate returns to evidence of excellent teaching during all the years of Maria's career, 12 years during which no one questioned her role modeling, and adds that Maria was not talking about sexuality to the students. But Ted argues that public knowledge of her sexual orientation would change her relationships with students.

This returns us to the argument, now articulated by Kate in #31, that only a few students and parents have complained. This same number could have complained about anything at all, or transferred for any reason at all, and normally such events would not be taken as reflecting diminished teaching effectiveness, at least at significant levels.

Ted comes back with:

> But isn't that up to the school board? That the school board should decide what the community standards are? And in this case, the school board has decided that the community standards say that homosexual behaviors are not acceptable?

This leads to a new cluster and content inference field: school-community relations with mention of a city ordinance providing protected-class status to homosexuals.

We give the back-and-forth display of this next in Figure 11, including a new column on the very far right that records stimulated recall commentary.

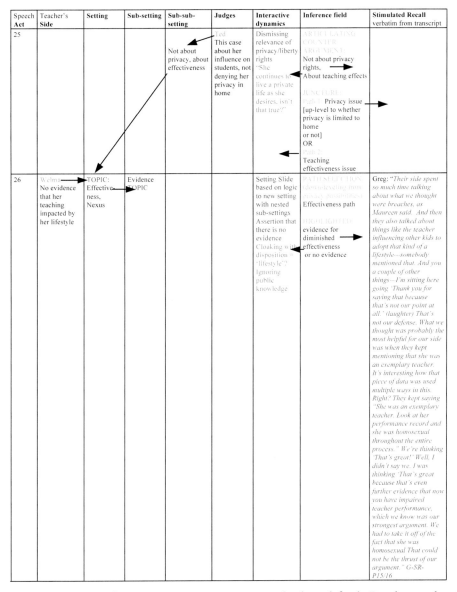

Speech Act	Teacher's Side	Setting	Sub-setting	Sub-sub-setting	Judges	Interactive dynamics	Inference field	Stimulated Recall verbatim from transcript
25				Not about privacy, about effectiveness	Ted: This case about her influence on students, not denying her privacy in home	Dismissing relevance of privacy/liberty rights "She continues to live a private life as she desires, isn't that true?"	ARTICULATING COUNTER ARGUMENT: Not about privacy rights, About teaching effects JUNCTURE: Path1 Privacy issue [up-level to whether privacy is limited to home or not] OR Path2 Teaching effectiveness issue	
26	Welma: No evidence that her teaching impacted by her lifestyle	TOPIC: Effectiveness, Nexus	Evidence TOPIC			Setting Slide based on logic to new setting with nested sub-settings Assertion that there is no evidence Cloaking with disposition — 'lifestyle'? Ignoring public knowledge	PATH SELECTION down-leveling from privacy-possibilities Effectiveness path HIGHLIGHTED: evidence for diminished effectiveness or no evidence	Greg: "Their side spent so much time talking about what we thought were breaches, as Maureen said. And then they also talked about things like the teacher influencing other kids to adopt that kind of a lifestyle—somebody mentioned that. And you a couple of other things—I'm sitting here going 'Thank you for saying that because that's not our point at all.' (laughter) That's not our defense. What we thought was probably the most helpful for our side was when they kept mentioning that she was an exemplary teacher. It's interesting how that piece of data was used multiple ways in this. Right? They kept saying "She was an exemplary teacher. Look at her performance record and she was homosexual throughout the entire process." We're thinking 'That's great!' Well, I didn't say we. I was thinking 'That's great because that's even further evidence that now you have impaired teacher performance, which we know was our strongest argument. We had to take it off of the fact that she was homosexual That could not be the thrust of our argument." G-SR-P15/16

Figure 11: The second effectiveness/nexus argument in back-and-forth Display, with stimulated recall (pg. 1)

Speech Act	Teacher's Side	Setting	Sub-setting	Sub-sub-setting	Judges	Interactive dynamics	Inference field	Stimulated Recall verbatim from transcript
27			TOPIC: evidence nuanced by temporal factor		Sally We don't know how this public knowledge impacts her teaching		UP-LEVELING to temporal factor evidence for continued excellence → or no evidence [implicit distinction between performance and effectiveness]	
28			TOPIC: ◄ Role model		Vivian She is not a role model for students, affecting classroom in negative way	Setting Slide to role model topic Teaming: expanding teammate's argument	UP-LEVELING, explication of public knowledge—effectiveness relation Role model as partial explication of adverse effect [Up-level: 1. Assumes role model links to sexuality status 2. What counts as adverse teaching effect? 3. What counts as evidence?]	
29	Kate She was a homosexual before, with exemplary teaching. No question of her role modeling then. She doesn't talk about sexuality in classroom					Assertion that teacher not talking about sexuality in classroom = not a role model with respect to sexual orientation	DOWN-LEVELING, peformance and effectiveness (inclusive of role modeling) equated [Up-level: Assumption that role model means behaviors in front of audience: what is "role model"?	
30				TOPIC: Definition of role model	Ted But it is public knowledge now, doesn't that change her relationship with students?	Challenging definition implicate sub-sub setting Use of questioning strategy (again by Ted) to make logical point	UP-LEVELING Performance vs. effectiveness distinction: Role model must be understood in terms of relationships OR Relationships with students is the issue rather than role model: OR Role model has to do with behaviors in view of audience → [Further up-leveling to role model cluster and adverse effects cluster]	
31	Kate → Three students asked for transfer – that can happen in any classroom for many reasons. Two parents out of a class of thirty. It isn't significant		TOPIC Evidence, numbers. Given Ted's definition of role model			Accepts Ted's definition of role model and broadens setting back to evidence topic	DOWN-LEVELING to evidence argument that would apply to either understanding of role model / effectiveness. HIGHLIGHTED: How ascertain a significant change in relationships? [Up-level relations between 1. role model, 2. relationships, 3. teaching effectiveness]	This might be where Maureen regarded as one of the two strongest points of the teacher's side? "Kate hinted at the disruption piece" M-SR-P15.

Figure 11: The second effectiveness/nexus argument in back-and-forth Display, with stimulated recall (pg. 2)

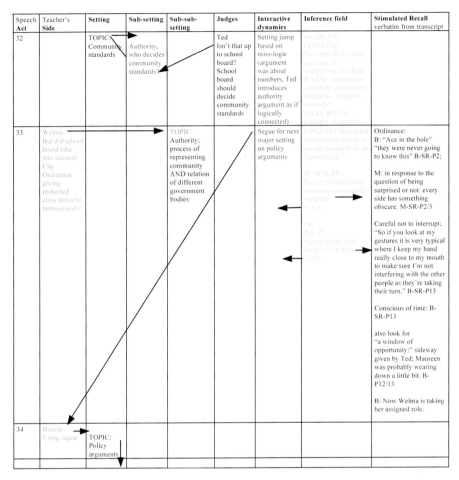

Figure 11: The second effectiveness/nexus argument in back-and-forth Display, with stimulated recall (pg. 3)

The argument can be followed in Figure 11 by simply reading statements made from the teacher's side followed by counterarguments on the judge's side. The way setting bids, sub-settings, and so on emerge during the argument is shown in Figure 11. The use of arrows pointing right and left in various places indicate how an argument could go from that point on. "Up-level" in the content inference field column is used to note what issues and assumptions are presupposed and thus could be drawn into argumentation next. **"Up-leveling"** marks a process that has actually up-leveled the field to produce new possibilities.

The argument over effectiveness this time is more complex than it was during its first appearance. A condensed version of this second argument over effectiveness would be as follows:

Second Effectiveness/Nexus Argument: Effectiveness Argument Interpreted in Terms of "Role Modeling" and Community Standards
(Speech Acts 25–32)

1. Teaching efficiency is in question (Ted)
   a. No evidence of poor efficiency or effectiveness **(entire career)**
   b. But that is **before public knowledge**, what about after? She is no longer a good **ROLE MODEL** for the classroom
      i. Prior to public knowledge, there were no complaints about role model, she has not talked about sexuality with children before or after public knowledge, therefore no evidence of negative role model (her **actions** have not changed)
         1. But public knowledge would change **relationships** with students
            a. Only small numbers
2. But that is up to the **school board**, representing the **community,** to decide (Ted)

Participants would seemingly be left with the following conclusions after this argument:

1. The concept of effectiveness could include being a "role model"
   Role model defined in terms of one's visible actions

   OR

   In terms of how one is interpreted given knowledge of one's sexual status and hence in terms of the relationships one is in

   Determine relationships by numbers: Small numbers not significant

   OR

   Any number significant
2. The school board determines the **community standards** and norms, and it finds homosexual behaviors inappropriate. Therefore, it determines this teacher is a **poor role model** for students, which means **adverse teaching effects**, which means **diminished effectiveness** and thus dismissal is appropriate

The argumentative process is diagrammed in Figure 12 below. We can see how much more of the content inference field is covered this second time.

BLUE = arguments from the teacher's side
RED = arguments from the judges
Arguments are given in order of their appearance during the debate

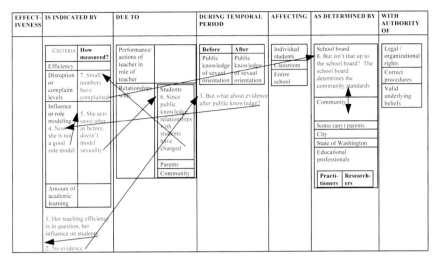

Figure 12; The second effectiveness/nexus argument

On Inference Chains and Up-Leveling

In speech acts 30 and 32, Ted gives arguments from the judge's position having to do with who has the right to make the decision in question. He argues that it is the school board's right to do so. But, on what basis could he be making this argument? The reasons in support of Ted's argument are implicit to the situation and within the intersubjective field, the content inference field, and thus something other participants and ourselves as researchers have access to. This is an example of what we call an "inference chain." The inference chain is *implicit* to Ted's assertion and is not directly related to the arguments we have discussed above, because Ted is introducing a new line of argumentation when presenting this assertion. Here is the chain implicit to Ted's last claim:

Ted's Inference Chain

> **G.** "Role model" is an accurate interpretation of effectiveness,
>
>> **F.** Role modeling is to be understood in terms of relationships rather than the actions of the role model,
>>
>>> **E.** Community standards are sufficient for determination of appropriate teacher role models,
>>>
>>>> **D.** The temporal period of interest is only the post-public-knowledge period,
>>>>
>>>>> **C.** Effectiveness has to do with effects on students,
>>>>>
>>>>>> **B.** The authority of the school board for making such determinations is not clear in this argument, but probably considered to be a matter of organizational hierarchy and rights
>>>>>>
>>>>>>> **A. The school board should/can determine community standards**

Notice that Ted's argument articulates a position on the last link—his argument could be challenged at any of the levels chained together. We number the steps of the chain in what looks like reverse order because Ted has not articulated his chain; he has rather articulated its conclusion. Ted might not even be fully aware of the full chain. But given the content inference field and Ted's claim, it is possible to up-level to assumptions required for his claim to be true. Hence we use a reverse alphabetical order in our diagram. Positions articulated at the same level do not presuppose each other but are combined conjunctively to support the articulated position at the bottom.

In Figure 13, we display this implicit chain on the effectiveness/nexus content inference field.

BLUE = Level of the assertion

BROWN = One level up: these positions must be valid if assertion level is valid

GREEN = Two levels up: these positions must be valid if brown level assertions are to *apply* to blue level

Positions at same level (= same color) work *conjunctively* in relation to levels below

⟶ Single arrows represent up-level relationships, the position pointed *at* is presupposed

◄ - - - ► Double headed arrows indicate conjunctive relations; one position does not depend upon the other but combined they are necessary for the level below

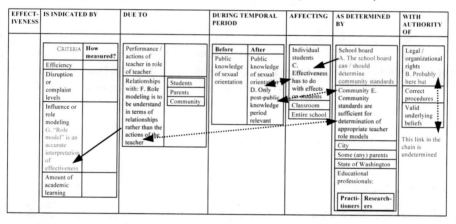

Figure 13; Ted's inference chain

In Figure 13, we see that every category of the content inference field is relevant to Ted's inference chain, and this would be the case for all inference chains. However, we only find one category in the field that is not determined in terms of what position one would have to take within it, for Ted's claim to be valid. Often many categories will be undetermined by the assertion that places them within a chain. This is related to the "multi-premise principle" in Robert Brandom's theory of implicit inference structures, pragmatics, and logic (Brandom 1998).

The general point is that all assertions in an argument will have some chain structure, but the chain will not always be clear. It will be clear, however, if the content inference field is well understood. Notice that the inference chain for Ted's claim takes positions within all the main categories of the effectiveness/nexus content inference field.

When analyzing arguments, we can look for implicated inference chains. The levels of the chains as well as the categories they address (e.g., in this case, categories include an interpretation of "effectiveness," a position on the temporal dimension, a position on who or what is affected) will be core structures to the content inference field within which a particular argument takes place.

The Third Effectiveness/Nexus Argument: Example of Partial Field Articulation

The third time the effectiveness and nexus issue was argued was in major setting three. This argument tells us more about content inference fields and how they operate within human interactions. Here are the relevant speech acts:

Teacher's Side	Judge's side
(34) BONNIE: May I please the court. We actually have three policy arguments that we would like to present, including the city of Tacoma's Ordinance. In the first bill it deals with is the Washington State Common School Provisions on "Employees Hiring and Discharge." The language in that declares that dismissing or discharging a teacher is really declared unconstitutionally vague if it is not coupled with actual adverse performance as a teacher. And clearly, the code recognizes that being homosexual, alone, does not constitute justification for dismissal of a teacher of Maria's caliber. (disrupted by Maureen)	
	(35) MAUREEN (interrupting): I still believe that the school board is arguing that she is being fired for being homosexual. From what I understand, from what was presented to us, the argument is one of the disruption and community standard.
(36) BONNIE: Yeah...Clearly in Tinker, the fear of disruption was not enough of an argument...and it simply talks about the extension of free association from political freedom to privacy right.... I think you have to make sure that you are not making a decision on the fear of disruption. There has not been any evidence.	
	(37) SALLY: The disruption has occurred that at least five families have been disrupted.
(38) BONNIE: They presented some objections. There are no evidences to indicate that there was a disruption in educational process in that classroom.	
	(39) MAUREEN: Couldn't changing classrooms be considered a disruption to a child's education?

Figure 14; The third effectiveness/nexus argument (pg. 1)

Teacher's Side	Judge's side
LAST QUESTION WARNING	BY PROFESSOR
(40) BONNIE: I didn't hear what it was.	
	(41) MAUREEN: Couldn't changing classrooms like some research says that remaining in the same classroom changes educational environment to be very disruptive to a child…couldn't changing classroom be determined to be disruptive for these children?
(42) BONNIE: I don't think there is any policy to support that changing classroom has been prevalent at this school for any student, whatsoever. And I think we made the argument earlier that I think students could be asked to be removed from a classroom for a variety of reasons. We don't see that as a valid argument in this case.	

Figure 14; The third effectiveness/nexus argument (pg. 2)

This argument can be condensed as follows:

Third Effectiveness/Nexus Argument: Effectiveness Argument Interpreted in Terms of "Disruption"
1. School board and community probably acted only out of **fear of disruption,** not actual disruption. Tinker case shows fear of disruption is not enough.
   a. Five families were actually **disrupted**
   b. There were some **objections**, no **evidence of disruption** to educational process in that classroom
      i. Transferring classrooms could cause disruption (to them? or to the whole class? not clear) according to "research" (no specific research cited)
         1. No evidence that changing classrooms has been prevalent (**numbers issue**)
         2. The transfers that did happen could have occurred for any reason (**nexus** between transfers and homosexuality)

The content inference field here undergoes some expansions in size and complexity with the added distinctions between **disruption** and **fear of disruption** as well as an implicit distinction, smuggled in by the judge's side and subsequently barely noticed, between **disruption of individual students** and **disruption of classroom educational processes**. Because this distinction was not precisely articulated, it remains an implicit issue, a sort of muddle, as the argumentation proceeds. We represent this muddle with dotted lines in the diagram below, to show implicit references to a different concept of legally significant disruption by Bonnie and the judges.

A main new item manifested within the effectiveness-nexus field here is attention to interpreting numbers: did the three transfers occur because of knowledge of the teacher's sexuality? Probably, but then three transfers made from a different classroom for an entirely different reason (later in the debate, Bonnie gave an example of a teacher mentioning evolution in class and getting three transfers as a result) probably would not have resulted in a teacher's dismissal. That provides additional argumentation that the **number** of transfers is too small to argue compromised teaching effectiveness. Three is within the range of acceptable transfer frequencies for a school. If this argument were accepted by the other side, then the only path for further argumentation seemingly open to them would be the argument that the teacher is a **poor role model** for students, based on **community standards**. In other words, Ted's final argument given in II above could seem to be the only way forward, according to the content inference field at this point.[11]

Here is the diagram:

BLUE = arguments from the teacher's side
RED = arguments from the judges
Dotted line connections show implicit, not articulated, relations
Arguments are given in order of their appearance during the debate

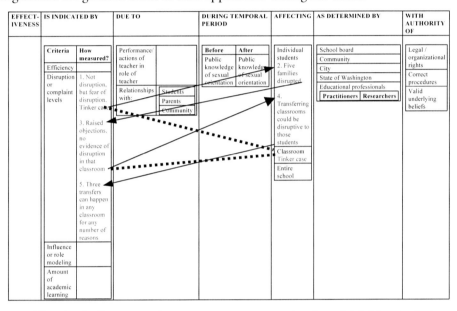

Figure 15; The third effectiveness/nexus argument: example of partial field articulation

IV. Summary and Conclusions

This chapter has presented some theory pertaining to the concepts of intersubjective space, logical-content inference fields, and illocutionary infrastructures. A way to understand "structure" was explained, as the compression, through learning processes, of temporal relations into simultaneous inferential relations involving possible subject positions within an intersubjective milieu. We argued that both the logic of contents, of what interactions are about, and the "deontic scoreboard" of illocutionary commitments and entitlements produce boundaries that enable actors to anticipate the position from which a next act will come, from another subject. Expectation boundaries also facilitate various degrees and levels of position-taking within interaction settings (one actor anticipating the anticipation of another actor for her own action, and so on). The theory of meaning underlying this is a form of communicative pragmatics. Anticipations are key structures in the instrumental learning processes emphasized in classical pragmatism because it is through anticipations that actions are related to consequences. When actions are not instrumental but communicative, anticipations are structured differently: in relation to a possible mutual understanding rather than to tangible action consequences. In this case, what is anticipated can be at least partially captured with the metaphor of intersubjective spaces within which various arrays of possible subject positions are assumed to be mutually understood.

We distinguished between illocutionary infrastructures and logical inference structures, relating this distinction to processes of objectivation. Illocutionary infrastructures, or "settings," involve identity-securing and identity-risking commitments that are performatively given, accepted, rejected, and negotiated while human interactions take place. We also introduced more theory with our concepts of "setting integration," "communicative structuration" and with a vocabulary to assist in the reconstruction of human interactions in relation to content inference fields.

These concepts and the theoretical discussions in this chapter can be used in any study of human interaction. Our illustration of how to reconstruct content inference fields from real qualitative data and then use them to better understand the interactions that implicated them could serve as stimulus and model for other studies by qualitative researchers. We hope that our various methods for displaying interactions and reconstructed fields may also be of interest to readers.

The goals of the project undertaken by both of us have not yet been realized. Our interest is in the relation between logical contents and illocutionary structures. And this relation should throw more light on the connection between the mode of being that is distinctive of personhood and how communicative reason emerges precisely in relation to this. Being a person is a process that involves acting for reasons rather than causes, being free, and being accountable and trustworthy. Personhood and communicative reason are equi-primordial emergent phenomena: as soon as there is communicatively mediated interaction employing normed symbols, there is emergence: the beginning of personhood and the beginning of communicative rationality. Being accountable to others rather than responding to something like a force of nature is only possible through communicative reason. And communicative reason is also the basis for human identity claims, both processes of individuation and processes of collective identity formation.

In analyzing mock debate data on the issue of firing schoolteacher Maria when she came out as a lesbian, we hoped to discover interesting relations between settings and logical contents. The illocutionary infrastructure of the interactions, we thought, would display the way in which illocutionary commitments have an intimate relation with human needs for identity security. Thus purely logical relations within the contents of this mock legal debate should be found to be subtly thwarted, hidden, or subordinated to moves made more for the sake of the identity of the actor than by the logic of the debate. But the opposite actually happened. Because the debate was a fictional one and because the roles performed by participants in the debate were explicitly defined and formally fixed, identity-securing acts were never really foregrounded. Instead the setting dynamics of this mock debate took a form that freed actors to concentrate on strategically using logic with the goal of winning the debate.

As a result, our analysis concentrated on content-inference fields. We did not reconstruct the "deontic scoreboards" of this debate any further than to note setting bids, negotiations, levels of nesting, and "setting slides" as we call them. Actors make use of setting dynamics to obscure, highlight, juncture, path-select, up-level, down-level, and dodge features of content inference fields. Their argumentation strategies used these fields and sometimes employed setting bids and so on in relation to the fields. But the setting dynamics were not centered about identity issues as we had expected. The "deontic scoreboards" were not very subtle and easy to reconstruct as their main features were formally set by the context (a mock debate). We hope to continue our analysis of logic, illocution, and intersubjective space so that the issues just coming to light in this first effort may be further illuminated.

Notes

1. "Intersubjective space" can be distinguished from "transpersonal" and we will address this a little further on in this chapter.
2. Notice that a person who acts compulsively and contrary to reasons to which others expect her to conform risks her subject-status only if she cannot provide a self-explanation in terms of these compulsions. If she can say, "You will have to get used to me. I act on impulse often and cannot control this," then her subject status is in no danger. Giving reasons, acting with reasons, and acting for reasons are ways to account for one's self from the position of other possible subjects, which in this case would be showing the ability to transcend, to be beyond, one's impulsive behavior by showing awareness of it.
3. Differences between possible meanings within a meaning field are structured by possible subject positions regarding the intention of the actor. For example, the difference between the possibility of sarcasm and sincerity in our example here is a difference in the possible intentions of the speaker. Intentionality is a tricky topic philosophically; it seems that intentions rarely precede actions, but more often come about through the endorsement an actor will or will not make for an act she has completed. The intention of the act seems to be built into the action impetus itself, because actions come up holistically and are usually learned, which means they internally anticipate how others will respond to them and what reasons the actor could give to account for her act in relation to these anticipated others. The idea of the prelearned action impetus and its internal composition is discussed at length in Carspecken, 1999. Meanwhile, intentionality is something that could perhaps be conceptualized in terms of acting from certain possible positions in intersubjective space; or even allowing acts to express from a certain position in intersubjective space. More work could be done on intentionality. We put in this footnote because "intentionality" has become an unpopular term in poststructuralist discourses. This is because those discourses assume it means having an intention, somehow, and then next choosing an act. But intentionality should not mean this at all and yet it remains important. Meanings cannot be understood, we argue, without the possible intention of a possible other subject constituting them. The actor's intention or the writer's intention need not be most important in an analysis of meaning—it depends on the purpose of the analysis. But some possible intention has to be in the picture when we conceptualize meaning. Another way to express that is to say that some possible subject position within an intersubjective space has to be in the picture.
4. Karl Popper presented his theory of three worlds in 1978 at the University of Michigan, as a Tanner Lecture on Human Values. The theory has been summarized and discussed by various philosophers since; a recommended summary and discussion of it may be found in Habermas's *The Theory of Communicative Action, vol. 1,* chapter 1.
5. This case scenario for the mock debate was modeled upon a 1977 Supreme Court of Washington State decision, Gaylord v. Tacoma School District (reference: Gaylord v. Tacoma School District, 559 P. 2d 1340; Wash. 1977). In the actual empirical case of 1977, the court upheld the dismissal decision. The court argued that since it can be inferred from the evidence that this teacher had engaged in homosexual activity, and that since such conduct can be reasonably expected to interfere with his fitness or ability to teach, the dismissal should be upheld. The case scenario used for the class debate was presented without any clarification on how Maria's lesbian status became public knowledge. The fictional case was set for the contemporary period and the gender of the teacher was changed from male to female.
6. This resulted in ten pauses of the tape with much discussion and explanation provided. In addition to the ten pauses with resulting discussion, the researchers had these three debate participants discuss what they remembered of their thinking and strategies prior to actually beginning the debate. This conversation, and the discussions that occurred with each pause of the video, were videotaped and the tape later transcribed for analysis.
7. This was recognized both by the researchers analyzing transcripts and the participants in stimulated recall who commented on this lack of development without the researchers even asking about it.

8. Different from the Continental legal system, the legal tradition in the United States is that the two parties have the primary responsibilities to bring evidence to court and establish their own arguments. Judges usually take the role of facilitators, asking questions and stimulating arguments. In the stimulated recall, judge Maureen explained her role as "to plant the seed but not necessarily keep going down one particular path." And it was also expressed from the judge's side that the goal was to be "fair" and also not to give arguments to either side to be used in the debate.

9. Bowers v. Hardwick, 478 U.S. 186 (1986).

10. Lawrence v. Texas, 539 U.S. 558 (2003).

11. In the stimulated recall, Greg, who was on the school board side, said that community norms and diminished teaching effectiveness were the "two dead horses" that his side had planned to strike "over and over and over again." At the end of the school board's rebuttal, the point that poor effects on any student at all would be grounds for dismissing Maria.

References

Austin, J. (1975). *How to do things with words* (2nd ed.). Cambridge, MA: Harvard University Press.

Brandom, R. (1998). *Making it explicit: Reasoning, representing, and discursive commitment.* Cambridge, MA: Harvard University Press.

Carspecken, P. (1996). *Critical ethnography in educational research: A theoretical and practical guide.* New York: Routledge.

Carspecken, P. (1999). *Four scenes for posing the question of meaning.* New York: Peter Lang.

Carspecken, P. (2003, August). Ocularcentrism, phonocentrism and the counter-enlightenment problematic. *Teachers College Record, 105*(6), 978–1047.

Giddens, A. (1979). *Central problems in social theory; Action, structure and contradiction in social analysis.* Berkeley & Los Angeles: University of California Press.

Habermas, J. (1984). *The theory of communicative action.* Vol. 1: *Reason and the rationalization of society.* Boston: Beacon.

Habermas, J. (1987). *The theory of communicative action.* Vol. 2: *Lifeworld and system. A critique of functionalist reason.* Boston: Beacon.

Habermas, J. (2000). *On the pragmatics of communication* (Maeve Cooke, ed.). Cambridge, MA: MIT Press.

Levi-Strauss, C. (1974). *Structural anthropology.* New York: Basic Books.

Piaget, J. (1971). *Genetic epistemology.* New York: W.W. Norton & Co.

CHAPTER TWELVE

The Descriptive Pronoun

BENETTA JOHNSON

Lan•guage (lăng′gwĭj) *n*.**1.a.** The use by human beings of voice sounds, and often written symbols representing these sounds, in combinations and patterns to express and communicate thoughts and feelings. **b.** A system of words formed from such combinations and patterns, used by the people of a particular country or by a group of people with a shared history or set of traditions (*The American Heritage Dictionary*, 1991).

It is not uncommon for research in education to utilize spoken language as a means for exploring the personal lives of human beings. Developmental theorists, such as Erik Erikson (1959), contend that the use of verbal language does not arrive until after a person has reached the capacity to understand symbols. As it is illustrated in the notation above, the definition of language includes the word "symbols." The symbolic nature of language allows for there to be meaning in expression through the use of body, sign, and various other nonverbal processes such as gestures, paralanguage, physical appearance, and written notations or images. Qualitative researchers often rely on language to address complex interaction across three domains—as phenomena of interest, medium of inquiry/analysis, and outcome. This chapter addresses the verbal replication of pronouns within a small group of African American women, illustrating how detailed attention to ordinary language can help researchers better understand the experiences of participants. The women within this study forged a shared understanding of their collective world through the symbolic means of verbal and nonverbal language. The research was able to engage with the participants as they disclosed, developed, and reconstructed their representative claims regarding their internal experiences. While each woman in the study was unique, among the women there was a shared desire to express a collective experience. Understanding how they managed their environments and understood themselves within particular social settings and systems is facilitated by understanding the meaning of their use of pronouns.

This chapter demonstrates that a close interpretation of the participant's use of pronouns can contribute to a richer, more critical understanding of the human experience. The inquiry process involved four African American women (Regine, Maxine, Khadija, and Synclaire) who were graduate students at a predominantly white university. Each woman within the study was an active participant with a psycho-educational support group that was conducted prior to her involvement within the research study. As a participant within a larger dissertation study, each woman was asked to take part in a structured focus group with one another. Prior to participation in the focus group, each woman was asked to complete an individual written activity that included her personal construction of a workshop outline and resource guide for individuals whom they considered to be similar to herself. In completing this activity, the women were open to decide what it meant to write for someone "similar to themselves." The structured focus group provided an opportunity for the women to talk about their completed products, personal implications that resulted from their workshop construction, and possible relevance to their current life positions. Following the focus group, each woman took part in two individual interviews that included asking her to develop an advertisement flyer for her proposed workshop.

One intention for these written activities included creating an opportunity for the women to express their academic experiences through slight distance (focusing on an "other" similar to self), more of a reflective third-person perspective on their own experiences coupled with a second-person normative perspective (Carspecken, 1996). It was within the focus group and individual interview process that each woman was asked to explore this distancing process and the actual presence that it had within the life experiences to which they were referring. Consequently, this presentation of distance and focus on a similar "other" allowed for expression and attention on the descriptive pronoun.

This chapter begins with a general discussion of language structure and qualitative research including an introduction to the descriptive pronoun. The next major section argues for an interpretive connection between emotionality and descriptive pronoun use. Examples from the study are introduced at this point. This part of the paper provides justification for utilizing a close critical analysis of the descriptive pronoun within qualitative inquiry. Once this justification is established, the chapter addresses how researchers might take account of descriptive pronouns in the data collection and analysis process and the dynamics of the descriptive pronoun, and clarifies the use of the descriptive pronoun. The descriptive pronoun is a refinement that emerged in this study from close analysis of the women's uses of pronouns.

Language Structure and Qualitative Research

One of the profound complexities of language is the way in which it has power within the human experience, even when full description is nonexistent. This is both an ordinary and extraordinary feature of human life. The inability, hesitancy, or evasion in fully describing an experience or circumstance provides an avenue through which the qualitative researcher can advance her understanding of life as it is experienced by the human being. Furthermore, it is within this effort to understand that the participant encounters an interactive opportunity that welcomes the exploration of her unique and rich experience.

Taking note of the intricacies of communication is not a new analytical landscape within qualitative research. One particularly relevant manner in which the recreation of meaning and experience is investigated is through the use of conversational analysis. This form of analysis, rooted in ethnomethodology (Lynch, 2000) considers two primary analytical foci, the investigation of interactive reciprocity and management of the conversation between participants (Gale, 2000).

Conversational analysis focuses upon the collaboration or absence of collaboration within communication. There appears to be a focus on how the speakers jointly share in the communication process. Focus is directed towards particular actions and parameters through which language is transformed (Sluzki, 1992). The various shifts within dialogue become germane foci to include such specifics as overlapped dialogue and transitional relevance place (Gale, 2000). It becomes important within this analytical method to consider how dialogue is constructed and organized (Have, 1986). While one method does not preclude or supersede another, the incorporation of a descriptive pronoun takes into consideration a different aspect within the dynamic of communication. This area of interest reflects a more representative view of expressed language. Given such, it is expected that there is an internally driven aspect of language that both reflects and represents a personal internal process that is specific to their unique experiences. Such an aspect of language serving as a human experience is further elaborated by such writers as Pain (2009), who discusses a process entitled "talk-in-interaction." Within her work, she addresses the transmission of knowledge from one person to another through the use of grammar. Pain (2009) considers language (as an ongoing, recursive process that is filled with continuous learning) to include a naturalistic aspect—namely, a human potentiality developed through interaction within an evolving environment. Pain's discussion of the human experience and its coupling with an ever-changing environment speaks to the presence of the unique experience of the language process.

The sentence, a unit of grammatical proportion, often includes numerous clauses, with a central focus of a specific subject. Within spoken language, the presented subject can be expressed either explicitly or implicitly. It is not uncommon for an explicit subject to later take an implicit form in order to decrease the amount of repetition or improve the quality of the sentence structure. Among English speakers, oral sentences can contain a combination of nouns, adjectives, pronouns, verbs, adverbs, articles, conjunctions, prepositions, and the like. But these structural elements alone cannot account for the profundity entailed within the spoken sentences—our understanding of one another is bolstered through the use of such gifts as dialect, tone, pace, and facial expression. Incorporation of these language components creates the opportunity for a juncture replete with human wonder, imagination, and newness. When thought of in this way, communicative language simultaneously links persons with a community of language users and produces uniquely personal expressions, ideas, and identities.

While the use of such language elements can provide indescribable benefits, there are many boundaries and constraints entailed in the use of words. It is, at times, assumed that the use of such pro-forms like the pronoun will unearth its meaning as the expression persists. Within qualitative research, an area of further intrigue becomes enlightened when the origin of this literal substitute is ambiguous. With respect to this study, it was the very nature of pronoun usage within such murky contexts that illuminated the human experiences of the women, which at times, were bound (but not determined) by our language limitations.

The Descriptive Pronoun

Linguistic Substitutions. The personal use of linguistic substitutions can be interwoven with the life journey and experiences of the speaker such that the substitution connotes not only the referent for which it is substituting, but also worldviews, stances, experiences, personal choices, and/or desires. For example, a researcher (like me) might "choose" to avoid use of the pronoun "I" in presenting her research findings (for example as this chapter aims to do). This choice reflects a (my) decision to leave out the use of the first-person pronoun in order to encourage readers' greater focus on the research participants and processes. The matter of choice is a complicated one in this chapter. Just as the use of personal, descriptive pronouns depends on one's personal experience and accessible resources, personal substitutions (those not specifically limited to language such as modes of transportation, nutritional access, and residential settings) also represent social constraint, limited awareness, lack of resources, and human obligation (all of which can have an impact on one's use of language). As such, the presence of substitutions within a person's life may represent a voluntary or involuntary occurrence. Descriptive pronouns offer patterned and significant interpretive material through the use of otherwise thought-of common pronouns. Their descriptive nature involves the way in which they carry narrative structures about the relations between the pronoun and the storyteller.

A major premise of any substitution is replacement and variation; meaning that, regardless of the lived experience, an alternative, in fact, exists, whether accessible or inaccessible. One could always have acted otherwise (Carspecken, 1996; Korth, 2003). Therefore, it should be of interest within the perspective of the qualitative researcher to consider the dynamics through which the use of a linguistic substitution is present when a participant is describing and disclosing her experiences. Because a substitution entails the presence of diverse options, it is relevant to consider how the participant shares her experiences and the linguistic expressions involved (Tannen, 2005). The following questions are worth asking:

- "Does the participant refer to herself?"

- "How does the participant refer to herself?"

- "What pronouns does she use to refer to others?"

- "What are the other linguistic options that could have been used by the participants in sharing their narrative?"

- "What is the possible meaning connected to the participant's use of this linguistic substitution?"

Identifying a Descriptive Pronoun. The use of a pronoun by a participant may or may not be relevant for intentional interest on the part of a qualitative researcher. Because the use of pronouns is largely commonplace within most languages, it is not unlikely for participants to include pronouns within his or her life narrative. As a result, the question of how to consider if further investigation is relevant becomes especially important in light of their abundant usage. Thus, it is important to reflect upon identifying the relevant factors useful in deciphering whether or not a particular type of pronoun usage warrants additional inquiry. Attention was drawn to the use of pronouns within the overarching study because of the participants' eloquent presentation of such words as "they" and "us" to describe the interpersonal dynamics within their academic relationships. In these presentations, the women addressed systems that they depicted as variously welcoming and disregarding of their unique existences.

He	I	She	Us
Her	It	Them	We
Him	Me	They	

Table 1 - Common Pronouns

Emotionality and Pronoun Usage. In his work to further understand the interactional processes between human beings communicating with each other, Kagan (1980) developed an approach to help people reflect on their interpersonal processes. As Kagan studied the impacting factors of human interaction, he found that interpersonal process recall, his theorized method for learning about communication, consisted of four critical dimensions, one of which includes affect. For Kagan, affect is characterized as "the music that goes along with the words" (Kagan, 1980, p. 32).

For most people, language is rarely devoid of feeling, whether expressed or subdued. The investigation of how a participant couples pronouns with feelings provides an avenue through which the process of personal pronoun usage can be further explored. The broad display of affect, impacted by cultural dynamics, can include the experience of sadness or joy, further identified through such distinctions as incongruent or restricted in full expression.

Usually, the observation of these affective dynamics of interactions are not absent of such unique attributes as facial expression, eye movement and gaze, posture, breathing pattern, body language, and intonation. For example, when using the pronoun "she," the participant may present an affective state that appears to denote frustration. This presentation of frustration is supported through the researcher's description of its observable expression. Within this particular example, the participant may speak the pronoun "she" through a closed mouth with teeth visible. His brow might exhibit tension and he may look upward as he completes his saying of the pronoun. This particular display of affect, exclusive to a specific content focus, may present a wealth of information that enhances the researcher's awareness about the participant's lived experience and the interpretive context within which his expression is meant to be understood. Descriptive pronouns imbibe whole narratives in terms of their relational meaning. Attention to this same level of detail is not unique to interpreting the meaning of pronouns—qualitative researchers use it to understand participants more generally. However, when these nonverbal characteristics are coupled with attributions associated with understanding why the pronoun is being used (in terms of its qualitative substitution and perhaps its vagueness), a richer set of interpretations emerges.

Emotionality and the Descriptive Pronoun: Justification for a Close Interpretation

Drawing on the analysis from the larger dissertation study, it becomes possible to see that an understanding of meaning requires a close interpretation of the descriptive pronoun. In this section of the paper, several different interpretations are developed in order to justify the researcher's attention toward grasping how pronouns help to express meaning. Specifically, the use of descriptive pronouns when coupled with the expression of emotion complicates the meaning in subjective ways. Such subjectivity includes references the participant makes to her own unique experiences and knowledge. In the examples to follow, participants' use of descriptive pronouns provided them with opportunities to speak to and about themselves through the voice of an "other," protecting themselves by depersonalizing specifically "harmful others." The findings of this study, then, justify further attention to the use of personal pronouns by participants. Within the following excerpt, there is a display of emotional/experiential distancing, through the use of the descriptive pronoun, to explore what appears to be an affectively laden life experience.

When "You" Refers to "Me"

> **REGINE:** I found a dissertation topic; I was like, you know, I don't know if I can do this. You know its okay.....because at one point, it was like, I'm the one who has to do this. And I came to the point like, it's okay if I'm, not the one to do it. If I do it it's great, I'm happy for anyone that writes the—but it's okay if I'm not. And so I had to let that take, you know, my purpose changed on that (*sniffles*). My purpose now I think is I don't know what it is. I mean, it's sort of like, I forget what it, again, it's continuing to evolve, like right now I mean I've set up these small goals, okay finish course work, okay if <u>you</u> finish <u>your</u> comps (*breaking of voice, eyes began to tear, she cries*), okay, finish <u>your</u> second set of comps, ok, and you know what I'm saying, that if I'm still feeling it, if I'm still feeling like yeah, this is it, then I'm gonna let it continue.

Here, Regine is responding to a question about academic goals and the freedom to change those. It is easily noted that Regine actively incorporated various pronouns to convey her message. Throughout this excerpt, Regine makes use of the pronouns "I," "you," "your," and "my," as well as a less common "one" and "anyone." Regine's pace and tone within this portion of her dialogue was rapid, highly inflected, and spaced, with short pauses frequently positioned throughout numerous portions of her dialogue.

While each use of a pronoun in itself is important data for greater understanding of Regine's experience, it is the use of her inclusion of "you" and "your" that seems to have a strong connection to the emotional content presented within this narrative. This particular excerpt begins with Regine consistently utilizing the pronoun "I" to represent her personal presence within the story. It is clearly her story. Regine shares internal dialogue, specifically sharing her feelings with regards to her personal perspective, presenting her thoughts about her peers' performance and accomplished tasks. What becomes evident as Regine continues to share her experience is a shift from the use of "I" and "I'm" to "you" and "your." During the exact moment where she begins to express herself through tears, her means of discussing "self" is relocated to a second-person position, with goals and ultimatums spoken by her to herself, but possibly not set from or for her. The anguish expressed presents a disconnect from her experience, creating a somewhat decreased personal association and identification with the felt experience. Within this excerpt, the descriptive pronoun is illuminated through the emotional affect presented through her tears and broken pace of speech. Specifically, the descriptive pronouns could be identified as "you" and "your." These particular pronouns have an emotionally laden component that may not be seen throughout other portions of Regine's dialogue, thereby increasing its likelihood of being descriptive.

Oftentimes the narrative surrounding the use of a pronoun provides clarity as to whom or what is being referenced. Because the actual pronoun, as it exists, is not exclusive to a sole referent, the pertinent dynamic, present within the use of that pronoun, increases its expression of meaning. In the example noted above, the use of the pronoun "she" was described in terms of an observation made by a researcher that coupled Regine's use of the pronoun. If such a method is further used within an investigation, it becomes important to distinguish a descriptive pronoun from one of lesser regard. Meaning that there are some uses of pronouns that may not lead towards greater understanding of meaning.

The attempt to compare the same pronoun across the participant's repertoire calls for a description of how that pronoun is personally used in light of the surrounding content. If the investigator becomes aware of a consistent pairing between displayed affect and pronoun usage, the inclusion of this pairing increases the possibility of a descriptive pronoun. Furthermore, the evidence of consistency, such as the participant's routine tendency to express an observably personal process through indefinite means, also increases the likelihood of a descriptive pronoun; particularly if this pattern seems present within numerous locations of the participant's account.

Depersonalizing the Experience—From Naming Them to "They"
Within the excerpt below, Maxine denotes a very personal experience that includes the description of an academic process she found emotionally taxing. Maxine is describing the situation where it seems as if she must choose between being authentic, or protecting herself in a relationship where the consequences could adversely influence desired outcomes. This situation identifies how she likely feels it necessary to mask her personal feelings in order to avoid risk—and maintain a professional relationship.

> **MAXINE:** And there's gonna be times when your department or your school's gonna have more power than you do. And it's gonna be times where you're gonna have to decide do you want <u>them</u> to dictate what's gonna happen, do you want to go outside of the school or the department and get help if your needs are not being addressed. Or do you want to get through that hoop. So that the ball's in your court again. And making that decision, and playing that game and being tactful putting this mask on, cuz sometime you know. It calls for you smiling at <u>someone</u> that's getting on your last nerve, um, cuz otherwise <u>they</u> might—although it's suppose to be a professional relationship <u>they</u> might take things personally.

Maxine's disclosure regarding her experience and the process of negotiating one's emotions in risky relationships highlights an important aspect of speaking about one's personal being through impersonal means. While Maxine is sharing an extremely heartfelt moment within her academic process, her use of language serves to remove the personal experience present within this struggle for power. Maxine's use of "them," "they," and "someone," places her adversarial opponent in a vague position. Her language may possibly shield her from the direct influence that she feels from these noted "others" who stand to impede her personal accomplishment. Given the power of this vague "other" within Maxine's disclosure, it is possible that the inclusion of specifics could create an additional experience of disempowerment. Therefore, it could be argued that Maxine's indirect language use creates an opportunity for her to share her personal experience through a mechanism less threatening to her internal perception of self.

One way of interpreting Maxine's use of a vague pronoun is that it circumvents her exposure to greater wrath from her adversary. If she maintains a nameless opponent, the threat may be understood by her as more general and less directed at her personally. Therefore, Maxine's removal of a person's name (generalized pronoun) reveals that this sort of experience, which happened to her, happens all the time between varying anonymous academic advisers and students. It is quite possible that by engaging in such language use, there is a presence of felt vulnerability and a desire to not fully expose her experienced circumstance for fear of possible harm. As a result, Maxine is engaging in a depersonalizing process of name omission, functioning as a form of self-protection against the possibility of future harm, thereby protecting herself from further felt anguish. Because specific identifiers have been removed from her dialogue, Maxine is somewhat shielded from fully recounting a particularly hurtful interaction. Therefore, she is able to share her story, limiting her opponent's influence on both her own interpretation of the story and potential future encounters. Perhaps this narrative usage ensures Maxine's ability to move forward with her daily tasks, decreasing the potential influence that this nameless other has on her personal sense of well-being.

Perhaps Maxine is actually referring to a specific person or group of people, but perhaps this pronoun indicates an experience that has become more generalized for Maxine. If it is possible to hypothesize that Maxine actually has a name for those whom she presents as nameless, then it is possible that she has experienced such interpersonal dynamics so consistently that a more generalized image has become a stand-in for her interpretation of all such experiences. In this case, in her own conceptualization of the experiences, the more anonymous pronoun, which seems to erase the names of those to whom she describes, might actually indicate this more generalizing experience. In other words, it may be possible that the specific names of people involved in the experience are not fully integrated into her interpretation of her experience.

What remains is a descriptor associated with a felt experience that continues to surface across various aspects of her academic experience, continually reminding her of the limits she consistently feels as a black woman in predominately white academe. This particular reading of Maxine's use of the descriptive pronoun encompasses the possibility that she has assumed a self-protective stance with regard to her own narrative. In other words, it may be that the use of a descriptive pronoun is part of a concealing process, limiting her range of affect for audiences where risk is a concern. Likewise, it is also quite possible that such omission is present within her internal experience, creating an internal process of denied affect. From her account, such interactional pattern may feel necessary to further proceed with her aspired goal acquisition. The use of descriptive pronouns, when the referent is not fully indicated or given, may indicate a variety of complexities entailed in the story/storytelling, exhibiting a possible sign of a taxing association in sharing one's narrative. The very fact that such interpretations can be developed creates added support that a close, pragmatic analysis of pronouns used by the participant has the possibility of illuminating aspects of the participant's experience that are worth further exploration.

The very exhibition of sharing a personal experience, impersonally, is worth further inquiry. This personal process provides further detail that the observed dynamic, whether present within a sterile interview room or observed within a naturalistic observation, produces greater claim to the personal experience attached to the participant's spoken pronoun. The emotionally laden presentation of an unclear pronoun calls for the attention of the qualitative researcher. It is within the nuances of this oxymoronic dynamic that clarity of an unknown becomes exposed. Mapping of perceived emotional expression and pronoun usage can create an investigative focal point that increases the researcher's understanding of ambiguous language.

Unresolved Emotional Conflict and "You"

Investigating the affect present within the participant's description of his or her experience is further developed when the consideration of "affect" as a verb is also included. As the researcher investigates the emotion present within the use of a pronoun ("affect" as a noun), it is similarly helpful to consider how the use of the pronoun influences the participant's disposition ("affect" as a verb). It is within the presence of affect that the distinction of a descriptive pronoun can be made. If a descriptive pronoun is used, it is likely that the presence of this pronoun, in particular settings and circumstances, has an influence on the participant's life experience and expressed narrative. Below is a written excerpt that was later discussed in an interview. Taken all together, it is possible to see how the use of a descriptive pronoun facilitated a tension for Regine between articulating a specific audience and behaving exclusively (which was morally complicated for her).

The following excerpt is drawn from a written task Regine completed as part of the study. As mentioned previously, Regine (as a study participant) was asked to develop a flyer for a proposed, hypothetical, workshop. In creating the structured advertisement, Regine was asked to complete the following query: "If you are …" This is what she wrote:

> **REGINE:** A parent and a graduate student and if <u>you</u> are feeling overwhelmed with managing <u>your</u> household, childcare, finances, social life, and meeting <u>your</u> academic requirements, attend this strategy-building, resource-sharing workshop.

The stem Regine and others responded to tacitly required participants to give more specification to an otherwise general audience for their hypothetical workshops. The task was included as part of the research process in order to encourage the women to share their personal academic experiences and routes to success. This was accomplished by having the women share their thoughts about how they anticipated being of assistance to someone similar to themselves. Once women completed the advertisements for the hypothetical workshop, they were interviewed about the ads. Regine was queried further in order to assist the researcher in gathering greater clarity into her circumstance. A central focus within this exchange was Regine's noted comment pertaining to how she gave voice to this prescribed "you," incorporating her understanding and vision of this "you" through her own experiences and identifications. With the interview as an opportunity to reflect, Regine is found apologizing for the flyer in the following excerpt:

> **REGINE:** I remember…that's the thing…, is it right for me to exclude? Or, right for me to like put this out and that could potentially exclude someone that might need help. And um, of course the answer for me is no. So that was just why I didn't, sorry.

Attempts to further conceptualize Regine's use of the word "sorry" involved making sure that emotionality was included in the interpretation. "Sorry," a word that is often used to express the emotional experience of regret, was a key indication that a unique emotional experience was present. Regine's words seem to suggest the difficulty of giving specific description to the prescribed pronoun as requested within the activity. What was found within this dialogue is an emotional reaction encountered during task completion. The emotional reaction seemed particularly linked to her efforts in deciphering who was being referred to by the use of the descriptive pronoun "you."

> **INTERVIEWER:** Okay, what did you say?
>
> **REGINE:** Sorry…
>
> **INTERVIEWER:** Okay.…why did you say that?
>
> **REGINE:** Um, I'm…think I said sorry, I'm pretty sure I said sorry, I'm pretty sure I said sorry because it wasn't as—one, I didn't feel like what I said was quite eloquent, and then two, sometimes, I think I need to…take either a humanistic stance or a more politi[*cal*]—which is—to me more political…more exclusive stance, um, because like I said, in—during the interview, I mean, I envisioned a black audience, so why not write about—on my flyer, (**INAUDIBLE**) a black audience…there's this other part of you like, well, you don't want to exclude anyone, because everyone needs help…I see straight-ass proof, and I know everybody…sometimes compassion needs to rule.

Regine left the "you" open, in part, because she could not resolve the conflict between unveiling her vision of a very particular "other" with whom she specifically identified with and felt compassion for. Additionally she held a concern of not excluding "others" who did not fit her own particular vision. The use of an imprecise "you" whose referent is open to the reader's interpretation and identification, allowed Regine to leave this conflict unresolved.

A Dynamic Developmental[1] Use of "You" Arises

One can understand Regine's unresolved conflict as locating her between a past and a future, where in the present she was unable to articulate her identifications through a more open, inclusive "you" and thus she also left the personal conflict intact. Given such, the proliferation of a descriptive pronoun can be understood and further investigated by the researcher through the use of a lifespan approach. If the presence of affect (both as a noun and verb) is pertinent for a particularly used pronoun, it appears unlikely that this pronoun would have a localized influence on the participant's life only during one aspect of their human experience. The presented emotion and influence of such emotion for the participant is likely to have developed throughout his or her life process, rarely to be experienced as a contained event. This is precisely what is meant by thinking of the pronoun as dynamic and developmental.

Because the presence of a descriptive pronoun merits a dynamic developmental interpretation, there are several points of consideration that can be further explored in order to gather additional information regarding participants' use of the pronoun (symbolic to a felt experience) in their storytelling. Before discussing who (both in unique and general terms) the actual pronoun represents, it may be helpful for greater information gathering if the researcher utilizes the pronoun discourse incorporated by the participant. Such utility may increase the participant's comfort in disclosing his or her own human experience, providing the participant with a transitional experience prior to being faced with direct inquiries regarding the subject of the descriptive pronoun.

Further exploration of this life dynamic is not restricted to, but can be additionally explored through, the following inquiries:

- How long has [descriptive pronoun: inclusion of pronoun used] been a part of your life?

- What is your earliest recollection of [descriptive pronoun]?

- What was life like before your awareness or felt experience of [descriptive pronoun]?

- How has the presence of [descriptive pronoun] influenced your life?

- Has the presence of [descriptive pronoun] changed for you throughout time?

- Currently, how does [descriptive pronoun] influence/affect you?

- How do you imagine your life would be without [descriptive pronoun]?

- Describe your envisioned future if there is a continued presence of [descriptive pronoun]?

As an adult woman, Khadijah made attempts at understanding her current experience through the conceptualization of her childhood and the limits of power and control when one is defined through a minority status. Khadijah seems to note a feeling of gained power in the awareness of this life dynamic.

> **KHADIJAH:** I think that there's a lot of power in knowing that,…<u>you</u> gonna feel like, oh my God, <u>you</u> gonna feel like <u>you're</u> 5 years old for a minute. <u>You</u> gon' feel like a lost puppy, <u>you</u> gon' just feel powerless. <u>You</u> know, and it like that's fine, that's okay. Just don't believe that shit….don't wallow in it, don't muddle in it. And that's probably really important for people to know.

As she mentions the word "you," it is likely that she is actually discussing her own personal experience and the journey she has endured in order to gain further clarity with regards to felt disempowerment. Here "you" refers to the self, but in a way that links the present with the past. The developmental aspect present within this excerpt depicts the inclusion of regression. Khadijah, a strong-willed woman in her own right, made attempts at understanding her current experience through an association that included her childhood journey. For Khadijah, her experience of childhood seems to largely depict vulnerability, isolation, and confusion. She depicts her own experience by using the historical me as stand-in for the present me.

Methodological Implications and Insights of the Descriptive Pronoun

Having just developed the methodological concept of "descriptive pronoun" and shared its analytic fruits, it becomes necessary to provide a detailed account of how one might elucidate descriptive pronouns methodologically. It also seems relevant to turn this analysis of the descriptive pronoun back onto the research process itself as a reflection. Included below is a specific description of the methods used to make the meaning of descriptive pronouns explicit. Further on is a reflection on the relationships between the researcher and the participants in terms of the use of descriptive pronouns. Both sections adumbrate the methodological implications of descriptive pronouns.

Patterned Disclosure and Location: Specific Methods

Particular methods and concepts for thinking about the interpretation of descriptive pronouns involve grasping the emotive and nonverbal aspects of expression employed by speakers in their use of pronouns with attention to the patterns, including contrasts, that such expressions exhibit. Researchers can use these patterns to grasp more refined interpretive details. In addition, researchers must work to "locate" the use of descriptive pronouns in the narratives of the participants. This involves thinking about the developmental, social, and political contexts of the pronoun uses. In this section of the chapter, specific methods for addressing patterned disclosure and location are described.

Patterned Disclosure

Arriving at the interpretations presented above depends on having information relative to the patterns and contexts regarding how the personal pronoun is used. Ethnomethodologists have developed strategies for noting how words are expressed including the pragmatic structures associated with the how (Schegloff, 2007). However, one need not turn to ethnomethodology to proceed. An essential component to locating a descriptive pronoun is keen observation and listening. Gathering data about the presence of a descriptive pronoun is enhanced when the researcher attempts to give greater focus and attention to the participant, in the present. This allows the active aspect of words (Searle, 1970) to be better grasped by researchers involved in trying to understand their participants' experiences. Such observation becomes a challenge if the researcher's main focus is dedicated to a thorough replication of her or his interview protocol versus an attempt at centering oneself within the interview process, taking greater note of the participant's nuances, in exchange for ensuring the delivery of contingency inquiries. While observation of the emotionality present within the descriptive pronoun can be attained through review of an audio record or written transcript, there are several aspects of the descriptive pronoun, such as a clenching of teeth or an observed increase in breath, which if not attuned to within the actual interview can become easily unnoticed within further investigation. Patterned disclosure refers to the interpretive nonverbal patterns that become part of how an actor's subjectivity becomes interpretable by social others.

Consideration of the participant's physical presence is one element of capturing the patterned disclosure and themes related to the descriptive pronoun. Although it could be argued that the physical presence of the participant could be obtained through the use of audiovisual equipment, it remains likely that particular aspects of the participant's physical expression could be easily lost if reliance on equipment alone is utilized by the researcher. It would not be beyond imagination for a visual recorder stationed to capture the participant's physical presence from mid-waist upward fails to notice the participant's incessant rocking of his or her left leg, a faint flaring of the participant's nostrils, or a concealed picking of the furniture's upholstery.

Observation of the participant's physical presence is itself a form of patterned disclosure. As the researcher takes note of the verbal story shared by the participant, incorporation of the physical narrative, displayed by the participant, will provide additional information as to whether the use of a particular pronoun is of a descriptive nature. In making such a distinction it will be helpful for the researcher to take note of how often the participant engages in such physical sharing when addressing a particular topic. This notation can be easily made with simple tic marks written throughout the researcher's notes, pairing the physical presentation with the verbal disclosure. This particular information will likely prove helpful during the clarification phase of the descriptive pronoun. It is not without saying that both the verbal and nonverbal information disclosed by the participant are of equal importance. Nevertheless, given the written nature of qualitative researcher, often supported by verbal accounts, it is not unlikely for the qualitative researcher to unintentionally ignore the wealth of nonverbal data present within the interview process. While the participant's verbal accounts can illuminate felt experience, it is also understood that the participant's life world can be expressed through nonverbal disclosure. Such disclosure likely illustrates a pattern and/or theme of a physical re-action likely to take surface during the actual life occurrence being narrated by the participant.

Location

An additional component of patterned disclosure found within the use of a descriptive pronoun rests within the noted position/location deciphered from the participant's story. Considering the question "What is the participant's life coordinates?" can provide further support for the descriptive pronoun. This idea of life coordinates or position is specific to a consideration of the participant's life world as it relates to the surrounding context included within partici-pant's noted experience. Because the participant's experience is likely to be influenced by the surrounding context presently available and/or unavailable to the participant, investigation of how this context surfaces within the participant's dialogue will create greater deciphering of likely patterns and themes specific to the descriptive pronoun. There are several types of "locations" that can provide further clarity into the descriptive pronoun. One such location includes consideration of the participant's developmental level. Others include sociopolitical, economic, gender, and so forth. In this study, the developmental and sociopolitical locations were prominent.

Developmental Location. A developmental position takes into account the participant's age, level of functioning, and socialized expectations with regards to their experienced develop-mental level. For example, in the United States, it is not uncommon for a teenager about to complete secondary education to be met with the expectation of being aware of his/her future aspirations related to college planning and career choice. This same teenager may also have the additional expectation of vacating his or her childhood home, with a likely parental/personal hope of self-sufficiency. While such expectations may be anticipated for this teenager, it is not a certainty that this young person will have the ability, motivation, will, or drive to meet such expectations. In considering this life dynamic and qualitative research, investigation of how the participant shares such a narrative can provide greater insight into the level of depth relevant for this life process.

After investigation of the interactions, if it is found that the participant shares this particu-lar life account in a manner that contrasts with other life accounts, it may be likely that the use of a descriptive pronoun is present. Merging the presence of a developmental position and the descriptive pronouns can create a wealth of information and knowledge for the researcher. The investigation of this merging can permit an opportunity for the researcher to gather additional information regarding the presence of the descriptive pronoun and the utility that the word has throughout the participant's lifetime. Within the above example, if it becomes apparent that the participant speaks of an other, mostly through the use of a pronoun, then it is likely that the identification of a descriptive pronoun can occur. Such an identification could be made through the researcher comparing this narrated experience to another experience largely men-tioned by the participant. If it is found that the participant seems to utilize more pronouns (or seemingly specific, unique pronouns) within one of the experiences, as opposed to the other, then it is likely that this particular experience, within a specific developmental position carries a descriptive pronoun.

Reflection upon the developmental location within the descriptive pronoun is important for gaining greater access into the participant's life experience. If the coupling of a developmental position and descriptive pronoun is met, the researcher has the option of making an attempt at describing the participant's interpersonal dynamics at that time. Through reconsidering the previously noted example, if it is found that the participant makes note of his or her parents through the use of "them" or "they," it may be possible that this verbal substitution reflects a desire for distance between self and parent. Grasping the probable interpretations would require comparing the participant's use of language with the content of other portions of the participant's narrative, which may include a discussion of his or her parents. Such comparisons are vital to the actual existence of the descriptive pronoun, particularly if the participant, when speaking of the same individual, utilizes varied pronouns invoking alternative relations across divergent contexts, for example, developmentally different stages in the person's life. Within a broader investigation, the researcher may be inclined to consider how the participant engages in the use of this descriptive pronoun along her/his life course. Through this investigation, the researcher may consider the evolution of a noted descriptive pronoun as the participant shares her or his life processes and developmental milestones. Such an analysis is expanded through the consideration of how the use of this descriptive pronoun relates to the personal and societal expectations relevant for that particular developmental location.

Sociopolitical Location. Becoming fully human involves a socialization process that occurs across the human experience. The socialization process is both personal (in that every individual has a unique set of experiences that mark the process) and social (in that the experiences and process link individuals with a social world and thus, the process will have shared aspects across individuals). These different socialization paths shape opportunity, access, and perspective. The process of socializing humans always involves the inclusion of rules and norms formally and informally established that influence the interactions between self and others. While the human being is influenced by the surrounding society, it is dually noted that a human being is not isolated from his or her own effort and determination in shaping existence. Although it can and has been argued that the human experience is not devoid of will, consideration of the socialization experience and human will are of equal importance. Like the developmental location, the sociopolitical location is also largely influenced by time. Sociopolitical location will always be tethered to a particular era of time that beholds the sociopolitical climate of a nation, state/province, town, city or neighborhood that has the possibility of transformation.

Politics, whether considered a subsection or an all-encompassing aspect of society, is frequently observed in various institutions such as schools, churches, hospitals, and corporations. The presentation of power that greatly influences the political climate of these institutions is significantly relevant for the descriptive pronoun. Understanding the descriptive pronoun is difficult to capture without consideration of the sociopolitical climate in which the words are uttered. It is within this context that greater appreciation and comprehension of the use of the pronouns becomes revealed.

Dynamics of the Descriptive Pronoun

In this section, I explore the participant and investigator interaction. This particular component of the chapter further elaborates on the unique experience of the descriptive pronoun, to illuminate the unique experience crafted between the participant and the investigator, supporting the notion that the internal aspects of language are present and accessible for inquiry. Though I could very well have chosen to use the term "I" to describe my presence within these interactions, you will notice that I stay with the traditional phrases such as "researcher" and/or "investigator." A central goal of this section is to highlight the participant-researcher dynamic through the voice of the participant with greater elaboration on her unique experience as depicted through language. Given such, the strength of the pronoun "I" is replaced with what is considered to be more complementary (researcher or investigator) to the presented task of enhancing the literary focus on the research participant. Though there is no way to avoid the privilege I have as the writer of the chapter, using the terms researcher/investigator is not meant to mask that privilege, but rather to temper it so that readers do not feel compelled to over-identify with the "I."

The Participant and Investigator Interaction

As the participant shares his/her experience with the researcher, there are various aspects of that interaction that can influence both the participant and the researcher. Because the qualitative research process relies on some form of interaction between the researcher and the participant, an understanding of how the descriptive pronoun surfaces within this investigative relationship becomes germane. Even within the naturalistic observation or more proximity enhanced researcher processes, the matter in which the participant and investigator are influenced and affected by the other is central to the work of qualitative research. Throughout the study referenced within this chapter, the interaction between the participants and the investigator was multilayered. The women who participated in the study were recruited from a two-year psycho-educational support group conducted by the researcher. Because the researcher and the participants shared similar demographic characteristics and interests, the researcher was also involved in various campus activities, clubs, and organizations that also included the presence of the women within the group. Given the levels of interaction and familiarity between the researcher and the participants, ignoring a similar dynamic present within the investigative process would have dismissed a central component within the women's research experience.

It is often helpful to begin this portion of the investigation through a consideration of the participants' and investigator's personal characteristics. Thoughtfulness dedicated to the similarities or differences present adds to the descriptive pronoun analytical process. It is considered that greater depth in capturing the experience of the participant is achieved if the researcher is able to take note of her or his personal experiences and the influence that his or her unique characteristics contribute to the investigative process. This interactional process is not specific to the demographic characteristics held by the participant and researcher. This interactional process also includes contemplating the manner in which the participants were recruited for the study and the influence of this recruitment process on the participant's presence within the project. Further consideration could include reflecting upon the type of interaction experienced by the participant and researcher, the setting in which the interaction took place, the type of response medium, as well as the amount of proximity between the participant and researcher. All of these interactional aspects can be further analyzed through considering the descriptive pronouns utilized within a given interaction. For example, it may be possible that a participant's use of certain descriptive pronouns is influenced by whether or not they chose the meeting location. Investigation of altered descriptive pronoun usage in varied settings can increase conceptualization and support for the presence of a descriptive pronoun.

As noted previously, the women who participated in this study were members of a support group conducted by the researcher. As a result, the women had an ongoing relationship with the investigator. Furthermore, the initial contact the women had with the researcher was mostly a result of their interest in a therapeutic process that focused on the life experience of black women in predominately white academe. Given such, there was an immediate similarity between the researcher and the participants as an effect of the common denominators of race, gender, academic standing, and interest in therapeutic process. The women within this study were selected by the researcher once for participation in the support group and again for solicited involvement in a research study. The observation of race and gender was vividly discernible for the participants and the researcher. This particular study incorporated one focus group and two individual interviews. The focus group, occurring first, took place in the same setting utilized for the support group. The women within the study were all a part of the same therapeutic support group. Such circumstance again addresses the aspect of the participant-investigator dynamic, which assists in creating the unique experience upon which the personal pronoun is shaped, even within the research process. As expected, given their level of previous exposure and involvement, the women were openly expressive during the focus group. While the setting dynamics held a level of familiarity for the women in the study, the setting for the individual interviews was selected by each individual woman. Setting differences also create the opportunity for comparing and contrasting the type of descriptive pronoun usage present within the varied settings.

In conjunction with the women expressing themselves collectively among each other, they also seemed to use language to articulate the observed similarities between themselves and the researcher. As the women shared their experiences with the researcher during the individual interviews, each woman chose to use varying combinations of "you know," "you know what I'm saying," "we," "us," and "our." In using these words and phrases, many of the women spoke in detail about their academic experiences as it related to academic politics, support, success, life stressors, transitions, and gender. While these life areas were frequently discussed by the women within this study, the topic of race was often an interview focal point that presented as a shared experience. During Maxine's incorporation of a racialized shared experience, she notes concern regarding the racial climate within her residing community.

> **MAXINE:** And when <u>we've</u> had incidences where, <u>our</u> agencies have been discriminated against, just because they're Asian, or <u>you know</u> at a night club, some black guy's getting beat down, afterwards, or, whatever it is, and um, racial slurs, it's like well, that's not everybody for sure but I've, I've seen people look at the good in X town more than the bad. Which, is nice to do, but, how realistic is it, and how can you really talk about diversity in a classroom where there's one, one minority student, <u>you know</u>, so I'm just sitting here like what, you mean our cultural restaurants on X street, yeah that's real diverse goodness, <u>we</u> don't even have Soul Food place here. But, I think it's very much a fantasyland.

While Maxine used the shared experience to further illustrate how black people are depicted, Synclaire made use of this form of discourse through her discussion of how she feels she can be an integral part of the legacy of black women academicians. During her discussion, she utilized the shared experience to further explain how having the support of a Black female faculty member improved her own experience and would likely enhance the academic process of future black female graduate students. She seemed to make claim to a shared experience, by implying that the researcher had an understanding of the black female graduate student experience.

> **SYNCLAIRE:** I pray that <u>we</u> pave the way to make it a little easier, for other black females who want to earn their Ph.D. That I'm able to be highly qualified to advise another black female through the process. To make it more meaningful…easier as far as being able to cope, not saying that the work would be easier, that the time that you put in to this will be easier, that you're, <u>you know</u>, your passion is gonna, it's, it's gonna be diminished or anything like that, but being able to help make it easier for you to navigate through the doctoral program…. I think sometimes <u>we</u>, <u>we</u>, um are matched with advisors who <u>we</u> feel very qualified in their work, but actually being able to navigate the system may not be as aggressive as you want them to be.

Regine also made mention of support systems while utilizing a discourse pattern of shared experience. As she provided details about leaving familiar settings and embarking upon new experiences and environments, she incorporated such words and phrases as "our," "we," and "you know." She made several parallels between us and them, black and white, new and old. It is during this presentation of dichotomies that Regine appears to place the researcher within an "us" category.

During Khadijah's candid discussion about race and graduate school admission, she clearly discusses her thoughts about how race is used to categorize black students. Within this discussion, Khadijah addresses the frequently quoted work of W.E.B. DuBois (1903/1989) and the talented tenth (p. 74). As she makes note of this historic work and its relevance to current events, she identifies through her use of language that this is a possible topic familiar to the researcher.

Through the women's use of language there was often a conveyed shared experience. It is considered that the women's ability to speak about such topics flourished as their levels of comfort increased. At times the women's use of such phrases as "you know what I mean" was utilized as a statement summarization point. While this expression abbreviated the women's statements, it also provided declaration of commonality that evoked a powerfully expressive presentation of a proposed collective. Although the challenge of slang and habitually employed language can dispute the interpreted meaning developed by the researcher, taking note of the frequency and presentation through which the descriptive pronoun phrase is utilized can support the interpreted meaning developed by the researcher.

Clarifying the Use of the Descriptive Pronoun: Toward Criticalism

Through the use of language, the women were able to openly display varying contradictions that were present within their thought processes. The analyses indicated contradictions about support systems, social issues, status quos, and racial dynamics. The surfacing of such contradictions became apparent through the varying forms of language used by the women. The rise of such contradictions produces greater depth in understanding the complexity of the human experience. As the women utilized writing, oration, and paralanguage within this study, clarification regarding their perspectives was considered via these varied communication mediums. As a result of their participation in the study, some of the contradictions were openly explored within the data-collection process. For some of the women, this exploration seemed to produce greater insight and reflection. For others, the notation of contradiction was not fully received. A short dialogue between the researcher and Khadijah illustrates this particular process:

> **INTERVIEWER:** Okay, from your response, you said—that's what I saw, sista's in the hood…. So my question is…how would they know that the workshop was developed exclusively for them in mind?
>
> **KHADIJA:** …Because of what I had on my flyer. If you're a first-generation college student, feeling overwhelmed and isolated, a person of color and feeling insecure about your academic capabilities.
>
> **INTERVIEWER:** What about in terms of, cuz when I hear the term "sista," I think of a black woman?
>
> **KHADIJA:** Yeah, that's what I think of.
>
> **INTERVIEWER:** Okay, so, what led to you not indicating that, that envisioned audience on your flyer?
>
> **KHADIJA:** I guess cuz it's just understood. On a certain level I think that, I think some things just don't have to be articulated. It's for everybody, it wasn't specifically for sistas, but I know that's who gonna come.

This particular exchange involves Khadijah's comment regarding her targeted audience. In noting her thoughts about who she saw within her audience, she indicated that she pictured "sistas from the hood." Further clarification confirmed that the audience she pictured when developing her workshop specifically focused on black women from inner cities. The contradiction within Khadijah's statement represents a disconnect between who she envisioned for her workshop audience and how she proposed to advertise for the workshop. Khadijah spoke in detail about the experience of black women within predominantly white academe and overall U.S. society. She was noted as discussing various racial and gender matters, specifically noting her concern for this particular subgroup. Nonetheless, when considering the possibility of her interest being publicly displayed, Khadijah seemed to illustrate some hesitancy with identifying this targeted audience.

This limitation in fully noting an intended audience was observed in all of the responses provided by the women regarding this topic. As Maxine shared her thoughts regarding this matter, she openly verbalized her cognitive process pertaining to this topic.

> **INTERVIEWER:** So your response…I see a bunch of me's. And I asked what do they look like? You said they look like me. And then my respond was, "they look identical?" And you said, to the "T"…so my question is, how would they know that originally the workshop was exclusively developed with them in mind…
>
> **MAXINE:** Well, that's tough because, I don't know if, well, as a new doctoral student…. I don't know that I would know that this is for me…because it says attention new doctoral students in X. And then it's, it's not until down at the bottom where it says concerns as a student of color. Well, that would have to change, that would have to change…. I'm actually visualizing myself going up to this flyer and looking at it and, and, and looking at it, and I don't know that I'm really getting a good feel that this is, this is for me.

In sharing her thoughts regarding this matter, Maxine provided the researcher access to some of her internal processes. Within this dialogue, Maxine is observed questioning her responses and dedicating substantial effort to considering the internal dynamic possibly present during her previous disclosure. Throughout her statement, Maxine's noted comment seems to be filled with numerous pronouns. Investigation of these words with the consideration of the descriptive pronoun allows for an extended analysis into the unique internal realm of Maxine's experience. This particular example provided by Maxine is given further support for the wealth of data housed within the use of what could be considered a mere pronoun. Maxine's selective use of pronouns within this disclosure provides a vast amount of information pertaining to her boundaries and areas of comfort when considering the topic of race within predominately white academe. It is within the query of her pronoun usage that Maxine begins to verbalize her noted experience.

The dialogue to follow this inquiry was strategically included within the data-collection portion of the individual interviews in order to obtain further clarification regarding the women's comments. It is considered that without this process of clarification, greater understanding into the use of the language presented by the women would have been restricted in terms of access to their personal process and internal dynamic.

When faced with an immense amount of information provided by the participant, finding a starting point to analyze qualitative data can be a challenging feat. The researcher's attempts at honoring the participant's life experience can further exacerbate the felt challenge encountered by the researcher. Given such circumstances, the possibility of becoming lost in a sizable sea of data can restrict the researcher from investigating the finer details present within the participant's shared experience. Incorporation of the descriptive pronoun provides an avenue through which the researcher can dedicate analytical observation to a finer detail of the participant's dialogue. The considerations of emotion and pronoun usage, developmental qualities, patterned disclosure, multiple observations, and clarification of the descriptive pronoun usage can assist the researcher in gathering greater support for the presence of this expressive phenomenon. What rests within the use of such language is the heavily laden human experience that is at times abbreviated and substituted for varying reasons, often unbeknownst to the researcher unless noticed and further queried.

Note

1. Developmental level references the life transformational spaces experienced by the human being. It includes such aspects as aging, changes in familial constellation, career and financial transitions, occurrences of consciousness, etc.

References

Carspecken, P. (1996). *Critical ethnography in educational resaerch: A theoretical and practical guide.* New York: Routledge.

Du Bois, W. E. B. (1903/1989). *The souls of black folk* New York: Bantam.

Erikson, E. H. (1959). Identity and the life cycle: Selected papers. *Psychological Issues, 1,* 1–171.

Gale, J. (2000). Patterns of talk: A micro-landscape perspective. *The Qualitative Report, 4*(1/2).

Have, P. ten (1986). Methodological issues in conversational analysis. *Bulletin of Sociological Methodology, 27,* 23–51.

Kagan, N. (1980). Interpersonal process recall: A method of Influencing human interaction. Houston, TX: Mason Media.

Korth, B. (2003). A critical reconstruction of care-in-action: A contribution to care theory and research. *The Qualitative Report, 8*(3), pp. 487–512.

Lynch, M. (2000). The ethnomethodological foundations of conversation analysis. *Interdisciplinary Journal for the Study of Discourse, 20*(4), 517–532.

Pain, J. (2009). *Not just talking: Conversational analysis, Harvey Sacks' gift to therapy.* London: Karnac Books.

Schegloff, E. (2007). Conveying who you are: The presentation of self, strictly speaking. In N. J. Enfield and T. Stivers (Eds.), *Person reference in interaction: Linguistic, cultural and social perspectives* (pp. 123–148). Cambridge, UK: Cambridge University Press.

Searle, J. (1970). *Speech acts: An essay in the philosophy of language.* Cambridge, UK: Cambridge University Press.

Sluzki, C. E. (1992). Transformations: A blueprint of narrative changes in therapy. *Family Process, 31*(3), 217–230.

Tannen, D. (2005). *Conversational style: Analyzing talk among friends.* New York: Oxford University Press.

The American Heritage Dictionary (2ⁿᵈ Ed.). (1991). Boston: Houghton Miflin Company.

CHAPTER THIRTEEN

Human Identity, Self-Narrative, and Negation

YI-PING HUANG AND PHIL CARSPECKEN

It is human being "that never is what it is and always is what it is not."—Hyppolite, 1974, p. 150

Consciousness, however, is explicitly the *Notion* of itself. Hence it is something that goes beyond limits, and since these limits are its own, it is something that goes beyond itself.—Hegel, 1977, p. 51

This chapter is about self-narrative and human identity, with special attention to structures and uses of negation in human identity claims. Narratives have a positive[1] form even when their structures are operating more implicitly than explicitly. They have "shapes" and can be distinguished from each other by type. But their unity is not captured in purely positive terms. Their unity has to do with human identity, and human identity is always "beyond itself" in some sense. A well-known expression for the human self in India is "neti, neti," meaning "not this, not that." It is what is not positive, what is not entity-like, what cannot be directly represented nor confined to a set of determinations. As we have quoted him above, Hyppolite writes that the self "never is what it is and always is what it is not." To understand the various manners and modes through which people claim their identities, something of much concern to most qualitative researchers, we need to understand identity-constituting negations.

Narrative is a primordial mode of knowing and representing. Attention to narratives by qualitative researchers for understanding and representing human lives and experiences has become widely accepted within the qualitative research community (for example, see Polkinghorne, 1988; Clandinin & Connelly, 2000; Ochs & Capps, 2001; Clandinin, 2007;). Of particular interest is the self-narrative: people telling stories about themselves. Self-narratives come up in considerations of human identity. The self-narrative is also a form through which people integrate their ongoing life experiences to make sense of and remember them. Moreover, at times and to different degrees, people interact with each other in ways that can be understood as "co-authoring" lived stories.[2] Hence a lot of qualitative data will be in the form of narratives, and at least some data analysis will examine narrative contents and forms.

"Narrative unity" is an expression that comes up in some of the literature on human identity. Alasdair MacIntyre (1981) uses the expression to refer to the "unity of a life" that individuals can strive for. Life is or can be a moral tale that people live out. Narrative unity has been claimed to be a "condition of personhood" (Christman, 2004). As we argue below, self-narrative unity is indeed a condition of personhood, but in terms of the capacity to claim unity and with structures and uses of negation involved. A human life as such is not a narrative. But when people consider their lives, talk about their lives, and simply talk about themselves, they do so in the direction of narrative integration. This can be quite different in form, for the same person, depending upon context and audience. But every time there is self-talk, we have claimed unity, and claimed human identity that exceeds the positive contents of this self-talk. Narrative unity can therefore be explored through understandings of negation and the negative. Human identity has transcending[3] features to it; it is the negative in relation to the positive stories it can tell about itself; it has to be given over, claimed, in part through referring to itself as something positive while also being beyond the determinations, the limits, necessary for the construction of anything positive.

During 2007 one of us, Yi-Ping Huang, noticed congruencies between uses of negation made by participants in her doctoral research when telling their life stories and Hegel's use of "negative" and "negation" in his *Phenomenology of Spirit* (1977). Yi-Ping explored the possibility of grouping types of negation used by people in claiming their identities into two main categories, inspired by the distinction made by Hegel scholars between first and second negation. In addition, Yi-Ping took inspiration from a number of other philosophers and social theorists to produce a complex meta-theory of human identity that presents new ways of understanding narrative unity and negation, distinguishes between different forms and levels of the third-person position people can take in relation to themselves, and does many other things as well (see Huang, 2008). In some new ways, this chapter builds upon a portion of that dissertation work. It is the result of collaboration between Yi-Ping Huang and Phil Carspecken. We begin with theoretical discussions of human identity and then explore four life-history narratives to illustrate and further explore the theoretical issues of interest to us. A "meta-theory" of human identity is a guiding proposal that researchers can bring into use when analyzing data, such that the meta-theory itself can be altered, refined, and further developed through the research process.

Part I: Theory

A. Human Being as Identity Claiming

Living within, Thematizing, Objectivating. Humans claim their existence performatively and continuously in and through meaningful actions, with or without (and most often without) linguistic representations. This is the feature of meaning and the existential foundation of personhood we call the "identity claim" (Carspecken, 1996, 1999a, 1999b, 2003). The manner in which a person is, the "being" of the human being, differs from the meaning that "being" has for us when discussing material things and physical states. Our usual concept of being, of existence, for physical things is related to seeing them and touching or grasping them. Their being is understood to not depend upon human knowledge of them. To exist in this sense is to be in principle something that can be "present" to a knower, present to consciousness. All forms of physical being are framed as existing as, or like, something that is independent of being known but that in principle could be known and known in the form of presence to consciousness.[4] Basic interpretative structures and concepts arise from this, as horizons of possibility for our forms of experience that are framed in terms of presence to consciousness. Our usual understanding of time and space are particularly fundamental for the ontology upon which we can understand the being of things that can be, but need not be, present to a knowing consciousness. To be present is to be here (in space), now (in time) for a knower. Consciousness itself is left out of the picture, although usual concepts of space and time do depend, at the end of the day, upon the tripartite distinction of space, time, and consciousness: here, now, and "I."

Human "being" is different. The being of a person is somehow within her actions (including thinking as a type of action) and as such it cannot be present to a knower because doing and knowing both have the human mode of being embedded within. In particular, the being of a human being cannot be present to itself, in that way that the being of a physical object can be present to a knower. And yet the very being of a person somehow includes its concern with itself, its "care" for itself as Heidegger (1962) formulated this. In Hegel's philosophy, the being of consciousness is its own quest to know itself and in this way affirm and validate itself. There is something right in this formulation that we find in human social phenomena: people are uncertain of their worth and value unless they receive consistent forms of identity-validating experiences. And it is arguable, with plenty of evidence on hand, that there is a desire in humans for a form of ultimate validation that, however, continuously eludes. This is a theme in spiritual traditions, in existentialist philosophy, in Hegelian philosophy, and in Eastern philosophies as well. We can also find aspects of it within our experiences of other people, including those who are participants in our research. The being of human beings somehow includes care about it, desires related to it, and the processes by which humans gain or construct some knowledge of it. So the being of human beings is not independent of the possibility of its being known, the way (we usually think) the being of a physical object is independent of its being known. Knowing, self-knowing, and being are intertwined in the case of this form of existence. Knowledge in this case is not simply knowledge about something that differs from knowledge, but instead partly is that of which it is about.

In a discussion of the specialized notion of intentionality used by phenomenologists, Heidegger uses the expression "living within the truth" and distinguishes this from knowing. We continuously experience "living within the truth," but do not grasp that we are doing so. To try to grasp it requires a temporal distinction and a special process: "thematization" (see Heidegger, 1985, p. 52[5]). Our "living within the truth" is always temporally prior to "intending" that truth; intending it always happens in a next moment when something that just was has become thematized or, we can say, objectivated.

For Hegel (1977).[6] this same structure is cast in terms of self-objectivating self-activity; living in the truth, if we use Heidegger's expression, is movement that can move towards knowing itself. Hegel distinguishes between "self-certainty" and "self-knowing" in a way that we find really helpful in understanding human identity as well as a host of other things. We experience self-certainty all the time, "live within it" but always without being able to "catch" it. This is very insightful, we think. It takes an argument made originally by Jacobi in Western philosophy to oppose Kantianism, and relocates it within a self-developing system. Jacobi had argued against the Kantian emphasis on conceptual knowledge, which fails to really satisfy true human needs, partly by stating that being can be and is known directly, irreducibly, and nonconceptually in feeling (see Gardner, 2009, pp. 6–8 for a decent discussion of this). All conceptual movements aimed for knowledge of God, the Good, and Nature rest on this ground, which is not itself conceptual. Shortly we will introduce the "I-feeling" formulated in philosophies from India, which is the same insight. In Hegel "self-certainty" is also something felt (and for him, fundamental to all concepts of being as well). Within moments of acting and moments of satisfying any desire at all, the self-certainty of "I am" is felt but then disappears in the flow of time. It continuously happens, is felt, through our actions and our satisfactions of desires, but as such it cannot be known to be true. It cannot be a conceptual form of knowledge. Embedded within all of our desires is the desire to know ourselves so as to affirm ourselves in an ultimate sort of way, to have self-certainty not only as a feeling, which is a kind of "living within the truth," but as an object of knowledge: a known truth. Human consciousness is the result of a development of this desire, to bring self-certainty into self-knowledge, which has led to the emergence of intersubjectivity. The felt certainty of "I am" is pursued for knowledge, by human beings, in the form of seeking recognition from another subject or subjects. It seems to us that identity claiming can be understood in a number of ways with the help of these thought forms articulated by Hegel, that can then be introduced within more contemporary forms of social theory.

Mahatattva, Ahamtattva, Cittatattva. Eastern philosophy is also rich with insights about the being of human beings. In philosophies from India, we have the distinction between "mahatattva," "ahamtattva," and "cittatattva," which are linked to the distinctions between "I am," "I do," "I have done" (see Carspecken, 1999b, essay 3, for a discussion of these distinctions in Indian philosophy). Here again we have the idea of feeling being, and feeling being much in the way Hegel seemed to understand it, as self-certainty. We feel our being within our living, our action. When we notice this "I feeling," it is already gone in time; it is always a "just was" feeling that had the certainty of "I am" within. Noticing is bare thematizing, and a temporal distinction is in place. We cannot have the "I feeling" present to us and notice it at the same time. We were living there, in our actions, but we are no longer there when the "I am" feeling, the mahatattva, is noticed. In Hegel's *Phenomenology of Spirit*, we have the formulation, "consciousness is desire in general" at a certain place in the dialectic (1977, #167, p. 165). The same idea is expressed with the theory of the distinctions between maha-, aham-, and cittatattva. What we are is a desire to merge within the ultimate self-certainty of the "I am" as well as the "I am" itself. We seek validation of our existing; and the orientation towards self-affirmation, validation, is how we exist. We can experience existential affirmations briefly through doing, acting, especially when we "flow" with our action and refrain from "thinking about ourselves," refrain from monitoring ourselves from the perspective of possible other subjects. That is the "ahamtattva," the "I do." It can happen, for example, when enjoying skiing and enjoying it most when not thinking about ourselves skiing, because then we can best feel ourselves through our action of skiing. All forms of "flow" seem to be about this, the ahamtattva, the joy of self-feeling through and as doing.

Cittatattva pertains to "I have done." So cittatattva is ultimately about self-narrative, autobiography. It is most certainly the result of thematizing, self-objectivating. We do not have to move all the way to self-narrative to find cittatattva because its form begins as soon as we attain even a very bare and implicit awareness of our action from the position of a possible other subject.

What we call the "identity claim" occurs at the interface of ahamtattva and cittatattva. Imagine enjoying skiing by having little self-consciousness, only a bare movement from living within the skiing and becoming just barely and nonconceptually aware of how that feels and immediately returning to living within the skiing, and barely aware again, as a sort of vibration of feeling-doing, aware of feeling-doing, back to feeling-doing. Then imagine a moment of becoming aware of your activity holistically, implicitly, as another subject would *experience* seeing you ski. This is the lowest form of objectivation, the purely performatively made identity claim. Here, within feeling, we have first-, second-, and third-person modes of experience unified as "I am this." Here "I am" is experienced in a more conscious way because it is embedded within an intersubjective structure, an "I am this kind of person" feeling configuration. Intersubjectivity is primordially moving between and juxtaposing other possible subject positions within feeling. It is primordially preconceptual.

The way we experience or would experience the actions of another person skiing just as we are now experiencing ourselves acting in that same way arise together as one feeling. It is a singular feeling. And next comes a very interesting structure within this experience: the possible other subject who could be observing us, whose possible experience of us from a different position is something we actually feel; this other possible subject might not experience us in an affirming way. We can feel affirming and negating positions in relation to ourselves, as we have felt them in relation to other people we have experienced acting, rather like we are within contexts rather like this one. And our desire for self-affirmation on this level of primordial feeling, this level of primordial intersubjectivity, can have the form of desiring another subject's feeling about us to be affirming or at least non-negating.

This is why it is the identity claim that is fundamental to human identity. In the most rudimentary mode of cittatattva, the mode of "I am what I have just shown by what I have just done," self-certainty is felt within the mode of a question, but in different ways and to different degrees dependent upon person and context and probably culture as well. It can feel like: "Other people would feel this if they were here; or if they understood"; "Other people should feel this, but maybe they don't"; "Other people do feel this" (a non-question but with the possibility of a doubt after a reflection); and all sorts of nuanced in-between forms of these question-feelings. A structure pertaining to why this mode of feeling is some degree of a question-mode is the structure of desiring a freely given affirmation from another subject whose regard towards us is something we cannot control. Philosophically, insightful arguments and phenomenological descriptions are given for this in the movement from the section, "The Truth of Self-Certainty," to the next section, "Independence and Dependence of Self-Consciousness: Lordship and Bondage" in Hegel's *Phenomenology of Spirit* (1977, pp. 105–112). Phenomenologically, we believe this to be something humans experience and can recognize when formulated. The freedom of the other subject for affirming or negating is crucial to the quest for self-affirmation. What is most wanted is an affirmation from a subject who could negate an identity claim but does not.

Cittatattva, "I am what I have done," is intersubjectively constituted. It is our experience of acting from the first-person position, made aware to us through possible other subject positions that we have internalized. Other possible subject positions are, of course, learned: contingent upon personal history and cultural milieu. Self-identity emerges as a matter of uncertain claims that can be affirmed or denied, and in this way self-identity is dependent upon others. We can find that we desire other people to feel certain ways in relation to ourselves, and our sense of their feeling will be affirming, negating or ambiguous with respect to our identity claims. This structure, however, is subject to a developmental process that will take diverse forms within a maturation process—an important point, but not one we can here pursue.[7]

B. From Performatively Made Identity Claims to Full Autobiographies

A Phenomenology of Performative Identity Claims. On a continuum of self-objectivations, we start with a bare and implicit sense, through a feeling, of what kind of person is indicated by our own actions. Structures that constitute possible kinds of persons are not fundamentally linguistic, although language use is necessary for most of them. The results of learning from using language to communicate with others are not most basically in linguistic form, but in the form of feeling configurations associated with possible action impeti that, *if expressed*, would take on linguistic expressions or nonlinguistic yet meaningful expressions (posturing, winking, frowning, and so on).

The most minimal form of self-objectivation is just a notch away from the ahamtattva. It is a singular feeling combining more than one possible subject position. It is a feeling not simply that we exist within our act, but that we exist as a kind of person. The unity underlying the singularity of the feeling juxtaposes subject positions in relation to a mode of activity. We do not usually act in "flow," but in pre-monitored action streams unified by an "I am such and such kind of person" claim.

So the singular feeling unifying many modes of meaningful action is the heart of the performative identity claim. It is a unity corresponding to the being of a kind of person, implicitly constructed from contingent cultural milieus, and corresponding to ways that we have experienced other people within our lifeworld. Structures juxtapose the distinctions in how we experience other people with how we experience ourselves so that what emerges experientially are singular "I am" feelings embedded within "I am such and such kind of person" feelings.

When qualitative researchers use the expression "embedded meaning" and even more "embodied meaning," the insight, we suggest, has to do with the first-person feeling-body: how we experience meaningful exchanges with other people from the first-person position on our own body. And the feeling configurations that come up in the feeling-body are for the most part intersubjectively constituted. They begin as a feeling, not yet a thought, that we have when just barely taking the position of a possible other subject in relation to what we are doing.[8] This is the identity claim at bottom. This is the performatively made identity claim. The singularity we can feel of our own identity claims when we make them is also something we can sense in other people. We can feel the claims to identity of others as we interact with them. We may not feel it the way they do, and thus may misunderstand them. We understand them through position-taking with other possible subject positions and understand them correctly to the extent that there is overlap in mutual position-taking. But accurately or not, we often feel identity claims from other people but respond to them according to our position within the interaction, culture, and personality. The felt identity claim of another person can be something threatening and thus something another person wishes to change in that other person (for example, when feeling that another person is "full of herself" and not liking it because of how it affects our own self-feelings).

The Full Autobiography. The other end of the self-objectivation continuum is a fully articulated autobiography. Performatively made identity claims can be challenged by others, and the person challenged is expected to be able to start giving a partial life-story. This is tied to accountability and responsibility in personhood. To be a person is to be a subject, not an object. That means a person does not just do things, but does things for reasons that she can give to others, if required to do so. Among the various types of reasons that can be given for an action is the partial autobiography. If you tell a person you will "get the job done" and receive a challenge in response—"Why should I trust you to do it? You don't seem very trustworthy to me"—the reasons you can provide for being trustworthy, a kind of person who is trustworthy, will be in the form of a self-narrative, a record of actions unified by a character you present as yourself. Identity claims are types of commitments.[9] They should be included, we think, within what Robert Brandom calls the "deontic scoreboard" of human interaction (Brandom, 1994).

Between self-narrative and totally performatively made identity claims are many levels of objectivation with language taking on increasing importance as we approach the full self-narrative. Performed identity claims can be partially reconstructed by listing out claimed person-attributes: "I am smart, and I am unpredictable, and I am funny, etc." The unity of the list of attributes within the singular feeling of the "I am…." is not reconstructed when we only list out adjectives like this. The performative claim can be further reconstructed if there is a way, given the culture and language and sometimes the creativity of the actor or researcher, to better represent it in words. "The macho man" for example, might catch an identity claim well. "The Southern Belle" is another culturally distributed expression that aims at the singularity of identity claims and not just the attribute list.

From those sorts of linguistic articulations we move into autobiography, self-narrative. All these forms of objectivation can only point at the unified identity claim and never fully capture it representationally, never represent it exhaustively in any way. At bottom it is existential and implicit, and different expressions can always be found to try to catch the same identity claim. People must recognize the claim through the representation. Autobiographies can be given just barely: "I'm the guy who burped really loudly during Schneider's lecture last year" and can be given quite extensively, as we tend to get when conducting life-history interviews in qualitative research and as in the case of published autobiographies.

C. First and Second Modes of the Negative in Human Identity Claims

> Consciousness is not a thing, a determinate Dasein; It is always beyond itself; it goes beyond, or transcends, itself. The transcendental requirement constitutes the nature of consciousness as such.— Hyppolite, 1974, p. 16

> …the tremendous power of the negative; it is the energy of thought, of the pure "I."—Hegel, 1977, #32, p. 19

The existential feature of performative identity claims and their always possible, internally entailed, further support in self-histories have a form that we can articulate with the help of more Hegelian formulations (Huang, 2008). In particular, the distinction between first and second negation emphasized in many commentaries on Hegel's texts seems to be recognizable in the ways that humans claim identity. Hyppolite expresses the core movement that takes many contextually specific manifestations in Hegel's philosophy as follows:

Yet the self never coincides with itself, for it is always other in order to be itself. It always poses itself in a determination and, because this determination is, as such, already its first negation, it always negates itself so as to be itself. (Hyppolite, 1974, p. 150)

In human actions, people cannot avoid claiming themselves in and through "determinations" that give finite boundaries to the kind of person they claim to be, distinguished from other kinds of possible persons that are contingently afforded by cultural milieus. This is the first negation. It is structural because claiming to be one kind of person will be claiming to not be other possible kinds of person, and one has to implicitly understand the whole structure of distinctions to understand the single claim. Identity-constitutive structures are contingent to cultural milieus and usually understood only implicitly by those who draw upon them, instantiate them, and often slightly alter them by acting meaningfully. Researchers have to grasp them implicitly by becoming familiar with the people and their culture and then reconstruct them into explicit linguistic representations as best they can.

All meaningful acts will have identity claims as part of their meaning horizons, but there is tremendous variability in terms of how foregrounded or backgrounded these claims are. If a person says to another, "I will be there tomorrow for sure; you really can count on me" the foregrounded portion of the meaning horizon concerns the promise to physically be somewhere in one day's time, somehow in support of the person addressed. But the criticizable validity claims constituting the meaning of this act are carried at different levels of a foreground-to-background continuum in the meaning horizon. We call this the "validity horizon" and it is part of a full meaning horizon (Carspecken, 1996, 1999a). Every claim in a validity horizon is criticizable. "I will be there tomorrow" is an objective claim concerning the future, in the foreground. Much more backgrounded is the assumedly shared understanding that this place exists, and that one can get to it. Also backgrounded are normative claims such as, "It is important to be trustworthy" and a less backgrounded value claim, "It's good to support friends." There are subjective claims such as, "I am sincere when I say this."

The identity claim, too, is criticizable. In this example, though we lack sufficient context to really precisely reconstruct the validity horizon as a whole as well as the identity claim, we can imagine a scene in which this is said such that the identity claim would be, "I am a solid, trustworthy colleague." It would be off the foreground but very close to the foreground. And it could be challenged as in, "Yeah, right! That's what they all say." Response to the challenge would most likely be articulation of a partial autobiography to assure the other person of one's character.

This identity claim mostly makes use of first negation: "I am a solid, trustworthy colleague" is a claim dependent upon contrasts with other kinds of people; untrustworthy ones and perhaps ones who are not colleagues. The claim exceeds the specific context of this meaningful exchange as all identity claims do.

So we see first negations in the structures that constitute "I am a such-and-such kind of person" claims. All of these type of claims carry "I am not this or that kind of person" with them. These claims are made performatively with or without language, and even when claimed with language, they cannot be captured fully through linguistic expressions. They are existential, implicit, "lived-within," at bottom.

The second negation Hyppolite refers to in the quotation above is much more difficult to articulate for most identity claims. An actor can and often does indicate through her acts that she is beyond finite determinations, including self-determinations. In many cases, this is like saying, "I am such-and-such kind of person; but more than that, beyond that." There are diverse forms of the second negation, acting so as to be mysterious, unknowable, and unpredictable for example. Second negation distinguishes the self from all positive forms, all determinations. First negations pertain primarily to the "me" and second negations primarily to the "I" as we will explain in more detail below.

Second negation has to do with such things as being able to change one's self, critique one's self, be responsible, be accountable, and judge one's self. One has to in a sense become other to one's self to do any of these things. Whatever can be said about a person by others or by the person herself, she will always be more than that. In Hegel's philosophy, this second negation is fundamental to the being of consciousness because consciousness is never an object or thing and therefore is never only the determinations it must self-claim, to be at all, about its self. It is always what it claims itself to be and not that, because beyond that, because able to take a critical position in relation to that, because able to change that in new actions.

D. Human Identity as Author and Critic of Self-Narrative

Consider this summary, in the quotation below, that Habermas gives of Wilhelm Dilthey's work. Habermas discusses Dilthey in two chapters of *Knowledge and Human Interests* and the quotation comes from there:

> the subject would be misunderstood if he were taken at his word and immediately identified with his manifest actions. As the art of rendering indirect communications understandable, hermeneutics corresponds exactly to the distance that the subject must *maintain* and yet at the same time *express* between itself, as the identity of its structure in life history, and its objectivations. The penalty of not doing so is being reified by those to whom the subject addresses itself. (Habermas, 1968, p. 166)

There is a lot of insight densely packed into Habermas's sentences, which squeeze together a number of sharp points articulated by Dilthey. Human identity is not the autobiography, or better, in plural, the autobiographies we can tell about ourselves, because articulated stories of one's self are self-objectivations. Linking this up with our discussion above, human beings need to claim themselves and in doing so objectivate themselves. Self-narrative is only one type of self-objectivation that is at the end of a continuum, and yet the possibility of giving one is crucial to personhood and entailed as a kind of commitment to provide backing in performatively made identity claims. Further, one of the key points in the quotation above, people must claim themselves in a way that distances themselves from all their objectivations. Human identity is mediated by, not identical to, its objectivations. We cannot resist quoting Hegel on mediation even though the quotation carries more implications relevant to human identity than we can go into here:

> For mediation is nothing beyond self-moving selfsameness, or is reflection into self, the moment of the "I" which is for itself pure negativity or, when reduced to its pure abstraction, *simple becoming*. (1977, #21, p. 11)

Dilthey argued that the autobiography is what synthesizes and unifies fully lived experience. Yet humans convey distance between "themselves" and their self-objectivations. Habermas puts the two features of human identity together succinctly by saying that humans claim themselves as both author and critic of their autobiographies.

The "I" as Action Source, Autonomous Self-Judge, and Member of Claimed "We" Positions. Author and critic, what does it mean? George Herbert Mead (1934) famously distinguished between the "I" and the "me" when discussing human identity, and it is clear that we also use this distinction as we have used it a few times above already. He also introduced the important term "generalized other." We change some of the ways that Mead and others use these terms while retaining the basic insights, in what follows.

The "I" is the claimed source of action and the self-judge one expects of a responsible, accountable person in general. As source, humans have an unknown potentiality for new actions and expressions. The flow of new actions, innovations, surprises, and so on suggest the "I" as source with unknowable potential. During the course of a life, a person self-realizes by accumulating a history of events that can be recounted as if one actor responsibly authored each of them. That is one characteristic of the "me." The "me" is human identity as experienced from the position of other possible subjects, the "I am such-and-such kind of person" claim is a "me" claim. The character of a self-narrative is a complex "me" claim too.

There is another sense to the "I": the "I" as self-critic rather than as author or source. The "I" involves the expectation that another person and we ourselves can and will give reasons for what we do when required to and criticize ourselves for what we have done or are doing, if appropriate. The "I" can operate from a claimed "we" position. A person can act and then give reasons for the act (with a variety of criteria but with moral criteria of most interest to us here) that she at least implicitly assumes any other member of a group, a "we" position, a generalized other position, would also give. A person can act and judge herself as the actor, as she would judge any possible member of a group who, in an identical situation, would act the same way.

The unknowable source of action has a transcending feature to it, and so does "I" as judge and responsible giver of reasons. The "I" takes a claimed "we" position in relation to its own acts. "We" positions are how we interpret Mead's expression "generalized other." It is by monitoring one's own actions from an assumed generalized other position, an assumed "we" position, that a specific "me" can be claimed and then self-judged, self-assessed. From the "we" position, a structure of many possible "me" claims is visible, and contrasts between the possibilities are what make the specific claim possible. So the generalized-other position is a culturally specific position, claimed and instantiated through meaningful actions, from which entire structures of "me" claims make sense. Why do we say that "we" positions are claimed? The reason "we" positions are claimed to be, rather than simply are, is that an actor can be mistaken about the positions from which others ascertain and judge identity claims, and also an actor can newly claim a valid "we" position as one others ought to occupy and endorse.

In distinction from self-realizing processes, human development of the "I" that takes "we" positions to self-judge and provide reasons is a self-actualizing process. The larger the "we" position taken in relation to one's own actions, the more the number and level of possible other subject positions go into it, the greater the degree of self-actualization. Habermas distinguishes between self-realizing and self-actualizing in a very similar way, in several places within Chapter 5 of *The Theory of Communicative Action* (1987).

When "We" Isn't Really "We": Self-Determination Struggling with Determination by Others; I-Me Configuration. Let's review something discussed above from a slightly new angle: The being of a physical thing is the being of something finite that can be represented through a combination of culturally supplied categories and terms. For example, we make claims like, "I own a

1993 Ford Mazda that has four doors, a turquoise color, and a prominent dent in its front bumper." What the car is can be approached by stringing together descriptive terms; the more terms used, the closer is our representation of this particular car. No description fully captures the particularity of an individual thing, but by combining more and more terms, we approach particularity.

Particularity is very important for human identity. People are motivated to claim and maintain it. To have recognition from others, humans claim themselves through implicit and explicit general terms, contingently available within cultural milieus. But they keep themselves distant from those terms partly because they are "general," shared with others, incapable of representing the absolute particularity of the "I am."

The various attributes, qualities, traits—determinations—ascribed to an identity are claims that come from both the person herself and from others who seek to define and position her. Human identity manifests within a sort of "substance" of person-representations that are contested. There is a struggle, a striving, in the being of a person, to have self-determinations rather than externally applied determinations; to be the "me" one claims and self-recognizes rather than to be what others claim one to be; to be the character one self-authors rather than a character in other people's stories about one's self. The contested milieus that identity claims have to make use of involve pre-given "we" positions from which people assess themselves and in relation to which people claim themselves. There can be and very often is a gap between available "we" positions and what comes from the unknown "I" as source. This is one way to characterize cultural power. It constrains self-recognition through inadequate identity repertoires that are inadequate because the "we" positions constituting them are not really "we" positions for groups of people.

"Determinations" that operate as epistemological structures, as ways of knowing something, specify whatever is known through contrasts to other possible, knowable things. Determinations in the knowing of a person to be a person are not only this but also existential substance, and they are used in a play or struggle between full self-determination and fully being subsumed within discourses, knowledges, and cultures dominated by others. Self-determination pertains to a claimed absolute particularity and uniqueness that cannot be captured by any set of categories and attributes. This is the "I" principle. It is the self-determination principle. It is the negative. It is never absent, but it can be obscured and minimized when self-determination is low, and determination by others—by ideologies, discourses, powerful majority groups, and cultural structures as a whole—is high. The culturally supplied categories and attributes are used for "me" claims, and "you/they" claims. Their use has to be in distinction from the "I," but the nature and extent of this distinction varies in ways of interest to the qualitative researcher.

Hence people can feel and often do feel as if their being is constructed and defined through the gaze and knowledge of others, but that is a feeling of oppression precisely because it contradicts the transcending feature of human being, which in turn is associated with an unavoidable push for forms and degrees of self-determination. The sorts of power-knowledges described by Foucault, the discourse-practices associated with criminology, pedagogy, sanity, sexuality (Foucault, 1965, 1973), do not provide evidence for fully constructed and in no way essential subjectivity, but rather exemplify I-me formations in which the "I" is submerged within an externally defined "me." The subject does exist with universal structures, but with many various forms and contents, and as a more or less integrated and consistent I-me configuration.

E. Human Identity and Diverse Forms of Negation

> ...the "I" is the *content* of the connection and the connecting itself. Opposed to another, the "I" which, for the "I," is equally only the "I" itself. (Hegel, 1977, #166; p. 104)

Negation features into identity claims in various ways. The "I" as source and as critic/judge cannot be directly, explicitly represented, but must be indirectly claimed through meaningful acts. The "I" as source pertains to the unknowable potentialities of a person for self-realizing qualities that distinguish and individuate persons. The word "I" alone cannot represent this, for it is empty, universal, and deictic. It is used within meaningful acts as a whole for identity claims that can be lexically represented in statements of the form "I am such-and-such kind of person." In autobiographies, the "I" is associated with a character who is said to have responsibly acted in various ways and have had various events and experiences happen to it. The "I" as self-critic, self-judge, is also the source of acts but special kinds of acts: self-reflective ones. Here action comes from a claimed "we" position to which the "I" is linked. But these acts also have consequences for "me" claims in that they demonstrate nuanced claims to accountability, integrity, and responsibility. A person with high integrity is a kind of "me."

Determinate Negations. Human identity is a matter of claimed "I-me" relations, the "I" component suggested negatively, the "me" in ways that can be articulated in positive terms. Thus negations in identity claims are similar in form to what Hegel called "determinate negation." Hegel explains what he means by determinate negation in a passage of his introduction to the *Phenomenology*, where he points out the limitations of skeptical consciousness:

> This is just the scepticism which only ever sees pure nothingness in its result and abstracts from the fact that this nothingness is specifically the nothingness of that *from which it results*. For it is only when it is taken as the result of that from which it emerges, that it is, in fact, the true result; in that case it is itself a *determinate* nothingness, one which has a *content*. (Hegel, 1977, #79, p. 51)

Use of the negative in identity claims includes something like determinate negation because something positive has to be claimed in order to indicate something beyond it. Precisely what it is that is positively claimed will be important for what is conveyed as "not" that.

Adaptations of the First and Second Negation Distinction. The initial thought behind using the distinction between first and second negation in studies of identity claims and self-narratives was inspired from readings of Hegel and applied by Yi-Ping Huang (Huang, 2008). Hegel's dialectics often emphasize two negations, two movements; and we have seen this in some of the quotations above. In his preface to the *Phenomenology*, Hegel writes about being, movement, and identity as follows:

> The movement of a being that immediately is, consists partly in becoming an other than itself, and thus becoming its own immanent content; partly in taking back into itself this unfolding [of its content] or this existence of it, i.e., in making *itself* into a moment, and simplifying itself into something determinate. In the former movement, *negativity* is the differentiating and positing of *existence;* in this return into self, it is the becoming of the *determinate simplicity*. (Hegel, 1977, #53, p. 32)

Every positive feature of a claimed existent is a specification of limits—of what the existent thing is not. The unity of the existent through its determinations, its first negations, coincides with the "I" of the one who knows the existent. But then in second negation, we come to understand that the existent is itself the process that has brought about its determinations.

> It is in this way that the content [of any particular knowledge] shows that its determinateness is not received from something else, nor externally attached to it, but that it determines itself, and ranges itself as a moment having its own place in the whole. (Hegel, 1977, #53, p. 32)

Hegel discusses being in general in terms of the movements of *Geist*, and few thinkers today consider being in general this way. But the movements Hegel attributes to *Geist* are recognizable as movements in human identity and consciousness; they are movements having to do with self-determination made with an opposition to external determinations. Human beings claim themselves and this requires specifying qualities and characteristics that, in turn, are constituted by structures of similarities and differences: negations and distinctions. This pertains to "first negation." But human beings also, as Dilthey emphasized, claim transcendence to those very self-applied determinations, qualities, and characteristics; and this roughly accords with the idea of second negation.

By first negation we refer to the structural constitution of the "me" portion of an I-me formation. All identity structures will have forms of first negation because they have to rely upon structures distinguishing person attributes in both culturally explicit and implicit ways. We can note a number of ways this can happen:

1. Claiming an identity implicitly by claiming *not* to be a different identity explicitly: "I'm not one of them!" "I'm not a tyrant, you know." "I'm not a fundamentalist."

2. Claiming an identity explicitly that is constituted by differences from other possible identities implicitly: "I'm a decent citizen." "I'm a kind and loving father." "I'm a brilliant scholar."

3. Claiming a positive identity explicitly that is more explicitly in negative relation to other positive identities: "I'm a solid working-class guy" can have a sense dependent upon a fairly explicit, but unstated, negative contrast with middle- and upper-class identities.

4. Claiming an identity by contrasting one's self negatively with what one used to be: "I was a real fool in those days: vain, materialistic, and selfish. I'm totally different now."

5. Claiming an identity by explicitly naming refinements in or growth from a past identity: "I was always very enthusiastic and still am, but I am less naïve now. You could say that I am now passionate but realistic."

Second negation is the indirectly referenced transcending feature of identity. We use it to refer to the ways in which people claim to be beyond positive characterizations, beyond types of possible person as afforded by a culture and its identity structures. We note a number of ways in which second negation can be at play in identity claims:

1. Acting with pragmatics that claim one's identity to be mysterious; i.e., "acting mysteriously."

2. Acting with self-referenced irony.

3. Laughing while talking about oneself.

4. Claiming a positive identity whose content includes second negation, such as "I'm a flexible, reasonable person willing to change."

These various modes we have here suggested, for claiming identity via forms of negation, are not meant to be exhaustive, of course.

Part II: Illustrations and Explorations

The data analyzed to illustrate and explore theoretical arguments made above consist of interviews conducted by one of us, Yi-Ping Huang, from four East Asian graduate students. All four were or had just been working as International Associate Instructors (IAIs, usually referred to as just AIs in what follows) in a university pre-service teacher education program (see Huang, 2008). These IAIs are all nonnative speakers of English, coming to the United States from South Korea (Jung), China (Yi-Pei and Ya-Chi), and Japan (Akiko). These names are pseudonyms to protect confidentiality.

Jung	South Korea	Novice AI teaching multicultural education
Yi-Pei	China (Taiwan)	Experienced AI teaching educational computing and early childhood education
Akiko	Japan	Novice AI teaching classroom communication
Ya-Chi	China	Novice AI teaching course in teaching methodology

Figure 1: the Research Participants

Data analyzed for this chapter originated from three interviews with each participant. Each individual interview lasted from 90 minutes to three hours. Data analysis was conducted both on what the participants said about themselves in their interviews and the identity claims made performatively by participants while responding to interview questions.[10]As discussed above, identity claims are carried by full speech acts. They are easily sensed, but often difficult to articulate. Reconstructing identity claims requires attention to both semantic (lexical) and pragmatic (for example, paralinguistic) features of speech acts. The interactions of the interviewee and interviewer were reconstructed in this way to articulate performed identity claims made by the interviewees with speech acts whose contents were about themselves and their life histories. It is important to note that the full analysis originally conducted by Yi-Ping Huang revealed many identity claims and structures underlying them that cannot be discussed explicitly in this chapter. We have named a performed identity for each participant that represents the most frequent, and interview-integrative, around which identity claims made during the interviewing process clustered. We examine the life-narratives provided by each participant with primary attention to the way they described their teacher identities chronologically.

Our interest was in exploring the negative in the identity claims made in self-narratives. What we found is rather complex. Identity claims were made by instantiating and claiming valid many entire structures simultaneously. Usually one structure would be foregrounded but dependent upon other structures that were more implicit and backgrounded. All identity-constituting structures have forms of first negation insofar as their positive terms have meanings partly (but not necessarily entirely) through not being other terms or possible terms in the same structure. It seemed worthwhile to us to only articulate these kinds of negative relations explicitly when they were explicitly made by participants or when they suggest importance for further analysis. Our focus in the analysis below, therefore, is on the structures employed for "me" claims. We also examine as best we can the way that the transcending features of self, the "I" over the "me," was indicated by our participants. In general terms, from the analysis of all participants, we found the following structures and processes:

Dimension, Milieu, Process	Structures; Forms of First Negation		Modes of Transcending; Second Negation
	Horizontal	*Temporal*	
PLACE DISTINCTIONS	U.S. culture/ Home country culture Fusing horizons, critical of both Fusing horizons without critique Endorsing home culture as distinctive	Moving to U.S. for new occupation Resulting in planned changes Resulting in unanticipated changes	*Self-actualizing emphasis:* Critic of both cultures Director of own life *Self-realizing emphasis:* Becoming more *in* U.S. culture Becoming more in *contrast to* U.S.
TIME	*Times within life history contrasted with each other* Forward as desire for change Back-ward as noting changes	*Time of interview contrasted with times in history* I am now what I have grown into I am now what I have always	• Laughing at self while talking • Sighing while talking • Talking to one's self to communicate to other • Acting out thought from past from first-person present • Vision metaphors; I see myself, look at myself, etc. • Modifying identity claim just made with new words

Figure 2: Negation Structures and Processes (pg. 1)

	Temporally Vertical	Temporally Horizontal	Self-Realizing Form
IDENTITY NESTING	*Finding* person identity over occupational identity — Via social awareness / Via psychological awareness; *Always* being person / Both identities develop / Only occupational identity	Levels in harmony | Levels in disharmony	*Self-Realizing Form*: Myself is unfolding, unfinished, non-determined larger form of self related to determined. **Self-Actualizing Form**: I am that which objectivates and analyzes, all determinations are nested below me
SOCIAL THEORY (Partial, participants')	*Positioning*: I am subject to my social location	*Self-reflection/ transcending in relation to*: I am critic and self-director in relation to my social location	By analyzing myself as socially positioned, I am beyond social determinations
PSYCHO-LOGICAL THEORY (Partial, participants')	Personal history shaped patterns | Culturally shaped patterns	Comparison method; my thoughts clarified in comparison with those of others	By analyzing my own psychological processes, I am beyond them
HARMONIZING	*SYNTHESIS*: By creating or finding new "me" — *DETACHING*: By withdrawing identification from action patterns		Positive forms of critic and author

Figure 2: Negation Structures and Processes (pg. 2)

Participants made use of distinctions on the basis of place, time, their own implicit social theories, their own implicit psychological theories, and the processes of identity nesting and harmonizing identity themes in tension. The ways that participants claimed themselves beyond their self-determinations are listed in the last column to the right of Figure 1. When talking about themselves as they were in the past and how this changed over time, participants distinguished themselves from their objectivations in ways specific to the "me" structures they invoked. Often this was in a form resembling determinate negations in which a transcending "I" was implicated by specific contrast to what was said about "me"-constitutive themes. In some cases, transcendence was claimed in the form of a positive "me" that directed and/or directs more determinate "me" forms nested within, creates a new "me" to resolve conflicts, self-realizes and continues to self-realize in uncertain and open ways, distinguishes itself from psychological processes it does not identify with, and so on. In the "time" row, ways that participants implicated themselves beyond the identity claims made in their talk, at the time of the interview, are included. The next chart gives special emphasis to the modes through which participants in this study claimed themselves beyond their self-descriptions:

	Participants who claimed transcending features of themselves this way
The self-director (psychologically)	Akiko: Controlling herself so as to not make subordinate identity claims Ya-Chi: Observing and not identifying with self-doubting patterns
The self-director (decision maker, author of life course)	Jung: Deciding to become a teacher to become a desired kind of person Ya-Chi: Deciding to move to U.S. to improve self-esteem Yi-Pei: Deciding to quit teaching as AI for reasons ascribed to her identity Akiko: Deciding to change career for reasons ascribed to her identity
Taking specifically determined other subject/group positions in relation to one's self	Akiko: Describing the kind of person she seems to be to Japanese audiences, contrasted with U.S. audiences, both contrasted to real self Ya-Chi: Taking position of supervisor of AI's to criticize herself as an AI.
The critic of identity-constitutive social and cultural positions	Akiko: critical of both Japanese and U.S. culture Jung: critical of role of education in social inequalities
The self-aware finder or constructor of a "me" identity; occupational identity specific	Akiko: A counselor, not a teacher Yi-Pei: A learning sciences person, not an IST person Ya-Chi: A consultant, not a teacher
The "I" always beyond all "me" identities	Jung: Continuous, consistent identity problematizing, especially after early portions of self-history
The self-aware chooser and endorser of a "me" identity; general person	Ya-Chi: Fully aware of traditional Chinese woman identity attributes and fully endorsing herself as a Chinese woman Akiko: Fully aware of and endorsing minority identity living in cultures dominated by others
The author and critic of the life-history interview	All participants claimed transcending features of themselves in this way

Figure 3: Modes of Claiming Self-Transcendence

We will now discuss each participant. Because of space limitations, we have truncated the discussion of each. Readers may consult Huang, 2008 for more extensive discussions of the participants in this study.

Jung

Throughout the research process, Jung presented himself as a very self-reflective and self-probing person. He stated explicitly that he would not wish to try to formulate who and what he is. During the interviews, he did not simply talk about the kind of person he was and is, but more fundamentally, continuously problematized each identity he attributed to himself when giving his life story.

Jung's autobiographical talk organized his life as an educator as a succession of teacher-identities. In condensed form and with concentration on his discussion of identities, his autobiographical account looks like this:

I WAS	I was a working-class man without power / I was not what I wished to be
I WISHED TO BE	I wished to be a powerful and mysterious male elementary school teacher / I desired what I was not and worked to become what I desired to be
I BECAME	I became an elementary school teacher, but found this identity wanting; I was an inexperienced and traditional elementary school teacher
AND WAS	I was not understanding of students and their lives and needs
I GREW INTO	After time I became an experienced, critical elementary school teacher; culturally sensitive and caring
I MOVED TO THE U.S.	When I came to graduate school in the U.S., I became an ineffective minority (Korean) instructor of multicultural education, a novice but open teacher
WHICH WAS/IS GROWING INTO	I was/am changing towards a more culturally aware and flexible minority teacher educator; a critical teacher educator
WHICH BECAME/IS NOW	I am a reflective, thoughtful and flexible AI
Self-Narrative Unity **"Jung the self-transcender"**	

Figure 4: Condensation of Jung's Self-Narrative

Jung's identity claims during his talk clustered consistently about what we call "Jung the self-transcender" because his talk about his personal history continuously displayed high levels of reflection, of distinguishing himself from what he said about himself, of making identity claims and then problematizing them.

In South Korea, Jung once identified himself as a powerless working-class male student. The figure of a "powerful and mysterious male elementary school teacher" that he had constructed from experiences as a young student drew him at that time. Self-transcendence was here located within the image of another, a type of person he was not. He wanted to become this type of person rather than remain powerless and working class, so he pursued this career and became an elementary school teacher. As Jung recalled,

J: I THOUGHT[11] being a teacher is the most powerful man.

R: A powerful MAN, not WOMAN,

J: Not woman—when I was an elementary student, more than 70% were males. You know teachers at that time was a privilege at that time and a mysterious person. ... Mysterious figure to me. So I decided to be a teacher. Being a teacher means powerful. To be a mysterious man

R: To be powerful—

J: To be powerful through my experiences. [Laughter] I know a lot of stereotypes about teachers and teaching. Teacher is an authority figure. Teacher is a very powerful man. So I wanted to be a teacher. And also it was accessible for me to be a teacher. ... Do I think this way now? No!

Jung's sense of himself as powerless and working class, and his desire to be different than this, to be a mysterious and powerful teacher, has a description in his life story structured by first negations. A positively articulated type of person, the powerless working-class student, implicates the structure of class distinctions. "Powerful" and "powerless" are given as additional attributes in binary negation of each other, but suggest the principle of transcendence, second negation, because "power" is used here to signify self-determination in contrast to the determinations of social location. "Mysterious" amplifies the transcendence principle—Jung compared himself as a powerless working-class student to an identity construction that represented both power and the unknown, the beyondness of self. Hence, as presented in the life story, a mode of being a person is defined primarily in terms of what it is not (but wishes to be), and the symbol of what is wished for leads Jung to his first choice of career. He was self-realizing, manifesting potentialities by becoming a teacher.

Work as an elementary school teacher brought unexpected experiences with it, which resulted in self-criticism and the development of a broadened sense of identity within a larger and more critical view of the world and society. Like other novice teachers, Jung had little experiential knowledge about teaching prior to taking on his first teaching job. He learned how to teach via experimenting, trying things out; and in this way, he learned through the consequences of his efforts. He recalled a particularly poignant experience he had, brought about by punishing one of his sixth-grade students for delinquency without considering, or even noticing the family background of this student:

J: I have so many these kinds of students. Some of them are failing ... I didn't know how to deal with it—when I had kids like them. One of my students, my sixth-grader, They didn't do well at school. So—I used physical punishment to deal with this issue.... I didn't know...his family situation. I tried to control with my third-grade teaching and he resisted and made me angry.... *Every kid should have this mandatory test at that time.*[12] I cannot find him. He was not there. So, I went to his house and broke the door. *I saw*—he has one room and *his five brothers and sisters.* He has to take care of them, his family. There is no income, except from the South Korean government. She was there tired. I didn't realize. I didn't understand. I made a mistake. I didn't understand at that time why he couldn't finish his homework.

Jung's description of himself during his early years of teaching again emphasizes a mode of first negation: being an inexperienced, unaware, and naïve teacher. Jung developed guilty feelings as a result of his punitive treatment of students like the one in the incident described above. He became aware that he had not been providing culturally responsive teaching. He changed as a result.

Jung's life story casts the next period in terms of self-actualizing, a process of finding a larger position from which to regard himself due to the self-criticisms that resulted from his beginning methods of teaching and disciplining students. The "me" feature of the identity he presents for this phase of his story is that of transformed teacher; a teacher who moved from being a novice and being naïve, becoming experienced, socially aware, and critical. Over time he became an experienced, critical elementary school teacher with a much broader understanding of children and families. The "we" position from which his identity claims were self-monitored and contrasted with other possible claims expanded. He concluded this part of his interview with remarks about how he changed: "You know teaching and learning is very limited.… education is not about education." Through self-actualizing, Jung generated more space within which his "me" could grow from close identification with the role of teacher to that of a socially aware and caring person.

When coming to the U.S., Jung, the former experienced and socially aware elementary Korean teacher, found himself in novice position once again. He was a neophyte in teacher education in a foreign land. He now had to teach student teachers, most of whom were non-Koreans, and teach them in English. He taught the multicultural education course in the teacher education program at his university. In the interview, Jung described himself as a novice teacher explicitly and went on to further qualify his identity and position as that of a "minority instructor." He was very conscious of his lack of experience and cultural understandings, and had to continuously think about what he ought to do in the many uncertain situations he experienced:

> I have to negotiate because I am aware that I am a stranger, because I am aware that I am less powerful than them [the students in Multicultural Education] in some ways. But I am an instructor. So I have to negotiate this with my students. Like—"Do I have to say this to my student?" For example—someone acted rudely. "Do I have to say that you are rude? Or ignore it? Or do I have to say something?" These are ALL—[Silence] something I have to negotiate—something I have to think and decide—and—if I were a—teaching in Korea, it may not happen. I may not need to negotiate.

Jung's talk about his identity issues during this period is talk about a person who was able to consider his own patterns and identity attachments with a willingness and openness to change himself:

> Whenever we discussed, we had different opinions and we just stopped. They don't want to listen to me. Maybe I don't want to listen to them. Maybe it's not just one direction. Maybe it's both directions.

The identity described is that of an open teacher who problematizes his own teaching. Also, with more teaching experience in the U.S., Jung was also able to identify the pros and cons of education in South Korea and in the U.S., rendering him a more culturally aware teacher educator. In the process of fusing Korean and U.S. interpretative horizons, Jung found yet a broader "we" position.

The frame of self-actualizing is given prominence in this portion of Jung's life story too. The "me" associated with it is explicitly problematized by Jung. He begins as a novice, minority teacher educator who is critically minded and uncertain, conscious of learning continuously from his efforts to teach. As Jung's university teaching continued, his teacher identity coalesced strongly about his flexibility, openness, and self-transcending nature. He did not wish to limit himself through self-definitions of being a certain type of instructor. For example, in relation to teaching philosophies, Jung said,

> I tried not to—elaborate it. What is my educational philosophy? This is my educational philosophy. This is not my educational philosophy. If I just decided which one, I may attach to it. And I don't like it. I just want to think more freely.

Attaching to an educational philosophy would be fixing himself in terms of an identity. Rather than making identity claims that would tie him to one camp or another, Jung avoided positive claims in this domain, identifying with the freedom of the position of being beyond "me" claims. By expressing a number of various positions on educational philosophy but not identifying with any of them, Jung preserved his uniqueness and autonomy through acts of second negation.

Overall, Jung's stories demonstrated moments of self-critiquing with different levels of self-awareness. What configured diverse (partial or full) life events into meaningful plots appears to be the self-critical and highly self-reflective Jung, who is beyond all definitions and labels.

Jung's self-history and his performative identity claiming during the interview are summarized in the following:

	"Me" Structures			Contrasts	Key Structures	Transcending Claims
WAS/WISHED TO BE	***Social positioning by class***			Horizontal contrast Explicit negative	Is/can be I/other person Class contrasts	Principle of transcendence located in Other
	I was powerless working class	I was not	Powerful mysterious male teacher			
	Implicit class contrasts	I wanted to be	Powerful mysterious male			
				Temporal contrast		Director of life
BECAME	***Occupational change***					
	Elementary school teacher					
	Unknowingly traditional and non-understanding of					
				Temporal contrast explicit negative		Social critic
GREW INTO	***Identity Nesting structure***			Nested Contrast, Finding, Becoming person over teacher	Traditional/ non-traditional; Socially aware not socially aware Person/ occupational role	Movement from teacher to person; aware of social location of teacher and critical
	Socially critical and caring person					
	Non-traditional teacher					

Figure 5: Jung Structures and Transcendence in Life Story (pg. 1)

		Geographical and Occupational contrast		
RESULT OF MOVE TO U.S.	*Identity Nesting structure* Open, flexible person Conjunction structure Ineffective & Minority & Novice Teacher	Nested Contrast	Conjunction structure Minority/majority & Ineffective/ effective & Experienced /novice	Openness quality, a person who changes via learning with attributes nested below
AM NOW	Flexible, open-minded person/AI "Jung the self-transcender"	Self-relation contrast	"I"/"me's"	Always beyond what can be said about me

Figure 5: Jung Structures and Transcendence in Life Story (pg. 2)

Yi-Pei

Yi-Pei organized her autobiographical account as two parallel successions of identities, one as a person and one as a teacher and academic. In condensed form and with attention to her talk about identities in chronological time her interviews can be summarized as follows:

	Person	Teacher, Academic Identities
I WAS	An unhappy person with problems, a secretary for assisting foreign teachers, a person living within a "smaller world"	
BUT I WAS	Not a "bootlicker" A person with integrity	
AND I WANTED TO BE	A serious intellectual, not a superficial "social" person	
SO I BECAME	Bringing out my serious intellectual self	A grad student of linguistics Enjoying life
WHICH LEAD TO	Moving to U.S.	Becoming an instructional technology student
AND ALSO		A university AI in the U.S.
NESTED WITHIN	A serious and intellectual person, manifested	
WITHIN THIS I WAS		A teacher-centered AI
BUT BECAME		A learner-centered AI, caring about students
AND AWARE OF	No leadership skills	Disqualified teacher, Not able to lead students, Not enough knowledge, More a learning sciences person than an instructional technology person
RECONCILED BY	A caring person	A caring consultant Not, rather than, a teacher
SO I QUIT	Was idealistic, Now realistic Am culturally aware	
GROWING INTO	A realistic and culturally aware person, with bigger heart and broader view	A struggling AI, not intending to continue teaching
AND NOW HAVE BECOME	More mature, happy, big-hearted and free person living in a larger world	More identified with general person traits than as a teacher
Self-Narrative Unity **"Yi-Pei the detached, rational, self-objectivator"**		

Figure 6: Condensation of Yi-Pei's Self-Narrative

The identity claims made by Yi-Pei when talking about herself autobiographically clustered about what we call "Yi-Pei the detached, rational self-objectivator." She consistently discussed herself as if analyzing another character altogether.

> When Yi-Pei became a secretary and teacher in a Chinese college, she soon found she loathed her job as a secretary who was obligated to assist foreign teachers, because she felt that the job positioned her as what she called "a social person," a person who would use others as a means to her own ends. She said she was not a "bootlicker" and yet the job pressured her in that direction. Her talk of her identity at this time emphasized the negative, what she was not and yet positioned to be, which is a mode of first negation in relation to the "social person/bootlicker" identity. Implicit was the positive claim of being a person with pure mind and dignity. Because of this she was unable to fulfill her responsibilities as secretary very well.

Although Yi-Pei found ways to resolve the tension between who she was and wished to be, and her job responsibilities, her desirable self—a serious intellectual—had not been reaffirmed; so she stepped down from the position to study linguistics at a prestigious graduate school in China. The positive, desirable identity claim of "I am a serious intellectual" reoccurred in our interview whenever Yi-Pei mentioned her learning at school. This claim was positive and foregrounded, but implicated implicit first negation as she juxtaposed her secretary job and graduate school learning via the contrast between social people and serious intellectuals. As she explained, "After my college, I decided, 'Okay! At graduate school, I will focus on academics. I don't want to do this [secretary job or be a social person] any longer.' So, I hide my past. I never tell people that I was very active in school at the time. … So, basically I was just studying and enjoying life." To maintain the identity of a serious scholar, she did not tell people about what she had done previously. She did not have a way to reconcile, within her new and fully endorsed identity, what she had done in the past (and the identity implications of this) with who she claimed to be during this new phase. At least she did not have a way to reconcile these opposed identities that she could trust others to recognize. And so she hid her past.

Yi-Pei continued with graduate work after her studies in linguistics by moving to the U.S., to pursue her doctoral degree in educational technology. To her surprise, she fell in love with education. Her interests in education combined her love of language and technology, her eagerness to share her passions for these subjects, as well as finding herself to be a "service person." She described herself during this period as a service and research person.

Yi-Pei then juxtaposed her teacher identity in China and in the U.S. When teaching in China, Yi-Pei emphasized her accurate performance in English, rather than her students as learners because, she said, the Chinese students held more accountability than teachers. What changed were not so much the topics of what she taught—technology or language—but the values she upheld. That is, she valued learners, learner-centered approaches, and learning more than before. She became a caring and responsible teacher who was devoted to making a difference in student life. As she said, "Yes, that is one of the things that I think American education has changed me, or at least the department I was in changed me." Yi-Pei differentiated herself from her past identity as a teacher-centered educator (explicit first negation) to a learner-centered one (implicit first negation). This transformation suggests a process of self-realization, bringing out more of her service orientation and her capacities for caring and being open. The process of fusing interpretative horizons from China with those she discovered by living and working at her U.S. university broadened the "we" position she used in self-analysis, which pertains to self-actualizing movements. The caring, learner-oriented values she found by working in the U.S. also served as standards by which to self-judge her performances.

In the U.S., Yi-Pei was not simply a teacher, but also a teacher educator who facilitated pre-service teachers to become future teachers. Although Yi-Pei had had teaching experience in China, the experience of teaching undergraduate students in the United States was difficult. Students were unmotivated, "immature," and they expected to receive good grades without hard work. They were often uncooperative, leaving Yi-Pei feeling out of control. Given her new endorsement of learner-centered teaching and her discovery of caring and service-to-other values, Yi-Pei experienced her difficulties with teaching as deficiencies within herself. She said that in order to satisfy diverse interests and needs, teachers need to be leaders. And she did not feel she had leadership qualities. In her own words:

> As instructors really have control and you should really have leadership and I realize I'm not very good at leadership. I'm better at consulting with students instead of …when there are multiple styles of learning,… students. I feel I'm not so good at it.

Yi-Pei explicitly differentiated herself from good teachers with excellent leadership skills, a mode of first negation. But she also claimed an identity positively, in this case both in the sense of having names for it and in the sense of valuing this identity positively, as a way to contrast herself from good teachers without taking on a totally negative self-evaluation. She said she is a good counselor, a good caring consultant, rather than a good teacher. Her self-identification as an individual, caring consultant, rather than a public leader, occurred whenever leadership skills came up within segments of her life story. Her frustration with teaching led her to step down from the AI position.

After quitting her AI position, Yi-Pei was able to detach herself and reflect upon her unsatisfactory experience of teaching. In an interview, she said, "I think I have a more BALANCED idea about what a teacher should do and what a student should do," and "I think I just became too idealistic. They [the Educational Technology teachers] taught me to become idealistic. NOW I become a little more realistic." Yi-Pei describes herself her as, in general, a "more realistic person," detaching from the role of teaching. She no longer identifies as either a teacher-centered or a learner-centered teacher. By taking a broader third-person position, a "we" position from which to self-judge and self-describe, she distinguished herself from roles that had previously served more directly as identity criteria.

Looking back on her life story as a whole, Yi-Pei stated that she is now more mature, happy, and free. In her own words:

> Before I came to America I was not in a very good state, personal life…. Then, my Mom encouraged me to come here. Suddenly, I realized that the things you worry so much, you feel sad and suddenly you can put them behind you because the world is so big. You have unlimited possibilities in life. So, I really thank my Mom for encouraging me to come out and make me feel the things that I felt was the whole of my life, the whole part of my life, it becomes so many tiny things. For the things I was not happy about, now when I look back I can look back at them in a very realistic way or a very humorous way. So, I feel I have a broader heart after coming. I don't think it's the U.S. I think any person who comes to a different culture and who [is] open minded they will have the same experience.

By objectivating her past self as a character in her story, Yi-Pei, as the self-critic of her life, was able to reevaluate herself and feels able to redirect her life. While saying that she is a person

	"Me" Structures	Contrasts	Key Structures	Transcending Claims
WAS	Social positioning by occupation forcing surface personality Serious Intellectual as non-realized core self	Horizontal contrast Explicit negative	Real self/appearance; Authentic self / self-expressions; Inner self/Outer self; Intellectuals /superficial social people	"This is not me" Director of life
		Temporal contrast explicit negative		Director of life
BECAME	Occupational change • Linguistics grad student • Nonintegrated with past	Audience, social group contrast Hiding past self from new audiences	Past self and social world/new self and social world Real self/superficial self	Self-realizing director of life
		Move to U.S. Geo and job change		Self-realizing director of life
BECAME AFTER MOVE TO U.S.	Identity Nesting structure IST student and AI Teacher-centered; not thematized	Temporal and place contrast Partially nested contrast	Graduate student and AI in no contrast What I was in China/What I am in U.S.	

Figure 7: Yi-Pei Structures and Transcendence in Life (pg. 1)

			Temporal contrast	Teacher-centered / learner centered; I am/I should be;	Self-definer or discoverer
CHANGE WITH EXPERIENCES	Conjunction structure with negations				
	Learner centered AI & Idealist, not thematized	Not a leader			
	And:	Not a typical IST student			
GENERATION OR ↑ DISCOVERY OF "ME" STRUCTURES ↑	Positive self-constructed or discovered "me" contrast structures		Discovered or constructed contrast "me" structural distinctions	Teachers must be leaders/ Consultants need not be leaders; IST types into technology / Learning sciences types into cognition	
	I am not an IST type	But I am a learning sciences type			
	I am not a good teacher	But I am a good consultant			
			Quit Teaching		Director of life
AM NOW	Identity Nesting structure		Temporal contrast Some nesting	Previous self/current self Potential self/realized self	Self-realizing via self-expansion
	Big-hearted, happy person in larger world Realist not idealist				

Figure 7: Yi-Pei Structures and Transcendence in Life (pg. 2)

with a broader mind, she accepted but also negated her previous self in the sense that she claimed she was no longer narrow-minded or unhappy. She told her story as a person in the present who has a broader heart and who is happier than the person she had been. Making the comparisons between now and then she claimed herself beyond both performatively, in the second negation mode. The recalling claimed, but implicitly, that Yi-Pei self-critiques as a rational and reasonable person who can consider herself "objectively."

Yi-Pei's talk about herself would at times distinguish herself from an immediately previous implicit identity claim. For example, when explaining that she had grown and changed and become a larger person living within a larger world, she next said, "I think any person who comes to a different culture and … who [is] open minded they will have the same experience." By so doing, she denied any possible claims of taking credit for or having pride in the fact that she has grown and become a person she clearly feels good about being—she claimed herself beyond this with a remark indicating humbleness and rationality—the ability to consider herself as she would consider any other person.

Although quite common and recognizable, the ways that Yi-Pei monitored her identity claims that were implicitly carried by her interview talk, and then modified them with a next act, are interesting and illustrate the second-negation principle well. Each reference to a previously claimed identity so as to show herself beyond it demonstrated levels of self-awareness. Each new level of self-awareness implicated the transcending "I" as traced to a previously claimed "me"; the "I" as not-that-me, the "I" as determinate negation. This sort of talk demonstrated the self-actualizing movement.

Akiko

Akiko differed from Jung and Yi-Pei in that she maintained a strongly unified performative identity-claim cluster during her interview talk that she also applied to her autobiographical stories, as if deep aspects of her have never changed. Jung was consistent in problematizing his identities when discussing them, but did refer to himself in past years as having distinctive identities, different from who he is now. Yi-Pei claimed her present identity more explicitly than Jung and also contrasted it definitively from the identity attachments she had moved through during the course of her life. Akiko, on the other hand, presented herself as a "self-director," as having an identity based on controlling tendencies within herself to act too much in accordance with expectations of minorities and females. She is a member of a minority group in Japan, since she is Korean Japanese. And as an international student, she is in a minority within the United States. Very conscious of social inequalities and forms of cultural power, Akiko discussed her life history as if the most central components of her current identity were operative all along. Like Yi-Pei, she organized her life story in the direction of two parallel sequences of life experience. But there is an interesting difference. Yi-Pei talked of her changes as a person with some distinction from her changes as a teacher and academic, but Akiko talked about herself as a teacher moving through different jobs and experiences (similar to one of Yi-Pei's life trajectories), but also talked about herself as she is now, but with respect to different periods in her life. The same qualities are emphasized in different life periods. Here is a condensed presentation of Akiko's autobiographical talk:

	Identity Now (and probably forever), in past contexts	Teacher-Related
I WAS/AM	Not a typical Japanese woman A victim of social injustice One who transcends victimization, does not internalize inferiority	
NESTED WITHIN	A strong supporter, a supporting leader, caring about social injustice, A facilitative teacher	
NESTED WITHIN	Both minority and majority Like inner-city kids	
MOVING TO U.S. I BECAME		An uncertain inexperienced teacher without "room" to take position of students well; sunk within her own teaching: identity survival
AND GREW INTO		A certain and confident teacher understanding of students' needs
I EXPERIENCED TENSIONS	Heightened cultural awareness	I can't be both a fair and also a caring teacher,
I BECAME AS A RESULT		Changed to school psychology
NESTED WITHIN	Greater maturity, More critical of both cultures, open about judgments yet position of judge and director is solid	A student of school psychology
Self-Narrative Unity **"Akiko the utopian self-judge and self-director"**		

Figure 8: Condensation of Akiko's Self-Narrative

In her talk, Akiko's performative identity claims clustered about what we call "Akiko the utopian self-judge and self-director." Her self-talk included descriptions of ways that she controls herself or wishes to control herself to be consistent with her ideals. And she wishes to work in ways that support the socially and culturally disadvantaged.

Akiko referred to herself as "atypical" for a Japanese woman, from her years of living in Japan to the present day. She talked of herself in relation to sociopolitical contexts frequently, and emphasized care for others, presenting herself as a socially critical humanist. Her orientation towards herself was like that of a social activist who unites the personal with the political. For example, Akiko recalled an experience she had when a college instructor pointed out how her own speech transmitted the very gender inequalities with which she had been combating. She perceived herself, and desired to be recognized, as an autonomous and competent heroine who cared for others, and fought for social justice. Although she was not educated to act submissively, she was shocked to realize that she still unconsciously internalized the compliant role:

...the one thing I still remember is that I guess she [the college instructor] was asking what would you like to do after your graduate study, and I was kind of mentioning that I want to work with families. And I don't care volunteering.... And then she stopped me right away saying "Do you know what? ... You shouldn't be thinking just that you want to become a volunteer. You want to think in a different way. You're the one who is going to be the leader and in charge of stuff." I knew a society, kind of like women think, somehow we are raised to think more of supportive roles.... So, I am not necessarily that I wanted to become a supporter, but how I put stuff into words sounded exactly that way. I know my parents didn't raise me that way and then she knew that I wasn't that way either, but somehow it sounded like that and she corrected me right away. That's how you just said it, and that kind of made me think I never thought that I would say that kind of thing, but I just said it. So, I think I will remember that forever how she said it. I should be the one who is going to be writing the book and then using people to help people and not using but like I'm the one in charge. I should make it my goal to be that way.

Akiko displayed herself as positioned by culturally constructed gender and ethnic inequalities but not as one who would victimize herself; a victim but not a self-victimizer. She took a third-person position to critique who she was (a victim of distorted social norms) and narrate who she desired to become (a leader for social change), by re-evaluating her current "me" claims in relation to the utopian roles that she desired to take. Akiko was consciously devoted to self-realizing processes of unfolding more of her leadership potentials. Her modes of finding autonomy involved self-guidance to conform her ways of talking and her aspirations to her sociopolitical ideals. Akiko's expressions and self-critiques of various "me" claims were united under the control of an autonomous, capable, and responsible agent; as an "I" who not only self-critiqued but also redirected one's life plots.

Akiko generally took the attitude of a strong supporter or a supporting leader in different situations. She described her role to be that of a facilitator rather than a director in relation to her students:

I just think that is my personal philosophy. I like to be a facilitator, a leader. I want my students to participate as much as possible. I think I want them to initiate learning. Not that I'm pushing them to learn. I want them to learn so maybe that is why I am one step behind or beside and let them do what they need to do. That's how I see learning.

Related to the theme of a supporting leader was Akiko's ability to identify with both minority and majority, but more importantly transcend this either/or structure. For instance, Akiko felt compatible with inner-city students because they were both members of minority groups in the U.S. As she explained,

I guess in a way I kind of feel like I fit there a little bit [into the inner city] because...there are a lot of diversities. Not necessarily my background could be close to white middle class, how I [was] raised in Japan so that my upbringings cannot be the same as those kids—but being in the United States as [an] international individual—not that I've been like discriminated a lot but being I could be discriminated or like stereotyped because of how I look and where I'm from.... I could relate that experience to what those kids are going through inner city, you know, so that does kind of like, made me feel I could use that skill, like you know my experience to connect to those kids and then work through.

By taking a third-person external-absent position as a foreigner in the U.S., Akiko claimed that she was "not necessarily" like the majority of middle-class Americans nor was she completely like a minority who had been discriminated against. This was how she viewed herself as a minority who was lucky to grab the opportunity to succeed in the U.S. The way that she shifted, in the talk quoted above, from a performatively implicated typical American "we" position to a typical minority person position reflected a higher level of self-awareness, transcending the either/or structure (implicit second negation with different degrees of reflection). Akiko spoke of her life with identity claims that balanced autonomy with relatedness.

In the U.S., Akiko experienced difficulties and uncertainties as a novice university assistant instructor, much as all of the participants in this study did. In her case, changes were described as being congruent with her dominant identity claims as self-director. She became more confident and skilled after two years of experience. Part of herself had been immersed within a "survival identity" when learning to be an AI, but as soon as she was able to find "room" to consider the ideals and purposes of her educative work, she did so:

> …The AI position was something I'm teaching the pre-service teachers. So, that's something I have to kind of consider.… So, maybe not the first semester I started teaching I didn't have that much room for myself to be thinking about those kinds of things.… But I guess as I progressed more in this year I did… start out with the semester kind of say, "Okay, you guys need to be professional because you're going to be a teacher." So, I use a lot of my perspective to think about "When you're a teacher, how would you deal with this situation. If you are a teacher what would you expect from your students." So, I did take those…preservice teachers, more into consideration…

She moved from being sunk in her own teaching to an idealized position of teacher-educator as soon as she was able to. But Akiko came to believe that she was not the right person for this ideal. Again, she cast this self-assessment in terms that implied permanent features of who she is, was, and will be. During an interview in which she explained her self-assessment as someone not fully suited for being a teacher educator, she added: "Maybe those professors who have taught 25 years, they might have better grasp on what's the better way to teach. But I think for me even if I teach 25 years, I still feel the same way.… So, I don't think I ever feel like I'm so satisfied [with my teaching]."

A key reason for feeling unsuited for the role of teacher-educator resided in Akiko's critical-social commitments. She strongly believes in fairness and justice, and she strongly cares for others. Teaching, she felt, made it impossible to be true to both sets of commitments simultaneously. As she explained,

> I think that is a challenge for me. I don't know where to draw the line.… I can't be so cut and dried about those students [who were not doing well in her classes].…… I do more work as a counselor like showing to understand what individuals are going through. That's my passion and that's what I want to do. Sometime by teaching, giving them grades, being fair to others, I can't always be caring for individuals.

Akiko's experiences with teaching resulted in dilemmas between fairness and care. Her solution was to find resonance with the role of counselor rather than teacher and she changed her major to school psychology as a result. She identified herself more as a counselor who should and could empathize with each individual, which contrasted with a teacher's responsibility to be fair to every student in grading and other forms of assessment. In her mind, this self-identification differentiated her from "good" teachers; to be very empathetic with individuals made it impossible to be a good teacher. A first-negation identity constituting structure led her to change career plans because she could not find a way to be a good but caring teacher. So Akiko decided to aim for the career of being a school psychologist within an inner-city area of the

	"Me" Structures	Contrasts	Key Structures	Transcending Claims
WAS AND STILL AM	Nested Identity Structure Caring about social justice, aware of plight of socially positioned others Positioned as minority in Japan and trans-cending, aware of this, and non-traditional Japanese woman	Nested contrasts	Minority cultures/ Majority cultures; Socially unaware/ socially aware	Socially aware and critical; Beyond positioning via awareness of it
		Geographical and cultural change		
RESULT OF MOVE TO U.S.	Occupational change Identity sunk in trying to survive teaching			
WHICH INVOLVED	A certain and confident teacher, but as teacher: Justice and Fairness VERSUS Caring	Temporal contrast Nested structure with incompatibles	Justice/care; "I"/my values	Self-director, values in tension controlled
GENERATION OF "ME" CLAIMS	Not a teacher but a counselor	Temporal integration via career change	Teacher/ counselor	Self-aware, Self-director
I AM, STILL AM, NOW	Caring and working for justice, social critic and Beyond both Japanese and U.S. cultures In control of my self: A cultural minority, similar to inner-city kids in the United States	Culture & place contrasts	Self/culture	Utopian self-director Endorsed identity as minority AND beyond two cultures

Figure 9: Akiko Structures and Transcendence in Life Story

United States, combining her passion for social justice with her capacity to care for individuals in the counseling role.

Akiko talked about her experience of living as a minority person in both Japan and the United States as follows:

A: … I guess I've become critical to both cultures. That might be the best way to say it. I've become not critical in a negative sense but positive sense. I'm more aware the cultural values maybe I carry and I see in this country and maybe I do appreciate those values.…. But not necessarily I become to value more one aspect of the cultural value.

R: Could you give me an example, what do you value?

A: Here I would say like more freedom, openness and individualistic way. I guess I appreciate that more because that helps me to become more independent in a way. But at the same time I see the negative side of those values. So I'm not just saying I value those more than any other.

Akiko uses self-interrogation, located in a previous time, to complexly claim herself in ways structured primarily by negative relations. She uses interrogation in self-talk, rather than an adjective or phrase.

Ya-Chi

Ya-Chi told a story in which she moved from being a person with low self-esteem in China to a proud and happy Chinese woman in the United States. Ya-Chi was the only participant who affirmed an identity based on her ethnicity. Her pride in being a Chinese woman has everything to do with living and working in the United States, being Chinese for non-Chinese audiences. She plans to teach Chinese language in the United States for her career. Aspects of her cultural habitus that she took for granted when living in China have become central to her identity in the United States. Ya-Chi has a critical-reflective awareness of her identity attachments to being Chinese and female, and from the critical-reflective awareness she fully endorses those attachments with pride. The condensed version of her autobiographical story looks like this:

	Person	Teacher
I WAS/AM	A person with low self-esteem, because of "cruel" Chinese system and family expectations Not like my sister, not ranked well academically as was she	
THEREFORE MOVED TO U.S.	To improve self-esteem, to become like sister	To become a teacher
AND BECAME		A novice, inexperienced teacher, not knowledgeable of cultural differences
AND HAVE BECOME		A Chinese as a foreign-language teacher, A "pedagogy person" Not a literature or linguistics person A good teacher
NESTED WITHIN	A Chinese ambassador Proud of being reserved in Chinese way; proud of Chinese culture A person who knows what she wants with certainty Sees critically that she is passive and also that she is proud but endorses both traits fully	A proud and passionate CFL teacher in the U.S. A proud "pedagogy" teacher
Self-Narrative Unity **"Ya-Chi the proud self-realized Chinese woman"**		

Figure 10: Condensation of Ya-Chi's Self-Narrative

Ya-Chi's performative identity claims during the interview clustered around her pride and happiness in being a Chinese woman and Chinese as a foreign-language teacher. These were totally congruent with the contents of her self-story, the story of a person who found herself and found who she wants to continue to be, in the United States. We call this "Ya-Chi the proud, self-realized Chinese woman."

Ya-Chi's years of growing up in China were described negatively because she felt inferior to her sister and to other students. The Chinese elementary and middle-school systems had city-wide exams that publicly ranked students in relation to peers in their class, their school, and their city. In addition, as Chinese parents value and view children as their future hope, they would compare their children's achievements. Ya-Chi's sister always did very well in this system, but Ya-Chi did not. Her self-esteem and confidence were very low as a result. Ya-Chi described facing parental expectations and school competition as "stressful," "cruel," and "spiritually torturing." Her low self-esteem eventually led to her decision to study abroad, to prove that she could perform as well as her sister. As she recalled,

…my sister…went to the U.S. I want to be as good as her. So, I think being able to go abroad and study it is kind of proof of my capability of doing things which is as good as hers. You know, in Chinese family the parents, my parents are very traditional parents. They care too much about how my kids will be able to do and grade or ranks and they will compare their kids to other kids…Like my sister is a very excellent girl academically…and she was always…the top one in her class…. my parents assumed that I should be as good as she is. However, I was not.… It really made me very uncomfortable. I feel I cannot do very well or as good as my sister is. So, I wanted to do something to improve.

Ya-Chi's descriptions of herself prior to coming to the United States emphasized what she was not, not like her sister and not highly ranked in the school system. Her explicit self-ascriptions for this period foreground undesirable attributes and a desire to self-realize in order to prove herself. She decided to study abroad to show she was not as her Chinese family and peers regarded her, or as she thought they regarded her.

Ya-Chi pursued her M.A. degree in Teaching English to Speakers of Other Languages (TESOL) for its popularity in China and for her desire to improve her English. She explained this in the following passage:

> …It's kind of a popular thing to do to go abroad after graduation in Chinese Mainland.… By the way, my major was English and I wanted to practice my English and use it because I didn't feel very well about my English proficiency after my graduation from college. I didn't think I could do anything with that in Chinese mainland especially teaching in a grammar-translation approach. That is so stupid I feel. So, I wanted to improve my English.

Ya-Chi was unhappy teaching English with a grammar-translation approach. She was dissatisfied being an EFL teacher, being in the Chinese community of EFL teachers. She went to the U.S. to pursue self-realization, proving herself by bringing out more of her potentialities.

After coming to the U.S., Ya-Chi gradually gained confidence and began to take pride in her traditional Chinese female identity. As she said,

> Very passive. [Laughter] I can appreciate some good things about being a Chinese. For example, I saw Chinese ladies more…kind of reserved. But I appreciate kind of the reserve-ness. It's got a kind of beauty so I think I have kind of beauty so I'm pretty proud. [Laughter as if embarrassed]…Some of my characteristics which are also very typical Chinese characteristics. For example, I am kind of modest or maybe not very confident in that way. I am kind of Chinese in language education is kind of very unique because we value diversity so each culture can contribute to this diversity. I think I am one of them.

Ya-Chi used such positive words as "appreciate," "reserved," and "beautiful" to express her pride as a typical, traditional Chinese female. Being a Chinese woman became a distinctive identity to foreground only when in the United States, where the dominant culture is not Chinese. Ya-Chi differentiated herself implicitly from other nontypical and/or nontraditional women, and from Western women. She could individuate in this way, once she moved out of China to the West.

Ya-Chi is also proud of her teacher identity. As a CFL teacher, her career identity is congruent with her more general identifications, and she feels that she is good as a teacher of this subject. She is a valuable and also unique person in the United States, receiving positive recognition for these things. Ya-Chi said she envisions herself as a cultural ambassador or "cultural transferer," as she would like to share "the Chinese beauty" to the world, suggesting that she transcended her previous diffidence in EFL and that her uniqueness and self-worth were recognized and reaffirmed in CFL.

Ya-Chi's struggles as a CFL teacher led her to distinguish herself as one kind of CFL teacher within a set of other types. She calls herself a "pedagogy person" rather than a "literature" or "linguistics" person. As she explained,

> I learned TESOL. I learned some teaching strategies of language but actually those strategies are applicable in some other contexts. They could be useful in teaching English and Chinese. But most of the teachers I know who are teaching Chinese are not pedagogy persons.... They didn't learn a lot of strategies. They didn't learn about language teaching. Some of them are literature persons. Some of them are linguistics persons. They are very knowledgeable in the linguistic aspects of things and also literature things. But I am a pedagogy person.... But my advantage is that I learned some strategies that I use in the English class which can also be used in my Chinese as a foreign-language class and it is effective, absolutely. They are very effective in helping my students with learning and that is very satisfactory. In fact, it is very good.... So, when I found that using my way of teaching can be more helpful than the other teachers'. See! Comparison! That's too bad!.

Ya-Chi ends this talk by reflecting on what she just did, which was to compare herself to others with herself comparing favorably, and then she affirms her self-assessment after demonstrating awareness of it. She shows herself beyond a "me" claim she just made, shows this by demonstrating her understanding of a criticism that could be made of such a claim (because, for one thing, she was very critical of the ranking system in China), and then reaffirms that same "me" claim. This is an excellent example of second negation in identity claiming. The result of these movements is an I-me formation that clearly distinguishes "I" from "me" while also fully affirming the "me."

Ya-Chi differentiated herself in first-negation modes from other teachers (that is, a linguistic or a literature person) by identifying herself as a "pedagogy person"; she claimed that she was not a linguistics person nor a literature person, but a pedagogy person in TESOL, transferable to CFL.

Ya-Chi experiences herself radiating, fully and happily expressed, in CFL teaching. But she feels inadequacies still as a teacher educator as well as a non-native teacher in a foreign land, for want of experience. She talked about this as follows:

> [Sigh] I have so little experiences. I still—I don't think—If I were the curriculum designer of this course, I probably would not ask a non-native speaker with no experiences to teach this course.... Because experience is really important, especially the cultural. You do not share a lot in common with your students.

The self-affirming sense of who she is as a Chinese woman and a good CFL teacher make it possible for her to distance her identity attachments from these inadequacies. She uses a psychological theory, a theory of habits that work autonomously from one's identity, to achieve this detached and rational perspective on aspects of herself.

> ...I'm not very confident some of the times because I'm always thinking I'm not as good as others. That has become a kind of habit. That is really bad because when I was a little child I always had this kind of feeling that I'm not as good as others. Or I'm not as good as my sister or the other kids. This kind of thought is engraved in my mind.... So, probably because of that, I decided to go abroad. I was very determined to go abroad, to go to the U.S. to prove that I am not that bad. I still can go to the U.S. and study and things like that.

Finally, again, Ya-Chi's sense of pride, fulfillment, and enthusiasm for her future career, and love of what she does, all of which are in stark contrast to how she described her years in China, really stand out among the participants in this study. Describing herself now and looking towards the future, Ya-Chi distinguished herself from others as someone who is unusually fortunate:

…I KNOW what I want to do and that is a big thing in my life. Not everybody knows what they want to do in life. I like to be a teacher. I enjoy teaching things. I particularly enjoy teaching Chinese as a foreign language and because that made me feel very passionate. I know I can make a living by doing that. That is fortunate for me, compared to other people who can also earn a lot of money but do not like what they are doing.… I know what I'm doing and what I really like.…

	"Me" Structures	Contrasts	Key Structures	Transcending Claims
WAS	Social positioning by Chinese School System Ranking I was **not** — Like my sister; Well ranked in examination system (Unnoticed) I **was** Chinese		My ranking versus ranking of my sister and others she represents	
		Temporal contrast was, positioned by system; becoming, my own director; (self-relation contrasts)	Potential/actual	Director of life, I can become more
AFTER MOVE TO U.S.	*Conjunction of negatives structure*: Novice AI, **AND** Inexperienced AI, **AND** Not comprehending new culture	Horizontal explicit negatives	Experience/ inexperience; Foreigner/native	

Figure 11: Ya-Chi Structures and Transcendence in Life Story (pg. 1)

	Positive self-constructed "me" contrast structure; "I'm a good teacher":	Discovered or invented "me" structural distinction with horizontal contrasts	Types of EFL and CFL teachers	Self-definer or discoverer
GENERATION OR DISCOVERY OF "ME" STRUCTURES	I am not a literature or linguistics person | But I am a pedagogy person			
AND BECAME	Nested Identity Structure — A proud Chinese Woman and a person who knows what she wants and a person who does what she wants — A Chinese as a foreign-language teacher	Self-realizing New Audience is U.S. student population Some nesting	Past self and social world/ New self and social world Chinese/U.S.; "I" and I affirm as myself	Self-discoverer and realizer; Aware of Chinese/ U.S. cultural differences and chooses, endorses, affirms Chinese

Figure 11: Ya-Chi Structures and Transcendence in Life Story (pg. 2)

Part III: Concluding Comments

Within many qualitative research communities and cultural anthropology as a whole, terms used in this chapter act like triggers for quick dismissal. Examples include "transcending," "autonomy," "self-realizing," and "self-actualizing." Why has it become so popular to dismiss theory that takes subjectivity, the subject, personhood, consciousness, and similar terms to be nonreducible to something objective? Scientific materialists have long argued in favor of this reduction and continue to do so today. The growing field of cognitive science is dominated by the reductionist view. Those who work within and endorse postmodern and poststructuralist discourses make up large percentages of the qualitative research community and faculty working in cultural anthropology, women's studies, critical race studies, and cultural studies. Most of these people object to the reductionist view of cognitive scientists and scientific materialists (subjectivity, self, intentionality are all reducible to brain states); yet much the same figure of thought is employed when subjectivity, intentionality, autonomy, selfhood, and so on are reduced to an objectified conceptualization of power, of discourses, of texts. Instead of matter and the laws of physics, everything is reduced to discourse practices and power as if these things were very much like physical forces of nature.

Our chapter presents some theory about human identity that takes the vocabulary of subjectivity to be nonreducible and to be about crucially important aspects of human existence and life. The theory can be easily located with a communicative action framework, which avoids both the errors of the philosophy of the subject and of efforts to reduce everything to one form of objectivity or another. In fact, the theory presented here owes much to George Herbert Mead, Jurgen Habermas, and Robert Brandom, each of whom have recognized important insights in the classical works of Kant, Fichte, Schelling, early Marx, and others.

Popular doctrines about human identity and selfhood now include two related themes: "the subject is dead" and human identity is nonintegral, multiple, and fractured. The communicative action framework used in this chapter reinterprets both of these themes in terms of identity claiming. With human identity as a chronic process of making identity claims, it is easy to understand fractured and multiple selves in terms of inconsistent patterns of "me" claiming. It is not hard to reinterpret the "death of the subject" as a death of the idea of a finitely determinable universal form that all human selves are, or have. The reinterpretations are important because they preserve those insights that have emerged in Western philosophy from Kant through Sartre, and that argue against scientific materialism and reductionism, positivism and physicalism. The "I" of human selfhood cannot be reduced to any objective form. It was not "invented" during some late period of Western history (simply reading ancient texts from the Greeks, Romans, Indians, and Chinese will make this obvious). It is presupposed, in fact, in all knowledge claims, all theories, all communications including those that seek to deny it or reduce it. But the "I" is not an entity. The "I" has a mode of existence that differs from the way we normally regard the existence of physical objects and states. The "I" claims itself and then distinguishes itself from its claims. This chapter was an effort to delimit a number of arguments about human identity in relation to the negative and (but less fundamentally) narrative unity; and then to explore those arguments by examining qualitative data. We think more studies can be done on this to improve and develop our understanding of human identity and how to analyze it in qualitative research.

Notes

1. When the word "positive" is used in this chapter, it will mean something that an actor and/or knower can relate herself to, in distinction from "it," from the perceived object, the thought, the emotion, the memory, etc., unless we qualify use of the word to make it clear that it means something good in distinction from something bad. Anything that can be represented as distinct from an actor and/or knower from that actor's, and/or knower's first person position, is "positive." The terms "negative" and "negation" have their meanings in contrast with this sense of "positive."

2. There have been some discussions and disputes over whether or not human actions and interactions fundamentally enact narrative forms. Czarniawska writes, "life might or might not be an enacted narrative but conceiving of it as such provides a rich source of insight" (2004, p. 3). We find that narrative forms crop up implicitly when actions are self-monitored, and because self-monitoring is chronic to human action, narrative forms will sometimes guide an interactive sequence with all participants implicitly understanding and contributing to a story structure. But this is most definitely not always the case; self-monitoring will often result in different implicit possible narratives (ways the actor could explain the act to others) from moment to moment.

3. The idea of "transcendental" is not very popular within a number of trendy academic discourses at this time. But this seems to be due to misunderstandings of what the word means: it does not mean essence, nor a kind of mysterious entity, nor anything composed of a sort of substance. It means a condition for entities, essences, substances, etc.; that which specifically is not captured by such concepts and that such concepts must be distinguished from to have the sense they do. "Transcendental" references what cannot have a positive form of any sort but what at bottom all positive forms are distinguished from to be positive. It cannot be pictured. No image works for it. This is the point of departure for our use of "transcending," and our use will further develop the idea contextually.

4. Thus the postulated entities used in models by physical scientists are in the end metaphorical constructions based on what can be seen, touched, grasped, and so on. Energy, force fields, subatomic particles are postulated in models and then tested by making predictions. Each such postulated entity is like something that can be present to consciousness.

5. The footnote on the same page contains a well-articulated commentary by Theodore Kisiel, giving more clarity to the expression "living in the truth" and relating Heidegger's discussion of it in this text, *History of the Concept of Time* (1985) to his development of it later in *Being and Time* (1962).

6. Our summaries and paraphrases of aspects of Hegel's philosophy all come from *The Phenomenology of Spirit* (Hegel, 1977).

7. Not all people concern themselves too much, as adults, with the feelings possible other subjects have of them. The uncertainty of one's self and self-worth can take a variety of forms via developmental processes and can be framed within religious terms as well, where we may have an ultimate Other Subject position (God, monotheistic religions), a practice designed to learn how to consistently let go of all forms of concern for recognition (Buddhism and similar traditions), an ultimate Other Subject that is really an abstract generalized other projected into the future, and various other configurations as well.

8. We can extend the analysis to being in more passive mode and receiving a meaningful act from another. We will not take up more space to do that in this chapter, but the analysis would include our theory of meaning, which is that of having "next acts" on hand in relation to an act addressed to a second person whose position we are either in or can position-take with (as in reading or observing others interact).

9. In some of Habermas's essays published together as *Postmetaphysical Thinking* (1988), as well as in Chapter 3 in volume one of his *The Theory of Communicative Action* (1984), there are compelling arguments about the illocutionary significance of human identity, the "practical" sense in which people use the words "I" and "me" rather than the "epistemic" sense. The practical identity claim is claiming to be "such and such kind of person," in our own terminology, in relation and as a commitment to those with whom we interact. This is very insightful on Habermas's part and it improves on the mainly epistemic treatment of self-reflection we find in Hegel and other German Idealist philosophers. Connections between the practical and the epistemic self-relation can be explored, but this is another fascinating and potentially important theoretical concern that we have no room to explore in this chapter.

10. This double analysis of both what was said and what was conveyed in the way it was said resembles the notion of stories within stories discussed by Czarniawska (2004; and see White, 1973, who implicitly exemplifies the same thing).

11. The capitalized words indicate amplifying volume as if a participant emphasized them or made a contrast.

12. The words in italics are those that I summarized or paraphrased for the tape was incomprehensible, but all of these italicized were confirmed by my participants.

References

Brandom, R. (1994). *Making it explicit: Reasoning, representing, and discursive commitment.* Cambridge, MA: Harvard University Press.

Carspecken, P. F. (1996). *Critical ethnography in educational research: A theoretical and practical guide.* New York: Routledge.

Carspecken, P. F. (1999a). There is no such thing as "critical ethnography": A historical discussion and an outline of one critical methodological theory. *Studies in Educational Ethnography, 2,* 29–55.

Carspecken, P. F. (1999b). *Four scenes for posing the question of meaning and other essays in critical philosophy and critical methodology.* New York: Peter Lang.

Carspecken, P. F. (2003). Ocularcentrism, phonocentrism, and the counter-enlightenment problematic: Clarifying contested terrain in our schools of education. *Teachers College Record, 105*(6), 978–1047.

Christman, J. (2004). Narrative unity as a condition of personhood. *Metaphilosophy, 35*(5), 695–713.

Clandinin, J. (2007). *Handbook of narrative inquiry: Mapping a methodology.* Thousand Oaks, CA: Sage.

Clandinin, J. D., & Connelly, M. F. (2000). *Narrative inquiry: Experience and story in qualitative research.* San Francisco, CA: Jossey-Bass.

Czarniawska, B. (2004). *Narratives in social science research.* London: Sage.

Foucault, M. (1965). *Madness and civilization: A history of insanity in the Age of Reason.* New York: Vintage Press.

Foucault, M. (1973) *The Birth of the Clinic: An Archeology of Medical Perception.* London: Tavistock Publications Limited.

Gardner, S. (2009). *Sartre's being and nothingness.* New York: Continuum International.

Habermas, J. (1968). *Knowledge and human interests.* (J. Shaprio, Trans.). Boston: Beacon.

Habermas, J. (1984). *The theory of communicative action.* Vol. 1: *Reason and the rationalization of society.*. (T. McCarthy, Trans.). Boston: Beacon.

Habermas, J. (1987). *The theory of communicative action.* Vol. 2: *Lifeworld and system. A critique of functionalist reason.* (T. McCarthy, Trans.). Boston: Beacon.

Habermas, J. (1988/1992). *Postmetaphysical thinking: Philosophical essays.* (W. M. Hohengarten, Trans.) Cambridge, MA: MIT Press.

Hegel, G. W. F. (1977). *Phenomenology of spirit.* (A. V. Miller, Trans.). Oxford: Oxford University Press.

Heidegger, M. (1962). *Being and time.* (Macquarrie & Robinson, Trans.) San Francisco, CA: Harper.

Heidegger, M. (1985). *History of the concept of time.* Bloomington: Indiana University Press.

Huang, Y. (2008). *Understanding international graduate instructors: A narrative critical ethnography.* Unpublished doctoral dissertation, Indiana University, Bloomington.

Hyppolite, J. (1974). *Genesis and structure of Hegel's Phenomenology of Spirit.* Evanston, IL: Northwestern University Press.

MacIntyre, A. (1981). *After virtue.* Notre Dame, IN: University of Notre Dame Press.

Mead, G. (1934). *Mind, self and society.* Chicago: University of Chicago Press.

Ochs, E., & Capps, L. (2001). *Living narrative: Creating lives in everyday storytelling.* Cambridge, MA: Harvard University Press.

Polkinghorne, D. E. (1988). *Narrative knowing and the human sciences.* Albany: State University of New York Press.

White, H. (1973). *Metahistory: The historical imagination in nineteenth-century Europe.* Baltimore, MD: Johns Hopkins University Press.

CHAPTER FOURTEEN

Performance-Centered Research

From Theory to Critical Inquiry

CORINNE DATCHI

Since the early 1980s, critical ethnographers have tested radical ways to bridge the gap between science and social advocacy. Using performance as a research paradigm, they have started to rethink ontological and epistemological questions about the world, knowledge, inquiry methods, and the relationship between the observer and the observed in ethnography. Performance-centered research rests on a set of values, for instance, intimacy and involvement, that depart from the standards of distance and detachment between self and other in traditional ethnography. It also involves the redefinition of ethnographic fieldwork as a collaborative process of sensuous knowing wherein the researcher and the participants are co-performers in the enactment of cultural practices (Denzin, 2003; Conquergood, 2006). Performance-centered research emphasizes the centrality of the body as the means by which the ethnographer comes into contact with others.

In the past two decades, critical ethnographers have also begun to use performance as a way of reporting their embodied experience of others, thus departing from the dominant textual practices of academic research (Denzin, 2003; Alexander, 2005). As a method of representation, performances function to create a space where oppressed communities tell their stories in their own voice and thereby exercise citizenship (Olomo, 2006). They bring to light the relation between performativity and agency, or individuals' creative participation in the enactment of everyday life practices, social roles, and cultural scripts (McCall, 2000; Hamera, 2006). It is this relation between performativity and agency that I propose to unpack here, using ethnographically informed methods of inquiry to study the interactions of two psychotherapy dyads over the course of six individual counseling sessions.

Performativity

Theories of performativity make a distinction between being and doing, between the material reality of bodies and the performative expectations associated with race, gender, class, and sexuality in particular communities (Butler, 1990; Denzin, 2003; Halberstam, 2004; Jackson, 2004). For example, doing whiteness is separate from being white to the extent that it corresponds to the behavioral manifestation of the social value and meaning given to white skin (Alexander, 2004). The disarticulation of being and doing makes it possible to illuminate the performative nature of identity and to show that being/identity is a function of doing/performance, and vice versa. This recursive relation between being and doing may be most evident in the self-presentation of transgendered individuals whose enactment of masculinity and femininity often involve shaping or transforming the material reality of the body through the use of hormones and plastic surgery.

In making a distinction between being and doing, theories of performativity situate identities within a context-dependent network of social discourses, and describe how performances of self both participate in and challenge the reproduction of the gendered, sexual, raced organization of the lifeworld. Specifically, Butler (1990) suggests that individual identities develop from a continuous process of self-presentation wherein individuals strive to duplicate normative ideals of gender. She argues that gender ideals are a fantasy; that gender is both the process and outcome of the act of duplicating these ideals; and that the repetition of the performative act of making copies creates the illusion of origin and naturalness. Gender performances produce and establish sex as the biological nature of gendered subjects; they are the "discursive/cultural means by which sexed nature or a natural sex is produced and established as prediscursive, prior to the culture" (Butler, 1990, p. 7). However, gender is not the cultural expression of a sexual essence, and subjects do not exist prior to gender; they are constituted as gendered subjects through gender performances. Likewise, Halberstam (2004, p. 52) uses the term "real" to describe "that which exists elsewhere as a fantasy of belonging and being" and the term "realness" to refer to the "appropriation of the attributes of the real." The real (or the origin) is an ideal of being. Realness (or the copy) results from individuals' attempts to bring about the ideal. Realness is always an approximation of the real. The copy is never perfectly identical to the origin. It follows that the act of making copies simultaneously contributes to the reproduction and revision of the social discourses that establish specific forms of heterosexuality, femininity, masculinity, and whiteness as standards of being. Indeed, if the repetition of the act of imitating the real creates an effect of continuity and naturalness that conceal power relations and facilitate their reproduction, then repetition is essential to the reproduction of the ideals that the social system maintains in the form of institutions (e.g., heterosexual marriage). It also requires that individuals be granted the freedom to participate in the reproduction of the origin or the real; that is, that they exercise agency or their capacity for action.

The repetition of the act of duplicating the real is a communicative and interactional process wherein individuals do race and gender in relation to others. As copies of the original, performances of self produce an identity that is thinkable and namable and therefore legitimate and acceptable by others in specific cultural contexts (Jackson, 2004). When performances deviate from normative standards of being, they challenge the current conditions of intelligibility, and call for the reconfiguration of cultural matrices of meanings. In sum, the performative repetition of the act of making copies involves the possibility of modifying the normative standards of being that make identities intelligible, thinkable, and namable, in ways that could alter the raced, gendered, and sexual organization of face-to-face interactions in the lifeworld.

Using the principles discussed above, I will now look at the interactions of two psychotherapy dyads over the course of six individual counseling sessions. I plan to demonstrate how the performance paradigm makes it possible to highlight the cultural conditions and discursive background that provide a con/text[1] for the experience of the participants' identity in the counseling relationship. Psychotherapy has been defined as a process of social influence whereby counselors first create relational conditions that enable them to have an impact on clients' attitudes, expectations, and attributions (Strong, 1968; Schmidt & Strong, 1970; Strong & Dixon, 1971; Corrigan, Dell, Lewis, & Schmidt, 1980; Goodyear & Robyak, 1981; Dorn, 1984, 1986; Claiborn & Lichtenberg, 1989). The social influence model of counseling explains that counselors must occupy a dominant position in the therapeutic relationship to successfully modify clients' cognitions and improve their psychological, emotional, and behavioral functioning. It also posits that counselors derive their ability to influence from five bases of social power, and thus highlights yet does not elaborate on the idea that the social context may determine the relational process of change in psychotherapy (Goodyear & Robyak, 1981). I here propose a performative view of psychotherapy that builds upon the postulates of the social-influence model and specifically the assumption that individuals engage in presentations of self that aim at controlling others' perception of the social environment. I will argue that the counselor and the client engage in performances of self that serve to establish and support their position of authority with regard to the act of storying the self in psychotherapy. I purposely use the word "authority" in lieu of "influence" to suggest that the counselor and the client make claims about their position of authorship and ownership with regard to the narrative that develops from their conversation. I will focus on the performative aspect of the counselor and the client's interactions; that is, emphasize the cultural conditions of their presentation of self and examine how they repeatedly instantiate normative ideals of gender in ways that mobilize agency in the service of social reproduction. I also will consider the counselor and the client's capacity to establish a critical relation to the gender ideals they invoke and emulate.

To study the con/text or discursive background of the therapeutic interactions, I have built a monological and dialogical record based on my direct observations and interviews of an African American female counselor, Josephine, and her two Caucasian female clients, Clara and Sophie, using the methodology detailed by Phil Carspecken (1996) in *Critical Ethnography in Educational Research: A Theoretical and Practical Guide*. This methodology includes procedures of data interpretation, namely, the analysis of interactive sequences and the reconstruction of meaning fields wherein the participants' interactions are embedded, that serve to highlight the patterns of the therapeutic relationship; the position the counselor and the client create for themselves in the relationship; and their repeated instantiation of normative ideals.

Interactive sequences are characterized by people's agreement on the purpose, norms, and values that guide their activities. The beginning of a sequence is typified by the act of making a bid about the organization of the interactions. The act of making a bid often corresponds to individuals' attempt to create a different position for themselves in the relationship. The meaning field represents the range of possible meanings that are associated with individuals' actions. It also comprises individuals' claims about reality, which can be organized into four interconnected categories: objective, subjective, normative-evaluative, and identity claims. These claims say something about the norms, values, beliefs, and standards of being that individuals foreground and background as they negotiate their position in relation to each other; their analysis brings to light the counselor and the client's performances of self in the context of individual psychotherapy.

What follows is a description of the participants and a summary of the concerns that brought Clara and Sophie to counseling, which I provide to facilitate the reading of the subsequent analyses. The counselor, Josephine, is a first-year graduate student in her mid-20s enrolled in a counseling practicum class at a midwestern university. She describes her theoretical orientation as eclectic and primarily informed by interactional theories of counseling. The clients, Clara and Sophie, are in their early 20s. They come from the same region and socioeconomic background, and present different concerns ranging from relational conflict to symptoms of anxiety. Sophie is involved in a same-sex relationship, and Clara is single. Both Sophie and Clara work one or several jobs, and share a living space with relatives or friends.

Sophie seeks professional help to sort out her feelings and thoughts about her current romantic relationship. Dissatisfied, depressed, and stuck, she is eager to learn new ways of interacting with her partner, Anne. In counseling, she discusses how her economic situation limits her capacity to make choices; she talks about not having health insurance, stable employment, or enough money to take her partner out. Sophie is a self-employed massage therapist and a nanny. She works for a same-sex family, and looks after their 8-year-old son in exchange for room and board. In the course of psychotherapy, she explores her feelings about her employers' way of life, their parenting practices, and gendered behaviors. She also examines her beliefs about the nature of care.

Clara enters counseling upon the recommendation of her family. She is looking for assistance in making the transition from the rural hometown she has just left to start a new life free of drugs and alcohol. In counseling, she talks about the person she used to be (that is, a shopaholic, a kleptomaniac, a drug addict, a school dropout, and the child of alcoholic parents), and describes her efforts to make new friends in a new place, to keep a job, and to go to college. She also examines the characteristics of her relationship with men, and expresses her indignation with regard to daily acts of sexism.

The Performative Act of Storying the Self in Psychotherapy

In their interview, both Sophie and Clara make claims about their position of autonomy and authority with regard to the therapeutic conversation. In particular, they report making a mental plan of the conversation and selecting topics for discussion prior to their meeting with Josephine. They bring to counseling chosen elements of their experience that they highlight, recount, and weave into a story of the self that develops from their efforts to make meaning of their experience. From the therapeutic conversation, I have selected passages that illustrate the performative nature of the act of storying the self. Storying the self is performative to the extent that Clara and Sophie not only tell about, but also enact who they are and conjure up their lifeworld. It is an act of doing as well as an act of showing who one is, that both informs and is informed by the storying of the self. Hereafter, I use the words "re-present" and "re-presentation" in reference to the descriptive and creative quality of the act of storying the self, which both presents what is and produces a copy of what is.

In every session I observed, Sophie and Clara summon the presence of their peers, partners, colleagues, and relatives, by quoting their words, speaking their voices, and re-presenting past conversations. In so doing, they create a space within the boundaries of the therapeutic setting where they are the narrator and actor of the story of the self and where the counselor is an interactive audience of the client's re-presentation. In the example below, Clara tells about an instant-messaging conversation she had with her friend Dylan. She re-enacts the online talk in front of an attentive audience who nods, laughs, and frowns:

> **CLARA:** Because in a way, I'm kind of thinking he wants me to make him, *[Clara turns her left hand towards her and puts it on her chest]* he's trying to make me jealous. *[Josephine nods and says mm-mh.]* Mm, jealous of what? *[Josephine laughs.]* You know. And mm, *[Clara is looking down with her left fist on her mouth]* we kind of started talking, oh, he was like, he wrote me that he had a dream, he was like: *[Moving her head back and stretching her left arm with her hand open]* "I had a dream about you. We were making out the whole time. That's all we did. And I love you." Mm. Okay. *[Looking at Josephine. Josephine's head is tilted to the right.]* "You're crazy, you're beautiful, and I love you." I was like: "Okay." That just freaked me out. *[Josephine nods. She is frowning.]* So, I wrote him. *[Turning her head to the right, raising her chin towards the ceiling]* I was like: "That was a really weird dream you had." I was like: "You know. Why did you have that dream?" *[Clara scratches her right cheek with her right hand.]* And I told him, I was like: "You know. *[Clara is gesturing with her hands. She seems to be counting on the fingers of her left hand. Her right hand is tapping the fingers of her left hand. Josephine is nodding.]* I can't think about having a boyfriend or *[There is a laughter in Clara's voice]* having a lover on the side or anything like that. I can't think of anything about that right now. *[Josephine says mm-mh. Clara puts her left hand on the armrest. She is now tapping the armrest with her left hand while she is speaking.]* Like I'm sorry if it sounds selfish, but I want to focus on work, *[Josephine nods]* I want to focus on school and I want to focus on getting my bills paid. That's it."

As Clara re-presents her conversation with Dylan, she makes claims about her self and her commitment to change. She communicates that she is a responsible and ambitious person who works hard to pay her bills and to get an education. She also projects an image of self that describes her as astute, experienced, honest, and assertive. It seems that her position as narrator and actor of the story of the self gives her the authority she needs to take a stand about the kind of person she is.

Like Clara, Sophie re-presents her interactions with others in ways that summon their presence in the room. In the quotation that follows, she recounts the details of a past conversation with her partner, Anne, and directly refers to her role of narrator and actor, when she interjects "I lost my line, I lost the story":

> **SOPHIE:** [...] We were talking about power: "Well, give me some." And she was like: "You've got to take it." And mm. I lost my line. I lost the story. Oh. "Give me some of the power." And she's like: "Well, you've got to take it back. I can't just give it to you." And she said: "You have got to." I've got to start showing her who I am and start trusting her. And that's the only way that I'm going to get more equal power. *[Josephine says mm and clears her throat.]* 'Cause she feels like I don't show her who I really am. [...] I think she wouldn't like me if I showed her all of who I was.

As Sophie speaks Anne's voice, she takes at least two positions, hers and Anne's, a first-person and third-person position with respect to the re-presentation of the past. In other words, she tells the story of her relationship with Anne from at least two perspectives. She also re-enacts the conversation in a somewhat impassive manner: Neither smiling nor frowning, her face is without a distinct expression and her voice sounds flat and monotone, as if she had put her feelings aside. It is possible that Sophie's impassivity and multiple positions in the re-presentation of the conversation serve to support the truthfulness of her story by communicating that the client is able to suspend judgment and to look at facts objectively. In other words, the act of quoting others may correspond to Sophie and Clara's efforts to establish the authenticity and legitimacy of the story they tell, by taking both a first-person and third-person position with respect to oneself in the storying process.

Josephine contributes in varying forms and degrees to the performative act of telling who the client is. In the next passage, she participates in the narrative process by speaking Sophie's voice:

> **JOSEPHINE:** I'd like to point out that you're talking differently about your relationship now. *[Gesturing with both hands]* That the way you were talking about your relationship in the beginning was like: "We're staying together. We're together. We're together. It feels funny. I don't understand why it feels this way, but we're together. We're together. We're together." Today there is a shift. *[Sophie says mm.]* And you're telling me: "I want to break up with her. I just don't know how. And I don't understand why I feel like I need to stay in it." But you're speaking a lot more directly about the concept of waking up.

Josephine describes the client's internal experience as if she were the client: She shows Sophie sorting out her thoughts and emotions, struggling to make meaning of her internal process and to take actions, and working her way towards greater self-congruence. In so doing, she re-stories the client's experience and draws upon the theory that the authentic self is dormant inside the person and that change is a function of genuineness and self-awareness ("the concept of waking up"): Now that Sophie is paying attention to her feelings, she can act in ways that are true to her self, rather than go by the injunction "We're together, we're together." In reply, Sophie proposes to interpret her own actions, and thus resume a position of narrative authority at the same time as she rejects Josephine's bid to influence the storying of the self. In every session, Sophie maintains a dominant position with respect to the act of highlighting and weaving selected elements of her experience into a coherent and meaningful story; she changes the topic of the conversation and challenges Josephine's interpretations, thereby setting limits on the counselor's contribution to the narrative process. A similar pattern describes Josephine and Clara's interactions. Again and again, Josephine joins Clara in the process of storying the self by highlighting chosen elements of the client's story, by describing the client's internal experience, and by sharing her definition of the client's situation. When Josephine foregrounds her voice and gives her opinion, Clara changes the topic of the conversation and challenges the counselor's interpretations, as if these were perceived as a threat to the client's ability to story the self into a narrative that may enable her to accomplish her project of being. In the example that follows, Josephine participates in the storying of the client's new friendship by re-presenting Clara's lifeworld:

> **CLARA:** […] But, he was just kind of weird, *[Josephine scratches her chin]* 'cause *[Josephine says mm-mh]* like even my friends back home, if I had something like [the mouth problem I have now], they wouldn't be like: "Oh, I'm so worried about you."

> **JOSEPHINE:** *[Left hand is open, moving as she speaks]* Well, and any friend who's just a friend, *[Clara says mm-mh]*, I'm sure their reactions would be more like...

> **CLARA:** "That sucks."

> **JOSEPHINE:** *[Immediately after Clara]* "That sucks."

> **CLARA:** *[Laughing and nodding]* Yeah.

JOSEPHINE: "Call me when you can talk."

CLARA: *[Laughing]* Yeah.

JOSEPHINE: *[Laughing]* You know. Or like "I can bring you food." But it wouldn't be like *[In a lower and softer tone of voice, head moving to the side]*: "I'm so worried about you. I'm really concerned." [...]

CLARA: *[In a low tone of voice]* I know. That's why I felt, I felt so crappy when I kissed him. *[Josephine nods.]* You know. Damn. *[Clara is playing with a strand of hair, pulls her hair back, tapping her fingers as if counting]* I shouldn't have done that, you know. *[Buries her face in her hands.]*

JOSEPHINE: *[Making swinging movement with her foot]* Yeah, because that communicated what?

CLARA: That I like him.

JOSEPHINE: Right

CLARA: Well, more than a friend.

JOSEPHINE: More than a friend.

CLARA: Yeah. But I don't know. [...]

When Josephine quotes Clara and Dylan, she takes a position of influence with respect to the storying of the self by becoming the narrator and actor of the client's story. Her re-presentation of Dylan's concerns highlights the presence *in potentia* of alternative stories that are different from, yet connected with the story that Clara brings to counseling, to the extent that they inform the definition of Dylan and Clara's relationship: stories of real friendships, stories of deception and honesty, and stories of women's relationship with men. When Clara responds "that sucks" or "more than a friend," she anticipates what Josephine is about to say, and acknowledges the stories *in potentia*, at the same time as she foregrounds her voice and maintain a position of narrative authority. On the one hand, she agrees with Josephine that friends do not worry as much as Dylan says he does. On the other, she challenges Josephine's re-presentation of Dylan and Clara's friendship and disowns the narrative that develops from their conversation: the statement "But I don't know" indicates that she rejects the storyline that Josephine offers, that is, the idea that she might have been ambiguous with Dylan, or that she might have been duped, or remotely that as a woman she occupies a vulnerable position in the relationship. Indeed, Clara goes on to explain that she posted a message on MySpace that clarified her intent to remain single. She signifies that she is aware of Dylan's objectives and that she is not a fool. However, she admits: "I felt so crappy when I kissed him. Damn. I shouldn't have done that." Her confession takes on a dramatic aspect as she buries her face in her hands, a gesture that conveys remorse, embarrassment, and shame, and that says something about the person she is (that is, she takes responsibility for her mistakes; she acknowledges that it's wrong to deceive people; she is sincere and honest). As Clara performs the act of being genuinely sorry for kissing Dylan, she engages in a dramatic self-presentation that serves to establish the veracity and legitimacy of her identity claims and that enables her to take a stand with regard to who she is. Her performance of self also affirms her authority with respect to the therapeutic narrative that develops from the act of storying the self in the context of the counseling interactions. The therapeutic narrative overlaps with the story that she brings to counseling to the extent that it shares similar units of meaning. However, it is not the client's story. It unfolds as the client and the counselor call upon stories *in potentia* that the client owns or rejects.

Thus far, I have discussed how Sophie and Clara defend their authority and autonomy with respect to the act of storying the self in psychotherapy: They select stories *in potentia* that best re-present their personal experience. As they weave chosen elements of their experience into a story of the self, they compete with Josephine for a position of greater influence as to the production of meaning and the development of the therapeutic narrative. When Josephine describes her view of the problem, the clients respond in ways that suggest the story is theirs: They foreground their sense of ownership and affirm their narrative authority by speaking the voice of others and by re-presenting their lifeworld. In sum, it is through the performative act of storying the self that Clara and Sophie exercise their capacity to realize their project of being within the boundaries of the social con/text of the performance. I will now consider the extent to which this con/text circumscribes the act of storying the self in psychotherapy.

The Imperative of Genuineness

Sophie and Clara describe counseling as a process in which they lay out their feelings, thoughts, mistakes, and "all the little things that [they] store inside." They use words and phrases (for example, "putting everything on the table," "laying it all out," "purging") that define the act of telling about the self as an externalizing process akin to a confession and an act of cleansing. In addition, they associate this externalizing process with the concept of truthfulness. For example, Sophie suggests that therapeutic change depends on the client's ability to be completely honest and true to herself. Yet, she also recognizes the limits of sincerity and genuineness: "You have friends that you're not completely honest with. I mean you're not completely honest with yourself either." She intimates that individuals may be so engrossed in the management of impression ("saying something because of the way that it sounds or mm the way you think someone will take it") that they may not have the ability to tell the authentic from the fake. How then do clients achieve truthfulness in counseling?

Sophie and Clara attribute clients' genuine presentation of self to the counselor's perceived objectivity. They describe Josephine as an "outside party who actually knows that she's saying something that pertains to me" and "who sees everything objectively." They suggest that the counselor has access to the clients' true experience because she is a stranger who is not involved in the clients' daily life. Josephine concurs that she has the capacity to hear what is not said and to perceive the truth that is buried in the clients' story: "If they're saying something completely different, but what they, I know what they're *really* saying [italics added]." She also talks about her efforts to be impartial, to "set her filters down on the side," and to "turn off her judgmental [self] and just be open" as she enters the room. In sum, Josephine, Clara, and Sophie imply that the doing of genuineness is a relational process through which the clients accomplish their project of authenticity (i.e., to be true to oneself). They also suggest that authenticity is a function of objectivity and truthfulness (i.e., to be honest). Last but not least, they emphasize the objective, truthful, and authentic aspects of the therapeutic interactions in ways that minimize the social context of the counseling relationship. For example, Sophie states that counseling is "its own little world," a distinct space outside the clients' daily life. Clara claims that she would never have met Josephine had she not sought counseling, thus indicating that the therapeutic relationship is separate from the clients' lifeworld, contained in the confidential setting of the counseling room. Similarly, Josephine describes race as an insignificant difference in psychotherapy. In the next two sections, I further examine the act of minimizing the social context to understand its relational effects. I also reconstruct the meaning field of the participants' interview and interactions to uncover the cultural conditions that delimit the project of authentic being and the doing of genuineness in psychotherapy.

"Relationships are relationships": Genuineness and the Transparency of Race

> And, mm, with the way African Americans are portrayed in the media, and mm, I think that that can influence how [clients] are going to experience me the first time. [...] I feel like [race] fades in the background for my clients. Mm, but it does never fade in the background for me. You know. I'll always hear if they say something that's slightly racist, and even though they might not hear themselves saying it. Mm, I know that people have relationships, and relationships are relationships. I know that I can have functional relationships with anybody. [...] And mm. But I think for [the clients], it's beneficial if, if, if race just fades in the background. [...] I feel like we can have a very good relationship because they get past it pretty quickly and because it does fade away.

In the passage above, Josephine articulates conflicting statements about the relational effects of race and the visibility of the counselor's African American identity. When she declares that "relationships are relationships" and that she "can have functional relationships with anybody," she plays down the impact of race and other contextual factors on the organization of the counseling interactions; she also makes a claim about her ability to transcend human differences. On the other hand, she states that race is "something that has to enter people's minds," and implies that race matters, that it determines the clients' perception of the counselor, trust and comfort, and that she is continuously aware of the clients' biases. As the therapeutic relationship develops, race fades away, yet remains an organizing structure of the interactions. In the next example, Josephine suggests that the backgrounding of race works to counter the client's racial prejudices:

> I had a client who was I think 90, and I had to go see her at her house. And we talked over the phone many times and I told her when I was coming, and we had an appointment set, and I knocked on her door, and mm, she yelled for me to come in and I opened the door, and she said: "Oh!" *[Josephine laughs.]* And I was like: "Hi, I'm Josephine." And she said: "You didn't sound like a negro over the phone." *[Josephine utters a laugh.]* And it was really, it was really difficult. Because I was like, I was angry, but then I was like: "She's 90, Josephine, she's 90, you know, let it go, she's 90." And so, and so I did. And it was fine. And we had a good working relationship, but she felt very comfortable telling *me* [sic] really racist things about other black people. And I was like: "Wow, I don't need to hear this." But I didn't know how to tell a 90-year-old woman that she was offending me, and a part of me just felt like it wasn't even worth it.

When the 90-year-old white female client exclaims that "[Josephine] did not sound like a negro over the phone," she calls attention to her position of privilege as a white person relative to Josephine's social status as a young black woman; she proposes to define the counseling relationship in ways that reproduce racial relations of domination. Josephine decides not to respond to the client's racist comment, as if doing so would constitute an acknowledgment of the white woman's definition of the relationship and an acceptance of the racial arrangement of their face-to-face interactions. Instead, Josephine suppresses her anger, and focuses on the formation of the "working relationship" with the client. In other words, she opposes the client's initial definition of the relationship by foregrounding the professional character of their meetings. It follows that the backgrounding of race coincides with the foregrounding of expertise: race fades away; Josephine becomes the expert; and the white woman, the client. Josephine ceases to be the object of the client's racist comments; it is "other black people" who now are the target. In the front region of counseling, Josephine draws upon the structure of expertise to gain social influence; the client and she develop a working relationship where Josephine occupies a position different from other black people's oppression. Josephine also confines herself to a position of silence with respect to the racism that defines her interactions with the white woman in the back region of counseling.

It is noteworthy that Clara, Sophie, and Josephine did not openly address race-related issues in the sessions I observed; they did not discuss whether race had some bearing on their interactions, on the clients' perception of the counselor, on the clients' assumptions about self and others, and on the clients' expectations about counseling. The absence of frank conversations about race contrasts with the counselor's acute awareness of her status as an African American woman in the counseling relationship:

> I have to be very conscious [that] I'm African American female, mm, there're people, especially here, who I'm going to deal with, who have never had a conversation with an African American person before in their life. You know. And so, the fact that they're gonna choose to sit in a room with somebody who they probably haven't dealt with, how they feel about being with somebody from another, mm, ethnicity, mm, being in a confined space with somebody from another ethnicity. I would think they would go home and be, and just talk about their counselor and say: "Oh," if somebody, I don't even know how it could come up, but it would be like: "Oh, by the way, she's black." You know. And it would be something that *[pause]* didn't really *[pause]* matter to them. But I think that it's also really good, because I think it's giving them an experience where it's like, where they're working with somebody who's African American, and they can trust me, and mm, feel comfortable with me, and hopefully it's something that generalizes as opposed to, is isolated.

Josephine does not identify the race of the "people here who have never had a conversation with an African American person before in their life." Given that the local population is predominantly white and non-Hispanic, it seems reasonable to assume that Josephine refers to white clients. In the particular context of the community where she provides counseling services, Josephine describes her relationship with white clients as an opportunity to bring together individuals from different racial and ethnic backgrounds. She suggests that cross-racial encounters in the enclosed and private space of psychotherapy may generate feelings of anxiety in white clients who have had little contact with African Americans. She also intimates that it is her responsibility to be aware of race and to attend to white clients' initial discomfort by creating a climate of trust and by providing a therapeutic environment in which race becomes a human difference that does not really matter. On the one hand, Josephine may see counseling as the occasion to break down racial barriers and to promote cross-racial relations in her immediate social environment; she expresses her hopes that the counseling relationship will serve as a template for how whites may relate differently to African Americans. On the other hand, she suggests that the act of crossing racial boundaries requires that the counselor's blackness become transparent and that race become a neutral factor. This might explain why it is difficult for Josephine to imagine how white clients may discuss her racial identity with their family and friends ("I don't even know how it could come up.")

Given the social visibility of blackness in the U.S., it is striking that the clients should not mention Josephine's race during their interview. When Clara speaks of Josephine, she highlights the counselor's age and gender, and ignores her race:

> [W]ith her, like I was a little, you know, kind of iffy going in, 'cause I was: "Oh, she's not that much older than me." You know. I don't know that, but it seems like that. She looks young. But, then, right away I felt more comfortable after like the first 45 minutes with her. I was like: "You know what, she was just the same, you know, whenever, how long ago." [...] Yeah, just that she's a very nice, nice girl and I feel very comfortable with her, even though I don't feel very comfortable with people. I feel comfortable with her.

Clara does not talk directly about Josephine's race; however, she uses words such as "nice girl" whose informality may say something about her racial positioning in the counseling relationship. It is probable that Clara does whiteness as she defines the counselor as a very nice girl; she emphasizes sameness in age and creates for Josephine a peer-like position in the therapeutic relationship that seems to question Josephine's expert authority.

I cannot infer from the interviews or from the therapeutic conversations that Clara and Sophie deliberately avoid race as a topic of discussion. Neither can I conclude that the act of not talking about race signifies the clients did not see or think about racial issues. However, the lack of dialogue indicates that Sophie and Clara are not compelled by a hostile environment to examine their racial positioning in society. The absence of conversation about race is itself a probable instantiation of the doing of whiteness in which the white clients look through the counselor's blackness and ignore race as a contextual factor that shapes their face-to-face interactions. As an instantiation of whiteness, the lack of dialogue about race may allow the clients to affirm their narrative authority and to reject the black counselor's participation in the process of storying the self. In addition, it is possible that Josephine's perceived responsibility with regard to white clients' racial comfort and their ability to view race as an insignificant difference may be a characteristic demand of whiteness, a structural rule that supports the reproduction of social relations in which whites do not have to see themselves as raced. When race is viewed as a neutral difference, it may be easier for the white female client to "be comfortable" and to be herself with the black female counselor; the counselor and the client become "people who have relationships, and relationships are relationships"; that is, they are able to relate to one another in a genuine way, free of contextual influences. The transparency of whiteness is then a cultural condition of the performance of genuineness that itself supports the counselor's expert position in the counseling relationship.

In the sections that follow, I consider how the doing of genuineness may also involve the reproduction of gender ideals. I study Clara's description of her relationship with men and Sophie's definition of authentic acts of care, and show how the performance of genuineness is an imperative of psychotherapy that serves to establish the veracity and legitimacy of the clients' story of the self.

"That's not what friends do!":
Genuineness and the Doing of Gender

Clara's conversations with Josephine include many topics and recurrent themes that refer to the concrete manifestation of gender in Clara's daily life, such as men's patronizing attitude, men's use of anger as a means of intimidation, hooking up versus friendship, and Clara's angry and voiceless position in relation to men. In particular, Clara and Josephine focus on Clara's relationship with Dylan, whom she met online. In the following dialogue, Josephine calls attention to the true meaning of Dylan's actions and recommends that the client follow her instincts. In reply, Clara suggests that the gendered organization of her relationship with Dylan limits her capacity for action:

> **CLARA:** And then he told me last night, he was like: "I will do anything for you. Just tell me something to do." I was like: "What are you talking about?" He's like: "I want to return the favor of you being so nice to me." And I was like: "Just be yourself. You don't have to do anything. It's not your job to make me happy."

> **JOSEPHINE:** *[Speaking softly]* That's really good.

> **CLARA:** He's like: "I get attached to people too fast." *[Clara shakes her head up and down as if she was saying yes.]* And I'm like: *[Laughing]* "Obviously." You know.

> **JOSEPHINE:** Right.

> **CLARA:** And like it's so weird. I haven't even kissed him. Like it's just, he's, and that's why I feel me being nice to him is leading him on. *[Clara explains that she does not want to start a romantic relationship with Dylan.]* And I just feel bad. Like. Because if I don't talk to him, I feel like I'm being mean, but if I do talk to him, I feel like I'm leading him on. […] He's just a little boy. *[Clara shrugs her shoulders and laughs. Josephine laughs.]*

Clara communicates that she feels stuck as she attempts to influence the definition of her relationship with Dylan. Although she may follow the rule of "just being yourself," she cannot avoid "misleading" Dylan, because she cannot fully control the meanings that her actions convey: talking and being nice might imply that Clara accepts Dylan's definition of the relationship as something more than a friendship; to not talk would signify that she is indifferent, uncaring, and unconcerned about the relationship. Clara points to the transactional nature and the boundaries of the presentation of self. She also alludes to the impossibility of genuineness: just being oneself is a project that Clara carries out in the cultural context of her interactions with Dylan; it is bounded by Dylan's actions and the tacit rules that govern interactions between men and women in that context. The dialogue above helps to discern some of these rules: Clara should monitor the relational effects of her actions; she should be nice to Dylan and careful not to hurt his feelings. When Clara notes jokingly that "Dylan is just a little boy," she proposes a binary definition of their relationship: if Dylan is a little boy, then Clara is an adult who has matured and assumed many responsibilities since she moved to her new town. Clara's identity claim might give her more authority in the friendship; however, it also participates in the reproduction of the gendered arrangement of relationships where women have traditionally been responsible for the care of others, to the extent that Clara, as an adult, feels compelled to be nice and to protect Dylan, the little boy.

When Clara returns to the clinic for her next session, she reports that she kissed Dylan. In fact, she responds to Josephine's question, "How are things with Dylan?" in an incidental manner, as if the kiss was a trivial event that she could forget and laugh about:

> **JOSEPHINE:** How are things with Dylan?

CLARA: Mm, they're alright. I haven't seen him since last week. 'Cause, ooh, I was stupid, I made out with him. *[Laughs.]*

JOSEPHINE: *[Laughing, looking down]* That's not what friends do.

Clara invites Josephine to laugh with her at the same time as she admits to kissing Dylan. Her statement suggests that she feels contrite, sorry, embarrassed, and guilty for crossing the limits of friendship and for not being true to her words. (In the dialogue, it is "I" not "we" who made out.) Her remark also communicates that she understands the consequence of her behaviors; has acknowledged her responsibility; and has the ability to differentiate the good and the bad. Indeed, Clara's statement, "oh, I was stupid, I made out with him," is a confession that invokes moral values about relationships between men and women. So does Josephine's response: "This is not what friends do." Josephine's speech act is associated with many possible meanings: kissing Dylan was inappropriate; true friends do not kiss; a woman should only kiss the man she is dating; Clara broke the rules of friendship; Clara said that Dylan was her friend and that she did not want to have a romantic relationship with him; it is probable that Clara was not being honest or that she acted in ways that were not true to herself. Josephine calls upon the norm of authenticity as she comments on Clara's actions. She also accepts Clara's invitation to laugh about the kiss, thus indicating that she agrees on Clara's definition of the kiss as a small incident. The act of laughing defines the relationship as a friendly space where Clara can tell about her embarrassment and her remorse; it also conceals the counselor's evaluative stance as well as the norms that the counseling interactions draw upon. As they continue to speak about the kiss, Josephine engages in a parody of Clara and Dylan's relationship that also invokes the norm of authenticity:

CLARA: 'Cause [Dylan] asked: "Oh, is there something I can do?" I was like: "You can't do anything, like I can't even do anything." *[Josephine says "right."]* It's just, it's got to, like, you know, make it stay. And then, hopefully, it'll be gone, hopefully I'll be fine. But, he was just kind of weird, *[Josephine scratches her chin]* 'cause *[Josephine says mm-mh]* like even my friends back home, if I had [health problems], they wouldn't be like "Oh, I'm so worried about you."

JOSEPHINE: *[Left hand is open, moving as she speaks]* Well, and any friend who's just a friend, *[Clara says mm-mh]*, I'm sure their reactions would be more like ...

CLARA: "That sucks."

JOSEPHINE: *[Immediately after Clara]* "That sucks."

CLARA: *[Laughing and nodding]* Yeah.

JOSEPHINE: "Call me when you can talk."

CLARA: *[Laughing]* Yeah.

JOSEPHINE: *[Laughing]* You know. Or like "I can bring you food." But it wouldn't be like *[in a lower and softer tone of voice, head moving to the side]*: "I'm so worried about you. I'm really concerned."

CLARA: *[Still laughing]* Yeah.

JOSEPHINE: But we talked about what he is communicating to you. And it's very clear that he's communicating to you: *[Articulating and stressing each word]* 'I like you.' You know. And you're just like: 'Hey, I'm not ready.' *[Puts head on left hand, left elbow on armrest, rubs ear.]*

CLARA: *[In a low tone of voice]* I know. That's why I felt, I felt so crappy when I kissed him. *[Josephine nods.]* You know. Damn. *[Clara is playing with a strand of hair, pulls her hair back, taps her fingers as if she were counting]*. I shouldn't have done that, you know. *[Buries her face in her hands.]*

Paradoxically, Josephine re-enacts Dylan's behaviors to uncover the true meaning of his phony acts of care. She parodies the deception, exaggerates and thus distorts Dylan's actions, in order to establish the truth. In so doing, she blurs the boundary between the genuine and the not real, at the same time as she summons the normative ideal of authenticity. In response, Clara buries her face in her hands, a dramatic gesture that not only makes visible her feelings of embarrassment, but also functions to support the validity of her remorse as well as the truthfulness of her identity claims (that is, Clara is not the kind of girl who kisses any boy; she is a moral person who behaves properly most of the time). Clara's gesture abides by the imperative of genuineness and corresponds to the performance and reproduction of the ideal of authenticity. It follows that genuineness is a condition of the validation of the client's self-presentation; it intersects with the structure of gender to constitute the limits of the client's storying of the self.

Clara's story calls for a reconsideration of the concept of genuineness as a state of congruence between the presentation of self and the real self inside the person. It tells that Clara acted to protect Dylan's definition of the situation and to validate the image of self he was projecting, that of a caring friend who wishes to ease Clara's pain. The kiss is an instantiation of the gender norms that call upon women to return men's show of affection. Instead of causing embarrassment and challenging Dylan's romantic view of their relationship, Clara accepts the discomfort and the shame of a kiss that she does not fully consent to. Her story refers to the gender narratives that form the con/text of the kiss, and suggests that genuineness is something other than the act of being freely and deeply oneself, and that the authenticity and validity of the performance of self may depend on the reproduction of gender norms. So does Sophie's story of her relationship with Shawn, the 8-year-old child she looks after.

Genuine Care and the Reproduction of Gender Ideals

In counseling, Sophie talks about her efforts to create a nurturing, safe, and moral environment for Shawn. She cooks dinner, disciplines the child, stays up late to bake cookies for his birthday, and confronts Ken, Shawn's father's boyfriend, about his forceful parenting. These behaviors constitute Sophie's enactment of genuine care and gender ideals. For example, in the passage below, Sophie invokes the ideal of authenticity as she contrasts her caring style with Shawn's parents' laissez-faire attitude:

SOPHIE: [Shawn] was never told no, until like this year when [Ken and I] came into his life. 'Cause his parents had a very like: "Lolly doll. Let him do whatever he wants. He'll decide his own path." Which I think is good when he's a little bit older. But, you have to start out with boundaries and you have to start out, you know, you can't let kids decide whatever they want to do. [...] I mean, I do, I do discipline him. He has like a checklist of stuff that he needs to check with an X. And, mm, you know, I will, you know, I do put him in line, if he needs, if he's like saying things that are inappropriate *[Josephine nods]* or just being really, not saying please, or. [...] I think [Shawn's mother] has really inappropriate boundaries with him. [...] She is not even starting to look for a job, [...] she, mm, it's like, it's not just support herself, but she needs to support Shawn too. [...] I have a problem, because she's supposed to be an example.

[Josephine nods and says mm-mh.] And it's, she's showing Shawn laziness and dependency. [...] I'm not a parent and I'm not fully invested the way a parent would be with Shawn. [...] But I mean it just seems like there are certain things as a parent that you should sacrifice for your child.

Sophie's claims about genuine care include the following beliefs: Shawn's parents should be more involved and invested in their child's upbringing; they should teach their son good manners; if they truly cared about Shawn, they would focus their energy on him and set limits; a 7-year-old should have limited freedom; parents should be in charge; if Shawn's mother truly cared about Shawn, she would put her feelings aside and think more about Shawn's welfare; she would look for employment in order to support her son. These claims are unspoken statements that define familial normalcy in terms of eating meals and playing together, nurturing, disciplining, and teaching proper conduct and moral principles. They refer to the socially sanctioned motherly responsibility of steering children in the direction of social virtues (for example, industry and autonomy), and suggest that caring is genuine to the extent that it reproduces the social norm of motherly investment and selflessness. In the subsequent passage, Sophie defines genuine care more explicitly in terms of altruism and self-sacrifice:

SOPHIE: Yeah. And it's, I mean, *[There's a laugh in her voice]* he's not a nice kid. But, but he's, he's a child, and I have love for him, because he's a child. *[Josephine nods]* That's just, I mean, that's just what I do. And, huh. *[4-second silence. Sighing.]* I don't know. *[4-second silence.]* It's like when does, like me moving now would just be *[3-second silence]* so my comfort level would be better. *[Josephine nods.]* Mm. But that seems so much less important compared to his *[pause]* daily life. You know. *[Josephine nods]* And I don't necessarily even see him every day. *[Josephine says mm-mh.]* 'Cause a lot of the times he is already in bed when I get home. *[Josephine nods]* Or I just don't even stay there. I don't really stay there at all. It's cold and uncomfortable. So, you know, I'll hang out with him for a little while and then leave. *[Josephine nods.]* Mm. *[10-second silence]* I don't know, I guess that's all I really have to say about that. *[5-second silence]* 'Cause I mean I will. I'll stay there. *[Josephine nods.]* I have to. He needs *[Sophie is laughing softly]* someone who's normal.

JOSEPHINE: What is it that you provide him with? *[Josephine's hands are tucked underneath her right leg. She slightly pulls her right leg back on her left leg.]*

SOPHIE: I'm his friend. We hang out. And we have like a big art table with a bunch of craft stuff on it. And we do crafts together. Mm. I watch him play his computer games. That's what he really likes, is for someone to watch him play computer games. *[Josephine nods.]* [...] And I take him to school three days a week and that's like when we have our chance to talk. *[Josephine nods and says mm-mh.]* But, usually, he's just like *[Sophie's voice sounds deeper. She says something that I cannot make out and that makes Josephine laugh. Josephine rubs her collar with her right hand and then puts her right fist underneath her right jaw.]* Mm. So. I mean, I think that's really all that I provide him with is I, *[pause]* I hang out with him, *[Josephine nods]* which is what none of his other parents do. [...] I guess what I'm doing is trying to let him have as normal a childhood as possible.

When Sophie says that "Shawn is a child and that she has love for him because he is a child," she makes a claim about the kind of person she is: loving, selfless, loyal to Shawn, and dedicated to her role of caregiver. She suggests that she has the innate ability to care, and implies that caring is a natural and unconditional act. She stresses that she truly cares about Shawn by stating that her "comfort level seems so much less important compared to Shawn's daily life." Again, when she points out that she has accepted to live in poor conditions for the sake of the child, she communicates that her acts of care are genuine and that real caring involves altruism and self-sacrifice.

On the one hand, Sophie defines care as innate and natural. On the other, she calls it a moral duty, using the words "commitment" and "obligation" to define her relationship with Shawn: "I have got a commitment to go. I can't let him down." Sophie feels compelled to stay and look after Shawn. She also feels responsible for providing a normal familial environment. In the quote that follows, she shows signs of ambivalence about her perceived commitment to the child; it appears that she feels stuck in the position of care she occupies in Shawn's family:

> SOPHIE: But I feel like I have a responsibility to the, to the child. [...] Because his life is *[lingering on the word "so"]* so screwed up right now. And I'm about like the only normal female in his life. [...] But I don't, and I don't want to feel like I need to take on the entire responsibility, [...] but it is also the fact that he's not my kid, and because of that I know that I'll eventually get to the point where I resent it. Like having to treat him like he is my, not that he is my child, but that I have more of a responsibility for him than his step-dad's other friends do.

Paradoxically, Sophie communicates that her acts of care are both natural and mandatory. As she describes her responsibility to the child as an imperative from which she cannot break free, she points to the conflict she experiences between her caring nature and her obligation to care. This conflict calls for an examination of the concept of genuineness defined as the act of being freely and deeply oneself. Is Sophie being freely herself, a naturally caring person, when she puts a lot of effort into raising Shawn and when she accepts staying in a cold and damp room? Sophie's investment and self-sacrifice are actions that prove the genuineness of her caring disposition towards Shawn and that support the validity of her identity claims (that is, loving, selfless, loyal) in relation to the child; they also correspond to socially sanctioned behaviors that women have traditionally performed in relationships of care. In other words, the legitimacy of Sophie's story of the self seems to depend on her performance of genuineness, which itself is a function of the reproduction of familial normalcy and gendered ideals of being.

Sophie and Clara's stories of care and friendship indicate that genuineness corresponds not to a state of congruence with one's inner self, but to the doing of normative standards. They also suggest that the performance of genuineness as the act of being true to oneself or of "just being oneself" functions to conceal the gendered arrangement of social interactions. Likewise, Josephine's enactment of genuineness in the counseling relationship coincides with the fading of race and the reproduction of the transparency of whiteness. Clara, Sophie, and Josephine draw upon the ideal of authenticity to support their identity claims and to create a position of authority for themselves in relation to the narrative that develops from their conversation. At the same time as they enact and reproduce the ideal of genuineness, they choose and reject the stories *in potentia* that form the cultural con/text of their interactions, and thus exercise their capacity to act differently, namely their capacity to realize their project of being by producing a narrative of self that may or may not deviate from social standards of being.

Conclusion

In this chapter, I have used the performance paradigm to highlight the cultural conditions of the influence process in psychotherapy. I have proposed a performative view of the counseling relationship wherein clients select, recount, and weave chosen elements of their lifeworld into a story of the self that corresponds to their efforts to make meaning of their experience. I have argued that the counselor and the clients participated in the performative act of storying the self by means of which they not only described but also conjured up and re-presented the clients' lifeworld. They engaged in presentations of self that instantiated normative ideals of gender and race, and that worked to negotiate and support their position of authority with respect to the narrative that developed from their interactions. For example, I have noted that the clients' presentation of self invoked the normative ideal of authenticity and that the validity of the performance of self depended on its perceived genuineness, which itself was a function of the reproduction of gendered norms. The doing of genuineness intersected with the doing of gender in ways that restricted the storying of the self at the same time as it enabled the clients to author the therapeutic narrative and to take a stand about their personal project of being.

I have not examined the performativity of the research relationship or how the participants and I engaged in the doing of race and gender during the collection of data. This is an aspect of ethnographic research that warrants more attention. The performance paradigm provides a critical lens that makes it possible to examine what happens in the space between the observer and the observed and that helps to think about the effects of ethnographers' social positioning in the research relationship.

Note

1. The spelling of the word 'con/text' calls attention to the sociocultural narratives that form the background of human actions and that determine the range of meanings that these actions produce. Self-performances tell stories about the self that represent and/or challenge the sociocultural narratives of particular communities. They derive meaningfulness from the process of referencing their discursive background or con/text.

References

Alexander, B. K. (2004). Black skin/white masks: The performative sustainability of whiteness (with apologies to Frantz Fanon). *Qualitative Inquiry, 10*(5), 647–672.

Alexander, B. K. (2005). Performance ethnography: The reenacting and inciting of culture. In N. K. Denzin & Y. S. Lincoln (Eds.), *Sage handbook of qualitative research* (3rd ed.) (pp. 411–441). Thousand Oaks, CA: Sage.

Butler, J. (1990). *Gender trouble: Feminism and the subversion of identity.* New York: Routledge.

Carspecken, P. F. (1996). *Critical ethnography in educational research: A theoretical and practical guide.* New York: Routledge

Claiborn, C. D., & Lichtenberg, J. W. (1989). Interactional counseling. *Counseling Psychologist, 17*(3), 355–453.

Conquergood, D. (2006). Rethinking ethnography: Towards a critical cultural politics. In D. S. Madison & J. Hamera (Eds.), *Sage handbook of performance studies* (pp. 351–365). Thousand Oaks, CA: Sage.

Corrigan, J. D., Dell, D. M., Lewis, K. N., & Schmidt, L. D. (1980). Counseling as a social influence process: A review. *Journal of Counseling Psychology Monograph, 27*(4), 395–441.

Denzin, N. (2003). *Performance ethnography: Critical pedagogy and the politics of culture.* Thousands Oaks, CA: Sage.

Dorn, F. J. (1984). The social influence model: A social psychological approach to counseling. *Personnel and Guidance Journal, 62*(6), 342–635.

Dorn, F. J. (1986). The social influence model: An overview. In F. J. Dorn (Ed.), *The social influence process in counseling and psychotherapy* (pp. 3–15). Springfield, IL: Charles C. Thomas.

Goodyear, R. K., & Robyak, J. E. (1981). Counseling as an interpersonal influence process: A perspective for counseling practice. *Personnel and Guidance Journal, 59*(10), 654–657.

Halberstam, J. (2004). *In a queer time and place: Transgender bodies, subcultural lives.* New York: New York University Press.

Hamera, J. (2006). Performance, performativity, and cultural poiesis in practices of everyday life. In D. S. Madison & J. Hamera (Eds.), *Sage handbook of performance studies* (pp. 46–64). Thousand Oaks, CA: Sage.

Jackson, A. Y. (2004). Performativity identified. *Qualitative Inquiry, 10*(5), 673–690.

McCall, M. M. (2000). Performance ethnography: A brief history and some advice. In N. K. Denzin & Y. S. Lincoln (Eds.), *Sage handbook of qualitative research* (2nd ed.) (pp. 421–433). Thousand Oaks, CA: Sage.

Olomo, O. O. O. (2006). Performance and ethnography, performing ethnography, performance ethnography. In D. S. Madison & J. Hamera (Eds.), *Sage handbook of performance studies* (pp. 339–445). Thousand Oaks, CA: Sage.

Schmidt, L. D., & Strong, S. R. (1970). "Expert" and "inexpert" counselors. *Journal of Counseling Psychology, 17*(2), 115–118.

Strong, S. R. (1968). Counseling: An interpersonal influence process. *Journal of Counseling Psychology, 15*(3), 215–224.

Strong, S. R., & Dixon, D. N. (1971). Expertness, attractiveness, and influence in counseling. *Journal of Counseling Psychology, 18*(6), 562–570.

CHAPTER FIFTEEN

Narrative and Genre in Qualitative Research

The Case of Romanticism

AMIR MARVASTI & CHRISTOPHER FAIRCLOTH

Positivistic science texts are founded on the assumption that as factual reports, they do not require discernable narrators with a particular view of social reality presented to a specific audience. Evading the issues of narration, perspective, and audience reception, positivistic science presents itself as epistemologically transcendental, or as knowledge that rises above constraints of subjectivity and social context.

Post-positivistic qualitative researchers have rejected these knowledge claims to universal objectivity by showing that scientific texts themselves can be deconstructed and analyzed as forms of representation, or stories, in their own right. Recognizing that any given text, is a representation of knowledge or human experience implies that it:

- has a certain structure (such as a beginning, middle, and end)
- is embedded in social relationships (for example, the audience-storyteller relationship, and
- involves representational devices (such as metaphors, plots, and genres).

Thus "science" itself can be thought of as a "grand narrative" (Lyotard 1983) and consequently stripped of its transcendental truth claims. It is worth noting that this argument does not mean every knowledge claim is therefore false or fabricated, or, for that matter, useless. Far from it, knowledge claims are indeed practical and useful, despite being social constructions. For example, the claim that cigarette smoking does not cause cancer (though blatantly false) served the tobacco industry very well for decades. Similarly, regarding the truth value, accuracy, or validity of knowledge claims, a cautious post-positivism would not dismiss such issues out of hand, but instead it would simply point out that they cannot be judged in a social vacuum of space and time. The relatively simple but revolutionary idea behind a narrative approach to science (that is, narrativity) is that all knowledge claims are contextually embedded and perspectival.

There are, of course, many unresolved issues in this debate. For example, defining the very idea of a narrative is a tricky business. The average scholar can find herself mired in the endless disputes surrounding the problem of defining "narrative" before she even begins to collect the first bit of data (see, for example, Livingstone's discussion of "rival definitions of narrativity," 2009, pp. 26–28).

We wish to sidestep the sticky terrain of narrative analysis by assuming a relatively simple position: Narrativity is an analytic construct that can be applied to any text. It is not an inherent quality of any medium; rather, it is a way of apprehending the medium. Any given text can thus be analyzed it terms of its narrative qualities.

With this approach in mind, we want to take a closer look at the narrative of qualitative research itself. That is to say, we are interested in reading qualitative research reports as narrative constructions in their own right. As a whole, qualitative researchers have been fairly sensitive, particularly in the area of narrative analysis, to the constructive practices embedded in their research subjects' stories. Moreover, starting with Geertz' (1973) description of ethnography as "fiction" in the sense of being a construction of others' constructions, and continuing with James Clifford and George Marcus' *Writing Culture* (1986), there has also been at least some attention to representational practices among ethnographers themselves. (See also John Van Maanen, 1988; Margery Wolf, 1992; and others.) But generally, researchers tend to be interested in how narratives are used to represent the experiences of others and seem less inclined to think of their own research writings narratively.

In the next section, we (1) introduce the notion of narrative genre, in general; (2) define romanticism as a specific genre; and (3) offer an empirical analysis of how it is used in qualitative texts.

Narrative Genre

There is growing awareness among social scientists about the influence of genres on the way we communicate our ideas. For example, Daniel Just's "The Modern Novel from a Sociological Perspective: Towards a Strategic Use of the Notion of Genres" (2008) makes a strong argument for a more nuanced analysis of the narrative structures of novels and possibly using them "strategically" to frame sociological writing. In his words:

> Given the fact that one of the strengths of the novel is its ability to hide its all-absorbing logic behind the seemingly anti-generic absence of its own positive features, the strategic use of the notion of genres can expose this logic and thus open the possibility of a radically different type of narratives. (2008, p. 393)

Moving beyond Just's call to entertain the possibility of using genres strategically, in "The Inevitability and Importance of Genres in Narrative Research on Teaching Practice" Rosiek and Atkinson (2007) suggest that genre is essentially a ubiquitous feature of writing that can and should be critically assessed. In particular, Rosiek and Atkinson note narrative, or narrative genres, are not inherently innocent:

> If genres are the products of contingent historical processes, then genres cannot be considered innocent or neutral. They are neither natural nor inevitable. They highlight certain issues and elide others. The critical

question that needs to be asked, therefore, is what interests and priorities are served by a given genre? This critical inquiry becomes all the more important when the description of genres seems like it may give way to proscription—enforcement of a narrow selection of genres as norms. If the development of a genre of representation is being forwarded as a desirable aspiration within a field, then the motivations for and interests served by this advocacy need to be critically interrogated.... What is needed, therefore, is not the avoidance of genre per se but a self-conscious commitment to understanding genres as pragmatic programs of action whose consequences need to be critically tracked and continually reassessed. (p. 502)

It follows from these arguments that storytelling, whether practiced by research respondents or researchers themselves, is not a natural, universal, or transparent form of communication. Rather, storytelling and writing are culturally embedded practices and mediated by a set of factors, some of which might be discernable choices on the part of the narrators and others might reflect less obvious, nonetheless, obdurate, social conditions.

The concept of genre is then one way in which researchers can reflect on and reveal the regularity and persistence of textual practices. With this overall orientation in mind, we next examine the prevalence and use of the romantic genre in social science writing. After a brief introduction that locates romanticism within the boundaries of Western thought, we analyze its enduring influence on qualitative texts.

Romantic Genre in Social Science Writing[1]

Historically, romanticism has been associated with three relatively distinct movements in France, Germany, and Britain (Steer & White, 1994). In all three countries, romanticism emerged around the late 18th to early 19th century. Although each school embodied its own artistic interpretation and techniques, French, German, and British romanticism all involved a passionate exploration of the exotic and the mysterious. In many respects, the artist's emotions and the strange Other converged on the canvas or the text to portray a reality that transcended the boundaries of reason and logic. The exotic was particularly significant for artists of this period, because it symbolized the possibility of competing realities and different worlds of meaning.

Philosophically, romanticism is closely affiliated with transcendentalism, defined as "the idealistic system of thought based on a belief in essential unity of all creation, the innate goodness of humankind, and the supremacy of insight over logic and experience for the revelation of deepest truths" (*Merriam-Webster's Encyclopedia of Literature*, 1995, p. 1128). The emphasis on "the innate goodness of humankind" and the primacy of "insight over logic" jointly crystallize the utopian project of romanticism and its commitment to social change. Romanticism can also be regarded as a backlash against utilitarian rationalism, which reduces human cognition to a simple cost-benefit analysis for arriving at the most efficient course of action. The significance of this reaction for romanticists is described by Eagleton (1996):

"Imaginative creation" can be offered as an image of non-alienated labor; the intuitive, transcendental scope of the poetic mind can provide a living criticism of those rationalist or empiricist ideologies enslaved to "fact." The literary work itself comes to be seen as a mysterious organic unity, in contrast to the fragmented individualism of the capitalist marketplace; it is "spontaneous" rather than rationally calculated, creative rather than mechanical.... Literature has become a whole alternative ideology, and the "imagination" itself, as with Blake and Shelley, becomes a political force. Its task is to transform society in the name of those energies which art embodies. Most of the major Romantic poets were themselves political activists, perceiving continuity rather than conflict between their literary and social commitments. (p. 17)

As a whole, romanticism, as a style and a movement, was inspired by a set of historical, philosophical, and political events that centered on rebelling against the reduction of human ingenuity to factual analysis of causes and effects, a development that parallels the contemporary tension between qualitative and quantitative research.

Given this broad understanding of the discourse of romanticism, in the following analysis, we trace the influence of romanticism on qualitative writing. Our analysis is especially influenced by Dorothy Smith's (1987, 1990) work on how discourse mediates everyday practice and perpetuates "relations of ruling." According to Smith (1990),

> textual realities create a specific relationship between the reader and "what actually happened/what is." This relationship is organized not merely by choices of language and syntax: properties of the relations of ruling built into the text enter and determine the reader's relation to the realities constituted therein. (p. 89)

Borrowing from Smith's insights, we make the case that the romanticized representation of the participant in qualitative texts points to a taken-for-granted vision of morality and "relations of ruling" that are not inherently benevolent. The analysis rests on three foundational themes in the discourse of romanticism: (1) the lure of the exotic, (2) authenticity, and (3) the moral project. We treat these concepts as constitutive elements of the genre of romanticism and illustrate how they are used as narrative devices.

The Lure of the Exotic

A focus on the lure of the exotic has served as a vital component of the romantic literary style. Romantic authors and poets turned to the Middle Ages for themes, settings, and locales ranging from the Hebrides of the Ossianic tradition to the "Oriental" setting of Xanadu evoked by Samuel Taylor Coleridge (1916) in his unfinished lyric "Kubla Khan." Similar throughout these texts is a fascination with times and places far removed from the drudgery of mundane reality.

This style of writing has profound implications for the language of qualitative research because it directly affects the textual representation of research findings. Beginning with the classical works of the Chicago School to the present, the exotic has continued to lure researchers into strange worlds of estranged others. Consider Robert Park's plea for sociologists to take their minds and their notebooks to the natural settings of the urban world, outside and far removed from the security of their offices. Park urges the sociologist to personally visit the urban exotic.

> Go and sit in the lounges of the luxury hotels and on the doorsteps of the flophouses; sit on the Gold Coast settees and on the slum shakedowns; sit in the orchestra hall and in the Star and Garter burlesque. In short, gentlemen, go get the seat of your pants dirty in real research. (quoted in McKinney, 1966, p. 71)

Park exhorts researchers to see the different and exotic through visits to the flophouses, the burlesque, and the "slum shakedowns." In a decidedly romantic tone, Park pushes sociologists to see "what is really going on" and to view, firsthand, the strange and unfamiliar world of those they study.

Similarly, William Foote Whyte (1943) provided us with a pioneering example of romantically influenced ethnography in *Street Corner Society*, a seminal work that continues to inspire adoration and criticism in the field as evidenced by a special edition of the *Journal of Contemporary Ethnography* (Adler, Boelen, & Whyte, 1992). Although numerous methodological issues are implicated in the debate about *Street Corner Society*, Whyte's (1996, 1997) rebuttal to Richardson's (1996) questioning of his professional ethics is of particular interest here. Defending himself against the charge that the participants and their families were emotionally harmed as a consequence of his research, especially after one participant's (Doc's) true identity was revealed, Whyte (1997) stated,

> Clearly, some people were embarrassed by the book, but I could not find any evidence that I had seriously damaged any of them. The embarrassment of a few people may be a necessary price to pay for an intensive participant observer report that has been read by thousands of college students and others in the general public. Many professors have made the book required reading. (p. 34)

In this context, Whyte presented himself as the quintessential romantic hero, gallantly accepting both adoration and condemnation for a job he perceived had to be done. His defense invokes the romantic principle that the study of the exotic is a moral imperative in its own right. As Vidich and Lyman (2000) suggested, Whyte's research was "motivated by a sense of moral responsibility to uplift the slum-dwelling masses" (p. 51). His mission was to present the "human" side of the inhabitants of Cornerville to "respectable people," as the opening of the book indicates:

> To the rest of the city it is a mysterious, dangerous, and depressing area. Cornerville is only a few minutes away from fashionable High Street, but the High Street inhabitant who takes that walk passes from the familiar to the unknown.... Respectable people have access to a limited body of information about Cornerville.... Cornerville people appear as social work clients, as defendants in criminal cases, or as undifferentiated members of "the masses." There is one thing wrong with such a picture; no human beings are in it. (Whyte, 1943, p. xv)

Whyte's attempt to put a "human" face on an otherwise strange world is admirable for its eloquence and apparent sincerity, but his moral enterprise is founded on a dubious distinction between two spheres of life (that is, the respectable and the mysterious). It is this dichotomy that allows the ethnographer to offer the strange Other for inspection by the peering eyes of the familiar self. The gap between the two worlds remains a foundational feature of Whyte's narrative, putting him in the privileged position to attest to the seemingly surprising ability of Cornerville's inhabitants to be orderly and "human."

Inspired by the moral mission of normalizing the different in the service of the same, contemporary ethnographers continue to pursue the exotic, as indicated in this excerpt from Bruce Jacobs's (1999) ethnography of crack dealers:

> Qualitative methods provide a thoroughgoing exploration of the daily behaviors and careers of often hidden or hard-to-reach populations. Such methods allow researchers to decode the manner in which these persons and groups communicate and to describe a body of knowledge or cognition not easily understood by outsiders. (p. 11)

Similar to Whyte's work, the discursive foundation of this ethnography of inner-city dwellers is the presumed gulf between the familiar and the strange (i.e., "often hidden or hard-to-reach populations"). It is worth noting that empirical support for this chasm between the known self and unknown Other is itself textually accomplished. Such ethnographic accounts of the exotic begin by juxtaposing taken-for-granted order against reported chaos and end with a pacifying solution, taming the unknown in the reader's eyes. Consider, for example, the contrast between the introduction and conclusion of the following ethnography on male strip clubs:

> It is like a mob—what seems like two hundred women packed into a room, all moving together, scream-ing, chanting. The room is hot, crowded. It is difficult to move from one area to another. It is impos-sible to do so without rubbing up against (or being rubbed against by) one of the sweaty, nearly naked men—clad only in skin-tight briefs, slithering through the club. Dancers hug women and kiss them on the cheek. Women, often under the influence of some kind of alcohol, take advantage of their freedom to stuff dollar bills into waistbands, to touch and grab, as if on a dare—with a tentative, yet devilish expres-sion and usually with a squeal of delight. Such is the atmosphere of male strip clubs. The basic ingredients are the same: women, men taking off clothes, alcohol, and screaming. (Montemurro, 2001, p. 276)

> This research is important because we lack information on the way these and similar industries preserve order. Stereotypes about chaos in and "sleaziness" of strip clubs and rumors of rampant prostitution and drug abuse are called into question as The Hideaway [the research site] proved to be a profit-driven orga-nization focused on and providing an entertaining, "sensual" show while operating within the law. Future research might examine the ways in which social control functions in other deviant occupations, particu-larly in female strip clubs, to explore the existence of rules, and structure. (Montemurro, 2001, p. 301)

In this research, the sociological imagination lies in the narrative transformation of reported disorder into believable order, the textual taming of the wild. The opening paragraphs set the tone for the narrative transformation by signaling chaos and uncontrollable lust: "It is like a mob." Ironically, the remainder of the article is devoted to contradicting the introductory textual representation. Also, the use of the pronoun "we" is very telling in the conclusion. Presumably, "we" does not include The Hideaway's customers or staff but the "outsiders," or the equivalent of Whyte's respectable, normal society.

The immersion into the world of the exotic in effect has become a rite of passage for ethnographers and a formulaic feature of their work in sociology of deviance. For example, in her work with drug dealers, Patricia Adler (1985) described how she and her husband become involved in the "subculture of drug trafficking." Theirs is a story of gradual involvement in the exotic world of drugs. Although narrated in a detached, realistic tone, a romantic sense of the exotic seasons this work throughout, as seen in the following description of the research participants:

> Ben was also very tall and broad shouldered, but his long black hair, now flecked with gray, bespoke his earlier membership in hippie subculture. A large physical stature, we observed, was common to most of the male participants involved in this drug community. The women also had a unifying physical trait: they were extremely attractive and stylishly dressed. (p. 58)

It is important to note that the lure of the exotic here is not an incidental feature but the defining characteristic of the story, giving context and meaning to the more mundane re-search practices such as gaining entry and establishing rapport with the natives. To a degree, Adler's risky encounters and long-term relationships with members of the drug underworld are the story. The ameliorative effect of ethnographic research is best understood in relation to the seemingly relentless lure of the exotic, the romantic impulse that entices field workers to uncover supposedly mysterious, bizarre, and glamorous worlds. This is often done for the benefit of readers, who one can only assume are members of "normal society." As seen earlier in the case of Whyte's (1997) defense of *Street Corner Society*, this way of storytelling casts the ethnographer as the reluctant hero whose adventures allow "normal" readers to peer into the mysterious world of outcasts.

Examples of the unearthing of the strange are plentiful in ethnographies of the homeless. Here, stories of the exotic Others usually take the form of documenting their desperate attempts at normality, or their burning desire to be like the familiar self. Consider these excerpts from Elliot Liebow's (1993) *Tell Them Who I Am* and Snow and Anderson's (1993) *Down on Their Luck*:

> What has impressed us most about the homeless we came to know and whose stories we have endeavored to tell is their resourcefulness and their resilience. Confronted with minimal resources, often stigmatized by broader society, frequently harassed by law enforcement officials, and repeatedly frustrated by their own attempts to claim the most modest part of the American dream, they nonetheless continue to struggle to survive materially, to develop friendships, however tenuous, with their street peers and to carve out a sense of meaning and personal identity. (Snow & Anderson, 1993, p. 316)

> At first sight, one wonders why more homeless people do not kill themselves. How do they manage to slog through day after day, with no end in sight? How in the world of unremitting grimness, do they manage to laugh, love, enjoy friends, even dance and play the fool? How in short do they stay fully human while body and soul are under grievous assault? (Liebow, 1993, p. 25)

Undoubtedly, these notable scholars are sympathetic to the plight of the homeless; however, it is not their intentions but the textual representation that is the subject of criticism. In this mode of writing about the homeless, the harmful effects of capitalism on the poor are relatively unexamined. Instead, the presumably heroic efforts of the down-and-out to be a part of normal society, "to claim the most modest part of the American dream," become the focal point of the story. Romanticism, in this case, masks or diverts attention from other possible realities. It serves as a "collective misrecognition" (Bourdieu, 1990) that softens the harsh realities of life under capitalism and, in doing so, tacitly approves of the status quo.

The variations in its use notwithstanding, the lure of the exotic is synonymous with the appeal of ethnographic research. Unfortunately, this discursive practice runs the risk of perpetuating the moral distance between the ethnographer and the research subject. Like the photographic gaze described in *Reading National Geographic* (Lutz & Collins, 1993), the ethnographic gaze connotes the worthiness of the exotic as a topic of study while simultaneously signaling its failure and unfulfilled desire to imitate the familiar self.

Authenticity

This section begins by drawing a distinction between authenticity and autonomy to highlight the moral significance of the former for romanticists. Generally, autonomy or agency implies a sense of accountability and choice for one's actions. In contrast, authenticity suggests a sense of moral responsibility or "the actor's capacity to observe consistently a *self-imposed* principle" (Ferrara, 1998, p. 6). Although the two concepts overlap in some ways, they refer to relatively distinct realms of cognition and action. Romanticists are motivated by the belief that "the capacity for being oneself" is tantamount to the capacity for moral conduct (Ferrara, 1998, p.

8), and they search for the authentic in various people and cultures with the hope of revealing the nature of morality.

In this vein, ethnographic texts have become fertile ground for the crossbreeding of innovative literary and traditional scientific approaches in an attempt to better apprehend the authentic moral subject. Particularly, a group of ethnographers, loosely referred to as "emotionalists" by Gubrium and Holstein (1997), are ostensibly and deliberately self-absorbed. The emotionalists overtly advocate the use of, and reliance on, romantic themes.

> We live for feelings. Feelings lie behind, are the foundation of and the goal of, all thought. Feelings pervade thought, are fused with thought, inspire thought, and at the extreme, destroy thought. But feeling without thought is blind. Thought (reason, rationality) is the guide of feelings. . . . To present the whole picture we must begin with the beginning, the foundation and the end of all else: feeling. (Douglas, 1977, pp. 14–15)

In emotionalist research, the vague but intimate relationship between feeling and thought is often resolved in favor of the former. In essence, these researchers follow Rousseau's personal revelation that "I felt before I thought," or as David Silverman (1989) wrote, they seek "the impossible dream of transcending the discourses we speak/speak us" (p. 38). For the emotionalists, the authentic is located deep within the self and is brought to life through a romantic writing style that privileges and praises imagination over reason, emotions over logic, and intuition over science. Indeed, the emotional approach is quite deliberate about its romanticist leanings. In the words of Carolyn Ellis and Michael G. Flaherty (1992), the goal is to capture and evoke the complex, paradoxical, and mysterious qualities of subjectivity.

Reveling in the very methodology of producing a self-conscious narrative, for these researchers the textual production is a liberating act in its own right. They blur disciplinary genres and incorporate a "messier" style in their writing (see Ellis, 1991; Ellis & Bochner, 1992, 1996; Richardson, 1990, 2000), in an effort to "join ethnographic and fictional writing, the personal and the social, autobiographical and sociological understanding, and literature and science" (Ellis, 1993, p. 724). These exhortations have moved romantic qualitative researchers to openly share soul-searching journeys into their innermost beings.

For example, in her article "Multiple Reflections of Child Sex Abuse: An Argument for a Layered Account," Carol R. Ronai (1995) reported in vivid detail her personal tragedy as a victim of abuse. Her gut-wrenching descriptions of being violated are punctuated with a detached scientific tone. The changes in tone and style act as rhetorical devices that underscore the authenticity of the personal in juxtaposition to the professional. Ronai's multilayered approach effectively pulls the reader into her world and her memories of abuse.

Similarly, Lisa Tillman-Healy's (1996) work, "A Secret Life in a Culture of Thinness," takes the reader through a lifetime of experiences dealing with anorexia. To adequately express the depth and brutality of the exotic experience, Tillman-Healy used poems, reflections on everyday experiences, and at times "hard" social scientific facts to convey the authenticity of her experience. The goal, Tillman-Healy noted, is "to help you engage how bulimia feels" (p. 104); thus, "multiple forms are used to mimic the complex and multilayered nature of food addiction" (p. 104).

As moving and informative as these romantic accounts of authenticity are, they are not without their critics. For example, Regina Bendix (1997) saw the broader search for cultural authenticity as a quixotic effort to capture the essence of "pure" human existence. For her, this effort assumes a static and mythical view of culture that is incompatible with the actual com-plexities of social life. Similarly, Charles Taylor (1991) criticized "the ethic of authenticity" as a modern invention that places undue emphasis on self-awareness as both the instrument and the goal of morality at the cost of ignoring broader sociocultural factors that influence human behavior. In his words, the advocates of authenticity "see fulfillment as just of the self, neglect-ing or delegitimating the demands that come from beyond our own desires or aspirations, be they from history, tradition, society, nature, or God; they foster, in other words, a radical anthropocentrism" (p. 58).

The romantic preoccupation with the authentic self in qualitative research to some extent mirrors the scientific preoccupation with objectivity. Both romanticism and positivism assume a subject through whose gaze "truth" about an external world is accurately revealed, and in both cases, such a subject is a universal constant. Ironically, some avant-garde ethnographers take for granted the authentic self in the same manner their positivist rivals endorse universal laws that supposedly govern human behavior. In both cases, empirical reality takes a back seat to unexamined ideological assumptions.

The enthusiastic emphasis on subjectivity as the source of authenticity and truth needs to be revisited with a more critical eye. Clearly, the pioneering literary-oriented works that refer-ence the researcher self in the text have inspired ethnographers to challenge and to break away from the dominant positivist paradigm. Nevertheless, this approach raises its own epistemo-logical questions. For example, we may ask: What are the discursive sources of the "selves" from which we write? Simply writing from a subjective stance does not resolve the representational issues that fueled the formation of alternative standpoints. Richardson (2000) captured the reflexive relationship between discourse and subjectivity when she wrote,

> Language is not the result of one's individuality; rather, language constructs the individual's subjectivity in ways that are historically and locally specific. What something means to individuals is dependent on the discourses available to them.... Experience and memory are thus open to contradictory interpreta-tions governed by social interests and prevailing discourses.... Because individuals are subject to multiple and competing discourses in many realms, their subjectivity is shifting and contradictory, not stable, fixed, rigid. (p. 929)

Accordingly, an ethnographic subject that is not textually situated in, and critical of, the pre-vailing social conditions runs the risk of misrecognizing, or even masking, the "relations of ruling" (Smith, 1990) that mediate its expression. The subjective voice is not inherently free of dominant and oppressive discourses, no matter how emotionally, sincerely, or eloquently it is written. In defense of the subjective standpoint in qualitative research, Bochner and Ellis (1999) stated,

> We write a story in which we are featured as a main character. Sometimes, we provide no explicit analysis, no explanatory theory. "How can this be science?" you ask.... Narrative offers a divergent rationality. What makes narratives believable is the sense of reality they create, their intimacy, economy, accessibility, verisimilitude, and their capacity to evoke and promote identification, feeling, empathy, and dialogue. (pp. 491–492)

Again, we acknowledge that the narrative turn represents a break from the false subject-object duality embedded of positivism, but we pose a different question. Namely, how do we assess the emancipatory potential of the new texts? As sociohistorically located constructs, rhetoric and affect were used to legitimize the worst systems of oppression in the 20th century. For example, Joseph Goebbels's masterful manipulation of emotionality and rhetoric was instrumental in the rise of the Third Reich. Goebbels's position on the relationship between art and education is particularly instructive in this regard. Speaking to a group of German filmmakers in 1941, he advised,

> This is the really great art—to educate without revealing the purpose of education. . . . The best propaganda is that which, as it were, works invisibly, penetrates the whole life without the public having any knowledge at all of the propagandaist initiative. (Kaes, 1989, p. 5)

This quotation suggests that the methods of oppression and liberation are disturbingly similar. Aesthetically oriented texts are not immune from the relations of ruling that make oppression possible. In this context, far from being irritating, constant analysis and explanation are necessary safeguards against totalizing narratives.

The Moral Project

Social reform and a moral emphasis on individual rights in a rapidly developing world have been prevalent themes in the works of romanticists. During the late 18th and early 19th centuries, romantic authors were particularly critical of urban life and the conditions of the industrial city that Rousseau argued put "men in chains." Elaborating on this theme, William Wordsworth (1888), in "The Prelude," wrote of "the close and overcrowded haunts/ Of cities, where the human heart is sick" (p. 467). Similarly, William Blake (1989), in the poem "Milton," spoke to the "dark satanic mills" that dominated the countryside of his native England.

In the same vein, American sociology has long been concerned with a "moral salvation" of the social world. From its inception, social thought in America has had its roots in Christian religion, setting as its goal the establishment of a "Kingdom of God" on Earth (Vidich & Lyman, 1985, 2000). This orientation to the social world is obvious in the writings of Robert Park and other Chicago School devotees. Their works reflect a grand moral project to fight against the urban decay of the city.

> The great cities concentrate the great class which are being pushed to the wall. The rate of human wear and tear is dreadful in a great city. The great city draws in the best brains and brawn of the country all about. It is there that the great prizes are won but failure comes there too. Business failure but worse yet the physical failure of bad air, late hours, excitement, bad food, bad amusements, etc. All these tend to destroy mental and moral strength…. The cities kill off the masses just as the wars of the middle ages. (Church, 1965, p. 48)

Orienting their work to the "human junk" of modern society, the Chicago School concentrated on the social amelioration of the urban world and "the great cities" (Thomas & Znaniecki, 1918). Leading this movement was Park (1927/1973): "I made up my mind to go in for experience for its own sake, to gather into my soul… 'all the joys and sorrows of the world'" (p. 253; as cited in Ritzer, 1996). Park focused on what he considered to be a general institutional crisis in the world and sought for a "brotherhood of mankind" (Vidich & Lyman, 1985).

In *Street Corner Society*, Whyte (1943) echoed a similar moral tone as he commented on his own personal "interest in economics and social reform." Whyte discussed the importance of visiting Cornerville firsthand and observing its "problems" so that they may be "solved." To

Whyte, "it follows, therefore, that no immediate and direct solution to the problems posed for Cornerville can be a given" (p. xvi). One must go there, or as Park so bluntly stated, one must get the "seats of their pants dirty." He strove to see Cornerville not just as an Italian slum but as a complex and unique social structure whose study was a necessary step in carrying out the moral project. The moral emphasis is also apparent in contemporary ethnographies. For instance, Barrie Thorne's (1994) research is written with an ongoing concern over the ways and mechanisms through which gender is constructed through the socialization of children. Thorne ended her book urging us toward a moral evaluation of gender and its construction. In the moralizing tone that has become a characteristic feature of most ethnographies, Thorne stated that she shared with many others "the long-range goal of eliminating the gender typing of tasks and activities, of allocating opportunities, resources, and teacher attention to the social categories of students" (p. 159).

Similarly, an appreciation of others and creating a sense of community are recurring themes in many ethnographies that use writing as a means of giving voice to alienated others and the disempowered. For example, Tillman-Healy's (1996) article on bulimia ends by reminding the reader that the piece is written for bulimics as an account of "comfort and companionship." Its goal is to "maintain a critical attitude" about our culture and its stories and relationships of body, gender, and food. Tillman-Healy put forth her work as a moral project that "direct[s] us toward healthier bodies and more contented hearts" (p. 105).

Ronai's (1996) autoethnography, "My Mother Is Mentally Retarded," provides another example of morally oriented qualitative research. In this piece, Ronai spoke of growing up as a child of a mentally retarded mother and of the relationship with her mother. She depicted the dramatic climaxes and ambiguities of this life through an intense emotional tone. Referring to this article, Ellis praised Ronai for a story that "extends beyond herself, to the backstage of disturbed families" (Bochner & Ellis, 1996, p. 32). Ellis went on to suggest that Ronai's story opens up the reader to experiences normally not discussed within clinical literature and provides a better understanding of very real issues that families, whether "disturbed" or not, must cope with. The strongest support for the ameliorative effect of writing is expressed by Ellis and Bochner (1996), who suggested the very purpose of ethnography is no longer to write a "good" one but rather to write a "useful" one that can help to morally improve the social world. This can be seen explicitly, and in gripping detail, in Aliza Kolker's (1996) "Thrown Overboard: The Human Costs of Health Care Rationing," a moving account of her battle with breast cancer and the difficulties associated with an inadequate healthcare system.

The story is especially enlightening and timely, given the recent political debates on healthcare reform. Kolker asked, Is it moral to ration healthcare? In this sense, her work can be considered a "useful" autoethnography, offering an emotional argument against a failing healthcare system. Morally, Kolker's text provides an excellent example of giving voice to experiences that are shrouded in secrecy (Ellis & Bochner, 1992; Ronai, 1995).

Similarly, the issue of morality in ethnographic research has been of particular interest to postmodernists, whose position on the romantic moral project can be divided into the two categories of "skeptics" and "affirmatives." As Pauline Rosenau (1992) noted,

> The skeptics are political agnostics, proposing that all political views are mere constructions and generally avoiding advocacy of any type…. Affirmative postmodernists are more politically optimistic. They support a wide range of political and social movements and advocate pluralism and tolerance rather than dogmatic and partisan postures. (pp. 23–24)

Hence, some branches of postmodernism view moral emancipation as a worthy objective. For example, Jean-Francois Lyotard (1983), in *The Postmodern Condition*, alluded to the moral struggle against the shackles of modernity:

> Under the general demand for slackening and for appeasement, we can hear the mutterings of the desire for a return of terror, for the realization of the fantasy to seize reality. The answer is: Let us wage a war on totality; let us be witnesses to the unpresentable; let us activate the differences and save the honor of the name. (p. 82)

Postmodern ethnography, in particular, embraces Foucault and Lyotard's position on knowledge as being productive of power and reality. Referring to this orientation, Richard Rorty (1989) argued that in a liberal society, it is the responsibility of "text," whether it's a newspaper, film, poetry, or ethnography, to promote a "compassionate understanding" and to steer creative energies toward moral change and progress.

Following Lyotard's dissension with grand narratives of the past, postmodern ethnographers "critique science, realism, and the realist text" (Clough, 1992, p. 132; Denzin, 1997, p. 232). They denounce traditional narrative analysis and ethnography for being in the service of the modern technocratic state. Their differing standpoint epistemologies of gender, color, and sexuality promise to reverse this trend through the emergence of "messy texts." In a sense, for affirmative postmodernists, the moral project of romanticism does not lose its significance but becomes more immersed in conscious theorizing and esoteric terminology.

An important aspect of the romantic moral project is the notion of humanism, which advocates the oneness of humankind based on purportedly universal strengths, frailties, and desires. Skeptic postmodernists are especially critical of the humanist agenda. As Rosenau (1992) put it,

> The skeptics contend that humanism has been used to justify Western superiority and cultural imperialism.... Neo-colonialism was humanist in that it asserted a responsibility to educate primitive peoples, to teach them to read and write. But in most cases education translated into assimilation to the culture of the colonial power, teaching the reading and writing of a foreign language. Similarly, native people in America were moved to reservations because it was said they could not take care of themselves. (p. 49)

The shortcomings of humanism in qualitative research are underscored by Alexander Liazos (1972) in an article titled "The Poverty of the Sociology of Deviance: Nuts, Sluts, and Preverts." Referring to the labeling school's aim to "humanize and normalize the 'deviant,'" he pointed out the potential pitfalls of such well-intentioned efforts.

> A young woman who grew up in the South in the 1940's and 1950's told Quinn (1954, p. 46): "You know, I think from the fact that I was told so often that I must treat colored people with consideration, I got the feeling that I could mistreat them if I wanted to." Thus with "deviants," if in fact they are as good as we are, we would not need to remind everyone of this fact; we would take it for granted and proceed from there. But our assertion that "deviants" are not different may raise the very doubts we want to dispel. (p. 105)

Nevertheless, humanism continues to be a central theme in contemporary ethnography. Consider, for example, this excerpt from a participant-observation study of AIDS patients:

> Finally, this story shows how those who are often labeled as "deviant, aberrant, or pariahs" in our society are not really as different from the rest of us as many might think. I say this because the PWAs [people with AIDS] who reside at the Tahitian Islander [the research site] often want nothing more than a home, a family, friendship, and a chance to be remembered. And although it is easy to misunderstand a life that seems foreign, we must never overlook those reminders of humanness that might draw us all closer together. (Cherry, 1996, p. 26)

This passionate appeal for sameness glosses over a host of important considerations. It would be a statement of the obvious that people with AIDS are not all the same. They vary in income, race, sexuality, and nationality, and these differences tell us a great deal about who is afflicted with AIDS and who is fortunate to escape it and receive treatment for it. At a broader level, it may be that many "deviants" are different from "the rest of us." In many cases, it is the very struggle to preserve difference that results in their labeling as outcasts. In the course of bridging the gap between the familiar and the strange, romantic humanism normalizes exotic others in the service of the dominant culture, or "the rest of us." It prematurely dismisses differences in the name of a greater good (i.e., humanism).

Some ethnographers abandon any reference to the moral project of humanism altogether. Instead, they become immersed in data gathering as an end to itself. Bruce Jacobs's (1999) reflections on his research on crack dealers underscore the notion of ethnographer as the moral arbiter of the field.

> The researcher must decide when to shade the truth and when to be forthright, when to offer and when to omit, when to induce and when to lie back. Such judgments are subjective and context specific, as any ethnographer will tell you. They must be made with audience in mind, whether that audience is legal, academic or social. Each choice affects the kinds of data obtained and revealed. (p. 174)

The vision of subjectivity in this case is not founded on the authentic self, nor is a moral project at the center of this work. Instead, the investigation of the exotic here is viewed as a utilitarian enterprise that can be molded to suit the needs of various audiences, be they technocrats, laymen, or academicians. Thus, the romantic moral project in ethnographic text ranges from writing as a "moral site" (Richardson, 1990) to a market-oriented approach that meets the diverse needs of its readership (Jacobs, 1999).

Writing as Political Practice

Our analysis rests on a basic question: What is the influence of the literary genre of romanticism on the ethnographic text? Specifically, we reexamine the assumption that the literary form is a monolithic and neutral descriptive style that simply makes social science prose more reader friendly. The meaning of qualitative text does not serendipitously rise out of empirical reality or the imaginative mind of the researcher, but it is shaped by various genres and other social conditions. The goal is to unmask certain relations of power embedded in various descriptive styles. In this regard, our critique echoes the agenda of a newly established academic journal titled Ethnography and its stated mission: "the ethnographic and theoretical tracing of... how the interests and views of the powerful are often finally secured within the processes and practices which may seem to oppose dominant interests" (Willis & Trondman, 2000, p. 10).

Subsequently, we maintain that the three discursive elements of romanticism outlined here (the exotic, the authentic, and the moral) create a centrist or mainstream vision of social reality.

For example, consider how the exotic serves as a roadmap in the quest for authenticity. In this context, the exotic is researched to rediscover the authentic self. As Taylor (1991) suggested, what is disturbing about this "ethic of authenticity" is that it takes for granted the bourgeois ethic of individualism and presents it as the ultimate moral struggle.

The romantic focus on outcasts signals a mythical union of humankind regardless of situation or surroundings and reduces the complexities of social life to a self-centered search for the inner truth. The moral project of romanticism is to maintain the integrity of a totalizing view of humanity, to attest to and perpetuate its existence. The romantic discourse, as we have described it here, rescues rationality from the throes of its inherent contradictions by returning social outcasts to the humanist fold. In place of a thorough and radical critique of mainstream culture and its administrative apparatus, romantic descriptions of social problems paint colorful, optimistic portraits of human salvation. Romanticism as a discourse and a descriptive style in qualitative research glosses over the complexity of the postmodern life. It takes for granted the modern self as the source of truth and authenticity and retards the formation of alternative visions of morality and social change based on the myriad social influences that shape the postmodern self.

Our critique of romanticism as a narrative genre in the ethnographic text does not call for a return to either cold realism or abstract purity. Rather, our stance on this literary trope is akin to Foucault's (1984) position on rationality, which he described as a revolving door that "refers to its necessity, to its indispensability, and at the same time to its intrinsic dangers" (p. 249). Our discursive analysis does not debunk romanticism and its central themes, but encourages more experimentation with, and interrogation of, this discourse.

To some degree, we want to encourage new utopian projects. In recent decades, it has become less acceptable for sociologists to explore or propose radically new forms of social order, lest they be accused of adhering to an outdated grand narrative of social change. With few exceptions (see, for example, Feagin & Vera, 2001), researchers have been content with vague references to reforms that do little to transform modes of domination and existing relations of power. The emancipatory goals of the ethnographic enterprise can be advanced through moral projects that address a broader range of social issues and conditions. Although romantically inspired studies modestly point in this direction, their ideological ties with transcendentalism limit their full potential. Romantic descriptions urge readers to escape from social problems to an indefinable utopia with no, or very little, attention to the obdurate conditions that give rise to present realities. Vidich and Lyman (2000) referred to this condition when they wrote that "the postmodern sociologist-ethnographer and his or her subjects are situated in world suspended between illusory memories of a lost innocence and millennial dreams of utopia unlikely to be realized" (p. 59).

As evidenced by two special issues of the *Journal of Contemporary Ethnography* devoted to this topic (see Ellis & Bochner, 1996; Loseke & Cahil, 1999), the field is not lacking for new and alternative approaches to writing. By suggesting that the romantic devices used in constructing the ethnographic text may be elitist or exclusionary, our intention is to add another measure of self-reflection to the existing debate. In some ways, this is consistent with feminist scholars' critique of social sciences and academia. bell hooks's (1990) self-reflection on her role as an educator in mainstream academia can be particularly enlightening in this regard.

> These days when I enter classrooms to teach about people of color and the students are nearly all white, I recognize this to be a risky situation. I may be collaborating with a racist structure. . . . In such circumstances I must interrogate my role as an educator. Am I teaching white students to become contemporary "interpreters" of black experience? Am I educating the colonizer/oppressor class so that they can better exert control? . . . This challenge then confronts everyone who participates in cultural studies, and in other interdisciplinary programs like women's studies, black studies, anthropology, etc. If we do not interrogate our motives, the direction of our work, continually, we risk furthering a discourse on difference and otherness. (p. 132)

The reflexive and dialectical nature of ethnographic research has received much attention (Hammersley & Atkinson, 1983; Marcus, 1994; Atkinson, Coffey, & Delamont, 1999). In this chapter, we have applied these developments to the analysis of romanticism as genre found in qualitative texts. The analysis presented here, as inspired by Smith (1990) and Gubrium and Holstein (1997, 2000), points to how narrative representation is always mediated by discourse and genres; and that no text, whether positivistic, constructionist, or naturalistic, can be exempt from this general principle.

Conclusion

It seems an odd occurrence that researchers who are experts in analyzing narratives give little attention to their own narratives. Perhaps, that is in part because the whole idea of science, or the cloak of science, means assuming transcendent powers over other knowledge domains. The reluctance to apply narrative analysis to researchers' own texts may also be aided by the illusion of unrestrained creative writing. For example, when Jerry Rosiek and Becky Atkinson (2007) analyzed the different genres used by educators to convey their experiences to other educators, they faced opposition, not from the traditional science front, but from "methodological anarchists . . . [who] seem to resent and resist any suggestion of regularity or structure in these newly emerging approaches to educational research on the grounds that this structure will become part of a new hegemonic order, procrustean of other new research possibilities" (p. 500). Rosiek and Atkinson maintain that the opposite is true. Namely, they note that the analysis of genres leads to: (1) critical examination of narrative forms and resisting the temptation to create hegemonic texts, and (2) the establishment of standards for evaluating and improving narrative forms.

We agree with Rosiek and Atkinson that close examinations of how we use genres in our writing, far from limiting creativity, can lead to more deliberate use of narrative structures and aid in the creation of new forms of storytelling and analysis. As qualitative researchers, we need to relentlessly ask ourselves: What are the implications and the purpose of storytelling? What are the aesthetics or narrative devices used in our analysis, and how do they further our specific objectives?

Note

1. This chapter originally appeared under the same title in *Qualitative Inquiry* (Marvasti & Faircloth, 2002). The introduction has been revised for the purpose of the present volume.

References

Adler, P. (1985). *Wheeling and dealing: An ethnography of an upper-level drug dealing and smuggling community.* New York: Columbia University Press.

Adler, P. A., Boelen, W., & Whyte, W. (Eds.). (1992). Street corner society revisited [Special issue]. *Journal of Contemporary Ethnography*, *21*(1).

Atkinson, P., Coffey, A., & Delamont, S. (1999). Ethnography: Post, past, and present. *Journal of Contemporary Ethnography*, *28*(5), 460–471.

Bendix, R. (1997). *In search of authenticity: The formation of folklore studies*. Madison: University of Wisconsin Press.

Blake, W. (1989). *The complete prose and poetry of William Blake* (G. Keynes, Ed.). London: Nonesuch Press.

Bochner, A. P., & Ellis, C. S. (1996). Introduction: Talking over ethnography. In C. Ellis & A. Bochner (Eds.), *Composing ethnography: Alternative forms of qualitative writing* (pp. 13–45). Walnut Creek, CA: AltaMira.

Bochner, A. P., & Ellis, C. S. (1999). Which way to turn. *Journal of Contemporary Ethnography*, *28*(5), 485–499.

Bourdieu, P. (1990). *The logic of practice*. Stanford, CA: Polity.

Cherry, K. (1996). Ain't no grave deep enough. *Journal of Contemporary Ethnography*, *25*(1), 22–57.

Church, R. (1965). The economists study society: Sociology at Harvard, 1891–1902. In P. Buck (Ed.), *Social sciences at Harvard* (pp. 41–58). Cambridge, MA: Harvard University Press.

Clifford, J., & Marcus, G. (Eds.) (1986). *Writing culture: The poetics and politics of ethnography*. Berkeley: University of California Press.

Clough, P. (1992). *The end(s) of ethnography*. Newbury Park, CA: Sage.

Coleridge, S. T. (1916). *The rime of the ancient mariner, Christabel, and Kubla Khan*. Boston: Ginn & Co.

Denzin, N. (1997). *Interpretive ethnography: Ethnographic practices for the 21st century*. Thousand Oaks, CA: Sage.

Douglas, J. (1977). *Existential sociology*. New York: Cambridge University Press.

Eagleton, T. (1976). *Marxism and literary criticism*. Berkeley: University of California Press.

Eagleton, T. (1996). *Literary theory: An introduction*. Minneapolis: University of Minnesota Press.

Ellis, C. (1991). Emotional sociology. *Studies in Symbolic Interaction*, *12*, 123–145.

Ellis, C. (1993). Telling a story of sudden death. *Sociological Quarterly*, *34*, 711–773.

Ellis, C., & Bochner, A. (1992). Telling and performing personal stories. In C. Ellis & M. Flaherty (Eds.), *Investigating subjectivity* (pp. 79–101). Newbury Park, CA: Sage.

Ellis, C., & Bochner, A. (1996). *Composing ethnography: Alternative forms of writing*. Walnut Creek, CA: AltaMira.

Ellis, C. & Bochner, A. (Eds.) (1996). Taking Ethnography into the Twenty-First Century. [Special Issue of] *Journal of Contemporary Ethnography* 25(1): 1-168.

Ellis, C., & Flaherty, M. (Eds.). (1992). *Investigating subjectivity*. Newbury Park, CA: Sage.

Feagin, J. R., & Vera, H. (2001). *Liberation sociology*. Boulder, CO: Westview.

Ferrara, A. (1998). *Reflective authenticity: Rethinking the project of modernity*. New York: Routledge.

Foucault, M. (1984). What is enlightenment? In P. Rabinow (Ed.), *The Foucault reader* (pp. 239–256). New York: Pantheon.

Geertz, C. (1973). *The Interpretation of Cultures*. New York: Basic Books.

Gubrium, J., & Holstein, J. (1997). *The new language of qualitative method*. New York: Oxford University Press.

Gubrium, J., & Holstein, J. (Eds.). (2000). *Institutional selves: Troubled identities in a postmodern world*. New York: Oxford University Press.

Hammersley, M., & Atkinson, P. (1983). *Ethnography: Principles in practice*. London: Tavistock.

hooks, b. (1990). *Yearning: Race, gender, and cultural politics*. Boston: South End.

Jacobs, B. (1999). *Dealing crack: The social world of streetcorner selling*. Boston: Northeastern University Press.

Just, D. (2008). The modern novel from a sociological perspective: Towards a strategic use of the notion of genres. *Journal of Narrative Theory*, *38*(3): 378–397.

Kaes, A. (1989). *From Hitler to Heimat: The return of history as film*. Cambridge, MA: Harvard University Press.

Kolker, A. (1996). Thrown overboard: The human costs of health care rationing. In C. Ellis & A. Bochner (Eds.), *Composing ethnography* (pp. 132–149). Walnut Creek, CA: AltaMira.

Liazos, A. (1972). The poverty of the sociology of deviance: Nuts, sluts, and preverts. *Social Problems*, *20*, 103–120.

Liebow, E. (1993). *Tell them who I am: The lives of homeless women*. New York: Free Press.

Livingstone, P. (2009). Narrativity and knowledge. *Journal of Aesthetics and Art Criticism*, *67*(1), 25–36.

Loseke, D., & Cahil, S. (1999). Reflections on classifying ethnographic reflections at the millennium's turn. *Journal of Contemporary Ethnography* 28, 437-441.

Lutz, C. A., & Collins, J. L. (1993). *Reading National Geographic*. Chicago: University of Chicago Press.

Lyotard, J. F. (1983). *The postmodern condition*. Minneapolis: University of Minnesota Press.

Marcus, G. (1994). What comes just after "post?" The case of ethnography. In N. Denzin & Y. Lincoln (Eds.), *Sage handbook of qualitative research* (1st ed.) (pp. 563–574). Thousand Oaks, CA: Sage.

Marvasti, A., & Faircloth, C. (2002). Writing the exotic, the authentic, and the moral: Romanticism as discursive resource for the ethnographic text. *Qualitative Inquiry 8*, 760–784.

McKinney, J. (1966). *Constructive Typologies and Social Theory*. New York: Appleton-Century-Crofts.

Merriam-Webster's encyclopedia of literature. (1995). Springfield, MA: Merriam-Webster.

Montemurro, B. (2001). Strippers and screamers: The emergence of social control in a non-institutionalized setting. *Journal of Contemporary Ethnography, 30*(3), 275–304.

Park, R. (1927/1973). Life history. *American Journal of Sociology, 79*, 251–260.

Richardson, L. (1990). *Writing strategies*. Newbury Park, CA: Sage.

Richardson, L. (1996). Ethnographic trouble. *Qualitative Inquiry, 2*(2), 227-230.

Richardson, L. (2000). Writing: A method of inquiry. In N. Denzin & Y. Lincoln (Eds.), *Sage handbook of qualitative research* (2nd ed.) (pp. 923–948). Thousand Oaks, CA: Sage.

Ritzer, G. (1996). *Sociological theory* (4th ed.). New York: McGraw-Hill.

Ronai, C. R. (1995). Multiple reflections of child sex abuse: An argument for a layered account. *Journal of Contemporary Ethnography, 23*, 395–426.

Ronai, C. R. (1996). My mother is mentally retarded. In C. Ellis and A. Bochner (Eds.), *Composing Ethnography*. Walnut Creek, CA: AltaMira.

Rorty, R. (1989). *Contingency, irony, and solidarity*. Cambridge: Cambridge University Press.

Rosenau, P. M. (1992). *Post-modernism and the social sciences: Insights, inroads, and intrusions*. Princeton, NJ: Princeton University Press.

Rosiek, J., and Atkinson, B. (2007). The inevitability and importance of genres in narrative research on teaching practice. *Qualitative Inquiry, 13*, 499–521.

Silverman, D. (1989). The impossible dreams of reformism and romanticism. In J. Gubrium & D. Silverman (Eds.), *The politics of field research: Sociology beyond Enlightenment* (pp. 30–48). London: Sage.

Smith, D. (1987). *The everyday world as problematic: A feminist sociology*. Boston: Northeastern University Press.

Smith, D. (1990). *The conceptual practices of power: A feminist sociology of knowledge*. Boston: Northeastern University Press.

Snow, D., & Anderson, L. (1993). *Down on their luck: A study of homeless street people*. Berkeley: University of California Press.

Steer, J., & White, A. (1994). *Atlas of western art history: Artists, sites and movements from ancient Greece to the modern age*. New York: Parchment.

Taylor, C. (1991). *The ethics of authenticity*. Cambridge, MA: Harvard University Press.

Thomas, W. I., & Znaniecki, F. (1918). *The Polish peasant in Europe and America*. New York: Dover.

Thorne, B. (1994). *Gender play: Girls and boys together in school*. New Brunswick, NJ: Rutgers University Press.

Tillman-Healy, L. (1996). A secret life in a culture of thinness: Reflections on body, food, and bulimia. In C. Ellis & A. Bochner (Eds.), *Composing ethnography* (pp. 76–108). Walnut Creek, CA: AltaMira.

Van Maanen, J. (1988). *Tales of the field: On writing ethnography*. Chicago: University of Chicago Press.

Vidich, A., & Lyman, S. (1985). *American sociology*. New Haven, CT: Yale University Press.

Vidich, A., & Lyman, S. (2000). Qualitative methods: Their history in sociology and anthropology. In N. Denzin & Y. Lincoln (Eds.), *Sage handbook of qualitative research* (2nd ed.) (pp. 37–84). Thousand Oaks, CA: Sage.

Whyte, W. (1943). *Street corner society*. Chicago: University of Chicago Press.

Whyte, W. (1996). Facts, interpretation, and ethics in qualitative inquiry. *Qualitative Inquiry, 2*(2), 242–244.

Whyte, W. (1997). *Creative problem solving in the field: Reflections on a career*. Walnut Creek, CA: AltaMira.

Willis, P., & Trondman, M. (2000). Manifesto for ethnography. *Ethnography, 1*, 5–16.

Wolf, M. (1992). *A thrice-told tale: Feminism, postmodernism, and ethnographic responsibility*. Stanford, CA: Stanford University Press.

Wordsworth, W. (1888). *The complete poetical works of William Wordsworth*. London: Macmillan.

Methodological Explorations of Structural and Institutional Phenomena

CHAPTER SIXTEEN

Infiltrating Fundamentalist Institutions[1]

NURIT STADLER

Ethnography and Fundamentalism

Exclusive educational institutions and scripturalism (the literal interpretation of sacred texts) are widely considered to be hallmarks of fundamentalism (Ammerman, 1987; Antoun, 2001). Marty and Appleby (1991, p. 1) argue that "fundamentalism appears as a strategy or set of strategies by which beleaguered believers attempt to preserve their distinctive identity as a people or group. Feeling this identity to be at risk, fundamentalists fortify it by utilizing a unique set of educational institutions and a selective retrieval of doctrines, beliefs and practices from a sacred past."[2] These widespread assumptions are predicated on the study of different fundamentalist groups the world over (see Ammerman, 1987; Boone, 1989; Marty & Appleby, 1991; Sivan, 1991; Aran, 1993; Beeman, 2001).

Despite the abundance of research on fundamentalism, minimal attention has been given to the methods that are best suited for investigating the unique nature of this phenomenon, its institutions, and scriptural dynamics. In other words, there is scant knowledge on the way text-based communities study their canons, select their sacred texts, produce knowledge, and translate this information into the everyday behavior of their members. My objective is to help scholars develop effective ethnographic approaches for researching fundamentalist groups. As illustrated below, it is incumbent upon scholars to ask the following questions upon setting out to research a text-based community: How do fundamentalists interpret their sacred texts? How do they explain reality via their religious canon? And how can we improve our ethnographic methods so as to further our understanding of this phenomenon?

In the ensuing pages, I shall elaborate on the methodology I developed over the course of my fieldwork on Haredi (ultra-Orthodox) male yeshiva culture in Israel. The Haredi community in Israel constitutes an enclave of fundamentalism and male piety (Stadler, 2008). Most of the group's fundamentalist activities take place in the yeshiva—a seminary for advanced Talmudic studies that is designed exclusively for men. The top students at these institutions go on to become members of the elite, wielding authority through their position as rabbis, adjudicators, and scholars (Heilman, 1983, p. 1). In the Haredi study hall, the principles of traditional Jewish virtuosity are instilled in the male students via mastery of the Talmud and its commentaries. Furthermore, insofar as the ultra-Orthodox community is concerned, the yeshiva system guarantees no less than the spiritual and physical survival of the Jewish people (Friedman, 1993, p. 184).

My fieldwork was conducted between 1997 and 2003. During this period, I interviewed 42 Israeli ultra-Orthodox yeshiva students and rabbis.[3] For the purpose of carrying out in-depth interviews against a textual backdrop, I sought to construct a dialogical framework that suited the features of this group (cf. Mishler, 1986; Bruner, 1990; Seidman, 1991; Lambek, 1993, p. 19). With this objective in mind, I managed to secure key informants (see Krannich & Humphrey 1986, p. 477)—yeshiva students who took an active part in devising the research methods, especially the interview format and the selection of texts. These informants helped me incorporate the pillars of the Haredi yeshiva world—its religious symbols, texts, and methods of knowledge production and transmission—into the interview structure. In the pages that follow, I will demonstrate how this methodology took shape and expound upon the three essential Haredi traditions that were integrated into the ethnographic fieldwork: (1) the logic of the Yeshiva lesson wherein students are instilled with textual skills and come to master the community's canonical knowledge; (2) the praxis of debating central issues in Jewish scriptures, through which textual hierarchies are established; and (3) textual critique, an informal dialectical process that gives rise to new ideas. The ultimate objective behind amalgamating these elements into my ethnographic methods was to explicate the dynamics of Haredi scripturalism and yeshiva dialectics.

In my estimation, this approach enabled me to unearth multiple levels of meanings concerning the Haredi yeshiva world's fundamentalist nature, which otherwise would not have come to light. Above all, I discovered that texts and symbols created by religious authorities are neither fully accepted nor implemented in a literal fashion, but are often challenged and occasionally mocked, condemned, and replaced. These insights on the transformative elements of Haredi scripturalism are likely to enhance our understanding of the fundamentalist experience. Let me begin my analysis with a brief survey of the Haredi community in Israel.

Haredi Fundamentalism in Israel

The ultra-Orthodox or Haredi community in Israel has been described as a fundamentalist hyper-segregated, religious enclave (see Friedman, 1987; Heilman & Friedman, 1991, Rapoport, 1993; Sprinzak, 1993; Heilman, 1994; Soloveichik, 1994; Selengut, 1994; Stadler, 2002, 2004, 2008). The word "Haredi" is also used by the members of the community so as to distinguish themselves from other religious groups in Israel. Haredi is a Hebrew epithet for a "mortified" devotee and has also been translated as "those who tremble," a reference to Isaiah 66:5: "Hear the word of the Lord, you who tremble at his word" (Heilman & Friedman, 1991, p. 198). This appellation made its way to Israel during the influx of Haredi communities from Europe after the Second World War. Indeed, during the country's early years, the majority of its Haredi residents were Holocaust survivors.

Upon the establishment of the Zionist state, a new form of ultra-Orthodox fundamentalism evolved, a postwar variation of fundamentalism that was driven by the faithful's solemn desire to preserve a Jewish way of life that was wiped out in Europe. However, in contrast to the traditional Jewish system of prewar Eastern Europe where only a chosen few studied Torah on a full-time basis, the Haredi leadership in Israel decided that all its male members were to pursue a life of devotional study.[4] By the late 1940s and early 1950s, yeshiva students—"bnei torah" in Hebrew—were regarded as the final outpost of traditional erudite Judaism (Stadler, 2008). In light of the above, the Talmudic seminary, namely the East European–style yeshiva, has become the center for male worship and fellowship in Israel. Within its halls, devoted men reinterpret sacred codes, revive Talmudic wisdom, and strive to set themselves apart and protect the community from the temptations and distractions of modernity and secularism.

Concentrated in exclusive neighborhoods, Haredim maintain a separate culture and education system. Likewise, their distinct dress code and lifestyle sets them apart from the country's secular majority. As part of the ultra-Orthodox ideology to completely abstain from anything that is perceived as impure, Haredim adhere to, inter alia, stringent dietary restrictions and sexual prohibitions and perform an array of exclusive rituals (burial, marriage, etc.). Living within an enclave prescribes and circumscribes behavior, and most communal services, including religious (e.g., synagogues and ritual baths), commercial, welfare, judicial, and self-enforcement are provided within the confines of the community. In addition, marriages are prearranged and endogamic (Heilman & Friedman, 1991).

The yeshivas and "kolels" (Talmudic academies for married men) are the center of communal life. According to Haredi perspectives, authentic Judaism can only be fully realized and passed on to future generations in a yeshiva environment (Friedman, 1998). In Deuteronomy (6:7), God commands the faithful to study Torah "…when sitting at home and when on the road." This obligation has been elevated by contemporary Haredi interpretations to the extent that male enrollment in seminaries is deemed to be a vital part of belonging to the community and perpetuating its legacy. In the aftermath of the Holocaust, the yeshiva can be said to have supplanted the traditional Jewish community as the center of Haredi life (see Friedman, 1993).

The seminaries' rabbis control most facets of male socialization by means of age-old techniques, such as the "shiur" (lesson given by a rabbi) and the "kchevruta" (reviewing the shiur with a partner in the study hall). Transmitting both venerable and novel interpretations, these pedagogic frameworks preserve and produce knowledge on behalf of the entire community. As opposed to other text-based communities, Haredi textual and cosmological principles are dominated by male interpretations,[5] which regulate all spheres of life (cf. Heilman, 1983; Soloveitchik, 1994; Nagata, 2001; Antoun 2001). Most male Haredim (plural for Haredi) stay in the yeshiva until the age of 40 and do not participate in the Israeli labor force. As a result, the majority of the community lives in relative poverty, maintaining a modest lifestyle that is highly dependent on state support (Berman, 2000). In light of the above, the yeshiva is an all-encompassing institution, as its assorted functions—a place of worship and study, a framework for socializing and leisure, and a quasi-municipality that provides material aid, housing, and even psychic support—cover the full gamut of the individual's needs.

In return for these "services," a yeshiva scholar is expected to renounce all worldly concerns and fully devote himself to intellectual and spiritual pursuits. Interrupting this duty for any reason is considered a sin. The Torah is perceived to be the primary path of an ascetic life that enables its sojourners to withdraw from the material realm (Stadler, 2002). Therefore, participation in state apparatuses, such as the army (or other forms of national service) and the economic sphere is deemed to be a profanation of Torah study and thus in violation of the principal community taboo (Stadler & Ben-Ari, 2003; Stadler, 2004, 2008). As a result, the income of a typical "kolel" (married student) and his family is heavily reliant on government support (primarily the child allowance) and institutional stipends (see Caplan, 2003). Finally, the reclusive Haredi community is in perpetual conflict with society at large over issues such as religious observance, state duties, and economic independence (Berman, 2000).

Ethnography and the Problem of Scripturalism

This entire research project was strewn with obstacles. Upon deciding to conduct an ethnographic study on the complex dynamic of scripturalism in the fundamentalist environment of the yeshiva, I was immediately faced with the problem of how to penetrate and make sense of this closed society. My initial objective was to obtain interviews with young yeshiva students, for I assumed that they serve as key agents on behalf of the entire community in all that concerns the transmission of knowledge and the interpretation of codes of behavior. However, as a secular woman, my every step into the Haredi world is considered a violation of the community's moral code, for the mere presence of a woman is viewed as a distraction from Torah study. In consequence, the very foundation of the anthropological approach—the intimate encounter between researcher and interviewees—posed a threat to the community's sacred order, especially the prescribed relations between men and women (Stadler, 2008). Against this backdrop, I had to come up with a cautious and sensitive approach for securing the "honorary male right"[6] to meet with and interview students (Stadler, 2007). That said, gaining access to the students was not enough; I had to devise a method that would enable me to win over their confidence so that they would be willing to discuss their lives and experiences as contemporary Haredi yeshiva "boys" in a candid manner. Given the circumstances, I made two decisions that would guide me throughout the research phase: to use my exclusion to my advantage; and to model the interviews, as much as possible, on the Haredi pedagogical system (See Heilman, 2000).

Drawing on the works of other ethnographers (see Shostak, 1981; Krannich & Humphrey, 1986, p. 477), my first step was to locate a key informant who was willing and able to help me surmount the above-mentioned obstacles and penetrate this male-dominated world. I searched for someone who could accompany me to the sessions and minimize the tension of a Haredi male's encounter with a secular female anthropologist, on the assumption that, if the yeshiva students saw me talking with someone of their ilk, they would agree to cooperate. I was indeed fortunate enough to find a young yeshiva student who was ready to lend a hand. While discussing my goals with him, I realized that perhaps the most crucial challenge was to grasp the lexicon, norms, and world of ideas of my subjects' text-based community. More specifically, I had to determine the text hierarchies, the mechanisms of their sacred sources, and the ways in which these texts are encoded, translated, and arranged in the communal knowledge base, in order to ascertain how the Haredi leadership utilizes this same knowledge base to control its members' behavior (cf. Geertz, 1961, on Javanese family; Powdermaker, 1966, on Indianola; Shostak, 1981, 2000, on Kung women). These objectives warranted a new attitude towards the logic and content of the interviews. At this early juncture, I asked the informants that I managed to recruit to help me improve the interview framework for the purpose of enhancing the mutual dialogue and my comprehension of Haredi scripturalism. From this point on, some of the informants became full-fledged partners in all that concerned the design of the research tools. I would even go so far as to say that the corroboration with my informants and their contribution to my understanding of their text-based society is the main focus of this chapter.[7] In this respect, my key informants served as my "ticket" to the field. Likewise, they helped me draw the initial distinction between "the field" (places in the community) and "home" (everything outside of the Haredi sphere).[8]

At an advanced stage of this research project, I came to the realization that being a woman goes well beyond what Freilich (1970, p. 2) described as the "privileged stranger."[9] In *The People of the Book*, Heilman (1983) describes how he entered ultra-Orthodox Talmudic study circles in Jerusalem and throughout the U.S. Adopting the participant-observer approach, he sought to decipher the meaning of "lernen" (studying) by scrutinizing the experiences of those engaged in yeshiva practices. As a male researcher who is also familiar with the texts, Heilman was able to avail himself of what he dubs a "native as a stranger" method (1983, p. 9). However, since women are prohibited from even entering the study hall, my first objective was to find a key informant to help me gain access to the yeshiva world, be it by informal, surreptitious, or other means. As a woman, my presence among male yeshiva students engendered multiple levels of "strangeness," which paradoxically worked to my advantage. To begin with, as a secular person, I was of little consequence to my subjects and distanced from the Haredi world. Everything was novel and strange, so that I merited insightful explanations from my "hosts." Second, as a woman, I was automatically excluded from the world of sacred texts and thus found myself in the role of the ignoramus. Last, by virtue of my entrenched outsider status, I did not pose a threat to the yeshiva students' standing or culture (cf. Lomsky-Feder 1996; El-Or 1994, 2002).[10]

The Simulated Lesson—Yeshiva Ambiance and Scripturalism

Almost every sentence that a Haredi yeshiva student utters contains a reference to a sacred text, predominately biblical and Talmudic sayings (cf. Lambek, 1993, pp. 134, 137). By citing these texts, Haredim believe that they are embodying the word of God, just like a shaman speaking through a performer, a Sufi teacher animating the words of those who have seen the other world, or a Baptist hearing the spirit's voice (Keen, 1997, pp. 60–62). The powerful inclination to constantly employ the sacred hermeneutic tradition is tied to the students' berth in the community, their education, and the manner in which they perceive their cultural heritage and roots.[11] Familiarity with the Talmud is thus vital to any meaningful interaction in communal life. In order to fathom the logic and reproduction of meanings in a text-based community, the researcher must first decipher the status of a cited text, namely its different uses and the extent of its veneration and diffusion.[12] Therefore, it was imperative that I examine how texts are utilized and interpreted as well as the relationship between texts and their purported meanings (Stolow, 2004).

With these issues in mind, I turned to well-integrated yeshiva students for assistance in formulating my interview structure and questions.[13] The first measure we took was to adopt the traditional yeshiva lesson, the "shiur," as the format for all the interviews. The shiur is an elementary unit of Haredi fundamentalist training, as it is the means by which knowledge is acquired and transmitted from childhood onwards, particularly in the context of a male yeshiva. In this respect, the yeshiva is similar to the madrasa[14] in certain Islamic movements or Christian Bible-school lessons (Gellner, 1981; Antoun, 1989; Lambek, 1993, p. 136). All the interviewees explained that the shiur undergirds their learning process. What's more, they stressed that it is the primary framework for discussing Jewish texts, for acquiring the tools to analyze, interpret, and internalize ideas and methods, and for shaping their worldview (see Heilman, 1983, 1992, 1994).

Since the shiur is a principal venue for learning, disputation, and introducing ideas and texts, the use of its images and structures provided me with a firsthand look at the Haredi textual interpretation process. Consequently, my meetings with the students, particularly at the early stages of the research, were transformed into proactive textual study sessions, which enabled me to partake in both observation and interviewing at the same time. Texts for a specific lesson were selected in advance, according to jointly selected themes (especially livelihood, family issues, and various aspects of learning). This format enabled me to comprehend the process by which texts are selected and extrapolated textual knowledge is transmitted and adapted.[15] Before each meeting, I informed the interviewees of the topic and asked them to bring a selection of texts (from the yeshiva's collection or their home library) that they thought was most pertinent to the topic at hand. As a result, we began most sessions by reading canonical texts and the attendant interpretations of several rabbinical figures. Thereafter, a discussion ensued on the major disputes regarding that particular theme. For example, one interview commenced with the following passage from the Talmud:

> **THE SELECTED TEXT:** Rabbi Simeon B. Eleazar said: "In my whole lifetime I have not seen a deer engaged in gathering fruits, a lion carrying burdens, or a fox [working] as a shopkeeper, yet they are sustained without trouble, though they were created only to serve me, whereas I was created to serve my Master. Now, if these [beasts] that were created exclusively to serve me are sustained without trouble, how much more so should I be sustained without trouble—I who was created to serve my Maker! But it is because I have behaved evilly and destroyed my livelihood [that I must toil]. As it is said, 'your iniquities have turned away these things'" (Kidushin, 82a).

> **MY QUESTION:** Do the animals in this excerpt also serve as a metaphor? If we are just like the animals, then someone is guarding us from above because "they were created in order to be used by the Lord," and nowadays we live from day to day just like the animals?

> **THE INTERVIEWEE:** Yes! This is a very nice interpretation.... This is also insinuated in the Mishna (Kidushin), and your interpretation is excellent.... Nevertheless, we have to take this one step further and ask: Why do we need an occupation? Why should a person...train himself? We know it is indicated in the sacred sources—that's true. But if we are like the birds, then why work? Yet perhaps there's a different message here. We know that even birds go out and search for food. If not, they would die from hunger.... There is a fine balance in nature, and this is why things function.... Perhaps it is a proverb, but the message here is that ultimately if one works hard, food will be obtained...and you will thus be free of any concerns for livelihood.... You will not have to worry about tomorrow.... If we think about it, what is the purpose of an occupation? Is it about [attaining] economic security? Sure. Yet it also means that we haven't put our faith and trust in the Lord! Perhaps this metaphor is about letting you know that you must learn a trade, but you shouldn't rely on it; the only thing you can trust in is God.... He will sustain you like the birds...

As evidenced by these excerpts, the shiur-oriented interviewing structure elicited numerous ideas and pointed to myriad possible interpretations of and attitudes toward the Jewish canon. It is important to note that, even though my "teacher-cum-informant" related to and even complimented my interpretation, he clearly emphasized the version that is presently accepted by the community. Although he responded to my idea, his primary goal was to reiterate and bolster the standard view whereby those who place their trust on the sweat of their own brow are not true believers.

Throughout the fieldwork stage, I assembled the texts and interpretations that came up during the meetings into what I dubbed the study's "textual reservoir." Texts and knowledge from the same reservoir thenceforth constituted the starting point for every other interview.[16] In conducting these improvised lessons (like other facets of this study), I basically joined the yeshiva students in an activity—Talmudic study—that, in their own opinion, they do best. Drawing on Crapanzano's insights (1980), this mode of interviewing spurred on a dynamic process of knowledge creation between the ethnographer and the interviewee. Put differently, the shiur framework engendered a special ethno-space wherein both researcher and subject created, examined, and reflected upon the community's ontological environment. By virtue of this method, I essentially became an active participant in the field. While surveying his encounters with Tuhami, Crapanzano (1980, p. 11) described a similar dialogical event: "Not only did my presence, and my questions, prepare him for the text he was to produce, but they produced what I read as a change of consciousness in him. This produced a change of consciousness in me, too. We were both jostled from our assumptions about the nature of the everyday world and ourselves and groped for common reference points within this limbo of interchange."

In sum, by evoking and reshaping extant native processes for the sake of encouraging conversation and debate, I managed to mitigate the sense of unfamiliarity (being a woman), bridge the cultural gap (being secular), and thus extract knowledge.

Let me illustrate this approach with yet another example. As noted earlier, the present-day Haredi community has sanctified the ideal of devotion to yeshiva life, while generally discouraging its members from working, especially in the conventional Israeli labor market (Berman, 2000). I was interested in ascertaining how the community uses sacred texts to justify its outlook on work. This particular example is especially intriguing because most of the students averred that the most accepted rabbinical sources clearly imply that all devotees must earn their own keep. For example, one of the most oft-cited proverbs of the Sages regarding the balance between work and studying Torah reads as follows: "Any Torah which is not accompanied by work will eventually be nullified and will lead to sin. Ultimately, such a person will steal from others…" (Avot 2:2). That said, while broaching some of the most prominent texts in favor of earning a livelihood, my interviewees also emphasized Rabbi Shimon Ben Yohai's position on this topic: "…when Israel performs the will of the Omnipresent, their work is performed by others" (Berakoth 35b). According to many of the students' interpretation of Rabbi Shimon's statement, if a devotee dedicates his life to the study of Torah, others will fulfill his profane chores on his behalf. In response to my inquiries, the informants largely agreed that Jewish tradition shunned Rabbi Shimon's interpretation; nevertheless, they prefer his view because it dovetails smoothly with the situation that Israel's Haredi community in Israel currently finds itself in. This example demonstrates how reading texts with the students exposed their strategic wherewithal to pick out ideas and justify interpretations that suit their needs, even when the cited opinion is rejected by authoritative figures.[17]

Dialogue Through Scriptures: Uncovering Hierarchies

Knowing how texts are selected and interpreted is not enough to explain the dynamics of scripturalism and piety in fundamentalist groups. Besides being transmitted and memorized, textual knowledge can stimulate a vivid dialogue between a group's members. With respect to Israel's Haredi community, the dialogical nature of its text-based religiosity is assembled, codified, and recorded. Therefore, in order to reveal the text's significance to everyday life, I predicated my questions on the above-mentioned reservoir of texts or a "textual arsenal." In other words, texts that I had encountered during the lessons/interviews were catalogued, and I then availed myself of pertinent objects from this cache during the subsequent sessions as both a starting point for the discussion and to entice further dialogue. At the outset of each meeting, the first-time interviewees were surprised by my evocation of these texts, but their familiarity with the subject matter helped alleviate the initial awkwardness. Furthermore, the questions that I formulated on the basis of these texts goaded them into displaying their expertise. These tactics invariably sparked a comprehensive debate on the texts, which centered around prominent interpretations of the Sages (to include some Talmudic references), Maimonides, Rashi,[18] and later authorities. By dint of these scriptural dialogues, I revealed the conceptual organization and hierarchy of the texts that the Yeshiva students constructed and abide by. Instead of viewing fundamentalist scripturalism as merely a literal reading of texts that is translated into practical behavioral norms, I discovered that these young scholars reorganize and rank interpretations (cf. Antoun, 2001, pp. 39–40) for the purpose of altering different dimensions of reality. As the fieldwork progressed, both the hierarchy of the texts and the concepts and images that spring forth from them came to light. For example, during the sessions on biblical narratives and symbols that pertain to questions of work and livelihood, the interviewees exposed a belief in miracles or divine intervention that, in all likelihood, I would not have extracted using any other interviewing technique. For example, the majority of my participants cited the words of Maimonides—the 12th-century halachic scholar, philosopher, and physician—when explaining the ideal of work in the rabbinic textual tradition. Above all, they emphasized Maimonides's recommendations concerning the order in which the major decisions in life should be taken:

> After studying in one's youth, one should find work, then buy a home, and only then should one get married. Fools, on the other hand, marry first, then they buy a home if they have the money, and only late in life do they try to find a job. Or else they live on charity (Deuteronomy: V, 11; see also Aberbach, 1994, p.110).

This view contravenes the absolute renunciation of work and full-time devotion to Torah study that informs the present-day Haredi community in Israel, for Maimonides interprets labor as an ideal undertaking for balancing the sacred and the profane, namely the pursuit of a livelihood vis-à-vis Torah studies (Aberbach, 1994, p. 111). In defense of their community's praxis, most of the interviewees referred to the narrative of the "desert generation" and the appearance of manna from heaven in the Book of Exodus. I usually responded to these claims by asking them whether there were any other interpretations and inquired as to why they had failed to mention them. Moreover, I raised the modern-day controversy over secular society's criticism of the "unproductive" and even "parasitic" elements of the Haredi model. A young yeshiva student from Jerusalem explained that the challenges of modern life rendered the current Haredi system a necessity and drew an analogy between his daily life and the miraculous manna that fell from heaven. He began his soliloquy by reading from the Bible:

[A]nd the children of Israel said to them, "We wish that we had died by the hand of Yahweh in the land of Egypt, when we sat by the flesh-pots, when we ate our fill of bread, for you have brought us out into this wilderness, to kill this whole assembly with hunger." Then said Yahweh to Moses, "Behold, I will rain bread from the sky for you, and the people shall go out and gather a day's portion every day, that I may test them, whether they will walk in my law, or not" (Exodus 16:3–4; translation taken from *The World English Bible*).

The student then interpreted the biblical text and showed how it concords with his current state of being:

…You must understand that in the traditional literature our situation is equated with the manna from heaven… [A] person who has succeeded in reaching a virtuous position and is utterly dependent on God almighty falls under the definition of manna. This is a very high level that was only reached by the people of the desert. You must understand that for all of us [Haredim], the topic of manna is a very central subject in our lives…. [W]hat is manna? Is it spiritual nourishment that is combined with worldly goods into one package? Does manna contain any physical nourishment whatsoever? If it was merely spiritual, then Moses our Rabbi would never have survived solely on manna for forty days and forty nights [upon ascending the mountain to receive the Torah]…. Plainly put, our body is connected to our soul, and a person can attain a certain position where the purely spiritual principle dominates his life and body in such a profound manner that he will eventually survive exclusively from this spiritual nourishment…

This young Haredi thus considers manna to be a powerful metaphor for an idealistic life in which a person throws himself at the graces of God's divine guidance (Stadler, 2008). His interpretation of the manna narrative operates on two levels: first, it reorganizes daily life in accordance with what the student perceives to be the spirit of the Bible; second, it emphasizes the possibility of experiencing miracles in this day and age. As such, the only way believers can completely free themselves from corporeal constraints is by immersing themselves in the spiritual realm through studious endeavors. In this fashion, the interviewee reconstructed the community's spiritual level and its members' individual existence by detaching himself from temporal concerns (Stadler, 2002).

Text-based reasoning and apologetics is indeed the lynchpin of the current Haredi world-view. As a result, the community's quotidian practices are shaped, justified, and reinforced by means of a selective repertoire of texts and the views of contemporary rabbis. The participants' evocation of both traditional and private interpretations of biblical, Talmudic, and other venerated texts shed light on various trends in contemporary ultra-Orthodox society, such as the significant shifts in all that concerns Haredi attitudes to the labor market and the institutions of government (See Stadler, 2002, 2008).

Can Ethnographers Elicit Criticism?

Students of religion define fundamentalist communities as "enclave cultures," a distinct entity with defined cultural and moral boundaries that are surrounded by "walls of virtue," which protect the saved and morally superior from the "depraved" (Sivan, 1995). Similarly, according to Almond, Appleby, and Sivan (2003), Fundamentalists strive to prevent the devil's forces from contaminating the enclave (pp. 34, 36). In this sense, greater society is deemed to be polluted, contagious, and dangerous. As Sivan (1995) puts it, "The outside is all the more harmful as it makes it look as though it partakes of the same tradition as the inside, while being in essence its very negation" (p. 19). In light of the above, scholars tend to describe fundamentalism and its institutions as static, uncritical, and obedient (Stadler, 2008). However, the methods that were developed over the course of my fieldwork enabled me to unearth multiple layers of internal criticism as well as fervent aspirations for change in the yeshiva world among the participants in this study (see Kahane, 1988, pp. 213, 214, 216; 1997). The fact that the interview sessions centered around two or more students debating a text and expressing personal opinions that touch upon the essence of their text-based community afforded me with the opportunity to observe the informal, multitiered critical thinking that informs the yeshiva world. Over the course of the interviews, I discovered that one of the most effective means for exposing undertones of criticism was to suddenly intersperse a question while two or more students were discussing texts that touch upon controversial aspects of yeshiva life. This technique usually provoked the students into admitting that they objected to and were disgruntled over various aspects of Haredi society. For instance, at one meeting, the interviewees referred to the acute tension between work and sustenance:

> STUDENT 1: In Maimonides's eyes, is a full withdrawal from this world, namely avoiding work and dedicating oneself to studious endeavors, the highest state of Judaism, or perhaps…a kind of asceticism?

> STUDENT 2: Not really…. We can touch upon two issues here: We read that Maimonides emphasizes the need to earn a living, but not from the studious activity itself…. So he believes that the true believer is obliged to study, yet…it is unacceptable to gain money from it…, not from the Ministry of Religion, not from a yeshiva, or anyone else… [E]ven though you have no wife or kids and you live alone and want to earn money to support yourself, you must not [according to Maimonides] beg on the street…, you must not ask [for money] from the community… [Instead,] you [should]…find a job and earn a living…

This discussion on Maimonides's interpretation of the proper balance between work and Torah study exposed one of the most vexing tensions that yeshiva students bear. When confronted with questions about the implications of these interpretations on their everyday life, the participants responded by raising doubts, pointing to ambiguities, and offering criticism. The studious model of masculine piety is indeed firmly entrenched in the Haredi world, but most of the interviewees had developed a skeptical view about its purpose and legitimacy. Although they voiced their opinions in a cautious manner, they nevertheless revealed their frustration. While employing canonical arguments, they exhibited both reflexive and creative tendencies and tried to construct a new model of behavior and religiosity. The presence of other yeshiva students at the sessions created an environment in which they felt comfortable enough to express their criticism, contemplate new forms of religious knowledge, and articulate their longings. A survey of the literature indicates that the yeshiva students' propensity to harbor doubts and skepticism are indeed commensurate with those of the members of other contemporary religious communities. That said, it also bears noting that this sort of uncertainty does not necessarily reflect an abandonment or crisis of faith (Gabler, 2002). In any event, my subjects' critical views shed new light on potential friction, intergenerational gaps, and vicissitudes in fundamentalist groups.

Another example of this sort of tension surfaced during a discussion on military issues (Stadler, 2008). In Israel, yeshiva students are exempt from the army. Notwithstanding the Haredi community's strict prohibitions against military service, quite a few students wasted little time before raising doubts about the exemption from military and other frameworks of state service. Many interviewees, both young and old, do not object to the military on conceptual, religious, or moral grounds. What's more, quite a few exhibited great interest in the

Israeli Defense Forces, and some even displayed considerable knowledge of the army's structure, performance, functions, courses, bases, and commanders. Time and again, the argument was made that the asceticism and studious piety might have suited the post-war Israeli yeshiva world but, are no longer sustainable in the 21st century. In order to gauge this friction, I once again confronted the students with apposite sacred texts, such as Deuteronomy 20:5–7:

> And the officers shall speak unto the people, saying: Who is the man who has built a new house and has not begun living in it? Let him go and return to his house lest he die in the battle and another man dedicate it.

Students used this passage to challenge the Haredi ideal. Whereas many of the interviewees stressed that they understand the idea of withdrawing from society at large, they resented the fact that they are compelled to lead highly regimented lives, bereft of alternatives or personal choices. For instance, a yeshiva student from Jerusalem assailed the decision to exempt all yeshiva students from military service:

> [The Haredi authorities] have built a society with very unrealistic values. It may be alright for a select few, a few ascetics who enter a monastery and also decide not to marry…. But to say that everybody in a society, without exception, should study…, and that abstinence is part of this ideal, is simply unrealistic. This is not what is written in the scriptures, and it is unsuitable for human beings.

The Jerusalemite thus also referred to the Haredi emphasis on the virtues of married life. He argued that, by requiring young men to remain celibate, the rabbis might be leading students dangerously close to the Christian model of piety or to those Jewish ascetics whose zealous continence is condemned in the Hebrew Scriptures. In his estimation, the yeshiva's strict requirements do not suit all men and the cost of forcing this way of life on yeshiva students could ultimately endanger the community of faith. His opposition to the system was not limited to the problems of abstinence:

> When you stop to think about it, it is horrible that parents might recognize that their son may not be an outstanding student of the Talmud or not destined to become an exemplary rabbi, yet they nevertheless feel obligated to send him to the yeshiva because perhaps, out of the thousands who study, he might become one of the chosen few. I am not willing to pay this price…. Maybe from a leader's perspective, these things seem right; but as an individual, if I am true to myself, I should get up and leave.

From this student's perspective, the yeshiva model evidently constitutes both a personal burden and a disservice to the entire community.

The examples cited herein demonstrate that the use of methodological strategies that were attuned to the sensitivities of the scriptural culture at hand helped me reveal more about the community than I would have had I turned to other approaches. In particular, I attained a deeper understanding of the mechanisms of constructing and justifying new potential forms of Haredi religiosity. Not only were the yeshiva students' responses indicative of the complexity of scripturalism, but they exposed shifts and disagreements within Haredi society.

Conclusion

In this chapter, I have touched upon some of the problems of conducting an ethnographic study on fundamentalist institutions. Israel's Haredi community is currently in the midst of major changes. These developments have arisen not only in response to the country's general security concerns and uncertain future, but due to intracommunal challenges as well, as issues that pertain to the community's fundamentalist nature. In my estimation, the ethnographic methodology that was explicated herein is sensitive enough to grasp these sorts of shifts and shed light on the dynamics at work on the different social and cultural strata of text-based communities. Any study on a fundamentalist group should begin with an examination of its unique features and cultural influences as well as the consequences of these factors. Moreover, it is incumbent upon the scholar to develop sensitive ethnographic tools for accessing the group's sacred canon and other forms of collective knowledge, to include its hermeneutic techniques and the hierarchy among related texts and interpretations.

The examples I have cited from my ethnographic experience within the Haredi yeshiva world testify to the efficaciousness of this approach. In this particular study, informants played an instrumental role, as they helped devise an interview method that suits the features and constraints of the scripturally oriented yeshiva world. More specifically, the integration of elements from the traditional shiur (lesson) into the interview structure and the informants' initial recommendation of relevant texts to be discussed during the sessions elicited candid debates and contributed to the establishment of a "reservoir" of texts that my subjects were intimately familiar with. The focus on prompting a text-based dialogue enabled me to infiltrate and plumb the depths of this insular community. Whereas scholars of fundamentalism have hitherto pointed to literalism and inerrancy as the principal features of scripturalism, this chapter demonstrates the permeability of these ostensibly rigid borders. By investigating the manner in which the Haredi canon is interpreted and translated, I discovered that the justification of extant religious models is not the sole function of the community's sacred texts, for they also constitute a platform for textual criticism and reinterpretation, which challenge some of the community's taboos, prohibitions, and norms. More specifically, the development of a discerning, "tailor-made" ethnographic approach was directly responsible for the following insights on Haredi fundamentalism:

On account of their reinterpretation of canonical narratives and the incorporation of these innovations into their discourse, yeshiva students can be viewed as active agents of fundamentalism.

Yeshiva students are heavily involved in the complex process of text selection, setting hierarchies, and reordering meanings and symbols. In consequence, they are active participants in the ongoing process of adjusting communal knowledge to changing circumstances.

Yeshiva students cast doubt on their community's established interpretations. Moreover, their criticism attests to their interest in a wide range of topics that have nothing to do with textual constraints and canonical interpretations.

Another facet of students' role as agents for change is their involvement in the effort to adapt their society's notion of piety and the yeshiva world to the modern era.

These roles and activities point to the latent potential for significant change in the fundamentalist experience. For example, my interviewees' critical views on the accepted paradigm of the yeshiva student appear to be indicative of their personal desire, or fantasies, to reform certain aspects of their text-based society. According to Obeyesekere (1981), understanding religious fantasies can indeed shed light on communal transformations. Moreover, critical views can also induce a change in the textual pecking order. For instance, texts that glorify dedication to studious pursuits can be replaced by those that legitimize participation in frameworks of state (for example, enlistment in the army) or communal projects (for example, volunteering in philanthropic organizations). Not only can these dissentious opinions be viewed as a reshuffling of the status and hierarchies of texts, but also hint to a desire on the part of community members to loosen the grip of scripturalism and its ideologues on their lives.

My fieldwork in the ultra-Orthodox community touches upon questions that were broached by Anthony Giddens (1979) on the relation between agency and structure (as well as Levi-Strauss's [1966] insights on structure and subjectivity). Whereas Giddens argues that structure determines agency and action, in my estimation this relation is more complex than previously recognized. In this chapter, we have seen how criticism of the Haredi world is emerging from the very heart of the yeshiva structure. Although top yeshiva students are the main agents and primary beneficiaries of their group's fundamentalist ideals, they no longer accept the "authoritarian structure" of the yeshiva system. More specifically, students feel that they can no longer accept their passive role as transmitters of ideas, and many are questioning some of their community's core beliefs. For these very reasons, it is incumbent upon scholars to keep a close eye on this generation and the far-reaching changes that its members are fomenting in the Haredi world.

Notes

1. This chapter was edited by Avi Aronski, I would like to thank Avi for his work, friendship and encouragement through the work of this paper.

2. According to Marty and Appleby, "these retrieved 'fundamentals' are refined, modified, and sanctioned in a spirit of shrewd pragmatism: they are to serve as a bulwark against the encroachment of outsiders who threaten to draw the believers into a syncretistic, areligious, or irreligious cultural milieu. Moreover, these fundamentals are accompanied in the new religious portfolio by unprecedented claims and doctrinal innovations…" (1991, p. 1).

3. Most of my subjects are members of the Lithuanian stream. The name "litvakim" (Lithuanians) is used by both the public at large and the community itself, as it defines the group and distinguishes its members from other Haredi sects, primarily the Hasidim. This distinction has deep historical roots and stems from a major transformation in Jewish history: the rise of the mystic Hassidic movement in southeastern Poland during the mid-18th century, which soon spread throughout the country and further afield. The Hassids challenged the authority of the rabbis and their entire value system, not least traditional ultra-Orthodoxy's more restrained and less spiritual approach to observance. However, wide swaths of East European Jewry vociferously opposed the Hassidic worldview, especially in Lithuania, the seat of power of the famed Gaon of Vilna and his disciples. The Hassids' adversaries assumed the name "mithnagdim" (opponents). In Israel, this appellation has been dropped in favor of the above-noted litvakim, which emphasizes their legacy of erudition.

4. In the past (especially in East European communities), only a handful of prodigies dedicated their lives exclusively to the pursuit of Torah knowledge (see Ben-Sasson, 1984; Stampfer, 1995), whereas today all Haredi men in Israel are obliged to devote themselves to studying in the yeshiva (Soloveitchik, 1994). This turn of events has reinforced the stature of studious activities and the centrality of the text in everyday life. The most significant effect of this development is that, rather than learning codes of behavior through imitation (see Mauss, 1979, p. 101), Haredi norms are constructed and transmitted through popular interpretations of sacred texts (Soloveitchik, 1994; also see J. Boyarin, 1989). As it now stands, the regulation of Haredi life and its attendant norms are indeed grounded on the interpretation of sacred texts by highly trained male "prodigies" (Stadler, 2002).

5. Scholars (D. Boyarin, 1997; Friedman, 1987; Goldberg, 1987; Heilman, 1983, 1992; and Soloveitchik, 1994) have written about Jewish male literacy, textuallity, and the central role of males in their capacity as interpreters of sacred texts.

6. I elaborate on the development of this approach in "Ethnography of Exclusion: Initiating a Dialogue with Fundamentalist Men," *Nashim* (Stadler, 2007).

7. It is worth noting that yeshiva students only agreed to meet me late at night (at around 11:00 p.m.), after completing their daily routine. This condition underscores the ascendancy of erudition in the Haredi world and the fact that all other activities fall under the category of wasting time better spent learning (bitul torah). Taking advantage of the students' romanticiztion of late-night study was also part of my informants' strategy to "market" the interviews with young Haredim. More specifically, the khevruta format and the scriptural subject matter that informed these encounters enabled the informants to morally justify the time spent as a continuation of the participants' studious nocturnal activities. I elaborate on the development of this approach in my book, *Yeshiva Fundamentalism* (Stadler, 2008).

8. See Gupta & Ferguson 1997, pp. 12–15, and El-Or, 2002.

9. For a more detailed discussion on the priviliged outsider status I enjoyed in my ethnographic work, see Stadler, 2007.

10. This method also minimized what Bourdieu referred to as "symbolic violence," which rears its head in all interviewer-interviewee relations (1996, p. 19).

11. In her comparative study of Veda- and Torah-based communities, Holdrege (1996, p. 5) argues that sacred texts are not only considered a textual phenomenon, but a cosmological principle that is embedded in the very structure of their culture and reality.

12. A great deal has been written about the impact of literacy on social and cultural life (e.g., Goody, 1987). Given the permanence of written cultural forms in traditional societies, researchers have indeed stressed the fact that literacy may bolster the members' ability to objectively view and criticize these texts (e.g., Goldberg, 1987). However, the effect of these texts on daily life only merited scholarly attention with the burgeoning interest in fundamentalism and religious revival (see Ammerman, 1987; Marty & Appleby, 1991; Aran, 1993). Researchers have also discussed the relationship between fundamentalist groups and the media, focusing mainly on their use of printed material and visual technology (see Lawrence, 1989). Insofar as the Haredi community is concerned, the centers of their neighborhoods are lined with bookstores and small publishing houses, which cover every possible aspect of communal and individual life: the Sabbath, festivals, famous rabbis, moral education, and more. These shops are usually packed with people reading, inquiring about new books, or seeking advice on assorted topics.

13. As per Bourdieu's approach to the relations between aesthetic disposition and cultural capital, the ethnographer "…will not have the capacity to operate the arbitrary classification which, within the universe of worked-upon objects, distinguishes the object socially designated as deserving and demanding an aesthetic approach that can recognize and constitute them as works of art…" (1984, p. 39).

14. The term "madrasa" shares a common root with the term "dars," Arabic for lesson or instructions. The designated goal of the madrasa is to qualify "ulama" (literally, scholars), a class of clergy well-versed in the Islamic legal tradition. For further details, see Pedersen and Makdisi, 1986.

15. My approach is akin to what Tedlock (1983, p. 128) defined as "ethno-paleography," namely ethnographic research that is undertaken for the purpose of elucidating the archaeological record via ancient texts. In his study on Quiche Maya rituals in Guatemala, Tedlock utilized his subjects' knowledge of ancient texts as an eliciting device. He presented complete sentences and larger units of ancient texts before his Quiche consultant and inquired as to their possible meaning. For example, "Does the name Zipacna mean anything to you?" Or "Do you know of stories in which someone claims to be a maker of mountains?" Following in Tedlock's footsteps, I interspersed ancient texts into my own questions: "What is the meaning of the word 'hishtadlut' [making an effort] in your life?" And "What is the connection between 'hishtadlut' and *bitachon* [security] in present-day society?"

16. Similarly, Tedlock (1983, p. 134) presented his Quiche-speaking subjects with a glossary of archaic words when it became evident that his own Quiche vocabulary would not yield results. In my own research, the "textual reservoir" also enriched my native discourse skills, facilitated and softened the encounter with my subjects, afforded me access to several frameworks for knowledge production, and immediately stimulated the conversation about any topic, especially those that were discussed prior to the "lesson" at hand.

17. See Lehmann, 2001, for comparible religious phenomena in Brazil and Africa.

18. Rabbi Shlomo Yitzhaki (1040–1105) is the author of widely acclaimed commentaries on the Talmud and the Hebrew Bible.

References

Aberbach, M. (1994). *Labor, crafts and commerce in ancient Israel*. Jerusalem: Magnes Press.

Almond, G., Appleby, S., & Sivan E. (2003). *Strong religion: The rise of fundamentalism around the world*. Chicago: University of Chicago Press.

Ammerman, N. T. (1987). *Bible believers: Fundamentalism in the modern world*. New Brunswick, NJ: Rutgers University Press.

Antoun, R. T. (1989). *Muslim preacher in the modern world: A Jordanian case study in comparative perspective*. Princeton, NJ: Princeton University Press.

Antoun, R. T. (2001). *Understanding fundamentalism: Christian, Islamic and Jewish move-ments*. Walnut Creek, CA: AltaMira Press.

Aran, G. (1993). Return to the scriptures in modern Israel. *Bibliotheque De l'ecole des Hautes Etudes Sciences Religieuses, XCIX*, 101–131.

Beeman, W. O. (2001). Fighting the good fight: Fundamentalism and religious revival. In J. MacClancy (Ed.), *Exotic no more: Anthropology on the front Lines*. Chicago: Chicago University Press.

Ben-Sasson, C. H. (1984). *Continuity and change*. Tel Aviv: Am Oved [Hebrew].

Berman, E. (2000). Sect, subsidy and sacrifice: An economist's view of ultra-Orthodox Jews. *Quarterly Journal of Economics, 115*(3), 905–953.

Boone, K. (1989). *The Bible tells them so: The discourse of Protestant fundamentalism*. Albany: State University of New York Press.

Bourdieu, P. (1984). *Distinction: A social critique of the judgment of taste*. Cambridge, MA: Harvard University Press.

Bourdieu, P. (1996). Understanding. *Theory, Culture and Society, 13*(2), 17–37.

Boyarin, D. (1997). *Unheroic conduct*. Berkeley: University of California Press.

Boyarin, J. (1989). Voices around the text: The ethnography of reading at Mesivta Tifereth Jerusalem. *Cultural Anthropology, 4*(4), 421–339.

Bruner, J. (1990). *Act of meaning*. Cambridge MA: Harvard University Press.

Caplan, K. (2003). The internal popular discourse of Israeli Haredi women. *Archives de sciences sociales des religions, 123*, 77–101.

Crapanzano, V. (1980). *Tuhami: Portrait of a Moroccan*. Chicago: Chicago University Press.

El-Or, T. (1994). *Educated and ignorant: On ultra-Orthodox Jewish women and their world*. Boulder, CO: Lynne Rienner Publishers.

El-Or, T. (2002). *Next year I will know more: Literacy and identity of young Orthodox women*. Detroit, MI: Wayne State University Press.

Freilich, M. (Ed.) (1970). *Marginal natives: Anthropologists at work*. New York: Harper & Row.

Friedman, M. (1987). Life tradition and book tradition in the development of ultra-Orthodox Judaism. In H. E. Goldberg (Ed.), *Judaism viewed from within and from without* (pp. 235–255). Albany: State University of New York Press.

Friedman, M. (1993). The Haredim and the Israeli society. In J. Peters & K. Kyle (Eds.), *Whither Israel: The domestic challenges* (pp. 177–201). London: Chatham House & I. B. Tauris.

Gabler, E. (2002). Beyond belief? Play, skepticism, and religion in a West African village. *Social Anthropology, 10*(1): 41–56.

Geertz, H. (1961). *The Javanese family: A study in kinship and socialization*. Glencoe, IL: Free Press.

Gellner, E. (1981). *Muslim society*. Cambridge, MA: Cambridge University Press.

Giddens, A. (1979). *Central problems in social theory: Action, structure, and contradiction in social analysis*. Berkeley: California University Press.

Goldberg, H. E. (1987). Text in Jewish society and the challenge of comparison. In H. E. Goldberg (Ed.), *Judaism viewed from within and from without* (pp. 315–329). Albany: State University of New York Press.

Goody, J. (1987). *The interface between the written and the oral*. Cambridge, UK: Cambridge University Press.

Gupta, A., & Ferguson J. (1997). Discipline and practice: "The field" as site, method, and location in anthropology. In A. Gupta & J. Ferguson (Eds.), *Anthropological location: Boundaries and grounds of a field science* (pp. 1–46). Berkeley: University of California Press.

Heilman, S. C. (1983). *The people of the book: Drama, fellowship and religion*. Chicago: Chicago University Press.

Heilman, S. C. (1992). *Defenders of the faith: Inside ultra-Orthodox Jewry*. New York: Schocken Books.

Heilman, S. C. (1994). Quiescent and active fundamentalisms: The Jewish cases. In M. E. Marty & R. S. Appleby (Eds.), *Accounting for fundamentalism: The dynamic character of movements* (pp. 173–196). Chicago: Chicago University Press.

Heilman, S. C. (2000). Ethnography and biography, or what happened when I asked people to tell me the story of their lives as Jews. *Contemporary Jewry, 21,* 23–31.

Heilman, S. C., & Friedman, M. (1991). Religious fundamentalism and religious Jews: The case of the Haredim. In M. Marty & S. Appleby (Eds.), *Fundamentalisms observed.* (pp. 197–264) Chicago: University of Chicago Press.

Holdrege, B. A. (1996). *Veda and Torah.* Albany: State University of New York Press.

Kahane, R. (1988). Multicode organizations: A conceptual framework for the analysis of boarding schools. *Sociology of Education, 61*(4), 211–226.

Kahane, R. (1997). *The origin of post-modern youth.* Berlin: De Greuter.

Keen, W. (1997). Religious language. *Annual Review of Anthropology, 26,* 47–71.

Krannich, R. S., & Humphrey C. R. (1986). Using key informant data in comparative community research. *Sociological Methods & Research, 14*(4), 473–493.

Lambek, M. (1993). *Knowledge and practice in Mayotte: Local discourse of Islam, sorcery, and spirit possession.* Toronto: University of Toronto Press.

Lawrence, B. B. (1989). *Defenders of God: The fundamentalists revolt against the modern age.* San Francisco, CA: Harper & Row.

Lehmann, D. (2001). Charisma and possession in Africa and Brazil. *Theory, Culture and Society, 18*(5), 45–74.

Levi-Strauss, C. (1966). *The savage mind.* Chicago: University of Chicago Press.

Lomsky-Feder, E. (1996). A woman studies war: Stranger in a man's world. In R. Josselson (Ed.), *Ethics and process in the narrative study of life* (pp. 232–242). London: Sage.

Marty, M. E., & R. S. Appleby (1991). The fundamentalism project: A user's guide. In M. E. Marty & R. S. Appleby (Eds.), *Fundamentalisms observed* (pp. vii–xiii). Chicago: University of Chicago Press.

Mauss, M. (1979). *Sociology and psychology: Essays.* London: Routledge and Kegan Paul.

Mishler, E. G. (1986). *Research interviewing: Context and narrative.* Cambridge MA: Harvard University Press.

Nagata, J. (2001). Beyond theology: Towards an anthropology of fundamentalism. *American Anthropologist, 103*(2): 481–498.

Obeyesekere, G. (1981). *Medusa's hair, an essay on personal symbols and religious experience.* Chicago: University of Chicago Press.

Pedersen J., & Makdisi G. (1986). Madrasa. In C. E. Bosworth, E. van Donzel, B. Lewis, & C. Pellat (Eds.), *Encyclopaedia of Islam.* Vol. 5 (pp. 1123–1134). Leiden, Netherlands: E. J. Brill.

Powdermaker, H. (1966). *Stranger and friend: The way of an anthropologist.* New York: Norton.

Rapoport, D. C. (1993). Comparing militant fundamentalist movements and groups. In M. E. Marty & R. S. Appleby (Eds.), *Fundamentalism and the state: Remaking polities, economies and militance.* Chicago: University of Chicago Press.

Seidman, I. E. (1991). *Interviewing as qualitative research.* New York: Teachers College Press.

Selengut, C. (1994). By Torah alone: Yeshiva fundamentalism in Jewish life. In M. E. Marty & R. S. Appleby (Eds.), *Accounting for fundamentalisms: The dynamic character of movements* (pp. 236–263). Chicago: Chicago University Press.

Shostak, M. (1981). *Nisa: The life and words of a Kung woman.* Cambridge, MA: Harvard University Press.

Shostak, M. (2000). *Return to Nisa.* Cambridge, MA: Harvard University Press.

Sivan, E. (1991). The culture of the enclave. *Alpaim, 4,* 45–98 [Hebrew].

Sivan E. (1995). The enclave culture. In M. E. Marty & R. S. Appleby (Eds.), *Fundamentalisms comprehended.* Chicago: University of Chicago Press.

Soloveitchik, H. (1994). Rupture and reconstruction: The transformation of contemporary Orthodoxy. *Tradition, 28*(4): 64–130.

Sprinzak, E. (1993). Three models of religious violence: The case of Jewish fundamentalism in Israel. In M. E. Marty & R. S. Appleby (Eds.), *Fundamentalism and the state: Remaking polities, economies and militance* (pp. 462–490). Chicago: University of Chicago Press.

Stadler, N. (2002). Is profane work an obstacle to salvation? The case of ultra-Orthodox (Haredi) Jews in contemporary Israel. *Sociology of Religion, 63*(4): 455–474.

Stadler, N. (2004). Fundamentalism in social issues. In N. de Lange & M. Freud-Kandel, *Modern Judaism: An Oxford guide*. Oxford: Oxford University Press.

Stadler, N. (2007). Ethnography of exclusion: Initiating a dialogue with fundamentalist men. *Nashim: A Journal of Jewish Women's Studies and Gender Issues, 14*(1), 185–208.

Stadler, N. (2008). *Yeshiva Fundamentalism: Piety, Gender, and Resistance in the Ultra-Orthodox World*. New York University Press, New York.

Stadler, N. & Ben-Ari, E. (2003) Other-worldy soldiers? Utra-orthodox views of military service in contemporary Israel. *Israel Affairs, 9*(4), 17-48.

Stampfer, S. (1995). *The Lithuanian yeshiva*. Jerusalem: Zalman Shazar Center for Jewish History [Hebrew].

Stolow, J. (2004). Transnationalism and the new religio-politics: Reflection on a Jewish Orthodox case. *Theory, Culture & Society, 21*(2), 109–137.

Tedlock, D. (1983). *The spoken and the work of interpretation*. Philadelphia: University of Pennsylvania Press.

CHAPTER SEVENTEEN

Citizenship, Diversity, and Education

What a Structural Analysis of Textbooks
Can Tell Us About State Intentions

J. DEBORA HINDERLITER ORTLOFF

Since the fall of the Berlin Wall and certainly since the start of new millennium, Germany has been undertaking a sort of national soul searching when it comes to questions of citizenship. Long-held beliefs and their corresponding policies and laws, which regulated "who" could be and become German, have been challenged and changed. There has been a movement away from heritage-based notions of citizenship towards a more inclusive concept, which can, in theory, extend to nonethnic Germans. Likewise, immigration has been recognized as a necessary part of Germany's future. These policy changes and the fiery national debate that has accompanied them (Ortloff, 2007; Ortloff, 2011) have not necessarily included changes to citizenship education policy and practice. If the state is faithful in its intentions to embrace a multicultural and cosmopolitan notion of German citizenship, then education policy and materials must reflect this intention. Whether or not this is happening becomes an interesting question for researchers. The possibility that there is not consistency in the multicultural and cosmopolitan values of the state and existing educational policy/materials provokes critical interests. The conflict of values can be masked or ideologically covered over in such a way as to limit their availability to ordinary question by actors who might draw on, recapitulate or be affected by their instantiation. According to Parsons and Shils (1951), a strain can emerge when social facts toward and through which people act out values are at odds with paramount values. So in this case there is the potential for conflict between who is depicted as German and the possibility of who could be included in this depiction with through a cosmopolitan lens. (p. 174).

Social scientists have not found it easy to explore questions linking interpretive values with social structures through which an understanding of such conflicts might be made explicit (Giddens, 1990). This chapter demonstrates the use of framing theory to analyze the interpretive structures prevalent in educational texts with respect to German citizenship. Specifically, I argue that citizenship and diversity, two notions that have direct implications for the personal lived experiences of people living in Germany, must be interrogated in a way that exceeds (without negating) those lived experiences. "[U]nlike structural patterns in biology, the structural patterns of action systems are not accessible to [purely external] observation; they have to be gotten at hermeneutically, that is from the internal perspectives of the participants" (Habermas, 1987, p. 151). Yet patterns of social structure can have shapes and effects in the everyday life that are not part of what actors drawing on those structures purpose or intend. "…for in the enactment of social practices [both with respect to the production of texts and] more generally, *the consequences of actions chronically escape their initiators' intentions in processes of objectification*" (Giddens, 1990, p. 44, emphasis in original). Using framing theory allows textbooks to be analyzed for their tacit meanings with an emphasis on probing the underlying conceptual structures and normative meanings of the ideal citizen, meanings that are hermeneutically accessible and also not particularly intentional in the typical way that word is used. These structures and normative meanings can then be compared with the stated goals of Germany to promote an inclusive, cosmopolitan German citizenship.

The Analysis of Cultural Structures

Systems-Level Analysis

What is ultimately necessary in any systems-level analysis is the development, or more pointedly the extension, of social theory to help explain how the data in any given study function as representatives of the system or the lifeworld. What happens all too often in studies that focus on state- or institutional-level data is a simplified empirical explanation of how data "fit" a particular criteria. In order for any system-level analysis to be successful, a social theoretical framework explicating data as system must be undertaken. While this is not the focus of this chapter, it is important to note the place of social theory because framing theory seeks to explicate normative claims at the system level. Consequently without understanding the place of the data in the system, we cannot validly construct such an analysis.

Elsewhere, I have elaborated on the theoretical construct used in the larger study from which I am drawing data for this chapter (Ortloff, 2007; Ortloff, 2009a). For our purposes here, let me briefly summarize. Citizenship education is used by the state as means of institutionalizing a particular image of citizen as best or ideal (Gutmann, 1987; Ortloff, 2007; Engel, 2009; Engel & Ortloff, 2009). Drawing on the German case, Habermas (1996) argues that citizenship has been used as a means of both creating and enforcing an ethnocultural community. These communities, as Anderson (1991) points out, exist not through political or economic borders or treatises but through myths and symbols reproduced through institutions and discourses. Thus, in Germany the preservation of the ethnocultural citizenship standards would result in state mechanisms, in particular, education, actively creating and reinforcing myths and symbols of the nation-state (Anderson, 1991; Hobsbawm, 1992). What is essential for this chapter, which focuses only on explicating cultural structures, is in what manner the textbooks (as cultural media) reify a particular notion of citizenship that is uncritically at odds with stated goals. Structures become reified, in one way, when their value content is objectivated as unquestioned fact.

School textbooks provide a window into the content of how the education of citizens is conceived. In the case of Germany, because of the highly centralized[1] and controlled manner in which textbooks are chosen, it can be safely assumed that the texts illuminate state citizenship education policy at one level, at least. Framing theory can then be used to examine the active range of possible meanings both enabled and constrained through the reification of a defined citizenry as symbols of the nation-state as explained by Anderson (1991) and Hobsbawm (1992). According to Habermas, the analysis of cultural structures becomes particularly important when the lifeworld and the system have become sufficiently differentiated that they can reciprocally influence one another. Certainly, this is the situation in modern Germany. One way the system influences take their effect on the lifeworld is on and through the cultural structures. This process of influence is not one that is

> available as themes *within* the lifeworld, and thus it cannot be read off from the intuitive knowledge of members. On the other hand, it is also inaccessible from an external, systems-theoretical perspective. Although it comes about counterintuitively and cannot easily be perceived from the internal perspective of the lifeworld [such as by interviewing people], there are indicators of it in the formal conditions of communicative action [such as who is allowed to criticize the implicit claims to truth]" (Habermas, 1987, p. 186)

Methodologically, researchers might note where certain content is not being reflected upon or critiqued, where contradictions in the norms limit the way in which people can participate in their production. It is particularly interesting to examine cultural products, like textbooks, from the perspective of articulating the cultural structures that might be open for system-level influence because of their positionality with respect to formalized state goals. "One of the main tasks of the study of the text, or indeed cultural products of any kind, must be precisely to examine the divergences which can become instituted between the circumstances of their production, and the meanings sustained by their subsequent escape from the horizons of their creator or creators" (Giddens, 1990, p. 44). The goals of citizenship education that reflect a certain level of intentionality ought to be evidenced in the texts related to citizenship. However, the "meanings sustained" that exceed those intentions might not be so straightforward. Such meanings, then, could also be expected to be less directly accessible through the study of the lifeworld. Framing theory draws on the patterns of representation that are embedded in cultural material, but that might simultaneously carry unintended traces as patterns themselves. In my use of framing theory, which will be described thoroughly below, I use the idea of a magnetic pole to illustrate how the patterns of meaning have particular "fields" that draw interpretations in specific directions, as if hovering around meaningful magnets.

Data Collection and Analysis Process Summary

Before turning to explaining the framing theory analysis itself, let me briefly summarize the methodological steps taken in the overall study from which I am drawing data for this chapter.

Sample. Since the greater research project examined issues of citizenship, I collected a purposive sample of Bavarian social studies textbooks published between 1988 and 2005. I used textbooks, archived through the Georg-Eckert-Institute for International Textbook Research (GEI), and included any available general textbook for the Hauptschule and Realschule from 1988 to 2006 (intended specifically to capture the immediate pre- and post-unification period in Germany from Bavarian materials) that was approved for use in Bavaria. A list of the textbook series examined appears in the Appendix to this chapter. I compared the textbooks collected to lists of approved textbooks for the time periods sought, compiled both by the GEI archivists and the Bavarian education ministry.

Analysis steps. In order to select which portions of the textbooks to subsequently code, I used the state-mandated curricular guidelines to locate sections in each of the grade levels (5–10) which addressed issues of citizenship. The following curricular themes guided the textbook section selection: community involvement, intercultural learning, active citizenship (mündige Bürger), Europeanization, globalization, migration, rights and privileges of citizenship, Bavaria, and Germany. Ultimately I was not seeking to limit what was coded in the textbooks, rather to be sure that, across the five grade levels and 19 years included in the sample, I consistently identified the same concepts. Since these themes are identified in the social studies curricula[2] as running themes and overall learning outcomes, they were appropriate for guiding the initial selection of material for the content analysis. This selection process follows both Krippendorf (2004) and Neuendorf's (2001) suggestions for consistency in developing a unit of analysis. Once I completed the sampling and text-selection processes, I moved forward with the data analysis. This first-level emergent coding followed the standard procedures for qualitative coding (Glaser & Strauss, 1967; Lincoln & Guba, 1985; Hesse-Biber & Leavy, 2004; Shenton, 2004). This is an important step in any systems-level analysis because it allows truth claims to emerge unfettered by any system structure framework, such as official notions of citizenship. Once I completed the initial coding, I turned my attention to re-analyzing the now-coded data using framing theory.

The framing analysis, which will be explained in depth below, revealed a range of ways of describing citizenship in Germany in terms of diversity. These ways forwarded both highly exclusionary and inclusionary models of citizenship and often put forth a seemingly inclusionary model, which depended on exclusionary thinking in order to remain logical. Framing theory allowed me to explore nuanced concepts of citizenship, even when competing ideas were forwarded in the same textbook section. A traditional quantitative content analysis would not allow for this more implicit coding schematic. Examining the emergent frames for their normative power allows me, as Carspecken's (1996) suggests, to explicate structural relations to explain the findings. This is critical, particularly in this case, because the changes in citizenship and immigration take place at the national policy level, but education policy is created at the state level and enacted at the local level. By using framing theory, I am able to consider how, from 1988 to 2006, diversity and citizenship evolved as Germany moved, in formal ways, away from a monocultural and towards a multicultural self-definition, but still failed to fundamentally establish either a multicultural or cosmopolitan citizenship education.

Summary of Framing Theory as a Methodological Approach.

It has been useful to conduct content analyses of textbooks and curricula by drawing on framing theory as a methodological meta-theory—a guiding theory for methodological practice. Rein and Schön (1993) describe framing as "a way of selecting, organizing, interpreting, and making sense of a complex reality to provide guideposts for knowing, analyzing, persuading and acting." My own knowledge of framing theory comes through the work of sociologist Erving Goffman (1974). He proposed framing methodology as a microsociological analysis that invoked certain assumptions about the nature of the self and the place of meaning in the analysis. Goffman's approach, often characterized as semiotic analysis, emerged through his exposure to existentialism, and he acknowledges allegiance to European phenomenology, while taking into consideration the structuralism critique. Communication studies as a discipline has further developed framing theory, particularly in terms of application to public discourse. Communication theorists, though, also draw on phenomenology, particularly Schutz (1967), from whom Goffman's work also benefits (Embree, 1988). In the social sciences, framing theory has been applied broadly to questions of bias, electoral behavior, trends in pop culture, and media influence (Snow & Benford, 1988; Reese, 2003; Kuypers, 2009).

In this study, framing theory offers a means of examining citizenship education curricula, policies, and textbooks in a diverse set of contexts, and in a manner meaningful enough to reveal the nuances that concepts like citizenship necessarily require. For this dataset, a framing theory analysis is appropriate because there are a finite number of textbook series (19) that can be read closely and in comparison with each other (Dierkes, 2003). The theory probes how an issue is described and implemented and what relations of significance emerge. Through coding implicit frames, the range of perspectives not immediately obvious in the medium may be revealed (Gamson, 1997).

However, it is not merely the existence of implicit frames that are of interest at the system level. In fact, we would expect a degree of implicitness to be probed both at the system and lifeworld levels, which is why authors such as Carspecken (1996) and Lather (2000) have developed tools for examining tacit meaning within the lifeworld. The real power of framing analysis is in its ability to help understand the implicit claims of content for their normative power. What I mean by this is that framing theory can serve a dual purpose, functioning both as a substantive social theory and as a methodological meta-theory.

Framing theory explains a relation between the cultural conceptualizations and the texts of the culture as they relate to the everyday lifeworld of actors. The theory explains how people might "read" cultural products. Thus, it is my claim that this theory, often applied to the media's role in public-opinion formation, can be useful in examining textbooks insofar as textbooks, like media, prime consumers/teachers and students with a limited number of options. As Terkildsen and Schnell (1997) suggest, such priming can be found in subtleties of language use, of what is explicitly expressed or only implied. Similarly, curricula can be conceived as a state's expression of the cultural frames of citizen. In this sense, curricula frame an issue, in this case citizenship, and produce and maintain something like a magnetic pole on the meaning of citizen.

Using framing theory also allows analysis not only of culturally intuitive meaning, but also of normative frames as structural patterns. In this study, then, framing theory helps me identify unique values that have not yet been explicitly named as German. For example, the manner in which diversity is valued as part of the ideal German citizen has the potential to expand or even narrow the frame of German citizenship. Normative frames are important in Durkheimian terms because they reflect the potential to discover similarity in beliefs and values that would be necessary for even more complex social structures to function (Durkheim, 1899). Oyserman and Lauffer (2002) describe normative frames as representative of the most fundamental notions of humanity in a particular group. Thus, if Germans fail to recognize basic normative frames, such as the value of a diverse German society, a priori, it would follow that no amount of citizenship education or education policymaking could succeed in creating a shared multicultural identity, at least in the short term. Using framing as a methodology to code for cultural and normative images allows the implicit and tacit frames, used within a culture for making sense of cultural artifacts, to be put into practice.

In relation to citizenship education, this translates to explicating the frames that indicate how citizenship as a cultural construct is interpreted or read through the artifact of social studies texts and curricula. Consequently, framing theory allows for a substantive concept of citizen to emerge. Likewise, it is through framing theory that the critical nature of this inquiry can be captured, because framing theory, unlike other forms of content analysis, examines absence and silence as significant. When power is unequally distributed, as it is in the case of access to citizenship and rights in Germany, then we can expect nonprivileged members of the society to be silenced. Given this, the portrayal of diversity and citizenship will likely diminish the narrative of the non-German within the textbooks. As a methodology, framing theory then helps us to organize and interpret these explicit and implicit meanings and concepts.

Summary of Findings

The intentions of this chapter are to highlight the need to use qualitative research to interrogate system-level notions, such as citizenship. As such, I will summarize one key finding from the larger analysis (Ortloff, 2007; Ortloff, 2009b; Ortloff & McCarty, 2009; Ortloff, 2011) as a means of demonstrating this methodological point. Specifically, the framing analysis reveals a range of ways in which being German is possible. This chapter will explore the "Being Us" frame, which describes German citizenship as something historic and based on a shared ancestry. Citizenship and belonging are linked directly to an essential notion of Germanness. The frame is constituted by two sub-frames, which act as markers for the absence of diversity or diverse voices. See Figure 1.

Figure 1

This frame reveals that the idea of "Being German" enacts—at least to some degree—an ethnic category. In this case, implicit ethnoculturalism forms a central core (the "pole," if you will) of the German citizen in the textbooks by underscoring the idea that belonging at the state level is available only to a particular "citizen," not to all citizens. Consistently, and in a variety of sub-topics, citizenship in Germany is presented as white and Christian. Yet, what the Being Us frame conveys is not only these characteristics of race and religion (which are also substantively represented in the other frames), but that being German or, to some degree, European, is intractable. You simply are German by virtue of your birth, your heritage, and your shared values. This is what the interrogation of the system level can help us reveal. Not just the surface-level representations of Germans as white and Christian, but what those representations normatively mean for the state's conceptualization of the ideal citizen. Below, as a means of showing how system-level intentions can be explicated, I will provide the details for each of the subframes constituting Being Us.

Lack of Diverse Voices

In both the pre-unification and post-unification textbooks, diverse experiences, for example, the experiences of non-Germans living in Germany, are largely left out of the description of the German nation, despite their effect on its development. In the post-unification textbooks, especially those of the late 1990s, the difficulties of unification are described and the rosy picture of all Germans living happily in one nation is less idealistically portrayed. Yet even with the adoption of this more critical stance, the picture of the German citizen is not expanded to include non-Germans.

In describing life in West and East Germany, the textbooks highlight youth culture and economic recovery through 1989. Special attention is paid to the "economic miracle" in West Germany and protest movements in the 1960s. With the growing stability of the West German economy, the everyday German's life is described as dreaming of one's own house, traveling internationally, and being involved with group activities. Yet there is no mention of the Guest Worker immigration, either in terms of policy the fact that it was at least in part through these economic migrants' labor that the economic miracle continued (TRIO 9, 1997, 1999, 2004; Begegnungen 9, 1999, 2004) In the 9th-grade textbooks, because of the expanded curricular mandates, there is a separate chapter that focuses on migration that includes mention of the Guest Workers. Nevertheless, they are excluded from the description of the growth of the German nation.

In discussion of pre-unification Germany, youth culture in both East and West Germany is described. Not too surprisingly, the youth in West Germany are portrayed as being permitted (by the state, it is implied) to develop individually. These "young citizens," however, are clearly only ethnic Germans. There is no discussion of immigrants' experiences or discussion of youth culture in non-German groups. Any depiction of young non-Germans is relegated to chapters on foreigners or on Islam. This is true also with respect to depictions of everyday Germany. Take for example, TRIO 8, 1998, in which a series of citizens are asked what they want to know about city/state services (TRIO 8, 1998, 18). Diversity exists in terms of age and gender, but this representation of "citizen" forwards a white and Christian view of who these citizens are. We see this through the names, race, and occupations. Throughout the whole dataset, chapters and subchapters that focus on the local community or everyday life in Germany feature pictures or representative quotes from citizens who are universally white Germans. Immigrants and any nonethnically German residents of Germany are absent in this way, not only from the history of the FRG becoming a nation, but also from being young in contemporary Germany and from being included in activities undertaken by citizens.[3]

Life for the everyday German citizen, as portrayed by the textbooks, leaves out the lives of immigrants or other non-"German" groups. When we consider the normative frame being forwarded, what this means is not just the exclusion of non-ethnic Germans from citizenry, but the reification of "Germanness" on the part of the state.

Inclusion of Diverse Voices Superficially or Without Context

The Being Us citizen frame also includes diverse voices, but only in a superficial or decontextualized manner. Take for example the photograph at the start of a chapter in the Durchblick 8 book (2006, p. 51), which typifies the way non-German experiences are added to textbooks; namely, in a manner that provides students with no context with which to make sense of the depicted experiences. In this image, an older man, probably a Roma or Sinti (minority throughout Europe, referred to often as gypsies) or a Palestinian refugee, is pictured begging. It isn't easy, per se, to establish the ethnicity, but it is easy to assume this is not a "German."

He holds a sign that reads: "State-less, no home, not allowed to work." The picture is the cover page to the chapter on Germany as a social state wherein the disparity between rich and poor is highlighted. The man sits next to a boutique window in which a mannequin wears an expensive dress. The caption reads: poor and rich. The picture is not integrated into the chapter, nor is the fact that this person who lives in Germany is part, in some manner, of the German nation. Indeed, the experiences of immigrants, refugees, and migrants within the social state are not part of the chapter at all.

Throughout the textbook sample, most of the images of non-Germans living in Germany are in stereotypical roles, as vegetable sellers (cf. Durchblick 9, 1998, 77; TRIO 8, 1992, 44), beggars (see above), or the underclass. This typification is made very clear when we examine the images of the non-German in contrast to the pictures of the average German presented above. The average German is pictured as the everyday German citizen contributing to the well-being of the German state through voting, community service, work, and political leadership

These findings demonstrate that exclusionary forms of the German citizen are still central to the notion of citizen. However, neither the state nor the textbooks, as proxy for the system's intentions, comes out and says: "non-ethnic Germans don't belong" or "non-ethnic Germans are not a part of our community" or "You might live here, but you are not German." Without considering the content in terms of its implicit meaning as it relates to state notions of citizenship, the overall normative claim of who should be German is lost. The Being Us frame conveys that being white and otherwise typically German is a requirement for citizenship and because these characteristics are not learnable, acquirable characteristics, the Being Us frame serves to underscore that being German is immovable; you simply are German by virtue of your birth, your heritage, and your shared traditional values. From this perspective, becoming German is not possible. In this frame, we see a monolith of Germanness as an inherited ethnic (and inherently racial) trait emerges through the texts in a way that leaves no room for another means of Being Us.

Conclusion

Substantively, even with only a small portion of the data presented, it is easy to see that there is a serious contradiction between articulated Bavarian state citizenship education policy (which promotes an expanded, multicultural, or cosmopolitan notion of citizenship) and notions of citizenship promoted through educational texts. The Being Us frame shows that implicitly state intentions remain ethnocultural. This in turn translates to a system-level ideal citizen who is ethnically German, white, and Christian. Traditionally, qualitative research has excelled at detailed micro-level analyses that are situated in the lifeworld. However, many of the complex concepts explored in qualitative research, including for example citizenship, diversity, and belonging, are ultimately situated in the system. It is therefore important to develop social theoretical and methodological tools for probing system-level intentions. This chapter demonstrates one such means, framing theory, for this type of analysis. Ultimately, as Habermas (1987) makes clear, as the lifeworld diversifies, the system complexifies and they mutually influence one another. Consequently, a study of citizenship, or other concepts that rely heavily on system imperatives is incomplete when situated in only the system or the lifeworld. It is the interplay between the two that would provide the most complete picture of how citizenship and diversity manifest in educational policy and practice. Framing theory facilitates the explication of structures through which the system might influence the lifeworld. The findings of this study suggest that the cognitive content we find in texts indicating what it means to belong to the German citizenry is not consistent with German goals of cosmopolitan citizenship. Moreover, the patterns of meaning imply that a group of students who are being taught about being German citizens are conceptually not included in the representation of citizenship. This opens a space for cultural critique made visible through the use of framing theory to articulate the contravening structural patterns. Habermas (1987) wrote that "mechanisms that repress an actual conflict [between stated goals for a diverse citizenry and textbook representations of citizenry] by excluding it [the conflict] from the realm of situation interpretations and actual orientations and covering it up with illusions [treating the topics of citizenship as if they are devoid of heritage-based notions] have pathological side effects" (p. 229).

Appendix

TEXTBOOK SERIES
(GRADES 5–10 FOR THE *HAUPTSCHULE*
AND GRADE 10 FOR THE *REALSCHULE*)

1. Begegnungen Geschichte, Sozialkunde, Erdkunde.; Karl Filser. Munchen, OldenbourgAmbros Brucker; 2005, 1999, 1998, 1997.

2. Demokratie verpflichtet. Andreas Mack; Munchen, Oldenbourg, 2003, 1995, 1984 (used through 1994).

3. Durchblick/Bayern/Hauptschule. Hanne Auer, Braunschweig; Westermann, 2004, 2001, 1999,1998, 1997.

4. Forum: Sozialkunde, Realschule Bayern. Braunschweig: Westermann, Grundwissen Okonomie/Christine Fischer, 2004.

5. Geschichte, Sozialkunde, Erdkunde. Klett-Perthes (Terra). Harald-Matthias Neumann., 2004, 1999, 1998, 1997.

6. Politik-nicht ohne mich! Bamberg: Buchner, 2003.

7. Politik-Wie? So! Rainer Dorrfuss. Bamberg: Buchner, 1995.

8. Geschichte-Sozialkunde-Erdkunde: GSE; Hauptschule. Regesburg: Wolf, 1997, 1998 and 1999.

9. Sozialkunde/Bayern/Hauptschule: Regenburg: Wolf, 1994,1995.

10. Menschen, Zeiten, Raume/Barern/Hauptschule. Berlin: Cornelsen. 1999, 1998, 1997.

11. TRIO/Bayern/Hauptschule: Geschichte/Sozialkunde/Erdkunde, Norbert Autenrieth; Hannover; Schroedel, 1994, 1997, 1998 and 1999, 2004.

12. ZeitRaume: entdecken, erfahren, orientieren. Norbert Horberg. Stuttgart: Klett, 1997 and 1998.

13. Burger und Politik: ein Lehrund Arbeisbuch fur Sozialkunde, politische Bildung. Eduard Steinbugl. Darmstadt: Winklers Verl. Gebr. Grimm, 1995.

14. bsv-Sozialkunde. Ingrid Ziegler. Munchen: Bayer. Schulbuch-Verl., 1991 and 1992.

15. Denkanstosse: Sozialkunde fur die Hauptschule. Gunter Neumann. Kulmbach: Baumann, 1986 and 1987 [used through 1998]

16. Politisch denken, urteilen and handeln: ein Lehr- und Arbeitsbuch fur den politischen und sozialkundlichen Unterricht. Von Roland Herold. Wolfenbuttel: Heckner, 1982. [used through 1994].

17. Sozialkunde/ bearb. Oskar Buhler. Schulerarbeitscheft. Ansbach: Ansbacher Verl., Ges., 1986. [used through 1995].

18. Sozialkunde fur Hauptschulen in Bayern. Dieter Grosser. Braunschweig: Westermann, 1988. [used through 1995].

19. Burger und Politik: e. Lehr-u. Arbeisbuch fur Sozialkunde, polit. Bildung. E. Steinbugl. Darmstadt: Winkler, 1984. [used through 1992].

Notes

1. The choice of textbook content is centralized at the state level. Education is the purview of each individual state in Germany.

2. Refers to the Hauptschule and Realschule curricula for two school forms in Germany that equate roughly to our 9th and 10th grade. Both school forms are preparation for vocational training in blue-collar and technical fields.

3. In reality, it was not until 1998 that the more liberal citizenship laws would have allowed so-called foreigners to attain citizenship with voting rights. But the representation of citizens here is not just voting rights but participation in the community, attending festivals, bicycling, being involved in community groups. Foreigners remain, as the continued use of the term "Ausländer" reinforces, foreigners, and not a part of the citizen's community.

References

Anderson, B. (1991). *Imagined communities: Reflections on the origin and spread of nationalism*. London: Verso.

Carspecken, P. F. (1996). *Critical ethnography in educational research: A theoretical and practical guide*. New York: Routledge.

Dierkes, J. B. (2003). *Teaching portrayals of the nation: Postwar history education in Japan and the Germanys* (Unpublished Ph.D. dissertation). Princeton University, New Jersey.

Durkheim, E. (1899/1956). *Education and sociology*. Glencoe, IL: Free Press.

Embree, L. (1988). *Worldly phenomenology: The continuing influence of Alfred Schutz on North American human science*. Washington DC: University Press of America; Center for Advanced Research in Phenomenology.

Engel, L. C. (2009). *New state formations in education policy*. Amsterdam: Sense.

Engel, L. C., & Ortloff, D. H. (2009). From the supranational to the local: Citizenship education reform in Bavaria, Germany and Catalonia, Spain. *Journal of Curriculum Studies, 41*(2), 179–198.

Gamson, W. A. (1997). News as framing: Comments on Graber. *American Behavioral Scientist, 33*, 157–161.

Giddens, A. (1990). *Central problems in social theory: Action, structure, and contradiction in social analysis*. Berkeley & Los Angeles: University of California Press.

Glaser, B., & Strauss, A. (1967). *The discovery of grounded theory*. Chicago: Aldine.

Goffman, E. (1974). *Frame analysis: An essay on the organization of experience*. New York: Harper & Row.

Gutmann, A. (1987). *Democratic education*. Princeton, NJ: Princeton University Press.

Habermas, J. (1987). *The theory of communicative action.* Vol. 2: *Lifeworld and system. A critique of functionalist reason*. Boston: Beacon.

Habermas, J. (1996). The European nation state; its achievements and its limitations: on the past and future of sovereignty and citizenship. *Ratio Juris, 9*(2).

Hesse-Biber, S., & Leavy, P. (Eds.). (2004). *Approaches to qualitative research: A reader on theory and practice*. New York: Oxford University Press.

Hobsbawm, E. (1992). Mass-producing traditions: Europe 1870–1914 In E. Hobsbawm & T. Ranger (Eds.), *The Invention of Tradition*. Cambridge: Cambridge University Press.

Krippendorf, K. (2004). *Content analysis: An introduction to its methodology* (2nd ed.). Thousand Oaks, CA: Sage.

Kuypers, J.A. (2009). Rhetorical criticism: Perspectives in action. Lanham, MD: Lexington.

Lather, P. (2000). Against empathy, voice and authenticity. *Transgressive Methodology, 4* (Special Issue: Issues of Women, Gender, and Research), 16–25.

Lincoln, Y., & Guba, E. (1985). *Naturalistic inquiry*. Thousand Oaks, CA: Sage.

Neuendorf, K. A. (2001). *The content analysis guidebook*. Thousand Oaks, CA: Sage.

Ortloff, D. H. (2007). Holding to tradition: Citizenship, diversity and education in post-unification Germany, a case study of Bavaria. (Ph.D. dissertation). Indiana University, IN. Retrieved November 17, 2010, from Dissertations & Theses: A&I. (Publication No. AAT 3283958).

Ortloff, D. H. (2009a). Social studies teachers' reflections on citizenship education in Bavaria, Germany. *Race/Ethnicity: Multidisciplinary Global Perspectives, 2*(2), 189–214.

Ortloff, D. H. (2009b). Disenfranchisement and power: The role of teachers as mediators in citizenship education policy and practice. In R. Winkle-Wagner, C. Hunter, & D. Ortloff (Eds.), *Bridging the gap between theory and practice in educational research: Methods at the margins*. New York: Palgrave MacMillan.

Ortloff, D. H. (2011) Moving the border: Multicultural and global citizenship in Germany. *Educational Research, 52*(2), 137-149.

Ortloff, D. H. & McCarty, L. P. (2009) Educating for the globally competent citizen, the case of Germany. In G. Wiggan & C. Hutchison (Eds.), *Global issues in education: Pedagogy, policy, school practices, and the minority experience*. University Press of America.

Oyserman, D., & Lauffer, A. (2002). Examining the implications for cultural frames on social movements and group action. In L. S. Newman & R. Erber, (Eds.), *Understanding genocide: The social psychology of the Holocaust*. New York: Oxford University Press.

Parsons, T., & Shils, E. (Eds.). (1951) *Toward a general theory of action*. Cambridge, MA: Harvard University Press.

Reese, S.D. (2003). *Framing public life*. Mahwah, NJ: Lawrence Erlbaum.

Rein, M., & Schön, D. (1993). Reframing policy discourse. In F. Fischer & F. Forester, (Eds.), *The argumentative turn in policy analysis and planning*. London: Duke University Press.

Schutz, A. (1967). *The phenomenology of the social world* (G. Walsh & F. Lehnert, Trans.). Evanston, IL: Northwestern University Press.

Shenton, A. (2004). Strategies for ensuring trustworthiness in qualitative research projects. *Education for Information, 22*, 63–75

Snow, D. A., & Benford, R. D. (1988). Ideology, frame resonance, and participant mobilization. *International Social Movement Research, 1*, 197–217.

Terkildsen, N., & Schnell, F. T. (1997). How media frames move public opinion: An analysis of the Women's Movement. *Political Research Quarterly, 50*(4), 879–900.

CHAPTER EIGHTEEN

At the Queen Mother's Court

Ethnography in Kumasi, Ghana[1]

BEVERLY J. STOELTJE

Having arrived in Kumasi, I was eager to meet the Asantehemma, the Queen Mother of the Asante. My friend, a prominent American-educated businessman, John K. Ampofo, agreed to accompany me to her palace at Manhyia, located in the heart of Kumasi, the capital city of the Asante in Ghana. He provided a formal introduction, after which I offered my gifts. The Queen Mother had requested, through my friend, that I bring her a sweater from the U.S., which she was pleased to accept. She then received the European Schnapps that I had also brought for her, a convention always observed when paying a visit to a queen mother or chief in Ghana. After inquiring of me about my "mission" (a standard part of Ghanaian greeting ritual), she agreed to my research plan, informing me that I could observe her court, which meets at her palace every week. This was a good arrangement for her as well as for me, since she would have a visiting researcher associated with her, but she would not have me underfoot. (As I soon learned, queen mothers and chiefs are adept at managing people.) With this initial meeting my ethnographic study was launched, and I was soon attending the court each Tuesday from 10 a.m. until midafternoon.

Obtaining permission to carry out research in the court was the first step of my project. The next step was familiarizing myself with the Court—a formal body of men and a few women, all of whom dressed "in cloth" (yards of unsewn cloth carefully draped over the body). In a short time I observed that the court brings together elites and commoners to resolve disputes originating in the course of everyday life. Cases in the court involve verbal offenses, theft, marital issues, land boundaries, and other conflicts common among individuals who live in the Ashanti region, especially women. The court caters to women especially because it is a queen mother's court, and all queen mothers are charged with ensuring the welfare of women.[2] (The King of Asante holds a court twice a week that takes up the affairs of men.) Members of the court include the Asantehemma's several "akyeame" (linguists; singular "okyeame"), male elders of the court, other queen mothers, servants, an audience, and the litigants. This court and other courts based on the indigenous legal system utilize the specific body of law, belief, and practices identified by the Asante with the term "custom." Used to index ideas, rituals, taboos, beliefs, and norms derived from the precolonial era in Asante, the term is familiar and circulates widely.

In this court, the litigants stand before the court and narrate the story of their case. The elders and akyeame then question them in order to clarify the story and obtain further information. According to the legal scholar Robin West (1993), knowledge of the subjectivity of others is gained and pursued through metaphor, allegory, narrative, literature, and culture, and it is this knowledge that facilitates community, makes us social, and motivates us to attain justice (p. 262). Narrative (as well as other forms) is, then, the vehicle for expressing the self, for telling others of one's experience. Applying this perspective to the Asante, when a dispute has arisen, the court uses narrative to gain knowledge of the individuals and their conflict, seeking to understand the causes of the conflict. Such knowledge of those engaged in the conflict contributes to a sense of community that will then create the desire to bring about justice.

This paper argues that the Asante courts, focused on narrative as the fundamental vehicle of knowledge to be considered, enact community as they pursue justice. The organization of the court reflects Asante stratified society and the longstanding jural superstructure of the precolonial Asante state that recognized citizens' rights (McCaskie, 1998). Consequently, the court is built on hierarchy and status, and sustains a belief in male superiority. While these conditions of inequality undeniably characterize the court, they do not preclude the existence of community and a society in which any individual citizen has the right to tell her story and be heard by a body of authorities who attempt to follow the tenets of the Asante social order as outlined in the beginning of the 18th century and adapted successively into the present.

In choosing to concentrate on queen mothers, chiefs, and their courts, then, my goal was to carry out ethnographic research that would inform us about these particular institutions—their potential and their practices. Through careful attention to context and situational analysis, this chapter explores the performance of litigation in contemporary Asante social life. Moreover, this chapter discusses the relevance of reciprocity to ethnographic fieldwork and of cultural conventions and social status to reciprocal practices. Because every social group has developed its own specific social order and accompanying ritual practices that maintain that order, identifying the social and political context in every situation is fundamental to successful relations in the field. Consequently, in the next section I will address the context of my research with the Asante.

The Asante of Ghana

The Asante people are one of several groups who constitute a larger cultural and linguistic family known as the Akan, all of whom are settled throughout southern Ghana in different locations, including some in Ivory Coast. Known to Westerners as the people who weave Kente cloth and whose country is rich in gold, the Asante are a people with an illustrious history as a large and powerful state.[3] Located primarily in the Ashanti region around their precolonial capital, Kumasi, their political system of chieftaincy and the cultural practices of custom remain vital today for many Asante. Though English is spoken by those who are educated, almost everyone, whether educated or not, speaks Twi, the language of the Asante. Together custom, chieftaincy, the courts, and the language constitute a substantial body of knowledge upon which the social system depends. This is not to say that the Asante are limited to the body of knowledge known as custom; the majority of the Asante are comfortable living in a world that allows an ease of movement between Asante culture and modernity as it has been shaped in Ghana.

The Gold Coast, as Ghana was known under British colonialism, was not a settler colony; therefore the British did not send people there to settle permanently as they did in South Africa and Kenya, for example. Although the British sent administrators and set up "indirect rule" (using local rulers to collect taxes and govern the local people), introduced formal education, the British legal system, and the English language, the Asante continued to speak Twi and to maintain their cultural practices. The anthropologist Meyer Fortes described the Asante in 1947 as a complex culture that had retained a robust historical "vitality" in its encounter with change.[4] The Asante ability to retain a robust culture has continued to serve them well after independence (in 1957), and as the 20th century has moved into the 21st, and successive state governments have introduced policy changes, the Asante continue to speak their language and maintain their institutions with vigor.

Consequently, while today Ghana is a modern country in West Africa that holds democratic elections, maintains a modified British-style legal system, and supports several well-established universities where its young people are educated, some features of the precolonial Asante cultural system remain vital. Most prominent of these is the institution of chieftaincy, which includes queen mother, sub-chiefs, linguists, and a host of other supporting positions as well as a hierarchy of chiefs. Characteristic of this system of chieftaincy is a dual-gender system of leadership. At the head of each political unit are both a chief ("ohene") and a queen mother ("ohemma") who are not married to each other but are members of the same royal family. Further, the political leadership is replicated in each political unit. That is, each town, village, and division or paramountcy has its own chief and queen mother who have a place within the hierarchical system of chieftaincy. Paramount chiefs have responsibility for matters in their political division, and the chiefs and queen mothers of each town and village are accountable to the paramount chief of their division. In Asante, the King of Asante, the Asantehene, and the Queen Mother of Asante, the Asantehemma, are the ultimate authorities, positioned at the top of the hierarchy. The King of Asante, Osei Tutu II, is a well-educated young Asante, the biological son of the Asantehemma. He was a successful businessman in London until he assumed the position of King of Asante.

This system creates leadership in every location, with knowledge of local matters, including land use and marriage customs. It provides what has become a popular concept today—infrastructure—that supplements leadership in areas the state does not cover.[5]

Discourse on African Culture: Custom and Chieftaincy

Asante knowledge and its accompanying institutions, rules, and routines are represented by chieftaincy as a political system, and custom as belief and practice. Chieftaincy and custom were never completely displaced, but were subsumed and modified by colonialism and the forces of modernity.

Although the British incorporated the Akan system and modified it to their advantage, and Kwame Nkrumah opposed the chiefs when he became the first president of Ghana at independence (Rathbone, 2000), the precolonial traditional system has adapted to these larger political systems and found its place in contemporary social life. Though some Ghanaians and some Westerners debate the usefulness of chieftaincy in the modern world, considering it outmoded and an obstacle to democracy, others claim it to be the heart of Asante identity and essential to the maintenance of social life. (Participation in the activities of custom and chieftaincy is a matter of choice, and not all Asante individuals choose to participate.) My position does not include a defense of those individuals who exploit the institution for personal gain. Certainly there are such individuals, and they are a familiar feature of the landscape (see Stoeltje, 2010). However, the majority of queen mothers and chiefs are respected for their role as local leaders, in dispute resolution, and as the embodiment of Asante identity. A few chiefs are extraordinary leaders and forward looking in the interests of their communities. Such a chief is Nana Otuo Serebo II, the Omanhene of Juaben Traditional Area in the Ashanti region. A major paramount chief who is well educated, he was recognized by the United Nations with an award for the many benefits he has brought to the people of Juaben and the residents of his paramountcy, especially his work with local farmers, the Juaben Oil Palm Outgrower Assocation, a new market complex, and improved water supply. In addition he served on the advisory council to revise the Ghanaian Constitution of 1992 and in numerous other national advisory roles.

However, the topic of whether or not custom and chieftaincy are beneficial remains controversial if one is to judge from Ghanaian newspapers and blogs. Strong opinions on the subject often reflect personal issues such as whether the person expressing an opinion is a member of an Akan ethnic group or a different one. However, the larger question of the compatibility of chieftaincy with democracy has long been considered seriously by scholars, lawyers, and politicians. Nevertheless, in spite of the debates on the subject, chieftaincy is recognized by the state and is guaranteed in the Constitution, where it receives a chapter outlining matters it guarantees and specifying that the term "chief" refers to chiefs and queen mothers who have been validly enstooled.[6]

A key element in the discourse of independence in Ghana (1957), and especially of Kwame Nkrumah, the first president, and one that characterized much of the writing by African leaders at the time, was an emphasis on restoring African culture (Nkrumah, 1964). Since then much discussion among local people, scholars, politicians, and activists has been devoted to issues addressing what is African and what was introduced by colonialism, and further, what should be changed and what should be retained. Opinions on almost any specific subject differ dramatically based on a broad set of interests and ideologies. As numerous scholars in several fields have demonstrated, the labels "traditional" and "modern" have long been overused to simplify complex issues. Though the subject of a rich body of critical scholarship, they are no longer considered meaningful categories for explaining social conditions and practices. Nevertheless, they continue to be widely used for rhetorical purposes when individuals are striving to establish a political position. Neither do the categories "African" and "Western" solve the problem of making distinctions between what is detrimental and what is beneficial, though they are widely used also. The difficulty in making these judgments derives from the fact that some practices in African cultures are detrimental and some are beneficial, a matter of whose interests are being served. The same holds true for other cultures, including Western institutions and practices—some are beneficial while others are detrimental, depending on who makes the judgment. The process of formulating those distinctions is much more difficult than using a simple dichotomy of terms that equal good and bad. An example illustrating the detrimental and the beneficial in African culture as it played out in one woman's life appears in the recently published collection *Women Writing Africa: West Africa and the Sahel* (Sutherland-Addy & Diaw, 2005). Kate Abbam, a journalist who ran her own magazine in the late 20th century, campaigned for change regarding the abusive treatment of widows in Ghana. However, when her husband died, and she herself became a widow, she experienced the same treatment from his relatives that she had campaigned against. His family came into her house to inventory her husband's personal effects (with an eye toward claiming them), calling their actions "tradition." Some years later, she was made queen mother of her community, the position of traditional female leader according to "Akan tradition." Acting as queen mother, she then called on women to work for significant change (Sutherland-Addy & Diaw, 2005, pp. 48, 60–61). In her experience, Kate Abbam illustrated the distinction between two practices derived from African culture. She publicly campaigned against the detrimental cultural practice of abusing widows, and she assumed a culturally defined position of leadership that allowed her to campaign for change in abusive practices.

While aware of arguments on all sides of these issues, my position is consistent with that of Kate Abbam and other feminists who are capable of recognizing the beneficial as well as the detrimental in cultural practices. As such I have found the courts in particular are important for those many ordinary Asante who are seeking justice in their social lives. For local people who are engaged in farming land that has not been divided into private property, for those who follow custom (belief and practice) in their everyday lives, and those who cannot afford the time or the money to take their cases to the state courts, chiefs and queen mothers provide a space, the knowledge, and the authority for the performance of litigation concerning custom and local affairs.

Legal Systems

The encounter between the British and the Akan legal systems has produced several systems of law that exist simultaneously today. The presence of more than one legal system is not unique to Ghana or to Africa, but is a widespread phenomenon, especially among cultures that experienced colonialism. Although the upheavals and ruptures caused by colonialism have received considerable attention from scholars, anthropologists have noted the presence of continuities, as well as change, and especially so in recent years. In no domain is this more evident than that of legal systems.[7] Sally Engel Merry (2001) has observed:

> Through historical processes, particular cultural conceptions and practices become embedded in politically and economically powerful institutions such as legal systems. (p. 46)

Widely documented by both lawyers and scholars for more than a century, multiple systems have often been described with the term "legal pluralism."[8]

Dispute processes and the institutions through which they are enacted, which were long established before colonial powers arrived and introduced Western-style law, continue to function today in Ghana. While a healthy number of scholars and lawyers have been dedicated to the study of indigenous law in Ghana (and neighboring countries), a major Ghanaian figure is often overlooked in these histories. Before the British had even fully established themselves in the Gold Coast, John Mensah Sarbah's father sent him to England where he was educated in law and returned in 1887 to become the youngest barrister in West Africa. Soon after his return, he published two major studies of the Akan legal system: *Fanti Customary Law* (1897) and *Fanti National Constitution* (1906), both of which deal with the legal system of the Akan communities. (The Fanti are one of several related groups who are known collectively as the Akan; their political and legal processes follow the same patterns). This very early documentation by a Ghanaian trained in British law gave legitimacy to the indigenous system. Not the first notice of it, however, the Asante legal system was observed as it was performed by the first major British observer in Ashanti, T. Edward Bowdich, and recorded in his monumental published work, *Mission from Cape Coast Castle to Ashantee* (1819).

Not only is Kumasi the precolonial capital of the Asante and the second largest city in Ghana, but the Asantehene and the Asantehemma have their palaces on a hill designated as Manhyia. In accord with the principle of matching the important with the important, the Institute of African Studies from the University of Ghana also maintains an office and an archive at Manhyia. Additional important institutions are located across the street. There the National House of Chiefs has its large multistoried meeting house, and the Regional House of Chiefs for the Ashanti region meets in its own building. Paramount chiefs from throughout Ghana meet together to constitute the National House of Chiefs, and each region of the country has a regional House of Chiefs. Chieftaincy issues and disputes are taken up in these formal organizations that are officially recognized by the government. Ghanaian chiefs include individuals who are well educated and others who have little formal education. (Many paramount chiefs have college degrees, and a few have postgraduate degrees, while the chiefs in small towns or villages might have only a primary school education. Most chiefs do speak English, but many queen mothers do not). To become a chief or a queen mother, one must be in the lineage of the royal family in one's town or paramountcy. There are no requirements regarding education, although most paramount chiefs are educated through high school, and many have completed college degrees. Some chiefs are successful businessmen or lawyers or accountants while others may be engaged in occupations of lesser status and income such as farming or small businesses. Contemporary chiefs represent a wide spectrum of occupations and education, resulting in a situation where some chiefs are more knowledgeable than others about Asante culture and the norms that govern custom. The National House of Chiefs and the Regional Houses of Chiefs ensure that this knowledge is shared and put into practice, in addition to their duties of holding hearings when disputes have developed within chieftaincy.

Ethnographic Context and Reciprocity

As my research project focused on queen mothers, chiefs, and their courts in contemporary Asante social and political life, my method was ethnographic. Integrated with the ethnographic and shaping my decisions and the questions I asked, was my theoretical approach. Incorporating scholarship from the anthropology of law, ritual and performance, feminist anthropology, and postcolonial studies led me to ask questions concerning the degree to which a queen mother or a chief can exercise power and authority and over what kinds of issues, and exploring the opportunities available to ordinary people, female and male, for defining conflict and resolving disputes. Utilizing theories of performance, both verbal and event centered, allowed me to concentrate on the close study of each session of the court and its participants, and to identify and rely upon individual cultural specialists associated with the political/legal system.

While theories in the fields that shape research with contemporary societies have undergone dramatic change in recent decades as scholars consider the effects of power, the actions of the state, and other broad issues, ethnography remains the method of choice for researchers who study human beings as they accomplish their everyday lives in accord with the social systems they have created. Writing about contemporary ethnographic studies, Sally Falk Moore (2005) observes that anthropologists currently seek to follow the trajectory of moving, interacting, social parts and the ideas that accompany them, discerning responses to major changes and shocks in a system as well as to mundane, local practices and how they may be connected to larger-scale systems. In spite of the focus on the dynamics of changing circumstances, Moore finds that contemporary ethnographers continue to emphasize a concept fundamental to anthropological studies—context. She reiterates it by citing Richard Wilson's research on human rights:

> The universality of human rights (or otherwise) becomes a question of context necessitating a situational analysis.... human rights doctrine does get reworked and transformed in different contexts. (Wilson, 1997, p. 12, 13)

While context can refer to the immediate surroundings of a situation, it can also refer to the larger circumstances—the history and politics relevant to a specific setting or action. The ethnographer must be well aware of both levels of context, as the research topic and the individuals involved in it may be influenced by contextual factors at any level. Moreover, the ethnographer can observe the effects of contextualization in the actual performance of litigation as participants align what they are doing to particular others and dimensions of context (Bauman & Briggs, 1990).

In Ghana, as elsewhere, the residue of colonialism continues to create conditions and contradictions that influence circumstances. Even more important is the impact of globalization, creating the desire to emigrate, affecting relations with one's relatives and with Westerners, and sending people, money, and goods, legal and illegal, back and forth across the Atlantic. As in all locations, the role of the state is especially relevant. A repressive government may create an atmosphere that will discourage people from talking with a foreigner; on the contrary, such a government may slow down general activity, providing more time for people to interact with an ethnographer. In order to take account of the political context, an ethnographer must develop a sensitivity to silences and indirection, and cultivate patience and careful listening. To complicate matters even further, a stratified society such as the Asante creates specific challenges to the ethnographer, who must learn the protocol for interacting with those who occupy different positions in the hierarchy. Moreover, a major factor includes learning to recognize what can be expected from individuals who occupy various positions in the hierarchy, and what is then expected of the researcher.

In all instances, the ethnographer must follow the ethical guidelines set out by his or her discipline and others as well. But she or he must also recognize what is considered ethical and responsible in the host society. A key to that position is reciprocity. In Ghana, as in most societies, reciprocity is important, not only in the sense of exchange but also as recognition of status. Gifts are important in Ghana after a relationship has been established, or if visiting a very important chief or queen mother for the first, and perhaps only, time. However, unlike the ritual of gifting in the West, in Ghana opening the gift may be a private act, apart from the giver, and there may be no further acknowledgement of the gift. Many other forms of reciprocity are available to the ethnographer as well, ranging from photos to driving people if one owns a car or paying for taxis, to expressing appreciation with appropriate amounts of money. Most important, however, for the researcher in Ghana working with chieftaincy is that a visit to a queen mother or a chief requires one to arrive with a bottle of Schnapps as a gift. Though some practices are known and accepted such as the presentation of Schnapps, in most situations in Ghana, as elsewhere, the ethnographer must devote special attention to learning what forms of reciprocity are expected and/or appreciated at different levels in a social hierarchy. For example, if visiting a chief or queen mother of status, one must deliver European Schnapps, not the locally made kind. Moreover, if giving a queen mother a gift of cloth, it must be European, not Ghanaian or Nigerian cloth.

The ethnographer is equally as visible and perhaps more so than others in the research situation so it is essential to determine what is expected of her if she hopes to find cooperation. It was the Asantehemma's acceptance that permitted me to observe the courts, and I was careful to bring the correct gifts to her. However, it was with the help of the okyeame and the Dujanatoahemma that I was able to learn how the court operates, and I provided small gifts of appreciation to them. However, I was expected to provide a gift of money to the court as a body, which I eventually did, but until I did, one individual member of the court criticized something I did every day. Once I had made my gift, publicly, to the court, the individual was warm and friendly, and no further criticisms were directed my way.

Key Person and Research Networks

My friend who introduced me to the Asantehemma proved to be important as his sponsorship guaranteed my acceptance. However, he subsequently did not play a major role in my research because he was a businessman. Yet other individuals became essential to my project, individuals I consider to have been key persons in my research network. These key persons embodied authority on cultural subjects, and not only provided information, but gave direction to my research.

Although ethnographic studies often mention those who collaborate with the fieldworker, few studies have devoted exclusive attention to these research friends and partners. An early exception is the path-breaking collection *In the Company of Man* (1960), edited by Joseph Casagrande. In this volume, twenty of the best-known anthropologists of the mid-20th century, conducting fieldwork in different settings, provide the profiles of those who aided and befriended them in their research. In the words of Casagrande, they served the anthropologist "so well in the collaborative enterprise of field work. They are the prismatic lenses, as it were, through which we see refracted the life we would observe." (p. xii). One especially rich essay from that volume is Victor Turner's profile of his friend Muchona the Hornet, an Ndembu "doctor" of several curative rituals who knew many medicines and shared his knowledge of rituals and symbols with Turner (p. 340). Several decades later, the publication *Bridges to Humanity* (Grindal & Salamone, 1995) updates the earlier volume with new stories of intimate friendships in the field by contemporary anthropologists. Edited by Bruce Grindal and

Frank Salamone, the latter of whom was a student of Casagrande, the work emphasizes the relationship between the anthropologist and the local friend, described as "a closeness in the shadow of separate paths" (p. 99). In this collection, Kirin Narayan established a close friendship with Urmila Devi Sood, a woman storyteller in the Western Himalayan foothill region of northern India. Narayan explains that she was reminded of the "seminars" on ritual Turner described in his profile of Muchona as "Urmila Devi explained the meaning of the stories she told" (p. 92).

Grindal and Salamone (1995) point out that "So-called 'informants' may actually end up being research directors" (p. 85), and indeed, I often felt that Nana Osei had become my research director. When I first arrived at the Asantehemma's court, I became aware that the key individual in the administration of the court was the okyeame, Nana Osei ("Nana" is an honorific term). Friendly and welcoming, and generally at the palace, he was very soon directing me to key events, ideas, and individuals who would prove to be central to my research. These were sometimes attached to the court and at other times were completely independent of it. In all instances, however, he seemed to understand that my goal was to understand the workings of the court and the social system of the Asante. Being an accomplished administrator, as he instructed me about an event or an activity, he explained that I would also be giving someone a ride or assisting in some other way. With this arrangement, he could add to his prestige by providing transportation for those associated with him, and it brought me into contact with those individuals and inevitably led me to important rituals, narratives, and individuals, all of which expanded my research and contributed to my understanding (Stoeltje, 2009).

The pleading chief, Nana Amma Fobi Kufuor, also took me under her tutelage and explained the court to me after we became friends. I attended the court for some time before I approached her, as she was not available in the palace as Nana Osei was. Once we became acquainted, however, she invited me to her room in her family compound where she lived, near the palace, and out of which she rented cloth and paraphernalia for ritual events. While she held a very important position in the court, she had not always lived in Kumasi. She explained to me in one of our meetings that until she was required to assume the position of pleading chief (as it was a position always filled by an individual in her family), she had lived in London where she was a trader. In the course of our many visits, she showed me her several photo albums reflecting her years in London. Moreover, she always served me tea as we talked, and on one occasion she instructed me in the proper way to drink tea—the British way, with milk.

In her role as pleading chief, she is the final step in a case in court. When the decision has been made about a case, the guilty individual comes to the pleading chief to negotiate the fine, and then the case is finished. In contrast, Nana Osei is the initial point in a case. Individuals contact him at the palace to explain their problem and arrange a court date, and then he begins the court each Tuesday morning and moves it along from one case to another. These two individuals, then, are responsible for the beginning and the ending of each court session.

The Asanthemma's Court and the Social System

The opportunity to observe the Asantehemma's court proved to be fortunate indeed as the court is a central node in the Asante social system.[9] All chiefs and queen mothers, but especially queen mothers, are responsible for the resolution of conflicts in their town or division, but the Asantehemma's court in Kumasi is the only formal queen mother's court that meets regularly with a full body of elders and linguists. It was held in a three-sided room inside the walls of the Asantehemma's palace. As part of the room extended into the courtyard, the audience sat on the edges of the courtroom in the courtyard. After extensive talks with Nana Osei and Nana Kufuor, and many afternoons observing the court, I was able to grasp the dynamics of the court in its several dimensions. First and most obvious is the meeting of the court itself. An ordinary person, female or male, can bring a case to the court where he or she and the defendant plus their witnesses will tell the story of their dispute. This entire process I have called the performance of litigation. A second dimension involves the members of the court and the position they occupy. The court is constituted of the Asantehemma, male elders, akyeame (linguists), visiting queen mothers, servants, and an audience. The majority of the elders of the court are representing a village or an entity that is obligated to send someone to serve the court. Thus the relationship between the court and the surrounding population is institutionalized and defined with obligation. Third, the court is linked to other institutions in the culture; understanding how these are linked provides insight into particular cases—how they develop, why they have come to the Asantehemma's court, and at times where it must go from the court (Stoeltje, 2009). As in any culture, one has to understand the relationship between law and cosmology in order to understand what law or practice has been violated, what the procedures for determining guilt or innocence are, and how redress is to be accomplished (Rosen, 2006). These guidelines lead to explanations of the customs governing what is actionable, the rules of the court, especially those governing who can speak and to whom and when, and what the consequences are for the guilty person.

While the Asantehemma is the authority of the court and the final word on all cases, male elders interrogate the litigants and debate the cases, and akyeame (male and female) also question the litigants and pass on the information to the Queen Mother in a triangulated form of communication (Yankah, 1995).

Women and a few men bring their cases to the court for litigation and when they are called to stand before the senior okyeame, they must drop their cloth off their shoulder should they be wearing cloth, and take off their sandals, as signs of respect. Then, facing the okyeame, each of the litigants tells their story. The elders, the other akyeame, and the Asantehemma will hear the stories as told by the litigants and their witnesses, though the okyeame will repeat portions of it for the Asantehemma in his role as linguist for her. Most of the members of the court are experienced in these matters and know the field of custom that provides the body of law for the court. The litigants are considered to be commoners, and most are not educated, or if they are, they may only completed a few years of education. The members of the court are considered to be royals, the elites of the Asante, based on their birth. Some are educated and some are not. The language of the court is Twi.

Apart from the queen mother herself, the key figure in the court is the okyeame. A specialist in speaking, the position is formally recognized in all Akan cultures as the person who speaks for the chief or queen mother to any other person, and vice versa, repeats the words of others to the chief or queen mother (Yankah, 1995). To state the rule clearly and unambiguously, no one communicates directly with a chief or queen mother even though he or she may be present. The okyeame transmits the words of others to the chief or queen mother and their words to the intended audience. A queen mother or chief may have a number of akyeame, but one of them will have the major responsibilities for speaking and for supervising and implementing policies. She or he may be recognized as the chief of the akyeame. On some occasions, the queen mother may not be present, and the okyeame simply assumes the authority for the queen mother and speaks for her but does not sit on her stool or stand in her space. In certain cases if she is not present but is in the palace, the okyeame will leave the court and go inside the palace to consult with her before making decisions.

The ultimate authority of the court is unquestionably the queen mother, but the okyeame implements the procedures and rules and shepherds individuals through the processes of the court. The Asantehemaa has a total of six akyeame, male and female. A female okyeame may be asked by the Asantehemaa to travel to outlying villages to investigate cases that come to the court from there, and a female okyeame might also be asked to investigate a case in which a "woman is naturally advantaged," that is, a case that is essentially about women's affairs.

Asked if the female akyeame engage in the same processes of interrogation and discussion that the males do when they are present in the court, the answer from the men was that it is possible for the women to do what the men do but generally "their mind is not as sharp as ours," so they do not often speak when the men are present. Moreover, the men believe that the women are not as adept at reading between the lines in difficult cases as the men are.

However, in terms of the hierarchy of akyeame, the senior linguist is a woman (Esessuhemaa), and after her comes the Bomsuhene. Next is Okyeame Osei, who occupies the okyeame stool and is, therefore, a chief, and consequently he has responsibility for administering the court. He also maintains a room in the palace and is expected to be available at all times for those who wish to schedule a case or consult him on other matters. Following him is Okyeame Dawuro and the last in status is Okyeame Nsiah, who was appointed by the Asantehemaa.

Each of these elders in the court has been selected by one of several processes. On the west side of the court are the Konson (singular), and on the east side are the Kotimsi. As they represent the first kings, they come before the Nkonson (plural). They represent a total of 25 villages that are obligated to send elders to sit in the court (it is also compulsory for the villages of the Kotimsi chiefs to send a child to the palace to serve the queen mother). In addition to the elders who are sent from those villages that have a historical obligatory link to the queen mother, she can appoint individuals to serve in the court. In this capacity several of the queen mother's brothers serve as elders, and they assume a prominent role in the court proceedings.

Performance of Litigation in the Court

The significance of having a voice, a publicly recognized voice, and an authority who will listen and rule on a case can hardly be exaggerated. The conflicts that develop into a case reflect issues of paramount concern in everyday life: the use of farm land, money, sex, marriage, theft, and others. However, the majority of the cases are ones in which individuals use a verbal form governed by custom, examples being Curse, Insult, and Oath.

Before the court, both of the litigants and their witnesses perform the narrative that tells the story of their conflict, thereby entitling it. In cases involving the utterance of a verbal taboo, the first issue before the court is whether or not a verbal form was uttered, and once that is determined, the authorities proceed to explore the source of the conflict. Using the discourse of custom, the elders explain to the litigants what offenses were committed and what must be done to redress the situation. At that point the authority of the court has been confirmed and one or the other of the litigants has been declared guilty and must pay a fine or make a sacrifice or do both. (A sacrifice represents a major offense such as curse or oath. An individual must buy a whole sheep, an expensive animal, and give it to the court in order to redress the situation). However, in some instances, the individual must go to a specific river where a deity ("bosom") resides, or to another site where a deity resides and go through specific rituals there. In this lengthy process by which social conflict is transformed into narrative performance and examined by authorities, the members of the court debate issues of custom, interpreting it according to the knowledge they possess, and apply it to specific cases, interrogating the litigants and discussing the issues until they have arrived at a decision.

These issues and the verbal taboos that have been violated in order to bring a case to the court cover a wide range of social interaction. But the verbal offenses are not the only issues that evolve into a case for the courts. Land use and boundaries, marriage and sexual relationships, or accusations of witchcraft are all issues that come to the queen mother's court. The following cases represent the cases that might come before the court on a typical day.

(A) Two women are farming the same land and seem to work together cooperatively, but the mother of one of them has placed a curse on the land. With a curse on the land, the other woman, the litigant, cannot go to farm the plot. The authorities of the court tell them not to gather produce from the land until the next meeting of the court when the case will be taken up.

This case will require some time to resolve, as it involves a dispute over who has rights over the land, but also a curse, which will be a separate issue. It will have to be proven that the woman put the curse on the farm, and if it is proven that she did, she will have to go through the rituals to revoke the curse, a complicated and expensive procedure.

(B) A marriage is breaking up, but there are issues between the husband, wife, and her father that have brought them to the court. The couple went to Nigeria, and now the husband says he doesn't want the wife any more. She "advised herself" that the marriage was over (she concluded that the marriage was over) and told her father. The father then sent Schnapps back to the husband.

The father's procedure is not correct, since marriages, according to custom, are arranged between two families. Therefore the father is found guilty. The correct procedure would have been for him to contact the husband's family to confirm this and then send the Schnapps to the husband's family to complete the dissolution of the marriage. This reverses the procedure of creating the marriage, a process between two families at which the husband's family provides Schnapps to the wife's family.

(C) Two women married to the same man bring a case of insult and curse. They are the senior wife and the junior wife. The junior wife accuses the senior wife of insulting her by saying that she has a "bushy vagina." The husband appears, but seems to be very passive.

The senior wife is convicted of both the insult and also of placing a curse on the junior wife. To resolve the issue, she must slaughter one sheep (and give to the court), and she must return the following week to reverse the curse, a very serious offense that will involve a series of ritual acts and a considerable sum of money.

The issues in these three cases represent the three most common kind of conflict in the court: farmland, a marital problem that cannot be resolved, and two women in conflict over the same man. In Ghana, as in other African countries, many women are farmers. But southern Ghana is a tropical area, and therefore, the areas they farm tend to be small plots in which they grow foodstuffs. The majority of the land in the Ashanti region, and in most of Ghana, belongs to the stool of particular areas, and the chief is the steward of the stool (it is not private property). Individuals have rights to farm on the land, and the chief generally oversees the distribution of it to those who live in the area of the stool. Therefore the chief or queen mother who is enstooled in a particular area resolves most conflicts over land use. But in the case above, it is the curse that has qualified this case for the Asantehemma's court. According to belief, if a curse is uttered, it can cause death or some other dreadful occurrence. Therefore, according to custom, when a curse has been uttered, the individuals involved must bring the case to this court to determine if the curse was uttered. After that decision has been made, the individual who invoked the curse must proceed to revoke the curse. In the case above, the elders determined that no produce should be gathered from the farm until the curse could be revoked, as that might release the curse and cause death, whereas having come to the court, the action of the curse will be held until it can be revoked.

In the case of divorce, the couple was married in accord with custom, which means that the families met and the groom's family provided the bride's family with Schnapps and perhaps something more. According to custom, then, the Schnapps must be returned to the family in order for the divorce to be properly completed. So, in this case, it was the violation of custom that was the problem, and thus the reason why the case was brought to the Asantehemma's court.

In the third case, the two women are both married to one man, legal in Ghana and not uncommon in Ashanti. But they are engaged in a conflict over him, and one of the weapons in such a conflict is a sexually charged insult. Insults are actionable. Moreover, the senior wife cursed the junior wife, an even more serious verbal act that requires a sacrifice of a sheep and other actions at the site of the deity in order to revoke the curse. Given that the consequences are expensive and the party who utters the curse is going to be publicly judged guilty, one might ask why an individual would engage in insult, not to mention curse. One explanation offered to me by a well-educated woman emphasized the importance the culture places on a man. She explains that it is accepted in the culture that every woman should have a man, and she should bear children. However, there are more women in the country than men, so women compete for men. If one is in a competition for a man, and the man is already married or has taken a second wife, there is the possibility that heaping profanities on the "other woman" or delivering an insult or putting a curse on her will drive away the other woman, in which case the one who utters the insult or curse is victorious socially although legally guilty. She has used the power of taboo to her advantage, and she will get the man and the house and whatever benefits that brings with it. We might wonder what the role of the man is in such a situation. It is likely that he is complicit. If a man has a wife, but he has another girlfriend and doesn't like his wife, he might just ignore her, or even bring another woman into the house in the hopes that the first woman will simply leave. Exploring this perspective is consistent with Comaroff and Roberts' (1981) explanation that if dispute-settlement processes are to be explained, attention must be given to the disputants' ostensible motives, how they recruit support, and their efforts to influence the course of events (p. 14).

In all three of these cases, as in the majority of cases at the Asantehemma's court, the issue is one of custom. The source of the conflict in the cases of the court may range over the course of human behavior and the resources considered valuable enough to fight over; but in the course of the conflict, a violation of custom occurs such as a verbal form is uttered or some other violation of custom happens. Then the case comes to the court because it has responsibility for issues involving custom.

In the case below, two problems have converged. Two women are in conflict over the use of a plot of land. In the course of their conflict, one has accused the other of being the descendant of a slave. This is a serious taboo. Moreover, she also accuses her of being an animal (antelope), and that, too, is a serious taboo as it implies uncivilized behavior. The court insists on separating the issues as they will not deal with two separate issues in one case. The brief excerpt below, from a lengthy text (translated from the Twi), illustrates a defendant's story and the discussion among elders that reflects their difference of opinion, a situation that occurs frequently.

DEFENDANT: I grew up in the knowledge that my mother farmed a certain land on which kola nuts grew. There was an incident when complainant's mother caused the kola trees to be felled.

OHYEAME MENSAH: My Auntie ["Auntie" is a term of respect here], what we want to know is about the insult, please.

DEFENDANT: I was working on my farm one day when I saw this woman walk up to me to challenge me on the farmland. In the verbal exchanges she told me that I am an antelope and that I am the descendant of a slave who behaves like a royal, and I replied her in the same words because we have a common ancestry. She even had a machete and brandished it at me so I wanted to pick a stick to disarm her.

(Audience and elders laugh at her implied bravery and strength.)

OHYEAME MENSAH: Elders, these women here are royals of the Bretuo abusua. For them to desecrate the family in the bush is a violation of custom, which must be quenched with blood before we even proceed with the case.

(Majority of the elders concur.)

NANA AFRIYIE: Nananom, I think once we have started with the case and have called the witnesses, we can conveniently go ahead with it and slaughter the sheep afterwards.

(Elders argue among themselves for some time after which they refer the issue to Nana Akyeampong, whom they call Baffour.)

NANA AKYEAMPONG: I agree with those who say blood should be shed before we proceed with the case. I will not be part of the proceedings if blood is not shed.

[*The elders still discuss the issue and Nana Akyeampong relaxes in his arm chair with his eyes closed, tapping the floor with his right foot. Finally they submit to the view of Nana Akyeampong and the ahenkwa, and the women are asked to go to the market to get a sheep* [to be slaughtered as a sacrifice because the accusation is so serious a violation of a taboo.]]

When a person is accused of being the descendant of a slave, a sacrifice of a sheep must be made. A sheep is expensive, and sacrificing it means shedding its blood, and thus Nana Akyeampong's comment to that effect. This taboo was in effect in precolonial Ghana as well because the Asante had several categories of non-free people, none of which bore any similarity to what was known in the United States as slavery. In some instances a person considered a slave was captured in a battle with a different group of people, and could have even been a royal there. In those cases, the person is integrated into the family, and their descendants were not considered slaves. For these and other reasons, it is a very serious violation to make such an accusation. In this particular case, these women come from the same family, and both of them are considered royals, making it particularly disgraceful that they should engage in such insults and curses.

These cases, like all of the cases in the Asantehemma's court, index features of cosmology as well as the conflicts of everyday life. In his book arguing for law as a part of culture, Lawrence Rosen (2006) tells us that

> a key role of most legal systems, quite apart from addressing disputes, consists precisely in their ability to help maintain the sense of cosmological order.... If the categories by which we grasp the world actually maintain our world, and if, in the legal realm no less than many others, long-term order may be accompanied by a sought-after short-term disorder, then it is at the point where boundaries are delineated that the telltale role of law as cosmology may be most readily apparent. (p. 171)

Certainly the major role of the Asantehemma's court is to articulate and maintain the categories and the boundaries of custom. Their rulings consistently turn on whether or not custom has been followed, and even the procedure, as in the case above, must follow custom before the conflict can even be explored (a sheep must be slaughtered to compensate for the offense before it can be litigated.)

Conclusion

None of these analyses or observations would be possible without an understanding of the context in which the Asantehemma's court is situated. In all research situations, context is an essential component of the framework of the research. Beyond the context and equally important, however, are the rules of reciprocity and the system of hierarchy and status that must be understood if the research project is to succeed. Specifically, I was prepared with an understanding of the rules and the system for meeting the Asantehemma and gaining permission to do the research. She did indeed issue the permission to observe the court; but other individual members of the court were essential to understanding how the court operates, and I had to learn about those individuals and their status and therefore what was expected of me as a form of reciprocation.

At times individuals engaged in ethnographic research make assumptions about access to knowledge that fail to take into account these considerations. However, the individual who overlooks context, reciprocity, and status in ethnographic research runs the risk of failing to make a serious contribution with her research. This article has demonstrated the relevance of the Asante context, and the importance of the status of the individuals who are members of the court and those who bring their cases to court, as well as the issues that are brought before the court as defined by Asante custom. Moreover, it has pointed to the importance of reciprocity in all research relations.

Reciprocal relations create relationships that may become lifelong friendships, and they are often responsible for assisting the researcher not only to obtain data but also to understand and interpret it. The research participants who generously provided information and interpretation of the Asantehemma's court made it possible for me to understand how the courts function as a site where belief, gender, ritual, religion, law, family, oral traditions, politics, and economics come together, reflecting the experiences of ordinary people in everyday life. Litigants, elders, akyeame, the Asantehemma, the audience, all place on stage the performance of conflict for review and its resolution by the tenets of custom that reveal the categories and their boundaries.

While those who participate in the Asante courts are clearly committed to the social system represented by the label "custom" and administered through chieftaincy, there are many other Ghanaians who consider the entire system a great waste of resources and a form of exploitation. For those who aggressively press for signs of progress and want to replace the institutions of custom with those of modernity, the courts are simply a measure of the past. Yet these courts provide a site at which an individual, including an ordinary woman, can tell her story, whatever it may be, and receive a hearing. Curses, insults, accusations, and other verbal forms of abuse remain powerful in Asante culture, shaping social relations whether the subject is economic or sexual. Conflicts over land use continue to plague people who farm. Sexual and marital relations are central issues as they are in most cultures, although they are always defined by demographic influences and cultural expectations of what is desirable, what is acceptable, and what is actionable. Moreover, the correct procedure for accomplishing social business constitutes a major issue in every society. The Asantehemma's court and other Asante courts provide the authority that maintains the boundaries and defines the categories of correct behavior for those who believe in the social system known as custom, and they provide the opportunity for individuals to resolve disputes that are inevitable in any society. In all cases, the authorities apply the discourse of custom, discuss the issue, and arrive at a resolution of the dispute. Meanwhile, the disputants have not only arrived at a resolution, but they have had the opportunity to address their adversaries and express their narrative to an audience who takes them seriously. In the process, some of the litigants will have achieved a public restoration of face and an affirmation of self-worth. For as long as these issues are relevant, the courts offer an opportunity for the performance of litigation and the articulation of cosmology.

In the process of the entire court performance, the participants have not only narrated their conflicts, but they have shared the knowledge of themselves with others in the court who have listened, interrogated, commented, instructed, and judged the actions of the litigants, employing metaphors, analogies, and other cultural means of illustrating their point. Whatever the motives for the conflicts, this entire process, based on cosmology, history, and jural corporateness, held deeply in the culture, expresses community, a sharing of morals, of verbal forms, of stories, of understandings that assures all of the participants that one has a place in a society, and the society has the means to pursue justice. We might conclude that in this case, conflict facilitates community (West, 1993).

Epilogue

As mentioned above, however, globalization and the state have an impact on all of social life, and the Asante are no exception. When Osei Tutu II became Asantehene in 1999, and John Agyekum Kufuor, an Oxford-educated lawyer, became president of Ghana in 2000, change was felt throughout the country. After 19 years of the rule of J.J. Rawlings, the country experienced a new freedom, a vastly improved economy, and an energy felt up and down. Soon everyone had a cell phone and was wearing new cloth, and suddenly people were very busy, traveling and meeting and working. As the biological son of the Asantehemma and a busines man, Osei Tutu II turned attention to matters in the Ashanti region long neglected by the state. He established an Asante educational fund to improve the schools in the Ashanti region (which had suffered from a lack of funding), to be funded by Asantes, especially the chiefs, in the U.S. and the U.K. as well as in Ghana.

Of special interest, he completely remodeled the Asantehemma's palace, creating a new and beautiful space for the court to meet. When I returned in 2004, everyone in the court was wearing beautiful new white cloth, and the personnel had also changed. The female akyeame were present and running the court. Some of the same elders and akyeame from the 1990s were participating in the court, and some were not. Nana Kufour was no longer present as pleading chief, and Nana Osei did not take an active part in the court. The audience was much larger, but much less responsive. One of the cases involved a proposed new building, and architects dressed in suits and ties were present with their blueprints. Prosperity and kinship had transformed the space of the court, the cloth of the members of the court, and the community itself.

Notes

1. This essay is based on research in the Ashanti region of Ghana in 1990 funded by a year-long Fulbright Faculty Research Fellowship, and numerous return trips since then. I wish to acknowledge also a year-long residency as a Weatherhead Resident Scholar at the School of American Research (now the School of Advanced Research
2. See Stoeltje (1997) for a description of the Asante queen mother's position.
3. See McCaskie (1995) for a comprehensive history of the pre-colonial Asante state.
4. See McCaskie (2000) for a study of a specific village as it encountered modernity.
5. Financing the system of chieftaincy often represents a problem in today's Ghana. Recognizing this problem, the current government announced on August 13, 2010 that it plans to pay a small stipend to both chiefs and queen mothers (Joy On Line, 2009).
6. Constitution of the Republic of Ghana, 1992. pp. 164–168.
7. See Comaroff & Roberts (1981), Griffiths (1997), and Hirsch (1998).
8. See von Benda-Beckman (2003), the *Journal of Legal Pluralism*, and the biannual publications of the Commission on Folk Law and Legal Pluralism for studies of legal pluralism.
9. For a fuller treatment of the organization of the court, see Stoeltje (2002).

References

Bauman, R., & Briggs, C. L. (1990). Poetics and performance as critical perspectives on language and social life. *Annual Review of Anthropology, 19*, 59–88.

Bowdich, T. E. (1819/1966) . *Mission from Cape Coast Castle to Ashantee* (3rd ed.). London: Frank Cass & Co. Ltd. [originally published by John Murray of Albermarle Street].

Casagrande, J. B. (Ed.). (1960). *In the company of man: Twenty portraits by anthropologists.* New York: Harper & Brothers.

Comaroff, J., & Roberts S. (1981). *Rules and processes: The cultural logic of dispute in an African context.* Chicago: University of Chicago Press.

Constitution of the Republic of Ghana. (1992). Tema: Ghana Publishing Corp.

Fortes, M., Steel, R. W., & Ady P. (1947). Ashanti survey, 1945–46: An experiment in social research. *The Geographical Journal 110* (4–6), 149–79.

Griffiths, A. (1997). *In the shadow of marriage: Gender and justice in an African community.* Chicago: University of Chicago Press.

Grindal, B., & Salamone, F. (Eds.). (1995). *Bridge to humanity: Narratives on anthropology and friendship.* Prospect Heights, IL: Waveland Press.

Hirsch, S. F. (1998). *Pronouncing and persevering: Gender and the discourses of disputing in an* African Islamic court. Chicago: University of Chicago.

Joy On Line. (2009). Government to start paying queen-mothers monthly allowances. *Joy News/ Myjoyonline.com/ Ghana.* Retrieved from http://news.myjoyonline.com/news/201008/50666.asp.

McCaskie, T. C. (1995). *State and society in pre-colonial Asante.* Cambridge: Cambridge University Press.

McCaskie, T. C. (1998). Custom, tradition and law in pre-colonnial Asante. In E.A.B. van Rouveroy van Nieuwaal & W. Zips (Eds.), *Sovreignty, legitimacy, and power in West African societies: Perspecties from legal anthropology* (pp. 25–47). Hamburg: Lit.

McCaskie, T. C. (2000). *Asante identities: History and modernity in an African village 1850–1950.* London/Bloomington: Edinburgh University Press/Indiana University Press.

Merry, S. E. (2001). Changing rights, changing culture. In J. K. Cowan, M. Dembour & R. A. Wilson (Eds.), *Culture and rights: Anthropological perspectives* (pp. 31–55). New York: Cambridge University Press.

Moore, S. F. (2005). Comparisons: Possible and impossible. *Annual Review of Anthropology, 34,* 1–11.

Narayan, K. (1995). Shared stories. In B. Grindal, & F. Salamone (Eds.), *Bridge to Humanity: Narratives on Anthropology and Friendship* (pp. 85–98). Prospect Heights, IL. Waveland Press.

Nkrumah, K. (1964). *Conscienticism.* London: Heinemann.

Rathbone, R. (2000). *Nkrumah and the chiefs: The politics of chieftaincy in Ghana 1951–1960.* Athens, OH: Ohio University Press.

Rosen, L. (2006). *Law as culture: An invitation.* Princeton, NJ: Princeton University Press.

Sarbah, J. M. (1897/1968). *Fanti customary laws: A brief introduction to the principles of the native laws and customs of the Fanti and Akan districts of the Gold Coast* (3rd ed.). London: Frank Cass & Co. Ltd.

Sarbah, J. M. (1906/1968). *Fanti national constitution: A short treatise on the constitution and goverment of the Fanti, Asanti, and other Akan tribes of West Africa* (2nd ed.). London: Frank Cass & Co. Ltd.

Stoeltje, B. J. (1997). Asante queen mothers: A study in female authority. In F. Kaplan (Ed.), *Queens, queen mothers, priestesses, and power* (pp. 41–71). Baltimore, MD: Johns Hopkins University Press.

Stoeltje, B. J. (2002). Performing litigation at the queen mother's court. In C. Jones-Pauly & S. Elbern (Eds.), *Access to justice: The role of court administrators and lay adjudicators in the African and Islamic contexts* (pp. 1–22). The Hague: Kluwer Law International.

Stoeltje, B. J. (2009, Spring). Asante traditions and female self-assertion: Sister Abena's narrative. *Research in African Literatures, 40*(1), 27–41.

Stoeltje, B. J. (2010). Custom and politics in Ghanaian popular culture. In T. Falola & F. Ngom (Eds.), *Facts, fiction, and African creative imaginations* (pp. 60–74). London: Routledge.

Sutherland-Addy, E., & Diaw, A. (Eds.). (2005). *Women writing Africa: West Africa and the Sahel.* New York: Feminist Press.

Turner, V. W. (1960). Muchona the Hornet, Interpreter of Religion. In J. B. Casagrande (Ed.), *In the Company of Man: Twenty portraits by anthropologists* (pp. 333–355). New York: Harper & Brothers.

von Benda-Beckman, K. (2003). The contexts of law: Legal pluralism and unofficial law in social, economic and political development. In R. Pradhan (Ed.), *Papers of the XIIIth. International Congress,* Vol III, ICNEC.

West, R. (1992). *Narrative, authority and law.* Ann Arbor: University of Michigan Press.

Wilson, R. A., (Ed.). (1997). *Human rights, culture and context.* London/Chicago: Pluto Press.

Yankah, K. (1995). *Speaking for the chief.* Bloomington: Indiana University Press.

CHAPTER NINETEEN

Two Legal Research Stories

REBECCA RIALL

The lawyer researching the law is practical and focused. She wants to find legal sources that support the realization of her client's wishes. She must uncover any legal dangers that may befall her client, so that she may warn him away. She must make arguments that rely largely on existing primary legal authority rather than appealing to broader social contexts such as justice or outcomes. Law schools train attorneys to privilege reasoning based on linguistic constructs over moral or social reasoning (Mertz, 2007). Say the lawyer's client is a newly birthed nonprofit corporation, toddling towards federal tax exemption. The nonprofit will not be served by its attorney informing the IRS that a particular revenue ruling resulted from a limited cultural viewpoint and should not apply to her client. Instead, the nonprofit needs its lawyer to help it encounter the IRS on the IRS's terms for the purpose of receiving and maintaining tax exemption.

In some ways, for the qualitative social researcher, the scope of inquiry is expanded compared to that of the attorney conducting legal research. The social scientist can acknowledge the power wielded by parties at court, political players, and judges. She can seek the social contexts that serve—as much as any rational principles of "natural law"—to explain court decisions. She can acknowledge that a court order is not inherently more authoritative than a newspaper article, an oral history, a personal narrative. At the same time, she can understand the processes that drive legal thinking and understand how some stories, some arguments, some ethics come to weigh more than others.

This chapter will, briefly, describe an attorney undertaking legal research on behalf of a client, in hopes that this information may be of some use to social scientists seeking to understand legal culture. The topic of how legal research proceeds has been discussed in greater depth elsewhere, so I will provide only a simplified sketch. The main body of the chapter then switches track to show how socially relevant information—in this case, information concerning perpetual treaty rights of American Indians—can be uncovered through a critical qualitative research approach to legal texts, giving attention to social meanings, cultural contexts, and historical outcomes.

Part One: A Lawyer Doing Legal Research

Sally is a public defense attorney in the fine state of Diligence in the United States. Three years ago, upon graduating law school, passing a multi-day bar exam, and providing satisfactory evidence of her moral character, she was admitted to the Diligence Bar. Generally, she may practice only in Diligence unless she either passes a bar exam in another state (offered twice a year at most) or until she achieves a sufficient number of practice years and can be admitted to practice in a state that has entered a reciprocity agreement with Diligence.

Yesterday, Sally met with a new client, a kindergarten teacher charged with failing to report suspected neglect or abuse of a child. With three years of criminal practice behind her, Sally is already aware of the statutory elements of the charge: being statutorily mandated to report because of profession, having reasonable cause to suspect child neglect or abuse, and failing to report the possible neglect or abuse to police. Six months ago, one of the teacher's pupils told him he was being left home alone for days at a time, cared for by his 7-year-old sister. The child often showed up unkempt, but he usually attended school and even brought lunches from home. Because the child routinely invented fanciful stories, his teacher gave little thought to this particular tale. The teacher never followed up with the parents or reported the possible neglect, until a few months later when the nightly news reported that his pupil had been rescued from a house fire in the middle of the night. The parents were several states away, and no adults were in the home. When the teacher contacted the police to report what his pupil told him months before, he was charged with failing to report child neglect.

Even though she knows the statutory elements of the charge, Sally needs to define key parameters. For example, under what circumstances have courts found a defendant to have had "reasonable knowledge" of child neglect? Under what circumstances have they found reasonable knowledge does not exist? In answering this question, Sally will confine herself to cases in Diligence, prioritizing cases from its highest court and its lower-level, first-order appeals court—both of which set binding precedents on the trial courts—keeping in mind that high-court rulings trump those from the lower appeals court. She internalized these rules of precedence and binding authority in law school and does not even need to think about them. Even though Sally has confined herself to appellate rulings, there are hundreds of cases concerning this charge. Sally refers first to several state-specific practitioner's manuals, which provide summaries of the law at the time they were written. These manuals provide citations to cases that (at least at the time of writing) controlled outcomes. Sally reads the cases herself, searching a commercial database for any subsequent references to those cases that may overturn, clarify, or otherwise reframe them.

As she parses the cases, Sally begins to formulate a list of rules from each case and to consider how the rules apply to her client's situation—the "facts" of his case, which are undisputed by both the teacher and the prosecutor. In truth, the rules are qualitative and subjective, with the high court seemingly developing law specific to each set of facts it encountered. However, Sally must, as best as she is able, present her arguments as if the law of the high court were a logically consistent body, even when she must stretch to do so. The client will be best served if she can convincingly argue that his situation is fundamentally unlike those in which the defendant was found to have reasonable knowledge of neglect. However, she may not be able to do so. Arguments about broader social impacts of the outcome in her client's case are disfavored and weak compared to a simple argument applying prior rulings to her client's facts. In this way, Sally's research is narrower in scope than that of a qualitative researcher, and she focuses narrowly on the law as it applies to her client's case.

Part Two: Qualitative Social Research of the Law[1]

As I argued earlier, the legal research typically conducted by lawyers and qualitative social scientific research of the law are different creatures. It is true that some lawyers undertake social scientific research using qualitative methods. However, such research is usually undertaken to assess or influence policy writ large, not to win specific cases. This part of the chapter will give an example of qualitative social research into legal texts—treaties between American Indian nations and the United States—undertaken to understand a socially important matter. The research is social and qualitative in that it examines a set of texts within their broader legal and ethical frameworks, not as mere linguistic constructs, but as texts that impact human daily lives.

American Indian people often rely on treaties to safeguard certain core rights from the federal government, state governments, and local governments. Treaty-based rights sometimes allow tribes to avoid certain kinds of regulation that state and local governments might like to impose against the interests of tribes. At their essence, treaties reflect the deep history of our nations' sovereign status. Treaties are not made between national governments and municipalities. Treaties are not made between national governments and corporations. Treaties are not made between public and private actors, or among private actors. Rather, treaties are instruments of international law, and arise only between sovereigns. The existence of treaties attests to the sovereign status of American Indian nations, acknowledged by one another, by European nations, and by the United States.

That said, for three primary reasons, treaties between American Indian nations and the United States do not merit our undiluted veneration. First, treaties, as embodied in written documents,[2] commonly extol racist notions of "civilization." At least 60 treaties between the U.S. and Indian nations list "civilization" as a goal for the Indian nation, implying that the Indian nation lacked civilization, (see generally Kappler, 1904). Second, given the circumstances under which treaties were signed, treaty texts are colonial texts that reflect deceptive signatures by tribal citizens lacking due authority to sign for their nations,[3] the unequal ability of non-English-speaking Indian diplomats to verify that the written terms accurately reflected negotiated terms,[4] and a cornucopia of unsavory U.S. "negotiation" strategies.[5]

Third, many treaty texts state that the Indian nation involved has seriously curtailed its sovereignty. For example, the 1826 Chippewa[6]–U.S. treaty states:

> The Chippewa tribe…fully acknowledge the authority and jurisdiction of the United States, and disclaim all connection with any foreign power, solemnly promising to reject any messages, speeches, or councils, incompatible with the interest of the United States, and to communicate information thereof to the proper agent, should any such be delivered or sent to them. (*Treaty with the Chippewa*, Aug. 5, 1826 [Chippewa-U.S.], 7 Stat. 290, art. 8; see also Kappler, 1904, p. 270).

Similarly broad restrictions on diplomatic capacity are widespread in treaties between tribal nations and the U.S.[7] Such restrictions isolated tribes from potential alliances with one another and with other powers. Moreover, these restrictions impair tribal claims to international statehood since diplomatic capacity is frequently considered a marker of statehood under international law.[8] For instance, the treaty could prohibit Ojibwa delegates from meeting with U.N. Working Group on Indigenous Peoples if the U.S. deemed such a meeting incompatible with its interests (provided, of course, that their tribal governments decided not to break the treaty—a right the U.S. claims in regards to treaties, as will be discussed further below).

Because treaties are important markers of the sovereignty of our nations, they—like any national symbol—sometimes give rise to exaggerated claims. In Indiana, one frequently hears the claim that the Indiana state legislature must provide free college education to citizens of tribes that formerly possessed Indiana because, it is said, the U.S. treaties with all those tribes clearly specify a perpetual right to education. However, the written treaties between the U.S. and current or former tribes within Indiana's current jurisdiction don't require the state to do any such thing. One explanation might be that such a right was included in the treaty negotiations, but stricken from the written document by iniquitous U.S. agents. If this were true, such a right exists and may have survived into oral history even as it was omitted from the treaty texts themselves, since U.S. law admits that treaties must be construed as the Indian negotiators at the time would have understood them, (see, e.g., *Worcester v. Georgia*, 1832, 31 U.S. 515, p. 582). However, it is also possible that such a right was never part of treaty negotiations, and that treaties, particularly as powerful national symbols and as strong legal sources of rights, generate a folklore that, while justice oriented, is sometimes exaggerated.

The worth of treaties lies not only in their text, but also in the admitted obligation of the U.S. to interpret treaties so that "ambiguities occurring will be resolved from the standpoint of the Indians," (*Winters vs US*, 1908, 207 U.S. 564, p. 576). A primary source of ambiguity is the fate of treaty terms over time. For example, the Ottawa were promised a perpetual $2,400 annuity in 1808, (*Treaty with the Ottawa*, Nov. 17, 1817 [Ottawa–U.S.], 7 Stat. 105 art. 2; see also Kappler, 1904, p. 93); are they to be paid the meager sum of $2,400 per year today? Or would Ottawa negotiators have perhaps thought of $2,400 in light of the goods for which it could be exchanged, meaning that $2,400 should be adjusted upward to account for inflation? In 1855, 23 northwest tribes were promised a physician, vaccination, and "medicine and advice to the sick," (*Treaty with the Dwamish, Suquamish, Etc*, Jan. 22, 1855, 12 Stat. 927, art. 14; see also Kappler, 1904, p. 672). Today, are those tribes entitled to exactly that, or are they entitled to more substantial health care that is the contemporary equivalent of this provision?

We'll now examine perpetual treaty rights—that is, explicitly stated treaty rights that can potentially run forever. I argue that the treaty rights with the most value today—with the exception of reservation boundaries protected by treaty—are rights to natural resources, rather than any of the other forms of perpetual treaty rights, and that we need to generate theories of American Indian social, national, and personal rights that do not depend too heavily on these brief, often unfairly negotiated documents.

§ 1. Treaties Between Indian Nations and the U.S. Federal Government

Indian nations entered treaties with European sovereigns, colonies, and states within the U.S., as well as with other Indian sovereigns. However, this chapter is concerned only with formal treaty-making between the U.S. and Indian nations, which ended abruptly in 1871, (*Indian*

Appropriations Act, Mar. 3, 1871, 16 Stat. 544, p. 566).[9] Thus, I examined the 372 treaties recorded in Kappler's (1904) *Indian Affairs: Laws and Treaties*, Volume 2 (Treaties), excluding treaties to which the U.S. was not a party[10] and treaties between U.S. states and tribal nations (since according to the Constitution, Congress rather than the states has the authority to regulate commerce "with foreign nations, and among the several states, and with the Indian tribes," U.S. Const., art. 1, § 8). I also excluded treaties not ratified by Congress and post-treaty "agreements" that were included as appendices by Kappler. Although the excluded treaties and agreements are significant in their own right, they are outside the scope of this chapter, because their existence does not entail an acknowledgment of nationhood or sovereignty of tribal governments by the U.S. federal government.

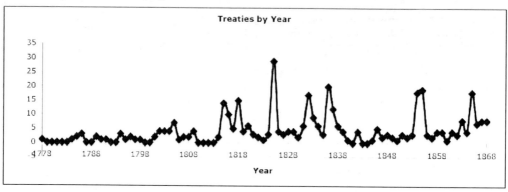

Figure 1 Annual number of ratified treaties between the U.S. federal government and tribal nations, 1778–1871

In the remainder of this section, I will discuss the history of treaties, from their negotiation through their post-ratification life.

A. The Treaty-Making Period, 1778–1871. The earliest treaty between the U.S. federal government and an Indian nation was negotiated and signed in 1778. Overall, from 1778 until 1868 (when the last treaty that would be ratified by the U.S. Senate was signed), treaty-making became increasingly common (see Figure 1, illustrating the number of treaties ratified per year during this period). Treaty negotiations also underwent significant spikes, particularly after international wars in which some Indian nations sided with other colonial powers than the U.S. (in Figure 1, notice the spikes after the War of 1812 and the U.S. Civil War, reflecting ratification of "conciliatory" treaties).

During this period, treaties between the U.S. and Indian nations were negotiated on the U.S. side by an executive treaty delegation pursuant to the President's exclusive constitutional authority to enter treaties.[11] Subsequently, the Senate could ratify—or not—the treaty. Tribes generally do not seem to have expected entry into force to depend on ratification by their own legislative bodies. Then, too, those tribal signatories who acted for personal benefit under false pretense of authority may have known that tribal legislative bodies would never ratify such treaties.

As Miller (2006) notes, the treaties frequently included language that purported to recognize diminished sovereignty of the tribal treaty partner, often following elements of the doctrine of the discovery, the legal principle by which European nations claim ultimate domain over non-European nations. It is unlikely that most Indian nation treaty delegates were conversant with European international law, so this duplicitous use of treaties to legitimize colonization further reflects the bipolar nature of treaties—they undergird our nations' sovereignty, but they do so only within the bounds imposed by a foreign power.

B. The Life of Treaties. Even after the creation of new treaties ended in 1871, tribes, states, and the federal government have vied with one another to interpret existing treaty provisions. Such disputes often find their way to the federal judiciary, although, as has been amply lamented elsewhere by many authors, federal courts are hardly neutral arbiters for fundamentally international disputes. Nonetheless, over the years, federal courts have promulgated rules of treaty construction. On balance, these rules do not favor tribes.

A particularly egregious judicial rule permits the U.S. Congress to unilaterally abrogate treaty terms without consequence, at least when Congress believes the abrogation to be in the best interests of the Indian treaty partner. This rule arises out of the *Lone Wolf v. Hitchcock* case (1903, 187 U.S. 553), in which Kiowa Principal Chief Lone Wolf challenged the U.S. taking of lands that had been reserved by the tribe in an 1867 treaty among the Kiowa and Comanche nations and the United States. Many treaties provide that further cessions of reserved lands will not occur or will only occur if some kind of consent from the Indian nation is obtained. In the case of the 1867 Kiowa and Comanche treaty with the U.S. (the treaty implicated in *Lone Wolf*), the condition for further land cession was a vote in favor of cession by three quarters of adult Kiowa and Comanche men (*Treaty with the Kiowa and Comanche*, Oct. 21, 1867, 15 Stats., 581; see also Kappler, 1904, p. 981). Stunningly, the U.S. Supreme Court held that even such an explicitly stated treaty right of an Indian nation is not absolute. Rather, in *Lone Wolf v. Hitchcock*, the court held that Congress could abrogate the Kiowa–Comanche–U.S. land-cession restriction—and other treaty provisions—without the consent of the Indian nation involved in order to allot portions of the land to individual Indians, unilaterally destroying the Indian nation's jurisdiction over land tenure.[12]

Admittedly, the potential for unilateral abrogation of treaty provisions is not unique to U.S. law concerning American Indians; the difference from other areas of law lies in the extent and results of abrogation of treaties between Indian nations and the U.S. *The Vienna Convention on the Law of Treaties* (United Nations, 1969), which sets out the predominant international legal expectations for treaties, considers several scenarios under which a party to a bilateral treaty might unilaterally terminate the treaty: impossibility of performance (art. 61); a "fundamental change of circumstance" (art. 62); or when a "new peremptory norm of general international law" develops that the treaty would violate (art. 64). Additionally, a serious breach of a treaty by one party "entitles the other to invoke the breach as a ground for terminating the treaty or suspending its operation in whole or in part," (art. 60[1]).

However, termination under *The Vienna Convention* entails consequences: the non-terminating party can seek judicial or arbitral remedy for harms, (art. 65-66). The general rule is *pacta sunt servanda*—agreements must be respected. Article 26 states, "Every treaty in force is binding upon the parties to it and must be performed by them in good faith." The power of abrogation that the *Lone Wolf* court gave Congress far exceeds the power of abrogation under general international law. The *Lone Wolf* Court differentiated Congressional abrogation of Indian treaties from its abrogation of "treaties with foreign nations":

Plenary authority over the tribal relations of the Indians has been exercised by Congress from the beginning, and the power has always been deemed a political one, not subject to be controlled by the judicial
department of the government.... The power exists to abrogate the provisions of an Indian treaty, though
presumably such power will be exercised only when circumstances arise which will not only justify the
government in disregarding the stipulations of the treaty, but may demand, in the interest of the country
and the Indians themselves, that it should do so. When, therefore, treaties were entered into between the
United States and a tribe of Indians it was never doubted that the power to abrogate existed in Congress,
and that in a contingency such power might be availed of from considerations of governmental policy,
particularly if consistent with perfect good faith towards the Indians. (*Lone Wolf vs Hitchcock*, 1903, 187
U.S. 553, pp. 565–566)

Moreover, the *Lone Wolf* court denied any judicial remedy for damages done by forced allot-
ment and sale of "surplus" lands to the U.S. ("If injury was occasioned…relief must be sought
by an appeal to [Congress] for redress, and not to the courts," *Lone Wolf*, p. 568). Congress's
legal story—that it "never doubted" its power to abrogate—was taken at face value, and the
Kiowa–Comanche legal story—that they absolutely doubted the power to abrogate—is ac-
corded no weight whatsoever.

That said, there is room for attacking the result in *Lone Wolf*. The right of a nation to hold
land exists regardless of the nation's treaties; this right may be restricted by treaties, but exists
independently of the treaties (except where lands are granted to the nation by a treaty in exchange for something else). The right to hold lands for itself may be expressed in a treaty, but
the right is not strictly a treaty right. Whether Congress can unilaterally abridge a fundamental
pre-treaty, unceded right of a sovereign nation is a different issue. A court that acknowledged
the inherent, robust, pre-U.S. sovereignty of Indian nations would likely have reached a different outcome on *Lone Wolf*. That said, *Lone Wolf* today is often read to give broad unilateral
powers to the U.S. Congress even on issues as serious as the rights of Indian nations to their
land, and such unilateral land seizures may not result in adequate or appropriate compensation
from Indian perspectives.

Even when courts award monetary damages for abrogation of an explicit treaty right such
as to land, (e.g., in *US v. Sioux Nation*, 1980, 448 U.S. 371, p. 422), monetary damages are inappropriate, inadequate compensation for destroyed treaty rights. As Wilkinson and Volkman
(1975, pp. 604–605) (among others) have argued, destroyed treaty rights—whether to land,
natural resources, activities, or something else—trample on sovereignty and diminish the ability to enjoy and determine national culture. To many tribal people, such losses are absolutely
incompensable. An economic value cannot, and should not, be placed on the sovereignty and
self-determination associated with land ownership or other rights,[13] but this is exactly what the
U.S. claims authority to do. However, given Indian nation–U.S. treaties' contested status in
international law, compensation for treaty rights can be better than nothing.

C. Rights Outside Treaties. A common belief among non-Indians is that treaties give rights to
Indian nations, with the corollary that it would comport Indian nations to be grateful for such
benevolent grants. Another common belief among non-Indians is that Indian nations have no
rights beyond those expressed in treaties.

These beliefs are illogical. As discussed earlier, most treaties memorialize exchanges: some
land here for a monetary or service payment; some rights at one location for rights elsewhere. It
would be a bizarre exchange indeed if one party to such an exchange had no rights to exchange

in the first place. Moreover, if we consider treaties as essentially contracts, in no contractual situation would we expect one party to give up every right not explicitly mentioned in the contract without at least some showing of intent. At the same time, a right mentioned in a treaty is generally better fortified against challenges than rights not mentioned in treaties. This is because treaties constitute inescapable evidence that both the U.S. and the Indian nation acknowledge the existence of treaty-based rights and have bargained over their forms.

§ 2. Perpetual Treaty Rights: What Are They?

As discussed above, treaty-based rights are important because, under U.S. law, they are currently more enforceable than Indian national rights not fortified by treaties, and their violation can lead to compensation—which, arguably, is at least some kind of minimal deterrent for violation. In broad terms, treaty rights are either perpetual or fixed-term. Perpetual treaty rights are treaty-based rights that could potentially survive forever. In contrast, fixed-term treaty rights are those whose end is clearly anticipated by the terms of the treaty. Given the advanced age of Indian–U.S. treaties, perpetual treaty rights have the greatest relevance to tribes today. Most fixed-term treaty rights have expired.

In treaties between the U.S. and Indian nations, one finds two general categories of perpetual treaty rights: those explicitly intended to last forever, and those with the potential to last forever. Within each of these categories, one can further subdivide rights into the categories of Figure 2 (see Figure 2). In large part, these rights are positive rights, although one also finds a few negative rights.

Despite the persistent belief among non-Indians that the U.S. "gave" tribes rights through treaties, treaties usually do not grant rights to Indian nations except when rights are being exchanged. Rather, treaties usually recognize rights that already existed. For example, the Makah Treaty of 1855, Article 4, reads:

> The right of taking fish and of whaling or sealing at usual and accustomed grounds and stations is further secured to said Indians in common with all citizens of the United States, and of erecting temporary houses for the purpose of curing, together with the privilege of hunting and gathering roots and berries on open and unclaimed land.... (*Treaty with the Makah*, Jan. 31, 1855 [Makah–U.S.], 12 Stat. 939, art. 4; see also Kappler, 1904, p. 682)

Before 1855, the Makah did not lack rights to do these things. A Makah fisher in 1854 did not daintily avoid lowering his hook because no treaty had granted him a right to fish. No 1853 Makah gatherer wistfully turned her back on berries because she lacked a treaty to permit her to gather them. The rights to fish, gather berries and roots, and so on existed millennia before the 1855 treaty. Article 4 is a mere recognition of these rights, partly made necessary because, in the 1855 treaty, the Makah ceded to the U.S. some of the land on which the Makah previously exercised these rights. Because the Makah otherwise relinquished all interests in the ceded land (*Treaty with the Makah*, 1855, 12 Stat. 939 art. 1; see also Kappler, 1904, p. 682), it was necessary to explicitly stockade these rights from the general land transfer. No new rights are created by Article 4; the U.S. did not fabricate rights out of air and kindly share them.

In other instances, however, rights were exchanged (such as when one tract of land was exchanged for another, although such exchanges were often unbalanced), and in only this narrow sense did the U.S. grant rights to tribes through treaties. In others cases, rights were extinguished rather than meaningfully exchanged.[14] The position of the treaties is always that both parties had some rights prior to the treaty. However, there is no reason that an ordinary right of a sovereign nation should be assumed not to exist merely because it is not expressly asserted in a treaty.[15]

Definitely Perpetual Rights	Potentially Perpetual Rights
Rights to natural resources	Rights to natural resources
Rights to education	Rights to education
Rights to goods, services, and payments	Rights to goods, services, and payments
Rights to reserved lands	
Political rights	
Rights not expressly ceded or modified by treaty	

Figure 2: Kinds of Perpetual Treaty Rights

It bears mentioning that rights not expressly given up by Indian nations remain in force. Any sovereign nation has some set of rights (whatever those may be) that it may choose to give up or to expressly articulate in a treaty. However, it would be a serious injustice to assume that any partner to a treaty has ceded rights beyond those expressly ceded. If this were the case, then treaty partners would be forced to state lengthily the rights they retained as sovereigns, with the smallest omission potentially leading to a vast unintentional abridgement of the nation's rights. Moreover, if we hold Indian nations and the U.S. to a single standard, then we cannot assume tribes have made implicit cessions of rights without also assuming the U.S. has made vast implicit cessions of rights.

The following subsections will characterize the perpetual rights acknowledged by treaties.

A. Unequivocal Perpetual Rights and Potentially Perpetual Rights. Some of the treaties describe "unequivocal perpetual rights," rights that have no ending condition and that are often facially described as "perpetual" or as running "forever." Others describe "potentially perpetual rights." These are set to terminate on some condition that may or may not occur. (Rights that will terminate upon some condition that is certain to happen—such as a specific date—are obviously not perpetual, but rather are fixed-term.)

An example of an unequivocal perpetual right (here, a right to an annual payment) can be found in the 1796 treaty between the U.S. and the "Seven Nations of Canada":

…the people of the state of New-York shall pay to them, at the mouth of the river Chazy, on Lake Champlain, on the third Monday in August next, the sum of one thousand two hundred and thirty-three pounds, six shillings, and eight-pence, and the further sum of two hundred and thirteen pounds six shillings and eight-pence, lawful money of the said state, and on the third Monday in August, yearly, forever thereafter, the like sum of two hundred and thirteen pounds six shillings and eight pence. (*Treaty with the Seven Nations of Canada*, May 31, 1796 [Seven Nations–U.S.], 7 Stat. 55; see also Kappler, 1904, p. 45)

Annual payments are common unequivocal perpetual rights; most of the treaties with such provisions specify a location for the payment, although the date for the annual payment in this treaty (as well as the use of British currency) is rarer, an artifact of the early date of this treaty. The intent of the treaty negotiators for the treaty to run "forever thereafter" is plainly stated.

Another example of an unequivocal perpetual right (this time, the right to various natural resources) appears in Article 4 of the 1855 Makah–U.S. treaty, quoted earlier in this chapter. Makah rights to hunt, whale, fish, and collect berries are described as "secured," and the treaty sets no date for their end. These unequivocally perpetual Makah hunting rights contrast with this statement of hunting rights in the 1806 Cherokee–U.S. treaty "elucidation":

> the Cherokee hunters, as hath been the custom in such cases, may hunt on said ceded tract, until by the fullness of settlers it shall become improper. (*Elucidation of a Convention with the Cherokee Nation*, Sept. 11, 1806 [Cherokee–U.S.], 7 Stat. 101; see also Kappler, 1904, p. 92)

The Cherokee rights to hunt on this particular tract do face possible termination. It is possible that the terminating condition will never occur (although, in this case—an unusual one—it is clear that the treaty authors expected that the condition would occur eventually), which renders this particular right a potentially perpetual right, rather than an unequivocally perpetual right.

More commonly, potentially perpetual rights are set to terminate on a condition that seems less likely to occur. An 1837 Chippewa–U.S. treaty offers an example, again concerning natural resource rights:

> The privilege of hunting, fishing, and gathering the wild rice, upon the [ceded] lands, the rivers and the lakes included in the territory ceded, is guaranteed to the [Chippewa] Indians, during the pleasure of the President of the United States. (*Treaty with the Chippewa*, Jul. 29, 1837 [Chippewa-U.S.], 7 Stat. 536, art. 5; see also Kappler, 1904, p. 492.)

Similar language in which a right is made dependent on the "pleasure," "discretion," or similar attitudes of U.S. officials (in some cases, Congress or an Indian Affairs agent) recurs throughout many of the treaties.

Potentially perpetual treaty rights might seem precarious, and perhaps they are. However, federal courts have—at least sometimes—taken a protective stance towards such rights.[16] At the same time, unequivocally perpetual treaty rights are more precarious than the treaties themselves suggest, given congressional willingness to unilaterally abrogate treaties.

B. Rights to Natural Resources. Rights to particular natural resources in national homelands are often culturally important; to many tribes, certain resources are gifts from the ancestors or from the resource itself. Moreover, resources endemic to a particular area are a reminder of a long cultural, national history in that place. It is telling that, despite the typical U.S. control of treaty formulation, some tribes' perpetual reservations of resource rights on lands otherwise ceded to the U.S. survived into written treaties.

Forty-nine treaties describe rights to use natural resources on lands otherwise no longer belonging to Indian nations (see Figure 3). Of those, a few treaties reiterate rights described in earlier treaties. In other treaties, Indian nations relinquish their hunting rights in exchange for compensation, although often very small compensation. For instance, under the 1863

U.S.–Eastern Shoshone treaty, the Eastern Shoshone ceded to the U.S. hunting rights they had previously reserved in exchange for an annual payment of $10,000 for twenty years (*Treaty with the Eastern Shoshoni*, Jul. 2, 1863 [Eastern Shoshone–U.S.], 18 Stat. 685, art. 5; see also Kappler, 1904, p. 849). (Interestingly, the cession is worded as if it were solely for Shoshone benefit due to "inconveniences" caused by white settlers.)

Resource Use Type	Number of Treaty Appearances
Hunting	34
Fishing	16
Use of waterways other than in fishing	3
Timber	2
Producing maple sugar	1
Whaling	1
Sealing	1
Gathering wild rice	1
Quarrying	1

Figure 3: Resource Use Rights Discussed in Treaties

Eight of the provisions for natural resource rights in ceded lands endure only while ceded land remains U.S. property. A typical example is this statement from the 1804 Sac and Fox–U.S. treaty:

> As long as the lands which are now ceded to the United States remain their property, the Indians belonging to the said tribes, shall enjoy the privilege of living and hunting on them. (*Treaty with the Sauk and Foxes*, Jan. 25, 1805 [Sauk and Fox–U.S.], 7 Stat. 84, art. 7; see also Kappler, 1904, p. 76.)

This is a potentially perpetual right, although given the widespread sales of ceded lands to U.S. settlers, the U.S. treaty delegates probably did not see it that way. Other terminating conditions for potentially perpetual rights to natural resources depend on the resource availability itself:

> [T]he tribes who are parties to this agreement…yet reserve the right to hunt on any lands south of the Arkansas so long as the buffalo may range thereon in such numbers as to justify the chase. (*Treaty with the Cheyenne and Arapaho*, Oct. 28, 1867 [Cheyenne–Arapaho–U.S.], 15 Stat. 593, art. 11; see also Kappler, 1904, p. 988.)

If the U.S. deliberately diminished buffalo populations and thus eliminated Cheyenne and Arapaho use rights to the lands "south of the Arkansas," could the Cheyenne and Arapaho recover damages? No cases of this nature have been litigated.

In some treaties, the perpetuation of the right depends on the behavior of citizens of the Indian nation exercising the right. For instance, the 1818 Quapaw–U.S. treaty predicates continued hunting rights to ceded lands on whether Quapaw hunters "demean themselves peaceably, and offer no injury or annoyance to any of the citizens of the United States" (*Treaty with the Quapaw*, Aug. 24, 1818 [Quapaw–U.S.], 17 Stat. 176, art. 3; see also Kappler, 1904, p. 160.) Hinging the availability of a resource to a whole nation on the (mis)behavior of even a few of its citizens could facilitate termination of the Quapaw hunting rights for less than honorable reasons. Such a right is rendered even shakier since the misbehaviors triggering the removal of rights are so vaguely described and since the treaty established no neutral forum for evaluating claims of "annoyance."

A few treaties predicate perpetuation of the right upon the wishes of the Indian nation itself. For instance, the 1858 Yankton Sioux–U.S. treaty preserves Yankton Sioux to quarry freely at a particular location to obtain red stone for pipes "so long as they shall desire" (*Treaty with the Yankton Sioux,* Apr. 19, 1858 [Yankton Sioux–U.S.], 11 Stat. 743, art. 8; see also Kappler, 1904, p. 779.) Of all the conditions upon perpetuation of a treaty right, this is probably one of the least onerous, although it is unclear what might happen to the right if, for instance, the Yankton Sioux temporarily stopped using the quarry, then later wished to revive the right.

Still other natural resource rights do not have any terminating condition. For example, the 1855 Tribes of Middle Oregon Treaty reserves to the Walla Walla and Wasco nations

> the exclusive right of taking fish in the streams running through and bordering said reservation…and at all other usual and accustomed stations in common with citizens of the United States, and of erecting suitable buildings for curing the same; the privilege of hunting, gathering roots and berries and pasturing their stock on unclaimed lands in common with citizens, is also secured to them. (*Treaty with the Middle Tribes of Oregon,* Jun. 25, 1855 [Walla Walla-Wasco-U.S.], 12 Stat. 963, art. 1; see also Kappler, 1904, p. 714.)

There are two different sets of rights in this provision. The first set concerns rights on reserved lands: there, the Walla Walla and Wasco nations have rights to all fish, and no one else has rights to any fish. The second set concerns rights off reserved lands, on "unclaimed" lands; these rights are "in common with citizens of the United States." Federal courts have held that rights held in common with non-Indian citizens of the U.S. can be regulated like the rights of those non-Indian citizens.[17] Moreover, these rights accrue to tribes, rather than to individual tribal citizens, so individuals who lose treaty-based rights have no right to sue on their own behalf in federal court, (see, e.g., *Whitefoot v. U.S.*, 1961, 293 F.2d 658, 663).

C. Rights to Education. The treaties, particularly by the late 1840s, evidence concern with "education," a concept often textually linked to intensive agriculturalism and Christianization in the treaties. For instance, the 1867 Cheyenne–Arapaho–U.S. treaty expounds:

> In order to insure the civilization of the tribes entering into this treaty, the necessity of education is admitted, especially by such of them as are or may be settled on said agricultural reservation, and they therefore pledge themselves to compel their children, male and female, between the ages of six and sixteen years, to attend school; and it is hereby made the duty of the agent for said Indians to see that this stipulation is strictly complied with; and the United States agrees that for every thirty children between said ages, who can be induced or compelled to attend school, a house shall be provided, and a teacher competent to teach the elementary branches of an English education shall be furnished, who will reside among said Indians, and faithfully discharge his or her duties as a teacher. The provisions of this article to continue for not less than twenty years. (*Treaty with the Cheyenne and Arapaho,* Oct. 28, 1867 [Cheyenne–Arapaho–U.S.], 15 Stat. 593, art. 7; see also Kappler, 1904, pp. 986–987.)

This statement is similar to many other treaty provisions concerning education in several respects. First, the tribe has agreed to send children of certain ages to school for an indefinite period. Secondly, the treaty authors—presumably the U.S. agents—clearly establish the educational goals of the reservation schools: "civilization" and "agriculture." In the treaty text above, the promise of education seems directed more towards U.S. goals of assimilating Indians as European-style farmers than towards Cheyenne or Arapaho goals for their own children, otherwise the treaty would not include parental pledges to "compel" attendance. Third, the U.S. promises to provide education for a minimum number of years, although, like this treaty, many treaties do not specify an ending point for the educational rights. (Some treaties do place a termination date on educational rights, and they are beyond the scope of this chapter.) Other treaties, like the 1826 Potawatomi–U.S. treaty, specify that the right continues as long as the U.S. desires ("as long as the Congress of the United States may think proper," (*Treaty with the Potawatomi*, Oct. 16, 1826 [Potawatomi–U.S.], 7 Stat. 25, art. 3; see also Kappler, 1904, p. 274).

The 1826 Potawatomi treaty is somewhat unusual in that the educational right is clearly intended as compensation for Potawatomi land and thus presumably is something the Potawatomi negotiators desired. Nonetheless, the U.S. claimed the right to determine how much education is enough and what form it should take. Sometimes a "manual labor school" was specified, (see, e.g., *Treaty with the Menominee*, May 12, 1854, 10 Stats. 1064, art. 3; see also Kappler, 1904, p. 627). In the 1826 treaty with the Potawatomi it was left to the U.S. President to expend the $2,000 annual education appropriation "as he sees fit."—rendering the educational rights as compensation of dubious value.

Education provisions in treaties differ markedly as to how education is to be funded. Some, like those in the 1826 Potawatomi treaty, require the U.S. to pay for education as an annual expense; this form of funding was most common through the 1830s. After the 1830s, as in the 1854 Miami–U.S. treaty, treaties usually promise to set aside some of the land otherwise ceded, then to sell it and deposit the proceeds (minus expenses incurred in the sale) in stocks, using the 5 percent annual interest to feed an education fund (e.g., see *Treaty with the Miami*, Jun. 4, 1854 [Miami–U.S.], 10 Stat. 1093, art. 2; see also Kappler, 1904, p. 641). With few exceptions, the terms of the education are to be set by "the President" (or, near the end of treaty making, the secretary of the interior) rather than by tribes themselves.

D. Rights to Medical Services. A relatively small number of treaties promise perpetual provision of medical services. Most such promises are directly stated. In one instance, the promise is indirect—the 1820 Choctaw–U.S. treaty promising to first meet the "wants of every deaf, dumb, blind, and distressed Indian" out of annual interest payments on land sales before making a general distribution of the interest payment (Treaty with the Choctaw, Oct. 18, 1820 [Choctaw–U.S.] 7 Stat. 210, art. 8; see also Kappler, 1904, p. 193). The plain meaning of "wants" would include medical care.

Most provisions for medical services and goods are more direct. For example, in the 1836 Ottawa–Chippewa–U.S. treaty, the U.S. promised the equivalent of $300 annually in "vaccine matter, medicines, and the services of physicians, to be continued while the Indians remain on their reservations," (*Treaty with the Ottawa Etc.*, Mar. 28, 1836 [Ottawa–Chippewa–U.S] 7 Stat. 491, art. 4; see also Kappler, 1904, p. 452). Under an 1868 treaty, provision of a physician to the Northern Cheyenne and Northern Arapaho similarly depends on continued reservation residence, (*Treaty with the Northern Cheyenne and Northern Arapaho*, May 10, 1868 [Northern Cheyenne–Northern Arapaho–U.S.] 15 Stat. 655, art. 7; see also Kappler, 1904, p. 1014). Other provisions do not depend on reservation status, but rather promise the services to the tribe as a whole.

Many of these healthcare provisions are potentially perpetual, rather than unequivocally perpetual. One provision mixes the forms—in an 1867 Comanche–Kiowa–U.S. treaty, the U.S. promised to employ a physician (among other personnel) for at least ten years for the Comanche and Kiowa Nations (expanded by a later treaty to include the Kiowa-Apaches). After that period, Congress could choose to discontinue employing the physician, but was bound to provide an additional $10,000 a year in educational benefits upon so doing, (*Treaty with the Kiowa and Comanche*, Oct. 21, 1867 [Kiowa–Comanche–U.S.] 15 Stat. 581, art. 9 & 14; see also Kappler, 1904, pp. 979, 981).

Medical care provisions—rather than provisions for the employ of a physician, construction of a hospital, or medical goods—are largely limited to fixed terms. In the few cases where they are stipulated to be potentially or unequivocally perpetual, these provisions rarely amount to substantial medical boons for tribes because they tend to be limited to small sums of money or to the employment of a single physician, or—in the rare cases of general provisions for "the infirm"— are simply carved out of a general tribal annuity rather than appropriated from U.S. coffers.

In most case, Indian nations currently have more substantive tools than treaties to receive medical care for their citizens, even when treaties do not provide for medical care: the Snyder Act, which led to the establishment of the Indian Health Service; the Indian Health Care Improvement Act; and the federal trust responsibility (the first and third being double-edged swords).

E. Rights to Other Goods, Services, and Payments. Some treaties promise an unequivocally perpetual annual payment or delivery of goods, or an often potentially perpetual service such as a blacksmith. However, many of these promises were overridden in fairly short order by subsequent treaties.[18] In many instances, the U.S. eventually bought out perpetual annual payments in exchange for one-time or serial payments for a discrete term of years. For example, in exchange for release from earlier promises of a perpetual payment or service, the U.S. treated to provide one set of clothing per person to the Ute, Brulé Sioux, and others annually for a fixed period of thirty years, (*Treaty with the Kiowa and Comanche*, Oct. 21, 1867 [Kiowa–Comanche–U.S] 15 Stat. 581, art. 10; see also Kappler, 1904, p. 979–980). Most annuities and promises of goods were set to a fixed term.

A few promises of goods, services, and annuities are potentially perpetual and were never bought out. In some cases, rights to goods and services have a minimum term after which they can be replaced with a payment, as in the *Treaty with the Cheyenne and Arapaho* (Jul. 25, 1868 [Cheyenne–Arapaho–U.S.], 15 Stat. 593, art. 10; see also Kappler, 1904, p. 987). Often potentially perpetual promises of goods and services were tied to dubious purposes. For example, in the 1790 Creek-U.S. treaty, we find:

> That the Creek nation may be led to a greater degree of civilization, and to become herdsmen and cultivators, instead of remaining in a state of hunters, the United States will from time to time furnish gratuitously the said nation with useful domestic animals and implements of husbandry. And further to assist the said nation in so desirable a pursuit, and at the same time to establish a certain mode of communication, the United States will send such, and so many persons to reside in said nation as they may

judge proper, and not exceeding four in number, who shall qualify themselves to act as interpreters...
(*Treaty with the Creeks*, Aug 7, 1790 [Creek-U.S.], 7 Stat., 35, art. 12; see also Kappler, 1904, p. 28)[19]

The agreement of Indian nations to advance in "civilization" recurs throughout the treaties, usually linked to animal husbandry and cultivation—even for Indian nations that had, in fact, pioneered cultivation of food crops long before European arrival. Such language bolsters the legal fiction that pre-colonial Indians were "savages," hunters who wasted land as wilderness—an argument advanced in the 1823 Supreme Court case *Johnson v. McIntosh*. In *Johnson*, the Court disingenuously claimed:

> [T]he tribes of Indians inhabiting this country were fierce savages, whose occupation was war, and whose subsistence was drawn chiefly from the forest. To leave them in possession of their country, was to leave the country a wilderness; to govern them as a distinct people, was impossible, because they were as brave and as high spirited as they were fierce, and were ready to repel by arms every attempt on their independence. (*Johnson v. McIntosh*, 1823, 21 U.S. 543, p. 590)

In this case, involving the competing land claims of whites, a case in which no Indian nation was party and in which no Indian nation was given the opportunity to present arguments, the Court ruled that Indian nations had only a possessory title to land, one that could be overruled at the whim of the supposedly conquering United States.

F. Political Rights. Two treaties, in exchange for cessions by Indian nations, give those nations political rights within the U.S. political system. These rights are truly grants (unlike, for example, most land "grants," which involve lands that already belonged to the Indian nation in question).

The first such treaty—which was also the first U.S. treaty with an Indian nation—promised that, with congressional approval, the Lenape (Delaware) nation and its allies might form a state and be represented in the U.S. Congress (*Treaty with the Delawares*, Sept. 7, 1778 [Delaware–U.S.], 7 Stat. 13, art. 6; also see Kappler, 1904, p. 4). Fifty-seven years later, U.S. treaty negotiators promised that "whenever Congress shall make provision," the Cherokee nation would be entitled to a congressional representative (Art. 8, *Treaty with the Cherokee*, May 23, 1836 [Cherokee-U.S.], 7 Stat. 478; see also Kappler, 1904, pp. 442–443).

Neither the Delaware nor the Cherokee nation ever exercised its right to U.S. congressional representation, although, in recent years, some have called for the Cherokees to do so (Rosser, 2005).

G. Implied Perpetual Rights? In limited cases involving water rights, tribes have been able to persuade courts to read rights into treaties that are not explicitly included in the text of treaties, but that are necessary to effect the treaty text (for example Winters v. U.S., 1908, 207 U.S. 564). Such a case differs from the proposition that rights inherent to Indian nations, unless expressly ceded, are retained by Indian nations. Rights that are not inherent to any nation might thus be implied by a court, based on treaty terms.

§ 3. Perpetual Treaty Rights Are Limited
Perpetual treaty rights, not counting perpetual rights to reservations (which were too often later treated away) are limited to a relatively small set of useful rights. There is not a substantial,

clear-cut treaty-based right to a college education. At the same time, because treaties must be interpreted today as the Indian parties would have understood them, we have a meaningful argument that some treaty-based rights, at least, should exceed the scope preserved in the written English manifestations of documents. There are unambiguous, meaningful, perpetual rights to culturally significant natural resources.

All this said, current U.S. law purports that treaty rights can be abrogated without the consent of the tribes involved. Treaties, in written form, often do not portray the actual understanding of the agreement by both parties at the time (and although under treaty construction canons, courts should consider the treaty as the Indian negotiators would have considered them at the time, this is a highly subjective area). Unfortunately, although treaties offer a safeguard for some rights and recognition of some form of Indian sovereignty and nationhood, they are limited in how much they can help tribes. The fact that treaties recognize sovereignty does not mean that sovereignty is dependent on the treaties for existence.

Conclusions

Qualitative social science researchers and attorneys typically possess different motivations for "researching" legal texts, meaning that the texts themselves can be examined through two markedly different lenses. As these two research stories show, lawyers undertaking legal research concern themselves primarily with realizing a client's goals, structuring arguments around legal textual supports. They are certainly aware of the broader social implications of legal texts.

Social researchers investigating the same texts may be more interested in identifying power relations, social contexts, cultural assumptions, and practical effects. At the same time, the two lenses may speak to one another: Legal texts constitute a rich body of data for social scientists, and social scientific research into the law can identify opportunities to modify or build legal theories to meet practical social and political needs. In the case of examining Indian treaties, we can use the treaties to identify limits of current law and identify theoretical gaps that create social harms. Qualitative social research into the law and legal work can inform one another, sealing gaps and serving important social needs.

Notes

1. The second part of this chapter, dealing with treaties, incorporates material written as an independent research project supervised by Judge Steve Russell (Indiana University, Bloomington Department of Criminal Justice). The author thanks Judge Russell for his critical suggestions and insistence on argumentative rigor in the original project, but also adds that he has not had an opportunity to review this final version of the second part, much less the whole chapter.

2. From here on, I will use "treaties" to refer to the written documents produced by the U.S. and ratified by the U.S. Congress, unless otherwise specified. This use excludes broader understandings of treaties, such as oral agreements about their content during negotiations.

3. An infamous example is the "Treaty of New Echota," *Treaty with the Cherokee* (Dec. 29, 1835 [Cherokee–U.S.], 7 Stat. 478); see also Kappler (1904, pp. 439–449). This "treaty" fraudulently professes that the Cherokee Nation have relinquished all lands east of the Mississippi to the United States; Id. (art.1; see also Kappler, 1904, p. 440). However, the Cherokee signatories were a faction of individuals absolutely lacking in authority to negotiate such a treaty under Cherokee republican law, as Cherokee Principal Chief John Ross wrote in his letter informing the Senate of the fraud and asking that they refuse to ratify the treaty (letter from Chief John Ross to the Senate and House of Representatives, Sept. 28, 1836, [Moulton, 1985]). Despite ongoing legal

and political protests by the Cherokee Nation and its citizens, the Senate ratified the fraudulent document as a "treaty."

4.   Those treaties involving tribes that lacked English-literate citizens are problematic because such tribes relied on U.S. interpreters—hardly neutral—to accurately translate and honestly state the written contents of the treaty. A particularly well-documented use of the English-literacy advantage for deception is discussed in Lehman (1990). Lehman documents that Oneida signatories agreed to one set of treaty terms, only to find out later that the written terms were radically different and amounted to vast unwanted land cessions. Although this instance involved New York, rather than U.S. treaty commissioners, the same potential for duplicity exists in many U.S–tribal nation treaties.

5.   Bribery of tribal officials is one such tactic and is implied in many of the treaty texts themselves. A significant number of the treaties provide Indian signatories or their families with gifts or private land grants. For instance, an 1818 Chickasaw–U.S. treaty promises cash gifts to many of the Chickasaw signatories upon its ratification (*Treaty with the Chickasaw*, Oct. 19, 1818 [Chickasaw–U.S.], 7 Stat. 192, art. 7; see also Kappler, 1904, p. 176). Robert J. Miller (2006) has demonstrated that bribery of tribal officials, coupled with a deliberate policy of indebting such officials to the U.S. "so that they would be inclined to consent to land sales to the United States" was explicit executive policy during at least Jefferson's presidency (pp. 86–89). Another dubiously ethical component of many treaties is special gifts—particularly of land—to interpreters or negotiators. For example, an 1861 Arapaho–Cheyenne–U.S. treaty includes gifts of 640 acres of land each to a U.S. interpreter and to the son of the other U.S. interpreter for the treaty (*Treaty with the Arapaho and Cheyenne*, Feb. 15, 1861 [Arapaho–Cheyenne–U.S.], 12 Stat. 1163, art. 7; see also Kappler, 1904, p. 811).

6.   The "Chippewa" of the treaty are, of course, the Ojibwa people. However, drawing as I did on the treaty's written, English text, I included the misnomer.

7.   I avoid the common term "Indian treaties" throughout since this moniker (1) casts Indian treaties as fundamentally different from other types of treaties, (2) lumps together highly heterogenous treaties between hundreds of nations and the U.S., and (3) might, from an Indian perspective, be better called "U.S. treaties," anyway.

8.   See, e.g., *Convention on Rights and Duties of States* (Dec. 26, 1933, 49 Stat. 3097, art. 1) stating that "The state as a person of international law should possess the following qualifications: a) a permanent population; b) a defined territory; c) government; and d) capacity to enter into relations with the other states." There are other theories of statehood under international law, but they are beyond the scope of this paper.

9.   Buried mid-document, appended to an innocuous appropriations line for the Yankton Sioux, Congress declared that tribes will no longer be considered "competent" for making new treaties. The unconstitutionality of this provision has been noted since the act's inception. See, e.g., Deloria & Wilkins (2000, pp. 65–66) discussing the opposition of some senators based on the constitutionally exclusive authority of the president to negotiate treaties and the Senate to ratify them—or not.

10. For discussion of a treaty between two tribal nations, see Haake (2002).

11. "He shall have power, by and with the advice and consent of the Senate, to make treaties, provided two thirds of the Senators present concur…," U.S. Const., art. 2, § 2, cl. 2. No distinction is made between Indian nations and European or other nations in the president's treaty-making power.

12. The historical context of *Lone Wolf* is discussed in depth in Clark (1999). Clark argues that, paradoxically, *Lone Wolf* also provides a framework for the U.S. to judicially recognize some extent of tribal sovereignty in that *Lone Wolf* acknowledged "the existence of tribes" (*Lone Wolf v. Hitchcock*, 1903, 187 U.S. 553, p. 111).

13. Moreover, the promise of compensation for abrogated treaty rights is coupled in U.S. caselaw with denial of compensation for national rights not explicitly recognized by treaties. *Tee-Hit-Ton v. U.S.* (1955, 348 U.S. 272). This places the U.S. Supreme Court at odds with most Indian people and nations, who believe—as would most citizens of any nation—that their nations have preserved any rights not clearly relinquished to another, and thus that rights not explicitly recognized in treaties are equally valid, binding, and compensable with rights not so recognized.

14. Of course, nearly any extinguishment of a right might be read as an exchange. For example, a robbery victim might be said to exchange his or her right to the stolen item in exchange for acquiring the right to be free of harassment by the robber. However, this is not a meaningful exchange because of the coercion involved. Similarly, some treaties purport to offer an "exchange" of rights (such as a right to ultimate jurisdiction for a right to "protection"), but the coercion is sometimes so extreme that not even a nominal exchange occurred. An ex-

ample of this is the 1849 Navajo–U.S. treaty, in which (examining only the face of the text) the Navajo extinguished their supreme jurisdiction, right to control passage through their territory, right to administer justice against non-Navajo in Navajo boundaries, and a host of other "rights" usually possessed by sovereign nations, (*Treaty with the Navaho*, Sept. 9, 1849 [Navajo-U.S.], 9 Stat. 974; see also Kappler, 1904, pp. 583–585). In return, the Navajo acquired rights for "the Government of the United States [to] grant to said Indians such donations, presents, and implements, and adopt such other liberal and humane measures, as said Government may deem meet and proper." Even if it were certain that the Navajo negotiators intended the treaty to read as it does, and that they were authorized by the Nation to make this kind of concession, the exchange is so unequal that it is not meaningfully an "exchange," Id.

15. That all pre-treaty rights of a nation continue to exist post-treaty unless the treaty explicitly states otherwise seems obvious and is the prevailing opinion among tribes. As David E. Wilkins and K. Tsianina Lomawaima note (2002, p. 141), this preservation of rights not clearly ceded is also necessitated as a canon of judicial treaty interpretation. Additionally, another canon of treaty construction—that treaties must be interpreted as the tribal signatories would have understood them at the time of signing (see, e.g., *Minnesota v. Mille Lacs Band of Chippewa Indians*, 1999, 526 U.S. 172, p. 196)—requires this preservation. However, as I argued earlier, the U.S. Supreme Court has not always recognized this persistence of rights not acknowledged by treaties (see, e.g., *Tee-Hit-Ton v. U.S.*, 1955, 348 U.S. 272).

16. See, e.g., *U.S. v. Bresette* (D. Minn. 1991, 761 F. Supp. 658), holding that Chippewa rights to sell migratory bird feathers were part of the 1837 treaty and were not abrogated by the *Migratory Bird Treaty Act*. See also, *Minnesota v. Mille Lacs Band of Chippewa Indians* (1999, 526. U.S. 172, pp. 189–194) where even an Executive Order demanding the Chippewa remove from and stop hunting and fishing on this land was held not to terminate hunting and fishing rights, because the Executive Order was not authorized by Congress. It seems the president must express displeasure in particular ways to terminate these rights.

17. The Supreme Court held that these rights can be quite thoroughly regulated in *Puyallup Tribe v. Dept. of Game of Wash.* (1968, 391 U.S. 392, p. 398): "the manner of fishing, the size of the take, the restriction of commercial fishing, and the like may be regulated by the State in the interest of conservation, provided the regulation meets appropriate standards and does not discriminate against the Indians" because the treaty in question did not mention the "manner" of fishing reserved by the tribe. Such a reading hardly constitutes construction of the treaty as the Puyallup negotiators would have understood it.

18. One striking example of this is the history of Miami annuities. The Miami entered fifteen treaties with the U.S. In 1803, the Miami and several other tribes were promised a total of 150 barrels of salt to be delivered annually. See, e.g., *Treaty with the Wyandot, Etc.* (Jun. 4, 1954 [Several Tribes–U.S.], 7 Stat. 75, art. 3); see also Kappler (1904, p. 65). In a series of treaties, the Miami were promised annual perpetual monetary and goods payments as consideration for land cessions. Perhaps the most elaborate promises were made in 1818, when the Miami Nation was offered "a perpetual annuity of fifteen thousand dollars, a U.S.-sponsored blacksmith and gunsmith, and 160 barrels of salt annually in addition to earlier annual payments." See, e.g., *Treaty with the Miami* (Oct. 6, 1818, [Miami–U.S.], 7 Stat. 190, art. 5); see also Kappler (1904, p. 173). Through several subsequent treaties, the annuities in goods and payment grew. In 1854, the U.S. paid the Miami $421,438.68 to relinquish all these annual payments and accept a fixed-period annuity in exchange. See, e.g., *Treaty with the Miami* (Jun. 5, 1854 [Miami–U.S.], 10 Stat. 1093, art. 3); see also Kappler (1904, p. 643).

19. From the text alone, we cannot determine the motivations of the two nations in including this provision. However, even at this early stage of U.S.–Indian relations, literate treaty negotiators for both sides sometimes wrote about the treaty process to their colleagues and allies. The primary Creek negotiator of the 1790 treaty was Creek "Emperor" Alexander McGillivray, an astute political actor advocating for both Creek sovereignty and his own personal interests amidst international intrigue involving the governments of Spain, the U.S., Britain, and the state of Georgia. For an account of machinations leading to the 1790 treaty, see Watson(2002).

References

Clark, B. (1999). *Lone Wolf v. Hitchcock: Treaty rights & Indian law at the end of the nineteenth century*. Lincoln: University of Nebraska Press.

Deloria, V. Jr., and Wilkins, D. E. (2000). *Tribes, Treaties, and Constitutional Tribulations*. Austin: University of Texas Press.

Haake, C. (2002). Identity, sovereignty, and power: The Cherokee–Delaware Agreement of 1867, past and present. *American Indian Quarterly*, *26*(3), 418–435.

Kappler, C. J. (Ed.). (1904). Indian affairs: Laws and treaties. Vols. 1–5. Washington, DC: U.S. Government Printing Office; available at: http://digital.library.okstate.edu/kappler/index.htm [accessed 1 March 2012].

Lehman, J. D. (1990). The end of the Iroquois mystique: The Oneida land cession treaties of the 1780s, *William and Mary Quarterly*, *47*(4), 523–547.

Mertz, E. (2007). *The language of law school: Learning to "think like a lawyer."* Oxford: Oxford University Press.

Miller, R.J. (2006) *Native America, discovered and conquered: Thomas Jefferson, Lewis and Clark, and Manifest Destiny*. Westport, CT: Praeger.

Moulton, G.E., (Ed.). (1985). *The papers of Chief John Ross, 1807–1839*. Norman: University of Oklahoma Press.

Rosser, E. (2005). The nature of representation: The Cherokee right to a congressional delegate. *Public Interest Law Journal, 15,* 91-152.

Seventh International Conference of American States. (1933). *Convention on Rights and Duties of States*. Washington, DC: U.S. Government Printing Office.

United Nations. (1969). Vienna Convention on the Law of Treaties, 23 May 1969, United Nations, Treaty Series, vol. 1155, p. 331; available at: http://www.unhcr.org/refworld/docid/3ae6b3a10.html [accessed 1 March 2012].

Watson, T. D. (2002). Strivings for sovereignty: Alexander McGillivray, Creek warfare, and diplomacy. *Florida Historical Quarterly, 58,* 400-414.

Wilkins, D. E., & Lomawaima, K. T. (2002). *Uneven ground: American Indian sovereignty and federal law*. Norman: University of Oklahoma Press.

Wilkinson, C. F., & Volkman, J. M. (1975) Judicial review of Indian treaty abrogation: "As long as water flows, or grass grows upon the earth"—How long a time is that? *California Law Review, 63*(3), 601-661.

CHAPTER TWENTY

Not So Obvious?

The Structural Elements of Caring:
An Example for Critical Qualitative Studies

BARBARA DENNIS (FORMERLY KORTH)

It is easiest, perhaps, to think of caring as a very localized, individual, relational activity that is nearly entirely about the specific people involved in its endeavor at a very particular time and place. Certainly, within our families and among our friends, this would be the intuitive way to think about caring. When we care for one another through our interactions, the caring is riddled with cultural norms and values that render it criticizable as any culturally patterned mode of interactivity might be. For example, why should it be the case that in my dissertation study, men received more care interpersonally than women (Korth, 1998, 1999, 2003)? In her critique of the scholarship on caring, Jaggar (1995) argued that care inquiry has not adequately addressed issues of its own critique—a critique that stands in relation to the interpretations offered up by those engaged in the caring. In general, care theorists have only begun to make refined connections between care and criticalism (for example, Eaker-Rich & van Galen, 1996; Luthrell, 1996). One way to begin such an endeavor would be to examine the structural elements of interpersonal forms of caring because it is likely the structural elements form threads in the links between the systematic engagement of caring activities and the interpersonal meanings of the caring.

For my dissertation (Korth, 1998), I conducted an ethnographic study interested in how six adult work friends navigated their individual and group identifications vis-à-vis involvement in their own particular friendship group. What I found was that their identity navigations, to a large extent, happened through caring. The caring was very personal and spanned a variety of activities from providing practical help and support to providing emotional sympathy and encouragement to smoothing things over when the interactions got rocky. I interpreted particular activities as caring because this was how the participants themselves made sense of those same activities. Reconstructive analysis (Carspecken, 1996) provided a way for me (a) to articulate the range of possible interpretations and the assumptions carried through those interpretations, and (b) to locate when actions were interpreted as caring (Korth, 2003). But there was something about the caring that was not articulated directly through the reconstructions of their interpretations of one another. These hermeneutic analyses were quite useful, but some questions remained. For example, the hermeneutic reconstructions did not get at the gender differences in the patterns of behavior.

This chapter focuses on the analysis of structural elements of caring and what such an analysis yields. The findings indicate that caring was comprised of cultural structures and patterns of effects that did not get clearly articulated through the hermeneutic reconstruction of the group's interactions, and thus required additional methods of analysis. This would not be uncommon in social research because all meaningful action is constituted in part by cultural structures and certainly, also, has the potential of producing effects that fall outside actors' interpretative expectations. By articulating the structures involved in the face-to-face patterns and habits of the group members, a new critique is possible. Critical findings are those that make explicit inequity, oppression, distortions to the communicative potential of participants, ideological influences and other such categories of impact on the autonomous, free and equal expression and participation of actors in engagement with one another.

On the level of hermeneutics, the study's findings indicated that these friends cared for each other in ways that, at least tacitly, mediated inequalities and distortions systematically at work in the culture they shared. The findings also illustrated that their caring activities served as an implicit critique of micro-cultural practices that (a) seemed to put people's dignity and sense of connection at risk, and, that also (b) seemed to hide ideological distortions/contradictions. For example, sometimes a group member told a joke that others did not think was funny. They laughed anyway because they did not want their friend to feel foolish. They pretended the joke was funny and pretended the teller was clever. They did this as a way of caring for their friend, but the caring also covered up a potential interpretation of the friend's identity and skill that would have marked him or her as somewhat less acceptable in the micro-culture. This example of caring among the friends itself points to a limitation in the micro-cultural boundaries of acceptable identities, behavioral repertoires, and so forth. Habermas (1987) reminds us that "[m]echanisms that repress an actual conflict by excluding it from the realm of situation interpretations and action orientations and [by] covering it up with illusions have pathological side effects" (p. 229).

There is another level of critique that has not been well-attended to in the scholarship of caring: Little to no efforts linking the interpersonal caring (caring achieved through face-to-face or direct interactions of people) to the cultural and ideological material that the acts both engage and (re)form. The structural analysis presented in this chapter moves forward from the hermeneutic critique to a structural critique. There have been a lot of concerns raised about care theory/research scholarship that indicates just such a need (Tronto, 1984, 1987; Hoagland, 1990; Jaggar, 1995: Korth, 1999, 2001; Goodman, 2008). Some critiques have been philosophical, suggesting that to theorize about the possibilities for caring within institutions without addressing the contrast between the ways activities are coordinated institutionally and hermeneutically is to invite a categorical error (Schutz, 1998). It is also clear that our caring activities can be riddled with, even while working against, the ideological elements of social life; yet caring analysis to date has not dealt with this problem. There are only a few examples in the literature where an analysis of caring has been used to explicate social inequities that the caring acts themselves seem aimed at countering (see Korth, 2001; Valenzuela, 1999 for examples). In fact, Jaggar (1995) argued that our caring actions may leave the very conditions underlying the vulnerability or need for care totally ignored or masked. Another theorist suggested that "Care is distorted whenever it compromised the autonomy of the recipient or the caregiver" (Clement, 1996, p. 27). Hoagland's (1990) work indicated that when children were cared for in ways that did not include some criteria other than the child asking for the care, those children were more demanding rather than more giving. The critical work on caring still predominately focuses on interactional analyses of caring, largely by applying definitions and criteria for caring to given encounters. In this chapter, I will illustrate one qualitative approach to analyzing structural elements of interactions and I will exemplify what such an analysis articulates in the context of my study with an adult friendship group. This analysis enunciates the kind of critical scholarship that seems presently lacking in the literature. I begin with a brief excursus on the topic of "structure" and "structuration." Then, I describe the methods used for this study. Following the methods sections, I present the findings. The chapter concludes with a call to expand our qualitative analyses to include these more systematic, counter-intuitive, structurally instantiated elements as a way of increasing the critical capacity of our qualitative research.

Structure and Structuration: A Brief Excursus

A well-acknowledged central problem in social theory involves how to adequately address the integration of social life as it comes about through the actions of autonomously engaged people acting as agents of their own life stories on the one hand, and as it comes about through the systematic coordination of action consequences and functions with momentum that exceeds the actors' purposeful engagement on the other hand (Willis, 1977; Habermas, 1984, 1987; Giddens, 1990). Willis (1977) wrote that class culture "comprises experiences, relationships, and ensembles of systematic types of relationship which not only set particular 'choices' and 'decisions' at particular times, but also structure, really and experientially, how these 'choices' come about and are defined in the first place" (p. 1). Habermas (1987) indicates that one's "goal-directed actions are coordinated not only through processes of reaching understanding, but also through functional interconnections that are not intended by them and are usually not even perceived within the horizon of everyday practice" (p. 150). These functional interconnections are part of what gets named through an analysis of structures. If social theorists limit their analysis to the lifeworld, that is, to the horizon of hermeneutic interpretations that constitute the form and substance of everyday communicative engagements, they will fail to grasp or describe "all the counterintuitive aspects of the nexus of social reproduction" (Habermas, 1987, p. 151).

If we are to say that there are effects of our actions that exceed our intentions, we need to talk a little bit about intentions. Most philosophers think of intentionality as subjective because there is a privileged epistemological distinction between the way I grasp my own intentions and the way some other person would grasp my intentions. Objectivity on the other hand, refers to the epistemological process that implies multiple access as its principle. Objectivity relates to the question of intentionality because it is the way in which we can understand the conditions of action claimed when we engage our intentions. To intend something or other, I must do so within a milieu of particular conditions I take to be objectively given; conditions you would also be able to identify, name, count, etc. using similar procedures. In other words, there are a set of conditions that structure people's interactions and that must be invoked if one's intentions are to be met or taken as sensible. Economic conditions, political conditions, and cultural conditions serve to structure our actions. In each of these cases, objectivity is the mode through which the conditions can be identified and described. Structural relations can be inferred from these conditions. Marx (1973) argued that every social fact with fixed objectified form "appears in a vanishing moment in the movement of society" (the conditions for acting). We need a way to conceptualize the structures that link the conditions of action with actors' intentions.

Structuralism

Saussure (1960) introduced the argument that all of the elements within a linguistic system can be connected via sets of contrasts and differences that constitute a "structure." Lévi-Strauss (1967) applied this contrasting structural approach to cultures. "Structuralist models of society…basically viewed social phenomena as the outward manifestation of grammar-like rules that actors articulate in their daily lives" (Carspecken, 1996, p. 179). Structures do not exist in space and time. Their existence is virtual and as such they cannot be observed, but must be inferred.

> Unlike structural patterns in biology, the structural patterns of action are not accessible to [purely external] observations; they have to be gotten at hermeneutically [in the first place], that is, from the internal perspectives of participants. (Habermas, 1987, p. 151)

This is not the same thing as Levi-Strauss's (1967) proposal that structures were merely posited mental models on the part of the observer (Giddens, 1990, p. 64). For Giddens, the structural reproduction of the social systems [social systems, for him, are "systems of social interaction" (p. 66)] implies people remembering how things should be done, social practices that are organized through the shared knowledge about how things should be done, and the presupposition that people are capable of doing things in the manner in which they should be done according to the social knowledge (Giddens, 1990, p. 64). These structures cannot be reduced to rules, prescriptions, formulas, or determinates of either their own reproduction or social action. Structures are recursively implicated in the social action of actors who could always have acted otherwise; actors whose volition cannot be discounted in either a practical or theoretical sense.

According to Carspecken (1996), "Cultural conditions of action are those that resource and constrain the volition of the actor" (p. 190). He continued on to assert that:

> Volition itself depends on cultural structures to exist …[and yet] [e]ach meaningful act … will usually reconstitute cultural structures and be a new creation to a certain extent" (p. 191).

The volition of actors (which as social scientists we get at through reconstructive analyses) will always depend on cultural structures, drawing on this structure with the effect of both reproducing it and innovating it in the same act. Carspecken (1996) advocates a social-science approach that includes examining the distribution of cultural themes, frequency of cultural themes, and currency of cultural themes. Doing this makes it possible for the social scientist to take the next analytic step and identify cultural structures that may be operating through actors' engagements with one another, but outside their mutual reflexive monitoring or intentions. Giddens's provides a theoretical model that can facilitate how we address this double-sidedness of structures which coexist through cultural conditions and through volition, but are themselves not determinate of either.

Giddens's Structuration

Giddens (1990) uses the word social system to include the "visual pattern" of social structure with its socio-reproductive continuities as patterns in space and time (p. 64). He advocates a structural analysis that "involves examining the structuration of social systems" (Giddens, 1990, p. 64). His concept of structuration requires us to take into account both the volition of actors and the conditions of action without falsely dichotomizing these or choosing between them in terms of priority.

Marx wrote, "The conditions and objectifications of the process are themselves equally moments of it, and its only subjects are individuals, but individuals in mutual relationships, which they equally reproduce anew" (Marx, 1973, p. 712). For Giddens, who draws on Marx, action and structure presuppose one another. They are not dualisms, but a duality. The duality of structure relates "to the *fundamentally recursive character of social life, and expresses the mutual dependence of structure and agency*. . . [in other words, the duality means that] structure is both the medium and outcome of the practices involved in social interaction through both society and culture, conditions for acting and acting." (Giddens, 1990, p. 69). "According to this conception, the same structural characteristics participate in the subject (the actor) as in the object (society). Structure forms 'personality' and 'society' simultaneously—but in neither case exhaustively" (Giddens, 1990, p. 70). Giddens said that it is a necessary feature of action that actors could have acted otherwise and that when they act, they do not merely and perfectly reproduce the structures and conditions for their acting. There is an interesting and important tension between the reasons people will offer up for their actions (for example, "because I cared about Grant") and all the additional explanations and contributions involved in producing the action as part of a stream of conduct (Giddens, 1990, p. 57). As a person is able to reflexively monitor her actions within a context of unacknowledged conditions of action and unintended consequences of action, the person is able to influence those same conditions and a critical effect is possible. That is, reflexive monitoring of these structural and systemic aspects of our actions affords us opportunities to critique the conditions and consequences of our actions for inequity, oppression, ideological distortion, and so on. Giddens (1990) produced what he called a stratification model of social action that (1) has the actor engaged in reflexive monitoring of action and (2) the rationalization and motivation of action (given through the hermeneutic situation) set within a context of unacknowledged conditions of action and unintended consequences of action.

This approach has some methodological benefits. If we want to get at the second aspect of his stratification model, we need a way to articulate the context of unacknowledged conditions and unintended consequences of action. The theory of structuration tells us that the structures are co-constituted through both the volitional and interpretive activities as well as the unacknowledged and unintended aspects of the action.

Methodology

The analysis presented in this chapter uses data from a larger critical ethnography that will not be fully reported on here (see Korth, 1998, 1999, 2003). I spent a year engaging with an adult work-related, friendship group. All the members of the group, including me, had some tie to the local university (hereafter referred to as "LU"). My original research question had to do with how these friends located themselves both as autonomous people and as members of the group. I found that it was through a variety of caring acts that they navigated their individual identity claims and their belongingness to the group, both at the collectively interactive level and through dyads.

Participants

I was a peripheral member of the group of friends who participated in my study. I had known each of them for about five years, but their friendships with one another were longer than ten years. Their ages ranged from 35 to 80 at the time of the study. Grant was the oldest member of the group and he had a stroke requiring extensive rehabilitation so he was unable to participate in the study past the third observation.

- Jim was in his mid-40s. He earned a Ph.D. in British literature and literary criticism from a prestigious Midwestern university. He was a professor at LU. He had served (in the past) as an administrator there. He was married to Jan at the time. Both Jan and I had taken classes as his student.

- Jan was in her early 40s. She has a graduate degree from LU and was a practicing psychologist's associate. She was a student of Helen's, Peter's, and Jim's. She and I took classes and internships together.

- Peter was in his 50s and had been at LU longer than any of the others. He earned two doctorates and a secondary teaching license. He was a professor of education at LU. Helen, Jan, and I had all been his student at one time or another.

- Helen was in her late 50s. She was the hostess of the group as the group tended to gather at her place on Friday nights. She earned her master's degree as a graduate student of Peter's and Jim's. She had been teaching psychology classes at LU since that time. I had taken a class from her and so had Jan. Stan was her son.

- Stan was in his 30s. At the time of the study, he was attending a local community college and living at his mother's home (Helen). He cooked for the group and helped his mother host get-togethers. He did not attend the lunch get-togethers.

- Grant was a professor emeritus at the same prestigious university where Jim earned his Ph.D. In fact, Jim had been his student. Grant served LU as an adjunct faculty member in literature and cultural studies.

Both Helen and Grant have passed away since this study was conducted. I remain in intermittent contact with Peter, but none of the others.

Design

I designed the study following Carspecken's (1996) five-stage critical ethnography. I went to lunch with the group every other Friday for a year, participated in Friday-night discussion get-togethers (on Fridays alternating from the lunches), conducted three group interviews, and multiple individual interviews (expect with Grant). Hermeneutic reconstructive analysis (Carspecken, 1996) of the particular caring interpretations among the friends led to an articulation of a modal typology of caring acts. The typology was composed of three interactive modes through which the caring acts were engaged. The caring actions described through the findings were not meant to generalize across friendship groups either in their interpretation or with respect to the mode through which they were engaged. However, the typology itself has been used in other contexts and, thus far, has been open enough to prove useful (Korth, 2001).

Basic Description of the Hermeneutic Findings

Some of the caring acts were interactively coordinated in explicit, overt ways where the caring motivation itself was quite candidly and openly available without discretion. I called this mode of caring "overt-explicit." An example of the kind of activity for this group was problem solving. While problem solving, participants openly acknowledged a problem and solicited the help of others in resolving the problem. Others openly offered potential ideas in the service of trying to help their friend solve the identified problem.

Some of the caring acts were interactively coordinated in implicit, overt ways; this mode was called "overt-implicit." These acts were engaged implicitly, from within other things being said or done, but they could at any point have been made overt and explicit as a part of the caring. An example of a kind of activity that was coded into this mode (for this group of friends) was "empathizing." In such cases, the caring was understood and responded to through implicit aspects of the interaction, although the caring motivations could have been made explicit at any time (this is why we would think of it as overt—the caring motivations and intentions were an overt feature of the meaning of the activities even when left unsaid). "The history of shared experiences among group members made it possible for actors to …[engage in caring] without having to propositionalize the range of needs or connective responses [appropriate to the situation]" (Korth, 1998, p. 105). "An implicit reference can become a symbol for a fuller, core expression" (Korth, 1998, p. 106). Acts that fell into this mode in the typology indicated the degree of intimacy and history the friends shared as well as the public conditions within which they were acting. Sometimes the caring was kept implicit largely so that others in the physical space would not be privy to the vulnerabilities or needs being cared for. Most often, the implicit nature of the caring was a direct manifestation of how well the group members knew one another and understood one another.

The third mode in the typology was "covert-implicit." The covert nature of these activities meant that the caring aspect of the action *only* entered the interactions implicitly. The participants engaged in recognizing tacit identity claims and subjective references of their friends along with understanding contradictory and/or oppressive normative structures at play in the setting. Caring for the identities and feelings of others forged the most direct link between the caring AND recovering one's full humanity (to use Freire's 1974 ideas) against the oppressive structures of a culture. Covert-implicit caring relied on implicit or tacit interpretations of meaning and required actors to refrain from naming the caring as such because this would forfeit its interpretability as caring. One example of covert-implicit caring encounters that was common among this group of friends was relieving tension. Here is a description by Helen:

> Sometimes if it looks like a particular exchange is getting a tad too intense or uncomfortable, we [the women in the group] step in and kind of diffuse it by, maybe just asking a stupid question.

We can imagine a context whereby someone might say: "Hey, I am getting worried that we are starting to make each other feel bad and perhaps we should figure out a way to proceed without doing that." This would have been an overt way of addressing the same need. Often, covert-implicit caring was engaged precisely because the overtness or explicitness would have called into the interpretive field a foregrounded negative, pejorative, or devalued identity (within the context of the group) or posed a challenge to accepted umbrella norms and values within the group. For this group of friends, to be overt and explicit in this instance would have meant acknowledging that people's egos are vulnerable to their ideas being accepted. And, to do that would have made the egos more vulnerable because it would have meant that they (as the participants) were not somehow okay enough with who they were to separate an assessment of their identities from assessments of their ideas. For this group, that would have been a challenge. The overt-implicit caring covered over the challenge, avoided it so to speak, and in so doing also failed to lodge a reflective critique of the vulnerability.

Analyses of Cultural Structures

It was the covert-implicit mode of caring that first piqued my interest in looking at examples of caring that seemed to cover up vulnerabilities; vulnerabilities that seemed to be the effect of some culturally distorted way of thinking about people. Thus, after, the hermeneutic description of caring seemed rich and complete enough, I then wanted to turn my attention to a more systematic understanding of the caring activities across the various instances of caring. To do this, I assumed a relative outsider's perspective toward the same set of data. I marked the observational data according to distribution, routine, and functional outcomes related to caring activities. Then, I re-examined the interview data for structural indicators—talk that seemed to point toward either localized patterns of effects and structures or an awareness among participants of cultural conditions as being in operation through their group interactions. I performed this analysis in order to describe conditions and consequences that might be structurally connected with the caring activities for this particular group of friends. Ultimately, the point was to locate structures which co-exist in the cultural conditions/unintended consequences and hermeneutic interpretations of the activities.

First of all, I began by marking the distribution of caring activities across group members. The distribution of activities is an effect that is not typically monitored for or taken up agentically by participants, although certainly actors can learn to pay attention to the distribution of activities. On the whole, the distribution is not intentionally produced by participants and so, in this way, can be said to be an unintended consequence of the interactions as they were regularly patterned or habituated. Recall the quote above by Helen: she was aware that women tended to offer stupid questions as a way of diffusing tension. This was her description of the distribution of acts (and it certainly did match what I found), but the distribution itself was not part of what the actors intended when offering up or accepting the stupid questions as a way of relieving tensions.

After being able to describe the distribution of caring activities, I looked more closely at what kinds of structural relations seemed involved in the distribution and organization of caring. The point of my analysis was to discover locally instantiated structural patterns (Giddens's ideas facilitated this). This analysis helped further clarify the conditions within which group members cared for each other, the manner in which caring was both liberated and constrained by the system of cultural resources, and the way in which an analysis of care was able to serve as a critique of social practices.

Giddens (1990) proposed two principal ways to study the properties of social systems. First he suggested that social scientists can "examine the constitution of social systems as strategic conduct"; that is, "to study the mode in which actors draw upon structural elements—rules and resources—in their social relations" (p. 80). In my study, this analytical approach made it possible to describe two broad structural complexes: "Structures of Expertise" and "Structures of Service." Second, Giddens (1990) advocated identifying unintended consequences of practices that are themselves chronically reproduced features of the social system (p. 80). One such consequence revealed by this analysis of care is the chronic reproduction of "experts" over and against others. This structure of valuing experts objectified attributes of intelligence and verbal articulation, and consequently reproduced a systematic division between those who were treated as "experts" and those who were not (and there were gender effects to this). Caring helped to reproduce this division because through caring, actors both (a) enacted identities that were positive and highly valued given this particular system of experts, and (b) compensated for/ covered inequalities that were perpetuated through these notions of "expert." In the findings section, I present the findings and the particularities of the analyses.

I used a variety of accepted strategies to validate the data and the analyses. These included using recording devices, double-checking the transcriptions, using long-term engagement in the field, multiple interviews, peer debriefers, member checks, negative case analysis, strip analysis, and examining the match between my analysis and participants' commentaries (Carspecken, 1996). I do not report on anything that did not survive these techniques.

Findings

There are three sets of findings that are reported here. First, I describe the objectification of needs that were open to caring in the friendship group. Second, I describe the cultural structures that resourced and constrained caring activities within this group. Third, I locate the unintended consequences that were the effects of caring among this group of friends.

Objectification of Needs

The objectification of needs as it occurs among this group of friends sets up the preconditions of reification from which more formal systemization of caring or institutionalized mechanisms of caring could be derived (Habermas, 1987, see chapter 6). By objectification what I mean is that a need is conflated for interpretational purposes to an objective correlate. We will see an example of this below. The objectification of needs tends to limit/hone the range of depth of interpretation engaged by the participants. I will illustrate how this happens.

The objectification process enables or resources caring because it makes it possible for actors to coordinate their activities around an operationalized focus to which each of the participants has, in principle, equal access (for example, focusing the conversation on a specific topic of concern to one of the participants). This process also enables actors to explicitly prioritize needs and corresponding responses; that is, they can order needs from most pressing to least pressing. Also, it is through the objectification of needs that the setting of these priorities can win the rational support of others.

The objectification process not only enables, but also constrains caring, because it can effectively limit the range of meaning enacted and the scope of needs that get taken up. The process artificially conflates feeling with condition, and norms with effects. This conflation could suppress the validity process as well by limiting what can be easily queried. Distortions in understanding can occur when the objectified claims are treated as if they constitute the whole interpretive field. This act of reification (equating an objectified claim with the whole interpretive field) conceals nonobjectified claims that might also be part of the interpretive milieu.

It's easy to see how this happens through events coordinated to meet practical needs. Practical needs (like money for lunch, a napkin to wipe one's hands, a ride back to campus when one doesn't have a car, a replacement drink when one's glass is empty, and so forth) were quickly matched with caring acts that were directly suited to meet those needs (Korth, 1998). Let's look at an example. We were eating lunch outside and we had been talking about Grant's recent trip to the Midwest. Grant cracked a joke and everyone laughed. Then, I made a bid for caring about a practical need:

> BARB: [Speaking to Peter.] Did you get a napkin? [Licks fingers. Am without a napkin.]
>
> PETER: [Looks at me.] Here. [Hands me a napkin lying beside his sandwich. Reaches insight the bag for another napkin.]
>
> [Helen looks under her sandwich for a napkin.]
>
> BARB: [Takes the napkin. Looks at Peter.] Thank you.
>
> PETER: I think she put one in there, right? [Digs deeper into his bag and pulls a napkin out.] Yeah.

This caring sequence was an insertion into the flow of an ongoing interaction. My bid isolated a need for a napkin and the way to meet the need by assuming a means-end appearance. The objective claims associated with my need for the napkin were most prominent in the range of possible interpretations and the connection between the need and meeting the need was easily grasped. If a napkin had not been available, then claims about the next best way to meet the need would have surfaced, still emphasizing the objective realm. Subjective claims (claims about my feelings) were not in the foreground. What if the following had happened instead?

> BARB: Oh, gosh. Look at this mess I'm making. And I don't have a napkin. This is embarrassing. [to Peter] Did you get a napkin?

In that example, a feeling of embarrassment was simultaneously linked to the condition of being without a napkin while eating messy food and so the objective correlate was "without napkin" or "needs napkin." The condition would have received attention and Peter would have probably handed me his napkin with the expectation that addressing the condition would simultaneously be caring for my feelings. If, in my expression, I had conveyed feeling more intensely embarrassed, then in addition to addressing the objectified condition (need for a napkin) someone would have probably cracked a joke (this was a common way of caring for people who were embarrassed among this group of friends) about how embarrassing it is for the whole group to have to take me out in public and this would have worked to dissipate my negative feelings of embarrassment.

Subjective claims were objectivated by hooking the claim either to the conditions (as was suggested above) or to the evidence required for claiming "what is." In the first case, I found, for example, that "feeling depressed" was consistently linked to the condition of "being out of work." Thus, feeling depressed was objectivated as "without work" (an objective condition). In the second case, the objectification was the effect of hooking the subjective or identity claim to objective evidence. Here is an example of how that worked among this group of friends. When Jan expressed feeling "dumb" or "inadequate," the other members responded by debunking the evidence upon which the feeling seemed based—treating her claim as if it could be queried via objective evidence about Jan.

Needs emphasizing normative expectations were also objectified. According to my study, normative needs were objectified as effects. For example, Helen expected her friends to take care of her by protecting her confidentiality when she spoke about difficult experiences at work. The normative claim involved was this: Friends should not divulge confidences outside the friendship circle. That normative claim was objectified for caring: We need to protect each other's confidences because if we do not, then outsiders can make damaging use of the information. Objectifying the need in this way served to truncate other possible aspects of the meaning—like perhaps Helen's feelings of worry and trust. The objectified (group) need for confidentiality was linked to potential, observable effects, namely that breaking confidentiality could have damaging effects because the information could be used by outsiders in harmful ways. To reiterate, the need was abstracted from a normative claim and conflated with a potential effect. What resulted was an objectification: Confidentiality is necessary because it keeps negative effects from accruing.

Through this objectification process, needs were abstracted from their more complicated claims presupposing the needs and then hooked with observable features (conditions, evidence, or effects) that involved and facilitated the principle of multiple access. The objectification process took on a quasi-mathematical structure. Here are the patterned forms of the objectifications enacted by this group of friends through their caring:

- Practical needs were identified with needs already objectified that immediately implicated "ends." The relation was structured through means.

- Subjective claims and identity claims were abstracted to needs and then objectified through a relation connecting the claim with either conditions or evidence.

- Normative claims were abstracted to needs and then objectified through a link with (potential) effects.

It is only through this kind of objectivating process that caring can take on the appearance of acts oriented toward consequences when the care originates as activity oriented toward understanding. If we appropriate insights from Habermas's (1984, 1987) *Theory of Communicative Action* and Giddens's (1990) treatise on the *Central Problems in Social Theory*, it would seem plausible to expect that the macro-system would only be able to lay claim to care-giving through this objectification process: abstracting "felt" needs from their presupposition in claims and structuring a relation between those needs and means, conditions, evidences, or effects.

Analysis of Structures

To engage in a structural analysis of the caring activities, I examined feedback loops that seemed already in place and primed for enactment. I looked for the routinized mechanisms of action that operated through caring activities to reinstate the caring or to thwart it. I identified two fundamental structural complexes through which caring was both resourced and constrained among these friends: Structures of Expertise and Structures of Service. These structures were strongly embedded in the group's interactions and could, in themselves, sustain an extensive exploration. Here, I limit my discussion of them to their involvement in caring. As Giddens (1990) suggested, these structures were simultaneously, yet unintentionally, reproduced as they were drawn upon in action.

Structures of Expertise. "Structures of Expertise" were broadly employed by this group of friends across many of their interactions. It was, perhaps, one of the most stable of all reiterated structures. "Structures of Expertise" supported the notions that intellectual expertise is valuable, earned, and relatively rare. In this particular group, Jim and Grant were most definitely thought of as "experts." This construction was reproduced through (1) the coordination of discourse strategies, (2) the hierarchical ordering of knowledge along discipline lines, (3) the concentric layout of participatory contrast sets, and (4) the counter-expert: an oppositional binary.

Expertise was something the group was able to recognize and describe. Peter, Helen, Stan, Jan, and I all explicitly expressed a desire to learn from Jim and Grant that was not reciprocally expressed by either of the two of them. Jim's and Grant's expertise assumed a "factual status" among group members. No other members enjoyed such a pervasive designation of "expert." Others' individual worth was measured against these experts. The elitism, lack of reciprocity, and inequality that were manifest in these structures were not part of their intentions with one another.

> **PETER:** It isn't a matter of him [Grant] trying to be the leader of the group or anything. Not at all. But because he is such a bright guy. So interesting.

The group's everyday discourse strategies interdependently contributed to the reproduction of the "Structures of Expertise." To clarify this, I wrote a skeletal third-person description of the flow of a discussion. Within this description, I used brackets to identify the discourse strategies employed. I follow the description with a record of some corresponding comments (drawn from the interviews) regarding the strategies used by Jim and Grant. These comments represent the ways in which individuals were aware of discourse strategies, an awareness that did not extend to grasping their systematic relations. None of the members articulated the interdependence of these strategies or their overall involvement in structuring "expertise" among group members. Here is the description:

> Everyone was sitting in Helen's living room, discussing a paper that they had read together. The paper was written by Barbara Hernstein Smith on communication theory. Grant had selected it for discussion. Grant read it aloud to the group. Jim and Grant had already read the paper and discussed it together [topic control]. After Grant finished reading the essay to the others, people started discussing various points raised by the author. Jim and Grant, critics of literature and well-read in linguistics, listened to the many positions and arguments put forth by others. They hung back in the conversation for a while, letting others talk [wait time]. Then, they entered the discussion, clearly not surprised by any of the ideas presented thus far [always already anticipating the ideas of others while they themselves were equipped with more novel, less anticipatable ideas]. When they began to talk about the essay, they did so by invoking the names of other theorists such as Bahktin, Chomsky, Stanley Fish, and Searle, without elaboration [name-dropping]. As Jim and Grant talked, they used what could be taken as ordinary words in highly technical ways. For example, Jim and Grant engaged Stan in an entire sequence about "interests" without clarifying their own more technical use of the "interests," which, unbeknownst to Stan, did not precisely correspond with his use [vocabulary specificity]. Sometimes one or the other of them, Jim or Grant, would launch into a monologue about an idea or the two of them would engage in a dialogue that excluded the others as talkers/contributors [monologues/dialogues] relegating them to the passive role of listener/learner. In the end, even though they entered the discussion later than others, Jim and Grant each talked more than anybody else [conversation monopolizing]. Moreover, they presented their ideas and critique modestly, taking great efforts to not sound haughty or overconfident of their own mental power [stylistics]. For example, Jim said, "Well, I don't know. It seems to me, and, uh, I could be wrong, that ..."

I isolated the following comments from the interviews to help pinpoint how these discursive strategies were at play and how other, non-expert members of the group were aware of the strategies.

Topic control	"Um, it was clear that the master [Grant, in this case] had spoken and he didn't really want much discussion on it." – Stan
Wait time	"And of course, Jim also waits like Grant [to speak], he likes to ponder." – Helen "Jim would wait [pause] and when we got through mucking around, after a while, maybe twenty minutes, half an hour had gone by, or something like that, then he would come in. He would be sitting there with a slight frown on his face, bent over, cogitating during much of that discussion. And then he would begin to hold forth. And he would try to pick it [the discussion] apart or comment on certain salient features of it for elaboration. Toward the end of the discussion, my, my understanding is that he is the one who comes in and tries to ties it all up." – Peter
Novel ideas	"But, I think because he [Grant] has such an interesting mind that when he speaks, the group just listens…. Not that we don't respect each other. Grant's viewpoint is never what you think it's going to be…. He has a torturous mind and sometimes it's difficult to follow him as he goes wandering down a path." – Jim
Monologues/ Dialogues	"I remember some passionate exchanges between Jim and Grant, for instance, in which the rest of us just kind of played audience while they were in that mode…. Oh, listening and trying to follow. I didn't always follow…. It's like watching a, a mini debate. So, you're not exactly a spectator, just trying to track what's going on there, rather than wanting to jump in, make a point, ask a question." – Peter
Monopolizing	"I do like to participate and I don't like not finding an entre for too long. Although I often will sit there, especially when Jim or Grant get going. I mean, they'll really hold the floor, sometimes for long periods of time with very little interruption. … I do appreciate what they're doing, and I like, and I do like to listen…but I do feel a desire to burst in sometimes and participate." – Peter

Figure 1: Discursive Strategies

Stylist devices were also used. For example, modest talk was considered appropriate among this group of friends. The more expert one was, the less one would put forth personal merit. Thus, modesty represented the stylistic understatement of expertise. Also, rhetorical questions facilitated topic control and indicated expertise. Experts provided answers to questions, used vocabulary in technical ways, and dropped the names of philosophers without explanation.

It was the combined effect of each of these discourse strategies that helped to designate Jim and Grant as experts. Disrupting these discourse routines could risk disrupting the "structures of expertise." Relations of complementarity work through these linguistic structures. Those complementary relations can be expressed through the following characteristics.

Experts	Non-Experts (everyone else—the complement of experts)
Topic control	Topic acceptance: need for topic was accepted/taken for granted; non-experts accepted the topics raised by experts as valid and important
Novel ideas	Predictable points of view: non-experts' best achievements involved (1) clear articulation of ideas rather than the composition of novel ideas; (2) the ability to appreciate novelty; and (3) an openness to the expert's new ideas
Monologues	Attentive (listening) learners: non-experts expressed interest—their interest is expected/taken for granted
Pondering (wait) time	Jumping right in: non-experts were willing to risk saying something foolish, jumping in without the apparent thoughtfulness or deliberation witnessed with experts
Asking rhetorical questions	Needing to learn: non-experts were willing to accept help in the learning process; operating under the assumption that they do not know all the answers
Providing answers	Asking questions, probing answers: non-experts were expected to express inquiring interest for which experts were able to supply answers

Figure 2: Stylistic Devices

Hierarchy of Knowledge. Expertise was also structured along academic disciplinary divisions. Hierarchical relations were assumed through these structures. Philosophy and literary criticism (from the humanities tradition) were most highly valued. Applied professional fields carried the lowest value. Vocabulary, knowledge, expertise, name-dropping, and viewpoints (which emerged through group interactions) assumed currency according to the discipline (or field) they reflected. For example, with respect to the name-dropping strategy, referring to well-known philosophers was more highly valued than referring to well-known educators. With this group, the hierarchy was like a series of ceilings. There were limits on the extent to which a very good idea reflecting knowledge in clinical psychology could be appreciated and valued within the interactions. That ceiling was lower than the ceiling accessible through a very good point that drew on knowledge in anthropology. Neither of these two disciplines had ceilings that approached the value of philosophy. These ceilings were not part of the actors' individual or collective intended consequences of interactions. The ceilings were arranged like this:

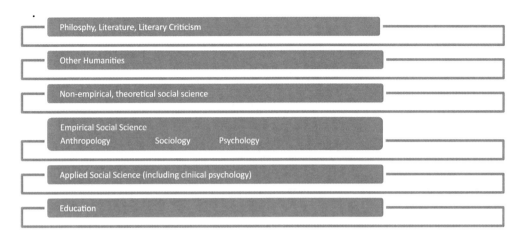

Figure 3: Hierarchical Knowledge Structure

Here is how group members talked about the hierarchy:

Peter: "I think also that there just simply has been no, no real attempt to explore what people like us [referring here to me and him—people in education] do. [Pause] Again, the themes are literary themes and philosophical themes. They are not ones like we, like we deal with in a lot of our lives." It's interesting that Peter said this, because, actually, Peter taught educational philosophy, so it's not as though Peter does not deal with philosophy; here even the range of what is considered "philosophical" has been determined by the structures of expertise such that Peter's educational philosophy does not count as philosophy, even in his own way of characterizing what is happening.

Stan: "He [referring to Jim] tends to comment in a philosophical way, which an indication of a man of great learning." Stan's comment here assumes that this hierarchy is an accurate reflection of one's expertise and learning.

Jan: "I just hope that I'm a valuable member. I hope that I'm able to add something to the discussion… most of the time I'm, I'm, I'm asking more than I'm commenting, or commenting on their explanations. I'm not as well versed in the literary parts as the main group is." Jan is indicating that she hopes her questioning is value-added to the discussion and her sense of herself as a valuable participant in the group discussion relates to this hierarchy of knowledge. We don't even get a sense here of what her knowledge is, just that her absence of literary knowledge means that the best she can do in the discussion is ask questions.

This hierarchy worked within the group to emphasize value relations across different domains of knowledge, ultimately positioning users of knowledge in an analogous hierarchy.

Concentrically Organized Participatory Contrast Sets. Concentrically organized contrast sets were also part of the "Structures of Expertise" and they were most identifiable through roles (hence they are named according to the most fundamental role configurations. Contrast sets comprised the domains of the circles as well as constituting the boundaries that marked off domains. There were three circles, which I labeled the inner expert circle, the middle participation circle, and the outer observer's circle. I will list each of the major sets involved in this concentric structuring.

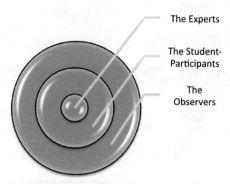

Figure 4: Concentrically Organized Contrast Sets

Jim and Grant were in the inner "expert" circle. The contrast sets that were associated with this inner circle included (1) various highly valued intellectual perspectives, such as Greek philosophy versus French structuralism; (2) role sets, such as "Proud Professor with His Prized Student" and "Intellectually Equal Sparring Partner for Grant"; and (3) historical experiences versus present experiences. These contrast sets were exclusionary and highly specific to the experts involved. The sets systematically excluded other participants, other academic perspectives, and others' experiences. Even though these sets were specific to Grant and Jim, they invoked common assumptions that were shared by other members as well. Some of those assumptions were articulated in earlier chapters of this text (for example, the assumption "we are, in part, our history"), and some of those assumptions dovetailed with the structures of expertise already described (for example, that philosophy is considered a highly valued intellectual discipline). While Grant and Jim acted from within the expert circle, Peter, Helen, Stan, Jan, and I supported the claims necessary to stabilize this set of contrasts ideologically.

The boundary between the inner circle and the next circle of student-participants was partially constructed through contrast sets that systematically limited access to expertise. Practically speaking, this boundary was not permeable—it was the least fluid and the contrast sets that generated the distinction between the expert circle and the student-participant circle were relatively stable. The contrast set involved in this middle student-participant circle were: (1) teachers versus learners; (2) the contrasting discourse strategies already described; and (3) getting serious versus "mucking around." The asymmetry across group members, which was an effect of these expert structures, was most visible through these contrast sets. These contrast sets corresponded to the expert/non-expert dichotomy spelled out above. Everyone except for Grant and Jim interacted most often from within this second ring. Grant and Jim were not excluded from this student-participant circle, but others were excluded from the inner expert circle.

The middle ring—student-participants—was comprised of the following contrast sets: (1) using humor versus serious attempts to be smart (according to Peter, one could always count on getting a laugh with a joke, but the worst thing one could do in the group was say something stupid); (2) voicing perspectives from the field of psychology in contrast with perspectives from the field of education; (3) hosting in contrast with being one of the guests; and (4) males in contrast with females. Three of these four relate quite obviously to one's activities within the group, but they move to decreasing flexibility in terms of reciprocity and access among participants whose interactions with the group are best described through this middle circle. Almost any of the participants could engage by using humor or by making a serious attempt to be smart; participants could not engage as either male or female, they were stuck with their socially assigned gender expression, which had structural effects on participation.

The first contrast set (using humor versus serious attempts to be smart) highlighted the most valued interactive skills among group members. Success with humor was more achievable for student-participants, and failure at acting smart was more devastating in terms of its results. Failed attempts at humor or being smart were, at times, taken up as bids for care. Also, humor was used to release tension (another act of caring among this group of friends). The use of humor was most often initiated by males.

The second contrast set involved interacting through disciplinary perspectives of lesser value than those exhibited by the experts. In this contrast set, psychological perspectives were considered more interesting and salient than educational perspectives. Almost anyone in the group could raise questions and comments from these perspectives, but they were distinguished from one another in terms of how they influenced the interactions.

The third contrast set (being host in contrast with being one of the guests) was generally a fixed contrast, though in principle this set could be reciprocated. In practice, Stan and Helen served the group as hosts. Stan and Helen drank the most alcohol and often would not have been able to drive home if the get-together had been hosted somewhere else. The hosts had special interactive privileges—they were considered necessary to the functioning of the group regardless of their assumed limitations in expertise. The group expressed appreciation for the hosting. Jan broke into this set by consistently bringing snacks along to the discussion sessions.

The fourth contrast set (male versus female) was fixed. Gender worked mostly to eliminate females from certain realms of discourse (sexist joking and lines of discourse, especially) and from initiating bids for explicit patterns of caring. Overall, the males dominated interactions of all kinds, including caring interactions. By dominated I mean produced more, controlled more, and controlled how much access one could have to the conversation. Helen exhibited rude-like behavior in attempts to work against the mark of gender, but Jan hedged participation and rarely initiated engagement in the discussion.

The boundary that marked this middle ring from the outer ring was a contrast set of interest (which marked the student-participant circle) versus non-interest (observers). This boundary was porous and could switch across topics and over time.

The outer ring (observers) is best understood through the following two contrasts: (1) the importance of real life in contrast with talk about ideas, and (2) putting up with the group in contrast with getting enjoyment out of watching group members interact. This ring was often presupposed by interactions that are structured through the inner and middle circles. The boundary set and expectations for participation pointed to the potential for members to act from a position that was structured by the contrast sets of this outer ring. Jan was the member most likely to act from this outer ring. I also acted from this outer ring in my role as ethnographer.

Counter-Expert: An Oppositional Binary. An oppositional binary worked probably from a highly tacit impetus to counter the "structures of expertise." Ultimately, the binary itself supported those structures of expertise, but they can be considered counter-expert because the activities were structured in opposition to the claims presupposed through the expert structure. For example, one time Grant dropped the name Bahktin (a philosopher) and Stan said, "Who the fuck is Bahktin?" He was told, "That's something you spray on sores" (referring to the antibiotic spray Bactine). These counter-expert oppositions were often not appreciated and resulted in sanctioning. Sanctions took the form of ignoring or limiting access to speak via politeness strategies, leaving open only rude- or belligerent-type behavior, or succumbing to the expertise. Bids for implicit forms of caring were sometimes offered. In other words, when someone acted through this counter-expert binary, they were interpreted as needing sanctioning or needing care. Oppositions included rude-like behavior (loud, insistent interruptions, for example), refusals to accept technical or jargonistic vocabulary, failure to acknowledge that experts knew more, and insistence on having the last word. Oppositional structures were accepted when they took the form of humor (which did not directly challenge the experts), but not when they represented serious attempts to outsmart the experts. Caring acts were more acceptable ways to counter the inequalities perpetuated through these structures of expertise than engaging in counter-expert activities. Stan was the member who engaged in counter-expert activities most often. Even so, during his interview he clearly espoused components of the structures of expertise in a way that made it seem that he was personally committed to them. He did not say things like "Jim and Grant know a lot, but so do I and what I know goes unrecognized" or "Jim and Grant think they are experts, but really other expertise is just not equally appreciated in this group." Instead, he said things like reported above: "He [referring to Jim] tends to comment in a philosophical way, which is an indication of a man of great learning." In other words, Stan acknowledged the structures of expertise as legitimate, thus his oppositional activities seemed to only tacitly suggest an awareness of a kind of oppression meted out through these structures.

Stan's response to these structures of expertise in interactions reminds me of Peter McLaren's (1986) work on the culture of pain. Stan did not articulate counter claims, but during interactions he acted as if he tacitly recognized the inequalities and felt pained by them, pained in ways that he did not express explicitly. Helen also participated in the counter-expert activities that seemed indicative of dissatisfaction. Helen's and Stan's interjections resulted in being cut off, failure to be recognized, and misinterpretations. Helen used ambiguity to retain some dignity in the group despite interactive sanctions. Stan's oppositional activities resulted in a standstill that left the experts intact and left Stan in need of care to save face. Both Helen and Stan set themselves relatively outside these expert structures through the binary. It was only Helen and Stan who expressed any sort of recognition of the oppressive, unequal effects of the structures of expertise. Furthermore, Stan rejected bids for caring for him that would have tied him to the structures of expertise. In this way, he also tacitly acknowledged the link between some interactively established needs for caring that served to simultaneously reiterate the oppressive structures of expertise. During his interview, Peter talked about a lack of reciprocity, but during interactions he consistently employed the structures of expertise and did not, at any point, take up counter-expert claims.

Summary and Speculation. I just articulated four componential clusters of the "Structures of Expertise." With respect to care, these structures of expertise emerge as a core explanation of inequality. Because "expertise" was a legitimate form of inequality, it was sustained even among friends who espoused strong democratic ideals. Expertise was legitimized, in part, through these very structures. Caring disrupted this legitimized form of inequality through implicit patterns when structures of expertise were directly involved, for example, through deferring intellectually.

On particularly common caring activity in the group, coded as "deferring intellectually," disrupted the potential negative consequences of the structures while reinstating them precisely because these caring acts were implicitly patterns. The disruption occurred because experts momentarily (and inauthentically) sacrificed their claim to expertise in the spirit of honoring the personal worth and dignity of the person (and disrupting the idea that expertise was more valuable than appreciating others regardless of their level of expertise). But the caring acts also reinstated the structures because the underlying assumptions that validated the category "expert," the legitimizing force, was not undermined for the group as long as the caring was left implicit. In this way, caring comprised a corrective for these particular structural inequalities, but fell short of dismantling them. Why not dismantle the offending structures? I speculate that at the time of this study, such a dismantling would have undermined significant and pervasive structuring of group interactions. The friendships might not have been able to recover after such an extensive shake-up.

The structures of expertise were similarly disrupted and, also, reconstituted through care that worked, in large part, to promote positive identities, because for this group, identities were deemed as "positive" given the structures of expertise. The positive identity claims, constructed according to notions of expertise, were not equally distributed. There was unintentional yet systematically limited access to those identity claims. That is to say, the recognition of those identity claims and ultimately the claiming itself was limited according to these structures of expertise. Nevertheless, through caring activities, Jan, Helen, and Stan did gain limited access to these specific positive identities. The validity of expert identities remained unquestioned, but access to those identities was given through caring. In this way, care momentarily recovered equality, but without de-legitimizing the systemic pattern of the asymmetry.

I want to speculate briefly on what might anchor these "Structures of Expertise" outside the face-to-face interactions the data give us. A system of academic experts has been legitimized through institutions of higher education. Consider these analogous trends. In the state of Texas, education courses are funded at a lower rate than courses in arts or sciences. Expertise is a marketed commodity in higher education. Expertise is recognized through the institution by much the same markings that got Jim and Grant recognized as the group's highest experts. The credentialing process includes prioritizing theory and research over practice, valuing breadth of knowledge in a specialized area, prestige of the university granting the degree, types of degree, and so on.

Structures of Service. "Structures of Service" denotes a cluster of systematically reproduced patterns involved in actors rendering services, services such as providing a place to gather, offering feedback on papers, and participating on faculty committees. Service was coordinated hermeneutically around objectified needs through two orientations. First, norms (convention or obligation) were used to explain why one would be willing to provide the service, and, second, means-end rationality was used to explain why the particular service provided was the best, most efficient way to meet the objectified needs. These structures were particularly useful for problem-solving and meetings practical needs. Also, these structures of service required and facilitated, at times, a systematic way to prioritize needs. Services were primarily interpreted as acts of care by participants.

Domains. "Structures of Service" were organized through domains of server/served relations. There were three domains of server/served relations marked by activities of group members. These were practical service, collegial service, and professional/institutional service. The domains differed primarily in terms of the binding force of the relation between server and served and the nature of the service itself (orientation toward the objective world implicated through the service). There were a few features that the three domains held in common. Service in any of the three domains was unidirectional for any given event. Also, those who were served were not seen as more powerful than the server, at least in the common use of the term of "power." The relation between server and served was not understood by actors to be the effect of coercive or persuasive uses of power nor as the effect of exchange. The server conceived of herself as freely offering to meet the identified need for the served person, group, or institution. Yet, there were interactive sanctions that might have worked behind the backs of actors to regulate these structures of service and in the case of professional and institutional service, pay was exchanged to secure a minimum expectation of service.

One server/served relation was practical with the most frequent example being a relation between host and group members. Services rendered within this domain included such activities as providing a place for group members to gather, supplying food and drink, attending to individual needs for comfort, and specific needs for such things as rides. The binding force in the relation between server and served was convention. Politeness strategies and skills were used to enact these services, but the main requirements for this service had to do with knowing and having what it took to meet the need (supply) and willingness. Members did not ascribe much skill to the rendering of practice service and yet, Stan began developing his talents in this area. He prepared special snacks for the group and was most attentive to the comfort and needs of guests. Jim was rarely the server in this domain. This set of services was less valued than other domains of service, but were nevertheless frequently made use of.

The second domain of server/served relations was collegial. Actors performed the following services in this domain: critiquing papers; covering classes for each other; solving professional problems; and providing professional support. Within this domain, only Jim, Grant and I were (historically speaking) served by others critiquing our papers. Peter expressed some resentment about this, so while he did not articulate the structural nature of these services, he did have a tacit awareness of them. He said:

> Just like we try to encourage Jim, You know, "oh, more stud with this novel [Jim was writing a novel.] Come back and read with us." [His tone sounds authoritative, almost miffed.] We reinforce the hell out of him, frankly. [Voice calm again.] And I think that was deserved, but there's been no reci—, reciprocation. Like he knows that I'm working on a manuscript.

Covering classes was only a possible service for Peter, Jim, Helen, and Grant, or me (not Stan or Jan). Moreover, Stan received only restrained support as a student, but not as a professional. Other activities in this domain were evenly distributed across group members. The binding force of the collegial relation was charm—individual commitments to the persons being served. A certain amount of skill was required to render collegial services. This domain of relations was least accessible to Stan and Jan and, therefore, caring activities that emerged through these services were correspondingly inaccessible to them.

This third domain was the most highly valued of the three. These first two domains differed from the third domain in two important hermeneutically knowable ways. First, the obligations that bound the server to the served through service were freed up if the intended receiver declined the service. In other words, the obligation was to offer the service with the understanding that one was willing and able to make good on the offer. If the offer was not accepted, then the server was not bound to the service. In her interview, Helen reported:

> With what Jim and Grace [a woman who did not participate in the study] were going through, they're still going through, I think that Jim's concern was that no group member stick his or her neck out [in support]. And that was sort of frustrating to members of the group. But once again, that was his choice.

In the previous domain, professional and institutional service, the server was bound to perform the service through moral principles and could only be freed of the obligation through a shift in moral interpretation or view. Service was conditioned through an institution or profession (an example of which is coming up).

A second difference between this third domain and the first two was that the service was considered a "good" thing to do in the first two domains, but the "right" thing to do in the third domain. That is, it was considered good by participants to provide a place for members to gather or to offer feedback on a paper, but it was considered right and obligatory to take one's place on a committee that served the institution. During a lunch get-together, Jim told Peter and me:

> I mean, from my point of view, I'm, **I am** [pause] ethically obligated to raise questions to, a-a-about violations of university policy. I mean, I don't have any choices.

Thus, the third domain of professional/institutional service was marked by server/served relations that were bound by ethics. While it was certainly true that these relations involved paid positions, the services of this domain were adhered to through ethical obligation rather than contract of service for pay. In fact, group members poked fun at each other about their inability to orient their own professional activities according to pay that would have, no doubt, resulted in them decreasing the amount and quality of their service within the institution. The kinds of activities that fell into this domain of service included, for examples, responding in a professionally supportive way to students and participating on institutional committees.

The professional relations constructed within this domain were comprised of more formalized institutions role sets that carried with them expectations for appropriateness. The binding force of these relations held regardless of the response of other actors involves in the institution or profession. In other words, the server could not be released from this obligation merely because others representing the institution declined to accept the service. Instead, rejection pushed the server toward an analysis of means. The obligation was reiterated through the instantiation of moral principles, for example, in policies or contracts that could be secured outside the face-to-face events of server and other representatives of the institution.

The server/served relations were initiated via a contract for work. Once in a while the contractual relations were foregrounded. This happened particularly when the need for employment had group members performing tasks to which they did not feel morally committed or maybe even tasks that seemed in opposition to their moral commitments. These tasks were forgiven by the group and were not counted as service here. For example, the administration asked Peter's academic division to do some work that Peter (and other group members) did not think was appropriate. Jim said,

> Yeah. Oh yeah. I mean there's no question! I don't in any way hold the division's faculty [especially faculty] responsible. They weren't. This wasn't something they chose to do. If the provost comes into a division meeting and tells 'em to do something, it's pretty likely they're going to do it!

Peter performed a task under administrative force and against his own good judgment. The task was not considered a service. Peter's service, instead, was enacted through his efforts to counter the task that he thought threatened the integrity of the institution. This service, you can see, was tightly bound by what Peter would argue was right or wrong. Caring was, at times, the interactive switching plate between acts initiated by external forces over and against acts structured by internalized moral force. Jim, Peter, and I engaged in sympathizing with one another and neutralizing negative thoughts and feelings in our interactions about Peter's situation.

Prioritizing Needs. The "Structures of Service" also revealed a patterned way of resolving conflicts regarding how to prioritize competing needs/requisite service. There were two operating schemes for making such a decision: personal and typological. I am writing of needs that were explicit and for which the group could target its services. Both mechanisms for prioritizing needs (the personal and the typological) resulted in a hierarchical ordering.

The first operating scheme (the personal) revealed an interesting conversion. First Grant's service-oriented needs, which were at some points in competition with each different person in the group, were always prioritized. Jan rarely explicated a need for the group to attend to, but when she did, her needs were prioritized. With both Grant and Jan, services were rendered if a need was expressed. Grant's service-oriented needs were prioritized because the needs were pressing (linked to his frail health and advanced age). Jan's requests for service were rare. For both people, their requests for services were most often met, and met as if the services were really necessary. Prioritizing needs beyond Grant's and Jan's was ordered according to amount of interaction power wielded within the group. Jim's needs were prioritized over Peter's and mine. Helen's and Stan's needs were treated as a low priority when they were in competition for service needs of other group members. Stan and Helen provided far more services than they received.

The needs were also ordered typologically. Practical needs intruded on interactions and they were addressed in the moment. Collegial needs were resolved before institutional-/profession-oriented needs when there was competition between bids. Usually these were ordered linearly so that each of the identified needs could be served according to its turn.

Services required by Grant were mostly practical with collegial needs running second. Jim received many services from group members in all three domains. In terms of frequency, Jim was the recipient of most of the services.

Summary and Speculations. Release from the demands to reach face-to-face consensus regarding service was achieved in the first two domains (practical service and collegial service) through routine practices and was powered by shared expectations of what was good. Release from the demands to reach consensus through face-to-face negotiations regarding service in the third domain was accomplished via policies and shared moral principles and powered by personal moral commitments.

Structures of service resourced explicit patterns of caring, especially problem-solving, sympathizing, and stimulating positive thoughts and feelings. These structures legitimized service-oriented roles that were compatible with certain caring roles in the group. These caring roles looked very similar to the ones Noddings (1984) studied as carer and cared-for: unidirectional for any given event, highly explicit, singular, specified meeting of needs. Structures of service resource interactive caring to meet needs one at a time. Multiple needs had to be met in a linear, prioritized fashion. The structures further limited caring by controlling access to server/served roles according to criteria that made access unequal.

This set of findings leads us to speculate on the complexities of serving others in an interactive context. Service cannot be thought of as a synonym of caring, but its structures will certainly influence the engagement of caring.

A related consequence worth speculating about is that maybe these structures of service make it reasonable for group members to accept university pay that is too low for living comfortably and doesn't adequately support one (given the years of invested education required) in the economic system by supplanting one's reasons for performing the service-oriented work with moral and conventional rationale. Praxis needs might be met by constructing one's self as a certain kind of moral person willing to commit regardless of compensation.

Analysis of Unintended Consequences

In this section, I want to shift the focus away from structures that resource or constrain caring toward the unintended consequences of caring as it was enacted among this group of friends. As members of the group cared for each other, some effects accrued that would not have been considered part of the intentional purposes of the actors. The unintended consequences were the byproducts of the acts brought about by distortions that intruded on the face-to-face interpretive milieu. Some of the effects would seem counter-intuitive to group members. Others would not. These unintended consequences were directly manifest in the reiteration of structures, but by presenting them here separately I hope to emphasize the image of effects that are distinct from the agency of actors—effects without the assignment of agency. In this way, the consequences take on a subjectless appearance.

The unintended consequences of caring in this group were related to (1) gender, (2) interactive engagement, and (3) interpretive field. Many of these unintended effects were one result of implicit type-caring among group members.

Effects Related to Gender. Distribution patterns revealed gender differences that were unintended consequences of engaging in caring activities. Distribution patterns were marked by gender differences. The men were more involved in explicit-type patterns of caring than women. The women were more likely to make bids for releasing tensions (one kind of caring common in the group) by asking what they thought of as a "stupid" question, while men were more likely to make bids for caring through humor. Men were more likely to meet leadership needs of the group than women. The women were more involved in implicit-type caring than they were in explicit patterns of caring. Fewer bids for caring were offered up on behalf of or by women in the group than on behalf of or by men in the group. These distribution patterns demonstrate that a specific kind of gender inequality was one unintended consequence of the caring.

One similarity that can be spotted in this distribution is that females engage in less opportunities for more publicly empowering patterns of caring (namely explicit-type caring and meeting leadership needs of the group) Moreover, females did caring in the group that did not afford them as many opportunities to claim the kinds of identities that were highly valued by group members (namely, smart and witty identities). Instead, witty and smart identities were claimed in other ways or when others were making similar claims simultaneously. Also, females did not claim interactive power over the caring acts themselves to the extent that males did, as indicated by the difference in the number of bids offered and the number of sequences closed. This finding suggests that caring patterns did not extensively allow females to overcome typical patterns of inequality obtained through discourse and leadership practices. Females claimed a broader range of identities through their caring than the males did. In contrast to females, identity construction of the males did not include, for examples, "I am an aware person" or "I am a nice person."

When females did make bids for caring, usually through implicit patterns, they intended to be involved in more complex forms of caring. Caring was the most frequent means through which women in the group entered the conversation.

Effects Related to Interaction Engagement. Caring had unintended effects on the patterns of interaction. For example, care regularly resulted in closing off conversation topics. This happened most notably, but not only, when arguments increased in intensity. A well-intentioned participant would jump in with a joke or silly question in order to diffuse the tensions. In so doing, the discussion at hand was derailed, but the good feelings and positive identifications among group members were, in part, protected.

Carspecken (1996) recommends that ethnographers examine interactive power using a typology he adapted from Weber. This typology distinguishes interactive power according to the manner in which the openness to dialogue and the extent to which subordinates are engaged have the capacity/freedom to assent to the superordinate or the manner in which force is used to secure actions regardless of assent—the most fundamental of which would be assent to the right of power over me (the subordinate). The superordinate stands in a strategic relationship to the subordinate(s). According to Carspecken (1996) following Weber, one type of power is coercion, where subordinates act in concert with the will of the superordinate in order to avoid sanctions or negative outcomes. This kind of power was not evidenced in this particular group with respect to caring. Another type of interactive power is charm. With this kind of power, the subordinate acts out of loyalty to the superordinate and in a way that diminishes the personal autonomy claimable by the subordinate. The superordinate would maximize the benefits of this loyalty for her own ends. Though certainly there was a lot of loyalty among the friends in this group, it lacked the strategic impetus and diminished personal autonomy to be recognized as a form of power. But the use of charm as power can be a bit ambiguous because it can accomplish more than bringing about a desired end. Many people asked me if caring was a form of power and I think the insight they might have been intuitively noting is related to charm. In this study, I did not ever find charm to be used solely as a form of interactive power. What I did find was that charm as a form of power was engaged primarily through the structures of service. What I mean by this is that the superordinate in the charm-power relationship was recognized as such through the structures of service and the outcome would be that the subordinate would acquiesce to the superordinate as a way of maintaining the service relations so entrenched in the group's habits.

In egalitarian friendships, we might expect little force of power to be involved with little demarcation of superordinates and subordinates. Also, we might expect that forced action without assent would not feel good among friends. A very close look at the interactions of this particular adult-friendship group suggests that interactive patterns seemed to reiterate traditional power relations. According to Carspecken's (1996) interpretation of Weber's typology, there are two subtypes of traditional power. One involves normative power. This is when the subordinate consents to the higher position of the superordinate based on cultural norms. In other words, the subordinate does what the superordinate wants because of norms that underlie the basic structure of the subordinate-superordinate relationship. The other type of traditional power involves interactively established contracts. In this type of power, the subordinate is acting to secure favors or rewards from the superordinate. The normative type of traditional power was the one that found its way into the interactions of this group of friends. The power differential distinguishing superordinates from subordinates was buttressed through the structures of expertise described earlier in this chapter and gender—both of which would be located as the normative type of traditional power. When care was invoked on behalf of superordinates, normative power was reiterated through the caring activities, but this was most certainly an unintended effect of the caring. For those group members who were subordinated to normative, care functioned as a momentary corrective to the power inequities. Care also functioned to buffer subordinates from the consequences of not doing what the superordinate wanted of them.

When caring acts did not reconstitute traditional normatively structured power relations (between superordinates and subordinates), the caring resisted these relations, pushing the group toward more egalitarian norms. For example, when a person deferred intellectually as an act of caring for their counterparts in the argument, the caring act itself pointed toward new norms capable of supplanting the normative power relations, like recognizing the worth of a group member outside the structures of expertise.

Effects Related to the Interpretive Field. One effect of objectifying needs so that others might help meet them is that this narrows the interpretive field of meaning. The most drastic narrowing of any field of meaning in an interaction comes through the process of reducing multiple claims to a single, unified objectivating claim. Some highly explicit patterns of caring required this, as this made meeting the needs more efficient and effective. However, it also resulted in distortions—through rejecting, negating or ignoring other claims potentially salient to the meaning.

Moreover, the process of objectifying claims solidified relations between care and certain feelings and/or conditions. Reinstantiation of these relations through caring could bring about reification. Data indicated that the following set of stabilized linkages were reinstated systematically through caring as it was enacted by this group.

- Care was hooked to fear—fear of particular effects of outcomes that included health effects (for Grant), fear of outside threats (unfriendlies at the university), and fear of disassociation (not wanting to lose the group).

- Care was hooked to discomfort—primarily as release for interactional discomfort and awkwardness.

- Care was hooked to identity formation—given group norms for modesty, care was a primary vehicle for constructing positive identities among the members.

What happens when caring unintentionally brings about the stabilization of such linkages? The communicative potentiality becomes truncated. This is a crucial finding. For example, when there was discomfort in the group, it was nearly automatically (and certainly habitually) responded to through caring. No one persisted in exploring the causes of the tension, the manner or reasons the tension came up, or the pattern of bailing out on the particular conversation at hand because of the tension. Certain caring actions were engaged (like cracking a joke) and the tension in the group was released. The effect of this was to leave behind any other features of the pragmatic horizon that might yield new responses to the tension or reveal others needs situated in the tensions.

Some highly explicit needs (like practical needs for tangible things such as napkins or water) were expressed through meaning fields that were already quite narrow and within which there was a distinctive gap between foreground and backgrounded claims. In these cases, care did not impose a narrowing of the meaning field. Once in a while, caring acts picked up on highly backgrounded claims that were coupled with highly explicit, highly objectified needs, and in these instances the care worked to broaden the interpretations taken up through the interaction by bringing those claims more into the foreground. Caring shifted the horizon of meaning with broadening effects.

Caring acts were capable of bringing about unintended shifts in the pragmatic horizon of meaning (for more on pragmatic horizons, see Carspecken, 1996, 2003). Sometimes when the horizon of possible interpretations was suppressed, the person being cared for was interactively disempowered because it would be subtleties in identity claiming that would get censored. This itself was an unintended consequence that also had unintended consequences. When identity claims were suppressed, the result was the reiteration and ordering of very specific identity relations/claims to the exclusion of others. Another unintended consequence was the reinstatement of implicit prioritizing of group identities, values, and needs, even when caring was not aimed to accomplish this. In some cases that resulted in reconstructing the kinds of effects related to gender and interaction that were previously described, for example, recapitulating the structures of expertise. By prioritizing group habits, cultural structures, and generalized needs, the explication of counter, individualistic needs was negated and abandoned.

Summary and Speculation. Unintended consequences result when the reflexive monitoring of participants does not include the full range of possible, plausible outcomes. When this happens, the salient questions include "Why?" and "What (if any) systematic exclusions are marked by the unanticipated consequences?" Among this group of friends, there were systematic limitations on valuing identity claims that, in turn, contrasted with the narrow range of identities valued through the structures of expertise and service. And yet, this limitation reflects a contradiction with group members' ideas that they are "accepted by their friends for who they are." The promoted identity claims coincide with the economic reward system of the university (paying literature professors more than education professors, for example). The re-instantiation of gender privilege well-cited as part of patriarchal vestige, certainly runs counter to how the group members would want to describe their interactions. And yet, these cultural conditions of sexism still supply background material for the group's interactions. It is helpful to be able to identify in a refined way how caring works against oppressive cultural conditions, but also works to reproduce those conditions.

Conclusion

The primary purpose of this chapter was to illustrate what an analysis of structures can contribute to critical qualitative studies and to describe one approach for conducting such an analysis. I used Carspecken's critical ethnographic methodology, which promotes beginning with hermeneutic reconstructive horizon analysis and moving into an analysis of structures that is informed by the reconstructive analysis.

In this study, I examined caring, which theorists like Noddings argue can only really be studied at the interpersonal level. Others have criticized care theory and research precisely because it has, until now, been unable to address questions like "What if caring activities reproduce conditions that are actually oppressive or distortive for the participants?" and "How can we judge the quality and content of caring in ways that go beyond the intentions of the actors?" By engaging in an analysis of structures involved in the caring activities of this group of friends, I was able to look more closely at the cultural conditions that both resourced and constrained the caring. I was able to articulate the structures that were both medium and outcome (particularly noted as unintended outcomes) of the caring. These unintended outcomes mark the contingent limits through which the friends were monitoring and interpreting their caring activities. A strong, critical social analysis will involve the hermeneutic reconstruction of meaning as would make sense to the participants and would simultaneously describe the cultural conditions through which volition is thought to emerge. This would be critical because it helps to locate disjunctures between agency and structure that inhibit our capacities to enact our full humanity (Freire, 1974). The findings could facilitate the critical awareness one acquires with respect to one's own oppression—this is what Freire (1974) called "conscientizacao." These structures can regularly escape the intentions and purposes of the actors who are involved in their engagement.

> Structural violence is exercised by way of systematic restrictions on communication; distortion is anchored in the formal conditions of communication action in such a way that the interrelation of the objective, social, and subjective worlds get prejudged in a typical fashion. (Habermas, 1987, p. 187)

This structural analysis is most meaningful if it does not abandon, but instead radicalizes, the understanding participants have of their own actions. "[W]hen pursuing forms of analysis that extend beyond the cultural horizons of the group you study, do so in a way that incorporates your [participants'] own insights and terminology." (Carspecken, 1996, p. 189)

Reflections

Critical researchers are "concerned about social inequalities, and we direct our work toward position social change" (Carspecken, 1996, p. 3). I care about conducting research that contributes to leaving the world better off. This requires careful attention to the lived experiences of those who willingly engage with us in inquiry (Korth, 2005). It requires democratizing the research process as much as possible, for as Carspecken (1996) put it, research "rarely has purely neutral effects with respect to human welfare. Making your research as democratic as possible, from start to finish, is the best way to help rather than harm" (p. 207). It also requires that the researcher reflect on her own positionality, experiences, and claims to truth (Korth, 2005).

In our modern sciencing, even our social sciencing, the "objective observer" has been the privileged, admired, idealized research. This object research is separate—distinct—from the objects of research. Post-enlightenment theories have variously challenged this modernist view (Carspecken, 2003). There has been sufficient challenge to the idea of the neutral observer who has no stake in the research. Critical research is expressly part of this challenge. As a critical ethnographer, my research is fundamentally oriented toward reaching an understanding with participants. This was even more keenly salient in the present study because the participants were my friends and colleagues.

I had individual relationships with each of the participants with varying degrees of intimacy. I was compatible with the group on issues of professional ethics, treatment of others, and politics. Moreover, I understood a lot of the background context with respect to the groups' interactive history and individual experiences. I was an outsider to the group in the sense that my wit and cynicism were no match for the others. I was not as well read as Jim, Helen, Peter, or Grant. I was the only member of the group who did not drink alcohol or eat meat.

I sought to democratize the research process by interviewing participants multiple times, by providing the participants with copies of transcripts and papers so that they could comment on what I was writing and contribute to it. I dialogued regularly with my friends about my interpretations and I remained open to their correctives.

There is no doubt that this study was simultaneously about others and about me—as friend and researcher.

> He [the social scientist] must already belong in a certain way to the lifeworld whose elements he wishes to describe. In order to describe them, he must understand them; in order to understand them, he must be able in principle to participate in their production; and participation presupposes that one belongs."
> (Habermas, 1984, p. 108)

This participation should not be through strategic aims, but rather as a communicative equal, open to what others believe, hope, intend, comprehend, know, and care about. "You [the qualitative researcher] sense a place for your self in the meaningful acts of other people that might threaten the habitual ways in which you construct your self" (Carspecken, 1996, p. 170). As I described the structures at work through the caring, I was describing this with respect to my own interactions with my own group of friends. I was co-producer. I must also turn this critical, reflective analysis toward my own engagements.

References

Carspecken, P. (1996). *Critical ethnography in education research. A theoretical and practical guide*. New York & London: Routledge.

Carspecken, P. (2003). Ocularcentrism, phonocentrism and the counter-enlightenment problematic: Clarifying contest terrain in our schools of education. *Teachers College Record, 105*(6), 978–1047.

Clement, G. (1996). *Care, autonomy, and justice: Feminism and the ethic of care*. Boulder, CO: Westview.

Eaker-Rich, D., & van Galen, J. (Eds.). (1996). *Caring in an unjust world: Negotiating borders and barriers in schools.* Albany: State University of New York Press.

Freire, P. (1974). *Pedagogy of the oppressed.* New York: Seabury Press.

Giddens, A. (1979/1990). *Central problems in social theory: Action, structure and contradiction in social analysis.* Berkeley & Los Angeles: University of California Press.

Goodman, J. (2008). Responding to children's needs: Amplifying the caring ethic. *Journal of the Philosophy of Education, 42*(2), 233–248.

Habermas, J. (1984). *The theory of communicative action.* Vol. 1: *Reason and the Rational-ization of Society.* Boston: Beacon.

Habermas, J. (1987). *The theory of communicative action.* Vol. 2: *Lifeworld and System: A Critique of Functionalist Reason.* Boston: Beacon.

Hoagland, S. (1990). Some concerns about Nel Noddings' caring. *Hypatia, 5*(1), 109–114.

Jaggar, A. (1995). Caring as a feminist practice of moral reason. In Virgina Held (Ed.), *Justice and care.* Boulder, CO: Westview.

Korth, B. (1998). *A reformulation of care as a pragmatic concept a qualitative study of an adult friendship group.* (Unpublished Ph.D. dissertation). University of Houston.

Korth, B. (1999). Ungendering the care/justice dichotomy: A critical reconstruction of naturalistically occurring acts of care and its relevance to feminist and methodological theory. Presented at the Journal for Curriculum Theorizing National Conference, Bergamo Conference Center, Dayton, Ohio, October 27–31, 1999.

Korth, B. (2001). The critical potential of care for locating inequalities and distortions in classroom culture: An example. Presented at the American Educational Research Association's National Conference. Seattle, WA, April 10–14, 2001.

Korth, B. (2003). A critical reconstruction of care-in action: A contribution to care theory and research. *The Qualitative Report, 8*(3), 487–512.

Korth, B. (2005). Choice, necessity, or narcissism: A feminist does feminist ethnography. In G. Troman, B. Jeffrey, & G. Walford (Eds.), *Methodological issues and practices in ethnography: Studies in educational ethnography.* Vol. 11. Oxford & London: Elsevier Ltd., 131–167.

Lévi-Strauss, C. (1967). *Structural anthropology.* (C. Jacobson & B. Schoepf, Trans.) Garden City, NY: Anchor Books.

Luthrell, W. (1996). Taking care of literacy: One feminist's critique. *Educational Policy, 10*(3), 342–365.

Marx, K. (1973). *On society and social change.* (N. Smelser, Ed.) Chicago: University of Chicago Press.

McLaren, P. (1986). *Schooling as ritual performance: Towards a political economy of educational symbols and hestures.* London: Routledge & Kegan Paul.

Noddings, N. (1984). *A feminine approach to ethics and moral education.* New York: Teachers College Press.

Saussure, F. (1960). *Course in general linguistics.* London: Peter Owen.

Schutz, A. (1998). Caring in schools is not enough: Community, narrative, and the limits of alterity. *Educational Theory, 48*(3), 373–393.

Tronto, J. (1987). Beyond the gender difference to a theory of care. *Signs: Journal of Women in Culture and Society, 12*(4), 644–663.

Tronto, J. (1994). *Moral boundaries: A political argument for an ethic of care.* New York & London: Routledge.

Valenzuela, A. (1999). *Subtractive schooling: U.S. Mexican youth and the politics of caring.* Albany: State University of New York Press.

Willis, P. (1977). *Learning to labour: How working-class kids get working-class jobs.* London: Gower.

The Critical Engagement of Qualitative Inquiry in the Social World

CHAPTER TWENTY-ONE

The Impact of Qualitative Research on the Lives of Child Participants

Possibilities and Challenges

ALBA LUCY GUERRERO & MARY E. BRENNER

There is an increasing interest in involving children in qualitative research that has been influenced by the recognition within the social sciences of children as active agents rather than as the objects of research (Christensen & James, 2008). As a consequence, there has also been a new interest in discussing the methodological and ethical implications of conducting research with children. Drawing on two qualitative studies with children in different contexts, we will focus on exploring the impact of qualitative research in the lives of children we research. Qualitative research is concerned with meanings constructed by people about events or people in social situations. Given that qualitative social research, particularly critical versions, is often done with marginalized and vulnerable populations, we need to consider the impact of the research process on our participants. This consideration goes beyond the individual informant's state of mind. Our research roles as both interviewers and participant observers can change the events and social contexts for those whose meaning we seek to understand.

The discussion presented in this chapter will show the lessons learned from two ethnographic research projects with nonformal education programs. Shooting Cameras for Peace (SCP) works with internally displaced children in Colombia. By focusing on the use of photography and narrative as identity artifacts of displaced children, the case study of SCP will discuss what it means methodologically, in theory and in practice, to conduct research that helps to transform complex feelings, experiences, and concerns into texts that make visible a sociopolitical situation while empowering research participants. Club Proteo is the subject of the other case study. This study involves describing a program in a low-income neighborhood in Southern California and examines how the use of educational technology and multimedia writing projects served elementary school children within organizational constraints and sometimes conflicting goals of the children and the other institutions that serve children. Both of these programs are affiliated with similar programs at other sites. Examples from these other sites will also be used to highlight some of the dilemmas that can confront researchers who are concerned with the potential impact of research on their research participants.

We are concerned with research as service that should bring benefits to its participants as well as to the researcher and society at large. From the point of view of the research establishment, research is intended to create new knowledge that contributes to the field by deepening understanding of the human condition and testing theories that have been incrementally developed by communities of researchers over time. The process of knowledge production is carefully monitored by a process of peer review for research publications and conference presentations, or in the case of graduate students, by faculty mentors who oversee a research project. Within this framework, the interests of the research participants are protected by Institutional Review Boards (IRBs) through the human subjects review process. Researchers are required to explain the risks to participants as well as the anticipated benefits of a research project. As long as major risks are ameliorated or agreed to freely by participants and the project has an anticipated benefit that outweighs relatively minor risks, researchers are given permission to conduct the research. The rights of the participants are presumably protected through informed consent, voluntary participation in the research project, and judicious handling of data to safeguard confidentiality. This process has been critiqued by a number of people because it seems to protect the researcher or the researcher's organization as much as the research participants themselves (Lassiter, 2005). Within this framework, the benefits of the research do not need to apply to the research participants themselves. In addition, dilemmas often arise that require researchers to make ethical decisions about the impact of the research on the participants that fall outside of the rather narrow parameters of the IRB approval process

In contrast to this traditional framework, our epistemological position draws from non-positivist qualitative research paradigms (critical theory and postmodern approaches) that consider research as a mutual interactive process of coming to know between researcher and participants. These theories are concerned with social inequality and issues of power (Carspecken, 1996). Our choices of research sites and research topics are influenced by our concerns with inequities and our recognition that research is both a social and personal activity. We acknowledge that a researcher's presence in a research context has implications and consequences for what is produced there (Emerson, Fretz, & Shaw, 1995). Even when researchers are not concerned with the impact of their research practice while doing it, their influence is always present. Therefore, researchers would be amiss if they failed to reflect on the ways the development and production of knowledge takes place. This chapter examines the role of research "subjects" involved in the process and the change for children, for communities, as well as for researchers. Cameron, Frazer, Harvey, Rampton and Richardson (1993) suggest that researchers need to shift the concept of "informants" from "research objects" to "co-participants." Similarly, Lassiter (2005) indicates the importance for ethnographers to see the people with whom research is done as consultants or even collaborators. While all these considerations apply in doing research with participants of any age, some play out differently when the participants are children. Questions regarding the impact of research on children participants will be carefully considered.

In this chapter, we begin by describing three main issues that arose while conducting our research that impacted the benefits of our research for the child participants. We then provide a brief description of each research project and the contexts in which they took place. Finally, we discuss how each issue became manifest within our research. We do not always provide a tidy solution to the dilemmas that arose, but reflect on the situations and the implications of the researcher's actions when doing research that serve and have the potential to change the community.

Issues in Doing Research with Children

In reflecting upon the impact of our research, we focused upon a number of issues that affected whether our research has had a beneficial impact on the children participants. The first of these issues, and the most encompassing, was that of power and empowerment. Even when researchers are concerned with the ethical implications of their practices and carefully reflect on their role, there is a potentially asymmetrical relationship between researchers and informants leaning toward the side of the researcher (Glesne & Peshkin, 1992). In contemporary contexts, this is of course compounded by the seemingly natural inequity in the relationship of adults with children. Thus, one of the magnified challenges of working with children is to break down the power imbalance between the adult researcher and the children (O'Kane, 2008) in order to create conditions that enable children to speak up. O'Kane suggests that in a context in which children's voices have been marginalized, researchers have to carefully find ways to understand children's experiences. Cameron et al. (1993) have argued that the use of interactive and non-objectifying methods make it possible to obtain a deeper understanding on the informant's experiences while creating opportunities for participants to engage in dialogue with their understandings of their own worlds. In this way, research participants have more control over both how they become represented in the texts created by researchers as well as the research process itself. Our use of critical theory has made us aware of the inequities experienced by our child informants and concerned about our role in ameliorating or reducing inequities.

A second issue that we considered is what roles the researcher takes on while conducting research. Cameron et al. (1993) note that the interactive aspects of qualitative research enable researchers to do empowering research, in part because it is natural for researchers to assume a variety of roles as do all people during social interaction. The authors challenge the assumption that the researcher holds absolute power over the powerless research participants. Dealing with power in research situations is complex because of the dynamics of local contexts and the fact that "the positions of all involved in fieldwork are shifting and variable rather than static" (p. 90). There are additional considerations when working with children. Fine and Sandstrom (1988) describe the roles that researchers can take with children along two dimensions—an emotional dimension relating to the degree of positive contact, and a dimension of authority in terms of how much direct control the adult can assert over the children. They assert that the ideal role is that of friend in which there is trust and positive affect but little explicit authority. However, the ability of adult researchers to act as friends is mitigated by the impossibility of an adult being a true peer and the need for researchers to assume adult responsibility at times with children.

The third issue we address is who actually benefits when doing research with children, particularly within organizational contexts such as those where we conducted our research. Lassiter's (2005) guide to collaborative ethnography defines some key aspects of collaboration. Of particular relevance to this chapter is his suggestion that research projects can arise from the concerns of the community instead of solely from the interests of the researcher. Similarly,

Cameron et al. (1993) suggest that empowering research participants necessitates a willingness to negotiate the purposes of a research project and to take on the agenda, at times, of the research participants themselves. But these authors also describe a variety of situations in which it is difficult to define who actually constitutes the "community" or in which there is dissension among individuals who might consider themselves part of the same community. In our case studies, we describe several dilemmas we faced when working with children. The definition of benefits to the children might differ between the adults within an organization and the children themselves. Additionally, at times the benefits to the organization itself might be in conflict with what the children want or need, as well as with what the researcher can provide.

Our studies are similar in that we chose to work with organizations that serve low-income children in neighborhoods that have few other options for out-of-school activities. However, they differ in critical ways in terms of the relation of the researchers to their research sites. The first author, Alba Lucy Guerrero, is a native of Colombia, but an outsider to both the neighborhood and the Shooting Cameras for Peace program. She had the opportunity to attend the program daily for several months, thus getting to know the children and the directors of the program in a very personal way. Mary E. Brenner, the second author, is one of the people responsible for running Club Proteo (along with her colleague Dr. Richard Duràn), although undergraduate and graduate student assistants did the day-to-day work and most of the data collection.

Case Study 1: Shooting Cameras for Peace

This study was conducted in a nonformal educational program, Disparando Cámaras para la Paz (DCP): Shooting Cameras for Peace (SCP), located in Colombia, specifically in Bogotá's outskirts, Altos de Cazucá. The program was a participatory photography project that provided vocational education to internally displaced children. The project started in 2002 as a personal initiative of an American documentary photographer who organized a photo workshop with 30 children who had been displaced from different areas in Colombia. His goal was to teach children how to document their lives with cameras. Since the beginning, SCP has had a close relationship with the international initiative AJA project located in San Diego, California. Initially, SCP was affiliated with the AJA Project whose mission was to provide "photography-based educational programming to youth affected by war and displacement; students think critically about their identities, develop leadership skills, and become agents of personal and social transformation" (AJA Project, December 2011.). The AJA Project supported two afterschool programs in San Diego and one in a refugee camp on the Thailand/Burma border. Although SCP had total autonomy and was administratively independent from the AJA project, the programs maintained a close relationship by fostering exchanges between children and staff involved in all the international locations.

At the time this research was conducted, there were approximately 60 children participating in the four levels offered by SCP. Participants were 9- to 16-year-olds and came from diverse areas of Colombia. The program was directed by a group of Colombian educators and photographers. The aim of the program was to provide a space for displaced children to reflect on their lives and changing culture, using photography as a means. The premise of the project was that spaces for meeting and artistic expression created opportunities for children to construct a positive future and creative life projects (Disparando Cámaras Para la Paz, 2003).

The classes were from Monday to Sunday, morning and afternoon, with the exception of Wednesday morning when the organization staff had their weekly meetings.

The curriculum of the program included four levels. In the first level, children were introduced to basic concepts of photography and built their own pin-hole cameras with materials on hand. During the second level, children learned photographic techniques and started taking and developing pictures. During the third level, children were taught about video, and focused on children's rights. The fourth level taught further photography techniques but focused on developing students' skills to become teaching assistants of preceding levels. Many of the students who began when the project first opened were still involved and had become "assistants" in the process of teaching photography to newcomers. An additional component of the program was the Project to Exchange Experiences between refugee and displaced youth participating in the programs of Thailand, the United States, and Colombia, in which children from the three locations were paired up to share letters and photographs.

The SCP photo workshops took place in a small house located in the midst of Altos de Cazucá, an impoverished area located in the outskirts of Bogotá. The area hosted approximately 20,000 internally displaced persons who lacked adequate protection and assistance from the national government (Norwegian Refugee Council, 2005). The neighborhood had a particular social and urban structure, which is common for neighborhoods on the periphery of Bogotá: a high-density population and a poor infrastructure (dusty roads; small houses made of brick, plastic, metal, and cardboard); lack of basic social services; and lack of parks and leisure facilities. Aside from inadequate living standards, the children and youth of Cazucá were threatened by being forcibly drafted into armed military groups, as well as murder by death squads that targeted young men and boys.

For internally displaced people from rural areas coming to the cities, a major problem is creating a new means of livelihood, especially for unskilled agricultural workers (Norwegian Refugee Council, 2005). With an unemployment rate over 50 percent, the informal economy of recycling materials, street vending, and domestic service have become the main alternatives for these neighborhood residents. Many of the children helped their families either by working on the streets or taking care of the house duties and younger siblings. The children's families were large and they shared minimal space. Just a few houses had regular building materials while the rest were made of recycled construction material.

Methods Used in Altos de Cazuca

Shooting Cameras for Peace gave cameras to displaced children for them to represent their lives from their perspective. During fieldwork, children were interviewed and asked to talk about their photos. Twenty-five in-depth interviews and four focus groups were conducted with children of different ages and from different times of involvement within SCP. The participants included children who came from different regions of Colombia. To elicit the narratives, Guerrero employed life-story interview techniques through open-ended questions, and used "photo-elicitation" strategies (Clark, 1999; Rich & Chalfen, 1999; Harper, 2002) to allow children to tell their own stories in a recursive way. The interviews focused on children's experiences in SCP, in the places they lived before, and the area where they live now, Altos de Cazucá. We asked questions about people and places that were important for them and also about their vision of the Colombian conflict and about how they envisioned their future. The interviews were conducted in different locations: the darkroom, the main classroom, a small porch in front of the house or in the playground, depending on the activities scheduled for the day. The interviews were conducted in Spanish and audiotaped for the subsequent analysis.

Case Study 2: Club Proteo

Club Proteo is ongoing, as an afterschool program that takes place at a Boys and Girls Club in a working-class neighborhood in Goleta, California, attracting 5- to 12-year-old children. The program is part of a larger collaborative called the Fifth Dimension that had the goal of establishing afterschool programs as research sites to explore alternative means of raising children's school achievement while incorporating emerging computer technologies (Cole & the Distributed Literacy Consortium, 2006). From its inception in 1994, the goal of Club Proteo was to make technology more accessible to the children of the local Latino neighborhood by incorporating bilingual literacy practices and family involvement through parent meetings and special events such as talent shows (Brown, Brenner, Duran, McNamee & Woodbridge, 2006). In addition, Club Proteo stressed exploration of community sites such as radio stations, businesses, and the nearby university through field trips and games such as scavenger hunts in the immediate neighborhood of the Boys and Girls Club. Although the goal was to support school achievement, the researchers purposefully set out to create a learning environment that was clearly different from school in that children had choices about what they wanted to learn and could incorporate their own interests into their activities.

Club Proteo initially began on two afternoons a week in the library of the Boys and Girls Club with computers donated by the researchers. Over time, the Boys and Girls Club expanded to include a dedicated computer lab and Club Proteo expanded to take place three afternoons a week. During Club Proteo time, the children were only allowed to use the computers for selected educational games, for writing projects, or other special activities planned by the researchers or the undergraduates who mentored the children as part of a practicum course at the university. In addition to using the computers, the children played board games with the undergraduates or sometimes did drawing or craft activities. Children were encouraged to try new games and activities through the metaphor of undertaking a journey of transformation.

In the prototype Fifth Dimension environment, which guided Club Proteo at its inception, there was a make-believe world created in the form of a maze of rooms. Each room had a choice of activities that children could master to move into another room with new choices. Each child had a toy animal that would move from room to room to mark his or her progress. The children followed the directions on "task cards" that detailed what they needed to do to become an expert at the game activities in each room. Over the years of Club Proteo, the maze transformed gradually. For a while each room represented a site in the community, many corresponding to the field trips taken by club members. After a few years, the maze was replaced by other metaphors for transformation. For instance, last year the new children in the club began as novice space cadets and as they gained expertise, they transformed into various types of space travelers to ultimately become expert astronauts. Writing has always been a part of the Club Proteo culture, although the focus of that writing has varied over the years. Like other Fifth Dimension sites, Club Proteo had an electronic figurehead/mascot whose name was Proteo. The children were encouraged to write to Proteo and received responses back either via email or printed letters. In some years, the children had pen pals at other Fifth Dimension sites in either California or Germany. Most recently over the past three years "distributed story writing" had been the focal activity for Club Proteo. In this activity, known as "traveling stories" to the children, a child would write a "chapter" to begin a story followed by a couple of questions about what was written. At this point, the original author or another child could add a second chapter. Some beginning chapters spawned three or four different stories by multiple authors. When story writing began, most stories were written and illustrated by hand. But over time, story writing had become a multimedia production as children learned to use the computers to produce PowerPoint texts, to search the internet for illustrations, to add sound effects and even basic animation to their creations. The title page for each story was posted on the wall of the computer lab. Each quarter there was a story festival in which selected children read and displayed their stories to the other children in Club Proteo, other members of the Boys and Girls Club, and sometimes the parents.

At the beginning, Club Proteo was designed to draw in the Mexicano children who lived in the immediate vicinity of the Boys and Girls Club, a low-income, high-density mixed residential and commercial area. There were no schools in the neighborhood and the children were bussed to several different schools. Flyers were distributed at their schools and in the housing projects near the Boys and Girls Club. Parents meetings were held bilingually but Spanish was typically the dominant language of the families that attended. In the early days, 20 to 30 children participated in Club Proteo on a regular basis, primarily from the two schools that served the neighborhood. As the Boys and Girls Club increased its investment in technology and was eventually remodeled to have a dedicated computer lab with 30 computers, the number and diversity of children who participated grew. At the time of this writing, Club Proteo served two distinct groups of children. The original targeted group was informally referred to as drop-in children. Their families paid a very small annual membership fee, and the children were allowed to come and use the many facilities of the Boys and Girls Club including the craft room, computer lab, game room, and homework help whenever the Club was open. The other children, referred to as daycare children, were enrolled in a more formal afterschool program for which their parents paid a monthly fee that included transportation from school to the Boys and Girls Club. These children had scheduled activities, including specific times they could come to the computer lab to participate in Club Proteo. Because of the monthly fees, these children tended to be from middle-class families. Over the course of a recent academic year, about 160 different children participated in Club Proteo from approximately 20 different schools.

Methods Used at Club Proteo

Daily events were documented at Club Proteo by undergraduates who wrote weekly field notes as part of their practicum course requirements. In addition, some undergraduates continued with Club Proteo through independent study courses and took on more responsibility for collecting specific kinds of data such as observational ratings of children's technology skills and demographic information. Over the years, there have been a number of more focused research projects at Club Proteo that have examined topics such as the development of writing skills in Spanish and English; the effect of Club Proteo participation upon gendered attitudes towards technology; the development of multimedia writing; mathematical learning; and incorporating science into Club Proteo through field trips and internet research. In addition to field notes, these projects have used focus-group interviews, analysis of children's written products, special tests, and focused observation.

Issue 1: Power and Empowerment

Shooting Cameras for Peace

Cameron et al. (1993) distinguish three components of empowering research: the use of interactive methods, the recognition of participants' agendas, and the sharing of expert knowledge. In the SCP research project, the use of narrative inquiry and children's photographs proved to be interactive tools that helped children to tell their stories while enabling them to create new understandings of their experiences. The photographs and written narratives were produced at the SCP workshops while the spoken narratives were produced in the context of the research interviews. The children's photographs provided clues to their concerns and identities. The themes covered in the photographs included: memory, future, family, fear, places, and self-portraits, among others. Both the photographs and the written narratives offered the possibility of perceiving the world from the viewpoint of the children. The photographs depicted children's loved ones, the streets they inhabit, their houses, their kitchens, their friends and also the disturbing presence of violence in their lives. In the next two photo-narratives, Rodrigo and Rosa portrayed in a personal way different fragments of their own reality. While Rodrigo captured an intimate moment in which his parents were kissing after reconciliation, Rosa composed a photograph of a boy playing dead to talk about the danger and violence of the area where she lived.

Figure 1. Photo-narrative by Rodrigo, 10-year-old.
Here my parents were fighting…because my dad had money and didn't tell my mom and spent it; they are not fighting any more.

Photography was a helpful tool for children to interpret their world and to express their concerns. Kids used the camera to communicate their likes and dislikes, to feature people, places, and things that matter to them in ways we as researchers otherwise might be unaware. While asking children to talk about their photographs benefited the children as they developed new understandings of their situation, it also benefited us as researchers by improving our sense of what was meaningful to them. To engage children in a dialogue about their photo-narratives, it was important to develop a trusting relationship with them. Guerrero spent approximately a month in the field attending the program on a daily basis before starting the interviews. By the time the consent forms for the interviews were collected, most children had already met and talked with the researcher. Developing a rapport with children was also facilitated by the fact that Guerrero was identified with the SCP teachers with whom they had already established a close relationship.

Figure 2. Photo-narrative by Rosa, 11-year-old.
In Pines they've killed lots of people, they've raped girls. For example last year they tortured a man, they cut him in half and left him naked. They've found girls dead there. Sometimes they rape girls and kill them afterwards and leave them there until they are found. That's why I took this photo.

The photos were a starting point in learning what was important to the children. Using the photos children had taken in the workshops, the researcher asked them to give a "guided tour" through their photos. The use of children's photo-narratives and photo-elicitation strategies helped children to feel comfortable during the interview. Since the work children did in SCP allowed them to vent their feeling, the researcher's inquiry was not disruptive; instead, it became an addition to this process of making sense of their past and present experiences. Children's written and spoken narratives provided another layer of insight into their shared values, beliefs, and knowledge about the world and their place in it. Seeing the photo-narratives created and asking questions about them allowed the researchers to enter children's worlds in new ways.

Glesne and Peshkin (1992) suggest that by listening, researchers provide a space for interviewees to reflect on their experiences and that interviewing is particularly suited for participants' self-exploration. While this applies with research participants of any age, the use of photographs and written narratives in interviewing children facilitated the reconstruction of the meanings of their personal and social experiences. Furthermore, children constructed new meanings not just about their previous experiences, but also about their role as social actors.

The images and stories created at SCP were powerful tools for educating the local, national, and international community about the experiences of displaced children. The photo-narratives created at SCP gave a visual voice to the suffering, struggles, and achievements of these children who seldom would be heard in other ways. The project, and particularly the images and narratives, gave children agency in their personal construction of self but also gave them an active role in the process of educating society about the consequences of conflict for the civilian population. During the research process, children spoke not only of the intimacies of their lives and the cultural context of their experiences, but they also gave a twist to the views of the conflict by placing themselves as subjects involved in the dynamics of awareness about the consequences of war in the civil population. In the following quote, Lina reflected on the importance of exhibiting children's work

> Thanks to the exhibition people are aware that not all people around here are the same, and that we had to experience the war but that does not make us bad people. In addition, photographs permit people to know how we live, where we live, how we behave and I also like that they can meet my family. Also, the fact that people read what I write makes me feel very good because it is like an outlet.

In the excerpt above, Lina discussed the worth she found in the public exhibition of children's work. She valued it as a way to have a voice, to eradicate stereotypes, and educate people about the reality of her community. On the other side, she prized the fact that she can express her own feelings. Especially striking is the confidence with which the children spoke about their photos, their assured tone of expertise, and their visible pleasure at being listened to. While the images reflected the severity and nature of the places where they resided, the narrative inquiry revealed how children transformed meanings to create distinctive images of themselves and their surroundings. Children's photo-narratives were not merely illustrative; they challenged the common depiction of displaced children as victims, locating them as subjects involved in the dynamics of awareness about the impact of war, urban violence, and poverty on civilians (Guerrero & Tinkler, 2010). The images and stories of SCP were personal, but talking about them gave children tools to reflect on their roles as agents of change within their communities. The visual material and the context of the research brought up the fact that their work at SCP reached beyond personal benefit to include their being active members in a society and the speakers for a community.

The research process using children's photos and narratives shifted from the frequent assumption that displaced children are passive and vulnerable victims, to recognizing them as agents in their own right. Photography emerged as an ideal strategy for breaking the silence and including children's voices and visions. The kind of photo-narratives children created at SCP allowed teachers, researchers, and other audiences to learn a great deal about children's perspectives while helping them to develop critical and interpretive skills about their circumstances.

Photography served as a useful tool for accessing children's "voices." Photo-narrative also gave an opportunity for children to challenge many of the negative stereotypes about their displacement conditions and the places where they live (Guerrero & Tinkler, 2010). Displaced children often have been portrayed in the media as either victims or villains. This project enabled kids to look back, confront, and create new images that portrayed the complexity of their lives. Photography was a prompt for dialogue among children about the gap between how they see themselves, how they think they are seen by others, and whom they wish to become. Images have the potential of establishing bonding, political awareness, and meaningful collective knowledge production among all participants involved in a research process (Pedersen, 2008). By changing their own images and challenging dominant discourses on their condition, children were creating opportunities for personal and community change.

Narratives have long been a tool to explore lived experience. The use of narrative in qualitative research is complex, but at the same time opens up new possibilities. Women in Croatia talked about how their experiences became a way to heal their suffering (Mimica, 1997). Similarly, Narrative Exposure Therapy (NET), a therapy program for treatment of child survivors of war and torture in Somalia, claimed that children reconstructing their own biographies would help to reduce post-traumatic stress symptoms (Euwema, De Graaff, De Jager, & Kalksma-Van Lith, 2008). In SCP, we witnessed the construction of narratives children created about their photographs, we asked the meanings about others they had previously done, and we constructed our own interpretations based on the ongoing dialogue we established with the children. Although the photographs were part of their photography workshops, the narrative inquiry provided a space for critical reflection on the circumstances of their lives and their own experiences. The research facilitated a process of moving from naive to critical consciousness (Freire, 1972).

The use of photography and narrative proved to be an effective tool to help underprivileged children break the silence concerning their experiences of displacement, and to engage them in a process of self-discovery and transformation that empowered them to become change agents within their families and communities. Displaced children's narratives also allowed outsiders to become aware of their ignored histories. Images and narratives, like projections of self, are highly relational constructions that expand the learning horizon of all participants including the researcher. The research provided the opportunity for constructing new insights and understandings for researchers and participants involved in the process. Photography and narrative as research tools promoted dialogue that exposed issues of injustice, inequality, and exploitation and that may eventually create social change.

Club Proteo

Although the children at Club Proteo also created narratives, their stories did not tap into their personal stories, and, thus did not directly give them a means to reflect on the meaning of their own circumstances and lives. An inherent part of the Club Proteo philosophy was to give children many choices of activities and topics. The undergraduate helpers and the site coordinator were there to support children in achieving their goals, whatever they might be. The Fifth Dimension prototype that was first employed at Club Proteo (Cole & the Distributed

Literacy Consortium, 2006) used two methods to direct children's activities more productively. The first was the use of the maze in which children would progress from room to room by achieving levels of expertise outlined in task cards. The second was through the influence of the club's mystical entity, Proteo (named after the Greek mythological figure Proteus who could change shape).

Although Brenner and the other researchers tried to use both of these to encourage children to write in accord with the goal of developing literacy skills, the children at the site were not motivated to do much writing through these mechanisms. Proteo's questions in his/her communications contained many probes about children's lives and families, but even the most frequent writers seldom went into much depth about their feelings or the difficult circumstances they might be facing at home. Because the program honored the children's right to make choices, the maze and the letters from Proteo have been de-emphasized in the club.

For many children, the attraction of Club Proteo came from learning to use technology in new ways or the opportunity to socially interact with peers and the UCSB undergraduates. The "traveling stories" satisfied the children's needs because they learned to integrate pictures, sound, and animation into PowerPoint presentations of their stories, often with the support of an undergraduate. As in SCP, the narratives were often stimulated by a picture, either one drawn by the child or an image found on the internet. Most frequently the stories revolved around popular culture such as superheroes, cartoon characters, or sports figures. In the past year, the children started hundreds of stories, but none of them directly dealt with the children's own lives. However, the site coordinator noted that he thought he could detect some of the stresses found in the children's homes in the types of stories they chose to write at times. Quite a few of the stories featured fighting or violence of various sorts that seemed to reflect the problems of the neighborhood, which is plagued by gang activity, drug use, and extremely crowded housing conditions. These connections were seldom written about by the undergraduates in their field notes. Unlike the intensive amount of time an ethnographer spends in interaction with the research participants, as in the case of SCP, the undergraduates came to the club once or twice a week over the course of a single academic quarter (ten weeks). Thus, they did not really have the opportunity to get to know the children or develop deep relationships. The site coordinator had such insights, but did not write weekly field notes like the undergraduates.

However, research revealed empowerment in the children's use and access to computers. Through observations of the computer room when Club Proteo was in session and when it was not, as well as focus groups with the children, Tinkler (2003) found that Club Proteo increased girls' usage of the computers and Club Proteo was their main place for getting access to technology. This finding was not a total surprise since during times when Club Proteo was not in session, the computers were dominated by boys playing competitive and frequently violent video games. Unlike what had been documented in the literature, both boys and girls saw themselves as having expertise in technology and computers were equally likely to be used by males and females during Club Proteo. Club Proteo supported children in learning a larger range of computer skills and the social environment was less male oriented both in terms of the allowed games (violent games were banned) and the large number of female undergraduates. Less expected was the observation that during times when Club Proteo was not in session, the middle-class Anglo boys managed to get an inordinate amount of time on the computers, particularly the most powerful computers. They figured out how to manipulate the sign-up sheet and used social pressure to force the other children into giving them preference for the best computers. The different social structure established during Club Proteo hours enabled both girls and lower-income Mexicano children to gain more equitable access to the computers.

In both cases, SCP and Club Proteo used interactive and nonobjectifying methods: photography and narrative at SCP, and the use of computers at Club Proteo. These methods created new opportunities for children to reflect on their understandings of their own worlds while simultaneously providing researchers new opportunities to understand children's interpretations of their experiences. The use of the research techniques also facilitated the formation of relationships in which children felt they could participate and express their own views and communicate their concerns.

Issue 2: Roles and Responsibilities of Researchers/Collaboration

Shooting Cameras for Peace

Researchers play different roles at different times (Cameron et al., 1993). Since qualitative research implies participation in the life of the community, it is common to face situations that researchers cannot predict or control. Guerrero became a regular participant in everyday and special activities at SCP. As she became more involved in the community, she found herself confronting uneasy situations she had not predicted and that created dilemmas and concerns about her role as a researcher and as an adult working with children. In areas affected by poverty, conflict, and violence like Altos de Cazuca, researchers might struggle with contextual constraints. In the next examples, Guerrero reflects on her experiences with practical and ethical difficulties in terms of dealing with situations in which she felt she needed to intervene, but found herself limited by contextual elements.

Fights related to romantic relationships were particularly frequent for youth in SCP. In one of the researcher's visits to the project, there was an incident in which Mireya, a 13-year-old girl, was hit and threatened with stabbing on her way to the project site. According to the children who witnessed the incident, it happened because the current girlfriend of Mireya's ex-boyfriend was jealous. All children agreed that Mireya should be careful because that girl would definitely attack her on her way home. The fight occurred just one block from the SCP workshop. When Mireya got to the workshop, she was scared and crying. At that moment, the researcher was the only adult person available to talk with her. The researcher tried to calm her down, assisted by Mireya's cousins, two girls of the same age who had witnessed the event. The two girls kept saying that something was going to happen for sure after the workshop. Guerrero felt powerless in her efforts to help Mireya, because she knew that it would not be possible to do anything that might guarantee Mireya's safety. The SCP teacher arrived and concluded that we would not be able to do anything directly. It did not make sense to walk Mireya to her house in a neighborhood in which we did not belong, in the context of high levels of crime and the presence of armed people. The SCP teacher and Guerrero suggested to the children and one community leader who lived close to Mireya's house that they walk with her on her way home in an effort to ensure her safety. We later learned that Mireya arrived home safely, but she did not come back to photography classes for the remaining two weeks that Guerrero was in attendance at the SCP workshops.

As an adult, Guerrero felt compelled to intervene, but the contextual elements of the situation limited her power for dealing with the situation. The circumstance positioned the researcher as an outsider, as an adult who did not have the power other adults might have in the community. The researcher experienced the failure of being unable to protect children from violence and hardship, which raised concern about fulfilling ethical responsibilities toward children. While solving the individual problems of research participants exceeds the aim of social research, these situations illustrate the unanticipated challenges a researcher can experience in terms of defining her role and responsibilities in fieldwork.

The everyday contact in the SCP workshops allowed the researcher to develop close relationships that encompassed, but also reached beyond the children to involve different members of the community including their families. The living conditions in Altos de Cazuca were very poor and unhealthy. With an unemployment rate over 50 percent, the informal economy of recycling materials, street vending, and domestic service were the main alternatives for these neighborhood residents. During a conversation with a mother about her employment possibilities, the mother commented that she would like to become a security guard, but she related she had not been able to save the money required to pay for the training classes (about US $35). She explained how beneficial it would be for her family's wellbeing of she could work as a security guard. She had worked for six months as a domestic servant and had been able to save about twenty dollars. Unfortunately, she lost her job and had to "put her dreams aside" because without a job, she was going to end up spending her savings. She just needed $15 more to be able to pay the training fees. The researcher contemplated the possibility of helping her financially, but the organization clearly restricted offering financial assistance because of problems that had arisen with the community in the past. Guerrero developed a close relationship with this mother, who volunteered to work in the workshops cooking for the children. The mother was always willing to collaborate in the SCP activities and Guerrero felt discomfort knowing that she could help this person with the money, but needed to respect the organization's policy. When working with poor populations, these are common situations that raise ethical dilemmas about the researcher's actions.

Club Proteo

The theoretical roots of Fifth Dimension clubs, and thus Club Proteo as well, are the sociocultural theories of learning that are traced back to the work of Vygotsky (1978). Organizers and researchers purposefully set out to create an environment in which children were intrinsically motivated to participate in a learning community. The undergraduates and the children were expected to play together as peers, although of varying capabilities depending upon the task. In terms of academic skills and problem-solving ability, the undergraduates were able to help the children with writing and certain tasks in the educational computer games. But the children were the experts in the ongoing activities of Club Proteo, because many of them attended for the whole year or longer, while most undergraduates participated in the Club for just eight or nine weeks. In addition, the children were more likely to know the rules for the computer games as well as the idiosyncratic quirks of the somewhat outdated computers. The peer status of the undergraduates was stressed through their designation as "buddies" rather than as tutors or mentors.

As described by Fine and Sandstrom (1988), the role of friend is useful in participant observation because it generates more trust and access to children's "hidden" culture (p. 17). Indeed, the undergraduates were quickly absorbed into the community each quarter and were usually engaged in activities with the children from their first day. As part of the practicum class, the undergraduates were taught to write field notes that became our major documentation of how the children were engaging in the activities and what they appeared to be learning. But this status as friend sometimes created difficulties for both the undergraduates and our research agenda. Discipline issues were rare, but sometimes arose in the form of inappropriate language, teasing between the children, or arguments about the rules of the board games. The undergraduates were often at a loss about how to deal with such issues because the children did not see them as authority figures who could stop annoying behaviors or put a halt to disputes. The undergraduates themselves felt uncomfortable in stepping out of the role as friend, particularly when their efforts were ignored by the children. In such cases the site coordinator, usually a graduate student or very experienced undergraduate, had the authority to take corrective measures. There was an ethical dimension to this situation for the undergraduates because they felt that as adults, it was their duty to intervene. This was often a topic in class discussions and in the forum on the class website.

The nature of Club Proteo made it difficult to collect other sorts of data such as measurements of individual learning, a requirement stipulated by funding agencies at times. Since the children voluntarily came to Club Proteo and were free to leave to participate in other activities at the Boys and Girls Club, the researchers were unable to mandate that children participate in any kind of testing. The children came expecting to have choices and they felt empowered enough to resist our entreaties to take a test, even if we tried to make it more play-like and nonthreatening. Although older children in other programs could understand that data collection and evaluation were important for the continuation of funding, the younger children in Club Proteo were not influenced by such programmatic needs. The research team tried using the undergraduates to collect individual data in a one-on-one situation, hoping that the children would trust their "buddies" enough to agree to participate. This did not work well at the beginning of the year because the relationships were new to both the undergraduates and the children. Some undergraduates who were more forceful in persuading the children to take a test subsequently had some problems in assuming the role of buddy/participant observer. At the end of the year, the undergraduates were more successful at encouraging the children to take some time out do an individual testing session, but the quality of the data was suspect. Often the children would do the minimum possible to satisfy their "buddy." There was also role conflict for the undergraduates because giving tests felt to them like a violation of their relationships with the children. In this instance and at many other Fifth Dimension sites (Cole & the Distributed Literacy Consortium, 2006), the interactive context was incommensurate with standardized data collection.

The examples described in the two research locations illustrate how unexpected situations in everyday interactions sometimes seem to push on our ethics as qualitative researchers. The cases also challenge the idea of the researcher holding exclusive power while illustrating the complexity of relationships researchers establish within the field. In research practice, the power distribution is affected by the institutional and social context, by the research agenda, and by the researcher's and participants' motivations.

Issue 3: Benefits for Who?

Shooting Cameras for Peace

There were a number of challenges we faced doing research to benefit children within organizational contexts. In a photography-based educational program for refugees located in San
Diego and affiliated with SCP in Colombia, Tinkler (2006) observed that there were some
instances in which the program staff changed or adapted children's photo-narratives to fit the
needs of the organization. She refers to a particular incident in which a Somali student had
taken a self-portrait covering her face with a veil. In the background of the photograph there
were chains blocking the entrance to a stairwell. The narrative that the student wrote for the
photograph was:

> My veil is my safeguard from this weird world. My veil is my key to heaven, to take the stairs, the chains
> represent the door to heaven. (Tinkler, 2006, p. 124)

However, the project staff published the photograph on their website with previous writings
the student had written in a different context in which she highlighted her difficult life experiences. The narrative read:

> Life has not been easy for me. Most people would look at me and automatically assume that I have had
> it easy. That my life has been normal. (Tinkler, 2006 p. 123)

The photograph of the girl with her face covered and the writing about her difficult life that
depicted her as an oppressed victim may have appealed to donors, but it was not an accurate
representation of the student's interpretation of the self-portrait.

Revealing displaced children's identities using visual methods in a context where threats
to their security are involved has profound ethical implications. In the SCP research project, pseudonyms for the names of all participants were used and faces in all the images were
blurred. However, responding to the organization's request, Guerrero did not change the name
of the organization (Shooting Cameras for Peace). The organization thought they could benefit from the research project when requesting financial support or as a way to publicize their
work. Guerrero's concern was that this situation could endanger the anonymity of the children
participants. Knowing the name of the organization, it would be easy to trace the research
participants. Depending on contexts and participants, there are different degrees of reciprocity
in qualitative research (Glesne & Peshkin, 1992). The organization staff was very supportive
before and during the fieldwork, giving their time, including the researcher in regular and
special activities, helping her to move around the neighborhood where she was not able to be
by herself for security reasons, and sharing their stories within the program. The researcher
reflected on her obligations with participants, and after discussing her worries with the organization staff, ended up accepting the organization's request.

Another dilemma the researcher confronted with the staff organization of SCP was their
request for an evaluation report on the organization's activities. Although the researcher clearly
explained that the study's objective was not to evaluate the program, the organization expected
to have an evaluation of their activities. When finishing the fieldwork, the organization staff
scheduled a meeting in which the researcher was supposed to share the main research findings.

The researcher explained that it was too early to make conclusions, but shared with them the type of data she had collected and explained how the data would be processed. The staff were a little disappointed that the researcher did not make specific recommendations and did not point out what they were doing right or wrong in the project. After finishing the research report, the researcher sent a summary document including the main findings to different members of the organization, but never received any feedback on this document.

Club Proteo

The intent of Brenner and her colleagues in starting Club Proteo was to set up a research site that would enable the study of learning outside the standard practices of classrooms. They believed that a fun environment with access to multiple sources of support (computers, undergraduates, engaging activities) would enable children to learn literacy, mathematical, and technology skills in different ways than through direct pedagogy. Studies at the site (e.g., Mayer, Quilici & Moreno, 1999) and at other Fifth Dimension sites (Cole & the Distributed Literacy Consortium, 2006) demonstrated that when compared to control groups, the children improved in mathematical problem-solving skills, language development, and reading. So the researchers felt secure that Club Proteo benefited the children because there was evidence that they gained academic skills relative to children who did not attend. And by choosing to attend Club Proteo, the children have indicated their interest in what is offered.

Though the researchers cannot claim that they have been able to develop a collaborative research agenda with the children, the children's participation has influenced what is done in Club Proteo, at times even resulting in a modification of the research goals. The researchers' initial interest in bilingual literacy development meant that they worked to recruit children who were already reading and who were allowed by their parents to come to Club Proteo on their own. After a couple of years, the older girls made them aware of a problem that was impacting their ability to attend Club Proteo. By fifth and sixth grade, the girls were becoming responsible for their younger siblings at the Boys and Girls Club, who were often just five or six years old. The computer games and other activities were not really appropriate for these younger children, who often felt left out or refused to enter the computer lab. On their own initiative, the girls started Club Proteo Junior, which had a much simpler maze and featured games aimed at young children. At that time, Club Proteo was running on just Tuesdays and Thursdays. The girls used Wednesday to run Club Proteo Junior. Over time, as the original girls went on to junior high school and shifted their interests to school-based activities, the researchers incorporated Wednesdays into the schedule and continued to buy software and games that were better suited to young children. In the past few years, younger children have constituted a much larger proportion of the club participants than in the past.

To date, the Boys and Girls Club has perceived benefits of Club Proteo and has reciprocated in various ways. Not only has the Boys and Girls Club given Club Proteo control over the computer room for six hours a week, they have helped in some years to pay for the site coordinator's salary and have always provided transportation for Club Proteo field trips. Administrators of the Boys and Girls Club have liked the educational focus in the computer lab and the fact that the research project brought in many undergraduate volunteers, 30 or so per academic year. Inevitably, there were limits to the Boys and Girls Club's ability to adequately provide the support that would enable Club Proteo to flourish. The computers were typically old, thus seldom able to run current software. As the economy worsened and the

Boys and Girls Club's financial base eroded, the Club had to cut back on the technical support they provided the computer lab. In the past year, almost half of the computers were removed because they were too old to fix. At most, six computers have been connected to the internet, thus limiting the children's ability to incorporate images into their stories and discouraging more children from participating in the writing activities.

Despite the effectiveness of the Fifth Dimension model instantiated in Club Proteo and many other sites, the goals of some hosting organizations have created tensions between the learning goals of the clubs and the research agendas of the university people. An early Fifth Dimension site at a library produced larger cognitive gains for the children than a very similar club in a Boys and Girls Club (Nicolopoulou & Cole, 1993). The authors attributed this difference to the varying "cultures" of the library and the Boys and Girls Club, namely that the children were more focused at the library, while at the Boys and Girls Club they shifted easily to varied activities when they became frustrated or bored. Despite the reported cognitive gains, the Fifth Dimension club at the library lasted only two years because of perceived incompatibilities with the larger mission of the library, but it endured at the Boys and Girls Club. A Fifth Dimension site at another Boys and Girls Club in Southern California ended, in part because the required research design for gathering data from a carefully controlled number of children conflicted with the Boys and Girls Club's goal of creating computer access to more children (Brown et al., 2006).

Another tension for some Fifth Dimension clubs, including Club Proteo, has been the need for evaluation. As mentioned above, it was very difficult to engage children in systematic evaluations of academic skills. The pressure for evaluation has arisen from several sources. Funding agencies often want to know what outcomes result from their investment. For instance, Club Proteo has received substantial support from the University of California. Initially such funding was framed within a university initiative of outreach to communities. It was sufficient to demonstrate that the club served a substantial number of low-income children. As economic issues have beset the university, there has become more of an emphasis on academic preparation, in other words, community-based programs were expected to prepare participants to attend a four-year college. This has forced the researchers to consider how to measure the children's progress on state academic standards. This problem has not been solved satisfactorily within the small financial resources that have had available. Some other Fifth Dimension clubs have been based at schools and this has provided these clubs with access to children's standardized test scores. At the same time, these clubs have been pressured to either align their programs more with state standards or to provide homework help. These programmatic changes can interfere with research goals and certainly conflict with the philosophical basis of the clubs, which are based on principles of choice and autonomy for the children. As Boys and Girls Clubs increase their partnerships with schools, a trend in some areas, these same pressures can impact more Fifth Dimension clubs in the future.

Although both of our projects took place within the context of organizations that had the goal of improving the lives of children, there were still conflicts between our research goals and other goals of the organizations. Further, the organizations themselves had expectations for the research, such as evaluative feedback, that were outside the ways in which we conducted our research and potentially counterproductive to our relationships with the children.

Conclusion

In this chapter, we have considered how research can benefit and empower child participants, but in ways that differ from the possibilities with adult participants. Through our case studies, we have tried to broaden perspectives on the power balance that exists between child research participants, researchers, and the contexts in which they work. As other authors have asserted, the use of interactive methodology provides opportunities to empower research participants in ways that would not be possible through observation or more positivist/quantitative methods. This applies to child participants as well. We showed some of the ways that children benefited and were empowered as a result of our research, but in our cases studies there were also limitations. In planning our separate studies, we did not set out to do collaborative ethnography (Lassiter, 2005) or research for social change (Shratz & Walter, 1995). Nor were we able to follow the advice of others such as Cameron et al. (1993) about ways to empower our research participants. For example, the children did not share our research agendas nor have opinions about what they would like to be the topic of research. Although they enjoyed interacting with the researchers, the children did not seek to gain expert knowledge or to directly benefit from the research activity itself. In addition, there were dilemmas created because as adults we felt additional responsibility to children and their families, yet in our roles as researchers, confidantes, and even friends, we had conflicts between what we would like to do for the children, what our research required us to do, and the constraints imposed by the organizations and community contexts in which we worked. Despite these challenges and limitations, research gives children a chance to make their voices heard and can provide greater opportunities to participate equitably in their community and society.

References

AJA Project (n.d.). *AjA Project Colombia*. Retrieved September 26, 2011, from http://www.ajaproject.org/html/organization.html.

Brown, K., Brenner, M. E., Duran, R., McNamee, G., & Woodbridge, S. (2006). Portraits of afterschool systems in flux. In M. Cole & the Distributed Literacy Consortium, *The Fifth Dimension: An afterschool program build on diversity* (pp. 34–65). New York: Russell Sage Foundation.

Cameron, D., Frazer, E., Harvey, P., Rampton, B., & Richardson, K. (1993). Ethics, advocacy and empowerment: Issues of method in researching language. *Language and Communication, 13*(2), 81–94.

Carspecken, P. F. (1996). *Critical ethnography in educational research: A theoretical and practical guide*. New York: Routledge.

Christensen, P., & James, A. (2008). *Research with children: Perspectives and practices*. New York: Routledge.

Clark, C. D. (1999). The autodriven interview: A photographic viewfinder into children's experiences. *Visual Sociology, 14*, 39–50.

Cole, M., & the Distributed Literacy Consortium (2006). *The Fifth Dimension: An afterschool program build on diversity*. New York: Russell Sage Foundation.

Disparando Cámaras para la Paz (2003). *El lugar que habito*. Bogotá: Dattis Comunicaciones.

Emerson, R. M., Fretz, R. I., & Shaw, L. L. (1995). *Writing ethnographic fieldnotes*. Chicago: University of Chicago Press.

Euwema, M., De Graaff, D., De Jager, A., & Kalksma-Van Lith, B. (2008) Research with children in war-affected areas. In P. Christensen & A. James (Eds.), *Research with children: Perspectives and practices* (pp. 189–204). New York: Routledge.

Fine, G. A., & Sandstrom, K. L. (1988). *Knowing children: Participant observation with children*. Newbury Park, CA: Sage.

Freire, P. (1972). *Pedagogy of the oppressed*. Harmondsworth, UK: Penguin.

Glesne, C., & Peshkin, A. (1992). *Becoming qualitative researchers: An introduction.* White Plains, NY: Longman.

Guerrero, A. L., & Tinkler, T. (2010). Refugee and displaced youth negotiating imagined and lived identities in a photography-based educational project in the United States and Colombia. *Anthropology & Education Quarterly, 41,* 55–74.

Harper, D. (2002). Talking about pictures: A case for photo elicitation. *Visual Studies, 17*(1), 13–26

Lassiter, L. E. (2005). *The Chicago guide to collaborative ethnography.* Chicago: University of Chicago.

Mayer, R. E., Quilici, J. H., & Moreno, R. (1999). What is learned in an after-school computer club? *Journal of Educational Computer Research, 20,* 223–235.

Mimica, J. (1997). *Psychosocial projects: Evaluation issues derived from forced migrants' and helpers' point of view.* Paper presented at the Conference on the Study of Forced Migration: Psychological, legal, humanitarian and anthropological interventions. Hvar, Croatia.

Nicolopoulou, A., & Cole, M. (1993). The Fifth Dimension, its play-world, and its institutional context: Generation and transmission of shared knowledge in the culture of collaborative learning. In E. A. Forman, N. Minick, & C. A. Stone (Eds.), *Context for learning: Sociocultural dynamics in children's development* (pp. 282–314). New York: Oxford.

Norwegian Refugee Council (2005). *Internal displacement: Global overview of trends and developments in 2004.* Nyon: Global IDP Project, Norwegian Refugee Council.

O'Kane, C. (2008). The development of participatory techniques: Facilitating children's views about decisions which affect them. In P. Christensen & A. James (Eds.), *Research with children: Perspectives and practices* (2nd. ed.) (pp.125–155). London: Routledge.

Pedersen, C. H. (2008). Anchors of meaning—helpers of dialogue: The use of images in production of relations and meaning. *International Journal of Qualitative Studies in Education, 21*(1), 35–47.

Rich, M., & Chalfen, R. (1999). Showing and telling asthma: Children teaching physicians with visual narrative. *Visual Sociology, 14,* 51–72.

Schratz, M., & Walker, R. (1995). *Research as social change: New opportunities for qualitative research.* London: Routledge.

Tinkler, T. (2003). *Boys and girls at Club Proteo.* (Unpublished master's project). University of California, Santa Barbara.

Tinkler, T. (2006). Transitory freedom: Political discourses of refugee youth in a photography-based after-school program. (Doctoral Dissertation, University of California, Santa Barbara, 2006). *Dissertation Abstracts International*, A67, 141.

Vygotsky, L. S. (1978). *Mind in society.* Cambridge, MA: Harvard University Press.

CHAPTER TWENTY-TWO

Trust. Listening. Reflection. Voice

Healing Traumas through Qualitative Research

GRACE GIORGIO

The traumatized [thus] dit and spin their testimony into forms which both they and their audience will find bearable. We become "survivors" [and] it becomes possible to see trauma as a sort of hard lesson rather than pure loss. (Tamas, 2009, p. 52)

A few weeks after publishing an article "Speaking Silence: Definitional Dialogues in Abusive Lesbian Relationships" in *Violence Against Women* (Giorgio, 2002), I received an email from a woman asking if we could meet. Like me, "Candace" was a survivor of lesbian battering. She was also a nursing student using qualitative research methods to study lesbian abusers.

I met her a few weeks later on a dreary winter afternoon. Older than I by about 20 years, she described weathering a difficult life. Over warm cups of tea, she told me about her experience. For more than 15 years, she had been with a woman who was a service provider at a battered women's shelter and had abused her nearly the entire time they were together.[1] Candace talked about how difficult it was for her to believe she was being abused, because her abuser convinced her that she was the violent one. For years she asked herself: how could this woman who loves me, loves all women, be so controlling, manipulative, and suspicious? The entire time she was in the abusive relationship, she felt she could not speak, fearing if she did, no one would listen. "The silencing," she quietly told me, "is just as you describe it."

"I cried deeply while reading your article. Someone else knew my experience and was writing about it," she said. Now, in her own research, she was finding her voice, speaking loudly, and people were beginning to listen. For Candace, qualitative research was becoming a catharsis, a truth telling, a shared witnessing of an experience once denied. In the moments of reading, writing, and researching, she was beginning to heal. It was a powerful moment in my research life. I had made an impact, one that helped someone like me. My catharsis in researching my experience was no longer my own.

On my way home that evening, I reflected on the other women I had met and written about, myself included, while conducting a qualitative research project on lesbian battering. I had been trained to conduct my interviews in ways that not only gained knowledge of lesbian battering, but also helped me and my participants find a place of healing. In our interviews, conversations really, I encouraged the participant to speak not only as a survivor but also as a victim. In doing so, she could experience the turning point in her identity, an epiphany that helped her tap into her healing process. As all battered persons know, healing from such trauma is not an overnight experience, but comes in incremental stages filled with triumphs and setbacks. Healing requires deep understanding of the self and the abuse. To heal, one must establish trust of self and others; find supporters who will listen as well as listen to oneself; reflect deeply on the trauma; and find one's voice in speaking about it.

Trust. Listening. Reflection. Voice.

I have always believed that qualitative research was filled with promise to help people heal. In most of my qualitative research and writing, this has been my desire and purpose: to promote individual and social healing from lived trauma. Healing, Judith Herman (1997) claims, comes from speaking about the trauma and in doing so asserting one's own order onto the confusion of the trauma, making sense of it, taking authority over it, and using it to help others understand their own. Herman outlines how feminist psychotherapy helps victims speak to heal, and in the healing eventually rejoin their communities safely and/or re-enter public life as an advocate to help others like them.

In this chapter, I explore how qualitative research as an investigative practice can be positioned for healing our traumas. I focus on how several qualitative research modes of inquiry, structured and unstructured interviews and autoethnography, become sites for truth telling(s), a narrative function equated with individual and social healing (Herman, 1997). By taking us into the multiple layers of lived experience and its varied vantage points, qualitative research expands our understanding of lived and shared traumas, revealing their multifold truths. I argue that qualitative research heals those who speak and write about the trauma, connecting the experience to the larger social and political world.

Norman Denzin and Yvonna Lincoln (1994) define qualitative research as a field of inquiry that "crosscuts disciplines, fields, and subject matter" (p. 1); it is an interpretive and naturalistic approach, with many methods—interviewing, participant observation, autoethnography to name a few—of which none are privileged (p. 3). Qualitative research is more than "getting a fix on the matter at hand" (p. 2); it is a posturing, taking "a strategic position" (Wolcott, 1992 as cited in Hamilton, 1994, p. 61), in one's inquiry. It is less about describing and explaining and more about strategic understanding for social good through a complicated and nuanced nexus of methods, approaches, conversations, and theories.

In all of its forms, qualitative research seeks in-depth understanding of lived and shared experience. Qualitative research in its deep reach into participants' subjectivities and identities (researched and researchers) revolves around theoretical reflections upon the self, other, and experience. Qualitative research questions how power operates in the formation of identities in the contexts studied, produces knowledge and understanding that can be used for individual and social healing. When we come to understand ourselves, others, and the conditions that create the experiences we have, we are better able to communicate across difference, better equipped to respect outcomes, and better prepared to heal ourselves as well as others. Denzin and Lincoln (1994) write, "The interpretive practice of making sense of one's findings is both artful and political" (p. 15). To this, I add that it is also healing.

Trust

I read the danger in her face. She leaned against the dresser, arms folded in front of her chest, waiting to see if I would take the apartment. Her eyes flickered with that glint of warning: "Don't get near me or you'll get hurt," but the lust between her lips suggested it would be worth it. It did not take me long to succumb to her. Within six months, I had left a life of safety, friendship, community, and freedom for one of jealousy, rage, captivity, and violence. My trauma resulted from more than the physical pain, of which there was plenty. My trauma also came from my believing I created it, that I wanted it. My trauma truly took deep root when my friends and community shunned me for going back to her time and again. Few listened to me; even fewer heard me. My own fears of losing what little self I held onto silenced me further. Eventually, I found a support group for battered lesbians. Speaking to others like me, hearing their stories, so sadly similar to mine, and our shared willingness to help each other brought me from the darkest days of my life to a place of hope and change. In my own healing, I began to own my "history" and feel a "renewed hope and energy for engagement with life" (Herman, 1997, p. 195). I eventually escaped my abuser by moving far away. Unlike some victims, I had choices. I chose to go to graduate school.

Even in my new surroundings, my healing was incremental and at times fleeting. I still jumped at the drop of a pin and cried myself to sleep at night. A major setback came when a feminist communication scholar told me flat out, "Women do not abuse." Yes, a dissertation was born, but this woman's ignorance and denial reminded me that I could not so easily escape my trauma. Because to heal, I would need to feel safe in my chosen community. It was years before I could comfortably date again, and honestly, it was no longer with women. My trauma, though compelling me to write about it, prevented me from entering my new home's lesbian community.

In "Three Ways to Lose Your Epistemology," Sophie Tamas (2009) describes trauma and its effects:

> Trauma responses are triggered by recognition of and surrender to unavoidable danger (Krystal, 1995). Trauma harms attachment systems based on the trust acquired in childhood, which underlies all relationships and faith (Herman, 1997). Its breach leads to disconnection, alienation, and the loss of a sense of self. Damage to faith and a sense of community is severe when trauma involves betrayal of important relationships. Outcomes of trauma include shame, doubt, guilt, feelings of inferiority, crisis in faith, oscillating intolerance to and outbursts of anger, self-isolation, and anxious clinging to others. We lose trust in ourselves, others, reason, logic, the laws of the natural world, human decency, and often in God. (p. 45)

Throughout my study of abusive lesbian relationships, which was grounded in in-depth, long-term interviews, my study's participants and I expressed our shared sense of loss of self and faith in our beliefs, losses that are at the core of the trauma from being abused. Each of us experienced shame, doubt, guilt, feelings of inferiority, and a crisis in faith in the lesbian community and its ethos. Women don't batter—men do. Women are victims of patriarchy. Lesbians don't fit into the battered women's paradigm because lesbian relationships are the most nurturing of all relationships (Wood, 1993).[2] Such doubt in self and community led each of us to self-isolation in which speaking about the abuse became impossible. For me and a few of my participants, our self-imposed silence eventually led to dissociation, which "appears to be the mechanism by which intense sensory and emotional experiences are disconnected from the social domain of language and memory, the internal mechanism by which terrorized people are silenced" (Herman, p. 239). Terrorized, we didn't even speak to ourselves.

In *Trauma and Recovery: The Aftermath of Violence—From Domestic Abuse to Political Terror* (1997), Judith Herman identifies a survivor's internal struggle of both wanting to speak and wanting to suppress the memory of the trauma as a "dialectic of trauma" (p. 1) and suggests that a survivor must surmount this dialectic to truly heal. Herman provides a process for clinicians to help victims overcome their traumas by identifying three stages of recovery: (1) establishing safety; (2) reconstructing the trauma story; and (3) restoring the connection be-tween survivor and her community. Each daunting stage prepares the survivor for the next. One cannot begin to speak about her suffering until she is safely removed from her abuser. One cannot begin to reconnect to others until she comes to a self-understanding of the trauma and her role in it.[3] However, as I have thus far suggested, speaking about one's trauma is never easy and always fraught with internal resistance. The traumatized are "those whose trust of memory and language has been so impaired by trauma that the very act that they are trying to bring to justice renders them unable to do so" (Levy, 2002, p. 874, as cited in Tamas, 2009, p. 45). Nevertheless, Herman argues that in order to transform ourselves from victims to survivors, we must speak; that speaking will transform our confusing and nonsensical experiences into something we, and others, can understand. When we speak, we assert our own order onto the mess of trauma; we regain control over our lives by acknowledging and sharing with others our own truths.[4]

Locating and creating safe places for speaking about trauma is essential to the process of understanding and overcoming trauma, its depths and effects on individuals and the social body. For some, the therapist's couch is such a place; for others, support groups; for a few, writ-ing is a refuge (Giorgio, 2009a). As a psychiatrist, Herman focuses on "the act of telling a story in the safety of a protected relationship" of the therapist/patient interaction, where together the participants weave a narrative of the patient's experience and feelings about the trauma (p. 177). According to Herman, "the fundamental premise of the psychotherapeutic work is a belief in the restorative power of truth telling" (p. 181); "its success: physioneurosis reversed by words" (p. 183). In essence, speaking about the trauma with guidance towards healing is a ca-thartic act. While the therapist's couch offers a safe environment for such work, qualitative re-search can as well, since it often involves interviews not unlike the therapist/patient testimony gathering. As praxis, qualitative research seeks and constructs narratives from lived experience such as trauma. When focused on traumatic experiences, it deepens our understanding of the trauma as well as helps the traumatized to speak, describe, feel, connect, conquer, survive, and thrive. As Phil Carspecken (2003) notes, "people are empowered when they feel understood, recognized and appreciated" (p. 1030).

Qualitative research, in its complex nexus of methods and theoretical foundations, helps victims relive and own their experiences through narrative reconstruction that the researcher (and sometimes the researched) writes about.[5] And yet the speaking and writing (though cer-tainly confined to methodology and professional standards) is rarely simple, quick, and neat. As it is with experiencing and healing from trauma, the qualitative research project's "meaning, interpretation, and representation are deeply intertwined" (Denzin, 1994, p. 504) and where the meaning itself is "radically plural, always open, and…there is a politics in every account" (Lincoln & Denzin, 1994b, p. 576). For the traumatized, "Belief in linear, progressive history becomes unsustainable" (Lather & Smithies, 1997 as cited in Tamas, 2009, p. 45). Narrating their experiences, my participants often expressed doubt about their memories and showed pity for their abusers. Untangling and mitigating the psychological and social effects of trauma through utterance (speaking and listening) requires trust in the research project from both researcher and researched. A critical approach,[6] I believe, is the qualitative researcher's entry to opening spaces for creating such trust.

Trauma Telling—A Qualitative Move

> Critical ethnography must make the effort to disrupt the traditional power of research by making as many features of the research as possible open to equal negotiation between all of those affected by the project. (Carspeken, 2003, p. 1021)

Herman argues that to heal, we need to integrate our traumas into a fully developed life narrative by telling ourselves and others about our traumas. In *The Wounded Storyteller*, Arthur W. Frank (1995) offers a historicity to the quest for understanding illness—or trauma, utilizing his own narrative structure for this historicity: the premodern, modern, and postmodern periods. According to Frank, in premodern times, those suffering "didn't know what it was. They went to bed and died" (p. 5); they accepted their fate without question. The modern period was marked by the knowledge that something could be done, but that something involved surrendering to authority, a doctor or therapist, and lacked a "personalized voice in storytelling of medical illness" (p. 7). Frank writes, "The modernist truths remain the basis of professional practice even on this side of the postmodern divide…. Ill people still surrender their bodies to medicine, but increasingly they try to hold on to their own stories" (p. 16). Conversely, Frank posits, "Postmodern experience of illness begins when ill people recognize that more is involved in their experiences than the medical story can tell" (p. 6); that there is more to illness than the diagnosis and more to healing than the medical intervention. A postmodern intervention for healing involves integration of one's experience of the trauma into one's life narrative. For Frank, a postmodern framing of illness moves beyond the medical practitioner/patient dichotomy (or researcher/researched) and opens up space for the traumatized to speak on their own and contest authority's powers to speak for them.

For Frank (and Herman), people tell trauma stories[7] not just to work out their own changing identities, but also to guide others who will listen. Trauma telling is for another just as much as it is for oneself: "Telling stories in postmodern times, and perhaps in all times, attempts to change one's own life by affecting the lives of others" (p. 18). Frank, like Herman, argues that we need to tell our stories "because the process of creating a story also creates the memory structure for the rest of our lives" (p. 61). This memory structure affords individual and social healing, since those who doubt their traumatic memories before speaking about them begin to feel that their experience was if not just as they recall, close enough for them to believe the experience was real and their feelings justified. When there is a collective memory structure around a shared trauma such as lesbian battering, a phenomenon that until recently was ignored and denied, healing of the social body begins. For Frank, for Herman, as for the qualitative researcher, telling the self-narrative is about more than the two people in the interview—it is about healing traumas shared in the social body.

Although Frank's notion of postmodern storytelling resonates with a critical approach to social science research, research positioned as "postmodern inquiry" is not without its limitations. Certainly, postmodernism challenges "mainstream social science research" (Carspecken, 2003, p. 980); however, its focus on "discourse practices and power" (p. 992) may be too open ended for the traumatized. As Tamas (2009, p. 48) writes,

> Our postmodern efforts tend to dwell on deconstruction and resistance rather than reconstruction and empowerment. As such they might, "exacerbate, rather than heal, the modern experience of rootlessness and meaninglessness" (Reason and Bradbury, 2006, p. 6). Making people feel disempowered is wrong if I have no better practical ideology to replace the one I have undermined. Postmodernists can hardly appeal to the modernist notion that truth, however painful, equals progress.

Postmodernism can seem like a never-ending quest for deconstructive knowledge, a practice for its own sake, solipsistic and without practical application. A research project designed to focus on lived and shared trauma needs to reach beyond questions of "truth," "power," and "discourse." The lived experience of suffering is embodied and internalized and in need of healing; trauma telling can promote healing, as Herman and Frank posit.

Qualitative research that is grounded in a critical approach can also allow for healing through projects that are "interactive rather than (a) controlling process(es)," aiming "for mutual understanding," (Hamilton, 1994, p. 67). Critical ethnography as a form of qualitative research allows researcher and participant to explore lived trauma through multiple lenses and multiple voices. A dialogic approach to the research moment allows participant and researcher "to gaze back at oneself through cultural categories" such as suffering, and "to be both an 'I' who gazes and a 'me' who is gazed upon" (Carspecken, 2003, p. 993). Critical ethnography operates through a dialogic theory of subjectivity and self—"an insight (that) captures what it is like to find oneself as a prisoner, a woman, a student, a patient" (p. 993), to which I add, a victim of trauma. Kincheloe and McLaren[8] (2004) outline recent innovations in critical ethnography, such as deconstructive ethnography, which "forfeits its authority" (p. 329), and reflective ethnography, which "rests on the 'declarative mode' of imparting knowledge to a reader whose identity is anchored in a shared discourse" (p. 328). Researching lived and shared trauma with compassion and respect for those speaking and those engaged in the trauma (survivors/readers/researchers) requires such critical approaches. Critical ethnography can be deployed for purposes beyond understanding and describing and towards deeper individual and social healing through shared trauma telling.

Critical ethnography provides a posture for opening the gates to healing traumas as a part of the research project. Through the fundamentals of critical ethnography—shared authority, conversational interviewing, even experimental or "new styles" (Fine, 1998)—qualitative research can be a productive, efficacious site for healing traumas. For instance, feminist interpretive methods (which continue to inform qualitative research), "punctuate women's voices as antidote to past subjugation of knowledge and experience...and offer a forum for women's experiences to emerge without succumbing to power imbalances and imposed categories (Jayaratne & Stewart, 1991; Reinharz, 1992, as cited in Jager & Carolan, 2009, p. 301). When the traumatized are able to voice their experiences without the interference of outside authority (their abuser, law enforcement, even their therapist), we reclaim our own authority over the trauma.

Listening

> Listening is hard but it is also a fundamental moral act; to realize the next potential in postmodern times requires an ethics of listening. (Frank, 1995, p. 25)

Relying heavily on interviewing, qualitative research requires deep listening to one's subject and oneself whether in participant/observation or through direct interviews with participants. My research on lesbian battering relied much on interviews with abused lesbians. The data consisted of interviews along with my own personal experience. Using qualitative research methods such as structured and unstructured interviews and autoethography helped me weave knowledge and interpretation into individual stories that were shared with the larger social bodies of the lesbian community, domestic violence advocacy, and gender and women's studies. Nevertheless, it was in the face-to-face interviews and conversations that my participants and I found our voices, explored our experiences of trauma, and gained insight into the experiences and into ourselves. In speaking, we found our lost selves, created new selves, and expanded the social dialogue about lesbian battering. In doing so, we each felt that, "Maybe this would help so that someone else wouldn't have to go through what (we) went through" (Jager & Carolan, 2009, p. 305).

In "Interviewing: The Art of Science" (1994), Andrea Fontana and James H. Frey outline the various forms that interviewing takes in the qualitative context. They write "interviewing can be used for marketing purposes, gathering political opinions, for therapeutic reasons, or to produce data for academic analysis" (p. 361), and explain the differences between the structured and unstructured interview. They critique the structured interview with its set questions, responses, coding, and reliance on a neutral interviewer, asserting the stimulus-response format, precise data collection, and rational responses overlooks emotional dimension (p. 364). The unstructured interview, they assert, lends itself more to a conversational flow that "immerses human to human" (p. 366).

I have had the opportunity to conduct both kinds of interviews and have found the simple face-to-face contact in both to create opportunity for researcher and researched to explore the human dimension of trauma. Still, Fontana and Frey have a point. The structured interview is limited and limiting. As a graduate student, I was asked to conduct interviews with parents whose children were in foster care but with whom the parents had visits with their children hoping to reestablish their family life. Foster care under those case circumstances was considered a temporary state as long as the parents could perform adequately with their children (caseworkers supervised the visits) and attend state-sanctioned courses to improve their parenting skills. Our study focused on the visits, which we videotaped. Before and after the visits, I interviewed the parents while a tape recorder recorded our conversation.[9] These interviews were structured with me as a "neutral interviewer" with a set of questions I had 45 minutes to complete the post-visit interviews—however, in some cases the interviews continued for longer than that.

Every parent I interviewed expressed heartfelt regret for his or her failure as a parent. Many were struggling with financial and familial resources. Most had what we call extreme drama in their lives: abusive partners, unstable and low-paying employment, hassles with the state, and drug and alcohol abuse. Some were domestic violence survivors or still being abused. Each interview was heart wrenching and cathartic. Nearly every participant digressed from the script, since the interview allowed the parent to reflect on her parenting, his interaction with his children, her hopes and fears for the future. My privilege was clear—my power not as intimidating as maybe a professor's—but to the parents I had something they didn't: social capital and a future. Although in the structured setting with a structured interview, a modern approach, I found myself in the postmodern conundrum: postmodern interviewing is concerned with the interviewer's influence (Marcus & Fischer, 1986, as cited in Fontana & Frey, 1994, p. 368). Thus, even in the structured interview event, the postmodern appeared, and for the better for me, my conversant, and the study as a whole (Fontana & Frey, 1994, p. 368).[10] As Fontana and Frey (1994) note, "Interviewing [is] undergoing not only methodological change but also a much deeper one related to self and other" (p. 373).[11]

In these moments, I reflected on my own role playing. Unlike my interviews with abused lesbians, with whom I shared an experience, I was different, and this difference could make or break the interview. As I prepared for each interview and moved through it, I reflected on the power differentials and worked to break them down. As Fontana and Frey suggest, how we present ourselves "leaves a profound impression on the respondents and has great influence on the success (or failure) of the study" to build trust/rapport (p. 367). I thought hard about how I presented myself, allowing my street smarts to inform my approach to the questions. I purged my vocabulary of theoretical terminology that might come off as obnoxious, and dressed in jeans and T-shirt. All of this helped, certainly, to promote a dialogue that went beyond the set of questions. Nevertheless, time and again, the parent thanked me for simply listening to her story. Many observed that they could open up, because I was not taking notes and not judging them as their caseworkers did. Instead, I demonstrated my interest in listening and hearing by adding my own questions to the questionnaire and following up with ideas, thoughts, prompts, and more questions about the experience, the children, the parent's work, family and hopes and dreams. Yes, I went off script, but no one seemed to mind, except on some days when we stayed at the lab longer than we planned.[12] This was the first time anyone had asked these parents about their feelings, their own traumas, without treating them as perpetrators of trauma.

As the parents opened up, they used the interviews to speak about their experiences with family services (DCFS). For instance, two women captured the sentiments of many others quite explicitly: "If you don't do as they say they'll put it down...and whatever they put down is what others believe."[13] And, "Once I'm done with these people, I don't ever want them in my life again. They don't have to worry about getting into my life again."[14] This participant expressed her desire to participate in the study because "I didn't do this because DCFS wanted me to. Not this right here. This was my doings, coming here. I thought it was a wonderful opportunity"[15] (to speak about her experiences). Other times, the participant made a confession: "Incest was rampant in our household when I was growing up. My father was molesting me. I was having sex with both of my brothers...and I myself victimized my little sister. And you're the first person that's ever been told that. Nobody else knows."[16]

The experience was invaluable to me as a researcher and human being, for I witnessed the power of listening to others who have so little opportunity to speak. For many, the interviews were "opportunities" to feel heard and to reflect on their lives. Still, despite these moments of self-revelation and release, these families' healing would take a much longer time than my participation in the research project. As Jager and Carolan (2009) note, "Clinicians who facilitate family-based services become witnesses to the multigenerational and repetitive crises of families who try to cope with painful experiences and cumulative trauma (Boyd-Franklin & Hafer Bry, 2000; Gil, 2006)" (p. 301).

Reflection

> My testimony needs to be more than my side of the story when my voice has so little air. It has to be *true*. (Tamas, p. 51)

Sydney and I sit on separate couches in her cramped living room. She self-consciously chain smokes, telling me the nicotine keeps her calm as she tells her story. Sydney is a 24-year-old white, working-class lesbian living on the outskirts of a college town where she grew up. Sydney confesses to not knowing many other places than this place she calls home. She describes how her father beat and abused her and her younger sister, and how her mother got them out of that household but not really in time. "We're fucked up now—especially me," she says with a shrug. She describes having to go see her father once a year. It helps keep peace in the family and since he's almost dead now she won't have to do it much longer. She just returned from one such visit—so the chain smoking is doubly necessary.

I met Sydney in a townie bar. We even flirted a bit until I found out her age. When I mentioned my study, her face twisted into a knot. "I know something about that, but you might not want to know it—because you may not believe me," she said. When I asked her why, she answered, "Because I'm butch and the girl who beat me up was femme." In my data collection up to that time, I had interviewed one other woman who identified as masculine, several androgynous, but no one outright butch, or "bull dagger" as Sydney liked to call herself. Another layer to the trauma of lesbian battering: lesbian identity and performativity shaped outsiders' perceptions and thus shaped a victim's sense of self.

Sydney expressed this loss of self in her community:

> Even now I cannot attend any lesbian anything around here because they talk about me to my face, behind my back. I'm the bad guy. I'm the wife beater. Don't date me. I'll beat you up. This is from Liz telling everybody I beat her up.

Later:

> I wanted to go to the local pride celebration but it was like I can't go there. No one will talk with me. Everybody will be standing there saying, "That's Sydney. Don't talk to her because she hits women" and I thought I am not going to that and it hurts because my friends didn't even want to listen.[17]

Over a series of interviews and conversations, Sydney and I explored our shared confusion over her abusive relationship. Even before I began to interview her, standing in line at a local deli where I later learned her ex-girlfriend worked, I overheard two young women talking about Sydney abusing Liz. "Gossip," I told myself. "Keep an open mind." During one interview, I told Sydney about this. "So, now you are on her side, right?" she demanded. "Not at all! She instigated the violence." Later during the interview, I asked her, "When did you really begin to believe you had been abused?" "Just now," she said. "Because, you're right, Liz instigated the violence. She was the abuser, not me." That moment was an epiphany, "that interactional moment that leaves marks on people's lives [and has] the potential for creating transformational experiences for the person" (Denzin, 1989, p. 15 as cited in Fontana & Frey, 1994, p. 369), released both of our doubts. Sydney was beginning to heal.

In the qualitative research interview, time and place stopped; the participant left her normal life by walking into my home, agreeing to be taped, and watching the tape recorder wheels spin her words into a place for another (me and my readers) to hear. The casual setting and shared understanding helped our unstructured interviews flow into constructive conversations. We began with the story, outlining the beginning, middle, and end if there was one yet. And then, much like what Herman (1997) suggests, we reconstructed not only what happened, "but also what she felt" (p. 177), at each juncture. Often I brought my own experience into the conversations; I certainly used my own experience in developing my questions and analysis. Such personal explorations allowed the participant to feel heard, respected, and not alone in her trauma. It also helped me feel this way. Over time, together we would explore the moment when the participant no longer identified as a victim—when she could use the word "survivor" to describe her sense of self: "When I could hear myself and not only her." "When I could listen to my inner voice that was telling me this was wrong and I needed to get out." "Right now, talking to you." These were some of the answers.

Voice

In these conversations and when interpreting them, "I constantly reflected on the power of one word—*voice*—that embodied the research process, my interpretations, and my inherent responsibility in publishing this research" (Jager & Carolan, 2009, p. 303). My concern with voice was multifold: victim voice, survivor voice, abuser voice, community voice, and researcher voice, each with internal and external attributes and consequences. I was interested in a confluence of shared and conflicting voices, internal and external. In the interviews, I asked my participants to experience a perspective taking that, as a survivor, I suspected they took privately. For instance, I asked my participant to tell me what she thought her abuser felt. Usually, the participant began by saying, "Who cares?" and then followed this answer with a series of reflections on her abuser's feelings—expanding the narration into a complex nexus of internal and external voices, each with their own truth: we loved someone who said she loved us but hurt us deliberately; our girlfriends did not know they were hurting us; instead, they too were trying to make sense of the relationship. We wanted to leave and we wanted to stay; she wanted us gone and she wanted us with her. In these moments, our compassion for ourselves and even our abusers grew. As Herman argues, the retelling of the experience, locating points of dissociation and rage, re-writing the experience into a truth-telling testimony helps the victim of trauma heal. In the conversational flow, my participants and I experienced placing order onto the mess of trauma. As Jager and Carolan write, "Together we wove narratives that incorporated both the pain and recovery from trauma into the construction of empowerment and trustworthy community connections" (pp. 304–305). Together, researcher and researched, we had begun to address empowerment and trauma recovery.

An Autoethographic Ending

The voice of trauma necessarily uses a language that borders the artistic and the actual. (Levy, 2002, p. 877 as cited in Tamas, p. 50)

I'm sitting with my husband on our kitchen stools after a long day of work. It is late, dark outside, and we are once again rehashing the same old argument that involves a terrible fear of abandonment. See, my husband's family not only rejected me. After much struggle about family loyalty and property, they also rejected him. It's been two and a half years since civil conversation has been exchanged between "Jack" and his mother. He has cut her off from his life as she has him from hers. The problem is that she now lives next door. There is no escape—only regrets and fears of more rejection.

I don't want to fight this fight again. We really only have each other and this day has been one of professional success for me. My second autoethnography, a short story about the family split, has received high praise from someone in my field whom I respect very much. The story will be workshopped in the upcoming Qualitative Inquiry Conference as an example of new and experimental autoethnography. I'm thrilled and have told Jack about it. Still, I also mentioned having lunch with a male colleague and this did not go over well. Fear of abandonment, a trauma, revisited once again. I decide it is time to change the subject. I will read the short story to him, something I have not done yet.

When I finish reading, I reluctantly look into his face. Does it only make him angrier? Does he feel I share too much with the outside world? Does he think my characterization of him and me and our situation wrong? Will it exacerbate our fight? Instead, he is crying—tears of release, our shared suffering rendered artistically. "The story is just as it happened," he says. The story, he tells me, helps him understand better than ever his own experience, his trauma of losing his family. "Keep writing about this," he tells me. And so here I am. At the end that is really only a beginning.

One may heal from a trauma, but this does not mean another will not come up in one's lifetime, as has been my own case. I had escaped an abusive relationship over ten years ago, and had researched and written about it in such a way that I feel healed from it. More importantly, I have been able to use my experience to help others, as an advocate, researcher, and writer. I had drawn the lessons of my past trauma to help others. I had reached stage three in Herman's schema. Qualitative research had helped me get here. And then another trauma—how could a family do this? How will I overcome the rejection and pain from being lied about and abused by his family? How can I help my husband heal? Will our marriage survive?

My first publication was actually an autoethnography, a performance piece that several campus groups used to educate students about abusive intimate relationships. Although I did not delve into autoethnography as my preferred form of writing until well after graduate school, in 1999 I felt I had found a creative and intellectual home. As a graduate student, I was being trained to conduct interviews and when possible incorporate participant/observation into my research. Fontana and Frey (1994) note, "Qualitative interviewing goes hand in hand with participant observation" (p. 363). Studying under Norman Denzin, I learned how "Postmodern ethnographers concern themselves with moral problems in the act of interviewing…with the controlling interviewer" and "increased concern for voices and feelings of the respondent" (p. 363). Yet, my study hardly afforded me the opportunity to observe my topic in action—all I had were my own memories, journals, and participants' words.

Since then I have come to see autoethnography as a new form of participant/observation where the researcher is both researcher and researched. Through autoethnography, I could include the other as co-author in our "narrative adventures" (Lincoln & Denzin, 1994b p. 577), which I did in "Living Lesbian Battering" (Giorgio, 1999). My participants not only had their voices in the piece, they also knew the piece was being performed for others. Autoethnography allowed me to create "experimental or messy texts, where multiple voices speak...often in conflict, and where the reader is left to sort out which experiences speak to his or her personal life" (p. 577). Autoethnography allowed me to incorporate the "multiple reflections" (Holman Jones, 2005, p. 770) of the internal and external voices of researched and researcher. As "an inventory of self and other on a journey through imitation and creation into movement" (p. 770), autoethnography invites "us into a lived and deeply felt experience" (p. 764).

"Living Lesbian Battering" (Giorgio, 1999) explored the multiple dimensions of lesbian battering through a scripted opening that introduced the characters and setting of my relationship followed by a series of scripts that denounced researchers' and advocates' ignorance about abusive lesbian relationships. In "The Hotline" (p. 7) my character calls a battered women's shelter after being raped by her girlfriend:

ADVOCATE: "Are you safe now?"

CLAIRE: "Yes, I'm home."

CLAIRE VOICE OVER: I say... my voice getting more distant from my body.

ADVOCATE: Are you hurt? Do you need to go to a hospital?

CLAIRE: No, but I want to press charges.

ADVOCATE: Do you know your assailant?

CLAIRE: Yes, I do, it's my girlfriend.

ADVOCATE: Excuse me? Your girlfriend?

CLAIRE VOICE OVER: She is repulsed by me. I know it. But I tell her how she entered my room with her keys and... she cuts me off.

ADVOCATE: Is this some kind of a prank? This is not funny. I do not appreciate your abusing the hotline number when we need it for...

CLAIRE: But she raped me.

CLAIRE VOICE OVER: I am crying, but the woman has the answer. I knew it all along.

ADVOCATE: Women do not rape.

CLAIRE VOICE OVER: And she hangs up.

The autoethnography concluded with a rewriting of the opening script as a third-person narration in which my character, as eventually happened in my abusive relationship, fights back by using her abuser's words and tactics to frustrate and repel her. In its multiple voices and epilogue, "Living Lesbian Battering" does what Ellis and Bochner (2006) suggest autoethnography should do: be an "unruly, dangerous, vulnerable, rebellious and creative" inquiry that "wants the reader to care, to feel, to empathize, and to do something, to act" (p. 433).

Autoethnography, I believe, is a form of qualitative research well suited for healing our traumas. In both of my traumas, lesbian battering and loss of family, autoethnography allowed me to negotiate my authority and to explore my many and shared traumas and truths. As I have written elsewhere, "autoethnography allows for deep excavation of our multiple truths, boundless experimentation with text and story, and their power to heal. One can explore the experience without having to give it an ending because, to be truthful, there is no ending to our traumas. We become our traumas, and our traumas become us" (Giorgio, 2009a, p. 160). In "The Wedding Dress" (Giorgio, 2009b), the autoethnography I shared with my husband that night, I used the short-story format to symbolically destroy that which represented Jack's family's intrusion into our marriage. Claire, the character representing me, burns her wedding dress, which Jack's sister made, in front of Jack, hoping he will value this symbolic act: creating a clean break from the family intrusion. He does.

As in my interviews with battered lesbians, in writing "The Wedding Dress" I struggled with voice. After experimenting with first person and a multivocal text, I decided to use close third person, because it allowed me to explore my inner struggle from an observational vantage point. When writing my experience in the first person, as reviewers suggested, I witnessed myself as a victim. In experimenting with close third-person voice, I found I could show my sense of victimization without succumbing to it. Recent psychological research of how people narrate their lives shows that "mental resilience relies in part on a kind of autobiographical storytelling, moment to moment, when navigating life's stings and sorrows" (Carey, 2007, p. 3). McIsaac and Eich (2004, as cited in Carey, 2007, p. 3) found that when people revisit a scene in the first person, the storytelling is more upsetting than when they do so in the third person, "as if they were watching themselves in a movie" or writing their experience as a story. Their research describes eighteen subjects who retold traumatic experiences in both first and third person: Third-person or "observational" scenes "were significantly less upsetting, compared with bad memories recalled" in the first person (McIsaac & Eich, 2004, p. 248).[18] With third-person narration, a tool I could use in autoethnography, I extracted my fears and decision-making and explored Jack's conflicted negotiating his family's struggles. Telling this story with an observational voice freed my imagination to create a symbolic gesture of breaking with Jack's family on my own terms. In writing "The Wedding Dress" and later reading it to Jack, we both began to heal.

I am not sure what Herman would think of autoethnography (is it too solipsistic?), but it is possible she would approve. Herman writes so effectively about the process of healing. Autoethnography, like qualitative inquiry in general, is about process: "The word qualitative implies an emphasis on processes and meanings…" stressing "the socially constructed nature of reality" (Lincoln & Denzin, 1994a, p. 4). I suspect Herman would appreciate autoethnography's political dimensions, since she writes, "These survivors recognize a political or religious dimension in their misfortune and discover they can transform the meaning of their personal tragedy by making it a basis for social action" (p. 207). Herman also writes: "Recovery based on knowledge that evil has not entirely prevailed and hope that restorative love can still be found in the world" (p. 211), opening up spaces for a qualitative approach to our traumas that is both forgiving and giving, a creative process whether in the interview or the autoethnographic script. In telling our stories, in their multiple qualitative and creative forms, we can find our own healing—researcher and researched, individual and social body, by "giving to others" (p. 209) as well as to ourselves. Qualitative research is an offering; it is a gift to the social body in its desire for understanding multiple and shared truths. In some ways, it is most compassionate, for it calls for trust, listening, reflection, and voice(s).

In this chapter, I have shared moments in my research when the traumatized have found healing in our many voices. I hope in your work, you and your participants also find healing.

Notes

1. This was not the first time I had learned of something like this. In my research pool of 11 battered lesbians, I had one participant who had been abused by her female partner who was a director of a battered women's shelter.

2. I encountered this theory in a Women's Studies course textbook my first semester of doctoral work three months after escaping my abuser. My research is now cited in this text to correct such assertions (though my name is misspelled).

3. When one is still living in the sphere of trauma, one experiences post-traumatic stress symptoms that outsiders cannot comprehend. This is why as in my data set, several survivors spoke about how no one in the community would listen to them; many thought they were the crazy ones. Without the marker of gender in the abusive relationship, the lesbian community and support services are confused over to whom to believe. Hence, re-entry to the community is often barred or eschewed by the victim.

4. These truths become a part of us, not all of us, a denial of the power of the abuser or torturer over us; hence, a transformation of self.

5. During my data collection, I shared the transcripts with my participants asking them to comment on and correct what I had gotten wrong. Although there were a few corrections, all participants expressed the simple desire to hold onto the transcripts and let me do the writing. I shared the final product, the dissertation, with my participants who wanted to read it.

6. By using the term "critical," I am drawing from Carspecken's (2003) in-depth exploration of what he calls the post-Enlightenment problematic in which he treats both postmodernism and criticalism as one broad orientation that together oppose "the worldviews of modernity within schools of education" and "are not singular discourses but rather discourse-clusters" (p. 979). Although I draw from Frank's linear historicity of illness telling, which moves from premodern to postmodern, I aim to describe qualitative research that is "critical" and though informed by postmodern thought, not steeped in it. Carspecken clarifies what is meant by criticalism ("a very complex and internally divided discourse with commonalities mainly concerning an emphasis on critical reason as opposed to positive theory" [p. 1015]). Criticalism asserts all knowledge is conjunctural and that knowledge is an evolving process. Criticalism, with its emphasis on validity claims, is less ocular and phonocentric in its approach to knowledge, representation, power, and self than is postmodernism—hence with more promise for social science research, according to Carspecken.

7. I interchange Herman's term "truth tellings" and Frank's "story tellings" with what I am calling "trauma tellings" to emphasize my focus on lived trauma. Herman and Frank are also referencing trauma (post-traumatic stress disorder and illness/suffering respectively) in their arguments and terminology.

8. Though Carspecken admits not knowing who coined the term "critical ethnography," from their personal discussions, Carspecken and McLaren believe it may have been McLaren in his ethnography *Life in Schools* (1989) (Carspecken, 2003, p. 1041).

9. Most of the study's participants were considered "motivated" and thus not fully representative of the numerous foster-care cases in our community. I never learned the outcome of any of the nearly 20 parents I interviewed over the duration of the study (approximately two years of data collection); however, I still have the transcripts, which continue to fascinate me. When meeting with parents prior to the visits, the conversations were limited to simple introductions and gathering of a few facts about the parent's perspective on the case.

10. See also Haight, Black, Mangelsdorf, Giorgio, Tata, Schoppe, & Szewczyk (2002); and Schoppe-Sullivan, Mangelsdorf, Haight, Black, Szewczyk Sokolowski, Giorgio, & Tata (2007).

11. Fontana and Frey ask readers to look at Fine (1998).

12. I recall several times the other researchers leaving me alone for the rest of the day to lock up the lab.

13. Anonymous parent, interview with Grace Giorgio, September 11, 1999, unpublished transcript, p. 7.

14. Anonymous parent, interview with Grace Giorgio, September 25, 1999, unpublished transcript, p. 15.

15. Anonymous parent, interview with Grace Giorgio, September 25, 1999, unpublished transcript, p. 15.

16. Anonymous parent, interview with Grace Giorgio, December 9, 2000, unpublished transcript, p. 27.

17. Sydney and Liz were together for several months before Liz began beating Sydney, who at first thought it was funny because with one stroke Sydney "could really hurt her." The beatings got worse, culminating in a near car crash that gashed Liz's head and bruised Sydney's arm. As Liz left the scene of the accident she yelled, "I got you now!" Sydney had no idea what this meant and walked home. Four hours later, the police came to Sydney's door and arrested her for attacking Liz. Eventually, the charges were dropped but by then Sydney's reputation was damaged in the community. Worse, she had lost sense of who was at fault for the violence.

18. My interviews with my participants were always framed in the first person. It would be fascinating to go back and interview those willing from a third-person perspective.

References

Boyd-Franklin, N., & Hafer Bry, B. (2000). *Reaching out in family therapy: Home-based, school, and community interventions*. New York: Guilford Press.

Carey, B. (2007, May 22). This is your life (and how you tell it). *New York Times*, pp.1–3. Retrieved October 1, 2011 from http://www.nytimes.com/2007/05/22/health/psychology/22narr.html?scp=1&sq=as+if+they+were+watching+themselves+in+a+movie&st=nyt.

Carspecken, P. F. (2003). Ocularcentrism, phonocentrism, and the counter-enlightenment problematic: Clarifying contested terrain in our schools of education. *Teachers College Record, 6*(5), 978–1047.

Denzin, N. K. (1994). The art and politics of interpretation. In N. Denzin & Y. Lincoln (Eds.), *Sage handbook of qualitative research* (1st ed.) (pp. 500–515). Thousand Oaks, CA: Sage.

Denzin, N., & Lincoln, Y. (Eds.). (1994). *Sage handbook of qualitative research* (1st ed.). Thousand Oaks, CA: Sage.

Denzin, N. (1989). *Interpretive interactionism*. Newbury Park, CA: Sage.

Ellis, C. S., & Bochner, A. P. (2006). Analyzing analytic autoethnography: An autopsy. *Journal of Contemporary Ethnography, 35*(4), 429–449.

Fine, M. (1998). Working the hyphen: Reinventing self and other in qualitative research. In N. K. Denzin & Y. S. Lincoln (Eds.), *The landscape of qualitative research: Theories and Issues* (pp. 130–155). Thousand Oaks, CA: Sage.

Fontana, A., & Frey, J. H. (1994). Interviewing: The art of science. In N. K. Denzin & Y. S. Lincoln (Eds.), *Sage handbook of qualitative research* (1st ed.) (pp. 361–376). Thousand Oaks, CA: Sage.

Frank, A. (1995). *The wounded storyteller: Body illness and ethics*. Chicago: University of Chicago Press.

Gil, E. (2006). *Helping abused and traumatized children: Integrating directive and nondirective approaches*. New York: Guilford Press.

Giorgio, G. (1999). Living lesbian battering. *Cultural Studies: A Research Annual, 4*, 3–18.

Giorgio, G. (2002). Speaking Silence: Definitional dialogues in abusive lesbian relationships. *Violence Against Women, 8*(10), 1233–1259.

Giorgio, G. (2009a). Traumatic truths and the gift of telling. *Qualitative Inquiry, 15*(1), 149–167.

Giorgio, G. (2009b). The wedding dress. *Qualitative Inquiry, 15*(2), 397–408.

Haight, W., Black, J., Mangelsdorf, S., Giorgio, G., Tata, L., Schoppe, S., & Szewczyk, M. (2002). Making visits better: The perspectives of parents, foster parents, and child welfare workers. *Child Welfare, 81*(2), 173–202.

Hamilton, D. (1994). Traditions, preferences, and postures in applied qualitative research. In N. K. Denzin & Y. S. Lincoln (Eds.), *Sage handbook of qualitative research* (1st ed.). (pp. 60–69). Thousand Oaks, CA: Sage.

Herman, J. (1997). *Trauma and recovery: The aftermath of violence—from domestic abuse to political terror*. New York: Basic Books.

Holman Jones, S. (2005). Autoethnography: Making the Personal Political. In N. K. Denzin & Y. S. Lincoln (Eds.). *Sage handbook of qualitative research* (3rd ed.) (pp. 763–791). Thousand Oaks, CA: Sage.

Jager, K. B., & Carolan, M. (2009). Locating community in women's experiences of trauma, recovery, and empowerment. *Qualitative Inquiry, 15*(2), 297–307.

Jayartne, E., & Stewart, A. J. (1991). Quantitative or qualitative methods in the social sciences: Current feminist issues and practical strategies. In M. M. Fonow & J. A. Cook (Eds.), *Beyond methodology: Feminist scholarship as lived research* (pp. 85-106). Bloomington: Indiana University Press.

Kincheloe, J. L., & McLaren, P. (2004). Rethinking critical theory and qualitative research. In N. K. Denzin & Y. S. Lincoln (Eds.), *Sage handbook of qualitative research* (1st ed.) (pp. 303–342). Thousand Oaks, CA: Sage.

Krystal, H. (1995). Trauma and aging: A thirty-year follow-up. In C. Caruth (Ed.), *Trauma: Explorations in memory.* (pp. 76–99). Baltimore: Johns Hopkins University Press.

Lather, P., & Smithies, C. (1997). *Troubling the angels: Women living with HIV/AIDS.* Boulder, CO: Westview Press.

Levy, S. (2002). "This dark echo calls him home": Writing father-daughter incest narratives in Canadian immigrant fiction. *University of Toronto Quarterly,* 71(4), 864–80.

Lincoln, Y. S., & Denzin, N. K. (1994a). Introduction. In N. K. Denzin & Y. S. Lincoln (Eds.), *Sage handbook of qualitative research* (Vol. 1) (pp. 1–17). Thousand Oaks, CA: Sage.

Lincoln, Y. S. & Denzin, N. K. (1994b). The fifth moment. In N. K. Denzin & Y. S. Lincoln (Eds.), *Sage handbook of qualitative research* (Vol. 1) (pp. 575–586). Thousand Oaks, CA: Sage.

Marcus, G. E., & Fischer, M. (1986). *Anthropology as cultural critique: An experimental moment in the human sciences.* Chicago: University of Chicago Press.

McIsaac, H., & Eich, E. (2004). Vantage point in traumatic memory. *Psychological Science, 15*(4), 248–253.

Reason, P., & Bradbury, H. (2006). Introduction: Inquiry and participation in search of a world worthy of human aspiration. In P. Reason, & H. Bradbury (Eds.), *Handbook of action research.* (pp. 1-14). Thousand Oaks, CA: Sage.

Reinharz, S. (1992). *Feminist methods in social science research.* New York: Oxford University Press.

Richardson, L. (1994). Writing: A method of inquiry. In N. K. Denzin & Y. S. Lincoln (Eds.), *Sage handbook of qualitative research* (pp. 516–529). Thousand Oak, CA: Sage.

Schoppe-Sullivan, S., Mangelsdorf, S., Haight, W., Black, J., Szewczyk Sokolowski, M., Giorgio, G., & Tata, L. (2007). Maternal discourse, attachment-related risk, and current risk factors: Associations with maternal parenting behavior during foster care visits. *Journal of Applied Developmental Psychology, 28,* 149–165.

Tamas, S. (2009). Three ways to lose your epistemology. *International Review of Qualitative Research, 2*(1), 43–60.

Wolcott, H. F. (1992). Posturing in qualitative inquiry. In M. D. LeCompt, W. L. Milroy, & J. Preissle (Eds.), *The handbook of qualitative research in education* (pp. 3–52). New York: Academic Press.

Wood, J. (1993). *Gendered lives: Communication, gender and culture.* Chapel Hill, NC: Wadsworth.

CHAPTER TWENTY-THREE

Word on the Street

Philosophy, Critical Ethnography, and Urban Youth Culture

KIP KLINE

> I think that philosophy is still rude and elementary. It will one day be taught by poets.
> —Ralph Waldo Emerson

Introduction: Philosophy and Ethnography in the 21st Century

Walter Feinberg (2006a, 2006b) has made one of the more recent connections between philosophy and ethnography. This relationship between the two was probably adumbrated by Peter Winch as early as 1958 (Winch, 2007) and has continued to be supported by more contemporary theorists such as Jürgen Habermas (Habermas, Cooke, & NetLibrary Inc., 1998). Feinberg (2006b) employed his version of the connection in his study of religious schools; he calls the confluence "philosophical ethnography" (p. 5). For him, "philosophical ethnography… suggest[s] an underexploited disciplinary hybrid that is beginning to emerge in educational research and that may have potential for helping to coordinate action in cases of inter cultural contact…" And he goes on to say that it "can be useful in circumstances where a single act or series of acts may carry competing meanings for different cultural groups, and where meanings and values may need to be negotiated" (p. 6). I do not think this is wrong, but it hardly breaks new ground in the confluence of philosophy and ethnography. In fact, I am not sure that one needs to be explicit about the use of philosophy to do what Feinberg wants "philosophical ethnography" to do. Ultimately, Feinberg's philosophical ethnography is a bit too rigidly formulaic in my view (it is outside the scope of this chapter to fully rehearse it here), but there is a great deal of importance in his contributing to the continuing conversation about the relationship between philosophy and ethnography.

I am perhaps most interested in Feinberg because my own particular locution of the confluence of philosophy and ethnography is, at first glance, similar. I have referred to my own study of so-called underground hip-hop artists in Chicago as "ethnographic philosophy" and more specifically "critical ethnographic philosophy." I am suggesting here a kind of doing philosophy through the use of critical ethnographic methods. My study of hip-hop, as critical ethnographic philosophy, produced a couple of distinct iterations of the connection between philosophy and ethnography. First, it revealed that critical theory and methodology and their relationship to philosophy can become a kind of meta-theoretical resource that, in this case, provided context for the study and perhaps important insight for ethnographers in general. Beyond that, the ethnographic work uncovered various ways in which hip-hop is connected to philosophy, and although it is grossly anachronistic to say so, this connection suggests Emerson was right. Hip-hop aesthetics and culture exist and have meaningful connections to philosophy. Additionally, engaging in philosophical inquiry through critical ethnography is an effective way to unearth connections between cultural phenomena and philosophy. We might think of the difference between these two iterations as related to the notion of ethnography as both medium and outcome. The first iteration reflects ethnography as medium, while the second iteration is an example of outcome. What follows is a discussion of both iterations. In the end, it seems that philosophy, ethnography, and urban youth culture are bound together in ways that are important to each of them individually since they are all concerned with basic questions and problems related to sociocultural life.

First Iteration: Methodological and/or Philosophical Issues

The rise of critical ethnography, marked by Paul Willis's *Learning to Labour: How Working-Class Kids Get Working-Class Jobs* (1977), strongly suggests a connection between ethnography and philosophy that could be explored toward fruitful ends. This confluence is underarticulated in Willis, but what is implicit in the text and in subsequent critical ethnography is a kind of uncovering of philosophical ideas embedded in a variety of social science inquiries. I will now address a series of issues that might all be considered to exist under the umbrella of the general idea of the intersection of philosophy and ethnography. Ethnographic philosophy seeks to maintain careful qualitative research methodology while conscientiously drawing on philosophical concepts to produce sophisticated analyses. Put another way, ethnographic philosophy seeks to honor both disciplines that make up its whole, not reducing one to the other. Ethnographic philosophy takes a cue from Jürgen Habermas's conception of the relationship between the reconstructive sciences and philosophy. "According to this approach, philosophy surrenders its claim to be the sole representative in matters of rationality and enters into a non-exclusive division of labor with the reconstructive sciences" (Habermas, Cooke, & NetLibrary Inc., 1998, p. 406).

The Lifeworld/System Distinction and Critical Ethnography

An examination of Habermas's discussion of the lifeworld/system distinction is an appropriate place to begin the elucidation of ethnographic philosophy, since that discussion makes a salient contribution to critical ethnographic methodology. Habermas introduces the concept of the lifeworld in his magnum opus, *Theory of Communicative Action* (1984), as "intersubjectively shared," and he claims it is "bounded by the totality of interpretations presupposed by the members as background knowledge" (p. 13). This lifeworld is a preinterpreted world whose entirety cannot be questioned by those within it. It is not a falsifiable world, since it cannot ever be fully objectivated for the purposes of a discussion in which it might be falsified. In fact, since the lifeworld is so basic to all meaningful acts within it, a member of the shared cultural community who questions the fundamental structures of the lifeworld would be thought insane or dishonest. For example, if I look at a nickel and tell you I see a square and you cannot convince me otherwise (namely that the shape of a nickel is circle), or if I point toward threatening storm clouds and tell you that I am looking forward to "the visitors," you would probably question my sanity. The lifeworld is then, a "lived culture" that constitutes both the medium and the outcome of action. These ideas also have relevance to the self, since people will often believe themselves crazy if others find them unintelligible.

A system refers to what Habermas considers to be the kind of human action that does not rely on communicative action for its coordination (as opposed to the lifeworld, of course). In other words, systems work to coordinate action between actors that are separated between space and time.[1] Societies are functionally differentiated into specialized roles of work/activity and thus, different institutions rely on other institutions to perform tasks they are incapable of themselves. This coordination constitutes a system. For example, doctors need factory workers to make their equipment, while factory workers need doctors when they are in ill health. Society needs teachers to educate and socialize children, and teachers need factory workers and doctors, and so on. Obviously, this system stands in contrast to the "lived culture" that is the lifeworld. The system can also be exemplified by the economic coordination of capitalist societies (this example and the Marxist criticism will be central to the discussion of Habermas's concept of "the uncoupling of the lifeworld and the system" below).

This lifeworld/system distinction should inform critical ethnographic methodology in significant ways. Certainly in critical ethnography we are seeking to explore the "lived culture" that is constitutive of the lifeworld and to provide analyses that uncover social inequalities in order to work toward positive social change and a refining of social theory (Carspecken, 1996). However, in order to do this, we must consider the impact of the system on the lifeworld (and obviously in order to do this we have to note the distinction). Habermas claims that the lifeworld of contemporary complex society is primarily "deformed" by system factors (This idea will be explored further below in the discussion of system colonization of the lifeworld.) So, the distinction between lifeworld and system is important for critical ethnographers who seek to refine social theory and ameliorate social inequalities. Of course, methodological questions are indicated by this discussion. Can we ever "observe" a social system if we are always already existing within a lifeworld? Developing an answer to this question is beyond the scope of this chapter, but Habermas begins to address the question by saying that access to social systems necessarily make use of hermeneutic processes and therefore systems analysis includes reconstructive methodology (yielding findings of different significance than analysis of the lifeworld).[2]

The Uncoupling of System and Lifeworld

The work of critical ethnographers can also benefit from an examination of the uncoupling of system and lifeworld. Habermas claims that both system and lifeworld grow as they are differentiated from one another (as in the social evolution of tribal societies to modern ones). As the rationality of the lifeworld grows, so does the complexity of the system (Habermas, 1987, p. 153). When this process reaches the stage of the modern society, the lifeworld that once was coupled with a scarcely differentiated social system gets reduced to a subsystem. At the same time, the system becomes more and more autonomous, with organizations connected through "delinguistified media" (that is to say, money, for example) that operate as steering mechanisms for "a social intercourse that has been largely disconnected from norms and values" (p. 154). Yet, systemic mechanisms are necessarily informed by the lifeworld. Thus, in modern societies, systemic mechanisms must be institutionalized, which results in bureaucratic (economic) spheres that are regulated solely by the aforementioned delinguistified steering media (money and power). Habermas adds that "Norm-conformative attitudes and identity-forming social memberships are neither necessary nor possible in these spheres; they are made peripheral instead" (p. 154).

This uncoupling of system and lifeworld depends upon "value generalization" and "reification." Value generalization refers to the process by which traditions, religions, normal and legal norms become culturally rationalized and move from the specific to the general. Here Habermas (1987) leans on Durkheim's ideas about legal development to assert the notion of "*universalization of law and morality* that brings with it a disenchantment of sacred law" (emphasis in original, p. 84). This value generalization is partially constitutive of the uncoupling of system and lifeworld, mainly as a precondition, as the increasingly complex system mechanisms can only be coordinated through more generalized norms. A good example of this is the traditional classroom that has specific rules that result in "mechanical solidarity" such as, a student must raise her hand to ask permission to speak or use the restroom. This is in contrast to a more constructivist classroom that produces "organic solidarity" that might employ more general rules that are interpreted in a given context, such as, "respect others" and "don't be rude." A related phenomenon within the realm of value generalization is the construction of trust in social relationships through generalizing categories. For example, the general category "doctor" comes to elicit trust in relationships and so on. So the growing complexity of systems depends on value generalization. Yet, as mentioned above, the lifeworld still informs systemic mechanisms. However, this happens through the reification of lifeworld phenomena where system differentiation causes "disturbances of its [the lifeworld's] symbolic reproduction" (p. 83). So the uncoupling of system and lifeworld depends on both value generalization and reification. This uncoupling eventually (and ironically, according to Habermas) reveals that "the rationalization of the lifeworld makes possible a heightening of systemic complexity, which becomes so hypertrophied that it unleashes system imperatives that burst the capacity of the lifeworld they instrumentalize" (p. 155). This provides an apt transition to a discussion of the "colonization of the lifeworld."

With regard to reification, what is fundamentally reified is a socially constructed "agreement" such as the agreement that money represents value, or the agreement that a formal position in an organization has a fixed relation of authority in relation to other formal positions. These reifications form the basis of system media, and with system media in place, we have the development of subsystems. The subsystems are not exactly reifications they are rather coordinated systems of action that depend upon reifications that have been substituted for communication.

Colonization of the Lifeworld

Habermas introduces the idea of the "colonization of the lifeworld" in Chapter 8 of *The Theory of Communicative Action*, Volume Two (1987). This notion is based on Habermas's evaluation of modern societies. He claims that systemic mechanisms of integration have replaced the lifeworld as a unifying societal force. This displacement happened alongside the diminishing of collectively held convictions that integrated society and is also tethered to the truncation of reason. In a modern society in which the system has colonized the lifeworld, "cognitive-instrumental" reason (a kind of theoretical reason conflated with technical reason) operates alone at the expense of aesthetic and moral-practical reason. This dominance of instrumental reason affects the everyday lives of people in modern societies since it creates subsystems that are nonnormative and are integrated only through the functional connection of action consequences (as opposed to communicative integration aimed at discursively producing a kind of "general will"). Clearly, these subsystems are merely objectifications in which the only appropriate form of reason is the cognitive-instrumental. Therefore, it is impossible to discursively and collectively argue for alterations in structures of power and economic opportunity through an examination of their normative implications that reduces individuals to self-centered actors. The result of this colonization is a general loss of meaning and freedom.

One particular example of this phenomenon that has salient implications for my own research of hip-hop culture is the welfare state. Habermas comments on this particular manifestation of lifeworld colonization. "The effects of this—to date, final—wave of juridification do not appear as side effects; they result *from the form of juridification itself.* It is now the very means of guaranteeing freedom that endangers the freedom of the beneficiaries" (1987, p. 362). The cognitive-instrumental form of reason exclusively dominates the subsystem of the welfare state, resulting in a theft of autonomy from the lifeworld and its subjects. Indeed when any government-controlled subsystem intervenes in societal problems, it does so through hegemonic hierarchy. In the 1970s, early manifestations of hip-hop forms of expression in the South Bronx were a direct response to such lifeworld colonization when once close-knit working-class black and Latino families were scattered into government project housing in order to make way for the construction of the Cross Bronx Expressway.[3] Of course, the result of this government subsystem intervention was a loss of meaning and autonomy. The early forms of hip-hop expression were attempts to seize both literal and discursive space in order to make meaning and construct a sense of autonomy. Put another way, these early hip-hop expressions can be taken as efforts to decolonize the lifeworld.

The Implicit System/Lifeworld Distinction in Paul Willis's Learning to Labour

Paul Willis's seminal work *Learning to Labour* (1977) is a fertile location for the exploration of the intersection of ethnography and philosophy. One salient example is that Habermas's system/lifeworld distinction lurks just beneath the surface in Willis's ethnography; specifically the idea is implicitly at play in the second part of the book, "Analysis." Here, Willis employs a number of bifurcated ideas (some more implicitly, others more explicitly) that can be conceived as approximating system/lifeworld distinctions. One of these is the "system"/"structure" binary in which the structure resembles "lived culture" or lifeworld, which is both the medium and outcome of action, as opposed to the "system," which is the production of patterned action that coordinates society across time and space. Related to this more implicit distinction is Willis's explicit use of "penetrations" and "limitations." Here Willis refers to the way the lived culture of the working-class "lads" can sometimes "penetrate" their conditions of existence (p. 119). Though Willis claims these "penetrations" are always "skewed" and "deprived of their independence," they are clearly associated with lived culture and therefore suggest a system/lifeworld distinction when taken together with the idea of "limitations." These limitations are the mechanisms that "confuse and impede the full development and expression of these impulses [that is, the impulses that constitute the 'penetrations']" (p. 119). This is one way we find the system/lifeworld distinction. A penetration and a limitation could in principle be related only to lifeworld domination, that is to say, dominant ideologies only, not clearly linked to systems. Penetrations into racism and sexism would have some of this character because although the two "isms" work to support system processes and arrangement, those processes do not absolutely need sexism and racism. They do, however, need classism, which is what Willis's inquiry is all about.

Further evidence that Willis's analysis implicitly makes use of a system/lifeworld distinction is the association of "creativity" with "penetration." This "creativity," Willis claims, is often constitutive of a penetration and is not an individual creativity, but rather a function of group activity. Additionally, it is not the result of "conscious intention." Here we see in the idea that collective and unconscious creativity informs "penetrations" another indication of a system/lifeworld distinction operating, albeit implicitly, in Willis's analysis of "the lads" and working-class culture. The system, for Willis, is social class and its relation to material production, which results in work conditions (as in factory work) that in turn produce a cultural response and this is where the distinction is most clearly at work.

Critical Epistemology and the Fact/Value Distinction

There are a number of features that distinguish critical epistemology from more traditional epistemological theories when applied to empirical studies of social life. To begin, it calls into question the paradigmatic status of sense certainty that is so ubiquitous in mainstream research epistemologies. In so doing, it takes seriously Husserl's phenomenological challenge to this sense certainty. However, critical epistemologists do not stop where the phenomenologists did with replacing the sense certainty of seeing an object as the ground for its truth with the not-dissimilar-enough certainty of experiencing phenomena; they also consider the poststructural/postmodern critique/deconstruction of presence found, most notably, in the work of Jacques Derrida. When the certainty of experience (or the certainty of pure presence) is dismantled (and Derrida's "trace" is all we are left with—and actually not even that, since this is the concept that "destroys its own name"), the phenomenological grounds for truth are dealt a philosophically fatal blow. So critical epistemology eschews both the sense certainty and phenomenological experience as grounds. Further, it resists the modified perceptual imagery embraced by some constructivists and naïve postmodernists. In their stead, critical epistemologists employ more communicative, holistic, predifferentiated imagery. This involves the recognition of what Phil Carspecken calls "cultural typifications" in which experiences are holistically recognized and not perceived.[4]

One cannot discuss critical epistemology without canvassing the fact/value distinction. It is in the location of this historically important and ongoing debate within methodological discourse that we find salient distinction between criticalists and non-criticalists with regard to epistemology. Phil Carspecken (1996) maintains a distinction between facts and values for critical epistemology. Instead of a naïve fusion of facts and values (again, accepted by some postmodernists and constructivists), he offers "value orientations" that do not determine the "facts" we uncover in the field. This kind of critical epistemology resists the notion that the ideology of the researcher inevitably finds its way into an inextricable relationship with the researcher's methods and findings. Instead, it operates with a more complex notion of the relationship between facts and values. Critical epistemologists do have value orientations that inform their guiding narratives for doing research. These value orientations clearly shape the kinds of studies critical ethnographers take up; however, they do not determine the empirical findings of their inquiries. In the end, Carspecken sums up the relationship between facts and values as "interlinked but not fused" in critical epistemology (p. 6).[5] How is it that facts and values are interlinked but not fused? All meaningful acts and thus all knowledge claims necessarily have three kinds of validity claims, so that it's impossible to assert only something objective, or only subjective, or only normative. It is only possible to foreground and background claims. So in the speech act, and this is the model we should map over to knowledge claims, we have an interlinking of the claims, including value claims when we emphasize facts, facts when we emphasize values, and so on. However, there is a necessarily understood analytic distinction between all three claims such that the response to a factual claim can always distinguish a factual component from a value component. But once again, the response will be in the form of a speech act and will have all the claims itself. Nevertheless, one can always respond to the response to make the analytic distinction between the various claims. This results in foregrounds to the acts progressively highlighting one claim in distinction from the others and it approaches purely objective, or subjective, or normative claims as limit cases. This is how these claims are interlinked and not fused. The distinction between them is understood by everyone with communicative competence and it is a distinction used to clarify meanings, refine scientific vocabularies, and so on. This is the kind of complexity Thomas Kuhn seems to have overlooked in *The Structure of Scientific Revolutions* (1996) when he suggested that values actually determine what scientists observe.

West and Kierkegaard

In addition to having previously noted the meta-theoretical relationship between philosophy and critical ethnographic inquiry, I turn now to a discussion of two more ideas from philosophy and their specific intersection with my own ethnographic inquiry. I discuss an idea from contemporary philosophy (West's "prophetic pragmatism") and one historical idea (Kierkegaard's "repetition"). I conclude with a preliminary discussion about validity in social science research and how "critical ethnographic philosophy" might go about validating its claims.

"Prophetic pragmatism," Cornel West's unique brand of neopragmatism, is a whole philosophical system, an explication of which is beyond the scope of this chapter. However, here I will deal specifically with an articulation of West's sense of the tragic found in "prophetic pragmatism" applying that idea to my ethnography.

The sense of the tragic in prophetic pragmatism is meticulously nuanced. It begins with the assertion that "tragic" is a polyvalent term. For prophetic pragmatism, the idea of tragedy is set apart from the Greek notion in which "the action of ruling families generates pity and terror in the audience" and is rather tethered to "a society that shares collective experience of common metaphysical and social meanings" (West, 1989, p. 227). Prophetic pragmatism's sense of the tragic emanates from what West calls the modern context of tragedy, "in which ordinary individuals struggle against meaninglessness and nothingness" within "a fragmented society with collapsing metaphysical meanings" (p. 227). This adaptation of tragedy to the modern context provides the criterion by which prophetic pragmatism accepts or rejects the sense of the tragic found in the various thinkers in American pragmatism.

Though West begins his genealogy of pragmatism with a celebration of Ralph Waldo Emerson, he is critical of Emersonian pragmatism's optimistic theodicy. West admits that Emerson did have a sense of the tragic, but

> [t]he way he formulated the relation of human powers and fate, human agency and circumstances, human will and constraints made it difficult for him … to maintain a delicate balance between excessive optimism and exorbitant pessimism regarding human capacities. (p. 226)

This balance is important for West, since without it there is no way to confront what he calls "the complex relations between tragedy and revolution, tradition and progress" (pp. 226–227). Prophetic pragmatism recognizes historical human atrocities and brutalities as well as "present-day barbarities." In fact, it is this recognition that requires of prophetic pragmatism a conception of the tragic. It must not avoid these facts of the human condition. Yet, for the prophetic pragmatist, the conception of the tragic is rooted in the modern context of tragedy, and for West this means not only the context of a fragmented society with collapsing metaphysical meanings, but also, and "more pointedly, the notion of the 'tragic' is bound to the idea of human agency, be the agent a person of rank or a retainer, a prince or a pauper" (p. 227).

Here the sense of the tragic found in prophetic pragmatism becomes profoundly attractive. It is both critical of Emersonian theodicy and yet gives primacy to the agency of all persons. West claims that the Reinhold Niebuhr of the 1930s best exemplifies this complex sense of the tragic. Niebuhr's

> struggle with liberal Protestantism … forced him to remain on the tightrope between Promethean romanticism and Augustinian pessimism. In fact, Niebuhr never succumbs to either, nor does he ever cease to promote incessant human agency and will against limits and circumstances. (p. 228)

Thus, prophetic pragmatism is unwilling to sidestep real and unavoidable human atrocities, some of which are admittedly not transformable; while at the same time maintaining "utopian impulses" through an unfettered belief in the agency of all persons. West anticipates that this may make his sense of the tragic seem a bit schizophrenic—an outlook in which human resistance to evil fails on the one hand, and the promotion of a quest for utopia on the other. However, West claims that "prophetic pragmatism denies Sisyphean pessimism and utopian perfectionism. Rather it promotes the possibility of human progress and the human impossibility of paradise." (p. 229). This is a subtle but profound movement away from a navigation between excessive pessimism and a pie-in-the-sky utopianism to a kind of paradigmatic shift that includes replacing the polar ideas with a singular conception of the evil in the world; an appreciable portion of which might be ameliorated through human agency, precisely because it is a product of human agency.

> Prophetic pragmatism is a form of tragic thought in that it confronts candidly individual and collective experiences of evil in individuals and institutions—with little expectation of ridding the world of *all* evil. (p. 228)

Now, consider the following passage from an interview with Melek Yonin, a pseudonym for one of the hip-hop artists in my ethnographic study. The context here is thinking about the meaning of commercially successful hip-hop artists/moguls versus the idea that hip-hop is essentially a resistance culture (the view from which Melek operates).

MELEK: P. Diddy hosts parties in the Hamptons as Jay-Z does. Which was kinda like this white playground. Which, in some ways is interesting and in some ways it becomes about class—wonder how many people of color are there, how many white people are there and I don't even know if it matters, but there are plenty of folks who will never be able to go to the Hamptons regardless of how many P. Diddys go. 'Cause the very nature of that economic system is to have the base be en masse and, you know, have those people working.… I mean, I don't know who P. Diddy's Hampton neighbors are, but I bet when they see him and crew come for the weekend or whatever, I bet folks were nervous and I think there's something really powerful in that and I think that that needs to happen too, but with the kind of music that they put out, it isn't about celebrating the mundane and the everyday struggles of day-to-day people, it's really, it's ultimately a song of capitalism…the overall systemic critique of capitalism has to acknowledge that there's only space for a certain number who will be at the top—and of course Jay-Z and P. Diddy in the scheme of things they make pittance compared to Bill Gates or other white men who will always be at the top. But if they can hang out together, you know, cool. I think Jay-Z and Donald Trump hang out at the same parties. But, I don't care. I mean, that doesn't mean that I have health insurance. And that doesn't make Chicago Public Schools better because P. Diddy has a house in the Hamptons.

An analysis of this portion of the interview certainly could benefit from an application of the sense of the tragic from West's philosophy.[6] Applying this philosophical idea to the words of the interviewee will have to be done delicately as to not dis-privilege the subject's voice. Yet, it seems apparent that in his words there is, implicitly, an assertion here that human atrocities and forms of oppression are not all transformable, while at the same time, Melek indicates that, on certain levels, even some forms of non-transformable oppression can be ameliorated and challenged and sometimes that happens through hip-hop "ways of being" and hip-hop expressions of which Melek himself is generally critical! We can better understand this with the help of the sense of the tragic in prophetic pragmatism. Some forms of oppression found in capitalistic societies may resist complete transmogrification ("white men who will always be on top"). Yet there is an emphasis on agency in Melek's assertion; human action within the oppressive system is not rendered meaningless ("I think there's something really powerful in that and I think that that needs to happen too"). So this reveals another way of thinking about philosophy and critical ethnography, since the subject here is himself the producer of philosophical ideas that can be reconstructed by the ethnographer. What I found in this particular case is that Melek, like Cornel West, "does philosophy." West's comes in a more traditional package, while Melek's philosophizing is the outgrowth of resistance to dominant ideologies through a particular aesthetic process that draws on his most personal experiences. Of course, there is much more analysis to be done here, but we can see that the application of this philosophical idea to qualitative research is fruitful.

Another idea from philosophy I have begun to use in the analysis of my ethnographic study is Søren Kierkegaard's "repetition." Repetition is first contrasted with the Greek notion of recollection. For Kierkegaard, movement must be a kind of forward movement and not the "retracing of steps" that is constitutive of recollection. Recollection undoes, whereas repetition produces. So the retreat of recollection (John Caputo [1987] calls it "antimovement") is simply another way out of the flux. Instead of staying with the flux, recollection suggests that we must retrace our steps out of it; that our goal is to recapture the eternity that always already has been. Its focus is on what has been lost, not on the "task" ahead. However, Kierkegaard's concept of time constitutes a direct contrast with that of the Greeks. Kierkegaard's "Christian time" considers eternity to have a futural meaning—"the life that is to come." For the Christian, time (or temporality) "means an urgent task, a work to be done," while metaphysics seeks its way out of time. In Kierkegaard's time, everything (or all eternity) hangs in the balance in each moment. This is the concept of time that is employed by repetition.

With this simplified articulation of Kierkegaard's repetition in mind, let us consider another passage from an interview with Melek. Here he is discussing hip-hop expressions as spiritual/ecstatic processes.

> **MELEK:** There are spaces to find within freestyle where you forget where you are and you forget how long you've been rhyming—the words just come. And, at its best, for me, it seems like you are really like a co-creator within the universe.... In a cipher when words are just being passed...it's just creation. I think, in recitation, that happens too sometimes...there are times when you kind of forget, you transcend that space. To me, sometimes, I'm speaking in that space, but I'm also speaking to and for my ancestors and for people who can't speak anymore or who wouldn't be able to be in front of that audience.

Here again we see an opportunity to apply a philosophical idea to analysis of qualitative inquiries. "Freestyle" is a hip-hop form of expression in which MCs or "performance poets" spontaneously rap and ad lib a "rhyme," most often in a group, a "cipher," in which the verbal baton is passed around a circle of poets/MCs. Melek's experience with freestyle is clearly a spiritual one in which time and space takes on new meaning, when "you forget where you are" and "how long you've been rhyming." It is interesting that Melek specifically mentions recitation as another means toward this spiritual end. Recitation necessarily involves repetition, and Melek is claiming that such repetition produces, not unlike Kierkegaard's repetition. This production includes a kind of identity in which Melek becomes the mouthpiece for his "ancestors and for people who can't speak anymore." Of course, there is much more analysis to be done, but it is clear that Kierkegaard's "repetition" will become another lens through which to view Melek's experience as a hip-hop artist.

After establishing the appropriateness of combining philosophical ideas with analysis of the results of qualitative inquiries, it is important to consider the concept of validity in social science research and how we might think about "validating" the use of philosophy in qualitative studies. To begin, critical ethnographers already lean on a philosophical idea when they use the concept of validity in their work. That is to say that we make validity claims in place of "truth" claims because our orientation toward "truth" is informed by the pragmatist notion of truth (or consensus theory of truth) that asserts all claims are fallible and we can only speak of truth with a small "t" and never with a capital "T." This, of course, will be no different when we "do philosophy" with our qualitative research. It is also important for researchers/philosophers to build bridges between their philosophizing and their subjects. Theories that are teased out or established philosophical ideas that are applied must be articulated to subjects in the study in a language accessible to them for the purposes of member checks and other measures critical ethnographers use to validate their findings. This will go a long way toward validating the use of philosophy in ethnography. Finally, researchers/philosophers seeking to validate the use of philosophy in ethnography must be prepared to experience Peter McLaren's notion of being "wounded in the field." This is especially important in the process of validating our claims to use philosophy in our research. Using philosophy in critical ethnography means, among other things, that we will likely uncover deep ways in which we as researchers are complicit in wielding some types of power. We will also likely uncover challenges to the ways in which we construct our identity (especially likely when, as in my own work, the philosophizing we do involves identity formation). Therefore, in order to validate our use of philosophy, we must be ready and open to being "wounded"; if we resist, our application of philosophy may evade validity.[7]

Having discussed a series of methodological and/or philosophical ideas using my study of the urban youth culture phenomenon of hip-hop, I now turn to the second iteration of the relationship between ethnography and philosophy mentioned above—the uncovered connection between philosophy and hip-hop.

Second Iteration: Hip-Hop and Philosophy

Philosophy belongs in the streets. Or so says William James (Darby & Shelby, 2005). And KRS-ONE.[8] Insofar as it is concerned with confronting the human condition "on the ground," philosophy has a multifarious connection with hip-hop culture, a connection that has reached some level of legitimacy in the academy if we take as evidence a book on the subject co-edited by a Harvard professor.[9] In general, this "philo-sophia" (love of wisdom) can be found at every stage of the hip-hop generation's proliferation, from the earliest trenchant pronouncements of Afrika Bambaataa's "Zulu Nation" to the so-called Golden Age of hip-hop when Chuck D and Public Enemy sketched the template for sociopolitically conscious rap. When hip-hop culture continued to grow in sophistication and manifestation in the 1990s, adding spoken-word poetry to its growing list of expressions, the love of wisdom expanded along with it, bound up in vocal packages of wit and witness, incisiveness and irony, satire and syncopation, all a cappella style. More recently, hip-hop culture's philo-sophia can be witnessed in its internal critiques by Saul Williams, Dead Prez, Sarah Jones, and others, along with so-called underground scenes that tell the stories of the local realities of Sly Stone's "Everyday People." Growing is the number of panel discussions, conferences, book and poetry readings, group discussions on hip-hop, inside and outside of the academy, while the number of university courses with previously implausible titles that include "Tupac," "rap," "hip-hop," or "hip-hop culture" is expanding in a variety of academic disciplines. Discursive pursuit of wisdom is not hip-hop culture's only manifestation of a connection with philosophy. The plurality in hip-hop's expressive idioms (from its early days, MCing, DJing, breakdancing, and graffiti art were all constitutive of "hip-hop") reveals a collage of performative action that unveils insight into the self-aesthetic relation through repetition and representation, techne, and technology.

I want to be clear that I am not claiming some precise equivalence between traditional academic philosophy and the urban youth culture phenomenon of hip-hop. However, it is reasonable to characterize hip-hop culture as being animated, in large part, by philo-sophia. Further, American pragmatists such as John Dewey sought to reconceptualize philosophy as cultural criticism and production, or put another way, to take it to the streets.

Any serious attempt at defining hip-hop or hip-hop culture must resist monolithic descriptions of its artists, artifacts, and audience. Mainstream media, politicians, teachers, and academics alike are prone to articulate severely truncated notions of hip-hop, the result of which has been a limited and dualistic discourse in the marketplace of ideas on popular culture. On the one hand, alarmists accuse hip-hop of a deleterious influence on youth. Hip-hop, to this way of thinking, valorizes violence and misogyny, derogates authority, and combines mindless lyrics with unoriginal music. These opinions are, in most cases, informed exclusively by media images, rap music videos, stereotypes of racialized, hypersexual bodies, and cursory examination of rap lyrics from commercial radio. On the other hand, progressives who defend hip-hop tend to limit their rhetoric to its counterhegemonic possibilities in sociopolitical terms. These arguments are largely focused on "conscious rap" or "knowledge rap," the lyrical content of which typically thematizes counterhegemony. This subgenre is not as commercially successful as other forms of hip-hop (although there are noted exceptions to this rule). The so-called Golden Age of hip-hop (roughly the mid-1980s to the early 1990s) and "underground" artists are the focus of this type of defense of hip-hop. This bifurcation of the discourse crowds out more complete examinations of hip-hop culture and serious aesthetic evaluation of its artifacts.[10] Richard Shusterman's venerable "The Fine Art of Rap," in his *Pragmatist Aesthetics* (2000) and Guthrie P. Ramsey, Jr.'s "Santa Claus Ain't Got Nothin' On This! Hip-Hop Hybridity and the Black Church Muse," in his *Race Music* (2003) are two such aesthetic examinations that should not get lost amidst the ubiquity of the more monolithic treatments of hip-hop. I discuss both works below and adopt and expand Shusterman's aesthetic categories for examining hip-hop as a postmodern art form.

Hard Livin' Mixed with Cristal Sippin': Hip-Hop as Culture

Examining hip-hop's connection with philosophy must begin by avoiding dualistic discourses and monolithic conceptions. Such avoidance can be achieved by making inquiry into hip-hop as a culture complete with multiple streams of style, rhetoric, values, sociopolitical commitments, and aesthetic sensibilities. Part of hip-hop culture is, no doubt, reinscription of hegemony through impetuous patriarchy and misogyny, glorification of conspicuous consumption, and perpetuation of racialized stereotypes. Another component of hip-hop culture is the counterhegemonic "conscious rap" complete with progressive and radical sociopolitical rhetoric. However, limiting the discourse to these two sides of the same coin is to treat hip-hop merely as a set of products and doing so necessarily fails to fully appreciate the culture qua culture. This mistake takes its most familiar form in the conflation of hip-hop culture and rap music. Rap music is not reducible to hip-hop culture, though it is a product of the culture. Other products have historically included graffiti tagging, breakdancing, and DJing, while later hip-hop became associated with so-called spoken-word poetry as discussed below. More important, hip-hop can be a description of something one does. Much like the sport of basketball has as its most commodified form or "product" the NBA (National Basketball Association), hip-hop culture has commercial rap music as its most recognized product. Yet, basketball is not limited to the product of the NBA, since anyone can enjoy shooting baskets or playing pick-up games at any local gym, park, or private residence with a hoop. In the same way, hip-hop kids can carry notebooks and scribble rhymes on trains and spit them in the school lunchroom or locker room or folks can gather in ciphers and trade rhymes or spontaneously freestyle at a party, all of which may bear only a tenuous resemblance to commercial rap music. Just as it is possible for people to enjoy playing basketball and be simultaneously critical of the NBA, there are hip-hoppers who are distinguishable from and are critical of commercial rap music.

Hip-hop cannot be reduced to rap music or to one particular rhetorical stream. There is, in my view, an internal conversation in hip-hop culture that is constitutive of its resistance to simple characterizations. Even within some commercially successful rap there are internal critiques of the misogyny and conspicuous consumption in hip-hop, or the general wackiness of some MCs. Though Shusterman (1997) gives hip-hop its most sympathetic and sophisticated aesthetic analysis, he characterizes this internal conversation as a set of "troubling contradictions."[11] Yet I take this kind of internal dialogue with which hip-hop operates as a characteristic that fortifies its status as a culture. Consider Brian Fay's conception of culture from *Contemporary Philosophy of Social Science: A Multicultural Approach* (1996). Here Fay builds on Kenneth Burke's (1957) idea of culture as conversation.

> Cultures are neither coherent nor homogenous nor univocal nor peaceful. They are inherently polyglot, conflictual, changeable, and open. Cultures involve constant processes of reinscription and of transformation in which their diverse and often opposing repertoires are re-affirmed, transmuted, exported, challenged, resisted, and re-defined. This process is inevitable because it is inherent in what it means for active beings to learn and apply cultural meanings, and in the ideational nature of culture itself. (p. 61)

We can also make sense of this internal and sometimes conflictual conversation in hip-hop through Anthony Giddens's idea of "structuration" (1986). The theory states that when agents act, they draw upon available cultural themes in the composition of their acts. The resulting acts will often produce innovations with respect to the way these themes are configured and claimed. The cultural milieu from which actors draw is called "structure" by Giddens, but at the same time he says that structure is nothing but the outcome of actions. Therefore, structure for Giddens is "the medium and outcome of action." Finally, because structure is always undergoing innovation, he calls the process by which cultural structures are continuously drawn upon, reproduced, iterated, and modified "structuration."

Fay's conception of culture and Giddens's theory of stucturation help us to understand hip-hop in ways that reveal certain criticisms of hip-hop to be misplaced. First of all, the internal conversation in hip-hop that is often conflictual shows that certain manifestations of hip-hop expression are indeed aimed at confronting those hip-hop iterations that would reinscribe various forms of hegemony. Also, Giddens's structuration makes sense of the way hip-hoppers constantly draw on a pool of cultural resources and produce innovations when they act. These innovations manifest themselves in hip-hop's rapid creation and transmittance of new variations in vernacular and sartorial style. This suggests that some criticisms leveled at hip-hop fail to recognize or appreciate its status as a complex cultural system within which actors draw upon cultural themes and produce innovations when these themes are claimed.

The Promise and Limits of Richard Shusterman's Pragmatist Aesthetics for Hip-Hop

Richard Shusterman (2000, p. 212) claims that hip-hoppers are "down with Dewey." By this he means that hip-hop operates with a pragmatist aesthetic that finds its most complete articulation in Dewey's rebellion against compartmentalization that creates hard oppositions like art/science, emotion/cognition, form/content, pleasure/truth. Hip-hop also aligns itself with Dewey's disputing the traditional identification of art with its material objects that produces the "museum concept of art" that Dewey criticized in *Art as Experience*. These ideas are rounded out by the connection between hip-hop and other Deweyan ideas about art including the challenge to the traditional hard line between high and popular art and his "challenge to the fetishization of art's objects [that] redefine[d] art in terms of dynamic experience and process." (Shusterman, 1997 p. 134).

Shusterman (2000) creates four categories for hip-hop in order to locate its place in pragmatist aesthetics: "appropriative sampling," "cutting and temporality," "technology and mass-media culture," and "autonomy and distance." In the same way that jazz created new art through the appropriation and metamorphosing of popular melodies, hip-hop lifts sonic units from a variety of sources including not only an array of musical genres but clips from speeches and sampled nonmusical sounds.[12] Yet hip-hop appropriation, as Shusterman (2000, p. 203) notes, divaricates from jazz in that it does not borrow "mere melodies or musical phrases—that is, abstract musical patterns exemplifiable in different performances and thus bearing the ontological status of 'type entities.'" Further, hip-hop has, since its inception, emphasized, thematized, and celebrated its borrowing and sampling, thus challenging the fetishizing of the idea (or ideology) of originality. It suggests a conception of art that celebrates the derivative and does not attempt to downplay or deny the idea that artists have always borrowed from one another. The hip-hop style of appropriation and creative metamorphosing suggests that "borrowing and creation are not at all incompatible" (Shusterman, 2000, p. 205).

Shusterman's next category is cutting and temporality, in which hip-hop's sampling and appropriation of sounds from previous recordings undermines the conventional notion of artistic unity and integrity. The emphasis in hip-hop is on open-ended continuation of artistic interaction with the object as evidenced by the endless collaboration, remixes, and reworkings found in hip-hop recordings. Shusterman finds another Deweyan aesthetic connection here as hip-hop suggests that art is more about process than product. This point is also illustrated by hip-hop's propensity toward an open concept of artistic ownership. In 2004, *Wired* magazine included a CD with its November issue that included tracks from hip-hop artists The Beastie Boys, Danger Mouse, and Chuck D released under the new "Creative Commons License," which makes it legal for anyone to manipulate the tracks for personal use. All the tracks are now available through the Creative Commons website along with the claim, "These musicians are saying that true creativity needs to be open, fluid, and alive. When it comes to copyright, they are pro-choice. Here are 16 songs that encourage people to play with their tunes, not just play them" (*Wired*, 2004).

Hip-hop is at once dependent upon and appropriated by technology and media. Kool Herc's use of commercial technology is part and parcel of the creation myth of hip-hop. Yet it is this same technology that allowed hip-hop to be reified and commodified. One result of this complex connection is an internal conversation in hip-hop about the merits and demerits of commodification and the attendant debates regarding commercial forms of hip-hop versus the so-called underground iterations. While some romanticize certain eras in hip-hop or its origins, or characterize underground hip-hop as the culture's purest form, there is also a well-known sentiment in hip-hop circles that an underground artist is simply another name for an artist without a record contract. Hip-hop artists are, like others who produce popular art, mostly looking to get their work in the hands (or ears) of as many consumers as possible. Another kind of technology, the internet, has been used as a tool for innumerable underground artists to put their work "out there" and in particular, the advent of the massively popular internet community, myspace.com, has become a vehicle for artists without contracts to promote themselves and their music. This relationship between hip-hop and technology is decidedly "postmodern" for Shusterman, and the postmodern challenges to modern artistic conventions are prefigured by American pragmatism, Dewey specifically.

Finally, Shusterman's category of autonomy is a further articulation of hip-hop's rebellion against the kind of compartmentalization found in modern notions of separate cultural spheres and the autonomy of the aesthetic. Hip-hop is replete with examples of artists who challenge this notion in their corpora. KRS-ONE is emblematic of this category, and Shusterman notes

KRS's simultaneous claims of status as teacher, poet, philosopher, and scientist. Shusterman concludes,

> Of course, the realities and truths which hip hop reveals are not the transcendental eternal verities of traditional philosophy, but rather the mutable facts and patterns of the material, socio-historical world. Yet this emphasis on the temporally changing and malleable nature of the real…constitutes a respectably tenable metaphysical position associated with American pragmatism. (2000, p. 212)

Shusterman's categories and aesthetic analysis amount to one of the most fruitful treatments the academy has produced on hip-hop. I adopted his categories for my own ethnographic study on philosophy, but I added one more: kinetic consumption. Hip-hop is meant to be felt and not just seen and/or heard. Performances are animated either implicitly or explicitly by the question "[do] you feel me?"—tantamount to asking an audience if it is connecting with the performer, if the text of the performance is resonating in deep ways with the audience. This connection, this feeling of the performer or the performance, unequivocally elicits some form of kinetic activity. It could result in dancing. It could manifest itself in intense vocal responses to the performance. It nearly always involves rhythmic head nodding. This study does much metaphorical head nodding to Shusterman's pragmatist aesthetics as applied to hip-hop. However, some of its limitations must be acknowledged. While Shusterman does discuss the sociopolitical aspect of hip-hop in as much as it relates to his aesthetic analysis, it is not fully theorized in his work. The connection between Deweyan metaphysics and hip-hop is a good start, and to continue in such a direction it is necessary to add the concept of the prophetic to the analysis. That is in part why this study is not content with an established connection between American pragmatism and hip-hop. The prophetism in hip-hop must be examined fully, and prophetic pragmatism will allow for this as well as being congruent with the rest of Shusterman's categories and analysis.

The other area in which Shusterman's project must be expanded is related to the locus of his inquiry. If pragmatist aesthetics reveals that hip-hop is "down with Dewey" in that it conceives of art as more fundamentally a process than a product, then inquiry into hip-hop culture must privilege an examination of process and not product. No doubt, rap lyrics are an indispensable part of studying hip-hop. Yet, Shusterman's examination relies too much on his reading of these hip-hop products. In order to move beyond this, it is necessary to closely examine process in hip-hop, and that requires more than a detached study of what hip-hop artists produce. In order to examine process, it will be necessary to live and walk with hip-hop artists, on the ground and in the streets. This kinetic consumption is another form of pragmatist rebellion against passive, museum conceptions of art and the mind/body dualism.

Conclusions

While it is not possible to cover completely the aesthetics discussion that resulted from my study of underground hip-hop artists, a couple of things should be clear. First, hip-hop culture exists and hip-hop aesthetic exists and both have real and meaningful relationships with philosophy. Second, doing philosophy through critical ethnography, or doing critical ethnographic philosophy, is a way to uncover such relationships between cultural phenomena and philosophy. Taken together with the conclusions from the first iteration above, that critical theory and methodology and their relationship to philosophy can become a kind of meta-theoretical resource; we can see that philosophy, ethnography, and the urban youth culture phenomenon of hip-hop overlap in a number of interesting and meaningful ways. Critical ethnographic philosophy is both a way to approach that overlap and to analyze it. Moreover, it seems the more the confluence of philosophy and ethnography is explored, the more powerful each becomes.

Notes

1. These ideas about "the system" as distinguished from the lifeworld come from *The Theory of Communicative Action*, Volume 2, Chapter 5 (Habermas, 1987).
2. Carspecken (1999) in "Five Third-Person Positions" also begins to explore this methodological question.
3. For a detailed account, see Rose (1994) or Chang (2005).
4. This summary owes much to Carspecken (1996). Examples of this type of imagery are provided in the first chapter of this text.
5. Also, for some additional perspective on this issue, see Korth (2005, pp 131–167).
6. It is also seems clear that this passage indicates a host of philosophical ideas that could be of benefit in its analysis.
7. It should be noted that additional, more practical suggestions for validating the use of philosophy in ethnography would certainly include the suggestions for validating meaning reconstruction in the normative-evaluative domain found in Chapter 8 of Carpecken (1996). In addition, see Lincoln & Guba (1985).
8. See especially the "Urban Inspirational Metaphysics" chapter in KRS-One (2003).
9. Tommie Shelby, co-editor of Darby & Shelby (2005) is John L. Loeb Associate Professor of the Social Sciences at Harvard University.
10. See Chang (2005), Forman (2002), Forman & Neal (2004), and Rose (1994). These works are examples of academic (or journalistic in the case of Chang) accounts of hip-hop that avoid treating it as a monolith. There is still more room for such complete and sophisticated treatments of hip-hop as the culture continues to grow and gain more influence over the larger popular culture while at the same time descriptions and evaluations of it continue to be oversimplified and truncated.
11. It should be noted that Shusterman goes on to claim that such "contradictions" are a result of "rap's rich plurality of styles" and "more fundamental contradictions in the socio-cultural fields of ghetto life."
12. "Sampling" refers to the process of electronically capturing any sound that can then be manipulated (usually by a keyboard or synthesizer) and assigned any pitch or rate of decay, etc.

References

Caputo, J. D. (1987). *Radical hermeneutics: Repetition, deconstruction, and the hermeneutic project*. Bloomington: Indiana University Press.

Carspecken, P. F. (1996). *Critical ethnography in educational research: A theoretical and practical Guide*. New York: Routledge.

Carspecken, P. F. (1999). *Four Scenes for Posing the Question of Meaning*. New York: Peter Lang.

Chang, J. (2005). *Can't stop, won't stop: A history of the hip-hop generation*. New York: St. Martins Press.

Darby, D., & Shelby T. (2005). *Hip hop and philosophy: Rhyme 2 reason, popular culture and philosophy* Vol. 16. Chicago: Open Court.

Dewey, J. (1935/2005). *Art as experience*. New York: Perigree Trade.

Fay, B. (1996). *Contemporary philosophy of social science: A multicultural approach*. Oxford: Blackwell.

Feinberg, W. (2006a). *For goodness sake: Religious schools and education for democratic citizenry*. New York: Routledge.

Feinberg, W. (2006b). Philosophical ethnography: Or, how philosophy and ethnography can live together in the world of educational research. *Educational Studies in Japan: International Yearbook, 1*, 5–14.

Forman. M. (2002). *The 'hood comes first: Race, space, and place in rap and hip-hop, music/culture*. Middletown, CT: Wesleyan University Press.

Forman. M., & Neal, M. A. (2004). *That's the joint!: The hip-hop studies reader*. New York: Routledge.

Giddens, A. (1986). *The constitution of society: Outline of the theory of structuration*. Berkley: University of California Press.

Habermas, J. (1984). *The theory of communicative action*. Vol. 1: *Reason and the rationalization of society*. Boston: Beacon.

Habermas, J. (1987). *The theory of communicative action*. Vol. 2: *Lifeworld and system. A critique of functionalist reason*. Boston: Beacon.

Habermas, J., Cooke M., & NetLibrary Inc. (1998). *On the pragmatics of communication*. Cambridge, MA: MIT Press.

Korth, B. (2005). Choice, necessity, or narcissism: A feminist does feminist ethnography. In G. Troman, B. Jeffrey, & G. Walford (Eds.), *Methodological issues and practice in ethnography* (pp. 153–198). New York: JAI Press.

Kuhn, T. (1996). *The structure of scientific revolutions*. Chicago: University of Chicago Press.

KRS-One. (2003). *Ruminations* (1st ed.). New York: Welcome Rain Publishers.

Lincoln, Y., & Guba, E. (1985). *Naturalistic inquiry*. Thousand Oaks, CA: Sage.

Ramsey, G. P. (2003). *Race music: Black cultures from bebop to hip-hop*; *Music of the African diaspora* (Vol. 7). Berkeley: University of California Press.

Rose, T. (1994). *Black noise: Rap music and black culture in contemporary America*. Hanover, NH: University Press of New England.

Shusterman, R. (1997). *Practicing philosophy: Pragmatism and the philosophical life*. New York: Routledge.

Shusterman, R. (2000). *Pragmatist aesthetics: Living beauty, rethinking art* (2nd ed.). Lanham, MD: Rowman & Littlefield.

West, C. (1989). *The American evasion of philosophy: A genealogy of pragmatism*. Madison: University of Wisconsin Press.

Willis, P. (1977). *Learning to labour: How working-class kids get working-class jobs*. New York: Columbia University Press.

Winch, P. (2007). *The idea of a social science and its relation to philosophy* (Routledge Classics). New York: Routledge.

Wired. (2004). The WIRED CD: Rip. Sample. Mash. Share. Retrieved October 1, 2011 from http://www.creativecommons.org/wired.

CHAPTER TWENTY-FOUR

(Participatory) Action Research and the Political Realm[1]

DORIS SANTOS

In her quest to understand evildoing, Hannah Arendt (1998) reflects, in the first place, on the things we human beings normally do. She claims that three fundamental activities are basic for us to live in this world: labor, work, and action. Labor refers to all those activities we usually need to do as biologically determined beings, while work is related to the activities we do to transcend such a biological temporality. From her perspective, eating and sleeping are activities we need to do in order to survive as biological organisms (labor), while the making of spoons and blankets is work. The third type of activity is action, that is, all that we do in relation to the other human beings with whom we inhabit the world. The human conditions underlying labor and work, which are life itself and worldliness, respectively, are different from the human condition that corresponds to action, namely, plurality; this is the condition by which we human beings are the same and distinct at the same time. These fundamental human activities are closely connected to the most existential conditions of all: birth and death, natality and mortality.

While German philosopher Martin Heidegger, Arendt's former PhD supervisor, regards mortality as man's defining characteristic (Heidegger, 1962), Arendt states that labor, work, and action are based on natality[2] since they preserve the world for the newcomers. She says that "the miracle that saves the world from its normal 'natural' ruin is ultimately the fact of natality...the birth of new men and the new beginning, the action they are capable of by virtue of being born" (p. 247). Of the three fundamental activities, action is the most closely connected to natality. That is, every time a person acts, he or she makes a new beginning from such an action.

From Arendt's perspective, and as a starting point for our reflections on participatory action research, every time we "do" things as researchers, they are not "doings" of the same sort.

For example, when we write a research report, we need to fabricate it using our hands and all the fantastic technological devices human beings have invented to materialize their thoughts and feelings. In other words, writing as a process of "materializing" human thoughts and feelings into tangible texts (printed or recorded objects) is the type of activity Arendt identifies as work. Different from what we can do with our hands as researchers, the words we speak and the actions we do are things human beings only do in between, without the intermediacy of any human handmade object; they are ephemeral and can only be remembered thanks to what storytellers do in written or oral ways. The most distinctive feature of speaking and acting, then, is that they embody the possibility of a new beginning insofar as the new can take place with them no matter what has been said or done before. This possibility of being born again and again through our words and actions is what is entailed in Arendt's general condition of natality.

Because of this, action is the political activity par excellence; natality, not mortality, is the central category for political thought, says Arendt. "The political realm rises directly out of acting together, the 'sharing of words and deeds.' Thus action not only has the most intimate relationship to the public part of the world common to all of us, but is the one activity which constitutes it" (Arendt, 1998, p. 198). So, political actions and political thinking are possible thanks to natality, although it does not necessarily guarantee them. Our birth as living beings, as well as our birth as political beings through our thinking, actions, and words, are possible thanks to the most general human condition of all, natality. Yet this does not mean that we become political beings just because we are born, biologically speaking. In turn, it follows that not every time we think, speak, and act do we bring about something new; potentially, we are able to, but this does not happen automatically. For this to happen, our actions need to be informed by the most political mental faculty of all, judgment, which allows us, according to Arendt (2005, p. 102), not only to organize and subsume the individual and particular under the general and universal, but also to make distinctions, for example, to distinguish right from wrong, the new from the old. Based on our judgments, our will can make those words and actions happen, that is, make them public, appear in front of other human beings. In short, though natality makes political action and political thinking possible, in the end it is up to each human being to make his words and actions bring about something new.

Although Hannah Arendt did not like to be called a philosopher and preferred the term "political theorist," her perspective has been considered unique in recent times. This may be because her perspective provides a refreshing air to the hopelessness emerging from complex contemporary life. In this essay, I use her perspective to analyze this account of what I believe to be one of the most meaningful research proposals in the social sciences. Participatory action research has been developed not only to contribute to finding out ways to improve life in a world sullied with wrongdoings. It also reveals, through its history and debates, the problems that contemporary societies suffer. In other words, the history or histories of participatory action research reveal, in some way, the problem I want to address here: to talk about participatory action research implies, from the political perspective described above, not simply taking for granted that our actions and words are bringing about new and better lives just because we have coined our doings under the "participatory action" label. Just a small amount of doubt about this can help us to make important and more insightful distinctions between what we advocate through participatory action research and what we "do." This questioning may also help to differentiate what participatory action researchers do that is different from what other researchers do. That is why the human condition of natality, as proposed by Arendt, is so powerful for this specific field of research. The human condition of natality reminds us that we can bring about something new anytime we judge it is meaningful to do so.

In this essay, I consider several versions of the origins of participatory action research in relation to what has been considered its main distinctive feature: its connection to the political realm. Exploring this distinctive characteristic will allow the identification of a current problematic situation with the words used in the literature to make reference to this type of research. Exploring this distinctive characteristic enables us to identify the problematical situation created by the discursive language about this type of research. Some concepts stemming from Arendt's political thought serve as an initial compass in this exercise. Close attention to the many ways in which the notion of participation is used in this discourse opens the way to a series of questions about current reflections and practices in the field. Here my main argument is that advancement in understanding "the political" of participatory action research has been undermined by an exclusive overwhelming attention to "the social" of participatory action research.

1. Action Research and Participatory Action Research

The history or histories of participatory action research, referred to in this first section as PAR, have been inextricably linked to the origins of action research (AR). This relationship has been characterized in different ways. Let us consider some of these historical accounts of PAR in relation to AR.

Although it is commonly thought that Kurt Lewin was the founder of AR, Altrichter and Gstettner (1997) argued instead for J.L. Moreno, for his work in 1913. They claim that although Moreno's direct influence on AR was small, his ideas and research strategies might have indirectly influenced the development of the concept by Lewin, who knew Moreno. Gunz (1986, p. 34), cited by Altrichter and Gstettner (1997), saw Moreno and Lewin in polarity and, maybe, complementarity: "Moreno, the committed actionist filled with intuition and charisma, and Lewin, the reserved social researcher of traditional style interested in logics and precision but on the brink of a paradigm change" (Gunz, 1986, p. 35). These different interests, personalities, and abilities would in time define different types of approaches to AR.

Greenwood and Levin (2007) point out that the diversity of activities today identified as AR cannot be linked to each other in ways as obvious as people might expect. Their genealogy of AR has great importance for this essay, since they connect the developments of AR to various conceptualizations of democracy. They address the origins of AR, among other issues, based on their concerns with "the political relationship between AR and conventional social research, the passive social role of universities, and the general lack of epistemological ambition and methodological attention in much AR writing" (p. xi). These authors celebrate, in this sense, the more ecumenical account of AR developments during the last two decades. Specifically, they refer to the efforts of academics such as Reason and Bradbury (2006), who gathered many strands of thinking in the field in *The Handbook of Action Research*. These efforts enable us to know more about shared references in the field of AR such as those of Karl Marx, John Dewey, Kurt Lewin, Jürgen Habermas, Hans Georg Gadamer, and Richard Rorty. However, these accounts have also helped Greenwood and Levin to identify what they regard as lacking in the handbook: "a critical discourse between different conceptualizations of AR or a contrast between different practices and findings" (Greenwood & Levin, 2007, p. 13).

Although Greenwood and Levin claim that the creation of this critical discourse can provide a more meaningful map of the varieties and trends in AR, they warn that this observation does not imply that AR activities lack the distinctive features that validate them being considered an intellectual and social movement. Recognizing that their account of the developments of AR is mainly defined by their experience as part of the Northern tradition of industrial democracy, they highlight the need for a convergence of Northern and Southern AR traditions in times when democratic practices are being compromised everywhere in the world. Here they acknowledge the contribution of Colombian sociologist Orlando Fals-Borda to activating this convergence with the world conferences he entitled "Convergence" in Cartagena, Colombia, in 1977 and again in 1997.

According to Greenwood and Levin (2007), the "industrial democracy" tradition refers to the first systematic and reasonably large-scale AR effort in Western industrialized countries. Based on Kurt Lewin's early work in the United States, this movement crossed the Atlantic and found resonances at the Tavistock Institute of Human Relations in London. Greenwood and Levin clarify that the major source of large-scale AR projects was in Norway in the Industrial Democracy Project, and these AR ideas were reinvented in Sweden and the United States as industrial management strategies. This widespread diffusion of AR has definitely been considered as an indicator of success in the history of AR. However according to Greenwood and Levin (2007), this historicizing is really a story about "the way fairly radical ideas for social change can be appropriated as management tools aimed at producing more efficient, rather than fairer organizations" (p. 15). For them, the concept of "industrial democracy" has lost its initial meaning. They also see "the same domestication processes" in two other AR approaches: the "Rapid Rural Appraisal" and "Participatory Rural Appraisal" or "Participatory Learning Analysis." From their perspective, these two approaches "unintentionally made participation into a commodity that was built into development strategies as a technique instigated by the funding agencies. This process is quite parallel to the co-optation of industrial democracy" (p. 15).

The early work of Kurt Lewin, who was trained in social psychology, was a so-called natural experiment. In this type of research work, "the researchers in a real-life context invited or forced participants to take part in an experimental activity" (Greenwood & Levin, 2007, p. 16). Despite its patterns of authoritarian control and its aim to produce a desired social outcome, Greenwood and Levin (2007) say that Lewin's thinking about experimentation in natural settings became the main strategy for the Norwegian Industrial Democracy Project.

In the 1970s, as a result of some cooperative work between the Tavistock Institute of Human Relations in London and the Norwegian Confederation of Employers and the Trade Union Council, a European study of industrial democracy was conducted to discover whether representative or participative models of democracy were more suitable to produce a high degree of employee control over their work. As expected, the findings confirmed that participative approaches to work organization could increase industrial democracy. Greenwood and Levin (2007) say that the core ideas in industrial democracy were picked up quickly in Sweden, the United States, and Japan. Three major conceptual schemes emerged from the Norwegian project: "sociotechnical thinking," "psychological job demands," and the idea of "semiautonomous groups." These conceptual schemes were coopted to optimize the efficiency of technological and social systems. These authors say that this diffusion route was possible thanks to the role played by research networks. However, they do not attribute its success to the academic channels: "the ideas diffused because 'they worked' and met strongly felt social needs" (Greenwood & Levin, 2007, p. 16).

According to Greenwood and Levin (2007), in contrast with the Northern historical route of AR, the Southern development of AR was a combination of democratizing efforts under conditions of overt oppression. They explain that most of the AR activities emerged in "some of the most undemocratic situations humans have created: massive colonial exploitation of Africa, Latin America, and Southeast Asia, the genocide/ethnocide of American Indians, the impoverishing of generations of Europeans who immigrated widely, and the enslaving of Africans in the West" (p. 29). They advise that many of the strands of this struggle against structural inequality came to be known as the Southern PAR, participatory research, and the civil rights movement. This appearance of PAR in the South is closely connected to interpretations of AR developments in other latitudes.

Kemmis and McTaggart (2005), for example, place PAR in the international setting as a contribution of a fourth generation of AR practitioners' works. These Australian academics present H. G. Moreno and Kurt Lewin as forming the AR first generation, with the British tradition mentioned by Greenwood and Levin (2007) as the second one. The third generation corresponds to a critical approach to AR made in works such as Carr and Kemmis (1986) and Brock-Utne (1980), as cited in Kemmis and McTaggart (2005). They consider PAR as the type of research being carried out by a fourth generation of scholars in the context of social movements in the developing world, including Paulo Freire, Orlando Fals-Borda, Rajesh Tandon, Anisur Rahman, and Marja-Liisa Swantz, alongside North American and British workers in adult education and literacy, and community development studies such as those by Budd Hall, Myles Horton, Robert Chambers, and John Gaventa. Based on this historical account, Kemmis and McTaggart (2005, p. 560) proceed to analyse PAR from a Habermasian perspective.

These two interpretations of the history of AR—by Greenwood and Levin and by Kemmis and McTaggart—both identify PAR as a particular type of AR especially linked to social movements in particular deprived contexts. However, when action researchers began to theorize "participation" as an integral component of any AR experience (Kemmis & McTaggart, 2005; McTaggart, 1997), this important qualifier initially distinguishing PAR from other AR appears to have been dropped. Through this theoretical exercise, researchers identified particular types of PAR such as critical PAR (Kemmis & McTaggart, 2005). This theoretical evolution began to blur the once-established distinctions between AR and PAR. We can see signs of this, from a different perspective, in some other recent accounts of AR developments.

Dick's three literature reviews (2004, 2006, 2009)[3] reveal that after more than a half of a century struggling towards scientific legitimacy, the field of AR has moved into a stage characterized by the explosion of applications of its theoretical and methodological principles to try to solve various social problems. Work on issues such as education, health, and organizational development has resulted in the consolidation of AR subtypes with their own legitimacy, for example, educational action research, community-based participatory research, and organizational action research. In relation to this explosion of applications of AR, Dick (2009) found that the boundaries between AR and closely related methodologies are fuzzy and are becoming fuzzier (p. 424). Dick advises that this can be seen easily, for example, in educational action research (EAR), which "ranges from quasi-experimentation (Sagor, 2000) through cyclic and participatory approaches (Mills, 2003) to the emancipatory approaches of people like Stephen Kemmis (e.g., 2001)" (Dick, 2004, p. 432). Dick also appears to see no difference between types of AR such as PAR and other proposals such as community-based participatory research (CBPR) (Dick, 2006, p. 444). By the end of his last literature review, he concludes: "My view is that good research is designed to fit the situation and the purpose. In a fast-changing world, that philosophy suits action research well" (Dick, 2009, p. 452). Positions such as his have been in the center of recent debates about what AR, or any one of its subtypes, is for (for example, Kemmis, 2006).

On the importance of "participation" in the field of AR during the last decade, Dick notes "growing attention to the practical details of participation and involvement" (2004, p. 425), and highlights several AR experiences developed from various participatory approaches. Acknowledging Reason and Bradbury's (2006) contribution to set AR as the umbrella term for participatory and action-oriented approaches, Dick provides evidence to support claims about the relationship of AR to issues such as participation, social action, and democracy. Here Dick offers an account of academic works on participation and the Scandinavian industrial democracy (Dick, 2004, p. 434); feminist participatory action research with an emphasis on social action, power, and collaboration (Dick, 2006, p. 440); the development of techniques applicable to community action research where public participation is one of the applications of democracy (Dick, 2006, p. 443); AR as a contributor to the shift from expert rule to the shared governance through a more democratic approach to politics (Dick, 2009, p. 428); and Youth Participatory Action Research, YPAR (Dick, 2009, p. 429). Finally, throughout these literature reviews, he questions the absence of material on building theory from AR (Dick, 2004, p. 425).

In this context, I believe we need to consider another perspective: that of a PAR practitioner of the South, who gained his perspective largely through a lifetime in the South.

Colombian Fals-Borda (2006a, pp. 353-354) claims the main motives for promoting PAR in the 1970s were not superfluous. One was to protest against "the sterile and futile university routine, colonized by western Euro-American culture, and so subordinating as to impede us from discovering or valuing our own realities" (p. 353). The other was to right wrongs—as he says, "to improve the form and foundation of our crisis-ridden societies by fighting against their injustices and trying to eradicate poverty and other socioeconomic afflictions caused by the dominant systems" (p. 353). But by 2006, circumstances on both fronts had changed. On the first motive he could claim, after ten PAR World Congresses, that PAR is now taught or practiced in at least 2,500 universities in 61 countries, many of which have accepted research theses on PAR topics and introduced postgraduate programs in this field. On the second, he would observe that although hard and cruel times have not ended, there are signs of a new horizon: "a different world, perhaps a more acceptable one than our generation has suffered" (p. 353).

In spite of these changes, Fals-Borda (2006a) wonders if it is progress or regress to know that the proposal to "investigate reality in order to transform it" through praxis in Third World countries has begun to become institutionalized. His concern is that institutionalization, although inevitable when ideas are widely accepted, "may lose something of its original cutting edges in the process" (p. 353). He thinks that universities and scientific institutions face a new challenge. In the first place, he cautions against reviving the right- or left-wing intellectual colonialism of either the North or the South (Fals-Borda, 2006a, p. 356).

In their 2003 study critiquing Eurocentrism, Fals-Borda (sociologist) with Luis E. Mora-Osejo (biologist) explain that although they were taught in the 1960s by prominent professors in the United States and Germany, respectively, they both had to relearn much of their disciplines back in Colombia due to the inadequacy of the very well-known frames of reference they had learned overseas for understanding and solving various problems in their home country. That is why, after 50 years of experience and study in tropical and violent areas in Colombia, they decided to "fly alone" (Fals-Borda & Mora-Osejo, 2003, p. 30). In their 2003 Manifesto, they combine an open and systemic contextual hypothesis with the concept of "endogenesis," a biological term that means "growth from within." They reason:

> as European and North American scientific paradigms have been conceived in the contexts of temperate zones and their historical, cultural and material development, they are similarly conditioned by those contexts in the determination of collective thinking and action.... Marx and his European followers should be understandably forgiven for their lack of knowledge of Latin American history and culture. (Fals-Borda & Mora-Osejo, 2003, pp. 32–33)

Having critiqued their own approach to Euro-American theories in their early years, Fals-Borda and Mora Osejo (2003) invite others to develop more endogenous paradigms rooted in every community's realities and circumstances. The more the researcher becomes involved in the knowledge of local realities through life experience or "vivencia," the richer and more useful this knowledge will be (pp. 32–33). PAR therefore emerged in these latitudes with a self-aware epistemic underlay, as a process of "knowledge accumulation" or "convergence"; "the harmonious reconstruction of the relationship of people and nature in our country implies a rediscovery of the peculiarities of our daily living and our socialization" (p. 35). While not pretending to ignore foreign knowledge, they invite formation of an alliance of North and South insofar as both are interested in similar problems and are motivated by convergent interests, two of which concern facing structural injustices and global defects of the modern world (p. 36). They conclude in this vein:

> With such objectives in mind, we can stimulate combined research-and-teaching attitudes and practices within and outside educational institutions which are able to overcome discriminatory distinctions, such as those between the academic and the popular, between the scientific and the political, and to stimulate self-esteem among our peoples and in our academic communities. (Fals-Borda & Mora-Osejo, 2003, p. 36)

Consequently, Fals-Borda (2006a) interprets the origins of PAR in the so-called Third World as an endogenous proposal based on an examination of local social, cultural, historical, and environmental roots in order to explain, describe, systematize, and transform contexts and existing conditions. This interpretation is shared by Rahman (2008), who presents a historical account of a South Asian trend in PAR that is closely connected to the articulation of people's collective self-initiatives in the field of rural development in India, Sri Lanka, Philippines, and Bangladesh. Rahman (2008, pp. 50–51) states that the first theoretical reflection on PAR can be found in the writings of Heinz Moser about a trend in Germany termed "emancipatory research." Yet he also claims that the origins of participatory (action) research relate to recognition of the autonomy of these endogenous proposals by the International Network on Participatory Research launched at a major conference on AR in Cartagena, Colombia, in April 1977. This network was the result of an initiative of Budd Hall of the International Council for Adult Education (ICAE) based in Toronto, Canada, and some of his colleagues, who exchanged ideas with Fals-Borda and intellectuals from many parts of the world.

Through this international exchange of ideas, PAR practitioners have tried out "advanced as well as much-applied principles and techniques, but also propose concepts and intellectual inventions of their own, appropriate and relevant to the realities that inspired them" (Fals-Borda, 2006a, p. 356). Fals-Borda (2006a) advocates the importance of PAR for universities and scientific institutions as they face current challenges, especially responding to the crises presented by neoliberal modernity. After overcoming strong debates about PAR—its validity, scientific rigor, the rhythm of theory and practice, the balance between subject and object, and ethical dilemmas of science and conscience—Fals-Borda remains firm. He insists that "as part of our scientific task, we have the political, objective and non-neutral duty of fostering the democratic and spiritual dimensions through more satisfying life systems. To this end, northern and southern scholars can converge and be soul fellows in the quest for meaning" (Fals-Borda, 2006a, p. 357).

These four historical accounts deepen our understanding of why PAR has become relevant in education. First, while the origins of AR are clearly defined by some researchers' interest in solving different social problems in different contexts of the world (Dick, 2004, 2006, 2009; Greenwood & Levin, 2007; Kemmis & McTaggart, 2005), the creation of PAR has been especially associated with some AR practitioners' understanding of their practices as inextricably linked to their political duty (Fals-Borda & Mora-Osejo, 2003; Kemmis & McTaggart, 2005; Fals-Borda, 2006a; Greenwood & Levin, 2007).

A second conclusion that can be drawn from these histories of AR and PAR is that it appears AR practitioners, including practitioners of PAR, find in participation an essential element to deal with the social and political dimensions of their research practice (Dick, 2004, 2006, 2009; Greenwood & Levin, 2007; Kemmis, 2006; Kemmis & McTaggart, 2005; Kemmis, Wilkinson, Hardy, & Edwards-Groves, 2009). Sometimes an emphasis on the political dimension leads AR practitioners to describe their research practice as PAR.

Finally, a third conclusion from these historical accounts of AR, and of PAR as one of its types, is that they provide evidence supporting the view that the practices of AR and PAR practitioners are informed by different ideologies associated with the social and political dimensions of their work (Dick, 2004, 2006, 2009; Greenwood & Levin, 2007; Kemmis, 2006; Kemmis & McTaggart, 2005; Kemmis, et al., 2009). However, as observed of contemporary higher education (Apple, 2005; Grundy, 2007), discourses and practices in the field of AR and PAR serve ideologies that are expected to be contested by the academic community (Greenwood & Levin, 2007; Kemmis, 2006).

Considering these latter evaluations of literature, from now on in this essay I use parentheses around the "p" in the acronym (P)AR referencing the two problematic situations so far identified. First, the parentheses refer to the type of AR where participation is considered an essential component, whether or not the research is described as PAR by their practitioners. Second, because different ideologies inform (P)AR discourses and practices, these parentheses also indicate that participation is regarded as a problematic term that presupposes (different) ideas of participation.

To analyse the developments of (P)AR, let us return to Arendt's political thought for some helpful ideas.

2. What Is Politics for Hannah Arendt?

Arendt (1998) goes back to the ancient Greeks for origins. She says that the foundation of the *polis* was the Greek remedy for the fragility of boundless and nontangible human relationships (p. 196).

> The *polis*, as it grew out of and remained rooted in the Greek pre-*polis* experience and estimate of what makes it worthwhile for men to live together (*syzēn*) namely, the "sharing of words and deeds," had a twofold function. [...] The *polis* was supposed to multiply the occasions to win "immortal fame," that is, to multiply the chances for everybody to distinguish himself, to show in deed and word who he was in his unique distinctness.... The second function of the *polis*, again closely connected with the hazards of action as experienced before its coming into being, was to offer a remedy for the futility of action and speech. (Arendt, 1998, pp. 196–197)

Arendt (1998) therefore interprets the political realm as emerging directly out of acting together (p. 198). She states that, properly speaking, the *polis* is not the city-state in its physical location but the organization of the people as it arises out of acting and speaking together, "and its true space lies between people living together for this purpose, no matter where they happen to be" (p. 198). From this perspective, action and speech create this space between the participants. This is a space, she says, "where I appear to others as others appear to me, where men exist not merely like other living or inanimate things but make their appearance explicitly" (pp. 198–199). However, she makes it clear that even though human beings are capable of actions and words, this space created by speech and action does not always exist; many people do not live in it.

Arendt (1998) says that the political realm is different from other spaces, that it "does not survive the actuality of the movement which brought it into being, but disappears not only with the dispersal of men [...] but with the disappearance or arrest of the activities themselves" (p. 199). She argues that what kills political communities is their loss of power. For Arendt (1998), power is what keeps in existence the public realm, that is, the potential space of appearance between acting and speaking people. "Power is actualized only where word and deed have not parted company, where words are not empty and deeds are not brutal, where words are not used to veil intentions but to disclose realities, and deeds are not used to violate and destroy but to establish relations and create new realities" (Arendt, 1998, p. 200). She claims the only indispensable material factor in the generation of power is humans living together.

Power is thus the human ability not just to act but to act in concert (Arendt, 1970). It belongs to a group, not to an individual. Power therefore exists only as long as the group keeps together: "When we say of somebody that he is 'in power' we actually refer to his being empowered by a certain number of people to act in their name. The moment the group, from which the power originated to begin with...disappears, 'his power' also vanishes" (p. 44). So power is what keeps people together after the ephemeral moment of action has passed, and, she adds "whoever, for whatever reasons, isolates himself and does not partake in such being together, forfeits power and becomes impotent, no matter how great his strength and how valid his reasons" (Arendt, 1998, p. 201). From this perspective, participation is inherently connected; in fact it is intrinsic, to the political realm insofar as this taking part in a collective situation makes acting together possible. The only limitation on power, Arendt says, is the existence of other people, which cannot be taken as accidental. Human power corresponds to the human condition of plurality, the fact that "we are all the same, that is, human, in such a way that nobody is ever the same as anyone else who ever lived, lives, or will live" (Arendt, 1998, p. 8).

In Arendt's view, the condition of human plurality is not only the conditio sine qua non, but also the condition per quam of all political life (Arendt, 1998, p. 7). Because of this, she claims that politics deals with the coexistence and association of different human beings who organize themselves according to certain essential commonalities found "within or abstracted from" an absolute chaos of differences (Arendt, 2005, p. 93). And she adds:

> As long as political bodies are based on the family and conceived in the image of the family, kinship in all its degrees is credited on the one hand as being able to unite extreme individual differences, *and*, on the other hand, as a means by which groups resembling individuals can be isolated and contrasted. (Arendt, 2005, pp. 94–95)

According to Arendt (2005, pp. 94–95), our political lives, although resembling our family lives, are constructed on a different type of tie (kinship). This new type of relationship leads to the fundamental perversion of politics insofar as it abolishes the basic quality of plurality. Politics arises in what lies "*between men*" (italics in original) and is established as relationships; this form of organization eradicates the original differentiation of each man. She emphasises that "politics organizes those who are absolutely different with a view to their *relative* equality and in contradistinction to their *relative* differences" (Arendt, 2005, p. 96, italics in original)

In her reflection on what politics is, Arendt (2005) says that our prejudices are always present when we talk about politics, although our shared prejudices are political too. She states that we cannot ignore these prejudices, since they indicate that in political terms, we do not know, or do not yet know, how to function in situations into which we have stumbled. In the 1950s, Arendt identified the hope and fear underlying our prejudices against politics as:

> the fear that humanity could destroy itself through politics and through the means of force now at his [*sic*] disposal, and, linked with this fear, the hope that humanity will come to its senses and rid the world, not of humankind, but of politics. It could do so through a world government that transforms the state into an administrative machine, resolves political conflicts bureaucratically, and replaces armies with police forces…. However, if we understand politics to mean a global dominion in which people appear primarily as active agents who lend human affairs a permanence they otherwise do not have, then this hope is not the least bit utopian. (Arendt, 2005, p. 97).

But for Arendt the problem is not having prejudices; she recognizes that we must have them since we cannot have original judgments about everything. In a broader sense, she identifies all prejudices we share as political insofar as they are "something that constitutes an integral part of those human affairs that are the context in which we go about our daily lives" (Arendt, 2005, p. 99). Prejudices are different from personal idiosyncrasies since they exist outside of experience, which is why Arendt believes the task of politics is to dispel them. However, there is something that prejudices share with judgement: the way in which people recognize themselves and their commonalities. Someone with prejudices, Arendt (2005) says, can always be certain of having an effect on others. This is why prejudices play a major role in the social arena, while what is idiosyncratic hardly prevails in the public and political spheres.

Arendt sees that in every historical crisis, prejudices begin to collapse because they can no longer be accepted. They become closed worldviews or ideologies with an explanation for everything, pretending to understand all historical and political reality (Arendt, 2005, pp. 102–103). In this view, what distinguishes prejudice from ideology is precisely this claim of universality since prejudice is always partial in nature, while an ideology shields us from all experience by providing a complete view of the world confronting us. Ideologies state clearly that both our prejudices and our standards of judgment are inappropriate and, because of this, we should no longer rely on them.

In relation to the modern crisis, Arendt claims:

> Regardless of how people respond to the question of whether it is man or the world that is in jeopardy in the present crisis, one thing is certain: any response that places man in the center of our current worries and suggests he must be changed before any relief is to be found is profoundly unpolitical. For at the center of politics lies concern for the world, not for man.... If we want to change an institution, an organization, some public body existing within the world, we can only revise its constitution, its laws, its statutes, and hope that all the rest will take care of itself. This is so because wherever human beings come together—be it in private or socially, be it in public or politically—a space is generated that simultaneously gathers them into it and separates them from one another.... Wherever people come together, the world thrusts itself between them, and it is in this in-between space that all human affairs are conducted. (Arendt, 2005, pp. 105–106)

From Arendt's point of view, the only activity that goes on directly between human beings without the intermediary of things, and corresponds to the human condition of plurality, is action. (Arendt, 1998, p. 7) She says that action is unique in that it "sets into motion processes that in their automatism look very much like natural processes, [...] action also marks the start of something, begins something new, seizes the initiative" (Arendt, 2005, p. 113). She believes that action cannot be eliminated in spite of its instrumentalization and the degradation of politics into a means for something else (Arendt, 1998). While frailty is the main feature of human relationships, uncertainty becomes the distinctive character of human affairs (p. 232). Only because human beings are capable of acting, of starting processes on their own, is it possible to conceive both nature and history as systems of processes.

Arendt therefore emphasizes that "men never have been and never will be able to undo or even to control reliably any of the processes they start through action.... And this incapacity to undo what has been done is matched by an almost equally complete incapacity to foretell the consequences of any deed or even to have reliable knowledge of its motives" (Arendt, 1998, pp. 232–233). The remedy against this irreversibility and unpredictability of the process started by acting, Arendt claims, is one of the potentialities of action itself. While the possible redemption from irreversibility is the faculty of forgiving, the remedy for unpredictability is the faculty of making and keeping promises (Arendt, 1998, pp. 236–237). Both faculties, she states, depend on plurality since forgiving and making and keeping promises need to take place in the presence and acting of others. And she adds:

> But trespassing is an everyday occurrence which is in the very nature of action's constant establishment of new relationships within a web of relations, and it needs forgiving, dismissing, in order to make it possible for life to go on by constantly releasing men from what they have done unknowingly. Only through

this constant mutual release from what they do can men remain free agents, only by constant willingness to change their minds and start again can they be trusted with so great a power as that to begin something new. (Arendt, 1998, p. 240)

However, there is one form of living together that needs action not to happen; this is the main demand from the social realm. For Arendt (1998), historically speaking, the rise of the social coincided with the transformation of private care for private property into a public concern:

> The emergence of society—the rise of housekeeping, its activities, problems, and organizational devices— from the shadowy interior of the household into the light of the public sphere, has not only blurred the old border line between private and political, it has also changed almost any recognition of the meaning of the two terms and their significance for the life of the individual and the citizen. (Arendt, 1998, p. 38)

In this perspective, society continually demands that its members act as if they belong to a big family, which has only one opinion and one interest; the most social form of government, in this sense, is bureaucracy (Arendt, 1998, p. 40). Society excludes the possibility of action on all its levels. Instead, "society expects from each of its members a certain kind of behaviour, imposing innumerable and various rules, all of which tend to 'normalize' its members, to make them behave, to exclude spontaneous action or outstanding achievement" (p. 40). In modern times, she says, the social realm has conquered the public realm, making the social and the political realms much less distinct. Understanding "politics" as a function of society, and action, speech, and thought as primarily "superstructures upon social interest" has made it impossible to perceive any difference between "the social" and "the political."

Inherent in the human ability to make a beginning, which is in turn inherent in the fact of being born, is freedom, which is the meaning of politics. Arendt (2006) states that freedom becomes the direct aim of political action: "[t]he *raison d'être* of politics is freedom, and its field of experience is action" (p. 145). Arendt says that freedom is possible, politically speaking, when there is a common public space where human beings can meet, in other words,

> [A] politically organized world into which each of the free men could insert himself by word and deed.... Without a politically guaranteed public realm, freedom lacks the worldly space to make its appearance.... Freedom as a demonstrable fact and politics coincide and are related to each other like two sides of the same matter. (Arendt, 2006, p. 147)

Arendt (2005) emphasizes that the principles of action that inform our thinking about politics have barely been questioned. Instead, questions have centered on identifying "which polities and forms of government represent the best of human communal life" (p. 197). Since the end of the 18th century, lively discussion has considered "the possible advantages and disadvantages of monarchy, aristocracy and democracy and/or some polity that could mix monarchic, aristocratic or democratic elements in a republic" (p. 197).

Arendt (2005) also provides an interesting interpretation of various attempts by the ancient Greeks to oppose the polis. One of these attempts was Plato's foundation of the Academy:

> This act stood in opposition to the polis because it set the Academy apart from the political arena, but at the same time it was also done in the spirit of this specifically Greco-Athenian political space—that is, insofar as its substance lay in men speaking with one another. And with that there arose alongside the realm of political freedom a new space of freedom that has survived down to our time as the freedom

of the university and academic freedom…. The free space of the Academy was intended as a fully valid substitute for the marketplace, the agora, the central space for freedom in the polis. In order for their institution to succeed, the few had to demand that their activity, their speech with one another, be relieved of the activities of the polis in the same way the citizens of Athens were relieved of all activities that dealt with earning their daily bread. They had to be freed from politics in the Greek sense in order to be free for the space of academic freedom, just as the citizen had to be freed from earning the necessities of life in order to be free for politics. In order to enter the "academic" space, they had to leave the space of real politics, just as citizens had to leave the privacy of their households to go to the marketplace. Just as liberation from work and the cares of life was a prerequisite for the freedom of the political man, liberation from politics was a prerequisite for the freedom of the academic. (Arendt, 2005, pp. 131–132)

Arendt's understanding of the political realm as the space lying between people, and of politics concerning the organization that emerges from their acting and speaking according to certain essential commonalities (Arendt, 1970, 1998, 2005, 2006), provides us with some more elements to analyze some of the most important developments in the field of (P)AR.

3. Politics and (P)AR: Learning How to Act Together

From review of the most cited reference academic works in the field of (P)AR, it can be said that its practitioners and advocates have certainly been exploring different ways of organizing human beings' acting together, in theoretical and practical terms, and no matter the contexts and problems tackled and perspectives adopted. However, politically speaking there are two problematic situations that are closely connected to the themes discussed above.

First, it seems that, although the goals pursued through (P)AR concern the political realm, especially on "social issues, the discussions and understandings about the former are overshadowed, and sometimes misled, by analysis of the latter. This problem is easily evidenced when revising the wide range of approaches to the notion of "participation" in (P)AR. The second problematic situation deals with what some critiques of (P)AR have called a lack of internal and/or external coherence in this type of research. Specifically, the community of (P)AR keeps on being challenged to know more about (P)AR practitioners' and advocates' ways of acting together with the communities to which we address our efforts, and among ourselves.

In tracking how participation has been theorized in the field of (P)AR, I have identified a variety of approaches and proposals. All of them turn out to be "readings" of (P)AR from different theories in the fields of sociology, social psychology, and philosophy. I have organized the results of this literature review to highlight particular contributions to an understanding of what could be called "the politics of (P)AR." Below I discuss some of the problematic situations while addressing these contributions in relation to the notion of participation.

One of the most cited academic works in the field of (P)AR was written by the Australian academic Robin McTaggart (1997). This has become a classic since it was one of the first theorizations of (P)AR. McTaggart's main concern was to define what (P)AR is, what it is not, and in particular what participation means in this type of research. As he noted five years later in a study with Helbert Altrichter, Stephen Kemmis, and Ortrun Zuber-Skerritt, a definition of (P)AR enables practitioners and advocates to "move thoughtfully beyond the paradigm dominant in our research field and begin with our own questions" (Altrichter, Kemmis, McTaggart, & Zuber-Skerritt, 2002, p. 126). Certainly, McTaggart (1997) and other (P)AR practitioners and advocates have helped the (P)AR community to establish some initial borders to start posing its own questions. Before addressing some of these questions and their possible answers, it is important to highlight McTaggart's warning about the problematic use of the term "participation." He says that the term has been used in a confusing way, specifically, "in situations where people with different power, status, influence, and facility with language come together to work on a thematic concern" (McTaggart, 1997, p. 28). In my view, this problem also emerges as a result of the convergence within the (P)AR field of different worldviews, which include conflicting ideologies and theoretical frameworks.

Based on some standard dictionary definitions of the word "participation" and Rajesh Tandon's (1988) work on participation in research, McTaggart (1997) suggests that making a distinction between "participation" and "involvement" can help to solve the confusing use of the term in the field of (P)AR. In doing this, he reflects on participation and its role in the process of interest here: research. From his perspective, participation "means ownership, that is, responsible agency in the production of knowledge and improvement of practice" (pp. 28–29); whereas mere involvement creates an illusion of participation (McTaggart, 1997, p. 30). Proposing eight guiding principles for any (P)AR process, McTaggart (1997) defines (P)AR as "a political process because it involves people making changes together that also will affect others" (p. 36).

Eight years later, McTaggart with his Australian colleague Stephen Kemmis provided an extended definition for (P)AR as "a social process of collaborative learning realized by groups of people who join together in changing the practices through which they interact in a shared social world in which, for better or worse, we live with the consequences of one another's actions" (Kemmis & McTaggart, 2005, p. 563) Although the sense of the political in the first definition is maintained in the second, the language is not. In the second, the social is explicitly forgrounded in direct connection to the notion of the learning process that takes place in (P)AR. This change of emphasis in the new definition could infer that living and acting together needs to be learned and (P)AR serves in this goal too.

A contemporaneous academic work that has been used as a point of reference in the field of (P)AR and from which some important contributions can be drawn in relation to politics, is by another Australian academic, Yoland Wadsworth. She analyses each of the three components of the acronym (P)AR based on her story as a (P)AR practitioner. Besides reflecting on (P)AR as a cognitive process closely connected to processes of constructing knowledge for everyday life (the "R" component of the acronym), she focuses on the action-effects of inquiry (Wadsworth, 1998, p. 5). In this paper, she analyzes the participation element mainly as an issue related to the way groups of people can organize the conditions under which they carry out (P)AR (Wadsworth, 1998, p. 7). But for the present study, the most important part of her reflection on politics concerns her understanding of action as a "moving into the new," a "creative moment of transformation," which involves an "imaginative leap from a world of 'as it is' to a glimpse of a world 'as it could be'" (Wadsworth, 1998, p. 6). She says,

> Not only is research itself an action in and on existing situations, but it also always has consequences. Things inevitably change as a result of research…. Whether people then choose to continue as before or to change course means that the new situation will either be different from that before, or it will be the same. To "not change" is nevertheless action: some might call it inaction! (Wadsworth, 1998, p. 6)

Wadsworth's reflections on action as linked to people's creative moments are subsumed by her insights into participation in terms of the roles to be performed by participants in (P)AR in order to achieve the "creative change" (Wadsworth, 1998, pp. 8–12). Again refracting through the political lens used for the present study, we see that Wadsworth's reflections on the political dimension of action are overshadowed by her consideration of its social dimension. This can be the result of what Susan Noffke (2009) identifies as the power relations existing in social research (p. 7). In relation to these power relations in the sciences, Fals-Borda (2006b) rejects the academic tradition of using research mainly for career advancement. He says that (P)AR practitioners and advocates have to try "to theorize and obtain knowledge enriched through direct involvement, intervention or insertion in processes of social action" (p. 30). This entails not only ethical but also epistemological considerations.

Moving to more recent works that present reflections on participation in relation to politics, two types of contributions are relevant for the research proposed here. These are not the only academic works of this kind, but they could be considered as essential for the reflections on: (1) (P)AR and the public sphere (Kemmis, 2006, 2007, 2008; Kemmis & McTaggart, 2005); and (2) (P)AR and epistemology (Elliott, 2005, 2007, 2009; Fals-Borda, 2006a, 2006b; Fals-Borda & Mora-Osejo, 2003; Fals-Borda & Ordonez, 2007; Kindon, Pain, & Kesby, 2007; Noffke, 2009; Reason & Bradbury, 2006; Wadsworth, 1998).

Regarding (P)AR and the public sphere, Kemmis and McTaggart (2005) from a critical perspective define (P)AR as a social—and educational—process insofar as it is directed towards studying, reframing, and reconstructing social practices (p. 563). In their view, (P)AR is participatory, practical and collaborative, emancipatory, critical, reflexive, and transformative. Based on German social theorist Jürgen Habermas's theories, Kemmis and McTaggart (2005, p. 578) claim that (P)AR opens communicative space between participants, projecting communicative action into both the field of action and the making of history. This type of research generates "not only a collaborative sense of agency but also a collaborative sense of legitimacy of the decisions people make, and the actions they take, together" (p. 578). The relationships of participation are therefore a central defining feature of (P)AR insofar as it

> issues an invitation to previously or naturally uninvolved people, as well as a self-constituted action research group, to participate in a common process of communicative action for transformation. Not all will accept the invitation, but it is incumbent on those who do participate to take into account those others' understandings, perspectives, and interests—even if the decision is to oppose them in the service of a broader public interest. (Kemmis & McTaggart, 2005, p. 579)

Their advocacy of a critical (P)AR is intended not only as an "antidote" to avoid using this type of research to justify social programs, policies, and practices that maintain social inequalities, but also to insist that "people can still have hope of knowing what they are doing and doing what they think is right and, more particularly, doing less of what they think will have untoward consequences for themselves and others" (Kemmis & McTaggart, 2005, p. 599). This is why, from this critical stance, (P)AR must be capable of telling "unwelcome truths" (Kemmis, 2006). In Kemmis's (2008) words, praxis or "this right conduct in response to a particular situation at a particular time, informed by the agent's knowledge and by recourse to relevant theory and traditions" (pp. 131–132) leads participants to use a particular form of reason whenever they have to act in a complex situation (practical reason).

In relation to epistemology in (P)AR and its connection to politics, this has been another productive area in the field. Returning to Wadsworth's (1998) thoughts, she links "the moving to the new" of action with an exercise of imagination:

> Where existing situations benefit or promote some but disadvantage or subordinate others, then creative change may be construed as "political." As well, participatory action research does not conceptualise this as the development of predictive cause-effect theory ("if this, then that"). Instead, as in the slogan: "the future is made, not predicted," it is more like "what if we..., then maybe." *Possibility* theory rather than predictive theory. That is, human actors are both wilful and capable of thwarting research prediction, and wilful and capable of selecting and implementing theories or probabilities they want to see manifested! Conventional science sees this as undesirable "contamination" and "bias." Participatory action research sees this as a goal, and the stuff of which "real life" is made or enacted. (Wadsworth, 1998, p. 6)

From this perspective, one of the presuppositions about the type of knowledge constructed through (P)AR concerns an exercise of imagination so that possible worlds in the social realm can be envisaged through this type of research. This is something on which (P)AR practitioners and advocates agree. In fact, for Arendt (1978), different from re-presentation, which makes present what is actually absent, imagination "prepares itself to 'go further,' toward the understanding of things that are always absent, that cannot be remembered because they were never present to sense experience" (p. 77).

These reflections on the role of imagination in the construction of knowledge as a crucial aspect in the politics of (P)AR are closely connected to what has been addressed by Colombians Orlando Fals-Borda and Luis E. Mora-Osejo (2003). They claim knowledge that "grows from within" each context (endogenous knowledge) opens the way for useful discoveries and initiatives. For a Southern reading of this principle, they point out:

> We as insiders to the tropics are in a privileged position to produce, analyze and systematize this knowledge with the help and contribution of autochthonous peoples.... We know that environmental factors in the tropics are complex and clearly distinct from those of other world zones.... Extraneous and/or incompatible formulae are precisely the ones that in our zones have had negative environmental impact. (Fals-Borda & Mora-Osejo, 2003, p. 34)

However, Fals-Borda and Mora-Osejo emphasize that working to construct knowledge that "grows from within" must not be done while neglecting the knowledge coming from outside. Recognition of the plurality of knowledges in (P)AR needs to be understood not only as a convergence between popular thought and academic science (Fals-Borda, 2006b, p. 29), but also as an encounter between knowledge coming from the North and from the South (Fals-Borda, 2006a). From this perspective, it seems that participation is essential to (P)AR insofar as it allows the appearance of a plurality of knowledges among equals.

This invitation to recognize the plurality of knowledges in (P)AR has also been made by practitioners such as Kindon et al. (2007). They advocate convergence among disciplines as well as institutions. This represents a major epistemological challenge to mainstream research traditions in the social and environmental sciences insofar as "the latter assume knowledge to reside in the formal institutions of academia and policy" (Kindon, et al., 2007, p. 9). To cope with this challenge, they suggest a participation continuum for (P)AR: from passive participation to self-mobilization (Kindon, et al., 2007, p. 16).

As mentioned above, (P)AR is also challenged by the mainstream ways to construct knowledge in the scientific world. On this, Fals-Borda (2007) emphasizes that the most important aspect in (P)AR is empathy. As he expressed in his typical rational and emotional terms, "It seemed counterproductive for our work to regard the researcher and the researched, the 'experts' and the 'clients' or 'targets' as two discrete, discordant or antagonistic poles. Rather, we had to consider them both as real 'thinking–feeling persons' (*sentipensantes*) whose diverse views on the shared life experience should be taken jointly into account" (Fals-Borda, 2006b, p. 30). This perspective cannot identify higher or lower roles in (P)AR because, through participation, what was considered "the object of study" is now recognized as "the subject," which brings about a relationship among equals. (Fals-Borda & Ordonez, 2007, p. 11) Consequently, Fals-Borda (2006b) claims, (P)AR is not just a quest for knowledge. Values accompanying the dominant research paradigm, such as consistency, simplicity, scope, certitude, and productivity need to be together in (P)AR, along with values like altruism, sincerity of intent, trust, autonomy, and social responsibility (Fals-Borda, 2006b, p. 32).

Noffke (2009, p. 7), based on Sandra Harding's (1987) depiction of epistemology, says that the varied forms of (P)AR address in quite distinctive ways questions of "who is the knower," "what kind of things can be known" and "what strategies count as means to be legitimated as knowledge." Noffke's (2009) exploration of these considerations has led her to identify three emphases in (P)AR practices that she believes correspond to three distinct but interconnected dimensions of (P)AR: the personal, the professional, and the political. She explains:

> My primary concern in using the "dimensions" construct was to find a way to explore the multiple layers of assumptions, purposes, and practices without creating an implicitly hierarchical set of categories which could be used to prioritize or even dismiss some forms of action research in comparison to others. Instead, I sought a way to see the complexities and interconnectedness across the dimensions. While all forms of action research (and indeed all research) embody the political, I felt that what was needed was a way to see the complexities of work in action research, rather than to find the form that is "just right." (Noffke, 2009, p. 8)

Her interest in making distinctions between these layered dimensions of (P)AR turns out to be a useful resource to understand (P)AR practices, for example, in relation to "who is the knower" (a person) and "what is to be known" (i.e., a profession), among other possible interpretations. Though Noffke (2009) aligns her way of thinking to Appadurai's (2006) understanding of research as connected to the human being's capacity to aspire, and illustrates a variety of manifestations of the political dimension of (P)AR, she provides very few clarifying elements to make a distinction between the political and the social in (P)AR. In some way, it can be said that she has treated the political realm and the social realm indistinctly (Noffke, 2009, pp. 11–12).

About "what strategies count as means to be legitimated as knowledge," Noffke (2009) states that, no matter the variety of methods and methodologies used by (P)AR practitioners, all of the latter share an epistemology that sees knowledge as essentially connected to practice (p. 21). John Elliott (2009) agrees on this latter point, but has a different perspective on methods and methodologies. Addressing the relationship between knowledge of universals and knowledge of particulars in (P)AR, Elliott (2009) offers the critique that social sciences have tended to assume that these knowledges are discrete forms of knowledge with their own distinctive methods of inquiry. He expresses his disappointment about the way the methodological discourse of the social sciences has distorted (P)AR practical philosophy; this has generated, in turn, a battle between the qualitative and the quantitative paradigms (p. 37). Aligned with Rorty's (1999) thought, Elliott (2009) states that all science is a form of practical reasoning and that this is what constitutes the democratic process of inquiry that characterizes (P)AR. Elliott (2005, 2007, 2009) and Kemmis (Carr & Kemmis, 2009; Kemmis, 2005, 2006, 2007, 2008;

Kemmis & McTaggart, 2005), through different perspectives and routes, argue for the creation of spaces for inquirers to engage in conversation with each other, the material condition for the community of (P)AR to generate knowledge.

Finally, and on the relationship between knowledge and action, Elliott (2009) says that "our capacity to recognize the unique and novel features of a case that are nevertheless ethically significant depends on their use. Becoming capable of recognizing the unanticipated when it occurs depends on the anticipations provided by universal rules of thumb, in Nussbaum's words, or action hypothesis" (p. 34). He also emphasizes that future action cannot be derived merely from a transformed consciousness (Elliott, 2005, p. 361). The space for exercising democratically informed agency comes from a political struggle to create material conditions for a free, open, and democratically constructed practical discourse to emerge as context for professional action (Elliott, 2005, p. 363). Referring to the field of education, he says he is convinced "that 'critical self-reflection' is an integral feature of action research, conceived as a systematic organisation of action that is aimed at the realisation of an educationally worthwhile and socially just learning process for students" (Elliott, 2005, p. 365). Like Fals-Borda and Ordoñez (2007), Elliott (2005) argues that (P)AR implies no specific methods of inquiry since methods are context bound and will be operationally shaped in the light of the problems that are presented in the context (p. 370).

One last contribution to an understanding of participation in (P)AR as related to the political realm is presented by Reason and Bradbury (2006). They define action research as "a participatory, democratic process concerned with developing practical knowing in the pursuit of worthwhile human purposes, grounded in a participatory worldview which we believe is emerging at this historical moment" (p. 1). This is perhaps the definition that gives participation a central role in (P)AR. Reason and Bradbury (2006) find in the metaphor of participation a basis for a more creative and constructive worldview:

> The emergent worldview has been described as systemic, holistic, relational, feminine, experiential, but its defining characteristic is that it is participatory: our world does not consist of separate things but of relationships which we co-author. We participate in our world, so that the "reality" we experience is a co-creation that involves the primal givenness of the cosmos and human feeling and construing. The participatory metaphor is particularly apt for action research, because as we participate in creating our world we are already embodied and breathing beings *who are necessarily acting*—and this draws us to consider how to judge the *quality* of our acting. (Reason & Bradbury, 2006, p. 7)

With this understanding of (P)AR, Reason and Bradbury (2006) sketch the characteristics of this participatory worldview as:

> the *participatory nature* of the given cosmos whose form is *relational and ecological*. Since we are part of the whole, we are already engaged in *practical being and acting*…. Thus our science is necessarily an action science, which draws on *extended epistemologies* and continually inquires into the *meaning and purpose* of our practice. (Reason & Bradbury, 2006, p. 7)

For these authors, the political imperative is not only that researchers consider their subjects in a different way or that they act ethically; it is also about the democratic foundations of inquiry and of society (Reason & Bradbury, 2006, p. 10). They conceive of (P)AR as an educative endeavor in so far as it is necessary for humans "to learn more about how to exercise power and position legitimately in the service of participative relationships, to find ways in which politicians, professionals, managers can exercise power in transforming ways, power with others rather than power over others" (p. 10). In similar spirit, Reason and Bradbury (2006) advocate that due to the condition of our times, human inquiry should not so much search for truth but seek to heal, especially "to heal the alienation, the split that characterizes modern experience" (p. 11).

New elements emerge from this review of (P)AR perspectives on participation: first, a wider perspective of "the whole," in which human beings partake or participate; second, and aligned with previous reflections, (P)AR is seen as a site for learning, but here to learn how to exercise power; and, third, the need to understand (P)AR as healing. Reason and Bradbury's (2006) ecological understanding about (P)AR inspires questions about the relationships between (P)AR practices and other types of social and political practices.

4. Some Final Words

The questions emerging from this analysis could be innumerable; in the meantime, this account of what could be called some "politics of contemporary (P)AR" leads us to conclude that, in theory, (P)AR is clearly defined in terms of its practitioners' political commitment to the communities with which they work and the broader society to which they belong. If we consider the blurred relationship between "the social" and "the political" in (P)AR, as shown through this chapter, it seems that nowadays much more is being said about the social than about the political in the field of (P)AR. This could be because of the more evident interest in solving problems related to social inequalities through theories of this sort, as well as the constraints imposed upon (P)AR through the social realm itself.

The various histories of AR reveal that (P)AR emerged in times and places when democratic practices were being compromised, and social researchers started considering their role in contributing to the restoration of such practices to help bring about expected/desirable social changes. Drawing from Hannah Arendt's perspective of politics, we could say that, in the case of (P)AR, its origins are directly related to political actions aimed at restructuring the social realm. However, as suggested in some of these accounts, some of these restructuring attempts have been used to "normalize" people's actions and words towards achieving the dominant groups' goals.

In this sense, the advocacy for more socially just societies needs to be taken—and given— cautiously as it is a type of discourse both informed and used ideologically. Though social justice matters have been the starting point of many (P)AR experiences, they have become part of a variety of ideologically informed discourses that attempt to impose their actions and words. Again drawing from Arendt's conception of political, when this happens, the actions and words aimed at generating the social changes are no longer political, as they lose the power that originated them. And, although people have participated, their actions could be considered merely social rather than political.

These historical accounts of (P)AR also reveal that, while trying to restore or introduce democratic practices to achieve more socially just societies, (P)AR practitioners have been asked to meet the scientific community's requirements of rigor to obtain legitimacy. That is, (P)AR practices began to be "normalized" in turn by the scientific community itself. And, once (P)AR was considered a legitimate form of social research, it began to be used as an effective means to achieve a diversity of goals informed by various ideologies that give participation different flavors.

From an Arendtian perspective, the politics of (P)AR—that is, the coexistence of different human beings who organize themselves according to certain commonalities through (P)AR—have been neither identified nor articulated in these histories of (P)AR. On the one hand, the scientific view of the world challenges (P)AR to find ways to recognize the plurality of views of the world that go beyond the scientific worldview. Unfortunately, it can be said that the scientific worldview has become an ideology with a claim of universality that impedes us (P)AR practitioners from other experiences and views of the common world. Action, as the only activity directly between human beings without the intermediary of things, is shaped by what is acceptable and feasible in the scientific world. The irreversibility and unpredictability of actions that characterize the political realm result in being "managed" in (P)AR.

On the other hand, the social dimension of (P)AR has affected it to a great extent. As expressed in some of these historical accounts, the existing relationship between the researcher and the researched, as well as the everyday more bureaucratic practices attached to contemporary research, have served to empty (P)AR words of their earlier meaning. Unfortunately, normalization of research practices disables participants' actions and words from being the main feature of the research process. It seems that even though the goals pursued through (P)AR concern the political realm, especially on social issues, and even though important insights are now in the literature to inform understanding of the relationship between (P)AR and the political realm, the understandings and discussions of this relationship have been overshadowed, and sometimes misled, by the social component of (P)AR.

Notes

1. This chapter draws on my PhD thesis entitled "On New Beginnings: Natality and (Participatory) Action Research in Higher Education," which is supported by Universidad Nacional de Colombia and an International Postgraduate Research Scholarship (IPRS) at Charles Sturt University, Australia.

2. *Natality* was coined for the first time in Arendt's doctoral dissertation on the concept of love in Saint Augustine, with supervision by existential philosopher Karl Jaspers. According to Vecchiarelli and Stark (1995) some of the key terms in Arendt's dissertation include *natality* as a key term jointly with *caritas, memory, foundations, free will, narrative, society*, and *the world*. They say that *Love and Saint Augustine* provides a provocative glimpse into the implied "context for Arendt's phenomenology, especially, in relation to her reflections on the social source and moral ground for action in the public realm." For the last time, in her reflections on Willing, published after her death in *The Life of the Mind*, Arendt cites Augustine's God's creation of man as the introduction of new beginnings in the world: "This very capacity [the will] for beginning is rooted in *natality*, and by no means in creativity, not in a gift but in a fact that human beings, new men, again and again appear in the world by virtue of birth."

3. Dick's three extensive literature reviews were aimed at identifying the various themes and trends emerging from the published material (paper and online) in the field of action research in three specific periods: 2000–2003, 2004–2006 and 2006–2008. All the materials reviewed were selected subjectively by the author, as he states at the outset, according to whether he considers the material useful, thought-provoking, or helpful for addressing present and futures issues in the field (Dick, 2004, p. 426).

References

Altrichter, H., & Gstettner, P. (1997). Action research: A closed chapter in the history of German social science? In R. McTaggart (Ed.), *Participatory action research: International contexts and consequences* (pp. 45–78). Albany: State University of New York Press.

Altrichter, H., Kemmis, S., McTaggart, R., & Zuber-Skerritt, O. (2002). The concept of action research. *The Learning Organization, 9*(3), 125–131.

Appadurai, A. (2006). The right to research. *Globalisation, Societies and Education, 4*(2), 167–177.

Apple, M. (2005). Doing things the "right" way: Legitimating educational inequalities in conservative times. *Educational Review, 57*(3), 271–293.

Arendt, H. (1970). *On violence.* San Diego, CA: Harcourt Brace & Co.

Arendt, H. (1978). *The life of the mind. The groundbreaking investigation on how we think.* San Diego, CA: Hartcourt.

Arendt, H. (1998). *The human condition.* Chicago: University of Chicago Press.

Arendt, H. (2005). *The promise of politics.* New York: Schocken Books.

Arendt, H. (2006). *Between past and future.* London: Penguin Books.

Brock-Utne, B. (1980). What is educational action research? *Classroom Action Research Network Bulletin, 4*, 10–15.

Carr, W., & Kemmis, S. (1986). *Becoming critical: Education, knowledge and action research.* Waurn Ponds, Victoria, Australia: Deakin University Press.

Carr, W., & Kemmis, S. (2009). Educational action research: A critical approach. In S. Noffke & B. Somekh (Eds.), *Sage handbook of educational action research* (pp. 74–84). Los Angeles: Sage.

Dick, B. (2004). Action research literature: Themes and trends. *Action Research, 2*(4), 425–444.

Dick, B. (2006). Action research literature 2004–2006: Themes and trends. *Action Research, 4*(4), 439–458.

Dick, B. (2009). Action research literature 2006–2008: Themes and trends. *Action Research, 7*(4), 423–441.

Elliott, J. (2005). Becoming critical: The failure to connect. *Educational Action Research, 13*(3), 359–373.

Elliott, J. (2007). Reinstating social hope through participatory action research. In D. Santos & M. Todhunter (Eds.), *Action research and education in contexts of poverty: A tribute to the life and work of Professor Orlando Fals-Borda* (pp. 33–48). Bogota: Universidad de La Salle.

Elliott, J. (2009). Building educational theory through action research. In S. Noffke & B. Somekh (Eds.), *Sage handbook of educational action research* (pp. 28–38). Los Angeles: Sage.

Fals-Borda, O. (2006a). The North-South convergence: 30-year first-person assessment of PAR. *Action Research, 4*(3), 351–358.

Fals-Borda, O. (2006b). Participatory (action) research in social theory: Origins and challenges. In P. R. H. Bradbury (Ed.), *Introduction: Inquiry and participation in search of a world worthy of human aspiration* (p. 362). London: Sage.

Fals-Borda, O., & Mora-Osejo, L. E. (2003). Context and diffusion of knowledge: A critique of Eurocentrism. *Action Research, 1*(1), 29–37.

Fals-Borda, O., & Ordonez, S. (2007). Investigacion accion participativa: Donde las aguas se juntan para dar forma a la vida. Entrevista con Orlando Fals-Borda. *Revista Internacional Magisterio, 26,* 10–14.

Greenwood, D., & Levin, M. (2007). *Introduction to action research: Social research for social change* (2nd ed.). Thousand Oaks, CA: Sage.

Grundy, S. (2007). Killing me softly: The audit culture and the death of participation. In D. Santos (Ed.), *Action research and education in contexts of poverty: A tribute to the life and work of Professor Orlando Fals-Borda* (pp. 71–82). Bogota: Universidad de La Salle.

Gunz, J. (1986) *Handlungsforschung. Vom wandel der distanzierten zur engagierten sozialforschung.* Vienna: Braumüller.

Harding, S. (1987) Introduction: Is there a feminist method? In S. Harding (ed.), *Feminism and methodology.* Bloomington: Indiana University Press.

Heidegger, M. (1962). *Being and time* (J. M. E. Robinson, Trans.). London: SCM Press.

Kemmis, S. (2001). Exploring the relevance of critical theory for action research: Emancipatory action research in the footspteps of Jürgen Habermas. In P. Reason & H. Bradbury (Eds.), *Handbook of action research: Participative inquiry and practice.* London: Sage.

Kemmis, S. (2005). *Participatory Action Research and the Public Sphere.* Paper presented at the CARN-PRAR Conference, Nov. 4–6, 2005, Holland.

Kemmis, S. (2006). Participatory action research and the public sphere. *Educational Action Research, 14*(4), 459–476.

Kemmis, S. (2007). From popular science to public spheres. In D. Santos & M. Todhunter (Eds.), *Action research and education in contexts of poverty: A tribute to the life and work of Professor Orlando Fals-Borda* (pp. 101–117). Bogota: Universidad de La Salle.

Kemmis, S. (2008). Critical theory and participatory action research. In P. Reason & H. Bradbury (Eds.), *Sage handbook of action research: Participative inquiry and practice* (2nd ed.) (pp. 121–138). London: Sage.

Kemmis, S., & McTaggart, R. (2005). Participatory action research: Communicative action and the public sphere. In N. Denzin & Y. Lincoln (Eds.), *SAGE handbook of qualitative research* (3rd ed.) (pp. 559–604). Thousand Oaks, CA: Sage.

Kemmis, S., Wilkinson, J., Hardy, I., & Edwards-Groves, C. (2009). *Leading and learning: Developing ecologies of educational practice*. Paper presented at the 39th AARE Conference.

Kindon, S. L., Pain, R., & Kesby, M. (2007). *Participatory action research approaches and methods: Connecting people, participation and place*. London & New York: Routledge.

McTaggart, R. (1997). Guiding principles for participatory action research. In R. McTaggart (Ed.), *Participatory action research: International contexts and consequences* (pp. 25–44). Albany: State University of New York Press.

Mills, G.E. (2003). *Action research: A guide for the teacher researcher* (2nd ed.). Upper Saddle River, NJ: Pearson.

Noffke, S. (2009). Revisiting the professional, personal, and political dimensions of action research. In S. Noffke & B. Somekh (Eds.), *Sage handbook of educational action research* (pp. 6–21). Los Angeles: Sage.

Nussbaum, M. (1990). An Aristotelian conception of rationality. In *Loves's knowledge*. Oxford: Oxford Univeristy Press.

Rahman, A. (2008). Some trends in the praxis of participatory action research. In P. Reason & H. Bradbury (Eds.), *Sage handbook of action research: Participative inquiry and practice* (pp. 49–62). London: Sage.

Reason, P., & Bradbury, H. (2006). Introduction: Inquiry and participation in search of a world worthy of human aspiration. In P. Reason & H. Bradbury (Eds.), *Sage handbook of action research. Concise paperback edition* (pp. 1–14). London: Sage.

Rorty, R. (1999). *Philosophy and social hope*. London: Penguin Books.

Sagor. R. (2000). *Guiding school improvement with action research*. Alexandria, VA: Association for Supervision and Curriculum Development.

Tandon, R. (1988). Social trasnformation and participatory research. *Convergence, 21*(2–3): 5–14.

Vecchiarelli, J., & Stark, C. J. (1995). Rediscovering Hannah Arendt. In J. V. Scott (Ed.), *Love and Saint Augustine* (pp. 113–233). Chicago: University of Chicago Press.

Wadsworth, Y. (1998). Paper 2: What is participatory action research? *Action Research International, 19*. Retrieved October 1, 2011, from http://www.scu.edu.au/schools/gcm/ar/ari/p-ywadsworth98.html.

Contributors

Mary E. Brenner is an anthropologist who looks at the effect of culture on learning, particularly in the area of mathematics. She combines ethnographic research on students' everyday lives with school-based research to find methods of instruction that will enhance the academic achievement of students who have traditionally underachieved in American schools. She has done research with diverse populations including Native Hawaiians, Native Alaskans, and Latinos as well as several cross-national studies in Africa and Asia. In addition, she has helped to create and evaluate a number of summer and afterschool programs that engage students in environmental science and technology activities. These informal education programs help to bridge the gap between children's out of school lives and the increasing demands of formal schooling. She has also written about using different qualitative research methodologies in educational research. Dr. Brenner is a Professor in the Department of Education at the University of California, Santa Barbara.

Svend Brinkmann is Professor of Psychology in the Department of Communication and Psychology at the University of Aalborg, Denmark, where he serves as co-director of the Center for Qualitative Studies. His research is particularly concerned with philosophical, moral, and methodological issues in psychology and other human and social sciences. He is author and co-author of numerous articles and books, among them *InterViews: Learning the Craft of Qualitative Research Interviewing* (Sage, 2008), *Qualitative Inquiry in Everyday Life* (Sage, 2012), and *Qualitative Interviewing* (Oxford University Press, 2013).

Lucinda Carspecken is the author of *An Unreal Estate: Sustainability and Freedom in an Evolving Community,* (published in 2012 by Indiana University Press,) and has several journal articles in press on the self and on alternative communities. She teaches Qualitative Research Methods and Life History Research at Indiana University.

Phil Francis Carspecken is Professor of inquiry methodology and philosophy in the School of Education, Indiana University. His interests are in philosophy and social theory, as related to inquiry methodology.

Corinne Datchi is an Assistant Professor at Seton Hall University in the Marriage and Family Therapy Program. She is the former Chair of the Section for the Advancement of Women in the Society of Counseling Psychology. She also serves as Editor of *The Family Psychologist*, the bulletin of the Society for Family Psychology. She studies women's issues in the crimminal justice system, gender and violence, transgender identities and relationships. As a licensed therapist, Dr. Datchi has integrated her research methodology with the principles and demands of therapy.

Barbara Dennis is Associate Professor of Qualitative Inquiry in the Inquiry Methodology Program at Indiana University. She has broad interests in the critical theory and methodological practices intentionally focused on eliminating sexism and racism from cultural ways of knowing and being. Most of her work practical work focuses on the gift of consciousness-raising through inquiry. This is coupled with theoretical interests in the limits of knowledge and identity and concepts of validity and truth.

Melissa Freeman, is assistant professor of qualitative research methodologies in the College of Education at the University of Georgia. Her research focuses on critical, hermeneutic, and relational approaches to educational research and evaluation, the role of dialogue in the construction of meaning and understanding, and social class relations within the discursive practice of parental involvement. Her most recent research focuses on the relevance of philosophical hermeneutics for social research and the use of alternative elicitation and analysis strategies in interviewing and focus groups. Her work appears in *Qualitative Inquiry, Educational Researcher, Cultural Studies ↔ Critical Methodologies*, and *Defending Public Schools: The Nature and Limits of Standards-Based Reform and Assessment*. She is the co-author, along with Dr. Sandra Mathison, of *Researching Children's Experiences* (Guilford Press, 2009).

Dean Garratt is Professor of Education in the Faculty of Education and Children's Services at the University of Chester, UK. His qualitative methodologies include phenomenological-hermeneutic, post-structural and psychoanalytic as he takes a critical approach to educational policy, applied sociology of sport, and citizenship theory.

Christopher Faircloth is Assistant Professor of Sociology at Xavier University of Louisiana. In addition, Faircloth has served as a National Institute on Aging Post-Doctoral Research Fellow at the Boston University Gerontology Center, and a Senior Research Health Associate with the Veteran's Administration Rehabilitation Outcomes Research Center. His primary research interests are in the "chronic illness experience," health disparities, a sociology of the body, social psychology, and qualitative research methods. Faircloth has edited or co-edited two volumes, one on the aging body, and a second on medicine and masculinity. He is currently working on a third focusing on the mind and medicine. In addition, he has published numerous articles and book chapters.

Melissa Freeman is assistant professor of qualitative research methodologies in the College of Education at the University of Georgia. Her research focuses on critical, hermeneutic, and relational approaches to educational research and evaluation, the role of dialogue in the construction of meaning and understanding, and social class relations within the discursive practice of parental involvement. Her most recent research focuses on the relevance of philosophical hermeneutics for social research and the use of alternative elicitation and analysis strategies in interviewing and focus groups. Her work appears in *Qualitative Inquiry*, *Educational Researcher*, *Cultural Studies ↔ Critical Methodologies*, and *Defending Public Schools: The Nature and Limits of Standards-Based Reform and Assessment*. She is the co-author, along with Dr. Sandra Mathison, of *Researching Children's Experiences* (Guilford Press, 2009).

Grace Giorgio's research focuses on qualitative research methods and narrative theory as forms of healing traumas. She teaches public policy and gender communication courses at the University of Illinois.

Alba Lucy Guerrero received her Ph.D. in Cultural Perspectives and Comparative Education with and emphasis in Qualitative and Interpretive Research at the University of California, Santa Barbara. She is interested in the contributions of education to social and political development in transnational contexts. Her research interests include educational equity, language and culture, education community relations, informal education, and qualitative research methods. Her dissertation looked at the ways displaced children by the war in Colombia created and recreated the meanings of their physical and cultural worlds through their participation in an educational photography-based project. Prior to coming to UCSB I worked as a research consultant for international agencies and local NGOs on issues of educational change and social development.

Michael G. Gunzenhauser is an associate professor of Administrative and Policy Studies at the University of Pittsburgh, where he studies issues of equity and social justice in education. He focuses on ethics, philosophy of education, and qualitative research methodology. He is the author of *The Active/Ethical Professional: A Framework for Responsible Educators,* published in 2012 by Continuum Press. His philosophical work about research methodology has been published in *Qualitative Inquiry, Review of Higher Education, Educational Foundations,* and the *International Journal of Qualitative Studies in Education.* He co-edits the journal, *Philosophical Studies in Education.*

Debora Hinderliter is Director of Assessment and Assistant Professor in Social Sciences at Finger Lakes Community College in Canandaigua, NY. Her research interests include: global citizenship, educational policy, assessment and evaluation. She enjoys working with both K-12 and higher education faculty on developing research, evaluation and assessment practices that are empowering and actual.

Yi-Ping Huang is an assistant professor at National Chengchi University, Taiwan. She is interested in exploring epistemology and ontology of (narrative) identity with a strong connection to Eastern philosophy. Her research interests also include conducting qualitative research to facilitate teaching/learning English as a medium of instruction in response to the internationalization of higher education.

Benetta Johnson, a native of Missouri completed her Bachelors of Arts at the University of Missouri-Columbia. She went on to obtain a Masters of Education in Community Counseling from the University of Georgia and later attained a Doctorate Degree in Counseling Psychology from Indiana University-Bloomington. Benetta primarily works as a psychologist in the Indianapolis area focusing her clinical work on women's issues and trauma. She has been blessed with a loving husband, caring siblings, family and devoted friends.

Kip Kline is Associate Professor of Education at Lewis University. His recent work applies existentialism and postmodernism to philosophy of education and philosophy of youth. He has previously published on the intersection of philosophy and hip-hop aesthetics.

Staffan Larsson, Ph.D. 1983, has been professor at Linköping University in adult education research since 1993. He has contributed significantly to the establishment of ethnographic research in the Nordic countries. He has also conducted research and published articles in the following areas: negotiations in adult education classrooms ("Paradoxes of Teaching", "Initial Encounters in Formal Adult Education"), study circles and folk high schools ("Seven aspects of democracy as related to study circles," "Folk high schools as educational avantgardes in Sweden"). Larsson received the Ahlström Award for the article, "An emerging Economy of Publications and Citations" in 2011 and presented fourteen lines of reasoning about pedagogy for adult learners in a book in Swedish (2013). With a start in 1998 he and a colleage initiated a web-based master programme in "adult learning and global change" run in cooperation between universities in four continents; a programme that is still running. Larsson has also been Chairperson for the Nordic Educational Research Association 2001 - 2004, member of the Committee for Educational research, Swedish Research Council 2007 - 2009 and chairperson for a network for research on popular education 1997 - 1912. Larsson now focuses on art after retirement in 2012.

Lai Ma earned her Ph.D. at Indiana University in Information and Library Science. Her research includes work in social theory with emphasis on understanding information systems in contexts of culture and more general social system processes and trends. She has also made contributions to methodological issues in the study of information production, distribution, take-up and large scale action coordination. Lai Ma currently lectures and researches at University College, Dublin.

Dan Mahoney is an Associate Professor at Ryerson University, Toronto, Canada and is also a sociologist with an interest in the social, cultural and interpersonal context of family life. Dan teaches and conducts research in the areas of health, research methods, and family studies. His methodological interests in family-based research include interpretive ethnography; self-reflexive storytelling; and thematic narrative analysis.

Amir B. Marvasti is Associate Professor of Sociology at Pennsylvania State University, Altoona. His research focuses on the social construction of deviant identities in everyday life. He is the author of *Being Homeless: Textual and Narrative Constructions* (Lexington Books 2003), *Qualitative Research in Sociology* (Sage 2003), *Middle Eastern Lives in America* (with Karyn McKinney, Rowman and Littlefield 2004), and *Doing Qualitative Research: A Comprehensive Guide* (with David Silverman, Sage 2008). His articles have been published in the *Journal of Contemporary Ethnography, Qualitative Inquiry, Symbolic Interaction,* and *Critical Sociology.*

Cathie Pearce is a research fellow at the Institute of Education. Perviously, she served as a Senior lecturer in Education for four years at Manchester Metropolitan University. Her Ph.D. dissertation is titled *Experiencing and Experimenting with Pedagogies and Research.*

Heather Piper is a Professorial Research Fellow in the Education and Social Research Institute (ESRI) at Manchester Metropolitan University, UK. Her research interests involve qualitative methods, conceptual critique, and a basic interest in troubling the common place. She has been publishing work that examines the problems of policy and practice os adult acting in loco parentis roles in schools, childcare facilitaties, and coaching.

Rebecca Riall is an attorney and a PhD candidate (expected December 2013) in anthropology at Indiana University. She practices law in Louisiana. Her current research is a legal anthropological examination of the state recognition of American Indian nations and groups.

Doris Santos has an MA in Linguistics and has done MPhil studies at the Universidad Nacional de Colombia. She has a PhD from Charles Sturt University, Australia. She conducts participatory action research, critical ethnography and critical discourse analysis research projects on higher education issues. She is a member of the Collaborative Action Research Network (CARN), the Association of Latin American Discourse Studies (ALED), the International Association of Argumentative Studies (ISSA) and the Australian Association for Research in Education (AARE).

Nurit Stadler is a senior lecturer in Sociology and Anthropology at The Hebrew University of Jerusalem, her principal research interests are fundamentalism, text-based communities, ultra-Orthodox Judaism, Greek-Orthodox and Catholic rituals in Jerusalem and the Galilee, Marian veneration in Israel/Palestine, and contemporary rituals at female shrines. In the book *Yeshiva Fundamentalism: Piety, Gender and Resistance in the Ultra-Orthodox World* (New York: NYU Press, 2009), she assayed the reconstruction of fundamentalist masculine piety amid the daunting challenges of modernity through the prism of the Israeli ultra-Orthodox yeshiva world. As demonstrated therein, the changes in Israeli society have forced the Haredi community to redefine the concepts of family, work, and civil society as well as its relation to the army. Her second book, *A Well-Worn Tallis for a New Ceremony* (Brighton, MA: Academic Studies Press, 2012), explores recent developments in voluntarism, citizenship, domestic life, and the notion of freedom in the ultra-Orthodox sector. Over the past few years, she published some of the findings from her long-term ethnographic study on the cult of Mary in Jerusalem. Her article "Between Scripture and Performance" (published in Religion 2011) takes stock of the Jerusalem Dormition Feast – an annual Marian celebration along a canonical route.

Within this framework, the article explored the difference in how the ecclesiastical hosts, local devotees, and foreign pilgrims celebrate and envision this Orthodox feast. Lastly, Stadler give a wide range of courses on sociological theory and anthropology of religion at The Hebrew University.

Beverly J. Stoeltje is Professor Emeritus of Anthropology and of Folklore and Ethnomusicology at Indiana University. She has been affiliated faculty with the African Studies Program, American Studies, and Gender Studies. She conducts ethnographic research in Ghana on the contemporary institution of Chieftaincy in Asante, focusing on the roles of Queen Mothers and Chiefs. Her work concentrates on the anthropology of law as it relates to the Asante legal system, especially performance in the traditional courts. She has published numerous articles in professional journals and chapters in books on her research in Asante and has co-edited Beauty Queens on the Global Stage with Colleen Cohen and Rick Wilk. Her publications also include articles on North American rodeo as ritual and festival, and on women of the American West. Her areas of expertise include gender, ritual and festival, legal anthropology, and nationalism, all with an emphasis on performance and relations of power.

Ian Stronach was appointed Professor of Education in the Faculty of Education, Community and Leisure in December 2008. Additionally, He is Co-Director of the Centre for Educational Research and Evaluation Services (CERES). Pervious appointments include Research Professor at the Institute of Education, MMU and Professor at Stirling University. He is a well-known scholar in the area of qualitative inquiry, having recently edited a special section of the International Review of Qualitative Research. His books include *Don't touch!' The educational story of a moral panic* (Routledge, 2008, with H. Piper) and *Globalizing education, educating the local. How method made us mad* (Routledge 2010).

Sunnie Lee Watson is faculty of Learning Design and Technology in the Department of Curriculum and Instruction at Purdue University. She received her dual major doctorate in Educational Policy studies and Instructional Systems Technology at Indiana University, Bloomington. Her research interests focus on critical systems theory/thinking for educational change and research, use of web-based technology tools for multicultural and peace education, and international technology policies and leadership for digital equity. She also specializes in the creation of personalized learning environments.

William R. Watson is an Associate Professor of Learning Design and Technology in the Department of Curriculum and Instruction at Purdue University. He is the director of the Purdue Center for Serious Games and Learning in Virtual Environments, which conducts research on and provides support for implementing, designing and developing educational video games and virtual environments for learning. Watson earned a Ph.D. in Education and a M.S. in Information Science from Indiana University. His research interest focuses on the critical, systemic change of education to realize a learner-centered paradigm, including the application of technology such as video games, virtual environments, and learning management software in order to create customized and personalized learning environments.

Ran Zhang is an associate professor in the Graduate School of Education, Peking University, China. She earned her undergraduate law degree at Peking University, an M.S. in International and Comparative Education and a double major Ph.D. degree in Educational Policy Studies and Educational Psychology at Indiana University. Over the past few years, she has won many awards and grants, including a Chinese Government Award for Outstanding Student Abroad (2006-7), China Times Cultural Foundation Junior Scholar Award (2007-8), a U.S. National Science Foundation Doctoral Dissertation Improvement Grant (2007-9), and a National Junior Scholar Grant from the Education Program of the Chinese National Social Science Foundation (2010-12). Ran Zhang is presently teaching Education Law as well as Qualitative Research Methods at Peking University. She has published more than twenty articles and book chapters, and her dissertation "Confrontation or Cooperation: Spaces of Action for Student Grievance in Chinese Universities" received the CIES (U.S. Comparative and International Education Society) Higher Education SIG Best Dissertation Award (2009-2010).

Studies in the Postmodern Theory of Education

General Editor
Shirley R. Steinberg

Counterpoints publishes the most compelling and imaginative books being written in education today. Grounded on the theoretical advances in criticalism, feminism, and postmodernism in the last two decades of the twentieth century, Counterpoints engages the meaning of these innovations in various forms of educational expression. Committed to the proposition that theoretical literature should be accessible to a variety of audiences, the series insists that its authors avoid esoteric and jargonistic languages that transform educational scholarship into an elite discourse for the initiated. Scholarly work matters only to the degree it affects consciousness and practice at multiple sites. Counterpoints' editorial policy is based on these principles and the ability of scholars to break new ground, to open new conversations, to go where educators have never gone before.

For additional information about this series or for the submission of manuscripts, please contact:

Shirley R. Steinberg
c/o Peter Lang Publishing, Inc.
29 Broadway, 18th floor
New York, New York 10006

To order other books in this series, please contact our Customer Service Department:

(800) 770-LANG (within the U.S.)
(212) 647-7706 (outside the U.S.)
(212) 647-7707 FAX

Or browse online by series:
www.peterlang.com